TUTANKHAMUN'S FOOTWEAR

Studies of Ancient Egyptian Footwear

André J. Veldmeijer

With contributions by:

Alan J. Clapham, Erno Endenburg, Aude Gräzer,

Fredrik Hagen, James A. Harrell, Mikko H. Kriek,

Paul T. Nicholson, Jack M. Ogden &

Gillian Vogelsang-Eastwood

Sidestone Press

For my parents

Antje Veldmeijer-Wagt (1940 - 1988)

Marten Veldmeijer (1934-2011)

© 2011 André J. Veldmeijer

ISBN 978-90-8890-076-1

Published by Sidestone Press, Leiden
  www.sidestone.com
    Sidestone registration number: SSP67280003

Illustrations: Erno Endenburg & Mikko H. Kriek

Cover design: Karsten Wentink, Sidestone Press

CONTENTS

Preface	9
Introduction	11
The Discovery of a Tomb	11
Ancient Egyptian Footwear Project (AEFP)	11
Carter's System of Excavating	15
Methodology	16
Layout	16
Chapter 1 Context	19
Chapter 2 Preservation and Conservation	35
Chapter 3 Description	43
3.1 Introduction	43
3.2 Sandals	44
3.2.1 Sewn Sandals Type C	47
3.2.1.1 Variant 1	47
3.2.1.2 Variant 2	80
3.2.2 Sewn Sandals Type D (Imitations)	86
3.2.2.1 Variant 1	87
3.2.2.2 Variant 2	95
3.2.2.3 Variant 3	107
3.3 Open Shoes	109
3.3.1 Type: Partial Upper, Leather and Beadwork; Variant: Sewn Sandal Strap Complex / Foot strap	109
3.3.2 Type: Partial Upper, Leather and Beadwork; Variant: Foot strap / Instep Strap	121
3.3.3 Partial Upper, Leather; Variant: Front Strap / Toe band / Foot Strap / Instep Strap	130
3.4 Not Kept Objects	138
3.5 Additional Observations	139
3.5.1 Size	139
3.5.2 Use and Wear	139
3.6 Comparison	142

Chapter 4	The Materials		145
	4.1 Organic Materials		145
	4.1.1 Fibres (André J. Veldmeijer)		145
	4.1.2 The Presence of Silver Birch (*Betula pendula* Roth) (Alan J. Clapham)		146
	4.1.3 Leather (André J. Veldmeijer)		147
	4.2 Inorganic Materials		148
	4.2.1 Glass and Faience (Paul T. Nicholson)		149
	4.2.2 Gemstones (James A. Harrell)		149
	4.2.2.1 Identification in the Footwear		149
	4.2.2.2 Origin		149
	4.2.2.3 Foreign		150
	4.2.2.4 Manufacturing of Gemstone Beads and Inlays		150
	4.2.3 Gold (Jack M. Ogden)		151
	4.2.3.1 Introduction		151
	4.2.3.2 Goldwork in Ancient Egypt		152
	4.2.3.3 The Gold in the Tomb of Tutankhamun		153
	4.2.3.4 The Gold in the Footwear		153
	4.2.3.5 The Technology		155
Chapter 5	Socks (Gillian Vogelsang-Eastwood)		165
	5.1 Introduction		165
	5.2 The Construction of the Socks		165
	5.3 Socks Versus Gauntlets		167
	5.4 Comparative Items		167
Chapter 6	Contemporary Footwear: A Survey		169
	6.1 Introduction		169
	6.2 Sandals		169
	6.2.1 Yuya and Tjuiu		169
	6.2.1.1 Sewn Sandals Type C		172
	6.2.1.2 Sewn Sandals Type D (Imitations)		180
	6.2.2 Nefertari		184
	6.2.3 Amarna		187
	6.2.4 Other Sandals		187
	6.3 Shoes		187
Chapter 7	New Kingdom Sandals: A Philological Perspective (Fredrik Hagen)		193
	7.1 Introduction		193
	7.2 Lexicographic Typology and Material Culture		193
	7.3 Symbolism and Ideology		198
	7.4 Economic Role and Manufacture		198

Chapter 8 Footwear in Late New Kingdom Art — 205
    8.1 Two-Dimensional Art — 205
        8.1.1 Manufacturing Footwear (André J. Veldmeijer) — 205
        8.1.2 The Identification of Depicted Footwear (André J. Veldmeijer) — 207
        8.1.3 Footwear in Domestic Indoor Spaces: An Incursion into Amarnian Iconography (Aude Gräzer) — 208
            8.1.3.1 Introduction — 208
            8.1.3.2 Footwear in Indoor Spaces — 209
            8.1.3.3 The Royal Couple — 213
            8.1.3.4 The Royal Children — 218
            8.1.3.5 Dignitaries — 220
        8.1.4 Footwear Outside Domestic Areas: Some Remarks (André J. Veldmeijer) — 221
    8.2 Three-Dimensional Art (André J. Veldmeijer) — 224

Chapter 9 Discussion — 225
    9.1 Typology — 225
    9.2 Philology — 228
    9.3 Art — 228
    9.4 Revision of Previous Work — 228
    9.5 Non-Fibre Footwear: Foreign and Unique? — 229
    9.6 Status — 230
    9.7 Finally — 231

Notes — 233

Bibliography — 251

Appendices
    I Abbreviations — 265
        I.A Abbreviations Used in Chapter 7 — 265
        I.B Other Abbreviations — 266
    II Glossary — 266
    III Concordances — 270
        III.A Footwear Tutankhamun — 270
            III.A.1 Carter's Number — 270
            III.A.2 Exhibition Number — 271
            III.A.3 Special Registry Number — 272
            III.A.4 Temporary Number — 274
            III.A.5 JE Number — 275
        III.B Footwear Yuya and Tjuiu — 276
            III.B.1 JE Number — 276
            III.B.2 CG Number — 277
            III.B.3 Special Registry Number — 277
    IV Tables — 279

Index — 302

Authors — 309

PREFACE

The study of archaeological footwear started in 2004 and includes several collections, as will be explained in the introduction. Ever since the start, the project grew continuously and the study of the many objects has only been possible due to the kind collaboration of many colleagues.

I am grateful to Dr Zahi Hawass and the Supreme Council of Antiquities for permission to access the footwear collection in the Egyptian Museum, Cairo and Luxor Museum, Luxor. I thank Dr Wafaa El Saddik of the Egyptian Museum, Cairo and the museum authorities (Mokhtar Abdu, Nariman Abd El Fatah Azab, Ibrahim Abdel Gwad, Abeia Elshamy, Hala Hassan, Nesma Ismail, Zienab Tawfik) and Dr Samaa Ahmed Ali of the Luxor Museum for their nice collaboration.

I also thank the authorities of the various other collections that allowed me to study material under their care: Ägyptisches Museum und Papyrussammlung, Berlin – Ashmolean Museum, Oxford – British Museum, London – Metropolitan Museum of Arts, New York – Museo Egizio, Turin – Museum of Fine Arts, Boston – National Museum of Antiquities, Leiden – National Museums of Scotland, Edinburgh – Oriental Institute Museum, Chicago – Petrie Museum of Egyptian Archaeology UCL, London – Roemer- und Pelizaeus-Museum, Hildesheim – Sammlung des Ägyptologischen Instituts der Universität, Heidelberg – World Museum, Liverpool.

Many people helped: Kathryn Bard, Giovanni Bergamini, Gary Brown, Caroline Cartwright, Subhadra Das, Denise Doxey, Dina Faltings, Claudia Farias, Rodolfo Fattovich, Klaus Finneiser, Elizabeth Goring, Jac. J. Janssen, Barry Kemp, Hugh Kilmister, Josephine Kuckertz, Lesley-Ann Liddiard, Barbara Magen, Jaromir Malek, Frank Marohn, Geoffrey Metz, Gillian Pyke, Stephen Quirke, Maarten Raven, Pamela Rose, Bettina Schmitz, Jeffrey Spencer, Raymond Tindel, Eleni Vassilika and Helen Whitehouse.

Christine Lilyquist was so kind to send me her photographs of the sandals on Tiuju's feet; I benefited much from these and the accompanying notes and discussion. I also benefitted from discussion about the more specific purpose of the tomb with Salima Ikram; fortunately, she was so kind to write the two first paragraphs of chapter 1.

Furthermore, I thank Mikko Kriek for his artist impressions and reconstructions and Adri 't Hooft and Erno Endenburg for photographing. Erno is also thanked for his technical drawings and assistance in the field. The Netherlands-Flemish Institute Cairo (NVIC) is acknowledged for their invaluable help. The Griffith Institute, Oxford, has been extremely helpful and I am indebted to them for allowing me to publish the Burton photographs.

The Michela Schiff Giorgini Foundation has partially funded the research in the Egyptian Museum, Cairo; other collections have been visited due to funding by The Netherlands Organization for Scientific Research (NWO) and Fam. J. Endenburg (Texel, The Netherlands). I thank the British Museum and Vivian Davies for financially supporting the photographing of the footwear collection by Adri 't Hooft. The Petrie Museum is kindly acknowledged for allowing me to use their photographs.

I am indebted to James Harrell who checked the description of Tutankhamun's footwear on grammatical errors; Joanne Ballard checked the entire text for which I am truly grateful. Of course, any remaining errors are all my own responsibility. Geert Jan Engelmoer is acknowledged for his invaluable help!

Finally, I would like to take the opportunity to thank everyone who I forgot to mention for which my apologies and, last but not least, my colleagues who collaborated in this project.

André J. Veldmeijer
Amsterdam, November 2009

NOTE IN PRESS
(André J. Veldmeijer):

Five days before this manuscript went to press, the results of DNA research of several mummies, including Tutankhamun's, was published (Hawass *et al.*). For the present work, the surprising observation that Tutankhamun's left foot was a clubfoot (*Ibidem:* 642-643), is important. Possibly, the foot strap in his open shoes 021f & g, 021k & l and 270a was a solution to this condition, a suggestion which is currently being investigated and tested. The results are planned to be published later this year.

Hawass, Z., Y.Z. Gad, S. Ismail, R. Khairat, D. Fathalla, N. Hasan, A. Ahmed, H. Elleithy, M. Ball, F. Gaballah, S. Wasef, M. Fateen, H. Amer, P. Gostner, A. Selim, A. Zink & C.M. Pusch. 2010. Ancestry and Pathology in King Tutankhamun's Family. – Journal of the American Medical Association 303, 7: 638-647.

NOTE IN PRESS
(Aude Gräzer):

I mention the presence or absence of footwear as a social marker between officials. The following note can be added at p. 221 ("if we base our reasoning upon the coherence of the iconographical construction, sandals introduce here a slight social nuance between characters belonging to a same group"): Spence (2009: 174) noticed that "rank and status were at least in part modulated and expressed spatially within palaces, through proximity to the throne and residential suite and through the mode of access". In the light of the Karnak Edict of Horemheb, it appears that "free access was clearly a privilege, and the mode of access was carefully observed and regulated in a number of ways: speed, on foot or horse, with or without personal attendants, shoes and potential weapons".

Spence, K. 2009. The Palaces of el-Amarna. Towards an Architectural Analysis. In: Gundlach, R. & J.H. Taylor. Eds. 2009. Egyptian Royal Residences. Fourth Symposium on Egyptian Royal Ideology. London, June, 1st-5th 2004 (KSG 4/1). – Wiesbaden, Harrassowitz Verlag: 165-187.

INTRODUCTION

THE DISCOVERY OF A TOMB

One of the most important discoveries in Egyptology as well as in the archaeological science in general is without a doubt the tomb of Tutankhamun in 1922 by Howard Carter.[1] The discovery of this largely intact tomb still appeals to the imagination of many people, even after more than 85 years. Amazingly, even after so many years, much of the tomb contents has not been studied properly. Fortunately, Carter was far ahead of his time as an archaeologist for which the following statement is a good example (Carter & Mace, 1923: 124): "It was a slow work, painfully slow, and nerve-racking at that, for one felt all the time a heavy weight of responsibility. Every excavator must, if he have [sic] any archaeological conscience at all. The things he finds are not his own property, to treat as he pleases, or neglect as he chooses. They are a direct legacy from the past to the present age, he but the privileged intermediary through whose hands they come; and if, by carelessness, slackness, or ignorance, he lessens the sum of knowledge that might have been obtained from them, he knows himself to be guilty of an archaeological crime of the first magnitude. Destruction of evidence is so painfully easy, and yet so hopelessly irreparable." Another example of his professional attitude is the remark about the idea of some people that an object bought from a dealer is as important as a carefully excavated one (Carter & Mace, 1923: 125): "There was never a greater mistake. Field-work is all-important, and it is a sure and certain fact that if every excavation had been properly, systematically, and conscientiously carried out, our knowledge of Egyptian archaeology would be at least 50 per cent. greater than it is."

One of the first things Carter did was employing specialists, among which a chemist (Alfred Lucas) and a photographer (Harry Burton). This was good thinking: in contrast to what is generally thought, the condition of the objects was not good at all and most needed to be consolidated and conserved. This, together with other problems such as difficult political situations, made that it took 10 years to clear the tomb.

ANCIENT EGYPTIAN FOOTWEAR PROJECT (AEFP)

For the first time since the discovery of Tutankhamun's tomb in 1922, a detailed study of the king's footwear was conducted in 2007 and 2008 as part of a larger study into ancient Egyptian footwear, the Ancient Egyptian Footwear Project (AEFP). The present work, being one of the most important elements of the project, is a good opportunity to explain the project in detail for the first time.

The AEFP is a multidisciplinary, ongoing research (figure 1), consisting of the study of archaeological artefacts, iconography, philology and experimental archaeology and, where appropriate, ethno archaeology in order to better understand footwear's meaning and position within the ancient Egyptian society. An important aspect is to explore the influence of foreigners (Nubia, Near East, Mediterranean) on Egyptian footwear and, in a broader perspective, leatherwork.[2] Moreover, the project aims to function as point of reference for future research.

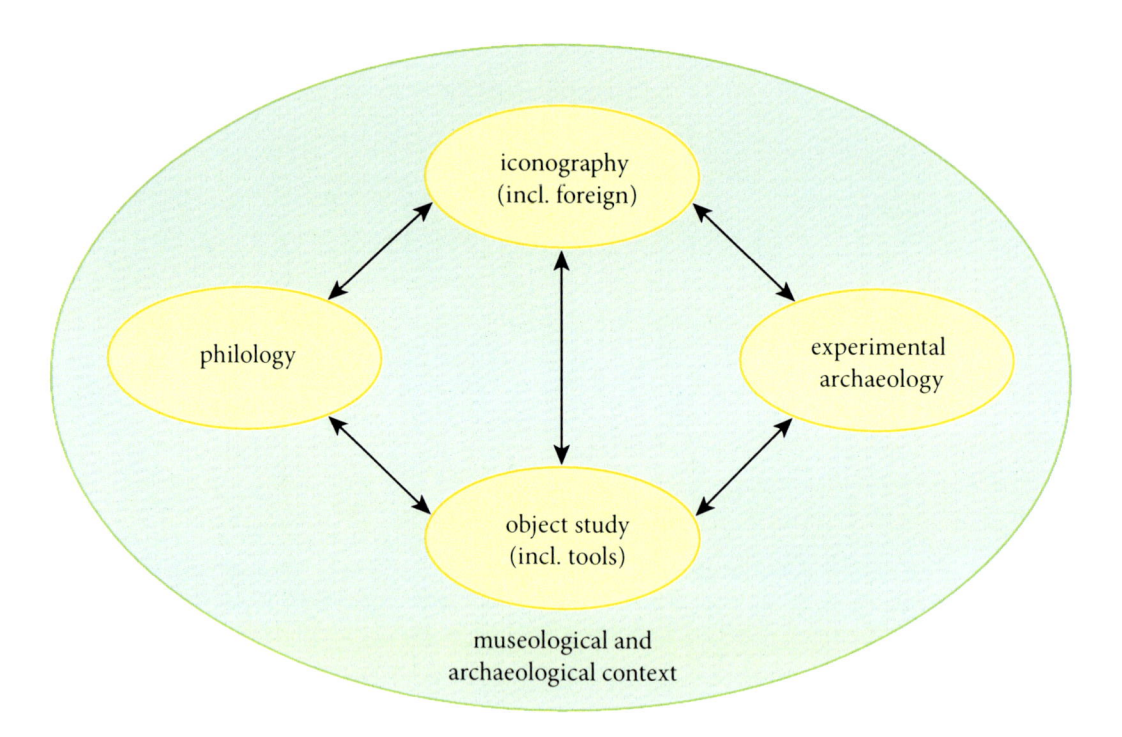

Figure 1. The Ancient Egyptian Footwear Project (AEFP) consists of several parts, which are intimately linked.

The basis of the research is the study of the archaeological finds (phase I).[3] One can only understand an object and put it into context with a thorough knowledge of the manufacturing techniques and its development. Phase II will deal with philological and iconographic information. Although phase I is still in progress, the textual and iconographic work has already begun as is evident from several of the chapters in the present work. The thus obtained information will, if necessary, be checked by experimental archaeology (which makes up phase III, together with ethnographic information): the remake of objects not only gives insight in the manufacturing techniques but the reproduced pieces of footwear allows us to study for example wear. Finally, anthropological data is needed to see, amongst others, what the consequences of going barefooted are and whether we can recognise this in the archaeological record. Moreover, it will give insight in the size of footwear.

The information of the AEFP will be combined with the results of the Ancient Egyptian Leatherwork Project (AELP; figure 2), the project of which includes experimental archaeology and chemical analyses of skin processing/paint and pigment. In the final phase, the results will be combined and interpreted in their entirety.

The objectives of the AEFP can be divided in two groups: the material culture (I) and socio-cultural aspects (II). The material culture consists of three components, addressing questions on the kind of materials (origin) and its processing before being turned into footwear (such as harvest and preparation). The second part will deal with the manufacturing techniques (*e.g.* stitching and coiling), the decoration (*e.g.* pigment/paint, appliqué work) and typology. Other characters, which are not part of the material culture *per se*, for example dating, will be ultimately included. The third part deals with the sandal-makers and their workshops, including the tools.[4] What do

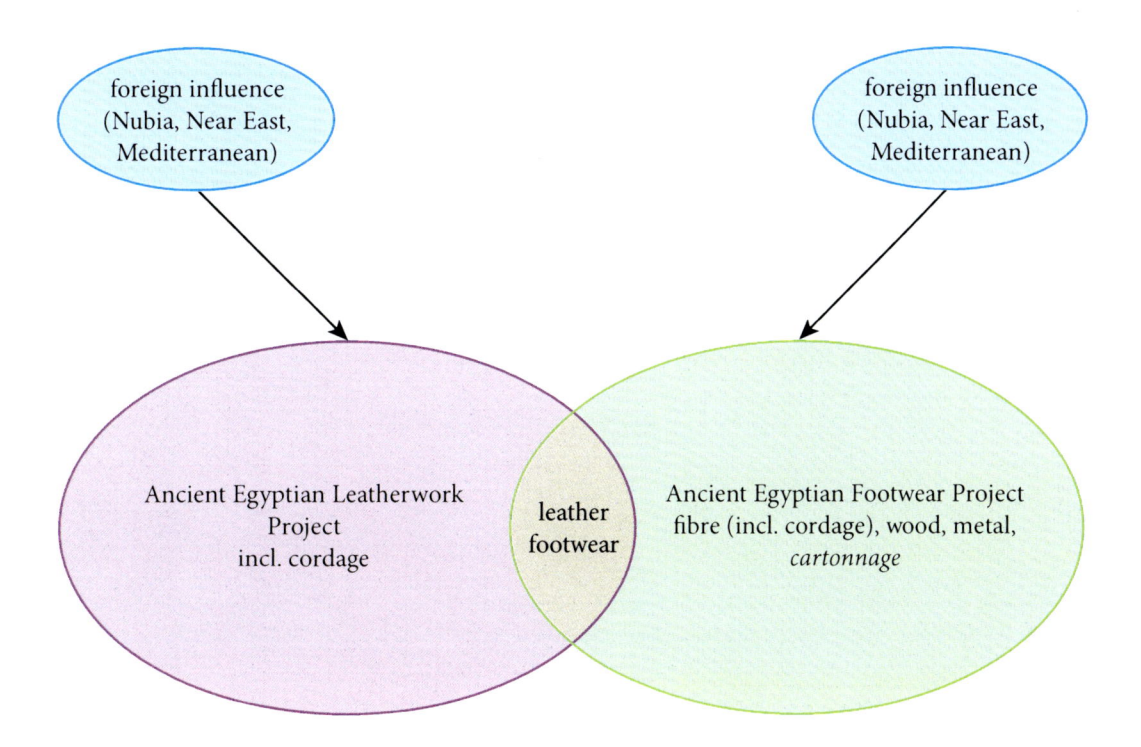

Figure 2. The relationship between the Ancient Egyptian Footwear Project (AEFP) and the Ancient Egyptian Leatherwork Project (AELP), showing that leather footwear is a shared group.

workshops look like and how can they be recognised in the archaeological record? If we recognise them, the information obtained from such spaces and tools needs to be combined with that from the artefacts themselves to elucidate production processes.

Socio-cultural aspects is a rather broad and loosely defined term, which includes topics such as the interpretation of the objects, the value of footwear within the community and society at large (in both a monetary and aspirational sense) and the organisation and status of the sandal-maker. Within these focal points, there are several points of interest.

Wich status had footwear within the community? This question goes along with the question how footwear is to be interpreted. For example, tomb sandals of wood or *cartonnage* are known to have been made especially for the funeral but was footwear, which could have been used in daily life, also buried with the owner? Important are, obviously, the finds in the tomb of Tutankhamun, even though these can hardly be representative for the society at large or possibly even for royal burials. Tutankhamun's footwear is also important with respect to foreign influence: closed shoes may have been a late New Kingdom (post-Amarna?) innovation brought by people from the Near East but recent research may point to a development from open shoes into closed shoes (Veldmeijer, 2009f; In press c). Indeed, it has been suggested that Tutankhamun's shoes are imported but these statements are not based on thorough research.

Sandal-makers are known from literature but how specialised was this profession? If referred to them, it is to those who produced leather sandals. Was this the same person who made other leather objects? And who made the fibre footwear: did the basketry maker produce sandals as well since the techniques of manufacturing fibre sandals partly overlapped with those of basketry? How are we to explain the absence of manufacturing of shoes in representations (and

13

the near-absence of depictions of shoes in general), whereas there are many examples known from the archaeological record and several texts mention 'enveloping sandals' (interpreted as 'open shoe'). What was the status of the sandal-maker and other people involved in this process?

How specialised was the craft of footwear manufacturing? Some types of fibre footwear do not seem to require specialist knowledge: could the people themselves have made these? Others, however, seem to have been made by professionals. Some of the footwear from Tutankhamun combines several materials, indicating that different craftsmen were involved: how was this organised?

How are we to explain the differences in detail? Are these due to regional differences and/or different production centres? Could, for example, the differences be explained by fashion or status or a combination?

Can we distinguish footwear for certain groups within the community? There are indications that royals wore other footwear. Also, texts refer to sandals for priests as well as sandals for men and women. We also know that children wore sandals: are these different, except, of course, for their size? What exactly are these differences? Closely related to these questions is how footwear was used. Can we recognise long-term use? Wear patterns as well as (extensive) repair gives much information. Could footwear be worn anywhere and at any time, a question that is closely related to symbolism. How are we to interpret the differences (if there are differences) if it comes to gender, religious scenes and wearing footwear inside or outside buildings?

On a less limited scale, we see that there are clear differences in footwear from Egypt, Nubia and the Near East (likely also the Mediterranean). We are fortunate, not only in having a large corpus of finds from Nubia, but with the preservation of possible Persian footwear (Elephantine) as well (Kuckertz, 2006[5]), the latter of which differs considerably from Egyptian (and Nubian) footwear. Moreover, foreigners are depicted relatively often (in Egypt as well as in their own countries) with footwear. How was Egyptian footwear influenced by this foreign footwear and if it was, how did this manifest itself? Can we detect differences on a more limited geographical scale, *i.e.* from one settlement to another?

The shape of footwear changed through time (but also other features, such as material and manufacturing techniques). By mapping this in detail a good insight can be obtained in the development (typology) and consequently, footwear might serve as an aid in dating. This, in its turn, could enable us to date footwear in collections of which the context and date are unknown.

In some cases, information can be obtained on the demography of the settlement. What does the footwear tell us about its owner and about the inhabitants of the community at large? What can we say about the relative wealth of them? Especially important for this question are the finds from Amarna, Qasr Ibrim and the Coptic monastery Deir el-Bachit, currently under study by the author.

There are several typologies of ancient Egyptian footwear, most of which are based on a limited number of archaeological objects.[6] Gourlay (1981a: 55-64; 1981b: 41-60) published a typology based on the material from Deir el-Medinah, making distinction between cordage sandals, sandals from palm/papyrus etc., and leather sandals. Although distinction is being made between sandals with an upper, they are regarded as a type of sandal (*Ibidem*: 61-62) rather than open shoe, despite the remark that the Type A sandal is turned into a shoe by adding an upper. Montembault (2000) has based the typology on the material housed in the Louvre, but most of the material is unprovenanced. Consequently, geographical information as well as date plays at best a marginal role. The typology developed by Leguilloux (2006) is more detailed and includes dates, but is based on the material from Didymoi, a Roman *caravanière* along the Coptos-Berenike route in Egypt's Eastern desert only and is therefore of limited use for Pharaonic footwear. In both typologies, the emphasis lies on the development of shape.[7] Goubitz *et al.* (2001), however, classifies European footwear on the basis of the fastening or closure method, which is used in the AEFP too. However, they note that in their work this "is not always consistently applied. In such cases priority has been given to recognisability." (*Ibidem*: 132). This method is followed by the AEFP. Using technological features, such as fastenings, and recognisability often goes hand in hand[8] but this relation is stronger in sandals than in shoes.

The AEFP first makes distinction, of course, between sandals, shoes, boots etc. made with different materials. These groups are divided into Categories, the differentiation of which is based on the materials in combination with manufacturing technology (for example fibre, sewn sandals, leather composite sandals etc.). These categories are, if possible, divided into Types, for which different criteria are used depending on the category. Finally, types can be divided into Variants. A typology should offer insight into the development of footwear, which can only be done after the incorporation of a large sample of, preferably, all periods of the history of Egypt. Moreover, dates as well as geographical distribution (provenance) will be incorporated. Since the first phase of the AEFP mainly deals with the manufacturing technology, these missing criteria will be investigated and incorporated in a later stage of the project.

The results of the study of the objects are published independently: phase I produces a series of papers with a strong focus on the manufacturing techniques, due to which the present work has such a strong focus as well. Consequently, it is necessary to emphasise that other topics will be discussed only in passing, to be dealt with in detail in a later stage of the project. Preliminary conclusions, however, will be presented.

CARTER'S SYSTEM OF EXCAVATING

All objects from the tomb of Tutankhamun, group of objects and every fragment was assigned a number (1-620; 5398 objects) by Carter. Within this numbering, subdivisions for objects within a numbered group were referred to by single or multiple letters. Whenever a further subdivision was needed, this was referred to by Arabic numerals between brackets. One group, however, which is important for footwear, differs and consists of 123 subdivisions. These are numbers 620 (1-123), the entry of 32 pairs of sewn sandals being 620 (119). The following numbers were assigned to the different part of the tomb (http://griffith. ashmus.ox.ac.uk/gri/4tut.html, accessed 6 May 2008): "Nos. 1 to 3 were from outside the tomb and the Staircase; No. 4 was the first doorway; Nos. 5 to 12 were from the Descending Passage; No. 13 was the second doorway to the Antechamber; Nos. 14 to 170 were from the Antechamber (No. 28 was the third doorway to the Burial Chamber); No. 171 was the fourth doorway to the Annexe; Nos. 172 to 260 were from the Burial Chamber (No. 256 was the King's mummy); Nos. 261 to 336 were from the Treasury; and Nos. 337 to 620 (123) were from the Annexe."[9]

Carter made meticulous notes on the objects on cards, which are preserved in the archives of the Griffith Institute, Oxford and are accessible at the Institute's website http://www.ashmolean.org/Griffith.html. Although his notes are, also for the study of the footwear, of the utmost importance, they are not without errors and not always as complete as one would hope. One should remember that the notes were made during the clearance of the tomb: a detailed research of the objects was planned for the future, but unfortunately never happened.

The notes clearly increase in importance due to Harry Burton's photographs, the low resolution versions of which are accessible through the aforementioned website of the Griffith Institute. The photographs are indispensable for the understanding of the construction of the so-called 'court slippers,' for example, but they also give good insight in the condition of the objects, which allows for comparison with the objects nowadays.

METHODOLOGY

In discussing the objects, reference is made in two ways: the 32 pairs of sewn sandals (620 (119)) will be referred to by their special registry numbers as Carter did not give them separate numbers. Some sewn sandals are referred to by their JE-number because they lack a Carter or exhibition number. The other items, however, will be referred to by Carter's number, as to simplify recognition in literature and Carter's card system. The heading and the tables include the full set of numbers.

In describing footwear, terminology[10] is after Goubitz *et al.* (2001). Terminology of knots is after Veldmeijer (2006; but see also Ashley, 1993) and for cordage terminology reader is referred to Veldmeijer (2005, but see also Wendrich, 1991 & 1999). The terminology that is used to refer to the various surfaces and sides of footwear is adapted from zoology and related sciences (figure 3): the ventral surface is the surface that faces the ground, and the dorsal surface is the surface that faces upwards; the lateral side is the side that faces outwards, and the medial side faces inwards. The front end or toe can be referred to as anterior and the back or heel as posterior, although these latter two will be used only when it would be confusing to use 'front' or 'back'.[11]

All objects, except the golden 'mummy sandals' have been studied first-hand by the author. The use of a magnifying glass (x 20), the usual measuring, writing and drawing equipment and a pair of pincers were the only tools used. James Harrell, Paul Nicholson, Mikko Kriek and Erno Endenburg

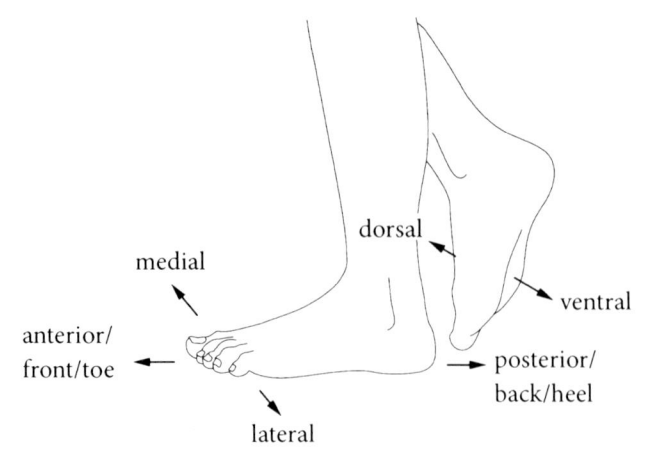

Figure 3. The directions of a foot as used in describing footwear. Drawing by M.H. Kriek.

made additional observations of the footwear exhibited in the showcase in 2008. Salima Ikram had a closer look at the marquetry veneer sandals as well as the isolated back strap in the fall of 2008. When possible, footwear was photographed from all sides, including the ventral surface. However, this proved impossible in some cases, hence the lack of images of this (these) surface(s). Moreover, the photographic conditions varied, depending on the working place within the museum, which forced us to process the photographs in order to obtain consistency in colour. The camera used is a Canon EOS 300D Rebel, 6.3 Megapixel. The objects could be photographed with a macrolens (Tamron 90/2, 8 DI CAF SP) in all cases. Most photographs have been made including a Kodak Colour Card. Due to the fragile condition of some pieces, detail photographs had to be done without this useful tool on occasion.

When quoting from sources, additions, clarification etc., which are inserted by the present authors, are placed between square brackets. The standard way of notation of ancient Egyptian texts is followed in chapter 7.

LAYOUT

Roughly, the book can be divided in two parts: the first part deals specifically with Tutankhamun's footwear. The first chapter deals with the context of the footwear, *i.e.* the tomb. The first section presents a description and discussion of the position of the footwear as found in the tomb by Carter and his team and includes a short explanation on the function of the tomb, with thanks to Salima Ikram. In chapter 2, the current condition of the objects is compared with their condition as found by Carter and his team. This is important in order to identify wear, damage during burial and post-excavation damage. The focus is on the condition in general; it proved less confusing to include more specific details with the description of the objects itself. In the third chapter, the footwear is described in detail of each object individually. However, the section that deals with the fibre, sewn sandals is prefaced with a general description since these sandals are much alike. Consequently, the description focus on details 'out of the ordinary,' as well as on their condition. After the description, a section with additional observations, such as size, compliments the description. Evidence for use and wear is discussed and the final section of chapter 3 presents a comparison. The different materials that were used in the footwear are discussed in more detail in chapter 4. Although in nature archaeological, additional information from two-dimensional art is included. Some of the materials are discussed in greater detail than others. The reason is the fact that some are better to deal with without detailed, microscopic research. For example, much can be said about the fibres, but the insight into glass and faience needs close examination, which has not been done (yet). This, however, is one of the future goals. The material-chapter includes a section on the gemstones by James Harrell, the goldwork by Jack Ogden, the glass and faience by Paul Nicholson and bark by Alan Clapham.

Although the tomb was disturbed and the necropolis officials restored the contents of the tomb, it is nevertheless important to take the associated objects into account. One group of objects, the socks, are obviously associated with footwear, which will be discussed in detail by Gillian Vogelsang-Eastwood in chapter 5.

In order to put Tutankhamun's footwear in wider context, the second part deals with 'non-Tutankhamun' topics. In chapter 6, some contemporary footwear is presented. From the objects from Tutankhamun's tomb, one could think that there was only very little variation in footwear in ancient Egypt. This is not true. There are indications that wearing footwear in the New Kingdom increased and with it, an increase in variation of types and variants. Examples from among others Amarna and Deir el-Medinah are shortly discussed. The footwear corpus from the tomb of Yuya and Tjuiu, however, are presented in detail, including descriptions and illustrations, which allow for a detailed comparison.

Philological evidence for sandals and the production of sandals in the New Kingdom by Fredrik Hagen is presented in chapter 7. The first part deals with the difficulties that surround any attempt at relating linguistic data to the material culture, but by comparing the archaeology of footwear with contemporary texts it is possible to suggest more accurate translations of problematic lexicographic elements. The second part consists of an analysis of administrative and literary documents that reveal aspects of the organisation and role of sandal-manufacturing both in institutional and private contexts.

In chapter 8, a survey of footwear in New Kingdom two- and three-dimensional art is presented, with a focus on domestic indoor spaces by Aude Gräzer. The manufacturing process as depicted is discussed shortly[12] after which the discussion focus on the types of depicted footwear: how are they depicted and how should they be interpreted. And if we succeed in that, are we able to recognise them within Tutankhamun's collection (and in the archaeological corpus at large). Moreover, who wore what type of footwear when?

In the discussion, the preliminary typology is explained. Attempts are made to put Tutankhamun's footwear in broader perspective, addressing questions on status, symbolism and the like. Thoughts will be presented whether his collection should be seen as unique for him only, or whether other Pharaoh's might have possessed a similar collection.

Since many people, the professional archaeologist and Egyptologist as well as the layman, is interested in the subject, I have tried to find a consensus between scientific and popular proza. The use of endnotes is one of these.

CHAPTER 1

CONTEXT

The lack of intact royal tombs leaves us with the question whether the 'ordinary' items (*i.e.* objects like clothing, furniture, and footwear as opposed to coffins, the mummy and the like) of tomb equipment had specific locations within the tomb, just as certain sacred objects had their own positions (Thomas, 1966: 278-285). Texts do not inform us sufficiently on this point either, so perhaps we can assume that there were very few rules regarding the non-ritual tomb goods.

The only virtually intact royal tomb ever found, that of Tutankhamun, also sheds no light on this question as the tomb had been violated and the location of objects disturbed, and, more importantly, the tomb itself was probably not made for royalty. Thus the positioning of objects therein could not follow any royal or religious protocol. This means that the precise find spots of objects are of little help to interpret specific functions, especially for the different footwear and related items. However, contents of single containers might arguably be related to one another, although there is no certainty in this.

According to several authors (*e.g.* Reeves, 1990a: 157), 93 pieces of footwear were recovered from the Antechamber, the Burial Chamber, the Treasury and the Annexe (figure 1.1). The number is based on Carter's entries; one (100d), however, is recognised as a piece of chariot, as were two others (054y, 085e) already identified as such by Carter himself (bringing the total to 90). They were entered as footwear in the system because Carter described two of them as sandal-shaped (054y and 085e) and the third one as sandal's sole (100d). When describing other parts of the chariots (Card No. 122rrr), object 122www is said to be equal to 054y. It is not entirely clear whether Carter meant that the pieces are the same or that one and the same object is marked 122www and 054y (as is the case with the sandal-shaped object 100d, see below).[1] Object 100d is, according to the description (Card No. 100d) an "Inner sole of a sandal of leather (?), covered with gold leaf on upper surface. Margin of 1 cm wide left without gold." It is renumbered by Carter as 122rrr.[2] The identification of 085e is uncertain as there is no description of it. It might be one of these three: 122ttt, 122uuu, or 122vvv.[3] The pair of sandals 373 has a separate number despite the fact that they were found on the floor of the Annexe, as were sandals 620 (119). It is not clear why Carter did so: possibly because their position clearly distinguish them from the rest and hence Carter was certain these two sandals were a pair. However, the pair has not been identified among the studied material and because the Museum's archival books state '620 (119)' and '373' together for 27 pairs (see below), it seems that upon entering the collection, the separation was not recognised.

The list of footwear from the Special Registry in the Egyptian Museum suggests the total number as 81 (see the concordance in the appendix), the number of objects which has actually been studied by the author.[4] Currently it is unclear what the reason for this discrepancy is. However, of two pairs (4286, 4287) only one sandal has been studied; the number (either A or B) suggests that the other was there at least at the time

19

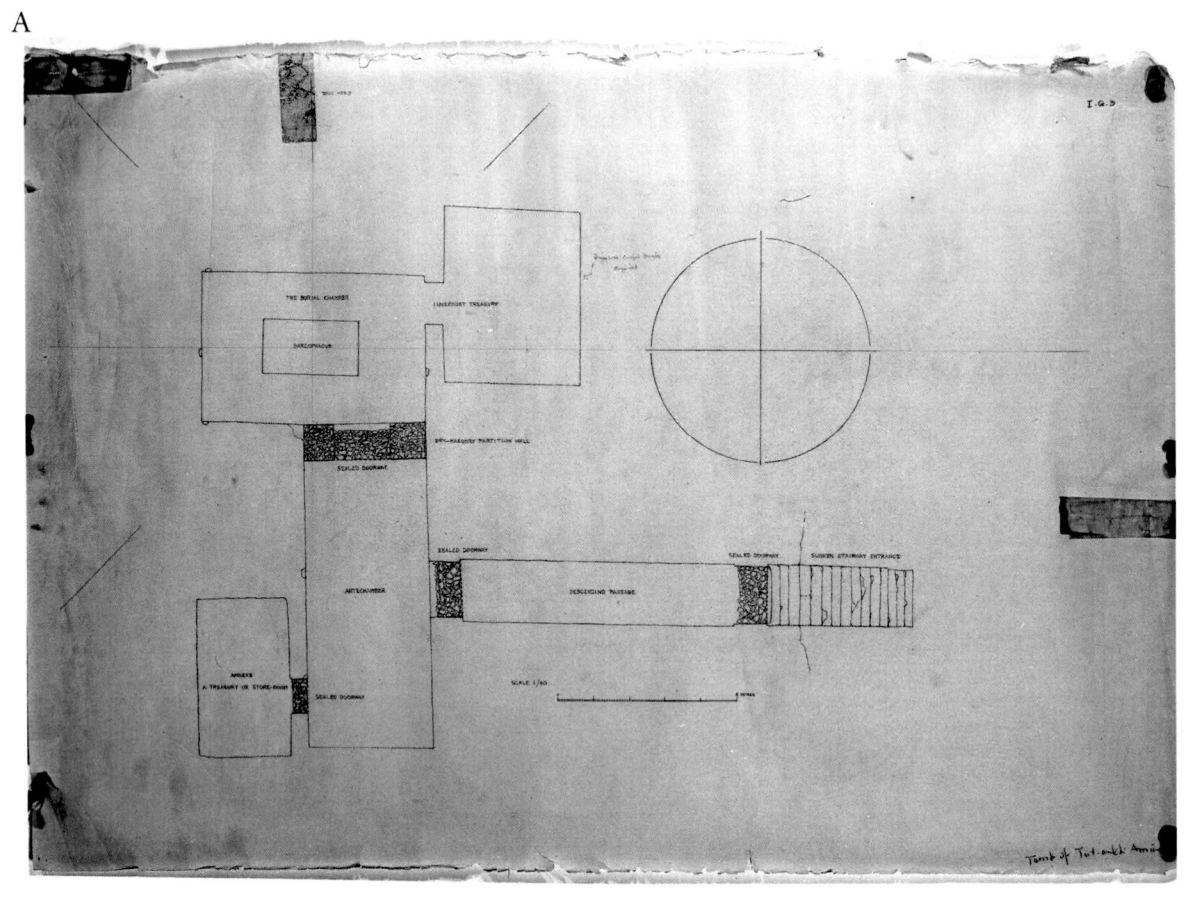

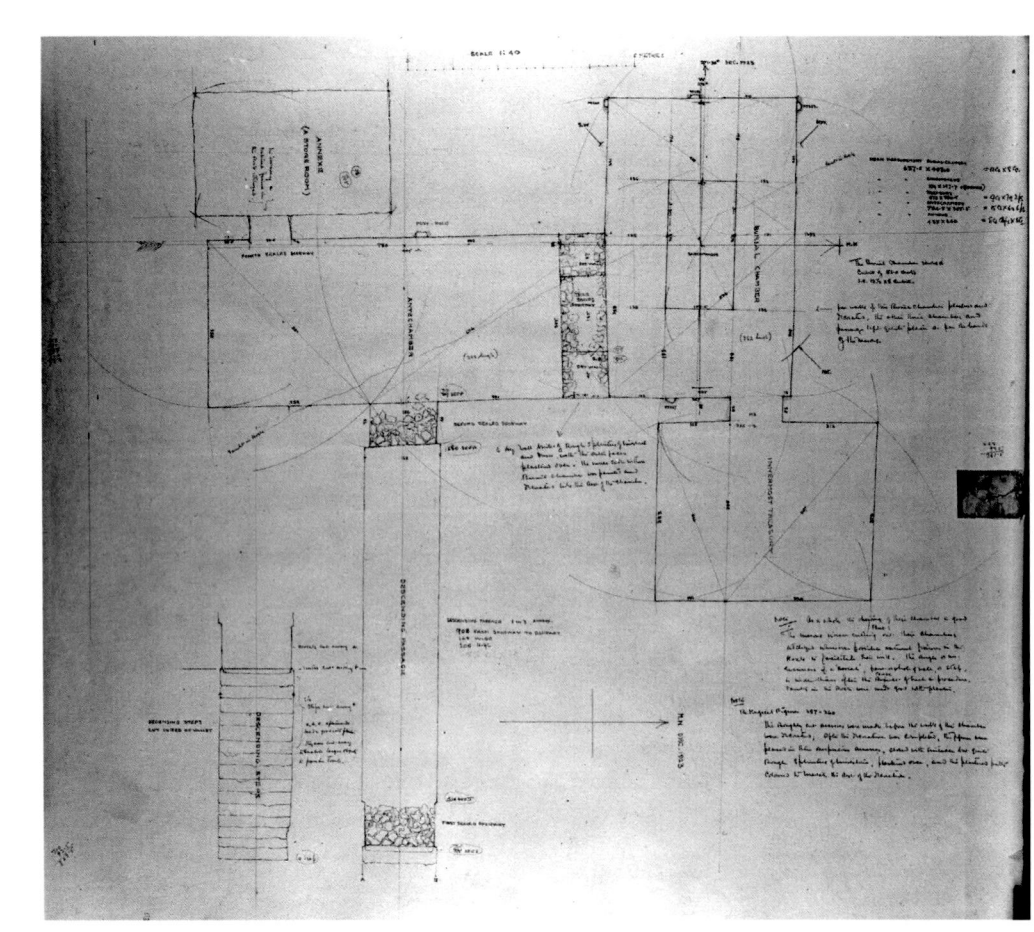

A

B

of registration. At least one entry of this group of sandals consists of only one sandal when found by Carter (2816),[5] which is the sandal with the decorated linen insole. When the entry is counted as 2 x 32 (pairs), this means at least one sandal too many (64, but because of the isolated sandal 2816, 63). Probably, what Carter meant by 32 'pairs', was 32 'entries', either pairs or isolated sandals, depending on how he found them. If, upon entering the museum, isolated sandals were put together (which might explain the pairs consisting of two left or two right sandals), a discrepancy arises.

Sixteen pieces of footwear have been recovered from the Antechamber.[6] Painted box no. 021[7] (figure 1.2A-E) contained nine pieces (021a & b; 021f & g; 021h & i; 021j; 021k & l). When opening the box, Carter and his crew found on the right (Carter & Mace, 1923: 167) "a pair of rush and papyrus sandals [021a & b], in perfect condition; below them, just showing, a gilt head-rest, and, lower again, a confused mass of cloth, leather, and gold" and on the left "crumpled into a bundle, there is a magnificent royal robe, and in the upper corner there are roughly shaped beads of dark resin." (*Ibidem*). The robe partially covered the left fibre sandal, which was taken away from under it, as can be seen in the photographs. Below the two fibre sandals lay, in the same orientation, the right sandal of pair 021h & i. Upon removal of the head-rest, robe, fibre sandals and leather sandal, the 'second layer' became visible. "Here, to begin with, were three pairs of sandals, or rather, to be accurate, two pairs of sandals and a pair of loose slippers." (*Ibidem*: 170). To be more accurate, this 'second layer' shows, to the left,

Figure 1.2. The various stages of unpacking box 021. A) First stage, showing sandals 021a & b. Photography by H. Burton. Copyright Griffith Institute, University of Oxford.

< *Figure 1.1A & B. Map of the tomb. Photography by H. Burton. Copyright Griffith Institute, University of Oxford.*

B

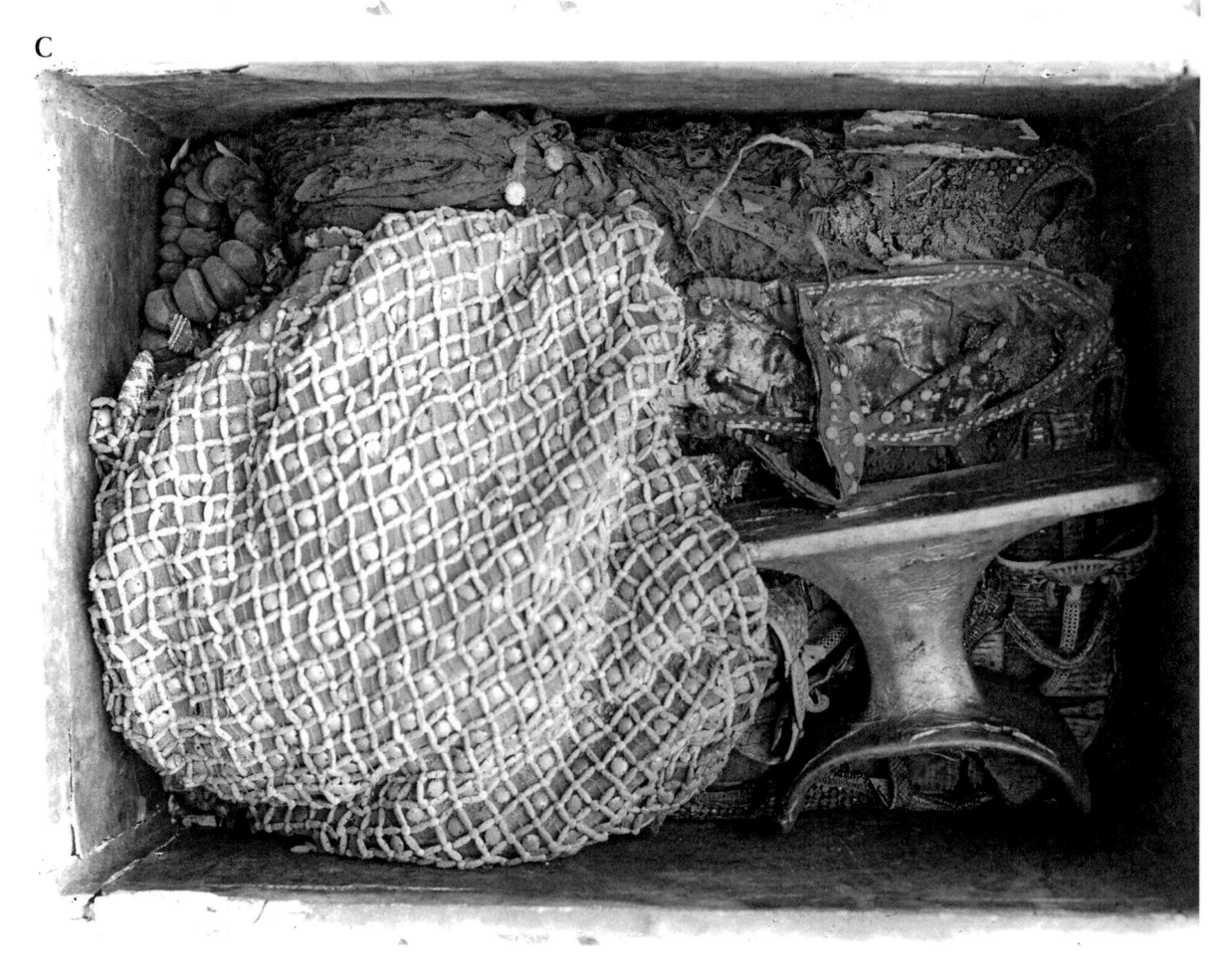

C

Figure 1.2. The various stages of unpacking box 021. C inset) The right sandal 021h & i. Photography by H. Burton. Copyright Griffith Institute, University of Oxford.

the left sandal of the leather pair 021h & i of which the right one was found in the 'first layer'. In contrast, this left sandal was positioned at a right angle to the right one and thus perpendicular to the box's length. The left shoe of the pair 021f & g lay at the opposite side and with its length also perpendicular to the box's length. It lay on top of the left shoe of the pair 021k & l. The right shoe of the pair 021f & g lay at a right angle to the left one and with its toe under it but over the left shoe of pair 021k & l and thus sandwiched between them. Next and slightly on top of it, against the long side, is the right shoe of pair 021k & l. This might indicate that the two pairs have been mixed up. Below 021h was a beadwork sandal (021j), which had fallen to pieces, and therefore no notes could be obtained of either size or ornamentation. "The beads were tiny disks of blue, red and yellow faience" (Card No. 021j). "Beneath the sandals there was a mass of decayed cloth, much of it of the consistency of soot [...] This [...] represents a number of royal robes. [...] There were at least seven distinct garments. [...] Bundled in with the actual garments there were [...] two faience collarettes of beads and pendants, two caps or bags of tiny bead-work which had almost entirely fallen to pieces, a wooden tag inscribed in hieratic "Papyrus (?) sandals of His Majesty," [see chapter 7] a glove of plain linen, an archer's gauntlet, tapestry woven in coloured thread, a double necklace [...]

< *Figure 1.2. The various stages of unpacking box 021. B) The right sandal removed, showing a head-rest; C) The removal of the left sandal reveals the right sandal 021h & i (see also inset above). Photography by H. Burton. Copyright Griffith Institute, University of Oxford.*

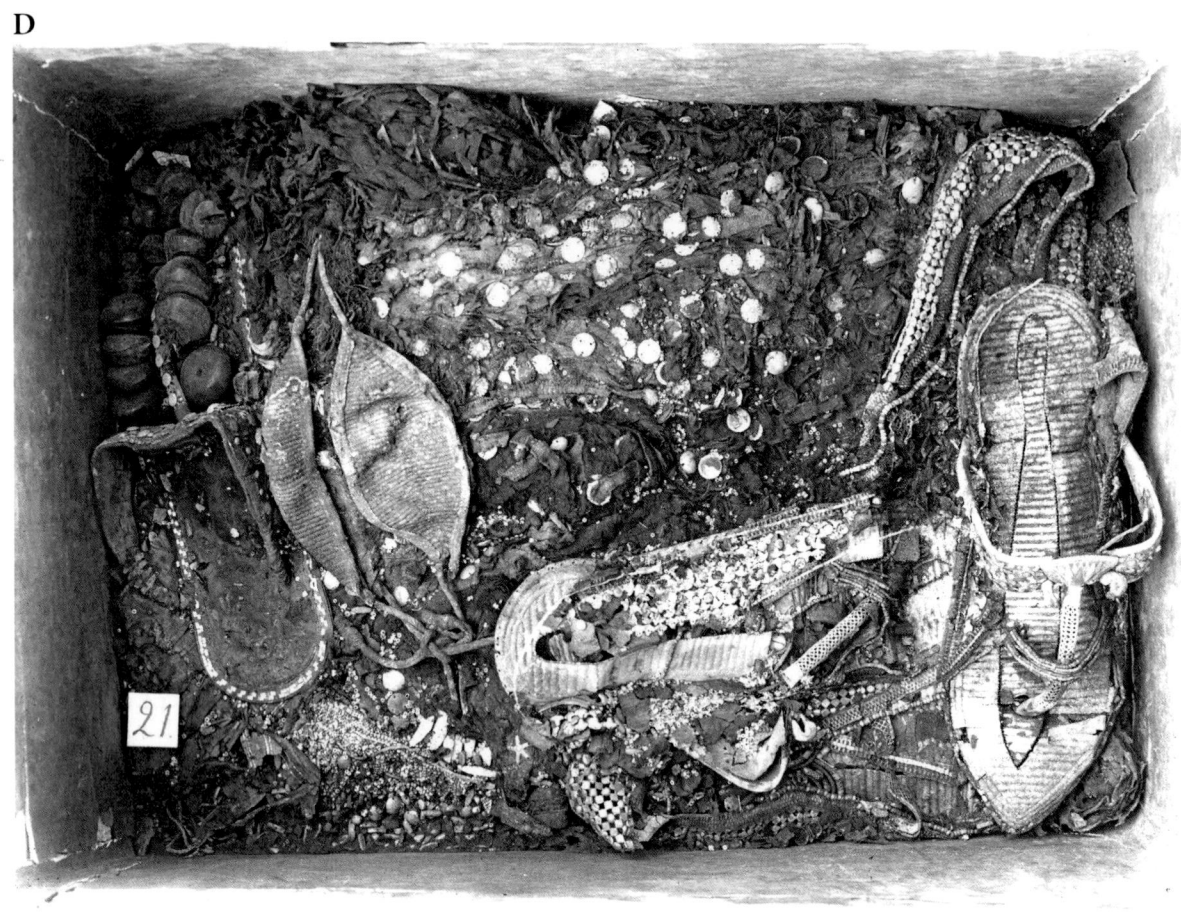

D

E

and a number of linen belts or scarves. Below the garments there was a layer of rolls and pads of cloth, some of which were loincloths and others mere bandages; and below these again, resting on the bottom of the box, there were two boards, perforated at one end for hanging, whose purpose is still doubtful" (Carter & Mace, 1923: 170-171; quotation marks in original).

The remains of a "leather (?) sandal with applied decoration in strips of coloured bark" (067b; Card No. 067b) was found on top of a wooden stool, 067a, which stood in the Antechamber "opposite the door, in front of central bed" (Card No. 067a). The stool was turned upside down (figure 1.3).

The badly preserved left sandal, made of leather (085c; figure 1.4) was also part of a miscellaneous group on the floor of the Antechamber, under the throne, resting on the remains of "reed matting" (Card No. 085). The sole was, according to Carter, in a very bad condition and hence not kept. The position close to 067b, might indicate that the two belong to each other (see section 3.4).

The bead sandal 085a (figures 1.3 & 1.4) was also part of the group, which in addition included the upper part of a stick (085b), a wooden label (085d) and "two fragments – fitting – of a shallow bowl of white (green?) faience. Found to belong to 170" (Card No. 085). The other sandal (147a), seen as the right sandal of the pair together with 085a (Card No. 147a), was found on the floor "under chariot wheels 131 & 132" (Card No. 147; figure 1.5), together with, ac-

Figure 1.3. Leather sandal 067b in situ in the Antechamber. Photography by H. Burton. Copyright Griffith Institute, University of Oxford.

< *Figure 1.2. The various stages of unpacking box 021. D) Upon removal of the royal robe, pairs of shoes 021f & g and 021k & l became visible; E) On the bottom among other things the imitation leopard-skin cloak. See Carter & Mace (1923: 166-172) for a detailed description of the stages of unpacking this box. Photography by H. Burton. Copyright Griffith Institute, University of Oxford.*

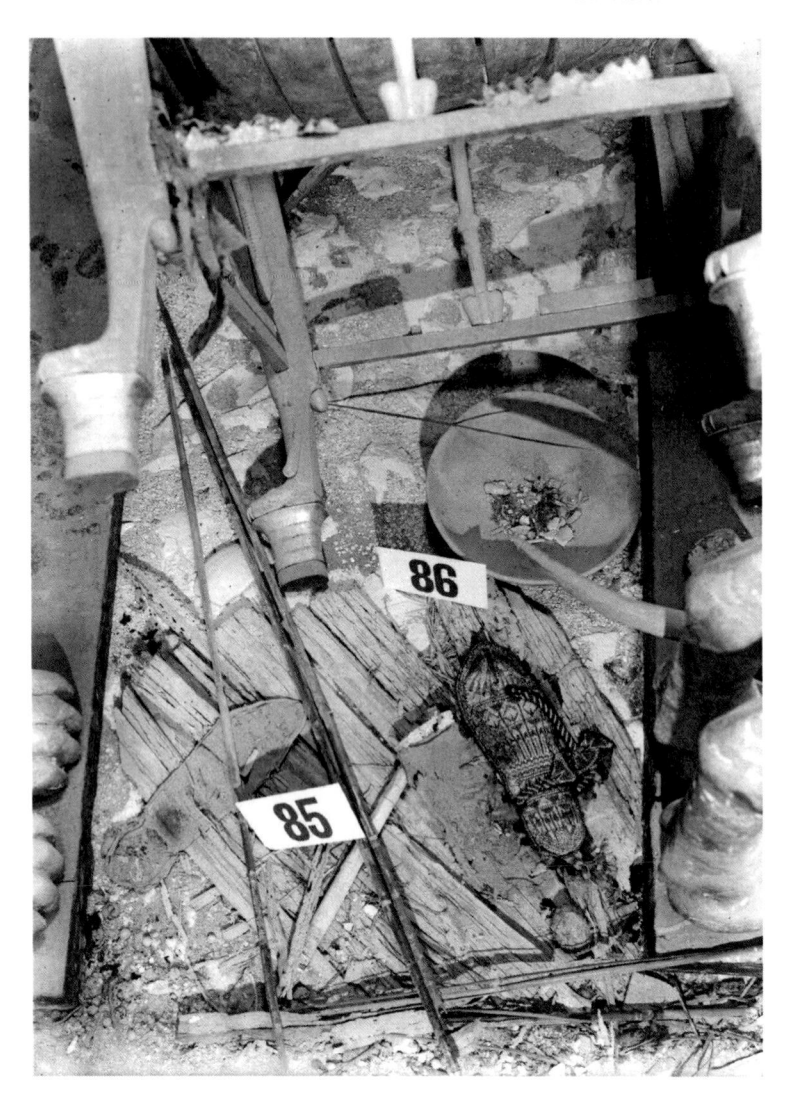

Figure 1.4. Carter referred to 085e (possibly the object next to bead sandal 085a) as a sandal-shaped piece of a chariot harness. To the left, sandal 085c can be seen, which might belong to 067b (see figure 1.3). Photography by H. Burton. Copyright Griffith Institute, University of Oxford.

cording to Carter's notes (*Ibidem*), a papyrus pad with rings, 5 arrow heads, a wooden model tool, a piece of sandstone grinder and a gold sequin from a robe(?).

Sandal 094a was found "On floor of chamber, under throne," (Card No. 094a) which stood under the Toeris couch (figure 1.6). It was found together with a wooden model of a hoe (Card No. 094a). Two sandals (104a & b) were found "On floor of chamber, near S.W. corner, between gold shrine and mouth of Annexe" (Card No. 104ab) (figure 1.7). Only one, 104a, was recovered; the other was in too bad condition to be kept (Card No. 104b). They were not a pair originally, judging from the difference in size (table 1).

The golden sandals on the king's mummy have a clear context and "were only intended to be beneficial for the dead king" (Carter, 1927: 138). Besides the gold sheet sandals, "each digit was enclosed in a separate gold stall" (*Ibidem*: 137; figure 1.8).

One pair of sandals (270a) was recovered from the Treasury. The pair was found in box 270 (Card Nos. 267-6, 270), which is a wooden box, painted white, with a vaulted lid. It is the third box from the west end of the Treasury, out of a series of five (figure 1.9). The contents of the box consisted (besides the pair of sandals) of the lid of box 269 and a stone anklet (Carter, 1933: 67). The linen, which is clearly visible in the photograph (figure 1.10), is not mentioned. It seems to be under the sandals inside the lid of box 269. The sandals and the linen were removed from the lid and the incomplete right sandal placed in approximately the same spot at the bottom of box 270, the reason for which is entirely unclear. This is

Figure 1.5 (left and below). Carter assumed that sandal 147a belonged to sandal 85a. Photography by H. Burton. Copyright Griffith Institute, University of Oxford.

98
88
97
96
99
87
95
94
93
92

110
107
105
106
103
104
108
111
109
113
115

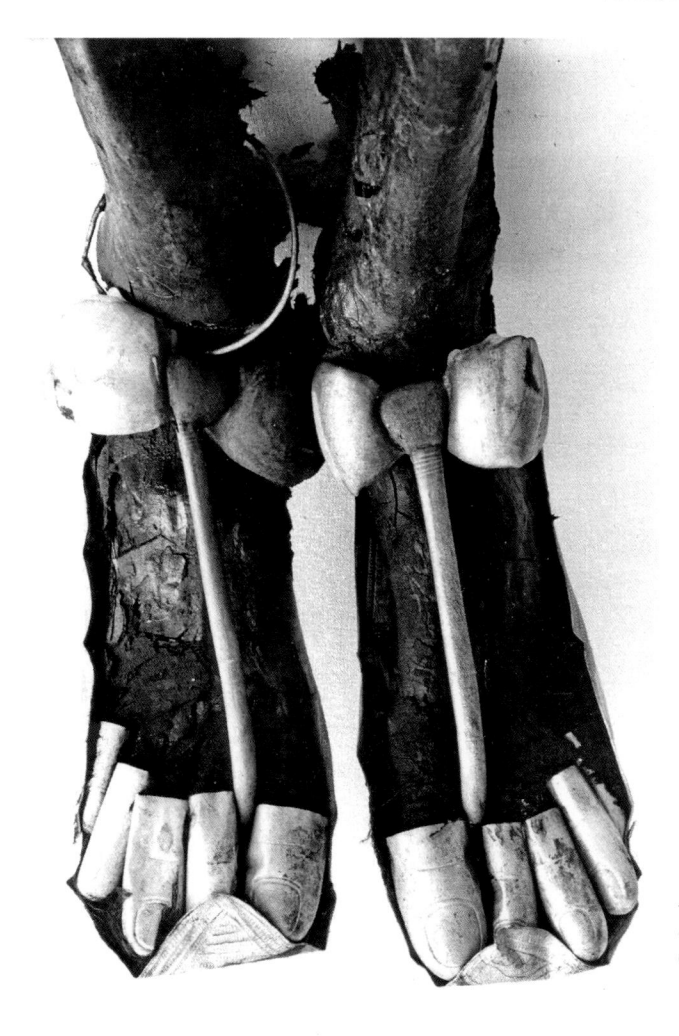

Figure 1.8. The gold sandals 256ll in situ on the mummy's feet. Photography by H. Burton. Copyright Griffith Institute, University of Oxford.

particularly unfortunate as the fluid, visible at the bottom nowadays (figure 2,1), is the result of post-excavation decay: no fluid is visible in Burton's photograph and both of the shoes are still in reasonable condition.

Sandal 367b was found in a wooden box in the Annexe. The box "rested on the top of a lot of baskets in front of the doorway [...], contained a quantity of miniature light and dark blue faience fore-legs of a bovine animal. In addition, thrown carelessly in, was an odd mixture of things: two crumpled-up gala robes, a pair of gloves, a pair [*sic*][8] of rush sandals, and a ritualistic turquoise-blue glass palette, which certainly did not seem to belong to the box." (Carter, 1933:

124). "The lid [was] found separate" (Card No. 367; figure 1.11). The pair of sewn sandals 373 was found on the floor of the Annexe, below the doorway, and is not visible in photographs (Card No. 373).

The pair of marquetry veneer sandals (397) was found in the Annexe (figure 1.12). "One of the sandals lying under basket 365 [...] but not visible in photos; the other sandal lying under basket 427 [...] also not visible in photos" (Card No. 397).

The strap complex 453b was found in the Annexe, next to box 453, which was "lying on [the] floor centre of southern end of [the] chamber between two alabaster vases Nos. 449 and 410" (Card No. 453). The strap

< *Figure 1.6. The right sandal 094a was found under the throne, which, in its turn, stood under the Toeris couch (137), not visible in the photograph, in the Antechamber. Photography by H. Burton. Copyright Griffith Institute, University of Oxford.*

< *Figure 1.7. The pair of sandals 104a & b was found near the entrance to the Annexe. Photography by H. Burton. Copyright Griffith Institute, University of Oxford.*

Figure 1.9 (left and below). Box 270 was the third in a series of five boxes, standing at the North side of the East and West axis of the Treasury, next to the Anubis on his shrine. Photography by H. Burton. Copyright Griffith Institute, University of Oxford.

Figure 1.10. Pair of open shoes 270a in situ in the box. Photography by H. Burton. Copyright Griffith Institute, University of Oxford.

complex is not visible in the photograph (figure 1.13).

The pair of fibre, sewn sandals 587c was found in box 587 in the Annexe "among a mass of miscellanea [in the] S.W. corner of [the] Chamber" (Card No. 587-1). According to Carter (Card No. 587-1), the roughly made wooden box, lacking its lid, contained besides the sandals, a leather cuirass, a faience thet-amulet and a violet ded-amulet (figure 1.14).

The entry 620 (119), 32 pair of fibre sandals, were scattered about the floor of the Annexe. It is not exactly clear how these were scattered; *i.e.* if they were still recognisable as pairs. The study of the objects reveals that several so-called pairs, were not pairs originally. There are several indications: one of a pair showing stitch holes for an insole but the other does not (4303). One pair consists of two left sandals (4307) and another pair of two right sandals (4289). In

> *Figure 1.11. The box in the Annexe with sandal 367b on top. Photography by H. Burton. Copyright Griffith Institute, University of Oxford.*

> *Figure 1.12. The pair of marquetry veneer sandals was found in the Annexe, under basket 365 and 427. The sandals are not visible in the photograph. Photography by H. Burton. Copyright Griffith Institute, University of Oxford.*

> *Figure 1.13. The strap 453b lay, in the Annexe, next to box 453 but is not visible in the photograph. Photography by H. Burton. Copyright Griffith Institute, University of Oxford.*

> *Figure 1.14. The heel of one of the pair of fibre, sewn sandals 587c in box 587 is just visible under the cuirass. Photography by H. Burton. Copyright Griffith Institute, University of Oxford.*

Context

Context

33

several pairs, the wear pattern clearly differs, which suggests that they do not belong together (*e.g.* 4301 and 4302). It is not clear whether this is because the excavators put two sandals, seemingly alike, together and registered them as a pair or that this happened already in antiquity. Remember that robbers entered the tomb at least twice; they might have thrown the fibre sandals out of their way in search for more precious items. The necropolis officials who cleaned up the mess might have put sandals of different pairs together, or, alternatively, did not bother to repack them and left them where they were, to be found by Carter so many centuries later. The latter explanation seems the most likely: why would the officials put two sandals together but still leave them scattered on the floor? We cannot entirely rule out the possibility that confusion of the items occurred after entering the museum, suggested by the '373-problem' mentioned above.

CHAPTER 2

PRESERVATION AND CONSERVATION

The condition in the tomb was particularly unfavourable for two types of organic materials: textiles and leather. According to Lucas (1927: 175-176) there had originally been "a considerable amount of leather in the tomb [...] but when found most of this leather was unrecognizable except from its position and chemical analysis, as it has become a black brittle, pitch like mass, parts of which at some period had been viscous[1] and had "run," and in several instances had dropped on to objects below, which it had cemented together. Judging from its position, what had been rawhide had perished more completely than tanned leather, thus the soles of sandals were in a worse condition than the upper parts. This destruction of the leather had been brought about by the combined heat and humidity of the tomb." (Quotation marks in original.) Carter (1933: 164) suggests "that the humid atmosphere created by [the] infrequent saturations caused chemical changes to take place among certain materials pertaining to the equipment – especially the leather and glues – which by process of evaporation deposited and formed this pink film [mentioned on p. 163] over everything." Some shoes were glued to each other and to other objects in the box in which they were found. Van Driel-Murray (2000: 303) explains the process of decay, saying that "In time, collagen and the oils and fats used in processing [oil curing] break down by hydrolysis in warm damp conditions (pH > 6.5) giving a black gelatinous mass, which dries to a glossy substance, resembling resin [...]." Moreover, and specifically of importance for the leather/metal shoes is that "Catalytic reactions with metals may cause similar gluey decay" (*Ibidem*). This especially seems to be the reason that so little is left of the soles whereas large parts of the leather upper are still present. It also explains why the back strap 453b, made partially of rawhide, is still largely intact and does not show signs of the black gelatinous mass, but rather the white yellowish colour, characteristic of this material.[2]

Additional damage to pairs 021f & g, 021k & l and 021h & i was caused by "their packing in the first place" (Carter & Mace, 1923: 170), showing "the metal toe-thong of one of the sandals [shoes 021f & g] had pierced right through its own leather sole and penetrated that of another which lay beneath it." (*Ibidem*: 135). The shoes 021k & l show a comparable condition. Also the leather sandals 270a suffered from their packing; the right one is still in the box in which it was found (figure 2.1). Note, however, that this is not the original situation in which the shoe was found (see section 1.1, *cf.* figure 1.10).

Carter and Lucas had sprayed the fibre, sewn sandals 104a with a solution of celluloid in amyl acetate (Card No. 104ab). The recovery of the pair of bead sandals 085a/147a was very problematic as the threading had rotted away for the most part. Carter & Mace (1923: 124) remark that, when lying on the floor, they looked in good condition, "but, try to pick one up, and it crumbled at the touch." So they treated the sandals on the spot "a spirit stove, some paraffin wax, an hour or two to harden, and the sandal could be removed intact."[3] The gold decoration of the pair of leather sandals with

35

Figure 2.1. The right open shoe of the pair 270a still lies in the box in which it was found by Carter. Note, however, that it was not exactly found like this: the open shoe was put in it (see text). See also figure 1.10. Photography by A.J. Veldmeijer. Courtesy of the Supreme Council of Antiquities / Authorities Egyptian Museum, Cairo.

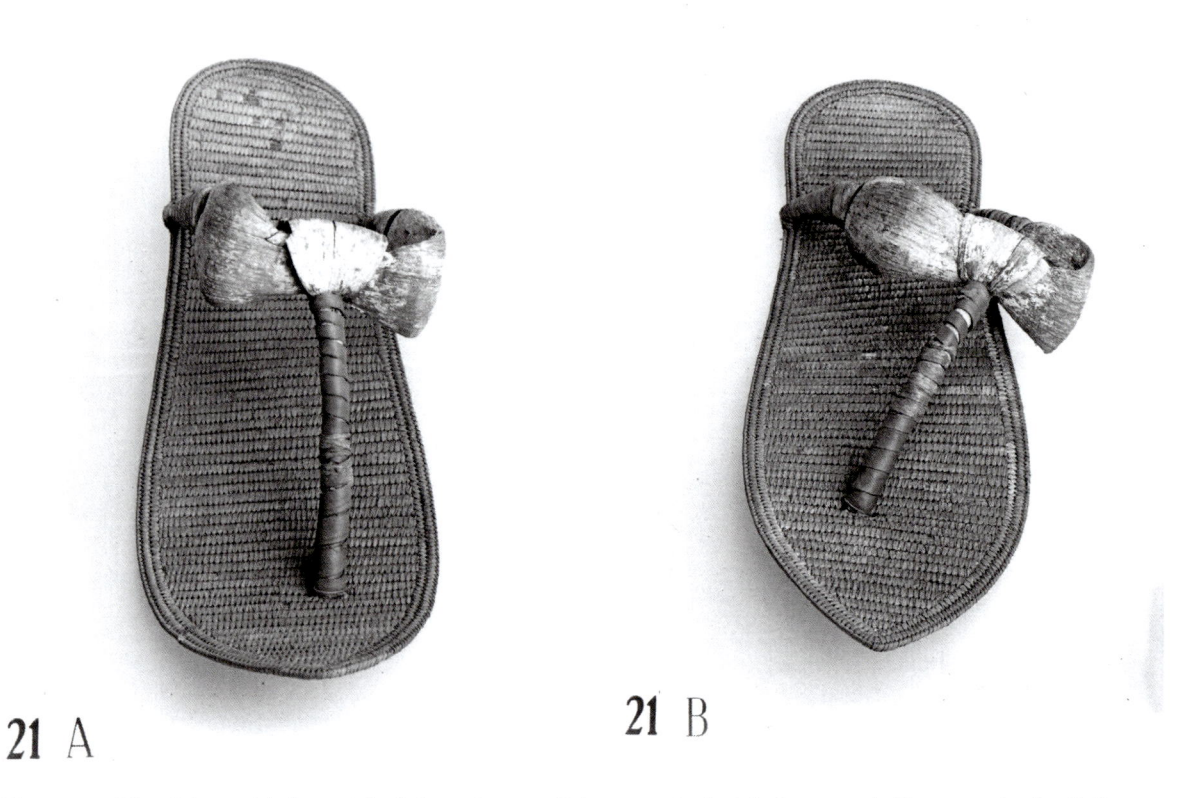

21 A   21 B

Figure 2.2. The right and left sandal of the pair 021a & b respectively (cf. figure 3.9). Photography by H. Burton. Copyright Griffith Institute, University of Oxford.

openwork decoration 021h & i were treated with a solution of Canada balsam in xylene, which was added to the "tops" by means of a pipette (Card No. 021i)[4] as were remains of heel and uppers of shoes 021f & g (Card No. 021f-20) and 021k & l (Carter & Mace, 1923: 170; Card No. 021k-26). The pair of fibre sandals 021a & b were only dusted off (Card No. 021ab). The condition of this pair, which were in excellent state when found, suffered quite a lot (figure 2.2, cf. figure 3.9). Although there are no comments about conservation related to the entry of 32 pairs of sandals, their current condition, being hard and inflexible, suggests treatment as stated for 104a.

After conservation, the footwear was packed for shipment to Cairo. The fragile specimens, such as the elaborately decorated shoes from box 021, were laid in bran (Carter & Mace, 1923: 176): the vegetable material was chopped to a very fine consistency (see figure 3.53). The objects were kept in classified groups.

The condition of especially the pieces which includes leather, viz. 021f & g (figure 2.3, cf. figure 3.62) and 021k & l (figure 2.4, cf. figure 3.67) and those of which consists mainly of leather, viz. 270a (figure 1.10, cf. figure 3.73) and 021h & i (figure 2.5, cf. figure 3.53) has worsened distinctly since they were recovered. If not stopped by conservation, the 'melting' of leather is continuous. Moreover, it is an irreversible process. But also the non-leather parts suffer. Numerous elements, such as the instep strap in pair 021k & l, have lost their coherence and lie loose on the soles. Moreover, the soles are

A

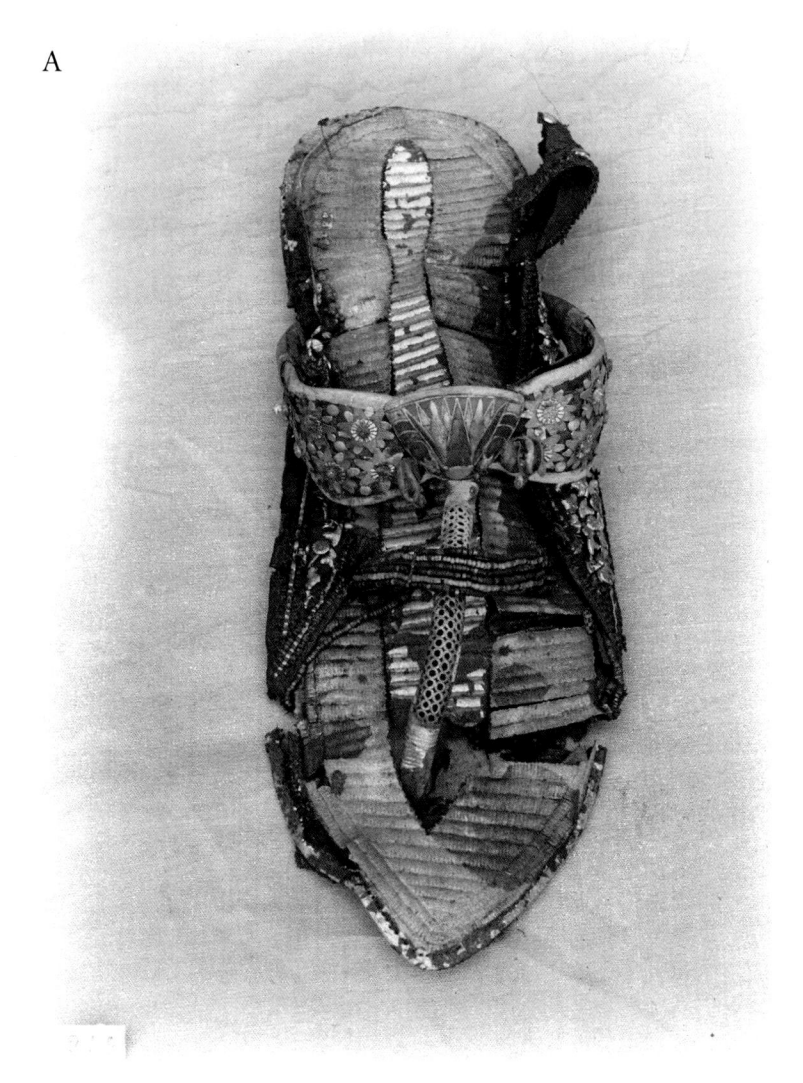

Figure 2.3A. Burton's overview photograph of open shoes 021f & g, and a detail (figure 2.3B, next page) taken shortly after one another. In figure 2.3A, the foot strap over the front strap is still intact; in the detail, however, the attachment is already broken (note also the many fragments lying around the shoe). Cf. figure 3.62. Photography by H. Burton. Copyright Griffith Institute, University of Oxford.

B

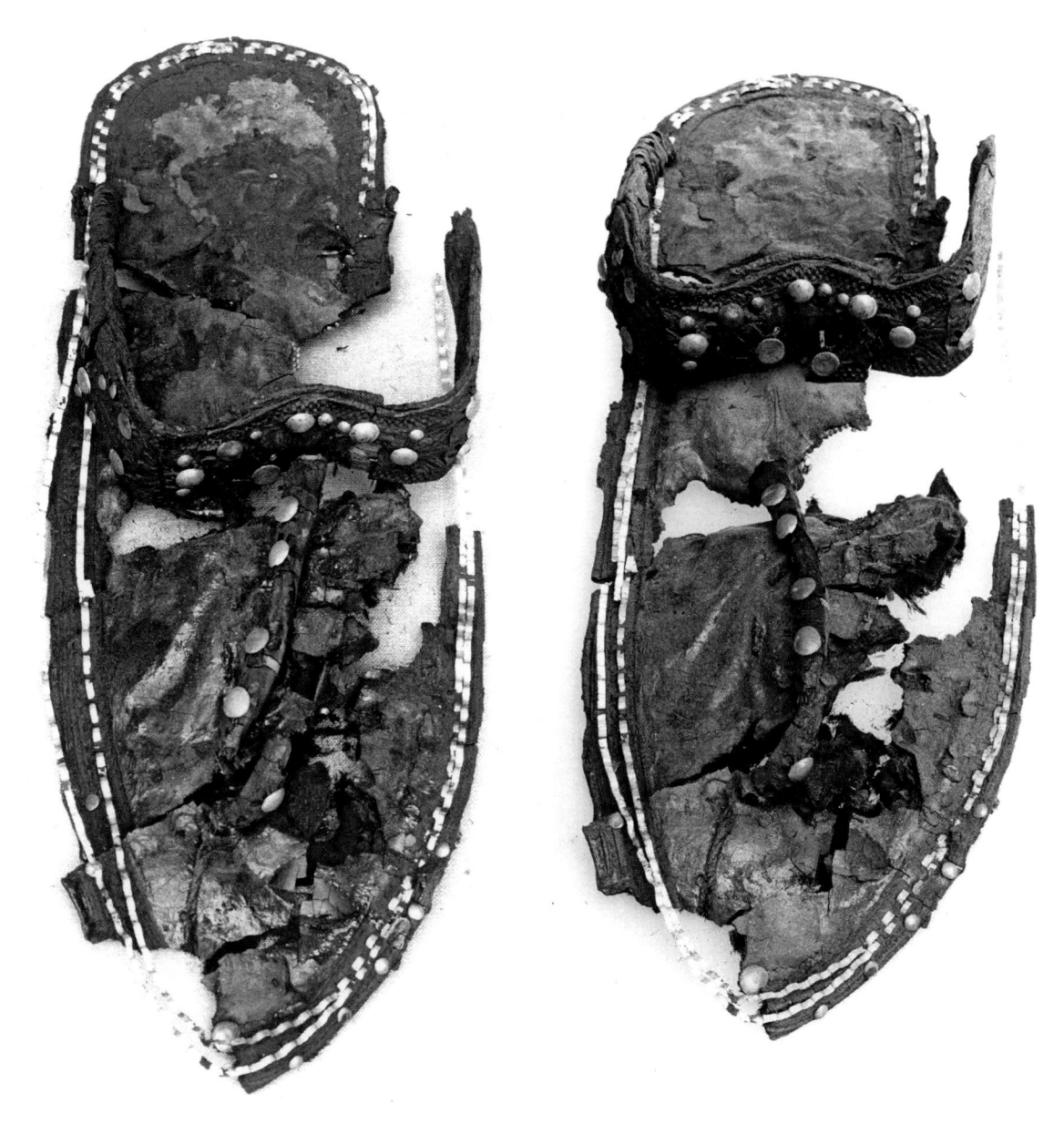

Figure 2.5. The leather sandals 021h & i already show deterioration immediately after recovery, visible in these two excavation photographs. Cf. figure 3.53. Photography by H. Burton. Copyright Griffith Institute, University of Oxford.

broken in several places and the upper has become almost entirely detached from the sole. The constant bumping into the showcase in the museum, the leaning against it etc., might be seen as an important factor of the shoes falling apart. Without any conservation and reinforcement (Carter has made it specifically clear that their treatment of the objects was only a first aid), they will continue to disintegrate: note, for example, that immediately after the recovery of pair 021f & g the foot strap was still in place

< Figure 2.3B. Detail of 023f & g. Cf. figure 2.3A (previous page). Photography by H. Burton. Copyright Griffith Institute, University of Oxford.

< Figure 2.4. Oblique dorsal view of the pair of open shoes 021k & l respectively as found by Carter. Cf. figure 3.67 and 3.68: many of the elements of the shoe (such as the foot strap) became loose after it was taken from the box; these are not shown in the excavation photograph of the shoes themselves. Photography by H. Burton. Copyright Griffith Institute, University of Oxford.

whereas in a photograph taken somewhat later, it had already lost its attachment to the shoe proper (figure 2.3).

The fibre sandals are stable, especially when they have been treated. Sandal 094a (figure 2.6, *cf.* figure 3.10) shows in Burton's photograph a complete, albeit slightly damaged, strap complex, which is nowadays entirely gone, save for some fibres of the front and back straps and both pre-straps. The sewing strips of the sole's transverse bundles show only slight damage since excavation. The sandal does not show signs of conservational treatment.

The condition of sandal 104a clearly worsened after excavation (figure 2.7, *cf.* figure 3.11). This might seem unlikely as the sandal was treated with a solution of celluloid in amyl acetate (Card No. 104ab), which was used for most other fibre sandals as well and with great success, but as ex-

plained previously, the condition of sandal 094a has worsened distinctly as well. The remnants of a transversely clad front strap, accompanying the sandal nowadays, does not belong to this sandal and is therefore not shown in figure 3.11.

Bead sandals 085a/147a (figures 1.3, 1.4 & 2.6) suffered enormously, but the condition of the 147a suffered especially: besides small damage, part of the heel broke off and the front strap, already broken when found by Carter and his team, has broken even further. Currently, the condition of the bead sandals is stable, which is due to the conservation.

The pair of marquetry veneer sandals (397) might have been treated too (personal observation together with Salima Ikram), but no records of this seems to exist.

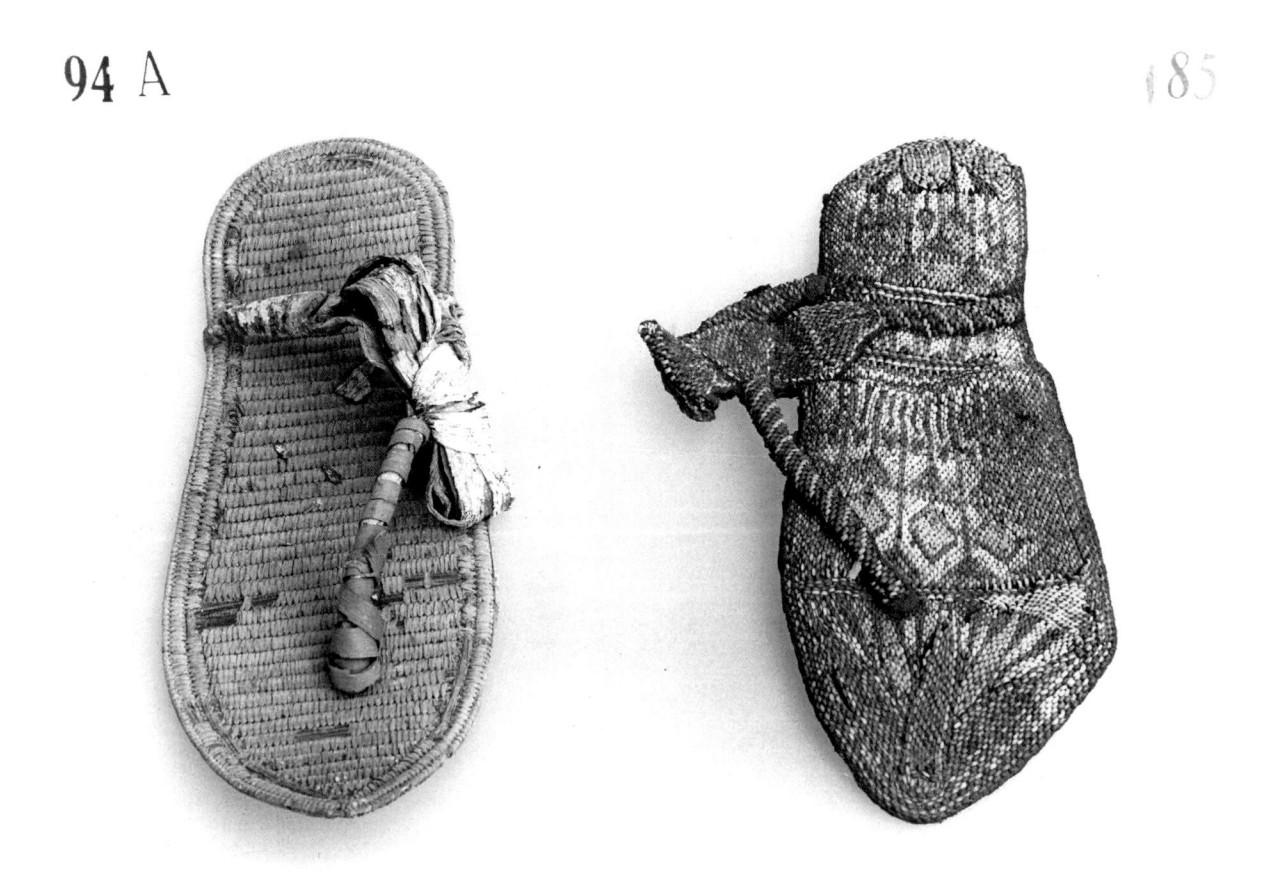

Figure 2.6. Sandal 094a (left) shortly after excavation. Cf. figure 3.10. To the right is bead sandal 85a (see figure 3.47). Photography by H. Burton. Copyright Griffith Institute, University of Oxford.

Figure 2.7. Sandal 104a, shortly after the recovery from the Antechamber. Cf. figure 3.11. Photography by H. Burton. Copyright Griffith Institute, University of Oxford.

CHAPTER 3

DESCRIPTION

3.1 INTRODUCTION

The category 'fibre, sewn sandals' is divided into four types (Veldmeijer, 2009a), which are referred to as Types A, B, C (all based on shape; figure 3.1) and D. Sewn sandals Type A have a rounded heel, constricted waist and expanded front, which terminates in a rounded toe. Lengthwise, they are symmetrical or nearly symmetrical and show no true indication of orientation (straight sole). Two variants are identified: plain soles (Variant 1) and soles with a leather treadsole (Variant 2).

Sewn sandals Type B have a rounded heel and a constricted waist from which, towards the front, the width expands. The lateral side, however, expands more distinctly

Figure 3.1. Artist impression of fibre, sewn sandals Type C. Drawing by M.H. Kriek.

than the medial side, which results in a pronounced big toe and thus the shape indicates the orientation of the foot for which the sandal is meant (swayed sole). Two variants are distinguished: Variant 1 is a plain sole and Variant 2 has a leather treadsole.

Sewn sandals Type C also have a rounded heel and constricted waist. Towards the front the width increases, but terminates in a pointed, (slightly) upturned toe part. Lengthwise, they are asymmetrical, and thus the sandals are swayed, but in general less clearly than those of Type B. Type C sandals can be divided into two variants: those with a plain sole (Variant 1) and those with a linen insole (Variant 2, only known from the tomb of Tutankhamun). There are many differences between the three types, besides their shapes, but in general one can say that Type C sandals are more refined than especially Type A in their manufacturing technology.

Type D sandals are typified by simulations of fibre, sewn textures in wood, metal, leather with plaster and gold foil, or a combination of these. Although some examples do not show a strong connection to one of the other types (for example some of Yuya's and Tjuiu's sandals, see below), usually, but not exclusively, Type D imitates Type C sandals.

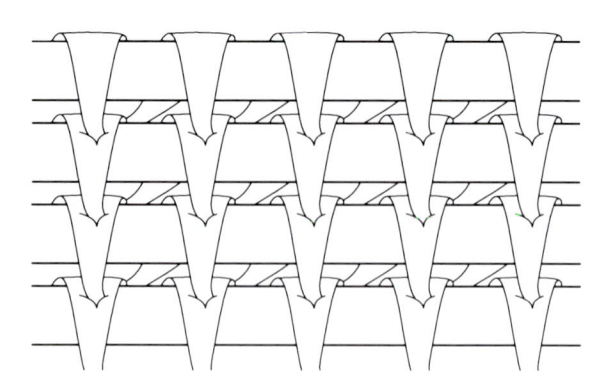

Figure 3.2. Construction drawing of the sewing technique in fibre, sewn sandals. Not to scale. Drawing by E. Endenburg / A.J. Veldmeijer.

3.2 SANDALS

All fibre sandals are Type C sewn sandals. The present work discusses the technology of the Type C sewn sandals in general terms, and with each individual sandal the description is limited to the condition together with deviating features. For a detailed account of the

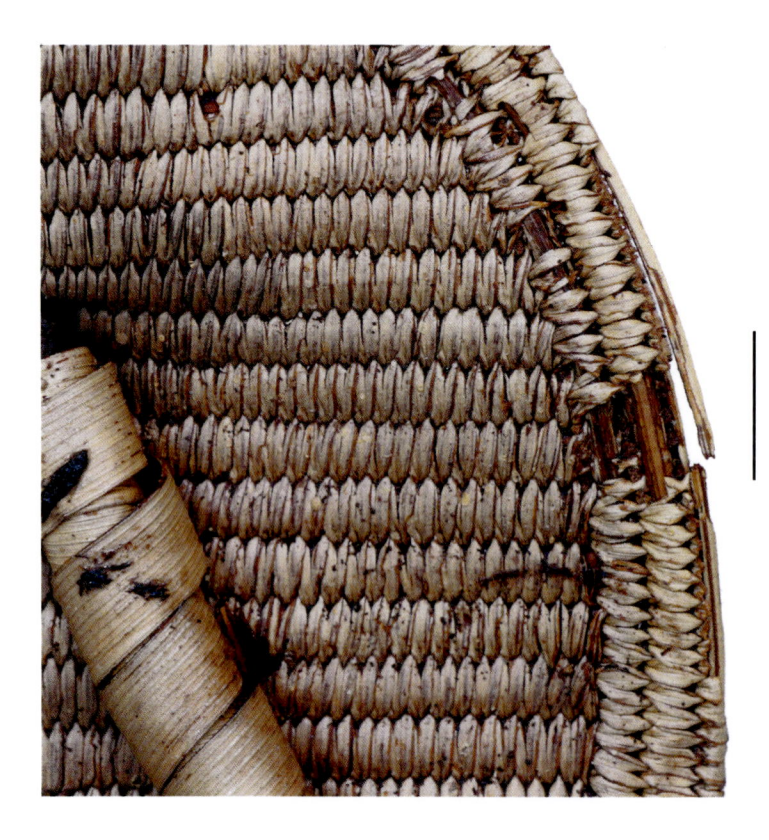

Figure 3.3. Detail of 1263, right, showing the triple edge along the perimeter of the sandal's transverse bundles. Usually, the innermost and middle rows sandwich the sole (cf. figure 3.4A). Scale bar is 10 mm. Photography by A.J. Veldmeijer. Courtesy of the Supreme Council of Antiquities / Authorities Egyptian Museum, Cairo.

technology of sewn sandals, the reader is referred to table 1, which summarises the technological details (see also Veldmeijer, 2009a). Except for Type D (imitations in other materials), the usual sewn sandals are made of transverse bundles of halfa grass (*Desmostachya bipinnata* or *Imperata cylindrica*),[1] which are sewn with strips of dom palm leaf (*Hyphaene thebaica*; figure 3.2). The perimeter of the sole proper is lined with an edge at right angles to the sole's fabric but in the same technique (*i.e.* cores, sewn with dom palm leaf; figure 3.3). In Tutankhamun's Type C sewn sandals and indeed likely in all other studied Type C sewn sandals,[2] the innermost and middle cores of the edge sandwich the sole (figure 3.4A). In the other types, only the innermost row sandwiches the sole's fabric dorsally and ventrally (figure 3.4B) whereas the middle one is placed against the sole's edge.

The strap complex consists of a looped pre-strap of palm leaf, which serves as reinforcement of the papyrus back strap. There is quite some variation in the length of the pre-strap, but in Tutankhamun's sewn sandals they are rather long and measure sometimes as much as 50.5 mm. In all sandals studied, the back strap is always pulled through the loop outside in.[3] The attachment of the back strap to the pre-strap is clad transversely with palm leaf strips (figure 3.5). Both are tied to the edge with the cladding (figure 3.6). The front strap is re-

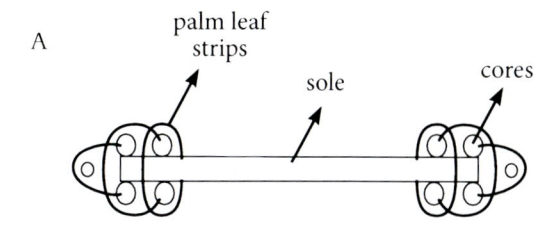

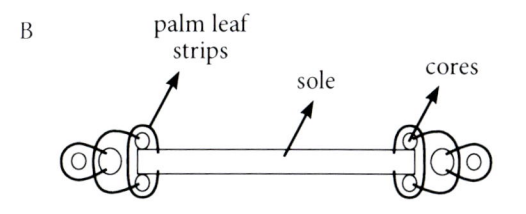

Figure 3.4. Edge construction in sewn sandals. A) In Tutankhamun's Type C sandals, as far as could be determined, the innermost and middle rows of the edge sandwiches the sole; B) In Type A and B sewn sandals, only the innermost row of the edge sandwiches the sole. Not to scale. Drawings by E. Endenburg / A.J. Veldmeijer.

ferred to as Type 5 (figure 3.7). It consists of a core of palm leaf, which is clad lengthwise with papyrus. Around this, a cladding of palm leaf is wrapped diagonally transverse. The front strap is inserted in a transverse slit in the sole, slightly off-centre to allow a good fit between the first and second toe. It is fastened at its ventral surface by means of a crown sinnet (figure 3.8). The inner core and papyrus cladding together form the crown sinnet. On the other end, the front strap is looped around the middle of the back strap (figure 3.7A). Although there

Figure 3.5. Detail of 587c(?), right. The papyrus back strap is pulled through the looped pre-strap (palm leaf). Scale bar is 10 mm. Photography by A.J. Veldmeijer. Courtesy of the Supreme Council of Antiquities / Authorities Egyptian Museum, Cairo.

Figure 3.6. Detail of 367b, showing the attachment of the pre/back strap by means of the cladding tied around the edge of the sole. Scale bar is 10 mm. Photography by A.J. Veldmeijer. Courtesy of the Supreme Council of Antiquities / Authorities Egyptian Museum, Cairo.

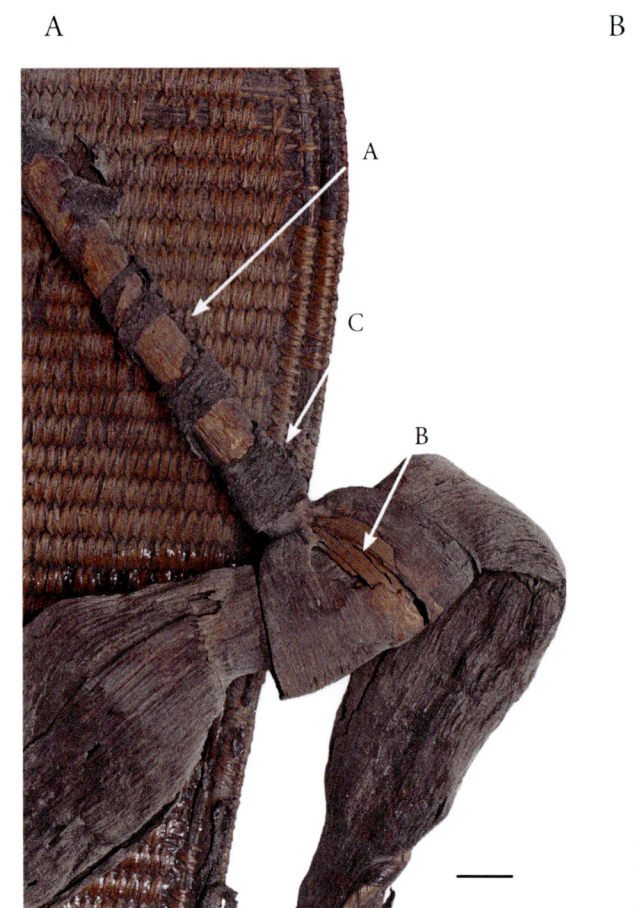

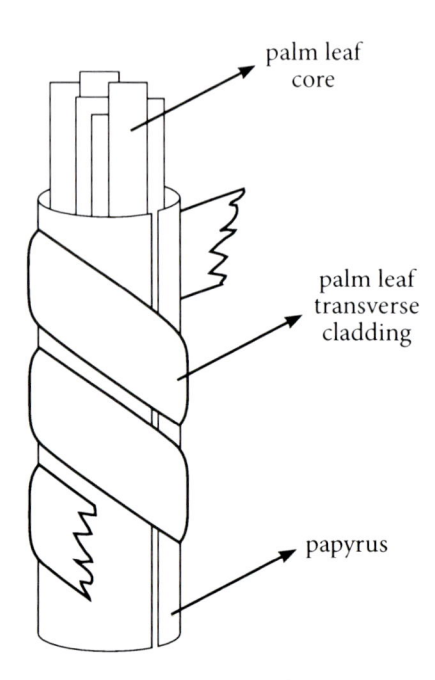

Figure 3.7. Front strap in Tutankhamun's sewn sandals. A) Detail of JE 62690, right. The front strap consists of a palm leaf core (A), a lengthwise papyrus cladding (B) and a transverse palm leaf cladding (C); B) Schematic drawing of the front strap. Scale bar is 10 mm. Photography by A.J. Veldmeijer. Courtesy of the Supreme Council of Antiquities / Authorities Egyptian Museum, Cairo. Drawing by E. Endenburg / A.J. Veldmeijer. Not to scale.

is variation in the front strap in terms of its core and cladding (Veldmeijer, 2009a), the basic construction is always the same; differences between the types are seen predominantly in the width of the straps.

After preparing the material, the grass bundles were made and the sewing could begin.[4] It seems unlikely that the bundles were cut to length individually. Instead, the bundles may have been cut to the approximate length, the shape of the sandal drawn on them (or indicated in another way) and then cut to fit the shape. It has been suggested (Veldmeijer, 2009a: 567-568) that it would have been more practical that the roughly cut bundles were sewn first and custom cut into the correct shape after fitting to the sole. This means that the stitches of the transverse bundles were left unfinished on the sides of the sandal and

A   B

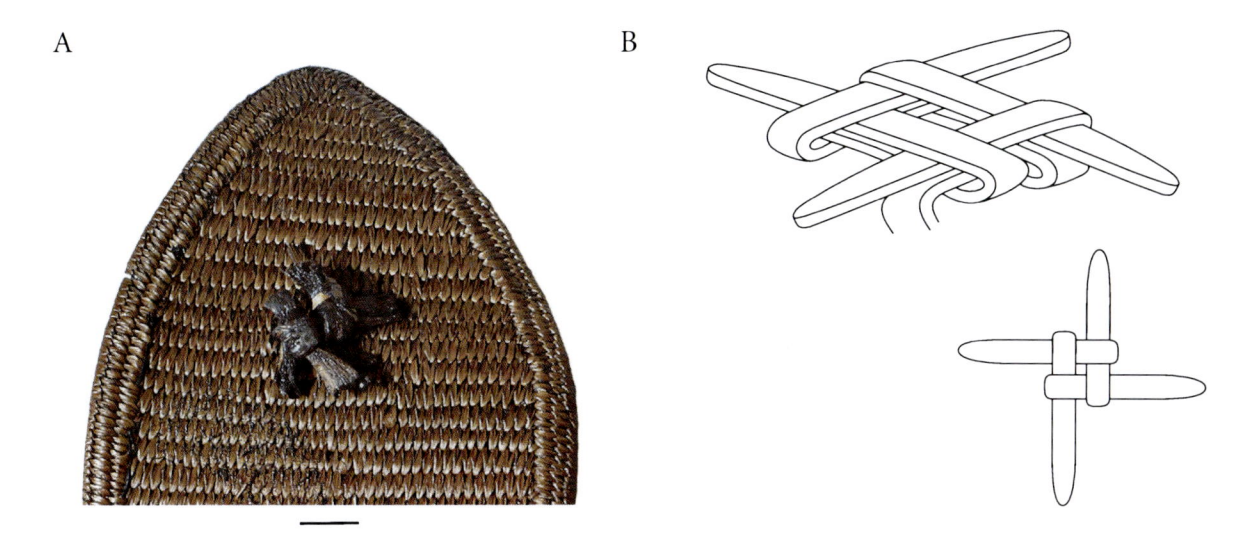

Figure 3.8. Fastening of the front strap. A) Detail of 4290, left, showing a largely intact crown sinnet at the ventral surface of the sole. Scale bar is 10 mm; B) Schematic drawing of a crown sinnet. Not to scale. Photography by A.J. Veldmeijer. Courtesy of the Supreme Council of Antiquities / Authorities Egyptian Museum, Cairo. Drawing by E. Endenburg.

secured by means of the innermost row of the edge, which, as described, consists of cores sandwiching the sole's edge dorsally and ventrally, followed by the rest of the edge. The sewing strip of one row was not used to continue sewing the next row, as the connections that would result from this method have not been observed. The point at which to stop sewing was estimated: at the edge, some stitches do not extend to the edge proper, exposing a small portion of the grass core (for example 4294bis in figure 3.24E). The sequence of construction is further suggested by the fact that the sewing strips of the edge are sometimes stitched through the sewing strips of the sole proper (see for example 4303 in figure 3.33C).

If the shape and measurement was marked, this may have been done with some sort of template[5] (which could also be a sandal or the other sandal of a pair) as the difference between the two sandals of a pair are usually negligible, especially in Types B and C.[6] Moreover, in a pair of sandals with swayed soles, they are always nearly perfect mirror image specimens.

In the final stage, the straps were attached: first the pre-strap[7] fastening to the sole (figure 3.6), followed by the attachment of the back strap (figure 3.5). Then the front strap, which was looped to the back strap (figure 3.7), was put through the sole and knotted (figure 3.8). Note that due to the thickness of the front strap, the opening between the bundles takes the shape of a slit. In Tutankhamun's Variant 2 sandals, however, the sole was first covered with the linen layer: the front strap goes through a hole in this layer, rather than the linen being laid down around it, which would have necessitated a cut. Moreover, at the back straps, the linen bulges due to the attachment of the straps, but this could also have occurred when the layer was added after the attachment of the back straps.

3.2.1 Sewn Sandals Type C

3.2.1.1 Variant 1

021a & b (2823; JE 62688; 911 [right] & 910 [left] respectively)

The pair, 021a being the right and 021b being the left one, is almost complete and are among the best made examples of sewn sandals from the tomb (figure 3.9A-C, table 1). Carter mentions that, besides "dusting off," they have not been treated (Card

Figure 3.9. Sewn sandals 021a & b. A) Left sandal in dorsal view; B) Right sandal in dorsal view; C) Right sandal in anterior view. Cf. figure 1.2A-E and 2.2A & B. Scale bar is 50 mm. Photography by A.J. Veldmeijer. Courtesy of the Supreme Council of Antiquities / Authorities Egyptian Museum, Cairo.

No. 021ab). The dorsal surface of the soles is intact save for some damage of the sewing strips. The sewing strips of the ventral surface show slight compression due to pressure from the owner's weight but are largely undamaged; the crown sinnet, which secures the front strap, is fibrous, which can be seen as an indication of friction with the ground. Due to the largely undamaged condition, it could not be established whether the middle row of the edge sandwiches the sole's fabric or not; the same is true for the material from which the cores are made.

The back strap in 021a is broken, showing on the medial side the complete pre-strap still *in situ* at the sole. On the lateral side, the pre-strap came off but it is still attached to the back strap. The lateral part of the back strap in 021b is detached from the pre-strap, which is still *in situ*; medially, the pre/back strap construction is intact, although the back strap and the cladding has shifted slightly, showing the lower part of the pre-strap. The back straps in both sandals show tiny holes, which are possibly due to insect activity. Note the light colour of the papyrus from which the back strap is made. This is the usual colour, seen in most preserved straps. However, sometimes the papyrus has turned a very dark brown, which must be due to the conservatives used, considering the fact that the discolouration is absent here. It is impossible to say whether the damage to the back strap is caused by wear or some other factor.

The front strap in 021b also shows a small length of cladding of a much darker colour, the edges of the strips of which are much damaged. Moreover, the cladding is rather loosened, which is not usually the case, as parallels suggest. It is possibly a remnant of an older cladding.

Vogelsang-Eastwood mentions (1994: 140), in the figure text of Burton's photograph of the left sandal, that the pair was covered with gold foil, but no indication has been found that confirms this statement. Moreover, Carter did not mention it, which he certainly would have done, as this would be a unique feature for this type of sandal: not one sewn sandal with a gold foil covering has yet been found (*cf.* Veldmeijer, 2009a). Vogelsang-Eastwood possibly interpreted the "white discoloration on papyrus parts" which Carter mentions (Card No. 021ab) as gold foil. Note that this discoloration is not visible nowadays.

094A (4284; 30 3 + 34 27; 3395; right)

Although the condition of this isolated right sandal is good (figure 3.10, table 1), it nevertheless shows, especially in the front third, damaged sewing strips at the dorsal surface. Damage to the sewing strips at the ventral surface occurs throughout. Moreover, the edge is rather damaged, especially but not exclusively, the innermost row.

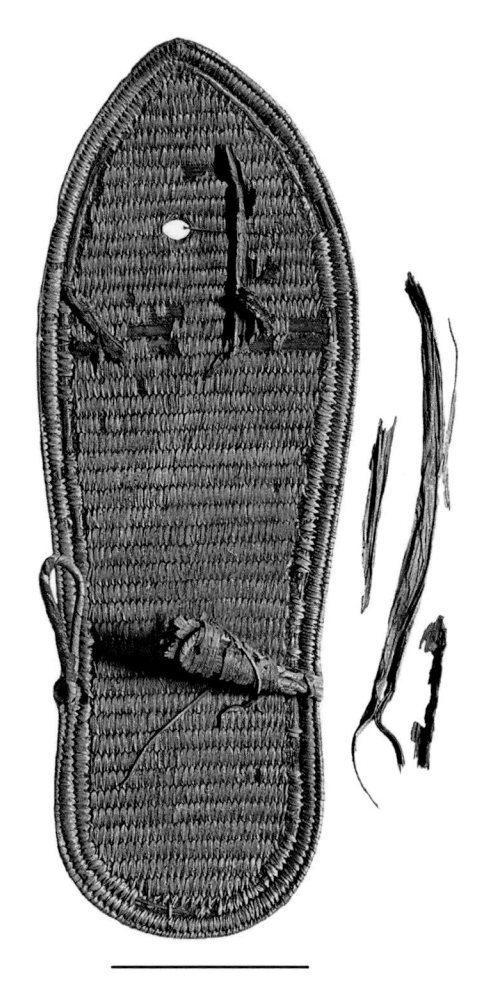

Figure 3.10. Right sandal 094a. Dorsal view. See also figure 2.6 left. Scale bar is 50 mm. Photography by A.J. Veldmeijer. Courtesy of the Supreme Council of Antiquities / Authorities Egyptian Museum, Cairo.

The strap complex is largely missing. The pre-straps, however, are intact, the lateral one of which still has the attachment of the back strap *in situ*, including parts of the cladding. The innermost of the three cores of the edge tapers slightly at the front (*cf.* for example 4285 in figure 3.16).

104a (4293bis; 30 3 + 34 45; 3413; left)

This left sandal (the right sandal was not kept, see above) is broken in two at about one third of its length (figure 3.11, table 1). Moreover, in several places the transverse bundles and their sewing strips are completely lacking and large areas go without the sewing strip (which is the case with the ventral surface as well). The edge is only intact for the larger part of the medial side of the sandal. The dorsal surface shows several black spots, which are remnants of 'melted' leather that had fallen on it. Note the slight curvature of the transverse rows at the heel.

The strap complex is largely missing, except for the intact pre-straps and two parts of the front strap (remarkably of different diameter and with a transverse palm leaf cladding of different width).

Although some places of the innermost row of the edge seem to show a core of palm, the majority of the cores consist of grass. The outermost core might have been made of grass as well.

587c(?) (2824; JE 62687; 1263)

There are no lists which link 587c with the exhibition number, the JE-number or the Temporary Number. We can, however, be certain that 1263 is not Carter's 373, as the dimensions do not fit the size stated on the card for 373. Most probably, the sandals with exhibition number 1263 are sandals 587c. The card for 587c does not give measurements.

The pair of sandals (figure 3.12, table 1) is of fairly small size, suggesting it was worn by the king when still young, possible around 10 years old. The dorsal surface of

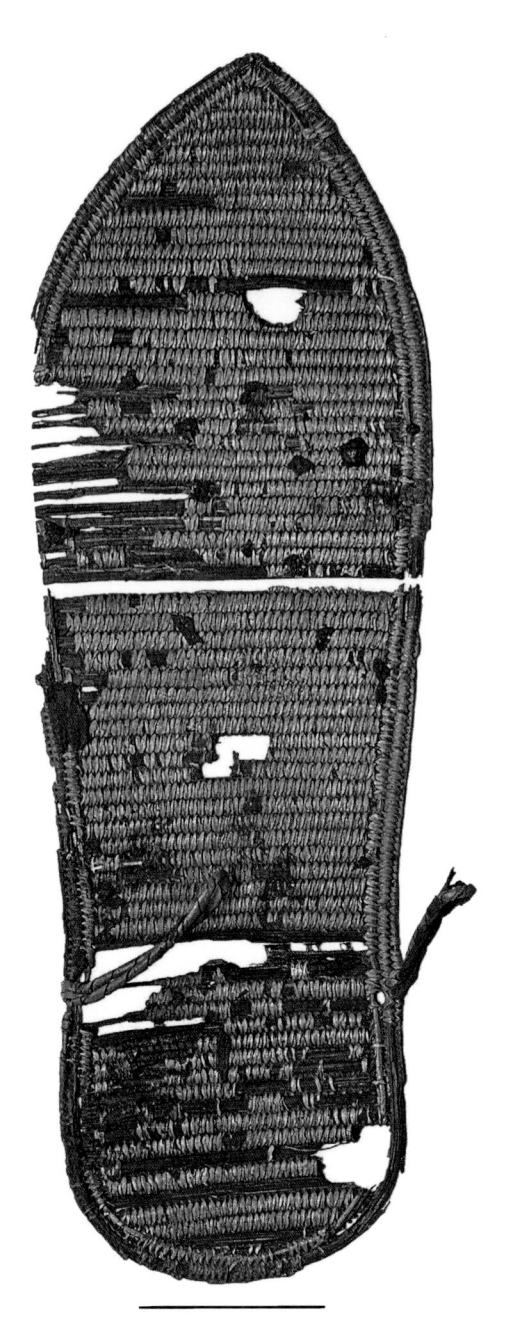

Figure 3.11. Sandal 104a in dorsal view. See also figure 2.7. Scale bar is 50 mm. Photography by A.J. Veldmeijer. Courtesy of the Supreme Council of Antiquities / Authorities Egyptian Museum, Cairo.

the right sandal in particular shows damage to the sewing strips, but it is restricted to three transverse rows and some isolated stitches. Several stitches of the ventral surface show damage but in the right sandal this is much less so than on the dorsal surface; the reverse is true for the left sandal. Large parts of the outermost rows of the edge of the right sandal lack the sewing strips entirely and occasionally the cores protrude.

A B C

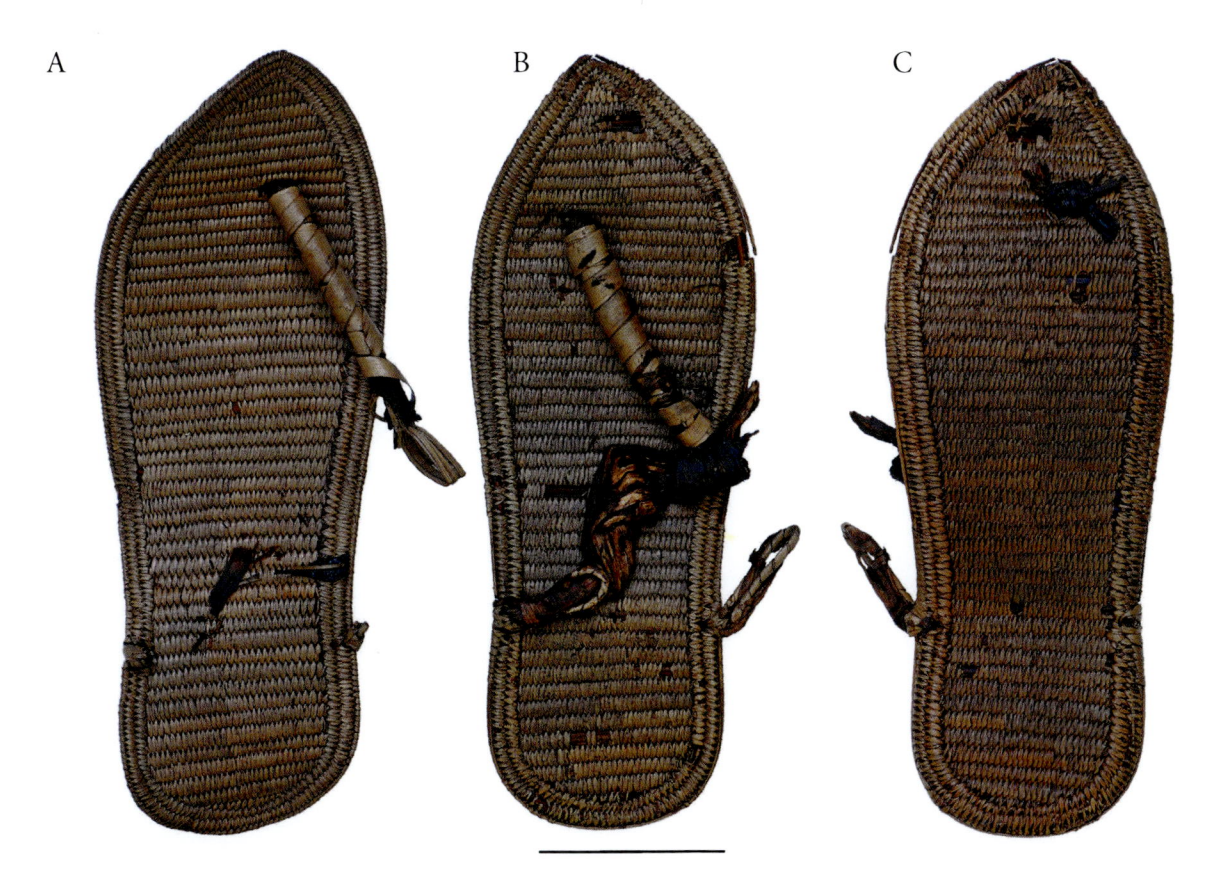

Figure 3.12. Pair 587c(?). A) Left sandal in dorsal view; B) Right sandal in dorsal view; C) Right sandal in ventral view. See also figure 3.5. Scale bar is 50 mm. Photography by A.J. Veldmeijer. Courtesy of the Supreme Council of Antiquities / Authorities Egyptian Museum, Cairo.

Less of the sewing strips of the inner two rows are lost, but there are still several damaged places. The core of the outermost row is possibly made of palm ("the fruit bearing stalks of the date-palm" Carter refers to on Card No. 373), but parts of it have been made of a narrow bundle of grass. The damaged state of parts of the edge suggests that the grass portions are repairs.

The strap complex in both sandals is incomplete. The left one lacks the pre- and back straps, but the attachment of the pre-strap to the sole is still *in situ*. The lengthwise cladding of (now darkly coloured) papyrus broke off before the attachment to the back strap. The loop of the palm leaf core for attachment with the back strap is largely intact. The transverse palm leaf cladding is largely complete, but loosened. Remnants of the original papyrus straps, probably originating from the back strap, still rests on the dorsal surface of the sole.

The strap complex of the right sandal is almost complete (see also figure 3.5), save for the lateral part of the back strap. The cladding of the pre/back strap attachment is largely lost, but remnants are still to been seen, the colour of which suggests it is also papyrus. The medial pre-strap is intact showing the attachment with the back strap being pulled through from outside inwards. The lengthwise papyrus cladding of the front strap is intact: the loop for the attachment to the back strap is still *in situ*. Also the transverse cladding is still largely intact, albeit loosened.

JE 62689 (620 (119); left)[8]

The toe part of this left sandal (figure 3.13A, table 1) is still bent in an upward position. The sewing strips of the dorsal surface show damage in various places, which is most prominent in the front half. The sew-

Description

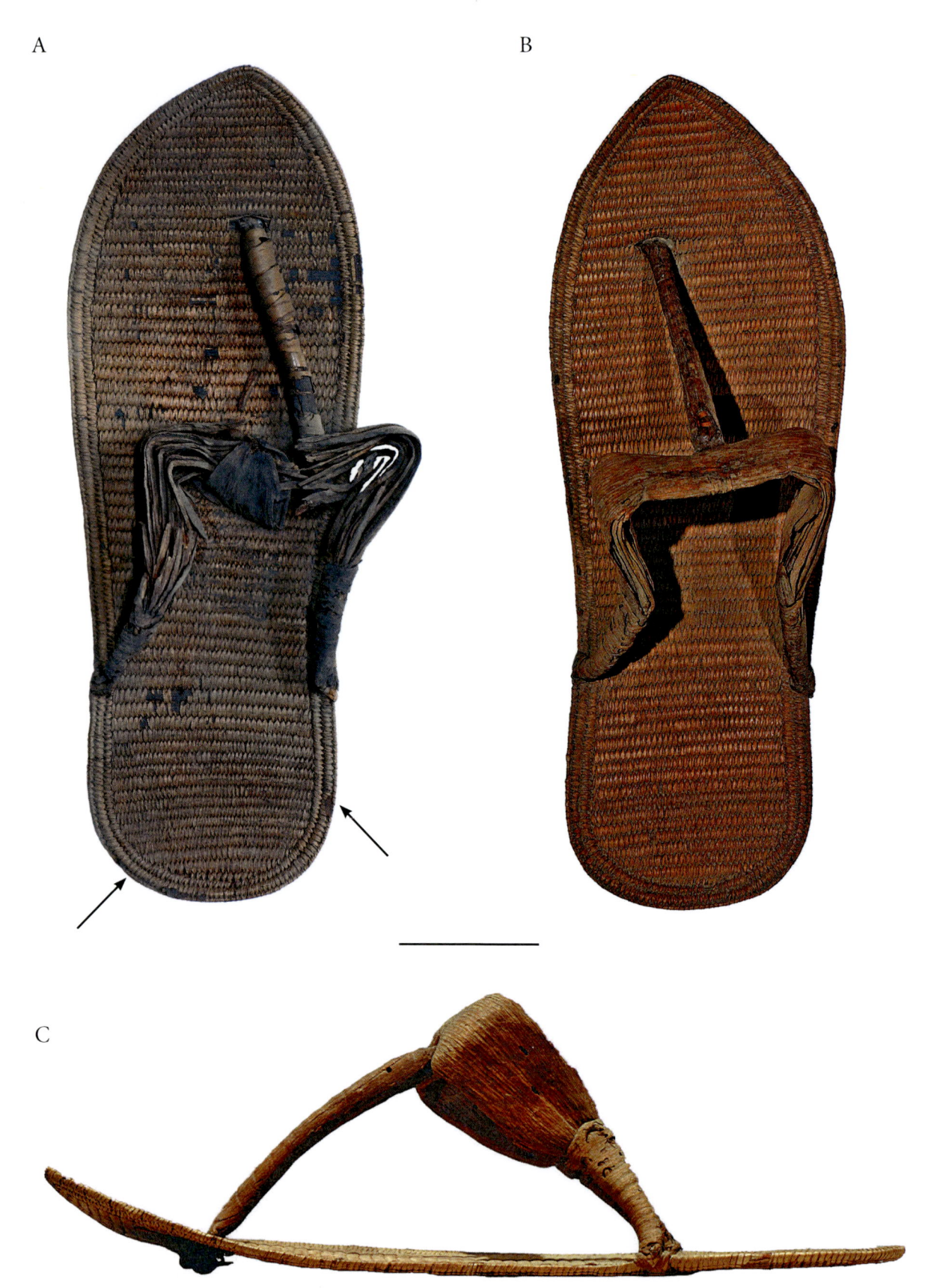

A

B

C

52

D

E

Figure 3.13. Pair JE 62689. < A) The left sandal in dorsal view; < B) The right sandal in dorsal view; < C) The right sandal in medial view; D) The right sandal in anterior view; E) Detail of the edge of the right sandals, showing remnants of flax stitches. The right sandal is discussed in section 3.2.1.2. Note the difference in colour between the left and right sandal (cf. figure 3.14). The left sandal is housed in the Egyptian Museum, Cairo; the right one in the Luxor Museum. Scale bar A-D is 50 mm; scale bar E is 10 mm. Photography by A.J. Veldmeijer. Courtesy of the Supreme Council of Antiquities / Authorities Luxor Museum and Authorities Egyptian Museum, Cairo.

ing strips of the ventral surface show comparable damage to the other sandals, *i.e.* it is only minor.

The strap complex is complete, albeit damaged. The front strap is still *in situ* in the slit in the sole, the crown sinnet of which secures it at the ventral surface.

Although the right sandal shows, as described below, clear indications of an insole (stitch holes and flax stitches), the left one does not. However, at the medial edge of the heel are small patches of finely woven textile fabric (arrows in figure 3.13A). Another scrap can be seen on the opposite side, albeit slightly more towards the posterior-most edge of the heel. Although no attachment could be identified, the fact that no other sandals have (patches of) textile attached seems to suggest that the patches in the sandal are not due to post-depositional circumstances but original.

The completeness of the edge prohibits identification of the cores. However, a small damaged spot suggests that the outermost is made of palm and the middle one consists of grass.

JE 62690 (620 (119); left and right)[9]

The left sandal (figure 3.14A-C, table 1) is in good condition and only shows some damage of the sewing strips on the dorsal surface of the outermost row at the edge of the heel. The ventral surface shows slight damage of the sewing strips. The condition of the right sandal (figure 3.14D) is slightly worse, showing several spots of damaged sewing strips, especially on the front part. The ventral surface is slightly damaged.

In the left sandal, the front strap is largely complete, although the transverse cladding is fragmentary. The papyrus loop for the attachment to the back strap is incomplete as well. As always, the front strap is inserted into the sole, but here the anterior side bulges slightly (figure 3.15), due to the weight of the owner, pushing the sole down and forward onto the crown sinnet, the shape

A

Figure 3.14. Pair JE 62690. A) The left sandal in anterior view; B) The left sandal in dorsal view; > C) The left sandal in lateral view; D) The right sandal in dorsal view. The right sandal is housed in the Egyptian Museum, Cairo; the left one in the Luxor Museum. Scale bars are 50 mm. Photography by A.J. Veldmeijer. Courtesy of the Supreme Council of Antiquities / Authorities Luxor Museum and Authorities Egyptian Museum, Cairo.

B

D

C

Figure 3.15. The bulging of the sole due to the pressure from the weight of the owner on the crown sinnet. Scale bar is 10 mm. Photography by A.J. Veldmeijer. Courtesy of the Supreme Council of Antiquities / Authorities Luxor Museum.

of which shows in the sole's fabric. This indication of a sandal's use is not often seen (other sandals showing this feature are JE 62689, 4286, 4287). Note the strongly upturned front, which is caused by pulling the front strap before fastening it to the back strap (the right sandal still shows this condition too).

The front strap of the right sandal is largely complete (palm leaf core and lengthwise cladding with papyrus), but the transverse cladding is largely incomplete and has turned into a black substance, which makes identification nearly impossible. However, the remnant close to the sole shows a textile structure. Its condition is comparable to that of the decorated textile insole of sandal 2816 (see section 3.2.1.2), and its deterioration therefore seems to be due to the conservatives used. The remnants at the attachment of the pre/back straps might be remnants of the textile insole, or perhaps more likely remnants of the cloth covering the straps. Although in other examples (JE 62689) the edge shows tiny stitch holes (nearly) throughout, this sandal seemingly lacks stitch holes and therefore a textile insole is unlikely; instead, the cloth might be a repair of the transverse cladding.

In the left sandal, the core of the outermost edge row consists of palm; the two inner rows are too intact to identify the material. Probably, these inner cores both sandwich the sole's fabric. The two inner cores of the edge on the right sandal are made of grass and both sandwich the sole.

The pre/back strap in both sandals is complete, although the cladding of the attachments shows some damage. Due to the completeness, it could not be established with certainty that the back strap is pulled through the pre-strap in the left sandal, but most likely it is as this construction is used in the right one.

| A | B |

4285 (620 (119); 30 3 + 34 19B [left] & 30 3 + 34 19A [right]; 3387)

The soles of this pair (figure 3.16, table 1) are intact, save some damaged sewing strips on the ventral surfaces in particular. In the right sandal, the edge has a small damaged spot on the medial side, close to the toe part. The bundles in the heel of the right sandal are slightly curved rather than exactly transverse. Moreover, the diameter of the various rows differs in the right one; in the left these measurements are nearly equal. There is also a distinct difference in the sewing of the two sandals, though not in the technique. The sewing of the right sandal is much closer and tighter than in the left sandal. Together with the slight differences in dimensions of the sandals, it seems likely the two were not a pair originally.

| C | D |

The left sandal lacks the strap complex entirely, but the attachments of the pre/back strap to the outer two rows of the edge are still present. Note that, on the lateral side, the outer row turns slightly inwards at the attachment, which is due to the tight tying of the straps to the edge. In the right sandal, the lateral pre-strap is still *in situ*, including the remnants of the back strap, which shows that the latter was pulled through the pre-strap outside in. The medial pre-strap is detached but still there.

The intact condition of the edges prohibits a clear view, but the core of the innermost two edges in at least the left sandal sandwiches the sole. The diameter of the three rows in the right one vary more than in the left. The innermost row of the edge tapers towards the front, ending in a sharper point than the perimeter of the sandal itself. This is often seen and seems to be due to the material used rather than an intended feature.

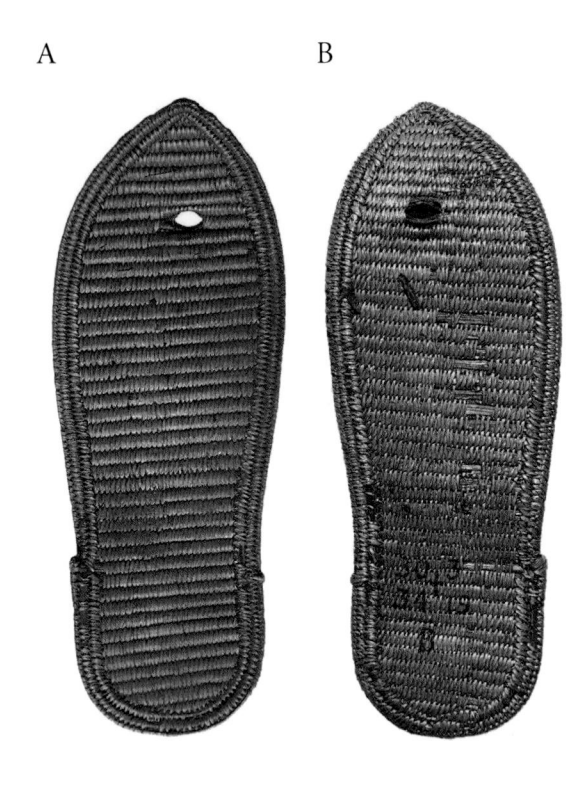

Figure 3.16. Pair 4285. A) Dorsal view of the left sandal; B) Ventral view of the left sandal; C) Ventral view of the right sandal; D) Dorsal view of the right sandal. Scale bar is 50 mm. Photography by A.J. Veldmeijer. Courtesy of the Supreme Council of Antiquities / Authorities Egyptian Museum, Cairo.

4286 (620 (119); 30 3 + 34 26A; 3394; right)

The right sandal 4286 (figure 3.17, table 1) is in good condition, showing no damage of

Figure 3.17. Dorsal view of the right sandal 4286. Scale bar is 50 mm. Photography by A.J. Veldmeijer. Courtesy of the Supreme Council of Antiquities / Authorities Luxor Museum.

the sewing strips on the dorsal surface, save for an isolated spot anterior to the front strap. The edge, however, is less complete and in various spots, especially on the medial side, the outermost row of the edge is missing.

The sandal is meant for the right foot, judging from the position of the front strap (slightly closer to the medial edge than to the lateral edge), but as in 4287 (see below), the position of the insertion is rather central. The quality of manufacturing is less than for the other sandals and is also comparable to 4287, where the width within a single transverse row also differs but less so. Moreover, the heel is rounded, rather than square. On the other hand, the difference in position of the medial and lateral pre-strap attachment is more substantial, and here not due to distortion of the sole. The heel part is slightly upturned, which seems to be due to post-depositional processes.

The knot that usually secures the front strap on the ventral surface of the sole is lost but the loop for the attachment to the back strap is still largely complete. The loop includes some scraps from the back strap. From lateral or medial view, the front strap shows a distinct bend at approximately a quarter of its length (seen from the sole) due to the fact that the inner core is broken. The transverse cladding is loosened. Again, a bulging of the area anterior to the insertion of the front strap can be seen (as in 4287, JE 62689, JE 62690; *cf.* figure 3.15), but far less distinct. The attachments of the pre/back strap to the sole are present.

The core of the innermost row on the edge might be made of grass with the outermost row of palm. Note that the intact condition together with the conservatives used prohibits a clear view.

4287 (620 (119); 30 3 + 34 24B; 3392; right)

4287 (figure 3.18, table 1) is a small-sized right sandal for Tutankhamun when he was about 10 years old. The sandal is in fairly good condition although several sewing strips on the dorsal surface are damaged. The ventral surface is intact. The sandal shows slight distortion on the lateral side at about the halfway mark along its length, which is possibly caused by post-depositional processes.

The sandal is less well made compared to much of the material found in the tomb. The transverse rows are roughly sewn, showing differences in width. At the heel especially, the rows are not transverse but slightly diagonal, which is also due to the fact that the width of a single row differs from the medial to lateral side of the sandal. Moreover, the sandal is a right sandal, judging by the position of the front strap, but its insertion in the sole is rather centred, albeit still slightly closer to the medial than to the lateral edge. The edge of the heel is square, rather than rounded, which seems to be the result of less care taken in making the san-

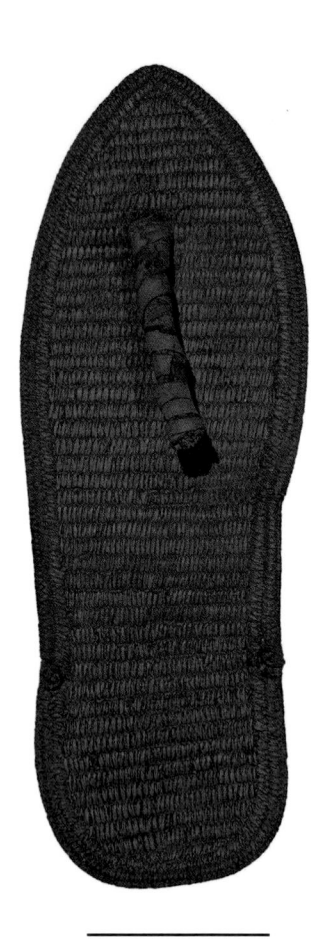

Figure 3.18. Dorsal view of the right sandal 4287. Scale bar is 50 mm. Photography by A.J. Veldmeijer. Courtesy of the Supreme Council of Antiquities / Authorities Luxor Museum.

dal. Note the decrease in width of the first row of the edge at the heel. The core of the outermost row of the edge consists of palm; the two inner rows are too intact to allow identification of the material.

The front strap lacks the loop for the attachment to the back strap. Moreover, the transverse cladding has loosened. As in JE 62689, JE 62690 and 4286, the shape of the crown sinnet that secures the front strap is visible as an impression from the ventral side of the sole, resulting in slight bulging of the sole's fabric anterior to the insertion of the front strap (*cf.* figure 3.15). The position of the attachment of the pre-straps to the sole is not quite symmetrical but this is possibly due to the above-mentioned distortion. These are the only remnants left of the pre/back strap.

4288 (620 (119); 30 3 + 34 22A [left])
& 30 3 + 34 22B [right]; 3390)

The damage to the sewing strips of the pair (figure 3.19, table 1) is mainly restricted to the dorsal surface but is, however, more severe in the right than the left sandal. The damage to the edges on the ventral surfaces is slightly more prominent than on the dorsal surfaces. Also, the right sandal has a damaged posterolateral edge and so lacks the two outer cores.

The strap complex is missing in both, but the right sandal has the lateral pre-strap still *in situ*, including part of the cladding. Remnants of the strap complex of the left one are concreted to the dorsal surface roughly between the attachments of the pre/back strap to the sole. Note the indentation of the edge at the attachment of the lateral pre/back strap in the left sandal, which is caused by the severe pulling of the strip. This is also visible at the medial edge of the right one but to a lesser extent. It is unclear what was used as the core material for the innermost row of the edge.

4289 (620 (119); 30 3 + 34 21A [right]
& 30 3 + 34 21B [right]; 3389)

The two sandals (figure 3.20, table 1) are registered as a pair, but are not truly a pair as they are both right sandals. Sandal 30 3 + 34 21B is broken in two just anterior of the front strap slit. A large part of the edge is damaged; it is entirely absent along the lateral side for about one third of the length (seen from the heel). Also on the posterolateral edge a small section is damaged, showing only the cores. The damage to the sewing strips is severe, especially on the front half. The other sandal, 30 3 + 34 21A, is better preserved. The dorsal surface of the sole also shows, however, damage to the sewing strips, which is predominantly restricted to the front half. The damage of the sewing strips on the ventral surfaces is negligible.

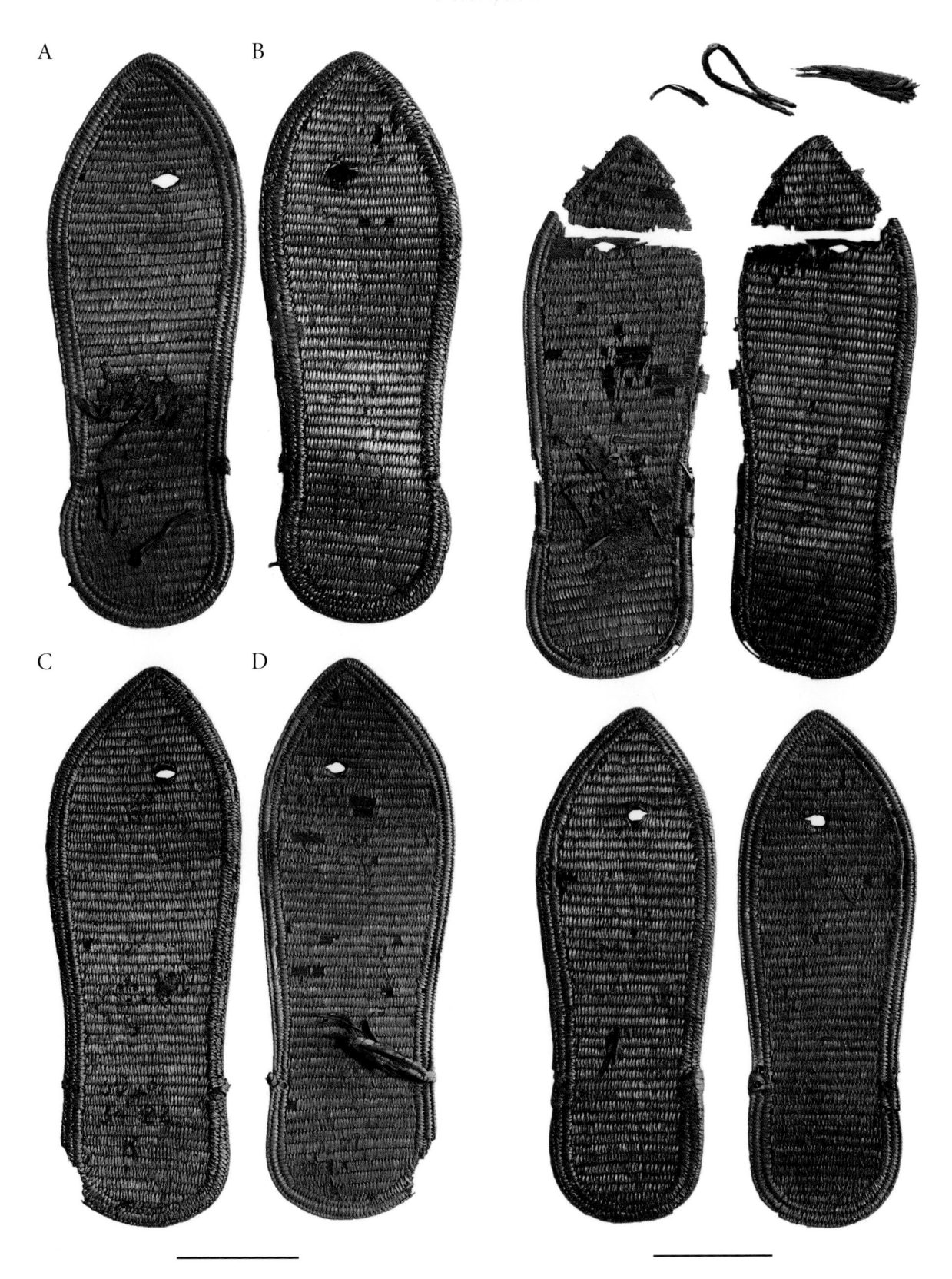

Figure 3.19. Pair 4288. A) Dorsal view of the left sandal; B) Ventral view of the left sandal; C) Ventral view of the right sandal; D) Dorsal view of the right sandal. Scale bar is 50 mm. Photography by A.J. Veldmeijer. Courtesy of the Supreme Council of Antiquities / Authorities Egyptian Museum, Cairo.

Figure 3.20. 'Pair' 4289. Dorsal and ventral view and ventral and dorsal view respectively of the two sandals, which are both for the right foot. Scale bar is 50 mm. Photography by A.J. Veldmeijer. Courtesy of the Supreme Council of Antiquities / Authorities Egyptian Museum, Cairo.

Only very small scraps remain of the strap complex, including one detached pre-strap of 30 3 + 34 21B and a portion of the back strap. The core of the innermost row of the edge consists, as in the middle row, of grass although some parts might be palm. If so, this could be an indication of repair.

4290 (620 (119); 30 3 + 34 23A [left] & 30 3 34 23B [right]; 3391)

Both sandals (figure 3.21, table 1) show some damage of the sewing strips on the dorsal surface, but it is more severe in the right one and occurs on the dorsal surface predominantly. Both sandals have patches of black material on their dorsal surfaces, which are the remnants of the discoloured papyrus strap complex.

The front strap in the right sandal is entirely preserved, except for the attachment to the back strap. The transverse cladding is slightly loosened. Of the back strap, a large fragment of the medial side, including the pre-strap, is still *in situ*. The lateral pre-strap is present, but detached; however, it still shows the attachment with the back strap, which is pulled through the pre-strap loop outside in. The strap complex in the left sandal is largely intact, but its condition suggests wear. The transverse cladding is, as in the right one, slightly loosened. The fastening of the back strap to the pre-strap is also loosened. Both sandals show an intact crown sinnet on the ventral surface.

A deviant detail is seen on the ventral surface of the right sandal. Here, a fragment of the palm core of the innermost row of the lateral edge comes out of the stitches and is attached with only several stitches over a short distance (arrow in figure 3.21C; figure 3.21E).

4291 (620 (119); 30 3 + 34 20B [left] & 30 3 + 34 20A [right]; 3388)

These are a well made pair of sandals (figure 3.22, table 1). The sewing strips in the left sandal show some damage at various points, the most substantial being at the heel where a small piece of core is gone, thus creating a hole. The ventral surface is less damaged. The dorsal and ventral surfaces of the right one are intact, except for the sewing strips of two transverse bundles on the ventral surface, which are entirely lost. The right sandal has a large tear on its lateral edge, ending in the slit for the front strap attachment. Moreover, the sole is not flat anymore but wavy.

Nothing is left of the front straps. Note, however, the relatively large, almond-shaped slit for the insertion of the front strap in the right sandal. Although most of Tutankhamun's sandals show much smaller holes, several have a comparably big hole to this one. Both sandals lack the pre/back strap, although the lateral pre-strap of the left sandal is still there; only the base of the medial pre-strap is preserved. The attachments of the pre/back straps are the only remnants that are preserved in the right sandal.

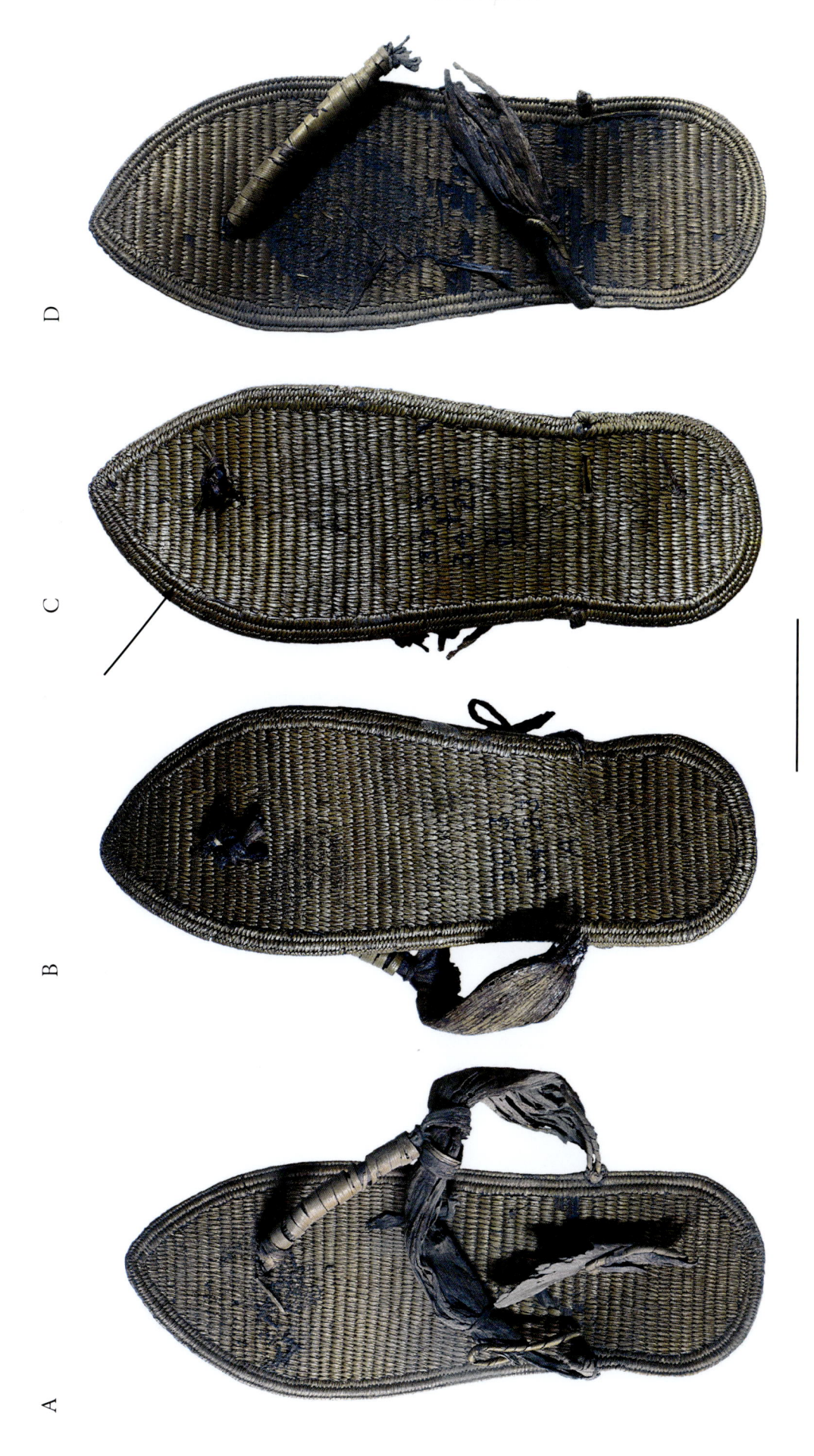

Figure 3.21. Pair 4290. A) Dorsal view of the left sandal; B) Ventral view of the left sandal; C) Ventral view of the right sandal; D) Dorsal view of the right sandal; E (previous page): Right sandal. A fragment of the palm core of the innermost row of the lateral edge protrudes from the sewing strips and is included in several stitches. Scale bar is 50 mm. Photography by A.J. Veldmeijer. Courtesy of the Supreme Council of Antiquities / Authorities Egyptian Museum, Cairo.

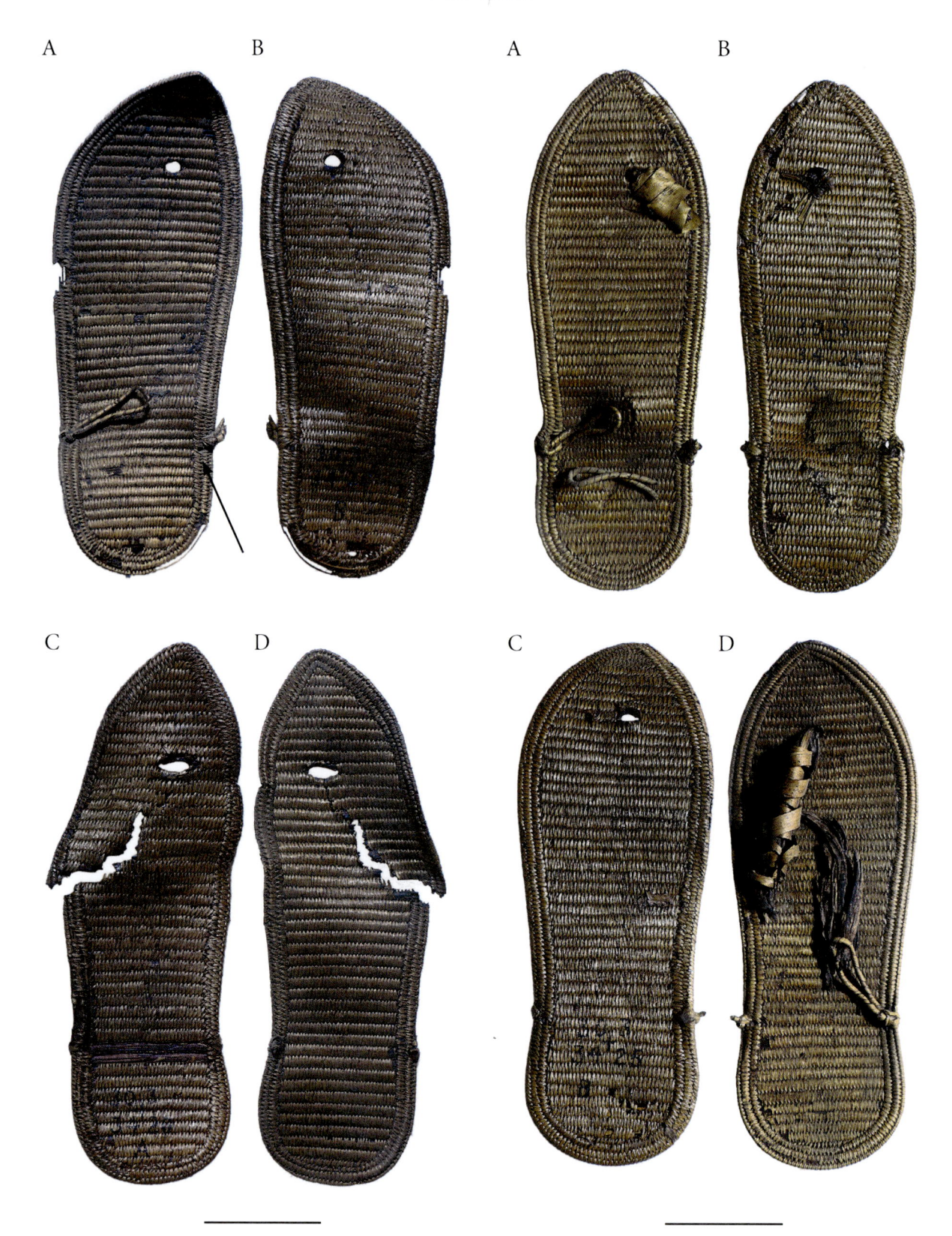

Figure 3.22. Pair 4291. A) Dorsal view of the left sandal; B) Ventral view of the left sandal; C) Ventral view of the right sandal; D) Dorsal view of the right sandal. Scale bar is 50 mm. Photography by A.J. Veldmeijer. Courtesy of the Supreme Council of Antiquities / Authorities Egyptian Museum, Cairo.

Figure 3.23. Pair 4292. A) Dorsal view of the left sandal; B) Ventral view of the left sandal; C) Ventral view of the right sandal; D) Dorsal view of the right sandal. Scale bar is 50 mm. Photography by A.J. Veldmeijer. Courtesy of the Supreme Council of Antiquities / Authorities Egyptian Museum, Cairo.

It appears that only the core of the innermost row of the edge sandwiches the sole, but visibility is hindered. On the medial side of the left sandal, posterolaterally to the attachment of the pre/back strap is a hole (arrow), the function of which is unclear.

4292 (620 (119); 30 3 + 34 25A [left] & 30 3 + 34 25B [right]; 3393)

The right sandal is slightly better shaped than the left (figure 3.23, table 1), showing a more distinctly constricted waist and a slightly more distinct toe due to a more rounded course of the front half of the lateral edge. Perhaps the differences are too small to conclude that the two were not a pair originally, but usually the two sandals of a pair are much more comparable (*cf.* Veldmeijer, 2009a). The toe of the right one still points upwards, with only slight damage of the palm leaf sewing strips on both surfaces. The damage of these sewing strips on the dorsal surface of the left sandal is even less, but there is an indentation and a short tear just anterior to the attachment of the pre/back straps, which must have been caused by a sharp object pressing into it from below. A small piece of the anteromedial edge is damaged, showing only the core of the outermost row. The cores of the inner two rows could not be identified due to the intact condition of the sewing strips.

Both pre-straps of the left sandal are preserved, although the medial one is detached. A small length of the front strap, including the insertion through the sole, is still *in situ*; it includes the cladding with a relatively wide palm leaf strip. As this strip is somewhat wider than usual, it might be a repair. The crown sinnet on the ventral surface is still intact. The front strap of the right one is almost complete, but lacks the loop for the attachment to the back strap. A short remnant of the lateral back strap is still *in situ* and is all that remains together with the lateral pre-strap.

4294bis (620 (119); 30 3 + 34 41B [left] & 30 3 + 34 41A [right]; 3409)

The dorsal surface of the right sandal of this pair (figure 3.24, table 1) is mostly intact, but has several damaged sewing strips. The damage to the dorsal surface of the left one is far more substantial, especially on the front half where several transverse cores are exposed. Also, parts of the edge are incomplete. The heel of the left sandal is slightly more rounded than the heel in the right one. The right sandal largely lacks the strap complex, but the attachments of the pre/back strap are still visible as well as a remnant of the front strap in the slit. The left sandal has only the lateral pre-strap *in situ* as well as the medial attachment of the pre/back strap (including a scrap of the cladding).

The core of the outermost edge is made of palm stalks. Visibility is hindered due to the intact condition. Open spots, however, suggest that the inner two cores are made of grass, although strips of palm seem to be part of the core as well. This conclusion, however, is based on the distinct difference in colour of the two materials.

4295 sr (620 (119); 30 3 + 34 36A [left] & 30 3 + 34 36B [right]; 3404)

For this pair of sandals (figure 3.25, table 1), the sewing strips on the dorsal surface of the right one do not show much damage, except for small patches of the edge (mainly the lateral side). The damage to the strips in the left sandal is more substantial. The wear of the sewing strips of the ventral sole is slight in both sandals.

The strap complex of the right sandal is largely lacking except for the two pre-straps, which are both *in situ*. Scraps of papyrus from the back strap are stuck to the dorsal surface. The strap complex of the left sandal is largely complete even though the medial side of the back strap is broken. The middle row of the edge might sandwich the sole, but the sandal's completeness prohibits certainty.

A B C

D

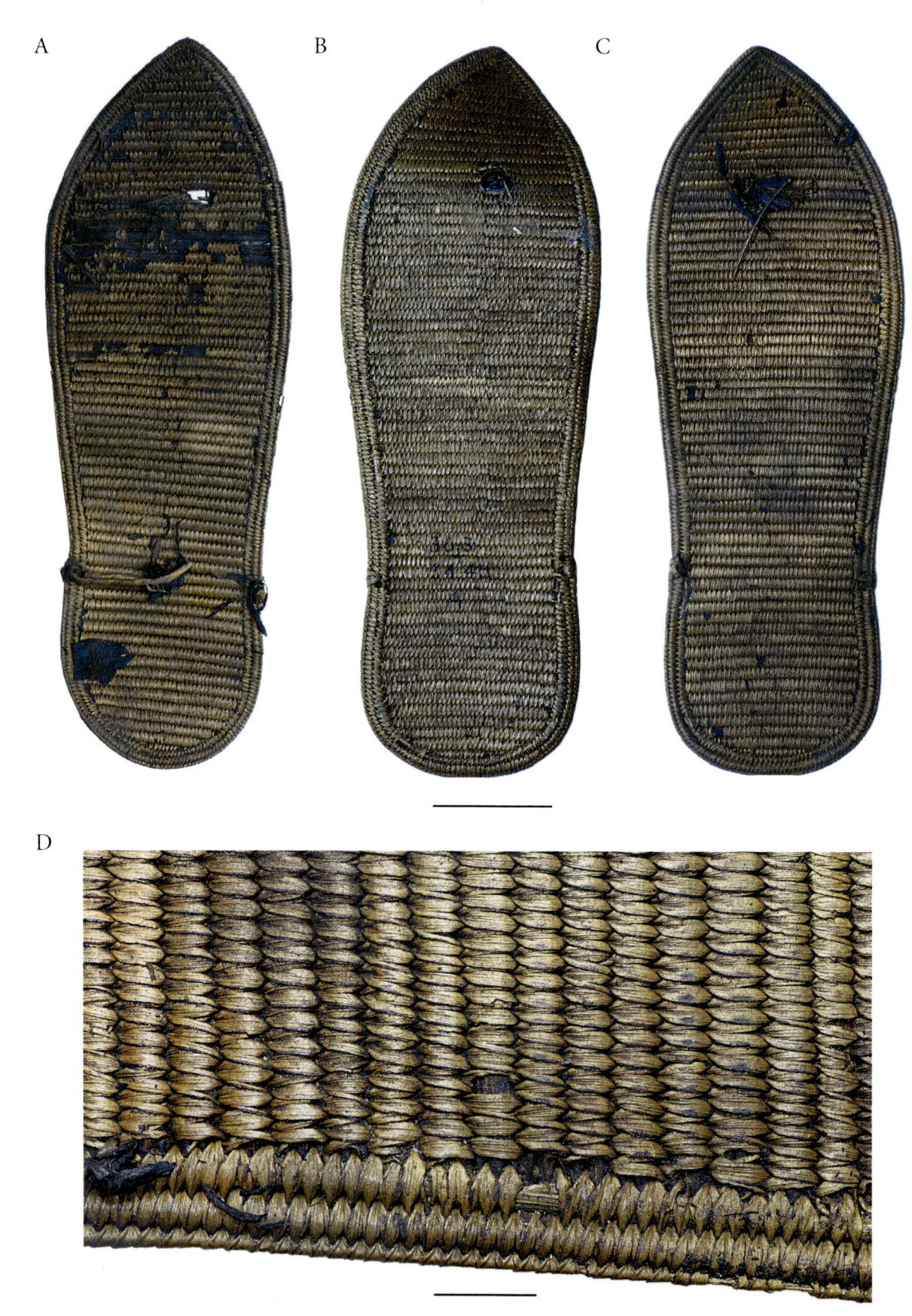

Figure 3.24. Pair 4294bis. A) Dorsal view of the left sandal; B) Ventral view of the right sandal; C) Dorsal view of the right sandal; D) Detail of the edge, dorsal view. Scale bar A-C is 50 mm; scale bar D is 10 mm. Photography by A.J. Veldmeijer. Courtesy of the Supreme Council of Antiquities / Authorities Egyptian Museum, Cairo.

A   B

Figure 3.25. Pair 4295. A) Dorsal view of the left sandal; B) Dorsal view of the right sandal; C) Detail of the lateral edge of the right sandal, dorsal view. Note the small hole with the pre-strap, which is due to the tight attachment. Scale bar A & B is 50 mm; scale bar C is 10 mm. Photography by A.J. Veldmeijer. Courtesy of the Supreme Council of Antiquities / Authorities Egyptian Museum, Cairo.

C

4296 (620 (119); 30 3 + 34 40A [left] & 30 3 + 34 40B [right]; 3408)

The left sandal of this pair (figure 3.26, table 1) shows less damage of the sewing strips on the dorsal surface; the damage instead is largely concentrated at the heel. In the right one, the sewing strips of the whole surface show damage, but less so at the heel. The ventral surfaces show comparable damage to that seen in other sandals (*i.e.* almost absent) although the left shows relatively more wear of the ventral and dorsal surfaces of the heel.

The strap complexes are largely lacking, leaving only the pre-straps, both of which in the left sandal are detached. The medi-

A   B

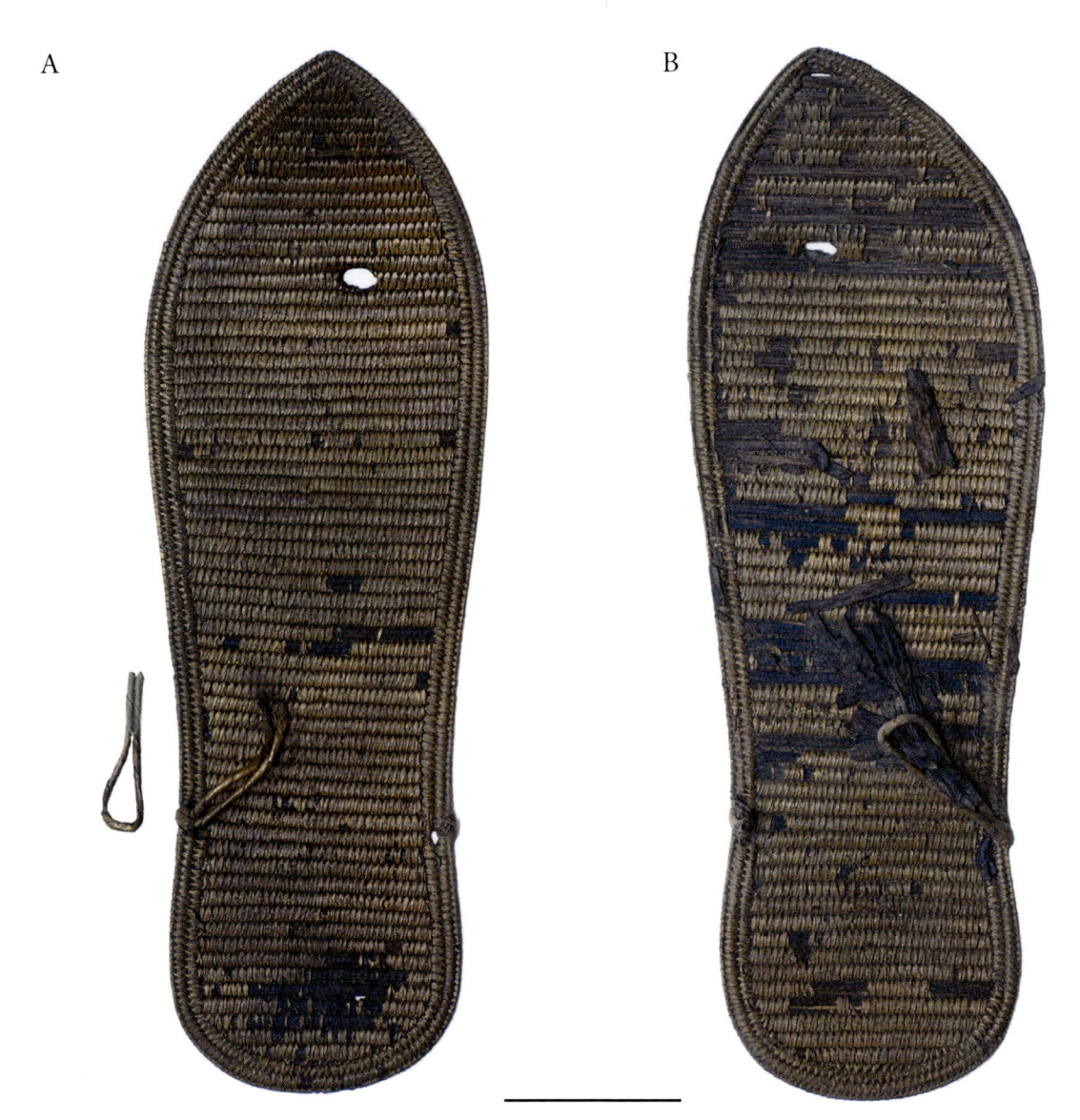

Figure 3.26. Pair 4296. A) Dorsal view of the left sandal; B) Dorsal view of the right sandal. Scale bar is 50 mm. Photography by A.J. Veldmeijer. Courtesy of the Supreme Council of Antiquities / Authorities Egyptian Museum, Cairo.

al pre-strap of the right one is detached as well, but the lateral one is *in situ*, and has a small remnant of the back strap in its original position.

4297 (620 (119); 30 3 + 34 37A [left]; & 30 3 + 34 37B [right]; 3405)

For this pair of sandals (figure 3.27, table 1), the dorsal surface of the left one shows only moderate damage to the sewing strips with the sewing strip along the edge largely complete (except for a small spot on the lateral edge close to the front strap slit). The dorsal surface of the right sandal shows large areas with the transverse cores exposed and the damage is slightly worse on the heel. In some spots, the sewing strips are entirely lost, including between the grass bundles. Moreover, various grass bundles are incomplete. The condition of the edge is comparable; it is broken and a small part is missing shortly anterior to the medial pre/back strap attachment. The damage to the sewing strips of the ventral surface of the left sandal is negligible, and the damage to the right sandal is similar to the damage of the dorsal surface.

A					B

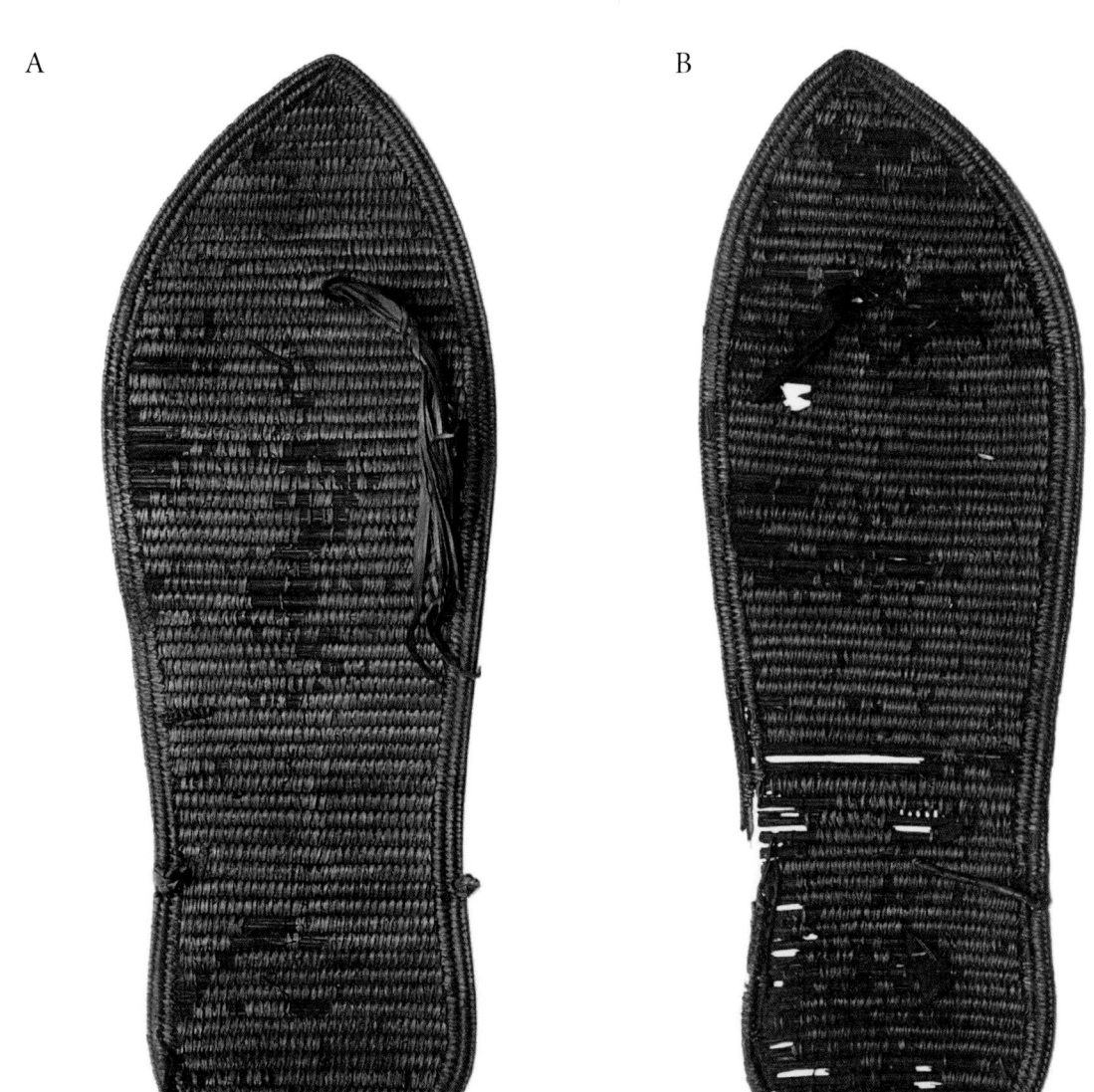

Figure 3.27. Pair 4297. A) Dorsal view of the left sandal; B) Dorsal view of the right sandal. Scale bar is 50 mm. Photography by A.J. Veldmeijer. Courtesy of the Supreme Council of Antiquities / Authorities Egyptian Museum, Cairo.

A small remnant of the palm leaf core of the front strap of the right sandal is still inserted into its slit. The lateral pre-strap is broken, leaving only half of the loop *in situ*. The strap complex of the left sandal is more complete, but still largely missing. The palm leaf core of the front strap is still *in situ* as is the crown sinnet on the ventral surface. Both attachments of the pre/back strap are present; one pre-strap is present, but detached from the sole proper (not in the figure).

4298 (629 (119); 30 3 + 34 29B [left] & 30 3 + 34 29A [right]; 3397)

Of this largely complete pair of sandals (figure 3.28, table 1), the left one particularly shows damage of the sewing strips on the dorsal surface, but this is still only minor. The damage of the sewing strips on the ventral surface is comparable to the other sandals and thus is minor as well. The strap complex is for the most part present in both sandals albeit much damaged. The front straps are detached from the sole, but

A   B

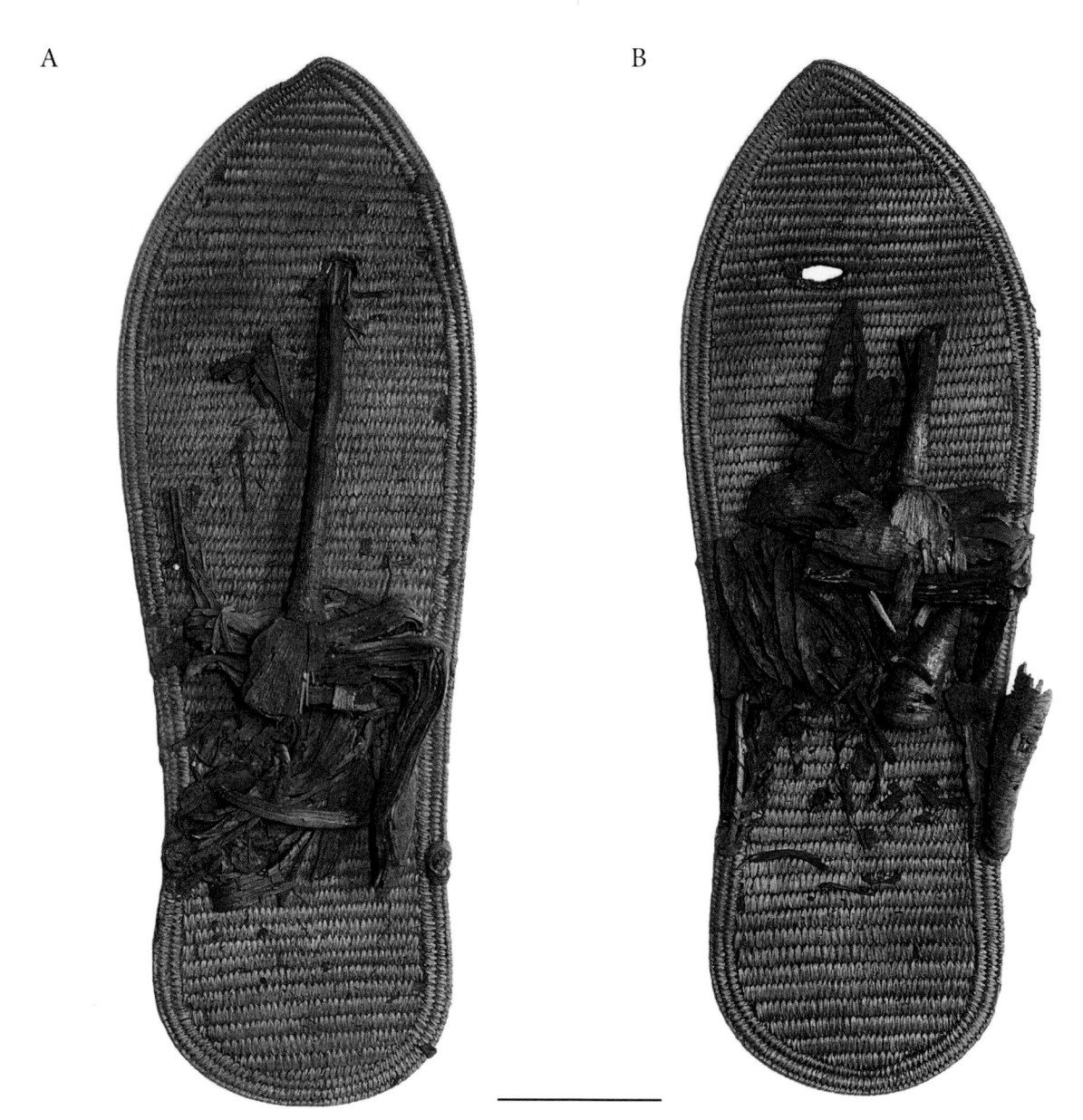

Figure 3.28. Pair 4298. A) Dorsal view of the left sandal; B) Dorsal view of the right sandal. Scale bar is 50 mm. Photography by A.J. Veldmeijer. Courtesy of the Supreme Council of Antiquities / Authorities Egyptian Museum, Cairo.

the loop to the back strap is still partially intact. The back straps are fragmented, but the common shape of this type can still be discerned. Only the lateral pre-strap of the left sandal is *in situ*. This one mostly lacks the back strap and all the cladding, but, on the side, the attachment of the pre/back strap remains. The right sandal's medial pre-strap has lost its cladding, but remnants of the back strap are still there. The lateral back strap does not seem to have been pulled through the pre-strap as in the other three pre/back strap attachments in this pair, but a clear view is obscured by the cladding. If so, it may indicate a repair. The fact that the pre-strap is still complete and *in situ* (again, in contrast to the others) might be interpreted as supporting this suggestion.

The cores of the innermost two edges cannot be identified and neither can their exact position in relation to the sole. The core of the outer row is made of palm stalks.

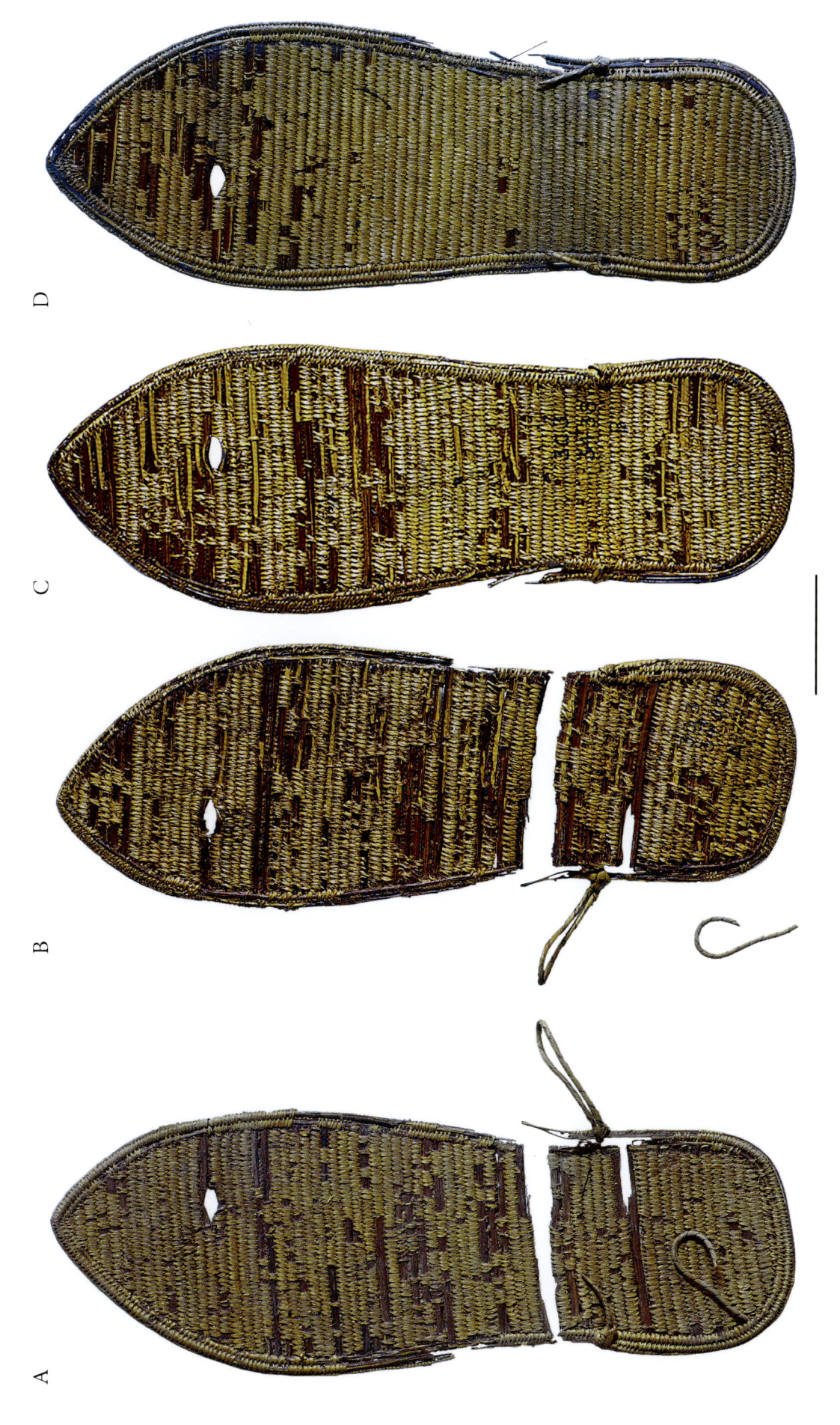

Figure 3.29. Pair 4299. A) Dorsal view of the left sandal; B) Ventral view of the left sandal; C) Ventral view of the right sandal; D) Dorsal view of the right sandal. Note the difference in colour compared to the other sandals. Scale bar is 50 mm. Photography by A.J. Veldmeijer. Courtesy of the Supreme Council of Antiquities / Authorities Egyptian Museum, Cairo.

4299 (620 (119); 30 3 + 34 38A [left] & 30 3 + 34 38B [right]; 3406)

The majority of the sewn sandals are of modest size, but this pair (figure 3.29, table 1) is substantially longer with its length being comparable to several of the shoes (see below). The left sandal is broken in two, shortly anterior to the pre/back strap attachment. Its heel is slightly squarer than in the right sandal. The dorsal surfaces of both show substantial damage of the sewing strips, but on the ventral surfaces the damage is even more severe. In the right sandal, however, it is mainly limited to the front third whereas it is throughout the entire length in the left. The ventral surfaces of both show severe damage of the strips throughout. This contrasts sharply with the damage in other sandals, which is much less and often nearly absent on the ventral surface.

Figure 3.30. Pair 4300. A) Dorsal view of the left sandal; B) Dorsal view of the right sandal. Scale bar is 50 mm. Photography by A.J. Veldmeijer. Courtesy of the Supreme Council of Antiquities / Authorities Egyptian Museum, Cairo.

A small patch of the lateral edge of the right sandal, shortly anterior to the pre/back strap attachment to the sole, lacks the outermost and middle rows. The sewing strips are absent in various places. The edge shows severe damage ranging from missing rows to missing sewing strips. The strap complex is absent, except for remnants of the pre-strap.

4300 (620 (119); 30 3 + 34 35B [left] & 30 3 + 34 35A [right]; 3404)

The dorsal surface of this pair (figure 3.30, table 1) shows the usual damage of the sewing strips but on a limited scale, as do the ventral surfaces. More substantial damage, albeit of small extent, is seen on the heel in the right sandal, where the sewing strips are lost in between the two transverse grass cores. There are several isolated stitches between the edge and the first row of the sole's fabric on the heel of the right sandal.

The strap complex of the right sandal is largely absent, although the medial pre-strap is still *in situ*, containing remnants of the back strap. The attachment of the lateral pre/back strap is all that is left of this part of the strap complex. Note the hole at the inner side of the attachment, which is caused by tightly fastening the strap to the outer two rows of the edge (*cf.* figure 3.25C). The strap complex of the left sandal is much more complete but severely damaged and fragmented. The lateral pre-strap is detached (including remnants of the back strap) but the medial one is still attached to the sole, containing the attachment of the back strap and scraps of the cladding. The front strap is still *in situ* in the slit, but detached from the back strap (although the loop is still visible).

4301 (620 (119); 30 3 + 34 33A [right]; & 30 3 + 34 33B [left]; 3401)

The dorsal surface of the right sandal of this pair (figure 3.31, table 1) is largely intact; the dorsal surface of the left shows only a few small spots of damaged sewing strips.

In one case, however, the strips are lost from between the grass cores as well. The edge of the right sandal is intact but the lateral edge of the left is damaged: the core sticks out of the remaining palm leaf stitches. It shows the usual construction consisting of grass cores for the innermost two rows (sandwiching the sole) and a core of palm stalks for the outermost one. The ventral surface of the left one shows negligible damage. The ventral surface of the right one, however, shows clear signs of wear: the transverse bundles at the heel and ball of the foot are compressed due to the weight of the owner and shows a dark discolouration (*cf.* 4302).

The strap complex of the right sandal is fragmentary: a remnant of the front strap remains in the slit as does the crown sinnet on the ventral surface. Another remnant is detached. The two pre-straps are present but detached; their attachments, however, are still *in situ*. For the left sandal, only the attachment of the lateral pre/back strap remains as well as the medial pre-strap with remnants of the back strap.

4302 (620 (119); 30 3 + 34 44B [left] & 30 3 + 34 44A [right]; 3412)

The sole of both sandals, registered as a pair (figure 3.32, table 1), are in good condition. The left one shows almost no damage to the sewing strips; the right one is intact. The left sandal has several damaged sewing strips at the ventral surface; the ventral surface of the right is intact. The sewing strips of the right one shows a distinct dark patina of the convex surfaces especially in the front part; the parts of the strips in between the rows show their original colour. The discolouration is due to the natural fats a skin produces and thus a clear sign that the sandal was worn. This seems to contradict the absence of damaged sewing strips, unless not much rubbing of the foot over the surface occurred.[10] The absence of the same patina in the left sandal also makes it questionable whether the sandals were originally a pair.

A   B

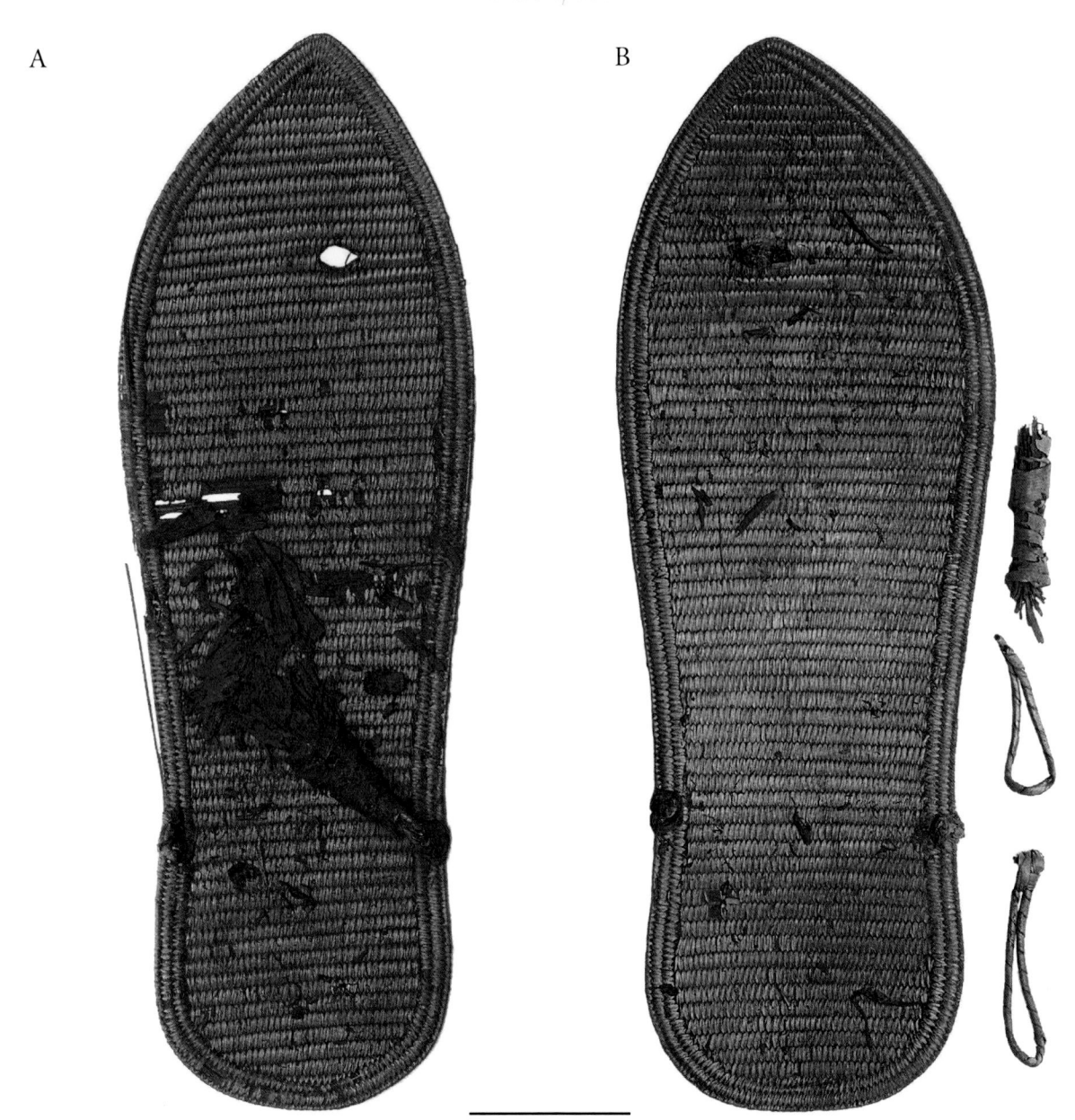

Figure 3.31. Pair 4301. A) Dorsal view of the left sandal; B) Dorsal view of the right sandal. Scale bar is 50 mm. Photography by A.J. Veldmeijer. Courtesy of the Supreme Council of Antiquities / Authorities Egyptian Museum, Cairo.

The strap complex is missing in both, although remnants of the insertion of the front strap are *in situ* in the slit in the left one. The crown sinnet still fastens the remnant. In both sandals only the attachments of the pre/back straps remain. The intact edges do not allow identification of the material and construction of the cores.

4303 (620 (119); 30 3 + 34 34A [right]; 3402)[11]

The dorsal surface of the right sandal 4303 (figure 3.33, table 1) shows large areas of damaged sewing strips, exposing the grass cores of the transverse bundles. The medial side in particular has suffered damage, in-

> *Figure 3.32. Pair 4302. A) Dorsal view of the left sandal; B) Ventral view of the left sandal; C) Ventral view of the right sandal; D) Dorsal view of the right sandal. Scale bar is 50 mm. Photography by A.J. Veldmeijer. Courtesy of the Supreme Council of Antiquities / Authorities Egyptian Museum, Cairo.*

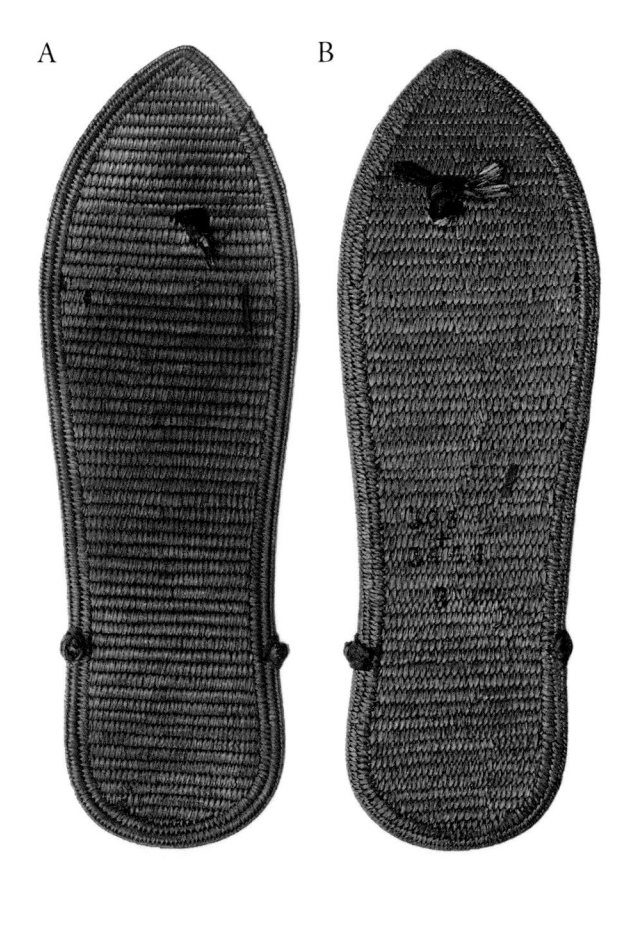

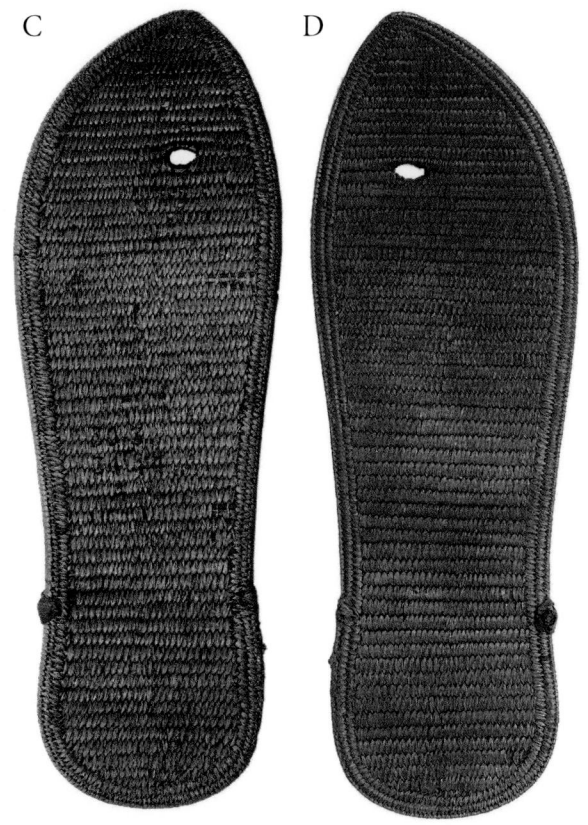

cluding the edge along which large parts have lost the sewing strips. The ventral surface shows relatively little damage as in most sandals. In the front half of the medial edge are black patches, probably 'melted' leather, which must have fallen onto the sandal.

The strap complex is mostly lost, although remnants of the front strap are still *in situ* in the slit and the crown sinnet is detached but still present. In between the pre-straps, which are still attached to the sole, are remnants of the back strap adhering to the dorsal surface. An isolated pre-strap (not illustrated), to which still a part of the back strap is attached, is registered with the sandal, but the origin is uncertain given that both pre-straps of the sandal are still *in situ*. Note the slight indentation at the attachment of the medial pre-strap due to the severe tying.

4304 (620 (119); 30 3 + 34 28B [left] & 30 3 + 34 28A [right]; 3396)

The dorsal surface of the left sandal in particular shows damage to the sewing strips. Both sandals (figure 3.34, table 1) exhibit small damaged sections along the edge: the left one at the anteromedial edge and the right one at the posteromedial edge. The damage on the ventral surface is comparable to most sandals and only slight. Note the slight diagonal course of the transverse bundles and, at the heel of the right sandal, a slight curvature.

The strap complex of the left sandal is present but entirely detached. The strap complex of the right sandal is more or less *in situ*: it is detached but still lying on the dorsal surface. Due to the strap's fragmented and fragile condition, the sandal's dorsal surface could not be properly cleaned of its accumulated dust. The strap's condition also hindered measurement of the maximal width of the back strap.

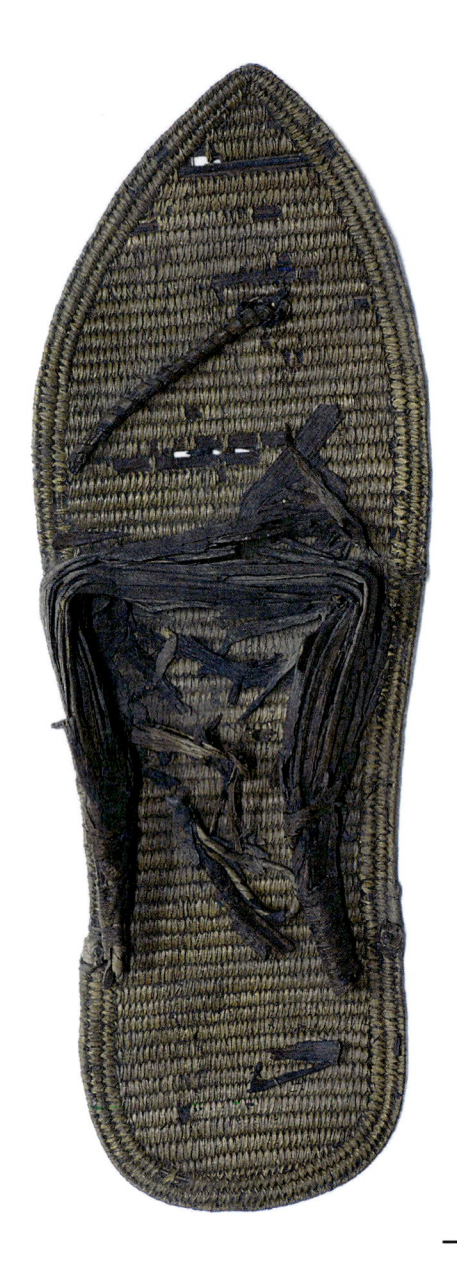

A   B

C

Figure 3.34. Pair 4304. A) Dorsal view of the left sandal; B) Remnants of the strap complex of the left sandal; C) Dorsal view of the right sandal. Scale bar is 50 mm. Photography by A.J. Veldmeijer. Courtesy of the Supreme Council of Antiquities / Authorities Egyptian Museum, Cairo.

< Figure 3.33. Pair 4303. A) Dorsal view of the left sandal; B) Dorsal view of the right sandal. Scale bar is 50 mm; C) The left one, described in section 3.2.1.2, shows stitch holes at the outermost row of the edge, indicating a, now lost, insole. Scale bar is 10 mm. Photography by A.J. Veldmeijer. Courtesy of the Supreme Council of Antiquities / Authorities Egyptian Museum, Cairo.

4305 (620 (119); 30 3 + 34 43A [left] & 30 3 + 34 43B [right]; 3411)

The dorsal surfaces of the pair of sandals 4304 (figure 3.35, table 1) show damage to the sewing strips. The ventral surfaces are nearly intact but the left sandal shows relatively severe wear at the heel. The toes of the soles are still slightly upturned.

The slit for the reception of the front strap in the left sandal is unusual in that it is nearly circular – typically the slit is almond-shaped, as seen in the right sandal. The strap complex of the right sandal is lost entirely, except for the attachments of the pre-straps. The lateral pre-strap, including the beginning of the back strap, is still *in situ* in the left sandal. The cladding, however, is largely lost. Of the medial pre-strap, only the attachment (including small remnants of the pre-strap itself) remains. Note the hole in the inner side of the attachment, which is caused by the severe tying of the pre/back strap to the edge (*cf.* figure 3.25C).

A

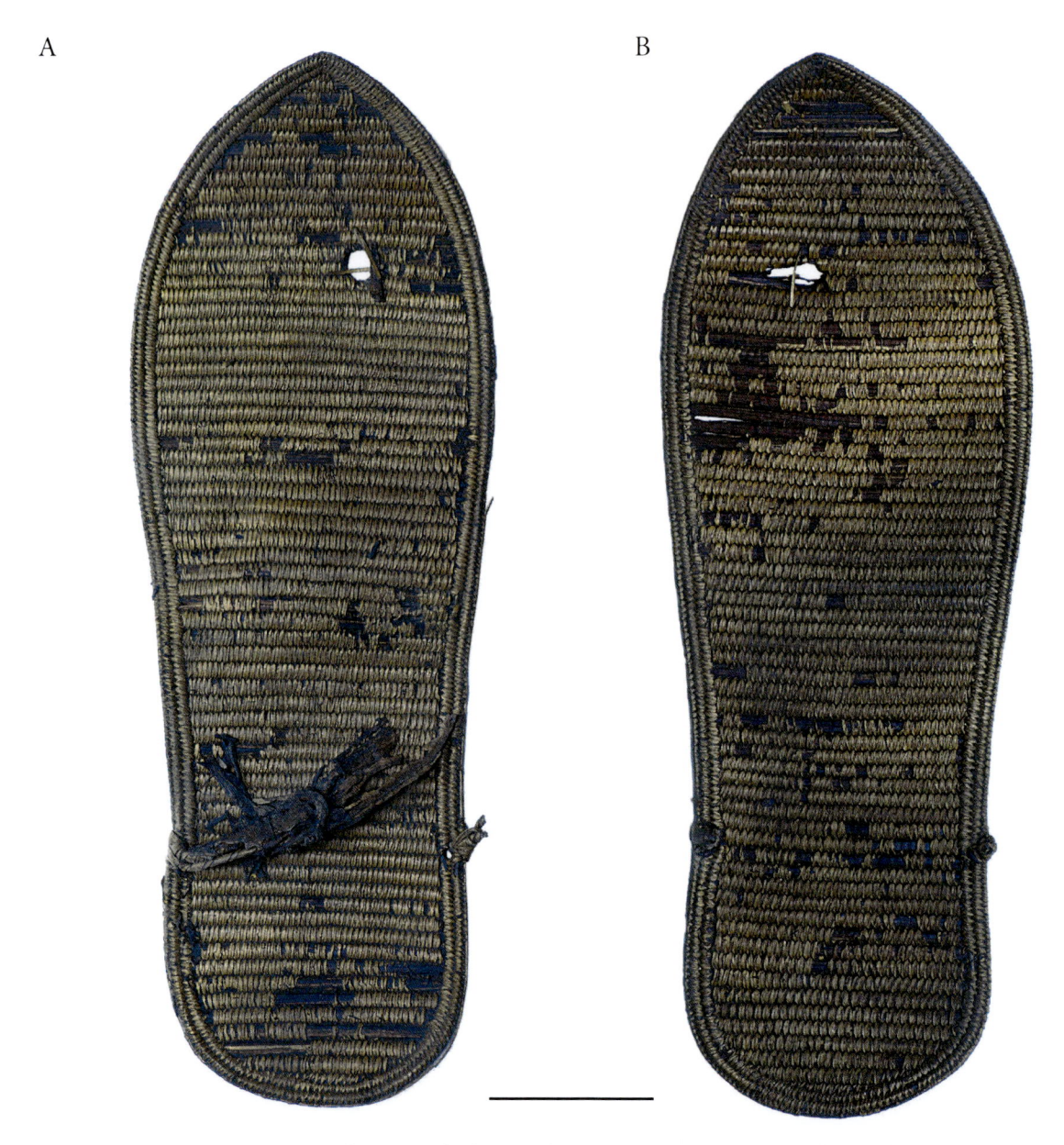

B

Figure 3.35. Pair 4305. A) Dorsal view of the left sandal; B) Dorsal view of the right sandal. Scale bar is 50 mm. Photography by A.J. Veldmeijer. Courtesy of the Supreme Council of Antiquities / Authorities Egyptian Museum, Cairo.

The edges are intact; therefore the sandal's construction lies hidden, but it seems to have grass cores for the innermost two rows (sandwiching the sole) and a palm stalk core on the outer one.

4306 (620 (119); 30 3 + 34 39A [left] & 30 3 + 34 39B [right]; 3407)

This pair of sandals (figure 3.36, table 1) shows slight damage to the sewing strips on the dorsal surfaces. The damage to the left sandal is slightly more substantial than to the right one but is largely limited to the front half whereas in the right it is largely restricted to the heel. The damage to the ventral surface is negligible. The edges are almost intact except for a few small spots where the sewing strips are lost, but from these it can be seen that the construction is comparable to most other sandals (*i.e.* the two innermost cores are of grass which sandwich the sole and an outer core of palm stalks). Note the curled toe of the left sandal,

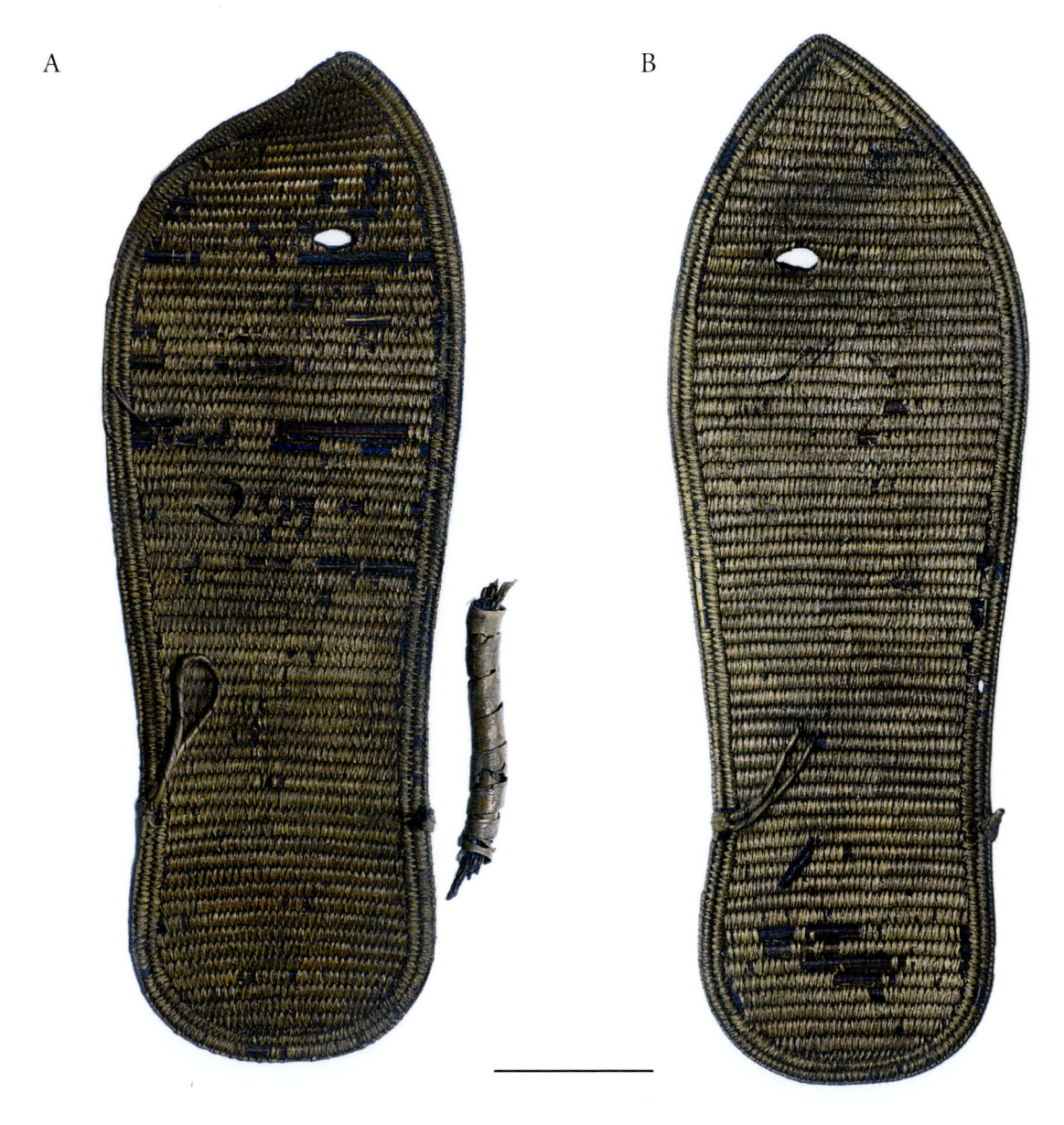

Figure 3.36. Pair 4306. A) Dorsal view of the left sandal; B) Dorsal view of the right sandal. Scale bar is 50 mm. Photography by A.J. Veldmeijer. Courtesy of the Supreme Council of Antiquities / Authorities Egyptian Museum, Cairo.

which seems to be due to post-depositional circumstances, judging from its strange curled shape.

The strap complex in the right sandal is absent, except for the broken medial pre-strap and the attachment of the lateral one. A remnant of the front strap for the left sandal is present, but detached from the sandal proper. The lateral pre-strap is present in the left sandal, but has lost its cladding; only the attachment remains for the medial pre/back strap.

4307 (620 (119); 30 3 + 34 31A [left] & 30 3 + 34 25B [left]; 3399)

The two sandals, which are registered as 4307 (figure 3.37, table 1), are both left sandals. The dorsal surface of 30 3 + 34 31A is nearly intact and the ventral surface shows no wear at all. The strap complex is largely missing, except for the medial pre-strap for which remnants of the back strap are still visible. The cladding, however, is entirely missing.

A

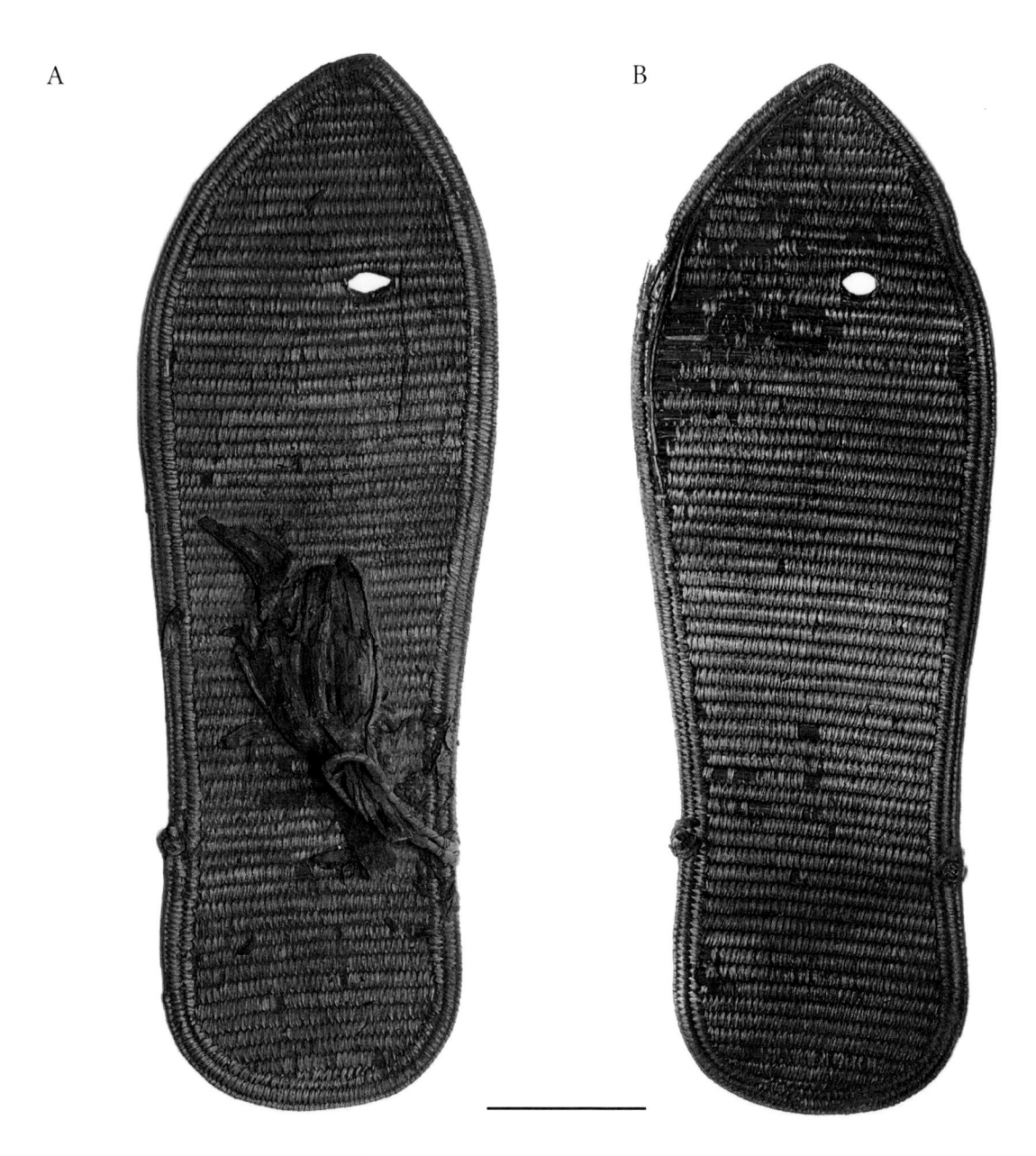

B

Figure 3.37. 'Pair' 4307. A) Dorsal view of 30 3 + 34 31A; B) Dorsal view of 30 3 + 34 31B. Scale bar is 50 mm. Photography by A.J. Veldmeijer. Courtesy of the Supreme Council of Antiquities / Authorities Egyptian Museum, Cairo.

Sandal 30 3 + 34 31B is even less complete and the dorsal surface shows, especially at the front, lost sewing strips. Moreover, the lateral edge of this damaged dorsal surface is damaged as well. Note the slight diagonal course of the transverse bundles. The strap complex is entirely lacking, except for the attachments of the pre-straps.

4308 (620 (119); 30 3 + 34 30B [left] & 30 3 + 34 30A [right]; 3398)

The left sandal of this pair (figure 3.38, table 1) shows several damaged sewing strips on the dorsal surface, but the wear of the strips on the right one is more extensive, with one bundle at the heel almost entirely exposed. The wear on the ventral surface is negligible. The width of the bundles shows slight, but rather large differences in dimensions for this type of sandals.

Figure 3.38. Pair 4308. A) Dorsal view of the left sandal; B) Dorsal view of the right sandal. Scale bar is 50 mm. Photography by A.J. Veldmeijer. Courtesy of the Supreme Council of Antiquities / Authorities Egyptian Museum, Cairo.

The strap complex of the right sandal is missing entirely but the attachments of the pre/back strap are still there. Several fibres of the straps are attached to the dorsal surface of the sandal. The strap complex of the left one is, in contrast, almost complete. The front strap broke off at approximately one third of the original length from the sole but the attachment to the back strap is still largely intact. The lateral pre/back strap is nicely preserved and still *in situ*. On the medial side the back strap has pulled out of the cladding and is broken off.

There are slight differences between the two sandals. The heel of the right one is slightly squarer and the transverse bundles of the heel part show a slight curvature, starting approximately at the attachment of the pre/back strap. At the front, the innermost row of the edge tapers whereas this is almost absent in the left sandal.

Except for the outermost edge of the right sandal (which has a core made of palm) the edge is intact and allows no identification of the core material. The inner two rows sandwich the sole.

4309 (620 (119); 30 3 + 34 42A [right] & 30 3 + 34 42B [left]; 3410)

Both sandals of this pair (figure 3.39, table 1) show slight damage of the sewing strips on the dorsal surface, including the edges (mainly at the heel). As in almost all sandals, the ventral surface shows far less damage relative to the dorsal surface, although in the left sandal this surface is slightly less intact.

The sandals lack the strap complex. The right one only shows the attachments of the pre/back strap. A small remnant of the medial pre-strap of the left sandal is still present, but it is, together with the part of the two cores to which it is attached, semi-detached from the sole. On the lateral side, a rectangular notch is apparent in the pre/back strap attachment area. Both the medial and lateral condition suggests that the straps were torn off with force.

4310 (620 (119); 30 3 + 34 32A [right] & 30 3 + 34 32B [left]; 3400)

For this pair of sandals (figure 3.40, table 1) the dorsal surface of the right one shows little damage of the sewing strips but still relatively more than the left sandal. The edges in both sandals are largely intact. Note the slight diagonal course of the transverse bundles in the right sandal. The ventral surface of the left sandal shows damage of sewing strips comparable to that typically seen. The ventral surface of the right one, however, shows clear indications of wear: the bundles are slightly pressed at the heel due to the wearer's weight and has a dark discolouration (*cf.* 4302).

The right sandal is entirely lacking the strap complex except for the lateral pre-strap, which is still *in situ*, and the attachment for the medial pre/back strap. There are several scraps of the front strap lying near the slit. The strap complex of the left sandal, however, is much more complete. The inner palm leaf core of the front strap is still present in the slit and secured with a crown sinnet. It is detached from the back strap, which is reduced to remnants and lying loose on the sandal's surface, but there are still remnants of the loop visible. The lateral pre-strap, however, still has scraps of the back strap *in situ*. The cladding is entirely lost. The medial pre-strap is still present.

3.2.1.2 Variant 2[12]

There are six sewn sandals with an additional sole, *i.e.* they have an insole made of linen or features that imply an additional sole.

> *Figure 3.39. Pair 4309. A) Dorsal view of the left sandal; B) Ventral view of the left sandal; C) Ventral view of the right sandal; D) Dorsal view of the right sandal. Scale bar is 50 mm. Photography by A.J. Veldmeijer. Courtesy of the Supreme Council of Antiquities / Authorities Egyptian Museum, Cairo.*

81

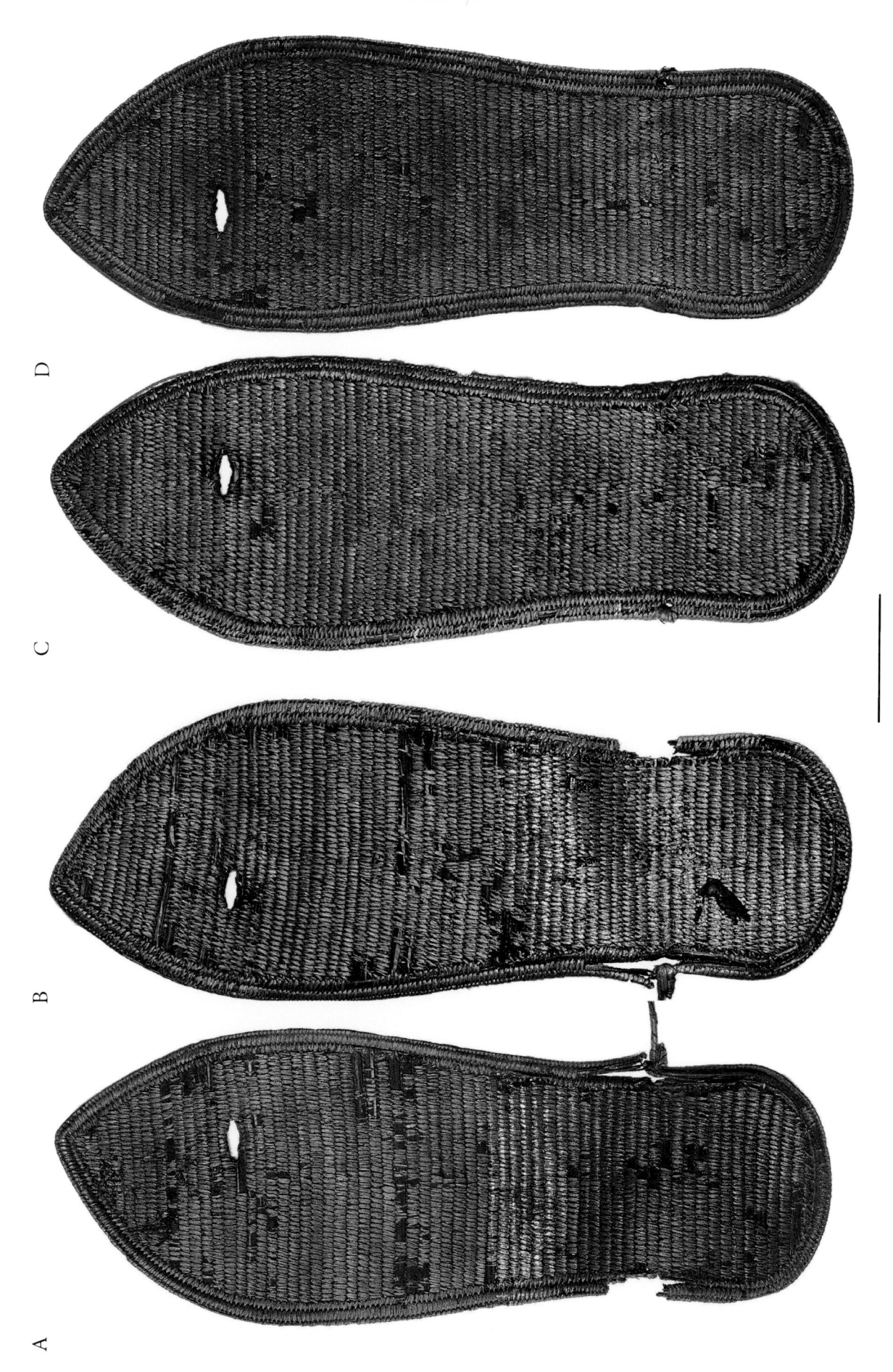

A	B

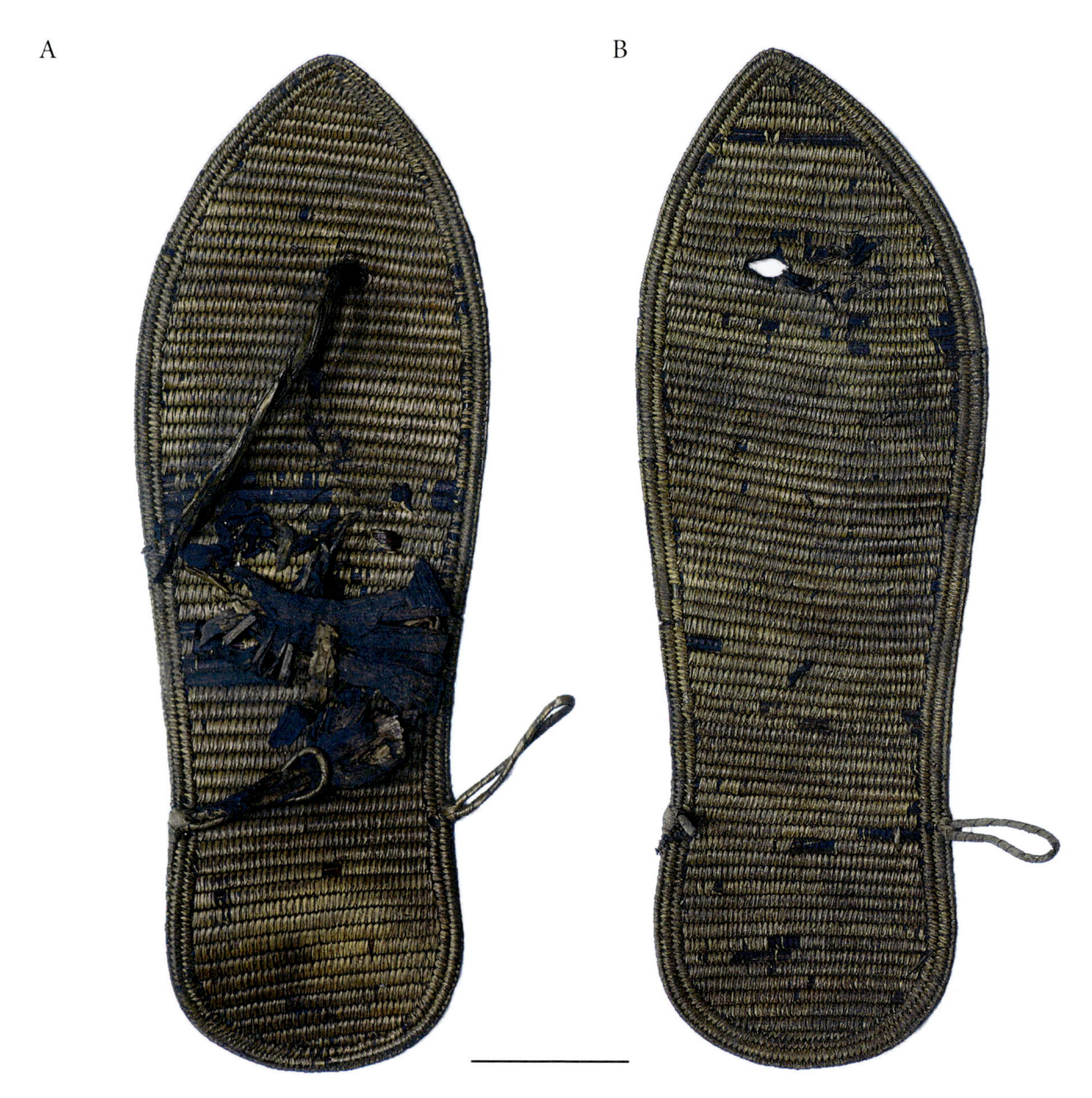

Figure 3.40. Pair 4310. A) Dorsal view of the left sandal; B) Dorsal view of the right sandal. Scale bar is 50 mm. Photography by A.J. Veldmeijer. Courtesy of the Supreme Council of Antiquities / Authorities Egyptian Museum, Cairo.

367b (2821; JE 62692; 1261; right)

This sewn sandal (figure 3.41 & 1.11, table 2), meant for the right foot, has an additional insole of extraordinary fine linen fabric, which is without decoration. It was not possible to identify the fabric by eye. The sole is attached to the treadsole by means of thin, running stitches which are, as far as they are preserved, situated at the treadsole's edge, or just inside it, and protruding from the treadsole's ventral surface (figure 3.41B). The flax stitches are neatly pulled through the palm leaf stitches of the treadsole, rather than stitched through them, as is the case of JE 62691 described below. The insole mostly follows the outer perimeter of the treadsole, but at the posteromedial side of the heel it is positioned slightly inwards from the edge proper (figure 3.41C). The edge of the insole is folded under and sandwiched between the insole and sewn treadsole, so that the fold's extension cannot be measured. No damage could be seen on the ventral surface of the sewn treadsole. The dorsal surface is obscured by the insole but the visible parts also show no damage.

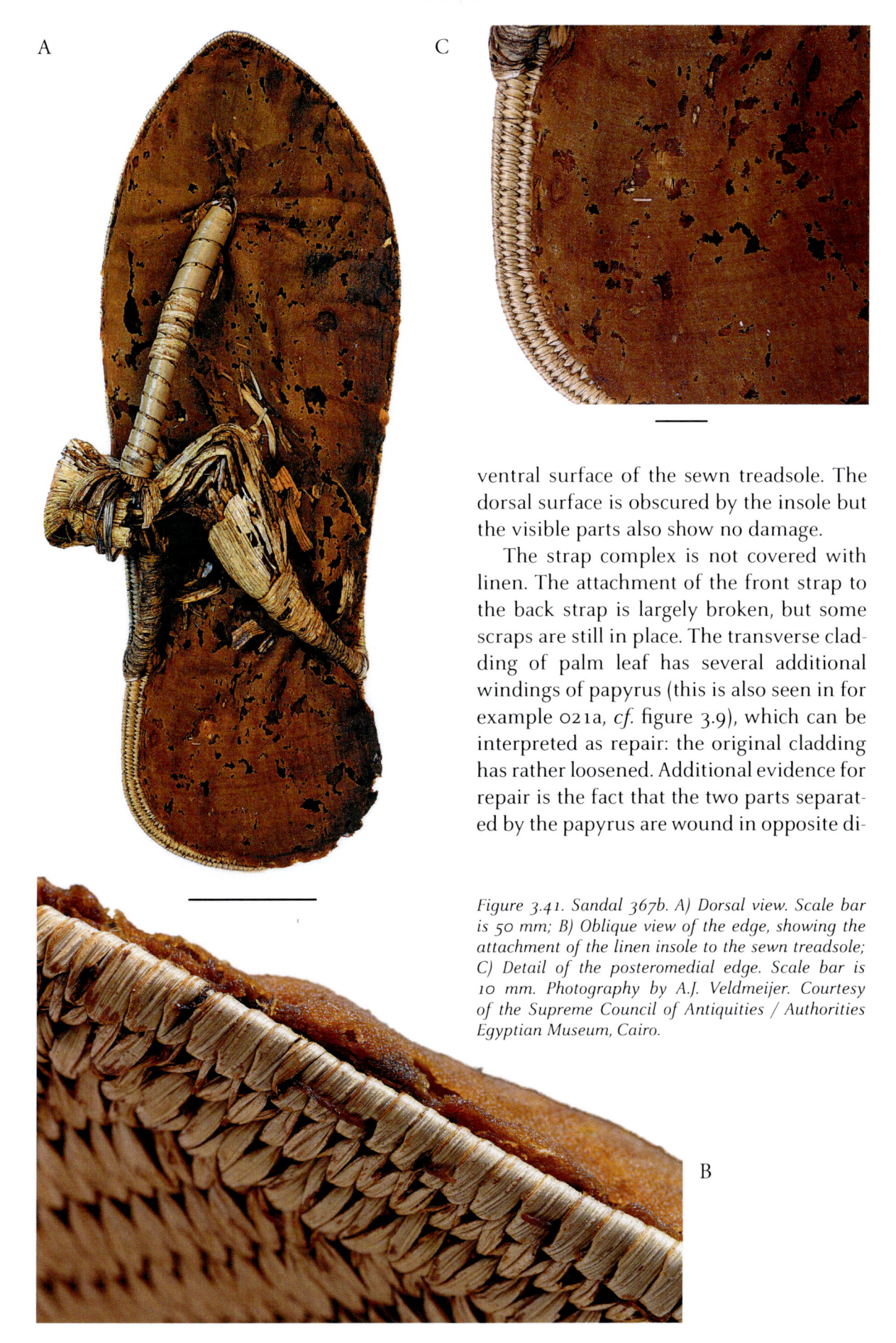

The strap complex is not covered with linen. The attachment of the front strap to the back strap is largely broken, but some scraps are still in place. The transverse cladding of palm leaf has several additional windings of papyrus (this is also seen in for example 021a, *cf.* figure 3.9), which can be interpreted as repair: the original cladding has rather loosened. Additional evidence for repair is the fact that the two parts separated by the papyrus are wound in opposite di-

Figure 3.41. Sandal 367b. A) Dorsal view. Scale bar is 50 mm; B) Oblique view of the edge, showing the attachment of the linen insole to the sewn treadsole; C) Detail of the posteromedial edge. Scale bar is 10 mm. Photography by A.J. Veldmeijer. Courtesy of the Supreme Council of Antiquities / Authorities Egyptian Museum, Cairo.

rections and are of slightly different width; usually, as parallels suggest, the transverse cladding is much more regular (see for example 4290 in figure 3.21). It is difficult to ascertain the construction of the pre/back strap, but apparently the pre-strap is positioned on the outside of the back strap, the latter seemingly not being pulled through the pre-strap loop. The lateral part of the back strap is mostly broken between the attachment of the front strap and the pre/back strap attachment. In contrast to most sandals, the cladding of the pre/back strap is done with papyrus rather than palm leaf.

The insole largely obscures the dorsal surface of the treadsole, including the edge, due to which the construction is not certain. Nevertheless, it seems to follow the common pattern, *i.e.* a palm core in the outermost row and grass cores for the inner two, which sandwich the sole's fabric.

2816 (620 (119); JE 62691; 1262; right)

This sandal (figure 3.42, table 2), meant for the right foot, is complete, including an undamaged strap complex. The single-layer, thin linen insole, however, is fragmentary. The fabric of the insole as well as the linen winding of the strap complex is coloured dark reddish brown to black. The weave of the fabric can only be seen on the back strap but it is impossible to give any details (figure 3.42C). The fabric follows the perimeter of the sewn treadsole: it is indented slightly inwards at the attachment of the pre/back strap. A small edge of the fabric, only few mm wide, is folded under the insole, thus being sandwiched by it and the sewn treadsole. The insole is sewn to the treadsole with stitches of flax that are pulled through the palm leaf stitches of the treadsole (figure 3.42D).

The technique of decorating the linen can no longer be established, but the 'high relief' of the decoration suggests needlework. Within Tutankhamun's tomb, applied needlework was also present in other objects (Carter & Mace, 1923: 172). At the heel, anterior to the back strap, the 'needlework' depicts the lotus and papyrus stem, tied with a reef knot, and this symbolizes the unification of Upper and Lower Egypt (figure 3.42B & inset). On the front part the decoration shows, according to Carter, African and Asiatic prisoners, but these are almost unrecognisable today (figure 3.42B).

The front strap is most likely Type 5, but with an additional layer of linen; the back strap is of a common type, but also with an additional cladding of strips of linen, each winding slightly overlapping the previous one.

JE 62689 (620 (119); right)[13]

Small spots along the edge's sewing strips, mainly from the outer core, are damaged in this right sandal (figure 3.13B-E, table 2). There is no damage of the sewing strips in the transverse bundles, or on the ventral and dorsal surfaces. The presence of remnants of flax stitches as well as empty stitch holes in the edge (usually between the middle and outer cores) suggests it had a linen insole originally of which nothing now remains. No remnants of the insole are visible within the stitches. Possibly, the insole was already lost before the sandal was placed in the tomb.

The transverse cladding of the front strap is gone, but the underlying lengthwise papyrus cladding shows the impressions of the winding. Although much of the loop attachment of the front strap to the back strap is lost, remnants are still visible. The fact that the front strap is, even without its cladding, still in place is due to the conservatives, which have fixed it. From both lateral and medial views, the front strap is distinctly bent. Anterior to the front strap's insertion in the sole, the sole bulges due to the impression of the crown sinnet (see also JE 62690, 4286, 4287; figure 3.15).

The pre-strap consists, as usual, of a loop, made of a twisted strip of palm leaf, and tied to the sole's edge. The papyrus back strap, however, seems to be attached on

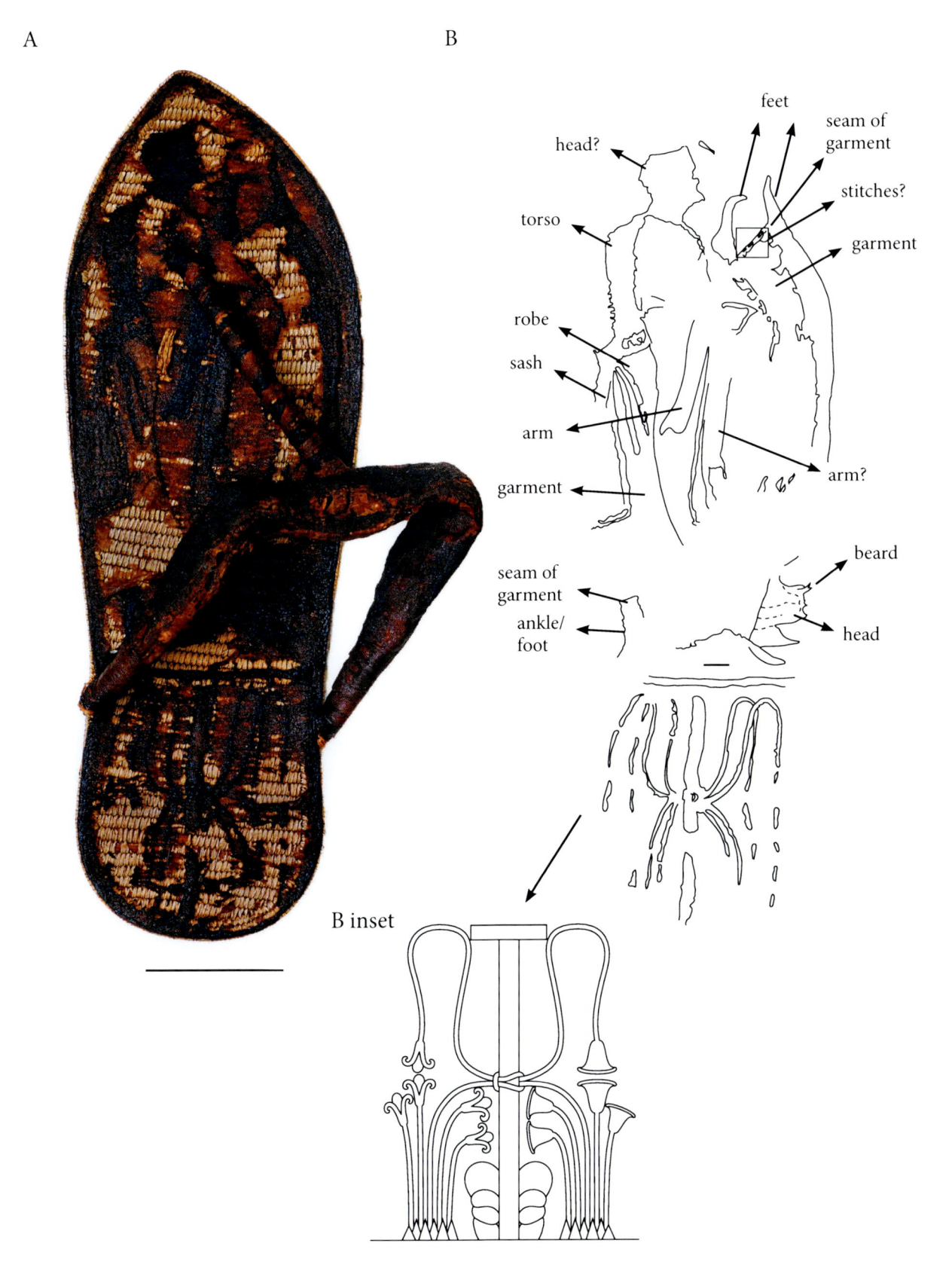

Figure 3.42. Sandal 2816. A) Dorsal view; B) The decoration of the linen insole. Although largely damaged, the two foes are still recognizable (cf. figure 3.43). At the heel the tying of the two plants (cf. inset). Scale bar is 50 mm; inset not to scale; > C) Detail of the clad back strap; > D) Detail of the treadsole's edge showing the stitches that secure the linen insole. Indication scale D: thickness of the sole is 5.3 mm. Photography by A.J. Veldmeijer. Courtesy of the Supreme Council of Antiquities / Authorities Egyptian Museum, Cairo. Drawing by A.J. Veldmeijer. Inset by E. Endenburg.

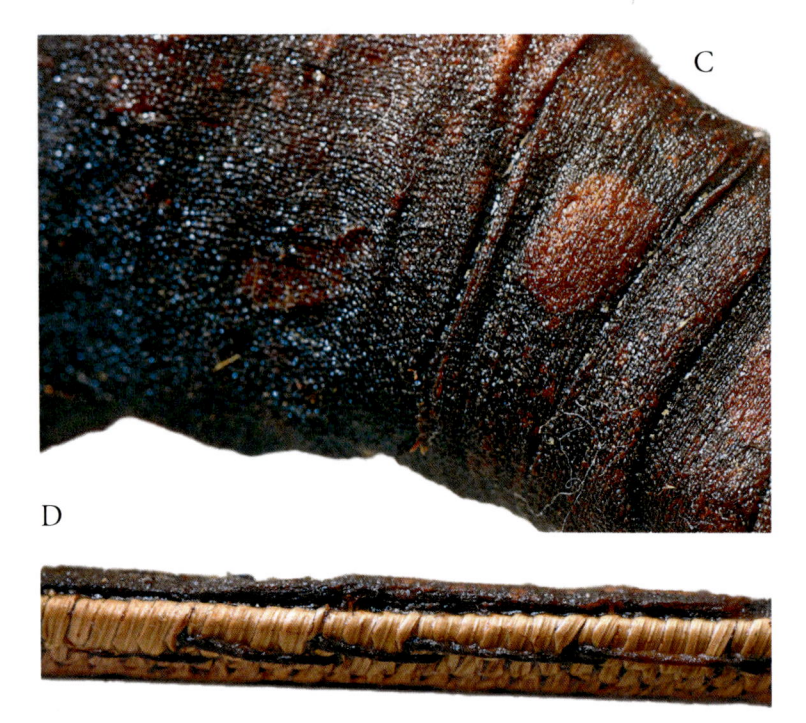

the inner side of the pre-strap, without being pulled through the pre-strap, after which the two are clad. However, it is not possible to be certain on this point, due to the largely intact cladding.

4303 (620 (119); 30 3 + 34 34B; 3402; left)[14]

There is occasionally clear evidence that two sandals registered as a pair were not, in fact, a pair originally. Pair 4303 (figures 3.33A & C, table 2) is such an example too: the left sandal discussed here, has evidence of an insole; the right one, discussed previously, has not. The left sandal is fairly complete, the dorsal surface of which shows, especially on the front part, damage to the sewing strips. There is also damage to the sewing strips along the edge, but very limited.

The edge, predominantly between the middle and outermost rows, shows stitch holes (figure 3.33C). Comparison with sandals having an insole suggests that these stitch holes are the result of the attachment of an insole. Nothing remains of the insole proper, however.

The strap complex is largely complete but in a fragmentary state. The front strap, still *in situ* in the slit at the front, is of a small diameter and made of strips of palm. A widely spaced, diagonal, transverse cladding holds the strips together. In this, it differs from the usual front strap, in which the palm leaf core is first clad lengthwise with papyrus around which a palm leaf transverse cladding is added. The strap might be incomplete, judging from the fact that the attachment with the back strap is lost as well. The back strap itself is still attached to the pre-strap, but is detached on the medial side. It is in its original position on the lateral side but is only connected by several fibres. Another pre-strap lies on the dorsal surface, the origin of which is uncertain as both pre-straps in the right sandal are still *in situ* as well.

3.2.2 Sewn Sandals Type D (Imitations)

Within the body of footwear of Tutankhamun are three variants of the Type D sewn sandals. Variant 1, imitations in wood, is represented by one pair of which the main material is wood. Variant 2 includes several different sandals, which resemble the fibre, sewn sandals mainly in shape, but the sewn fabric itself can at best be only vaguely recognised. Variant 3 is represented by the golden sandals.

3.2.2.1 Variant 1

Marquetry veneer sandals 397
(2822; JE 62692; 565) (figure 3.43)

Sole

The sole of sandals 397 (figures 3.44 & 3.45; table 3) is wood that is covered on all sides with a layer of gesso.[15] This layer, in turn, is covered with a thin layer of leather. It is clear that this latter layer is folded around the edges of the wood-with-gesso sole and its extension on the ventral surface is limited (as is usual with layers folded towards the ventral surfaces of soles) but to what extent is unknown. The extent to which it covers the dorsal surface of the wood-with-gesso sole is also uncertain, but there are several areas of damage which reveal a dark coloured layer underneath that seems to be leather. Consequently, the whole surface is likely to be covered with this thin layer.[16] The edge is covered with a strip of red bark, the extension at the ventral surface of which is unclear, but it certainly does not cover the whole surface. Possibly its extension is comparable to the extension of the leather layer.

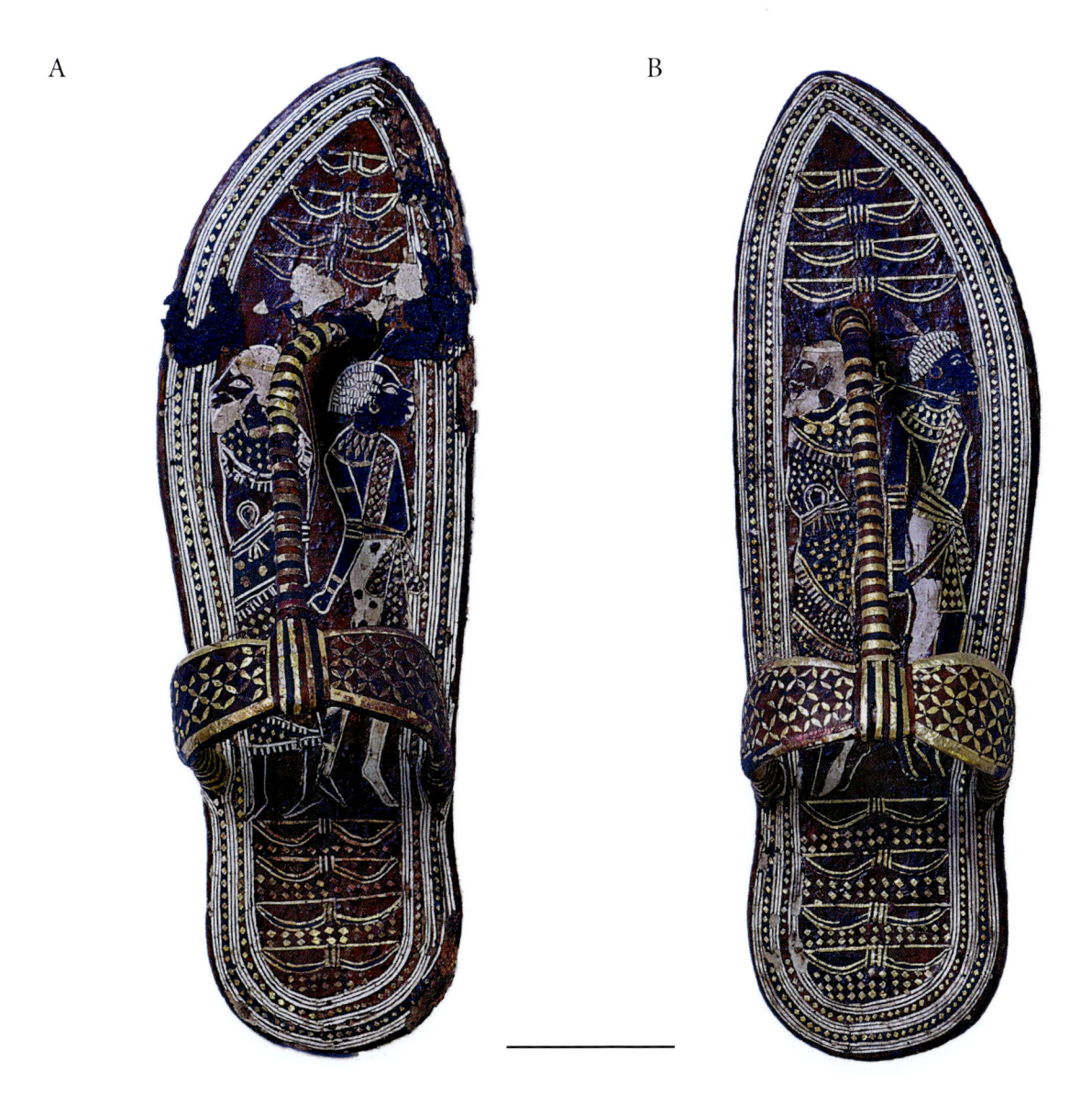

Figure 3.43. The marquetry veneer sandals 397. A) The left sandal in dorsal view; B) The right sandal in dorsal view. Scale bar is 50 mm. Photography by A.J. Veldmeijer. Courtesy of the Supreme Council of Antiquities / Authorities Egyptian Museum, Cairo.

Description

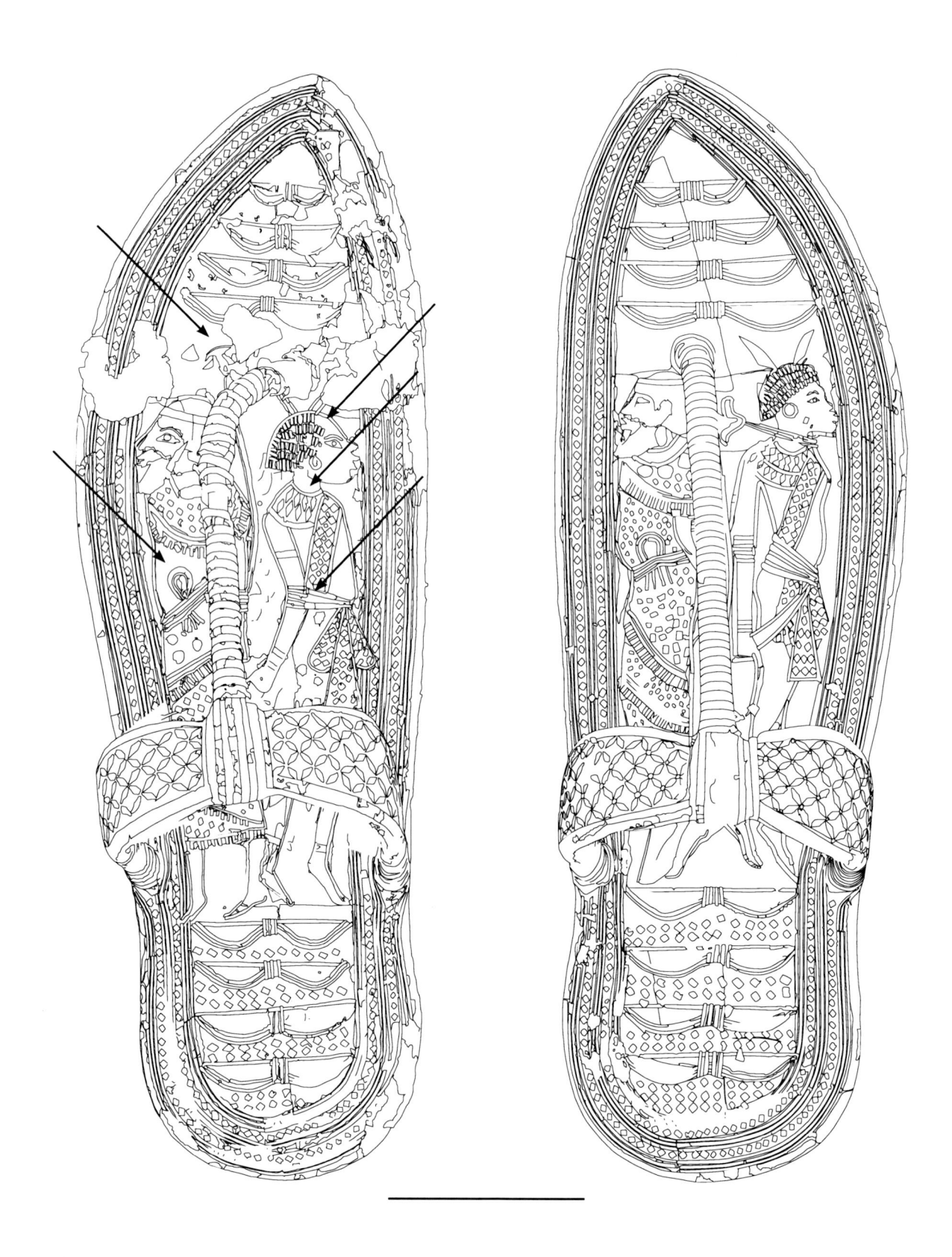

88

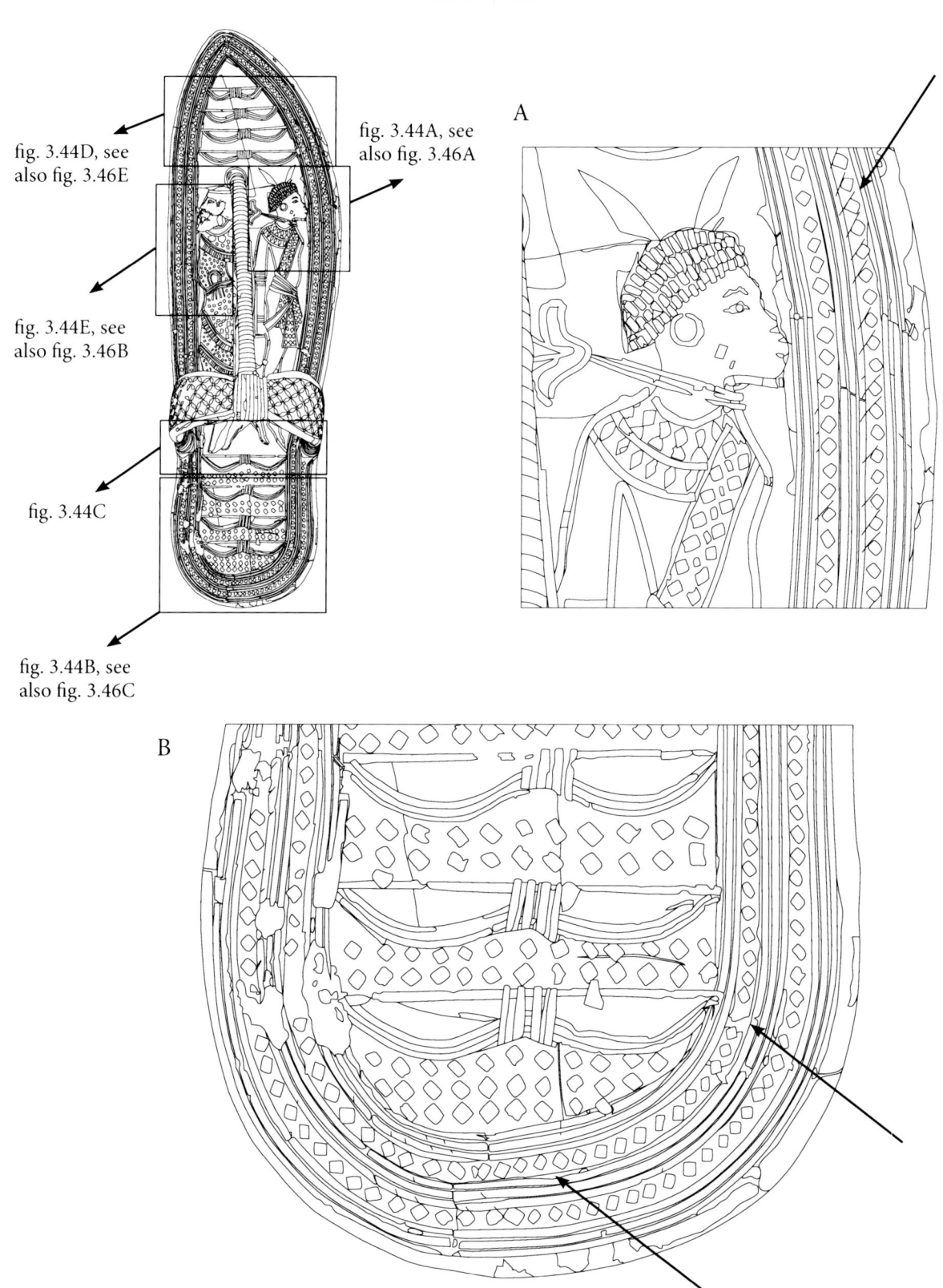

Previous page, above and next page: figure 3.44. The marquetry veneer sandals 397, overview. Inset: guide for the details. A) Detail of African prisoner of the right sandal. The arrow points to one of the many cuts; B) Heel part of the right sandal. The arrows point to the underlying, visible leather; C) Area immediately posterior to the pre-strap attachment of the right sandal; D) Front part of the right sandal, showing the four bows. The arrows point to the junction of several strips of bark; E) The Asiatic prisoner of the right sandal. The main differences of the images of the left and right sandal are with the prisoners and are marked by arrows in the left sandal of the overview (African prisoner: hair, tying of neck and arms, sashes; Asiatic prisoner: tying of arms, details of dress' decoration; see also figure 3.46). Scale bar overview previous page is 50 mm. Drawings by E. Endenburg.

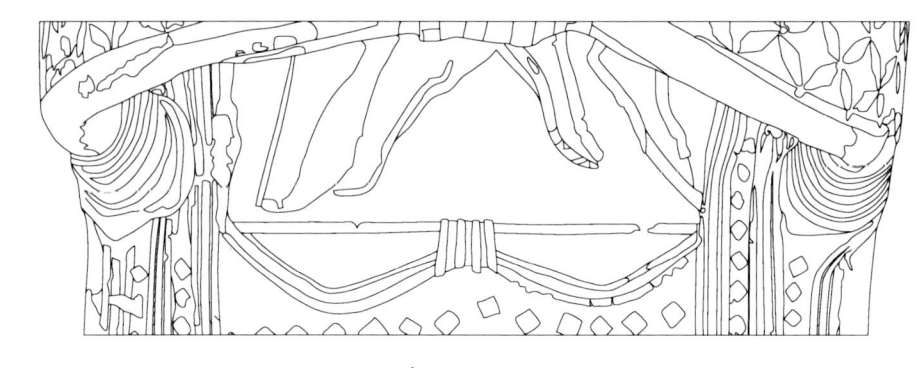

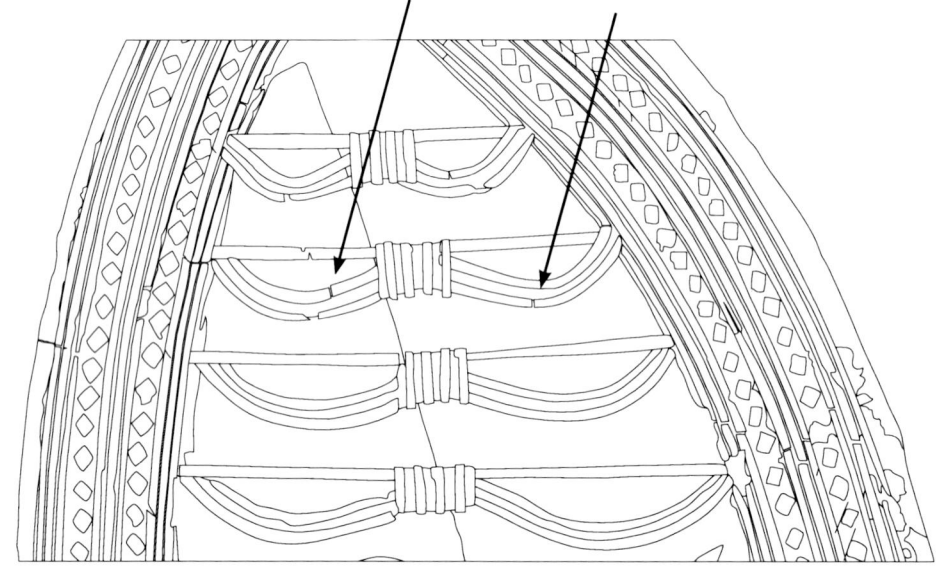

C

D

E

A

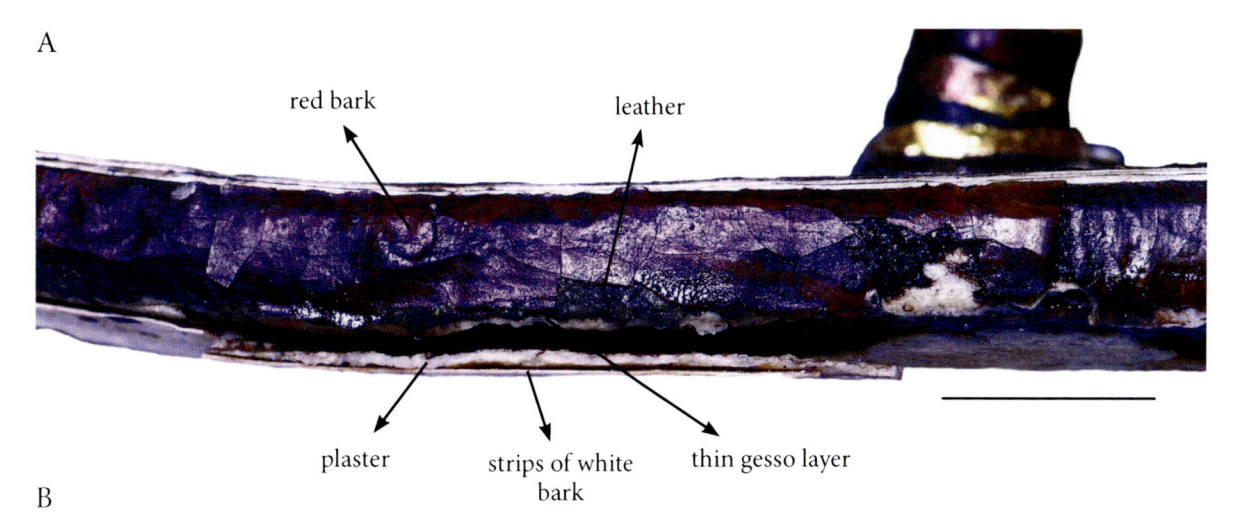

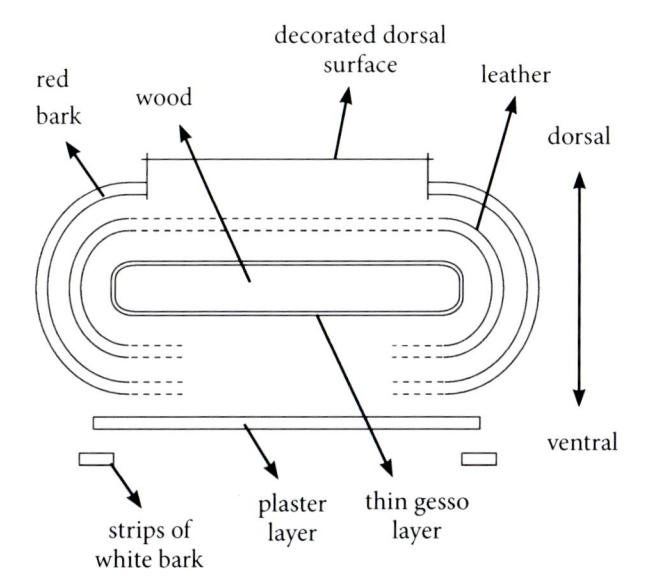

red bark   leather

plaster   strips of white bark   thin gesso layer

B

red bark
wood
decorated dorsal surface
leather
dorsal
ventral
strips of white bark
plaster layer
thin gesso layer

Figure 3.45. Detail of the marquetry veneer sandals 397. A) The sole seen from the side, showing the various existing layers (cf. 3.45B); B) The sole consists of a core of wood, which is covered with gesso on all sides. The dorsal surface is covered with a thin layer of leather upon which the decoration of the dorsal surface is applied; the edge is covered with red bark, extending to the ventral surface. A separate treadsole is attached; the edge at the ventral surface of the treadsole is neatly finished with a narrow strip of white bark. The dashed lines indicate that the extent of the layers could not be determined. Scale bar photograph is 10 mm. Photography by A.J. Veldmeijer. Courtesy of the Supreme Council of Antiquities / Authorities Egyptian Museum, Cairo. Drawing by E. Endenburg / A.J. Veldmeijer (not to scale).

On the ventral surface of the sole, the leather layer is covered with a thin plaster layer, sandwiching the leather and bark layers on their edges as they are folded over the edge of the wood-with-gesso sole. A small strip of white bark obscures the overlap. Carter mentions that the leather is green, which nowadays can still be seen in some spots, although the majority has turned black. Therefore, it is not clear whether the entire leather layer was green or that it was green only there where it was visible.

On the dorsal surface of the sole (figures 3.43 & 3.46), the red bark strip runs to the first[17] of the outermost set (there are three in total) of three parallel, white strips of birch bark (figure 3.44A & 3.46A-C). The strips run along the entire perimeter of the sole and are slightly separated, thus showing the leather. The width of these strips and the comparable strips of the middle and inner sets, as well as the strips used to form the figures vary in width but the average is about one mm. Each strip is not made of one continuous strip of bark but rather, several strips, as evidenced by the fact that several pieces do not always match exactly, and sometimes run over each other (figure 3.44D). The next row of decoration is a (green?) leather strip, on top of which are glued diamonds of white birch bark (about two by two mm, although several are slightly longer than they are wide), which are covered with gold foil.[18] Note that not all the 'diamond' ornaments in the sandal are diamond-shaped; there are many that are

91

rectangular and several with a more trapezoidal shape (see especially figure 3.46C). Next follows the middle set of three parallel strips of white bark, comparable to the first set. Following after this set, is a strip of red bark, which is like the strip of green leather, decorated with white birch bark diamonds and covered with gold foil. Here, since the bark strip is rather irregular in width, it is clear that it is put on top of the leather layer (see especially figures 3.44B & 3.46C). Next follows the innermost set of three parallel, white strips. On the right sandal (figure 3.44C), the first and second set of white strips curve around the lateral pre-strap attachment. However, the strips of the first two sets do not continue across the medial attachment of the right sandal: they stop at one side and then continue on the other. In the left sandal, both outermost sets curve around the pre-strap attachment (as in the lateral attachment of the right sandal) and the innermost set runs continuously inside the attachment (*cf.* figure 3.44 left and right overview). This might be an indication of construction by different craftsmen.[19]

An interesting feature, and especially well visible on the lateral edge of the right sandal (arrow in figure 3.44A) are cuts that follows one of the edges of the gilded birch bark diamonds of the first (outermost) perimeter row. These do not occur with all diamonds and mainly in one direction: from top right to bottom left although an occasional cut at right angles is present. It seems unlikely that these are the result of the cutting of the gold foil as this would not require much force. Instead, even though birch bark is easy to work with and quite soft, it might be the result of cutting the diamonds from a strip of bark while held in position (see figure 4.14). The technique seems to have been abandoned for the other side and the other sandal, where the cuts are far less numerous or even entirely absent.[20]

So far, all decoration has followed the sandal's perimeter. The decoration inside this decorative border is largely occupied by depictions of African and Asiatic foes and the eight[21] composite bows[22] (figure 3.44B & 3.46C). At the front there are four bows (figure 3.44D & 3.46E), each successively wider than the previous one, thus fitting the width to the border within the third (*i.e.* innermost) set of strips. However, some (the best example being the first (seen from the front) bow of the right sandal) were too big, or, alternatively, put too far towards the front, and the bow runs over the perimeter strips. This thus clearly shows the sequence in which the decoration was added. The bow strings as well as the outline of the arm[23] are made of strips of white birch bark covered with gold foil. The inner part of the arm is filled with a strip of (green?) leather. The grip is made with alternating strips of birch bark (covered with gold) and (green?) leather. Note that this scheme is not applied consistently in the same way: most bows have 'gold, leather, gold, leather, gold, leather, gold' (for example the first bow, seen from the front, of the right sandal) but some start with leather (for example the second bow of the right sandal). Also, some are composed of an uneven number of strips (for example the first bow of the right sandal); others are composed of an even number (for example the second bow of the right sandal). The strips that make the outline of the bows are continuous and thus the strips used for the grips run over them. Note, however, that on occasion these strips were not long enough and additional pieces were needed to complete the figure (arrows in figure 3.44D). The bows are secured on top of a red bark surface, which is cut to fit inside the third set of white strips, and this surface shows through the inner part of the bows (thus the area between the arm and bowstring). However, the red bark layer does not run underneath the Asiatic and African foes, described in more detail below, as can be clearly seen around the figures, where the layer has not been precisely cut away to make room for the figures (figure 3.44E). Moreover, several patches of red bark have been used to fill up gaps, for

Figure 3.46. Details of the dorsal surface of the right sandal of pair 397. A) The African prisoner; B) The Asiatic prisoner; C) Heel; D) Dorsal surface of the back strap; E) Front part of the right sandal; F, top & bottom) Lower part of the front strap of the left sandal. Scale bars are 10 mm. Photography by A.J. Veldmeijer. Courtesy of the Supreme Council of Antiquities / Authorities Egyptian Museum, Cairo.

example around the attachment of the front strap of the right sandal. The four bows at the heel (figure 3.44B) are similar to the ones at the front, although these four are more or less equal in size. In between them, however, are two transverse rows of diamonds (white birch bark, covered with gold leaf). In between the posterior-most bow and the innermost set of perimeter-line decorations are three of these transverse rows of diamonds. In the left sandal there is only one row of diamonds between the first and second bow, and two between the last bow and the perimeter decoration.

The heads of the foes (figure 3.44A & E; 3.46A & B) are made from white birch bark on which the details are added in leather, red bark and gold. The white area is produced by leaving the under-surface undecorated or, as for example with the eye of the Asian foe, cut out from the layer covering the surface. The knife cuts are clearly visible at the edges of the hair, beard and eye. The outline of the bodies is made of strips of birch bark (gilded as usual) and details added in different materials of various colours. Edgings of this material were not used where large, white areas were needed (the African dress). The foes on the right sandal are within the sandal's perimeter decoration; on the left sandal, however, they run partially over it (mainly the feet and lower leg of the Asian and the sash of the African; *cf.* figure 3.44). Although the overall layout is comparable, there are several differences in details in the figures (figure 3.44, arrows). One remarkable detail is in the left sandal where the Asian foe is tied with a rope ending in a lotus around his arms (the African foe is only tied at the elbow), whereas in the right, the African is tied with a 'lotus rope' around his neck with his elbows also tied (as are the elbows of the Asian foe).

Front strap

The front strap consists of a wooden core, around which is a relatively thick layer of gesso. At the insertion through the sole (figure 3.46F), this seems partly covered with a layer of leather, but this is in fact not the case: the leather is dripped on it from elsewhere (Card No. 397). Nothing is visible of the attachment on the ventral surface of the sole, due to the nature of the treadsole. The strap is decorated in transverse rows with white bark covered with gold foil, a strip of red bark, a strip of white bark with gold foil, (green?) leather, a strip of white bark with gold foil, etc.

It is clear that the front strap was inserted before the layer of red bark was added to the dorsal surface of the sole, a conclusion supported by the fact that this layer runs up to the pre-strap too. The decoration on the dorsal surface was added after the straps: at the back strap attachment, the leather runs up against the pre-strap and part of the perimeter decoration runs against it too. The fact that the bows and foes run over the perimeter decoration in some places shows that the decoration was built up, not only after the straps were attached, but from outside inwards. The decoration of the front strap itself was done after the attachment, as indicated by the fact that, as with the sole, the last strip runs over the red layer of the 'insole'.

Pre/back strap

The back straps are fairly complete in both sandals, thus preventing observation of the core. It is unlikely that the back strap is made of wood, like the rest of the sandal. Possibly, it is made of rawhide, which is suggested by a small damaged part of the outer surface of the back strap in the right sandal, showing the beige colour characteristic of rawhide.

The shape of the strap complex follows that of the Type C fibre, sewn sandals, although the front strap loop for the attachment with the back strap is nearly rectangular rather than triangular. It consists of rows of red bark, white bark with gold foil, green leather, red bark, etc. The attachment of the front and back straps cannot be ascertained.

A gesso layer covers, most likely, the entire surface, after which the posterodorsal and anteroventral edges and the ventral surface are covered with birch bark. The 'seam' between the edge and the ventral surface is covered with a narrow strip of green leather. In this, the construction differs from strap complex 453b (see below), which lacks the gesso layer.

Only the dorsal surface is decorated (figure 3.46D). The inner part is covered with red bark and a pattern of four diamonds of white bark, all overlaid with gold foil, around a centre of leather, with the whole thus resembling a bead-net pattern.

3.2.2.2 Variant 2

Leather and bead sandals 085a [left]/147a [right] (2825; JE 62686; 747)

This pair of sandals (figure 3.47, table 4) is relatively well preserved but has suffered since recovery. The leather is resinous in appearance and brittle. The left sandal is almost complete, but the first half of the lateral side has two semi-circular patches torn off. The posterolateral edge is slightly damaged as well, but to a far lesser extent. The right sandal is less complete, missing part of the heel. The strap complex is largely present, but broken. At the lateral front half, the edge is covered with a black substance, which might be 'melted' leather. Only the ventral surface of the left sandal could be studied as the right one is too fragile for handling. Due to boiled wax being poured over them as a conservative, the visibility of the sandal's details is reduced. Moreover, dust has adhered to the wax through the years, further obscuring the details. Adhering to the leather are remnants of what might have been packaging or material from an earlier museum display.

Sole

The shape of the sole closely resembles the shape of Type C fibre, sewn sandals. The treadsole consists of leather, the edges of which are bent upwards at a right angle and consequently obscure the outermost beads (partially, figure 3.48A). In doing this, it protects the fragile edges of the bead insole. The leather edge, detached from the treadsole at various points, is stitched with narrow leather stitches (or, alternatively, a thicker flax thread than used for stringing the beads), going through at least the outermost beads and apparently, judging from the line visible in some places on the ventral surface of the treadsole, back through the treadsole a few mm inside the edge proper (figure 3.48B). However, it cannot be entirely excluded, even though unlikely, that the edge was a separate, albeit very narrow strip of leather stitched onto the beads and under the treadsole (figure 3.48C).

The bead insole is stitched onto the leather, but it could not be determined exactly how, except for the previously-mentioned attachment to the edge. This might, however, be the only fastening. Additional points of securing the insole to the treadsole are the attachments of the straps, discussed below. The insole consists solely of coloured faience disc-shaped beads[24] in an elaborate design of lotuses and papyrus flowers, separated by transverse bands. They are strung with their flat surfaces against each other. Therefore the beads' edges form the surface facing the leather treadsole (figure 3.49). Each bead is passed through twice by thread. For any three adjacent rows of beads, these consist of one bead in the first row (A in figure 3.49), two beads in the second row (B in the figure) in between which the bead in the first row is positioned for half its visible diameter. The lower, third row (C in the figure) is the same as the first row and this process is repeated lengthwise as well as transversely with the result that each bead is surrounded by six other beads (figure 3.49). Taking the two threads coming from the bead in the first row and following it, one goes through the left bead in the second row whereas the other one runs through the right bead in the second row. In the third row, both threads turn inwards and pass through the same bead. This is repeated throughout the fabric. This simple but efficient technique allows the threads that emerge at the edge of the fabric to be used again in the opposite direction. This way of stringing beads was also the most common way of stringing closed beadwork in mummy netting (see for example Strecker & Heinrich, 2007: 222-224).[25] The stringing is done from side to side, which means that the sandal is built up either from top to bottom (anterior to posterior) or from bottom to top (there is no way of telling), but sewn sandals are always built from the heel forwards, for good practical reasons.

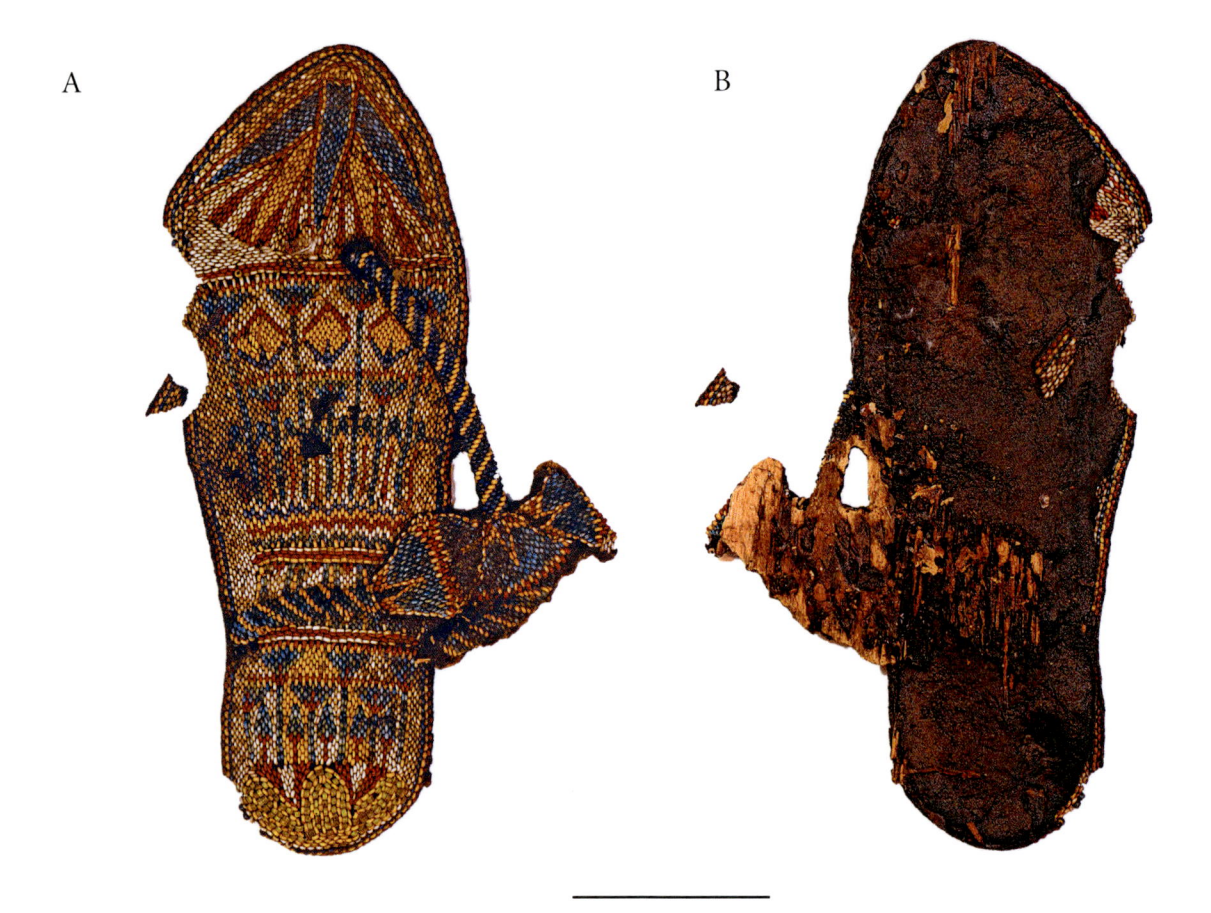

Figure 3.47. The bead and leather sandals 085a/147a. A) Left sandal (085a) in dorsal view; B) Left sandal (085a) in ventral view; C) Right sandal (147a) in dorsal view. Cf. figure 1.4 and figure 1.5. Scale bar is 50 mm. Photography by A.J. Veldmeijer. Courtesy of the Supreme Council of Antiquities / Authorities Egyptian Museum, Cairo.

The construction of part of the design proves somewhat enigmatic. Beads positioned at angles to the aforementioned pattern were fastened somehow, but one assumes that a similarly basic way of stringing was involved.

Front strap

The front strap and back strap are all one piece. The front strap consists of a core of leather onto which beads are attached in a spiralling pattern. The core is a lengthwise rolled strip of leather from the same piece of leather as the back straps, with right angle cuts (where it meets the back strap) which were rolled along the length of the core (figure 3.50). The core was then clad with the bead fabric. The edges of the leather might have been fastened together with the bead fabric. It is unlikely that the stringing technique was different from that used for the insole. The bead surface is made as a rectangular strip and the stringing tech-

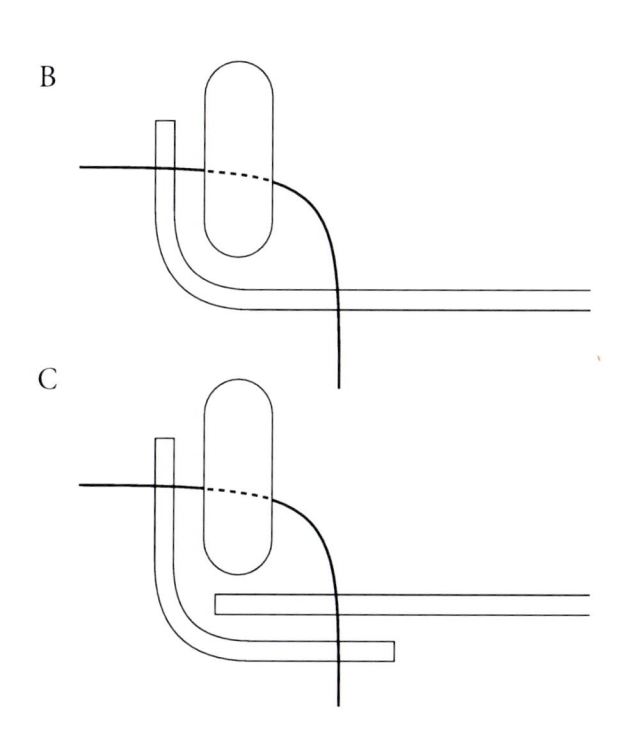

Figure 3.48A & inset) The edges of the leather treadsole protect the bead insole at its sides (cf. figure 3.48B); B) Probable construction of the in- and treadsole in 085a/147a; C) Alternative, but unlikely construction of the bead and leather sandals. Scale bar 3.48A is approximately 5 mm; scale bar inset is 10 mm. Photography by A.J. Veldmeijer. Courtesy of the Supreme Council of Antiquities / Authorities Egyptian Museum, Cairo. Drawing by E. Endenburg / A.J. Veldmeijer. Not to scale.

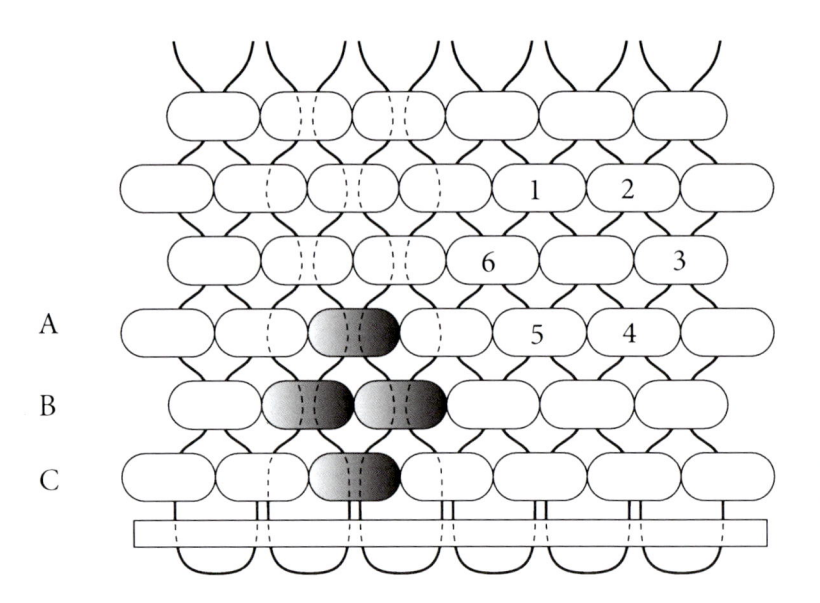

Figure 3.49. The bead insole in sandals 085a/147b. See text for explanation of A-C & 1-6. Drawing by E. Endenburg / A.J. Veldmeijer. Not to scale.

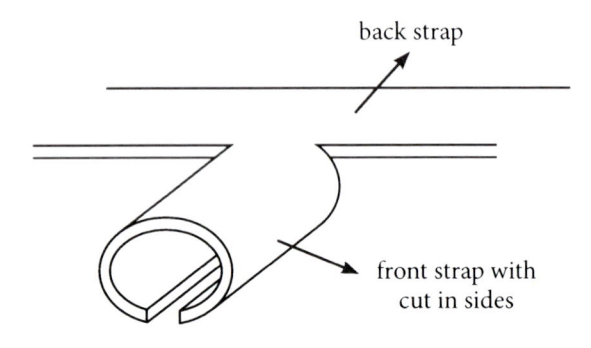

Figure 3.50. The leather core of the front and back strap is made of one sheet of leather. The front strap's leather is cut at the back strap and folded around to form a tube. The leather is covered with beads. Not to scale. Drawing by E. Endenburg / A.J. Veldmeijer.

Figure 3.51. The 'pre-strap' is sewn to the sole. Scale bar is 10 mm. Photography by A.J. Veldmeijer. Courtesy of the Supreme Council of Antiquities / Authorities Egyptian Museum, Cairo.

nique makes it possible to close it over the leather core without any problems. The core is inserted through the insole as well as the treadsole. Nothing, however, remains of the attachment on the ventral surface of the latter. The bead fabric has a spiralling design of bands of different colours and widths: two rows of blue beads alternate with one row of yellow beads.

Back strap

The shape of the back strap is the same as those in the Type C sewn sandals and consists of a leather layer onto which the bead fabric is attached. At the sides they taper into cylinders ('pre-straps'), which are comparable in design and construction to the front strap (*i.e.* a leather core, cut in and folded lengthwise). Remnants suggest that the leather of the 'pre-straps' was stitched to the dorsal surface of the leather treadsole rather than to the side or on the ventral surface (figure 3.51).

Leather sandals 021h & i
(4276; JE 62684) (figure 3.52)

This pair of sandals was much damaged when found (figure 2.5). Carter had already noted that the leather had turned into a resinous mass. The condition of the sandals,

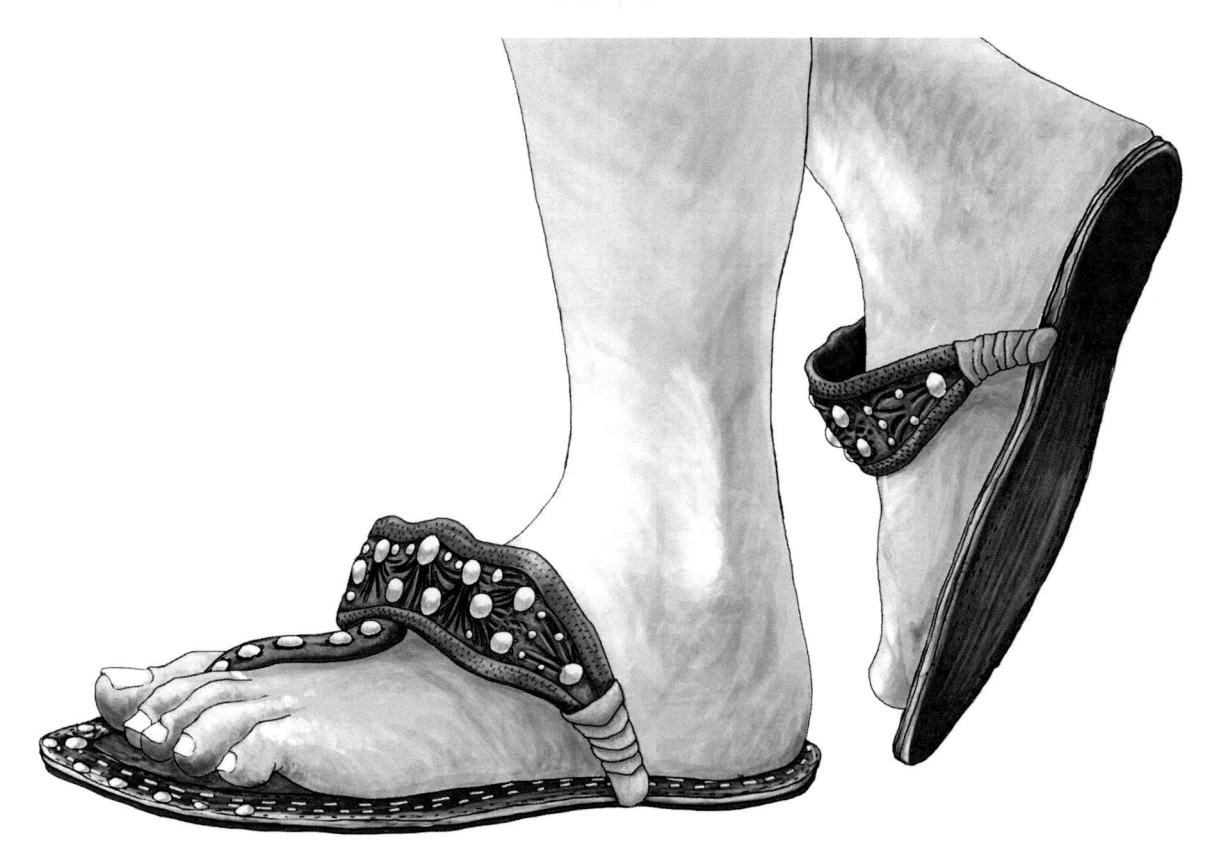

Figure 3.52. Artist's impression of leather sandals 021h & i. Drawing by M.H. Kriek.

however, has worsened distinctly since recovery, and as a result a thorough study is only possible after consolidation and reconstruction. The condition of the right sandal is worse than the left one and is now largely fragmented. It was decided to lift all the larger, loosely lying fragments to study some of the details. The major parts of the sandals, such as the soles and the straps, were not handled and hence some details remain uncertain.

Attached to the ventral surface of the treadsole are pieces of beadwork, which are parts of other objects from box 021 (possibly from the bead caps or bags mentioned by Carter on Card No. 021-2). The bigger, faience rosettes as well as the gold rosettes do not belong to the leather sandals either.

Sole

The sandals consist of an insole and treadsole of leather (figure 3.53 & 3.54A, table 5). The heel is rounded, the waist is slightly constricted and, towards the front part, the width increases, but slightly more to the lateral side than the medial side. The toe is pointed. The shape reminds one of the Type C sewn sandals. Along the perimeter of the insole is stitched a separate strip of leather, which is decorated with a double row of gold 'strips,' woven through slits.[26] This strip of leather is stitched on both edges (as in 270a, see figure 3.75A). It is uncertain whether the stitches penetrate both sole layers, but most likely they do so as to fasten them together. Carter (Card No. 021gh) observed that on the outside of this decoration ("at intervals of 2 - 2.5cm.") tiny gold hollow bosses are attached by means of loops soldered to their hollow sides (especially well seen in figure 2.5).[27] These are about "3mm. in diam." (Card No. 021gh). It is, however, unlikely that this 'boss decoration' extended further than about the front quarter of the sandal because there are no bosses preserved from this point back, and, moreover, there is no space to attach them as the strip's position

A

B

Figure 3.53. Pair of leather sandals 021h & i in dorsal view. A) Left; B) Right. Cf. figure 2.5. Scale bar is 50 mm. Photography by A.J. Veldmeijer. Courtesy of the Supreme Council of Antiquities / Authorities Egyptian Museum, Cairo.

> *Figure 3.54. Details of leather sandals 021h & i. A) Dorsal view of the heel of the right sandal; B) Oblique anterior view of the back strap; C) Side view of the back and pre-strap; D) and E) Oblique posterior view of the back strap. Scale bars are 10 mm. Photography by A.J. Veldmeijer. Courtesy of the Supreme Council of Antiquities / Authorities Egyptian Museum, Cairo.*

Description

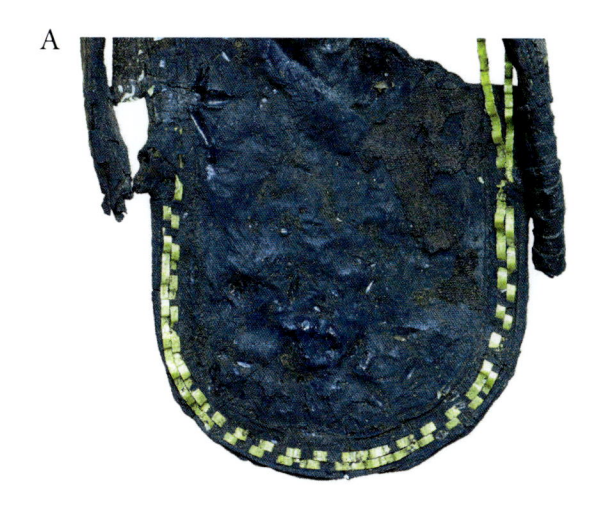

D

E

here is at the sole's edge. At the point of the toe is a larger boss ("7 mm. in diam.", Card No. 021gh; this is only visible in the *in situ* photo of the sandal in the box, figure 1.2C inset) and a similar one at the toe but inside the decoration strip with gold 'wire.' It is uncertain whether the bosses penetrate both soles.

Front strap

According to Carter (Card No. 021gh), the front strap is "a round stick, covered with leather(?)," but actually the core consists of palm leaf and papyrus, as also seen in fibre, sewn sandals, and is covered lengthwise with two strips of leather (figures 3.55B & C). The ventral strip, which was not visible originally, is, along its long edges, covered by the overlapping dorsal strip (figure 3.56). There is no evidence of stitching, which suggests that the leather is glued. The gold bosses (of the large variant mentioned previously) that adorn the dorsal surface, do not penetrate the entire thickness as the attachment is not visible on the ventral surface. The bosses are attached in the same way as seen in shoes 021f & g, *i.e.* with split

> *Figure 3.55. Fragments from the leather sandals 021h & i. A1-2) Fragment of the front edge; B) Piece of front strap; C1-2) Dorsal and ventral view of a front strap. Note the cut-out petals of the flower; D1-7) Fragments of the back strap's openwork layer; E1-2) Fragments of the sides of the back strap; F) Back side of the openwork layer, showing the attachment of a gold boss; G) Example of attached beadwork. Scale bar is 10 mm. Photography by A.J. Veldmeijer. Courtesy of the Supreme Council of Antiquities / Authorities Egyptian Museum, Cairo.*

A1　　　　　　　A2　　　　　　　　　　　　　B

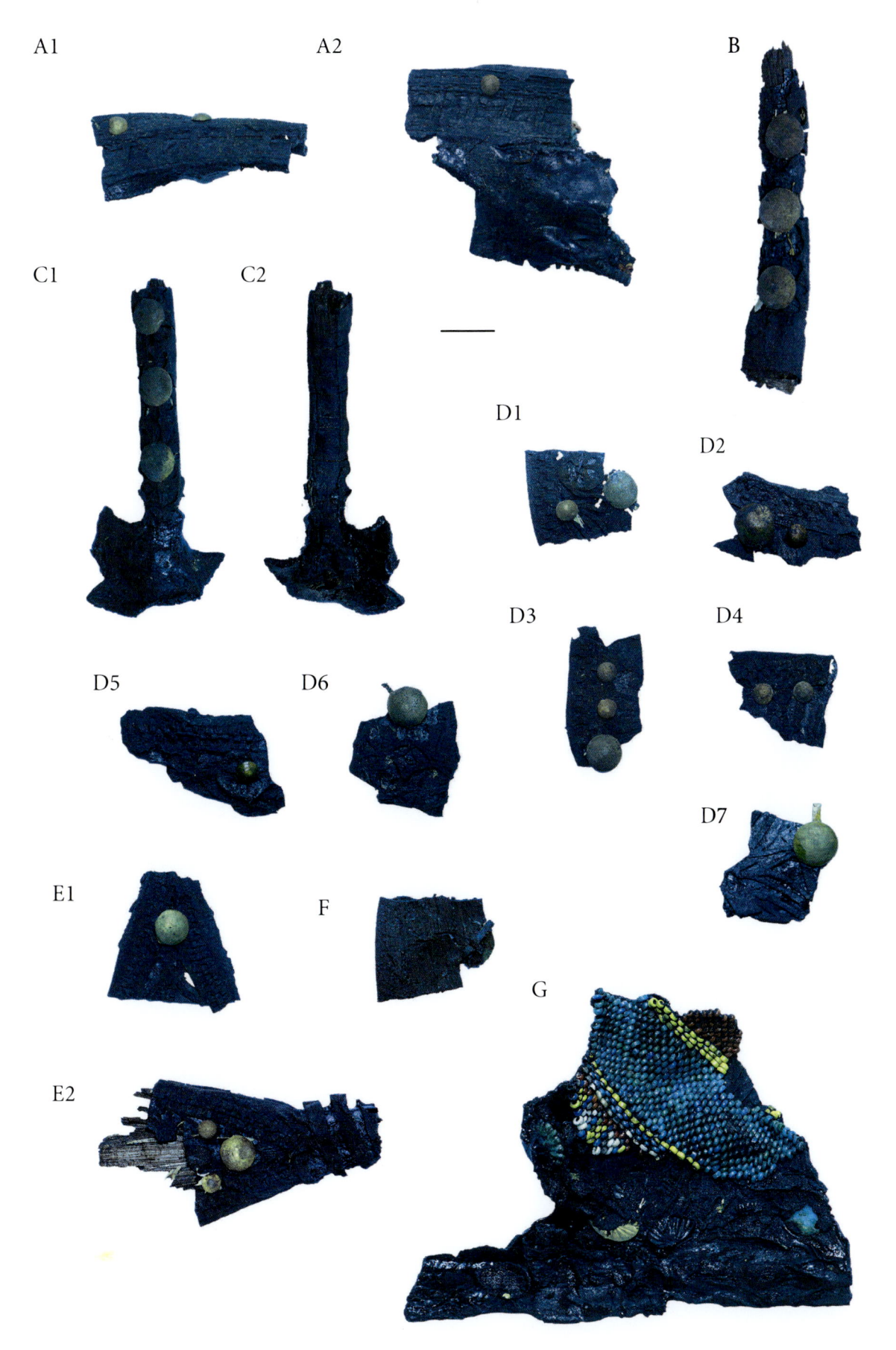

C1　　C2

D1　　D2

D3　　D4

D5　　D6

D7

E1　　F

E2

G

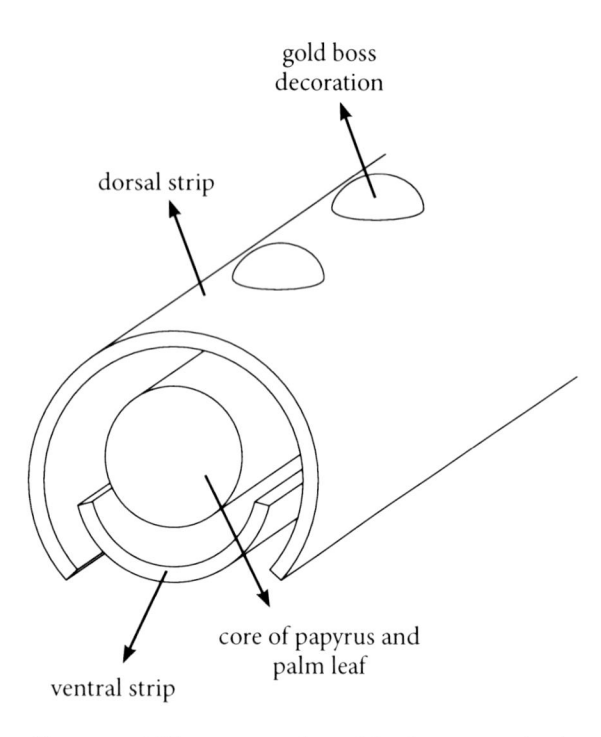

Figure 3.56. The construction of the front strap in the pair of leather sandals 021h & i. Not to scale. Drawing by E. Endenburg / A.J. Veldmeijer.

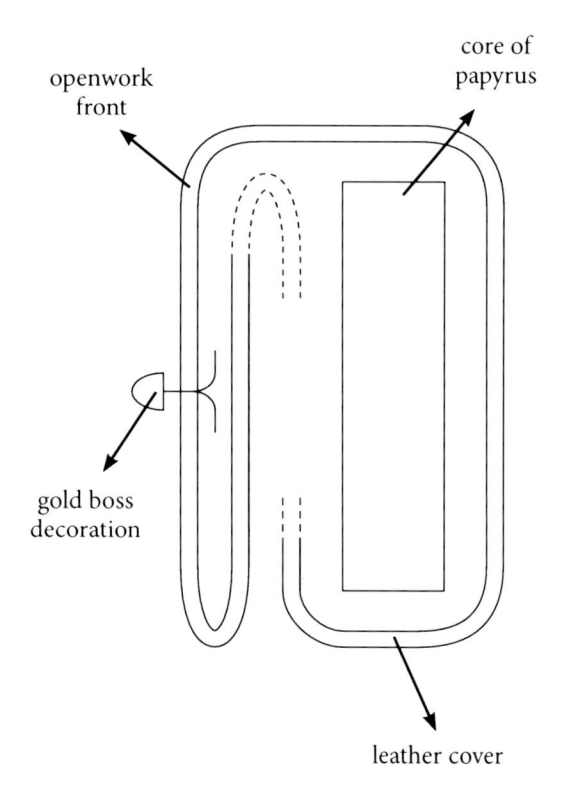

Figure 3.57. Construction of the back strap in the pair of leather sandals 021h & i. The length of the extension is uncertain, hence the dashed line. Not to scale. Drawing by E. Endenburg / A.J. Veldmeijer.

pin attachment (see section 4.2.3.5). Here, the bosses are inserted through the dorsal layer of the leather and the papyrus core and their hooks are obscured by the ventral layer of the leather. The bosses form the centre part of flowers, the leafs of which have been cut out in the leather (figures 2.5 & 3.55C1).

The attachment to the sole is uncertain. A thickening is visible at the front of the now isolated strap. It would seem that this is a separate strip of leather, which is involved in the attachment to the sole. Moreover, it seems that the sole's leather extends around the core of the front strap, but the condition of the leather does not allow observation of the construction. As in fibre, sewn sandals, the palm leaf core and the papyrus cladding are both looped around the back strap (figures 3.54B & D). The loop is triangular in shape. Note that the front strap's core is looped over the back strap's leather covering. In one of the fragments, the tied strap, before its looping the back strap, is still *in situ*.

Back strap

The shape of the back strap is the same as for the traditional Type C sewn sandal back strap (figures 3.54B-E) and so needs no further description here. At least part of the construction can be identified (figure 3.57). The back of the papyrus strap is covered with one layer of leather, which is folded around the dorsal and ventral edges. It covers the front of the back strap as well and is folded at the ventral margin, thus creating a second layer. The lower layer, *i.e.* the one covering the papyrus, is plain but the second layer is of elaborate openwork leather (with lotus designs) and decorated with gold bosses of both the larger and smaller diameters mentioned previously (figures 3.55 D-F). These are hooked through the openwork layer only.

Along the dorsal and ventral edges are three rows of slits, cut in an offset pattern. Although other examples have these slit-pattern decorative features with one or more gold strips woven through them, the slits here seem to act as the decoration itself: there are no indications that something was woven through them. The construction of the tapering piece of leather on the ventral surface of the back strap is enigmatic. It covers the front strap loop and acts, according to Carter (Card No. 021i), as reinforcement. The fold of the leather over the dorsal edge of the papyrus is clearly visible, but nevertheless it seems to be connected to the rest of the leather. On the sides, the back straps end in tubes, which imitate the pre-strap in fibre, sewn sandals with a strip of leather wound around the tapering end of the back strap. This construction is common in leather sandals (*cf.* for example Veldmeijer, 2009i). The attachment to the sole is not clear.

Strap complex 453b
(2817; JE 62683; 1259)[28]

Entry 453b (figure 3.58, table 5) is an isolated but complete strap complex that imitates the straps in fibre, sewn sandals. However, the loop of the front strap to the back strap is not triangular but rectangular, and in this resembles the marquetry veneer sandals described in section 3.2.2.1. It is not clear how the front strap is attached to the back strap.

The back strap is made of rawhide, with a ventral surface (when attached to the sandal) covered with relatively wide strips of birch bark (figures 3.59A & B). The dorsal surface, however, is not covered with this white material but instead with red bark. The sides of the back strap and the pre-straps do not have a foundation but rather, the leather and bark with gold leaf are applied directly onto the rawhide. The decoration of the front strap consists of strips of (likely) green leather, red bark and yellow gold (or reddish gold in several cases) on white bark, some of which are not closed on the ventral surface. A relatively wide strip of white bark is applied lengthwise, covering the ends of the coloured and gold strips (figures 3.59A & C).

The anterodorsal surface is decorated with two *wedjet*-eyes with two *nefers* at the inner side (figures 3.59D-F). The eyebrows are made of two narrow strips of gold leaf on white bark separated by a strip of green(?) leather. The outlines of the eyes also consist of bark and gold foil with the eye itself made of white bark. Note the details in the corner of the eyes, which was accomplished by cutting away the bark to reveal the red brown bark underneath. The pupil in one of the eyes is inlaid with a slightly darker coloured material, possibly also bark. The lighter surface of the eye has been cut out,

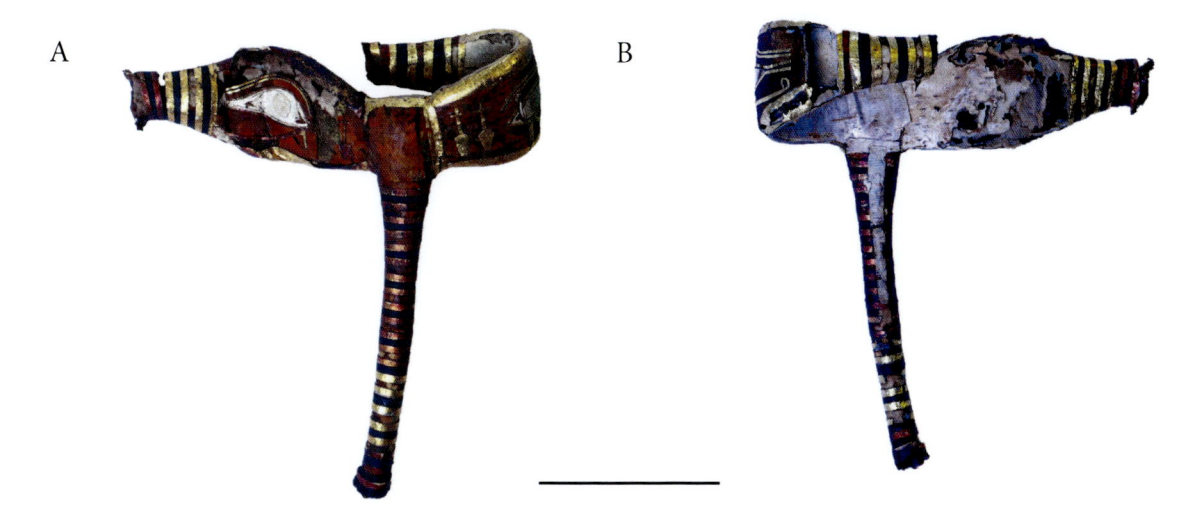

Figure 3.58. The isolated strap complex 453b, made with rawhide, birch bark, bark, leather and gold foil. A) Front view; B) Back view. Scale bar is 50 mm. Photography by A.J. Veldmeijer. Courtesy of the Supreme Council of Antiquities / Authorities Egyptian Museum, Cairo.

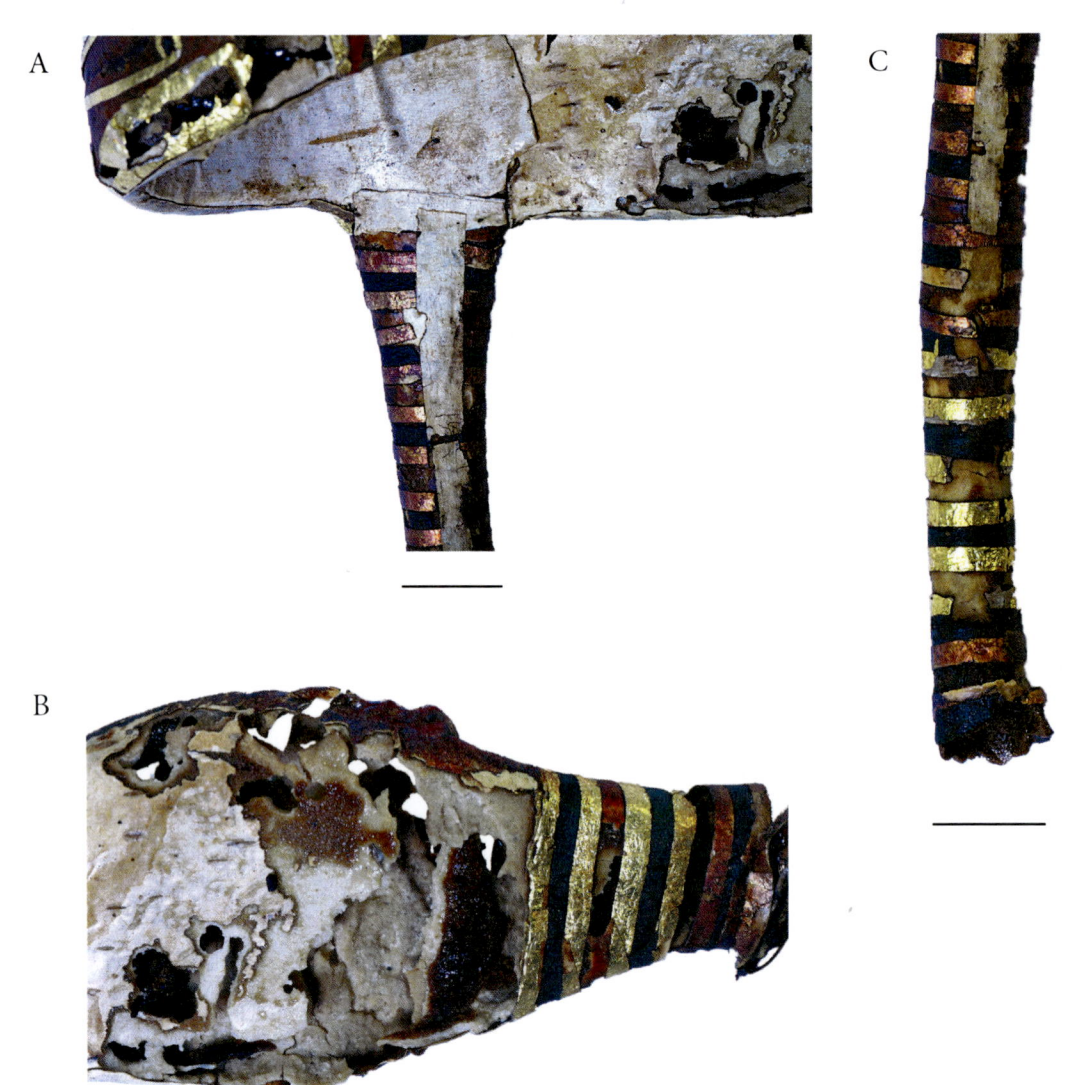

Figure 3.59. Details of the isolated strap complex 453b. A) Attachment area of the front and back strap, seen from ventral; B) Back of the left side; C) Lower part of the front strap, ventral view; D) Detail of the nefers; E) & F, next page) Detail of the wedjet-eyes. Scale bars are 10 mm. Photography by A.J. Veldmeijer. Courtesy of the Supreme Council of Antiquities / Authorities Egyptian Museum, Cairo.

E

F

as clearly suggested by knife cuts (see especially figure 3.59E). The *nefers* are made of white bark with gold foil. The long edges of the back strap as well as the intersection where the front strap loop meets the back strap, are overlain with gold foil on bark (figure 3.59D).

Note that the covering and decorations are similar in both the combination of materials and construction techniques to the marquetry veneer sandals (397): *i.e.*, white bark covered with a layer of gold foil, red bark and (possibly) green leather on the pre-straps.

3.2.2.3 Variant 3

256ll (3503/3504; JE 60678/60679; 327)

This pair of sandals, made of gold plate and found on the mummy's feet (Carter, 1927: 137; figures 1.8 & 3.60, table 5), are good examples of the Type D, Variant 3 sewn sandals. The heel is rounded, the waist is constricted and the width widens from this point towards the front (especially on the lateral side). The sandal terminates in a pointed toe, which is slightly off centre, thus creating a slightly swayed sole. It was bent over the toes, thus imitating the shape of fibre, sewn sandals closely. However, the condition is caused by the mummy wrapping rather than an intended feature (*cf.* Derry, 1927: 151-152). This is also evident from the fact that the edges and heels were folded over. After removal of the sandals, the soles have been straightened (*cf.* figure 1.8 & 3.60). The heel is slightly asymmetrical in the longitudinal plane: the posterolateral curvature is more pronounced in both sandals. This suggests that one sandal was cut from the gold plate and then placed on the plate to cut the other. In order to get a right and left sandal, the 'dorsal' surface of the template had to be put face-down on the future-dorsal surface of the other, the outline traced, and then cut. Alternately, the template was placed with its 'ventral' surface on top of the future-dorsal surface and

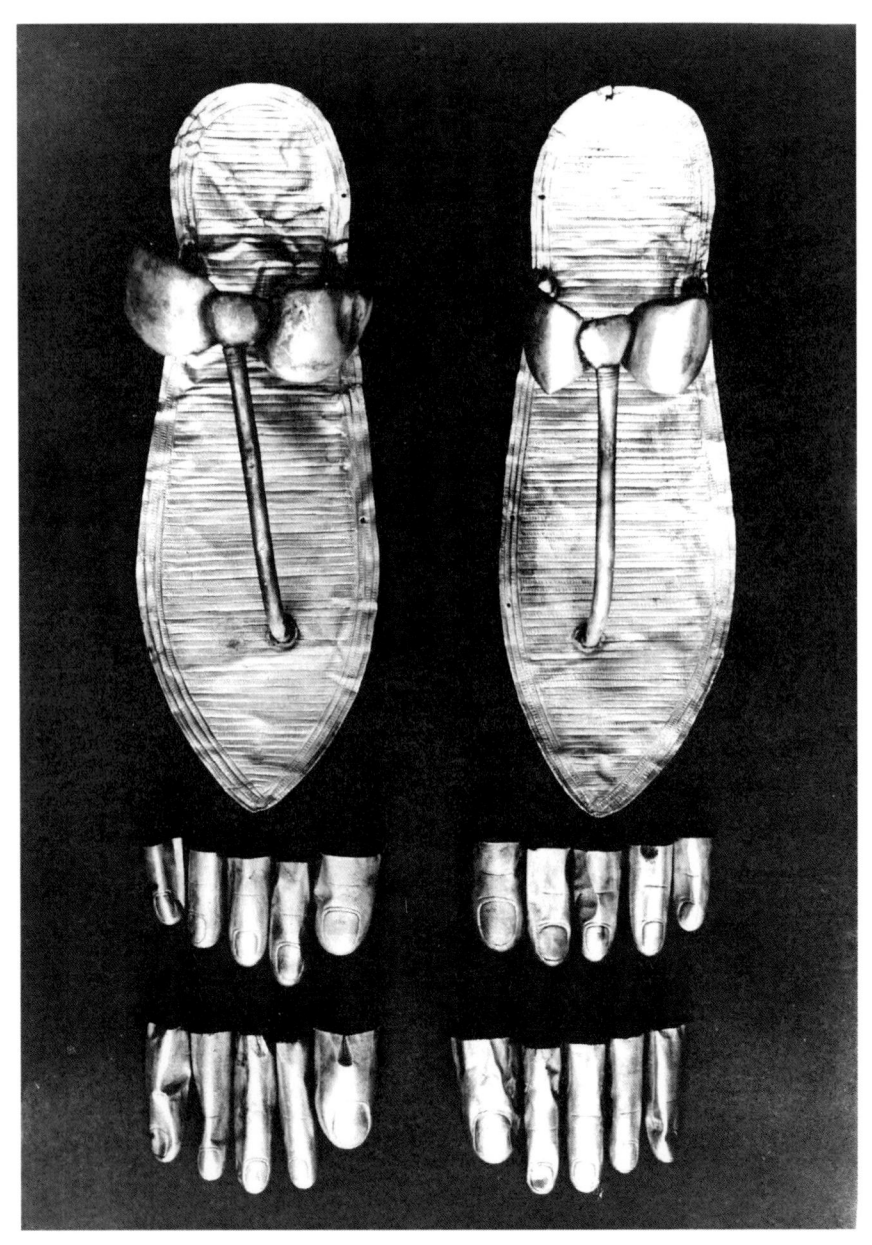

Figure 3.60. The golden sandals 256ll, which simulate fibre, sewn sandals, together with the gold toe and finger caps. Cf. figure 1.8. Photography by H. Burton. Copyright Griffith Institute, University of Oxford.

then cut, but in this case had to be turned over with the other surface upwards after cutting. The transverse bundles are embossed as well as the sewing strips (*cf.* the insole in shoes 021f & g, figures 3.63A-D & F). The edges of the sandals consists of a triple edge of which the sewing strips are visible. Moreover, "the inside borders of the soles are pierced with three holes for a purpose unknown." (Card No. 256ll).

The strap complex consists of a gold rod, going between the first and second toes, and running towards the backs strap as in the Type C sewn sandals. The tying of the front strap just before looping to the back strap is indicated with embossed transverse lines. The front strap is inserted through a hole in the front of the sole and does not seem to have been secured. The back strap is also put through the sole. Note the two indentations in the medial back strap of the right sandal.

A thin gold wire bangle was found at the right ankle of the king's mummy. As Carter said (Card No. 256mm), the purpose is unknown, but it does not seem to have had a connection with the sandal.

3.3 THE OPEN SHOES

3.3.1 Type: Partial Upper, Leather and Beadwork;
Variant: Sewn Sandal Strap Complex/Foot strap[29]

021f [left]/021g [right] (2818; JE 62680; 341) (figure 3.61 and guide on page 111)

This pair of shoes (figure 3.62, table 6) is in fragile condition and has largely fallen apart (*cf.* figure 2.3). The poor condition severely limited a thorough study, and only after consolidation and reconstruction might it be possible to study certain elements, such as the ventral surface of the treadsole. No loose lying parts were lifted.

Sole

The sole, the shape of which resembles fibre, sewn sandal Type C, consists of a leather (or rawhide) treadsole of which almost nothing remains: the leather has turned into a resinous mass. This treadsole is covered with a thin sheet of gold (figures 3.63A-D), serving as an insole, the edges of which are folded around the treadsole (figure 3.63J). The width cannot be determined, hence the dashed line in figure 3.65. The surviving remnants of the treadsole also show, on its dorsal surface, transverse 'bundles' (figure 3.64). Without a doubt, the surface was made in this way because if it were not, the voids in the corrugated gold sheet (the transverse bundles) would crush down onto the flat dorsal surface of the leather treadsole due to the weight of the owner.

The centre part (figure 3.63A), following the outline of the sandal, is isolated now, but this is due to the fact that the closely spaced stitch holes were torn along the sewing perforations into a long cut from forces exerted on them. It clearly shows the characteristic semi-circular remnants of the holes. Such an applied force is probably the reason for

Figure 3.61. Artist's impression of open shoes 021f & g. The line drawing on page 111 guides the reader through the text and figures. Drawing by M.H. Kriek.

A B

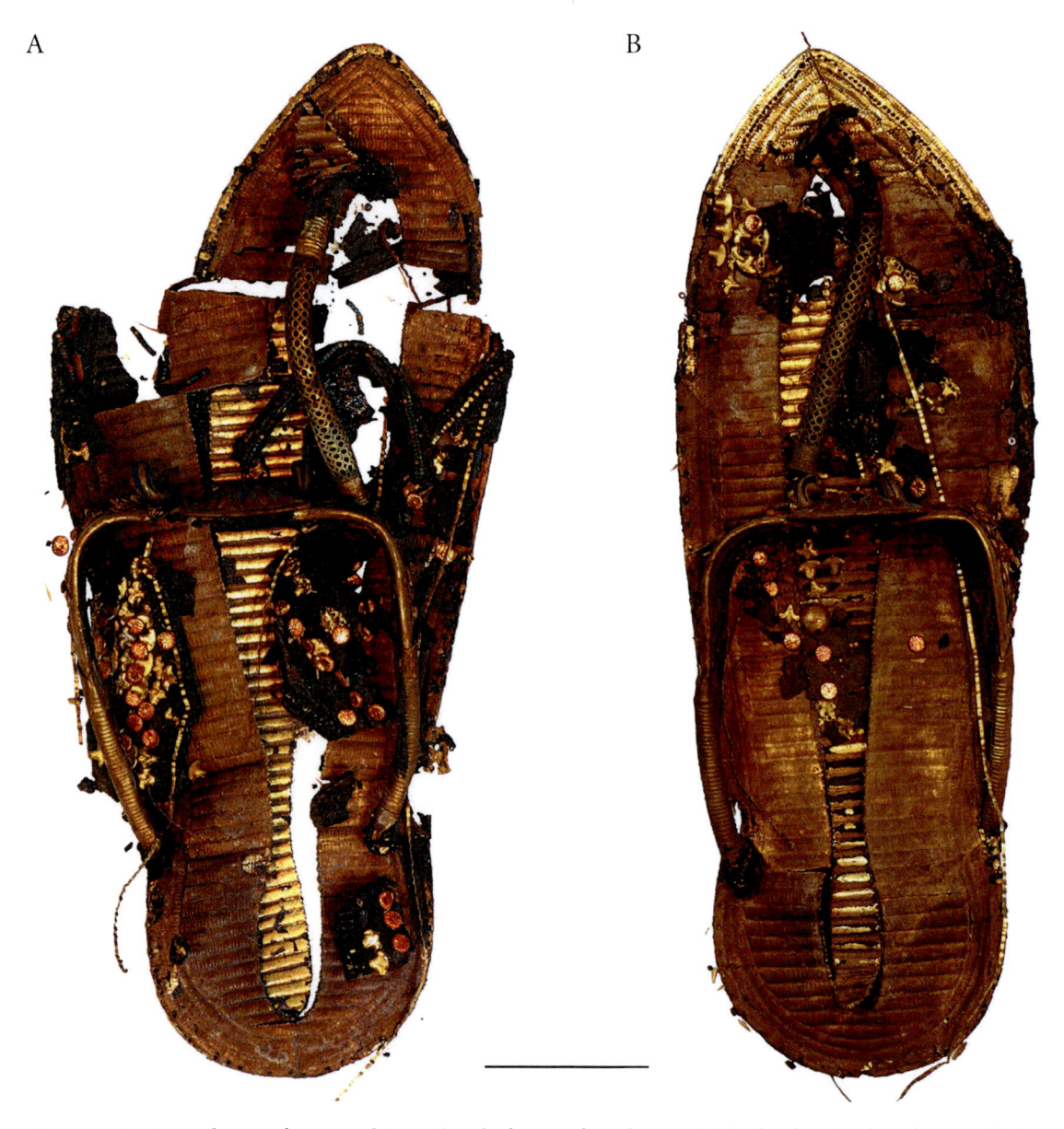

Figure 3.62. Pair of open shoes 021f & g. A) Left shoe in dorsal view; B) Right shoe in dorsal view. Cf. figure 2.3. Scale bar is 50 mm. Photography by A.J. Veldmeijer. Courtesy of the Supreme Council of Antiquities / Authorities Egyptian Museum, Cairo.

the fact that, in some places but not along the entire length of the cut, the edges of the holes of the broken stitch holes have been pushed downwards. Note that in Burton's photograph (figure 2.3) the centre part was still largely *in situ*. The surface shows the embossed transverse bundles in a continuous line with the outer part indicating that the sole was made as a whole with the stitch holes punched into it afterwards. The transverse bundles of this centre part do not show the sewn palm leaf strips embossed in gold, but the outer parts of the sole do

show these details (figures 3.63A & B). This suggests that such details were added after the centre part was covered. The stitch holes were used to attach a leather layer over this centre part, remnants of which can still be seen in Burton's photographs.

The peculiar distribution of the yellow and dull gold parts needs some more attention but will be discussed in detail in section 4.2.3.3 and 4.2.3.4. The distinct difference in colour between the centre part and the rest of the sole must have led Carter to question the material of the outer part. How-

110

GUIDE to 021f & g

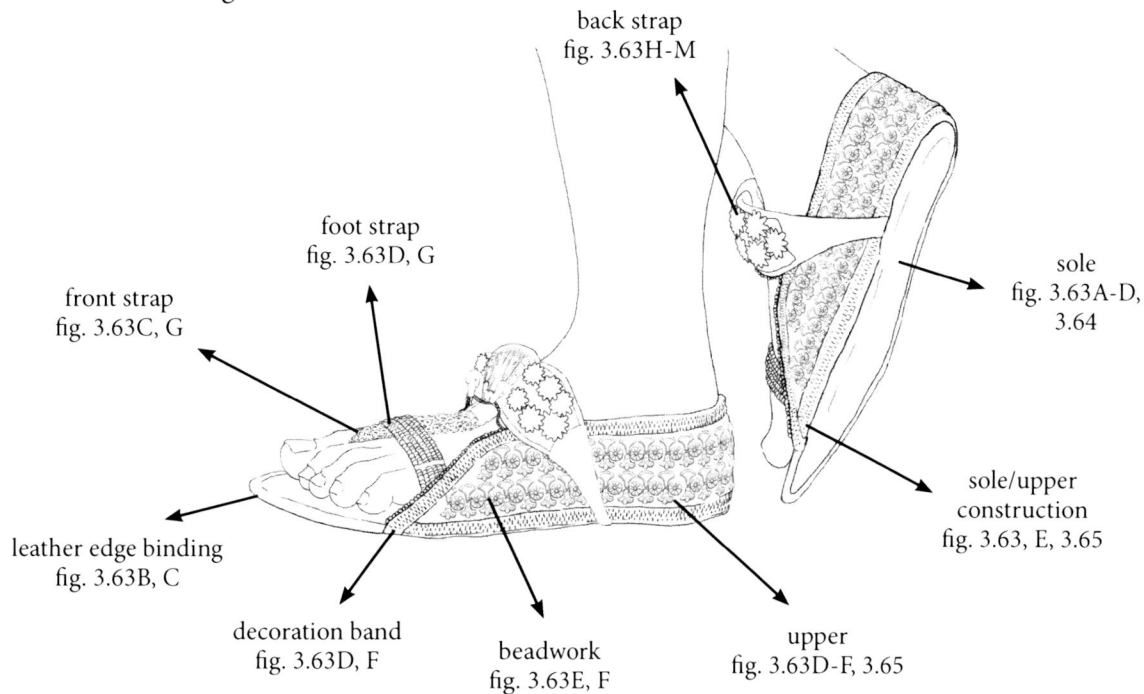

- back strap fig. 3.63H-M
- foot strap fig. 3.63D, G
- front strap fig. 3.63C, G
- sole fig. 3.63A-D, 3.64
- leather edge binding fig. 3.63B, C
- sole/upper construction fig. 3.63, E, 3.65
- decoration band fig. 3.63D, F
- beadwork fig. 3.63E, F
- upper fig. 3.63D-F, 3.65

ever, both elements show the bright yellow colour of gold as well as, to varying degrees, a light brown colour. The outer part predominantly shows the brown colour, with the exception of the front of the sandal, and the centre part is bright yellow. Also large parts of the edge still show the bright yellow colour of gold, and intact spots show remnants of the upper's leather, which apparently protected it. As will be argued, the colours seem to have been intended.

The gold insole shows the familiar fibre, sewn sandals Type C edge, consisting of three cores. Here, however, they were deliberately set slightly inwards of the sandal's edge (figures 3.63B & C), allowing for a small strip to attach the upper to the sole. Thus, the triple edge was not obscured, which suggests that it was important that it be seen, possibly in order to be recognisable as a sewn sandal. The edge of the sole has stitch holes at regular intervals (about 5 mm apart) along the extension of the upper. The stitch holes are more numerous in front of the upper and more closely-spaced. In fact, they are set so closely together that they almost touch, but

Figure 3.63 (next 5 pages). Details of open shoes 021f & g. A) The heel part, seen from dorsal, of the right shoe. Note the centre part; B) Front part of the left shoe; C) Front part of the right shoe; D) The start of the upper as seen in the left shoe; the band of decoration on the sole runs under the band at the top of the upper (inset); E) Sole and attachment of the upper in the left shoe; F) Left shoe, showing a small fragment of nearly intact upper. Note the back of the gold beads, showing different types of attachment; G) Left shoe. The bead-on-leather foot strap, showing the spacer bead that keeps the six strands of beads together. In the background the openwork gold front strap is visible. Indication scale: the beads have a diameter of 1.5 mm; H) Left shoe. The back surface of the back strap. Note the hooks, used to attach the duck heads as well as the daisies on the anterior side; I) Back view of the back straps of the right and left shoes, respectively. The back surface is covered with a thin layer of coarse linen; the hooks are hidden by means of a layer of leather, a remnant of which is just visible to the right. Note the torn cross section of the sides of the wooden back straps; J) Right shoe. Lateral part of the back strap; K) Right shoe. Detail of daisy (cf. figure 4.3); L) Right shoe. Detail of the triangular centre part, which clearly imitates the loop of the front strap in fibre, sewn sandals (cf. figure 4.12); M) Right shoe. Duck head. Note the small loop under the beak for the reception of the strand of beads. (cf. figure 4.13). Scale bars are 10 mm. Photography by A.J. Veldmeijer. Courtesy of the Supreme Council of Antiquities / Authorities Egyptian Museum, Cairo.

Description

D

D inset

E

113

Description

F

G

H

I1

I2

J

115

Description

K

L

M

nevertheless some are punched through the layer in pairs (figures 3.63B & C). In contrast to 021k & l, described in section 3.3.2, the row of stitch holes is largely intact and not turned into one continuous perforation (except for a small part on the left shoe, close to the start of the upper; Burton only photographed the left one, so the original condition of the right one when discovered by Carter and his team, is unknown). The stitch holes are mainly inserted through the outermost row of the triple edge, rather than the area presumably intended for that purpose next to it. These stitches in front of the upper served to secure the two sole layers, as remnants of stitches are still visible in some of the stitch holes. However, the stitches include a narrow strip of leather, covering the outermost edge of the sandal as suggested by the small surviving scraps. Without the aid of a microscope, it proved impossible to identify the material of the stitches. However, the upper is stitched to the sole by means of leather thong and it seems unlikely that another kind of stitching was used on this part of the sole.

Upper

When recovered, most of the lateral side of the upper of the left sandal was still *in situ*, the remnants of which are still preserved (figures 3.63D-F). It consists of one layer of leather with an additional layer of 'beads'[30] on the outer surface. The leather layer might have been thinner than the sole, but this could not be confirmed by measurements.

The upper begins at about one quarter the length of the sole, from the front on both sides (figure 3.61). The top edge (instep) runs upwards at an angle to a point under the back strap, after which it continues parallel to the sole, *i.e.* without a change in height. Its top is decorated with a band of leather, showing three horizontal rows of slits (figure 3.63D). Through the middle row, a narrow strip of gold is woven whereas the bottom and top rows show

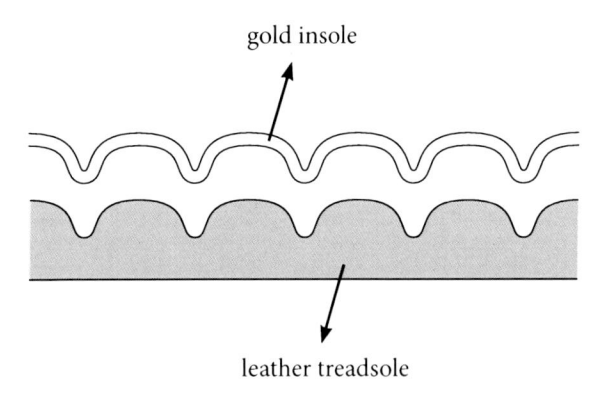

Figure 3.64. The dorsal surface of the leather treadsole in the pair of shoes 021f & g shadows the shape of the insole. Not to scale. Drawing by E. Endenburg / A.J. Veldmeijer.

small remaining scraps of what seem to have been a leather strip. The colour is not preserved, but undoubtedly it differed from the layer underneath. The leather band is stitched to the upper's leather immediately under the lower row of slits (figure 3.65), and although no remnants of the stitches are visible, the stitch holes are positioned in a straight horizontal line and at regular intervals, suggesting that a running stitch was used. The top band seems, in contrast to 021k & l described below, not folded but rather a separate piece. In Burton's photograph the sharp edge of the top of the upper suggests this because, had it been folded, the edge should be rounded. Moreover, one can see in several places in Burton's photograph, that the upper's leather protrudes slightly from the leather band. Alternately, it is possible that the fold, if it existed, has worn through. The way the leather band is attached at the top cannot be determined (hence the dashed line in figure 3.65), but it is fair to assume that it was done in the same way as at the bottom, *i.e.* with running stitches. Remnants suggest that the stitches were made of flax. The bottom of the upper shows a comparable decorative leather band that runs, at the start of the upper, under the top one (figure 3.63D). At the top, this lower band is attached to the leather of the upper as described for the band at the instep (*i.e.* with running stitches of flax). It was attached after the beadwork outer lay-

117

er (figure 3.63F). Because the band at the instep runs over this lower band, it was attached last, but most likely before the upper was attached to the sole. This is suggested by the front of the upper, including the top band, because it is folded around the sole's edge (figure 3.63D inset).

The outer surface of the upper is entirely decorated with gold rosettes, papyrus flowers and lilies, all of which are hollow on their back side, facing the leather layer. The edges of these beads are curved down slightly towards the hollow side (figure 3.63F). The rosettes though made of gold, have a red glow, greatly enhancing the decorative effect with the gold lilies and papyrus.[31] One horizontal row of beads consists of rosettes, with a lily between each rosette facing downwards and a papyrus flower facing upwards, touching the lilies (figure 3.63E). This is repeated throughout the horizontal row. There are two of these rows on the sides, but at the highest part of the upper, isolated lilies and papyrus flowers cover the small area between the full beadwork upper and the edge of the instep. Small though the lilies are, they show details embossed in them. The stitch holes have been punched from the back side, as evidenced by the raised edges of the holes on the outer, visible surface (figure 4.4). The beads are strung on z-spun flax thread horizontally as well as vertically (*cf.* figure 3.68A & G). Occasionally, the lilies were fastened to the leather, but it cannot be determined exactly whether there was a pattern or whether this was done at random. The lowest row shows four, and sometimes five, additional stitch holes in the downwards-facing lilies (figure 3.63E). The outermost of these stitch holes occasionally have been punched through the edge of the bead. In contrast to the holes for stringing the beads to each other, these holes are punched from the visible outer surface to the hollow back side. The holes were used for the attachment of the upper to the sole; *in situ* stitches show, however, that not all of them were used. This suggests they were made before attaching the upper to the sole. If punched while attaching the upper, there would have been no (or at least far fewer) empty stitch holes. Some of the beads are twisted at an outward angle, which can be interpreted as evidence of the fastening of the upper to the sole. The rosettes are not strung with the lilies but attached independently by means of the soldered eye at their hollow backs (figure 3.63F; see also figure 4.6). In addition, the rosettes are made with fine details.

According to Carter, and still visible in Burton's photograph (figure 2.3 and the beads top right in figure 3.63D), there was originally a string of disk-shaped gold beads (irregularly strung with intervals of two or three other beads), and red (carnelian), green (amazonite) and blue (lapis lazuli) beads, which line the instep. The attachment of this string of beads to the upper is obscure, but it seems reasonable to assume it was done in the same way as in 021k & l, described in section 3.3.2. Small fragments of this strand are still preserved, lying on the insole. It lined the front part of the upper and ran ventrally along the back strap through a small loop projecting from the ventral surface of the duck's beak, which will be discussed below.

Although most of the attachment of the upper to the soles is damaged, it is clear that the leather is folded over the edge, thus sandwiching the folded edge of the golden insole between it and the treadsole (figure 3.65). This is secured with a running stitch through the outer side of the upper and through the lower row of beads (figure 3.63E). Poor preservation prohibited study of the shoe's ventral surface, and so it is unclear whether the upper's leather is folded under the sole and then comes back over its edge with the upper end turning into the band with slits (hence the dashed line in figure 3.65). The lower band is positioned slightly above the sole's edge, which seems to suggest it is an independent element, unless it has worn through. If this is

118

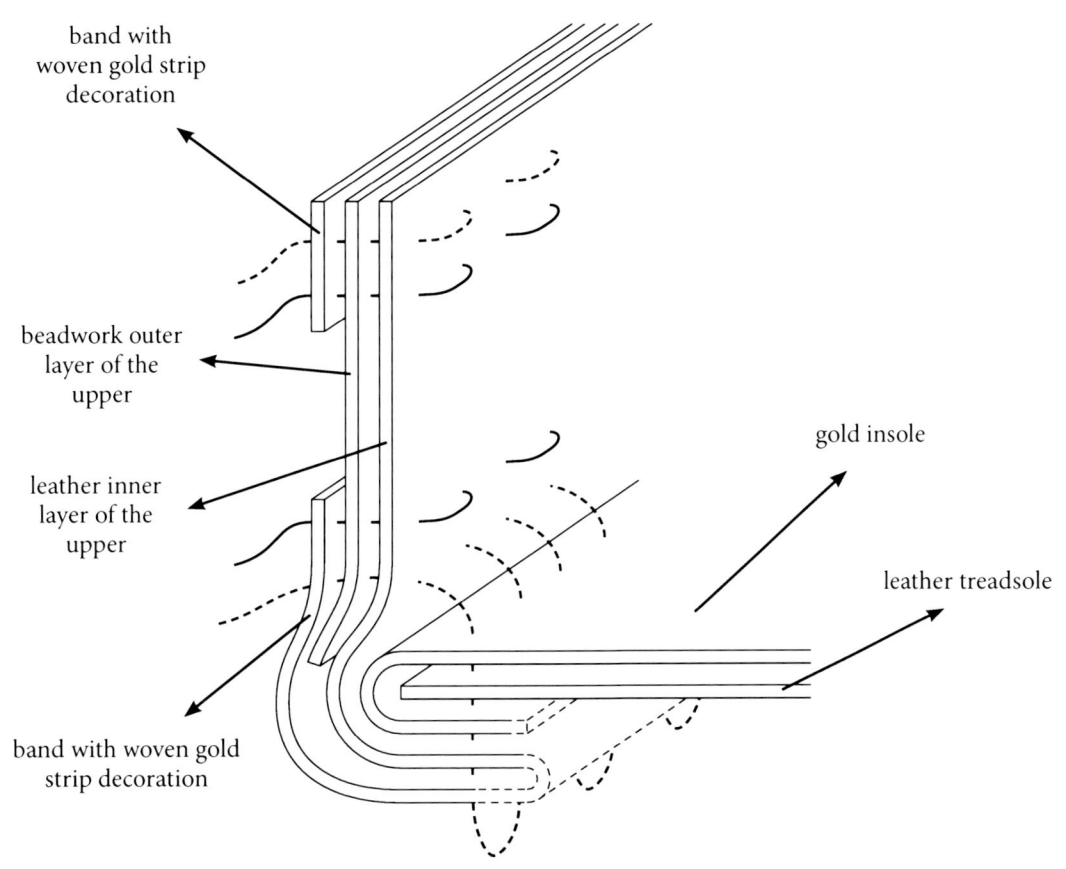

Figure 3.65. Sole/upper construction in open shoes 021f & g. Uncertainty is indicated by dashed lines. Not to scale. Drawing by E. Endenburg / A.J. Veldmeijer.

not the case, however, it is unlike 021k & l, where the lower band is an independent addition and the top one is made by folding the upper outwards (*cf.* figure 3.69).

Although the ventral surface of the soles could not be studied, the distance of the stitch holes to the edge allows the conclusion that the stitching was done through the folded insole. This has been done with running stitches, of an uncertain material but which is probably leather.

Foot strap

A foot strap runs over the front strap and is attached to either side of the upper, slightly anterior to the change in angle of the top edge of the upper (figures 3.63D & G). Although detached now, the remains show that six strands of tiny disc beads are attached to a foundation layer of leather. They seem to have been sewn to the leather only at the ends where it was also attached to the upper. This attachment to the upper, however, is obscure, but the stringing threads were most likely used to attach them to the edge of the upper. All strings have gold beads separated by intervals of five to seven gemstone beads.[32] Carter (Card No. 21f-20) describes the rows as of one colour, but the colours of the beads vary. The posterior row, imagining the attachment in its original position, consists of darkly discoloured beads, but in places one sees the original dark blue colour of lapis lazuli. The next row is predominantly made of green (amazonite) beads, with occasionally one of red (carnelian) and a gold bead. Again a row of dark beads follows and these have a more consistent shape than the beads in the posterior-most row. The fourth row is of a dark red brown colour (carnelian?), which likely is not the original colour (but this can no longer be determined). The fifth row is the same as the third row and is followed, finally, by a row of reddish-brown (carnelian) beads, similar to the fourth row. At one end of this construction, a lengthwise, six hole spacer bead was inserted in order to keep the strands of beads neatly in place (arrow in figure 6.63G). The material of this spacer bead is unclear, but it has the same reddish brown colour as some of the beads in the rows. Although not visible (anymore?), there might have been a second 'spacer' bead on the other side. It is interesting to note that the bead and gold ceremonial scarf, 2690 (Card No. 2600), not only consists of the same kind of beads, but also has similar spacer beads, although for the scarf these are made for seven strands of beads rather than six (Carter, 1933: 79).

Front strap

The front strap is made of a cylinder of relatively thick filagree gold, consisting of a pattern of connected gold rings (figures 6.63C & G, see also figure 4.8).[33] Inside, little remains of the core, but in Burton's photograph it was fully present (figure 2.3) and seems to have consisted of leather. The top and bottom are closed golden tubes that are embossed transversely with parallel lines. Remnants of leather around the bottom tube can still be seen. Since Carter (Card No. 21f-21) notes the presence of a hole for the front strap, it is likely the leather core went through the golden insole and was fastened on the ventral surface of the leather treadsole by means of a knot, an assumption that can no longer be verified. When Carter found the shoe, he noted (Card No. 21f-21) "The toe bar [front strap] had been bent and driven down into sandal [shoe] below by force used by priests repacking the box." Carter does not provide information about the attachment to the back strap, even though it was still *in situ*. Since the front straps are now detached entirely in both shoes, the fastening remains obscure.

Back strap

The back strap consists of two parts (figures 3.63H & I). The triangular centre part,[34] imitating the loop of the front strap for fastening it to the back strap in fibre, sewn sandals (see also figure 3.63L), is convex in the vertical as well as horizontal planes. The slightly glazy appearance visible on the back side, suggests that this triangular element is made of different material than the rest of the back straps (which are made of wood); it might be rawhide, but more research is needed to identify the material with certainty. At the bottom of this triangular part, remnants of gold leaf remain on the covering of this side. Two hooks on the upper corners of the triangle attach it to the back strap. Carter mentions on Card No. 21f-19 hooks on the bottom, but these are the ones fastening the duck heads. These hooks are not visible looking at the front, and thus have been applied before the frontal decoration of gold and inlay. The decoration represents a lotus in the middle, flanked by lotus buds with small crescent-shaped elements on top of those (figure 3.63L, see also figure 4.12). The frame runs around the perimeter of the triangle except along the top edge, where it is situated slightly below the edge proper (which is covered with gold sheet).

Carter (Card No. 021f-19) suggests that the back strap consists of two independent parts, but this can be challenged as it is clear, especially in the left shoe, that the back strap consists of one piece which is now broken into two (figures 3.63H & I). They are made of wood, the back side of which is covered with a layer of coarse flax cloth, which runs underneath the folded edges at the top and bottom of the gold sheet of the front. The exact purpose of the cloth is obscure since the pins, which attach the daisies[35] to the front (two for each daisy), are pushed through it. It does not serve a protective function. Over this, but also running under the gold edges, is a layer of leather (figure 3.63H). This layer protected the foot from the pins.

The front and sides of the back straps are beautifully decorated with gold daisies and bosses on a blue background mosaic of lapis lazuli (figures 3.63J & K). "These [...] twelve-petalled daisies [consist of a] centre boss of [...] tiny granules, about 50 granules to each boss, [...] of yellow gold. Below these [is a] circle[...] of red gold." (Card No. 21f-19 and 20). The first row of six petals is of dull coloured gold. Below this is a second layer of six petals in red gold, alternating in such a way that they are visible between the petals of the first layer. The two layers of petals are each cut from one sheet: the petals are not independent parts. In between the daisies are round bosses of yellow gold.[36]

Undoubtedly the most remarkable elements of this pair of shoes are the projecting duck heads that are situated at the lower edge of the back strap and flank the triangular centre part (the 'loop' of the front strap; figure 3.63M).[37] Made of gold and (semi-)hollow, they are attached by means of hooks through the back straps. These hooks are attached at the top and bottom of the duck's neck (figure 4.13), but it is not clear if they were fastened (and if so, how: a possibility is soldering). Alternatively, the heads may have been hooked onto them. The sides and top of the head and neck have blue inlays (possibly lapis lazuli or blue glass inlay imitating faience). The heads are well made, showing details of eyes and beak. Under the lower jaw there is a ventrally projecting loop for the strand of beads lining the lower edge of the back straps.

Pre-strap

The back straps fit, on each side, into the convex running pre-straps (figure 3.63J). Although they imitate the construction in fibre, sewn sandals, they are somewhat longer and more flattened in the lateromedial plane. They are made of golden sheets with the cladding simulated by embossing. The top part is rounded. They taper down towards the sole. The attachment to the sole is unclear due to the resinous condition of the leather surrounding the base. This, however, might be an indication that leather was involved as was suggested for the attachment of the front strap.

3.3.2 Type: Partial Upper, Leather and Beadwork;
Variant: Foot Strap / Instep Strap

021k [right]/021l [left] (2820; JE 62681; 912/913) (figure 3.66; see guide page 124)

The pair of shoes 021k & l (figure 3.67, table 7) is in fragile condition which limited its study. Only after consolidation and reconstruction can details such as the ventral surface of the sole and the inner surface of the leather layer of the upper, be studied. No loosely lying parts were lifted, except for the golden ducks, and nor was anything disturbed that was still in contact with other parts of the shoes.

Sole

The sole consists of a leather treadsole, of which only small fragments remain, covered with a thin gold sheet that acts as an insole. The insole imitates the fabric in sewn sandals, *i.e.* shows transverse bundles and is bordered with a triple core edge. In contrast to 021f & g, however, the sewn palm strips are not indicated (figure 3.68A, *cf.* figures 3.63A & B). Although not observed, the construction of the insole and treadsole compares with 021f & g (figure 3.64). The gold insole is folded around the treadsole on the edges (figure 3.69), but the width at the ventral surface of the treadsole cannot be determined, hence the dashed line in the figure. The attachment of the two sole layers is somewhat enigmatic. At the posterior part of the shoe, about three quarters of the way along the extension of the upper, holes have been made through the gold sheet (and without a doubt through the leather or rawhide treadsole) at regular intervals, roughly 5 mm apart (figure 3.68C). These are punched close to the sandal's edge and sometimes even at the very edge. Since the ventral surface of the soles could not be studied, it is not known how the stitches penetrate the sole: though unlikely, they might be stitched through the ventral fold of the insole as well (and through the

Figure 3.66. Artist's impression of open shoes 021k & l. The line drawing on page 124 guides the reader through the text and figures. Drawing by M.H. Kriek

treadsole), but since the extension of the fold is not known, there is a possibility that the stitches go through the insole and treadsole only (*i.e.* next to the fold of the insole). The upper was included as well, as will be discussed below. Some holes still have remnants of the stitching *in situ* and this is even more apparent in Burton's photographs (figure 2.4). These threads seem to be of the same type as the threads used in stringing the beads in the panel, which forms the outer layer of the upper. But here too, certainty could not be obtained.

On the front quarter, which is the part that tapers towards the toe, and starting from the termination of the upper, very closely spaced stitch holes line the edge (figure 3.68A). Indeed, they are punched next to each other so closely that it now forms a continuous perforated cut for the most part (small patches of stitch holes are still unbroken). On both sides of this perforation, the semi-circular shapes of the stitch holes characterise the original stitching. Nothing remains that can indicate the kind of sewing thread used. It probably held not only the soles, but also a narrow strip of leather, covering only the edge, as is seen in 021f & g.

The centre part of the insole, mimicking the contour of the sandal shape, shows comparable stitch holes to those on the front of the sandal: so closely spaced, they now form a continuous cut (figure 3.68A). Thus, the centre part seems a separate piece, as noted by Carter (Card No. 021k-25), but originally it was not. Additional support for this view comes from the fact that the simulated sewn fabric is continuous over the cut. On the same card, Carter mentions that it "seems to have been covered originally with some black substance", remnants of which are still visible. These are the remnants of a leather layer, stitched to the sole. In this, it compares well with the previously described pair 021f & g. The centre part might even have been stuffed with, for example, hair or plant fibre for increased comfort, but there is no indication of this. Although stuffing of soles is

A   B

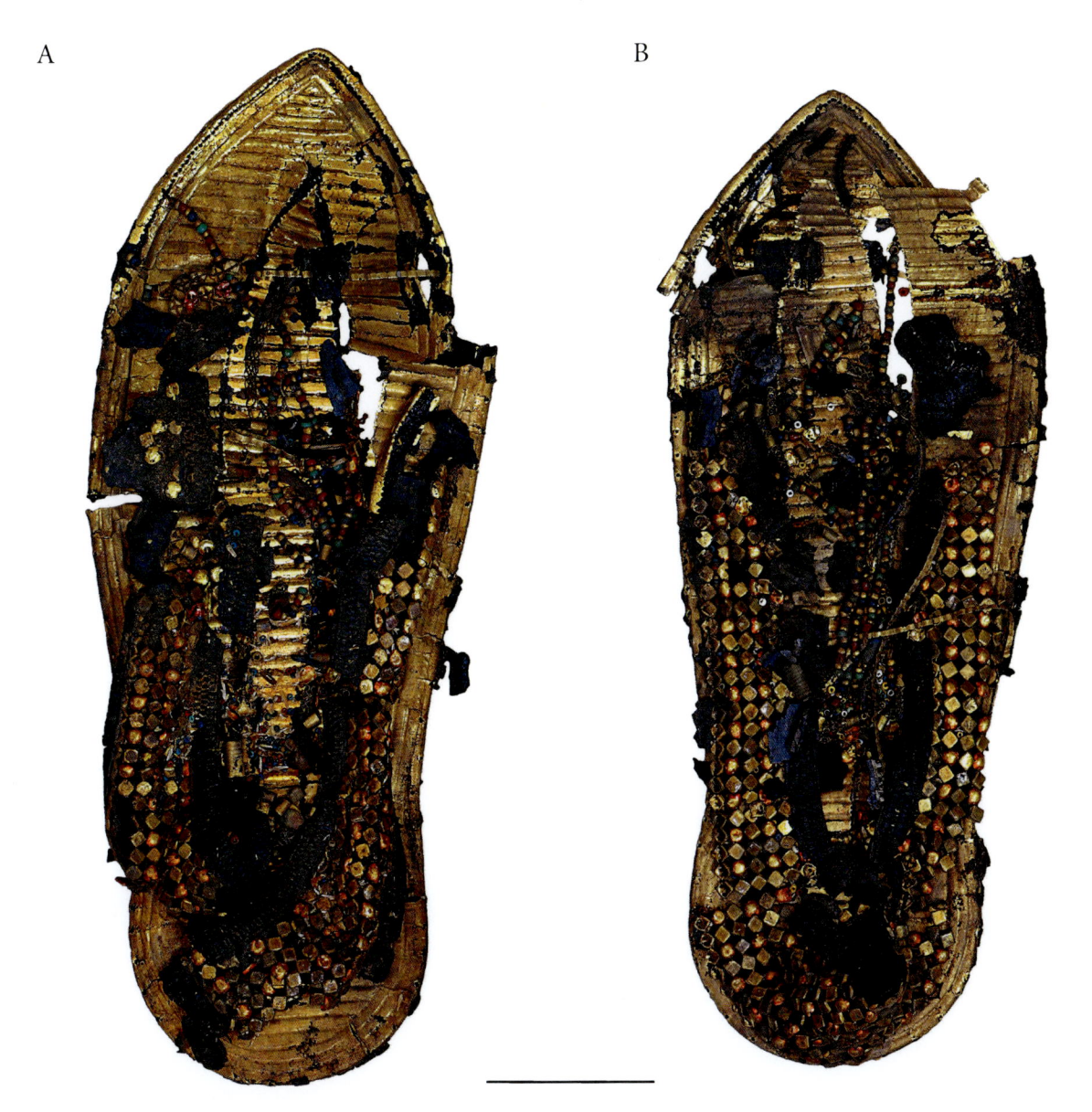

Figure 3.67. The pair of open shoes 021k & l in dorsal view. A) Left shoe; B) Right shoe. Cf. figure 2.4. Scale bar is 50 mm. The 'size difference' is due to the movement of of the front of the right shoe. Photography by A.J. Veldmeijer. Courtesy of the Supreme Council of Antiquities / Authorities Egyptian Museum, Cairo.

not common in ancient Egypt, it is certainly not unheard of as several leather composite sandals display such a feature (Veldmeijer, 2009i).

Upper

The upper consists of two layers. The inner layer is of leather and now has the same appearance as the sole, *i.e.* resinous, but is nevertheless better preserved. It seems to be slightly thinner, but due to the condition, this cannot be ascertained. At the top of the upper, around the instep, the leather is folded outwards, thus covering the outer upper's top rows of gold round- and diamond-shaped hollow beads (figure 3.68B). The beadwork upper is fastened on the lower edge, probably by means of running stitches, which go through two holes in each bead. The result is that there is an empty space between the top row of beads and the line where the leather is folded (grey arrow in figure 3.69). The presence of a row of running stitches at the lower edge of the band is certain; the presence of a row of running stitches at the up-

GUIDE to 021k & l

decoration band
fig. 3.68D, F

beadwork
fig. 3.68C, D, F, G

instep strap
(semi-circular panels)
fig. 2.4, 3.68D-F

sole
fig. 3.68A

foot strap
fig. 3.68A, 3.71

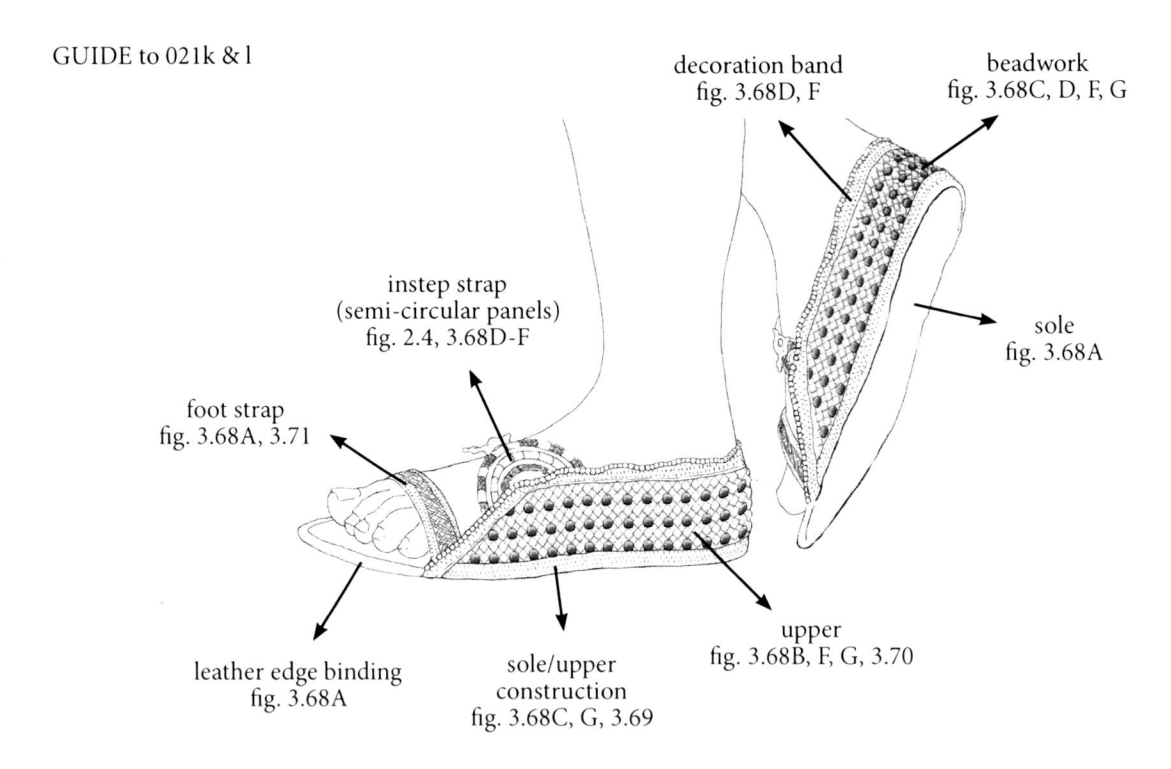

upper
fig. 3.68B, F, G, 3.70

leather edge binding
fig. 3.68A

sole/upper
construction
fig. 3.68C, G, 3.69

per edge is uncertain (hence the dashed line in the figure). The fold has three rows of slits parallel to the edge. The slits of the middle row are situated in such a way that they alternate with the slits of the upper and lower row. Carter does not mention anything being pulled through these slits, but the remains of a light coloured strip, which might be gold, are preserved in the middle row at the heel of 021k (figure 3.68B). However, small remnants of unmistakable gold strips are still *in situ* on the side. The narrow strips of gold lying in several places on top of the shoes clearly show the crimped pattern resulting from being woven through these slits. It is difficult to determine whether they were woven through one or more rows of slits, but most likely the latter, judging from the several, relatively long lengths of the strips lying about.

The lower part of the inner, leather layer of the upper differs. Here, the edge is not folded over the beaded, outer panel. Instead it is folded over the edge of the sole, thus sandwiching the gold sheet between it and the treadsole (figure 3.69), and so protecting it from damage due to use. Nowadays there are still tiny pieces showing this fold but in Burton's photographs (figure 2.4) larger pieces were still intact.

A layer of rows of gold round and diamond-shaped[38] 'beads'[39] forms the outer layer of the upper (figures 3.68B, C & F). At the heel, there are ten rows, but the sides

> *Figure 3.68 (next three pages). Details of open shoes 021k & l. A) Front part of the left sandal. The arrow points to the remnant of the foot strap; B) Heel part of the right shoe, showing the outer layer of the upper and the decorative band; C) The beadwork of the outer upper. The bottom row of beads angle outwards due to the tension from pulling the stitching thread so tight. Note the stitch holes at the edge of the sole; D) The instep was lined with a strand of beads (double arrow). The arrow points to an attachment of the filigree-with-leather-core element of the semi-circular instep strap; E) Solid golden ducks (or geese), act as buckle for the side panel; F) Transversely embossed, golden tube, remnants of the side panel. The arrows point to the remnants of fastening of the instep strap, consisting of 'woven' gold wire with a leather core, again in semi-circular shape to receive the 'duck-buckle' (see inset; note also the nearly intact foot strap (arrow)); G) Detail of the outer layer of the upper, showing the stringing of the beads. Scale bars are 10 mm. Photography by A.J. Veldmeijer. Courtesy of the Supreme Council of Antiquities / Authorities Egyptian Museum, Cairo. Inset 3.68F: Photography by H. Burton. Copyright Griffith Institute, University of Oxford.*

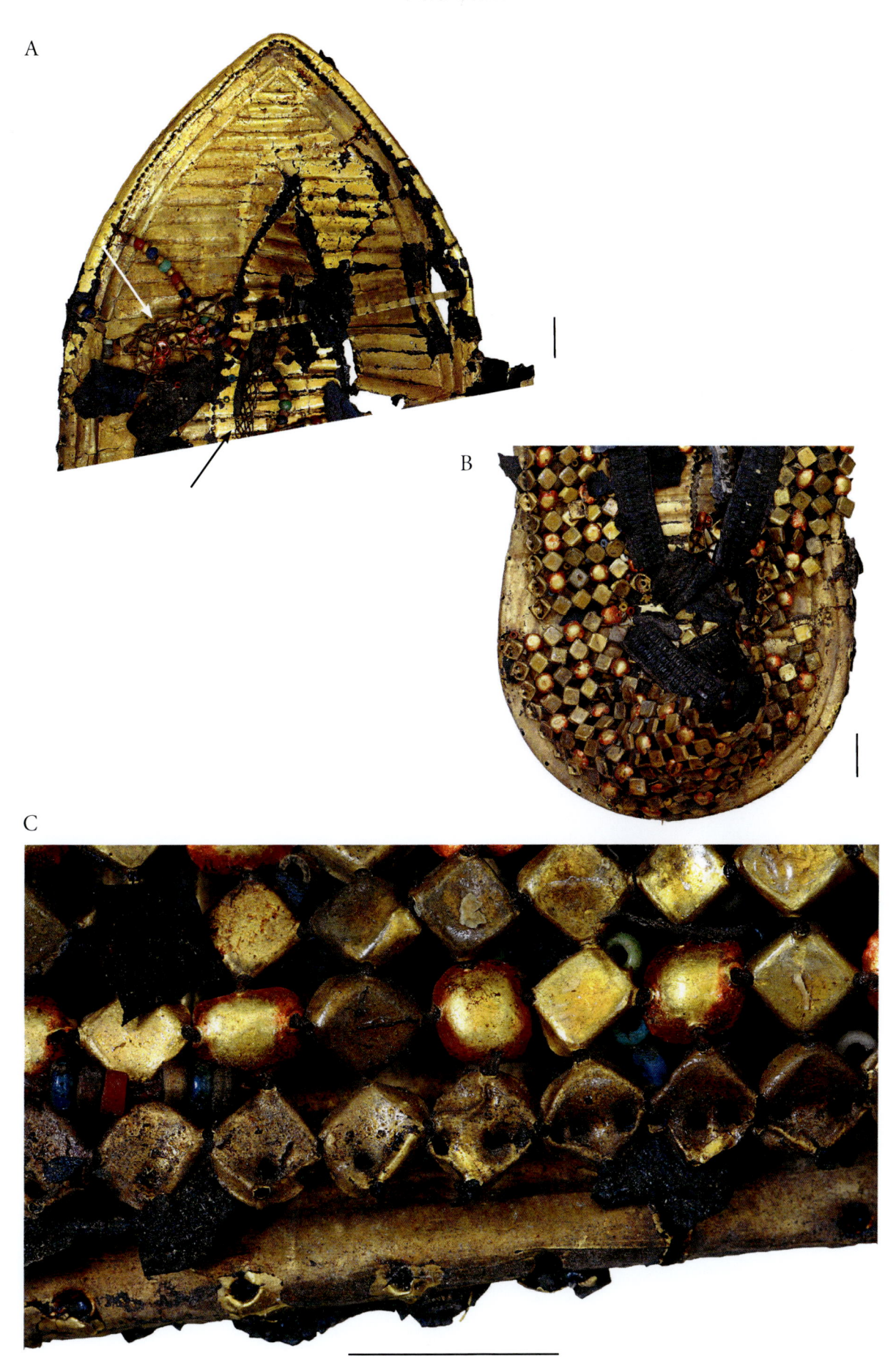

A

B

C

Description

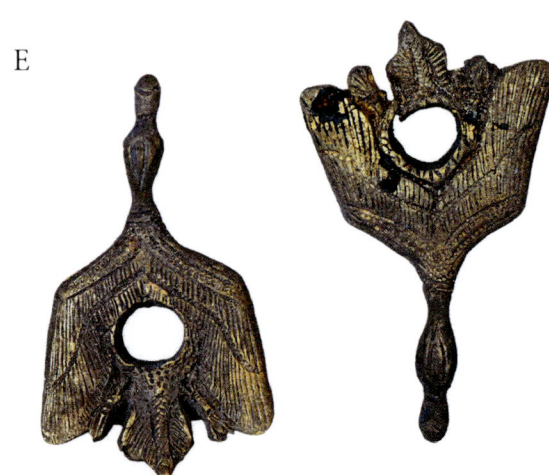

D

E

F

126

F inset

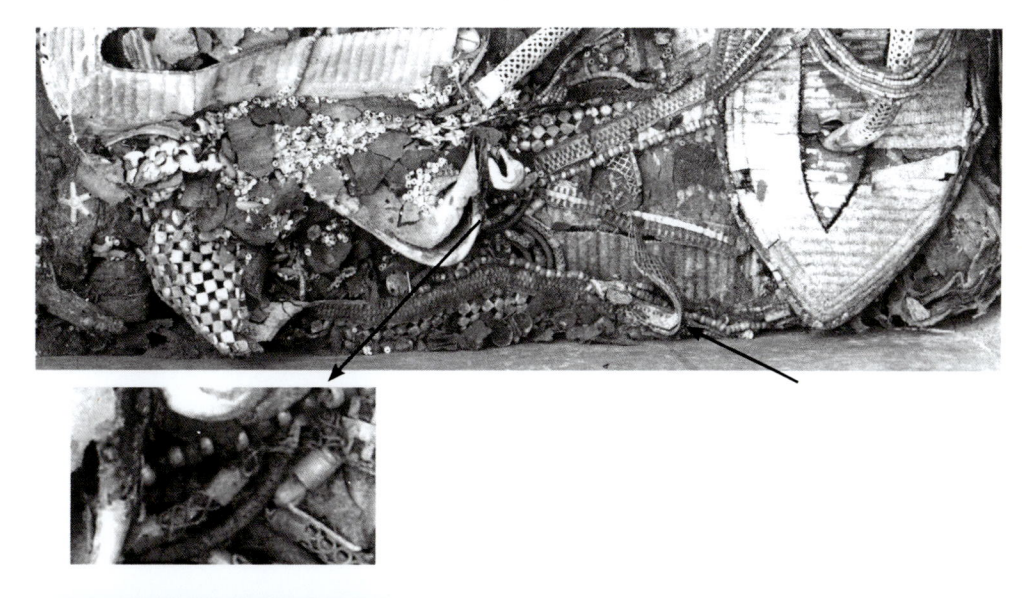

G

are made up of six rows close to the heel. The number of rows decreases continuously towards the front of the upper until only two rows are left. The horizontal top row consists of alternating round and diamond-shaped beads followed by a row of diamond-shaped beads only. The third row consists again of alternating round and diamond-shaped beads after which follows a row of diamond-shaped only, etc. The diamond-shaped beads are yellow but the rounds have a red tint (figures 3.68C & D). The gold beads are two-dimensional: only the sides are folded and the back is open (facing the leather inner layer). As a result, the sewing threads can be observed, and these run horizontally as well as vertically (white arrow in figure 3.68A; figure 3.68G). Consequently, each bead has four holes (one on each side) except in the upper and lower rows where they have two additional holes for attachment to the leather inner upper and the sole, respectively (figure 3.68C).

On the sole, a strip of leather consisting of four rows of slits parallel to the edge, which are arranged in the same way as described for the top of the upper, is attached to the outer upper with the intention of hiding the sole/upper construction. It is likely that only leather strips were pulled through these slits.

The three layers (*i.e.* the inner leather layer of the upper, the bead outer fabric and the folded leather of the upper's inner layer) must have been fastened with the same stitch to the sole. The thread would pass through a sole's stitch hole, then through both bead stitch holes, and finally back through the sole (figure 3.69). The whole sequence is repeated, running through the next bead used (see below) and so forth. However, if the stitches protruded from the ventral surface of the treadsole, they would be prone to wear, which might be an explanation for why most of the upper was already detached from the sole when the shoes were found by Carter. This, in its turn, suggests they were worn (often?).[40] The horizontal bumps in the beads as well as the outward folding of the decoration strip, suggests the stitching was done outside-inside and pulled relatively tight (figure 3.68C). The number of stitch holes in the lower row of gold beads does not correspond with the number of stitch holes in the sole and it seems therefore unlikely that all beads were used. This suggests that, because all beads in the lowest row were perforated (as well as in the top row), the beads were equipped with holes before being used in the construction (*cf.* 021f & g described in section 3.3.1.).

Around the instep is a strand of beads (figure 2.4) consisting of beads of gold, red (carnelian), dark blue (lapis lazuli) and green (amazonite), strung in the sequence green, gold, dark blue, gold, red, gold (*cf.* the strand of beads in 270a described below in section 3.3.3). The beads are roughly cylindrical, but are not all uniform in shape. The strand is fastened at six(?) points (excluding the attachment at the front of the upper) which are widely spaced and divided regularly over the instep. It is attached to the upper's leather inner layer, but exactly how can no longer be determined. However, the strand seems to be attached by stitching through the instep's edge, which firmly attaches one bead to the edge for reinforcement of the stitch.

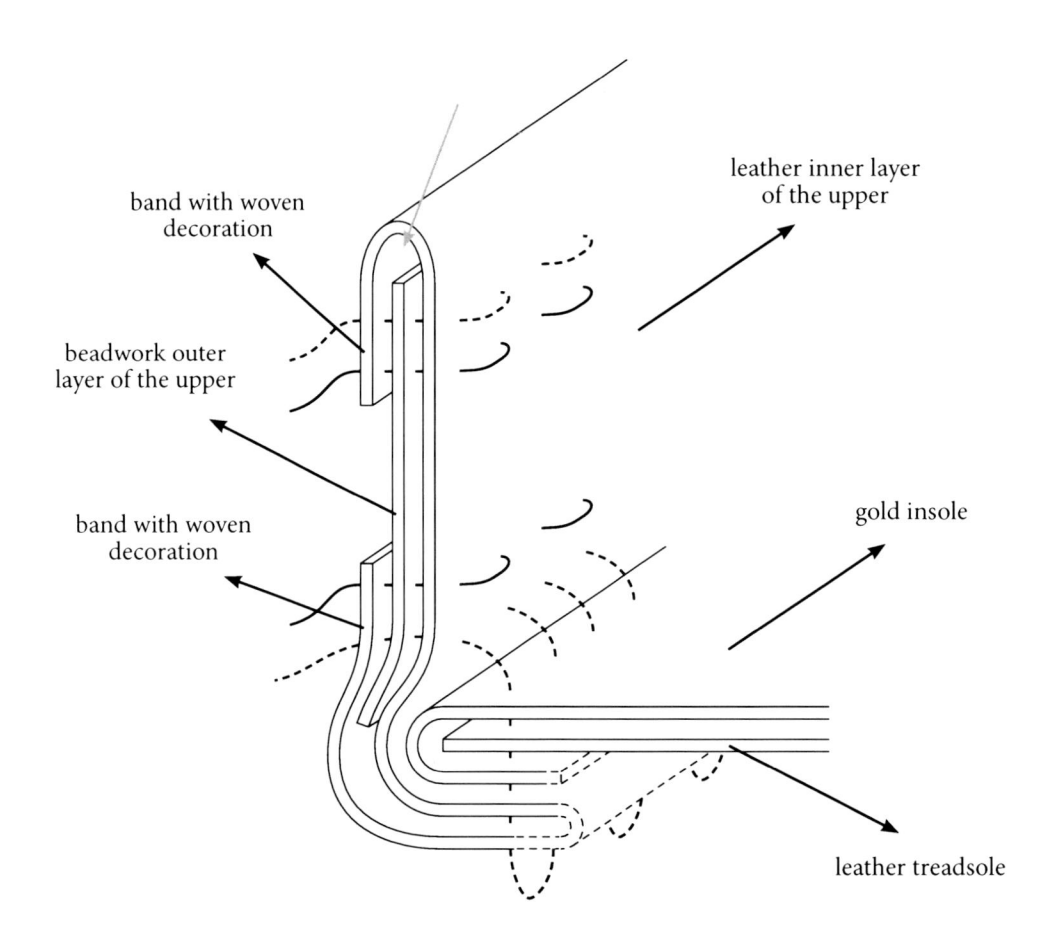

Instep strap (semi-circular side panel)

Carter (Card No. 021k-26) mentions semi-circular panels on "each side of shoe." Actually, each shoe had one big pane, which was attached on the lateral side of the upper and a smaller panel at the medial side. Today, these instep straps are entirely detached, but in the original photographs, one panel is still *in situ* (figure 2.4, *cf.* figures 3.68D & F), as well as its fastening. According to Carter (Card No. 021k-26) the panels consist of "broad bands," made of "lengths of gold filagree, fitting at ends into gold cylinders." These, however, are bigger panels; the smaller ones are made with different elements, as will be explained below. Actually, the filagree cylinders consist of sections of open worked disks, interspersed with gold tubes at regular intervals (lengthwise, four circles, a tube, again four circles, etc).[41] The cylinders have a core of leather, which were probably green, serving as reinforcement and enhancing the decorative effect. Possibly, however, the most important function was as an attachment (*cf.* the front strap in 021f & g, section 3.3.1). These leather cores must have been separate and attached to the upper after the filagree was strung on them. These leather tubes, consisting of a narrow, relatively thick strip of slightly twisted leather, are inserted through the edge of the fold, *i.e.* the dorsal edge of the instep (figure 3.70, *cf.* figure 3.68D). Thus they are sandwiched between the band with the rows of slits and the upper's inner layer. It cannot be determined anymore how it was fastened, but there is only one logical possibility: they are included in the sewing of this folded part of the leather and the upper row of beads of the outer upper. In between these rows of filagree are bands of leather. In contrast to the leather cores of the filagree work, these tubes consist of very thin, lengthwise rolled leather, the colour of which is still green. In the middle, at right angles to the semi-circular rows, runs, according to Carter, a similar tube of rolled green leather (figure 2.4), but the attachment to the rest of the panel is not clear. The solid gold duck[42] was fastened at the end of this, but exactly how is no longer possible to determine. Most likely the leather was pulled through the relatively big hole in the duck and secured by means of an overhand

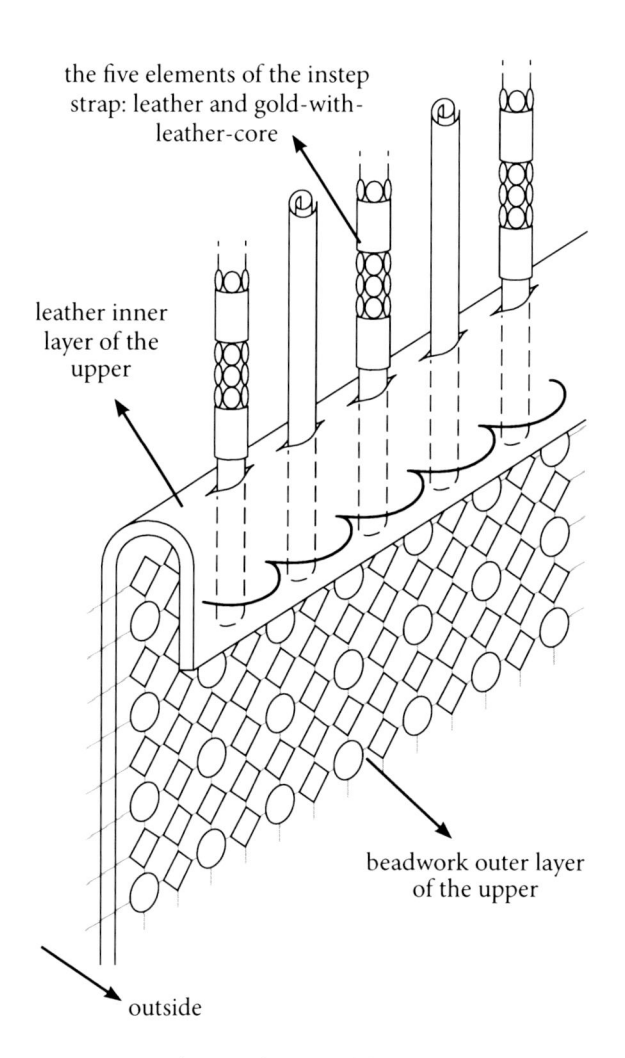

Figure 3.70. The attachment of the instep straps (semi-circular side panels) and their attachment on the other side (cf. 3.68F inset; not included here) in open shoes 021k & l (cf. figure 3.68D). The leather tubes that act as cores of the filigree work are inserted through the edge of the instep. Thus being sandwiched between the inner layer of the upper and the folded decorative band, the ends are fastened with the stitching that also fastens the decorative band to the inner layer of the upper. Not to scale. Drawing by E. Endenburg / A.J. Veldmeijer.

< *Figure 3.69. Sole/upper construction in open shoes 021k & l. Uncertainty is indicated by dashed lines. The grey arrow indicates the void between the fold of the leather layer of the upper and the beadwork outer layer. Not to scale. Drawing by E. Endenburg / A.J. Veldmeijer.*

knot.[43] The semi-circular panel was folded over the foot and the 'duck-toggle' was pulled through the 'semi-circular' panel at the medial side that most likely consisted of two cylinders. These, in contrast to the ones of the big instep strap at the lateral side, are made of latticework rather than soldered circles[44] but have a core of leather as well (figures 3.68F & 3.68F inset). Without a doubt, although not clearly visible, these leather cores are inserted in the fold in the same way the green leather cores of the big semi-circular panels were. The height of the panel is much smaller; nothing can be said about the width, as nothing except for some remnants (figure 3.68F inset), remains nowadays.

Foot strap

The most damaged parts of the shoes are the fronts and as a result the extension of the upper is not exactly clear. However, it seems to extend about a quarter of the way back from the front proper. In the *in situ* photographs (figures 1.2C, D & 3.68F inset) it is clear that there was a foot strap, still largley complete, of which only a scrap of leather with slits and latticework remains. Carter (Card No. 021k-26) mentions the "lattice work of thin gold wire," which is still among the remains of the shoe (arrow in figure 3.68A). Remnants of leather adhere to it. The leather was the lower layer on top of which was fastened the openwork lattice (figure 3.71), possibly with a separate strip of leather. The exact construction cannot be determined any more, but the light coloured line at the edges of the strap seems to have been stitched with running stitches to the leather layer, thus obscuring the edge of the gold lattice. The attachment to the sole is not clear. The gold strip, visible in the picture, does not belong to the foot strap.

3.3.3 Type: Partial Upper, Leather; Variant: Front Strap / Toe Band / Foot Straps / Instep Strap

270a (2819; JE 62682; 904) (figure 3.72; see guide page 133)

This pair of leather open shoes embellished with gold and beadwork (figure 3.73, table 8) is in an advanced state of 'melting', a process that began in the tomb. Burton's photograph (figure 1.10) already shows that the left one is the better preserved of the

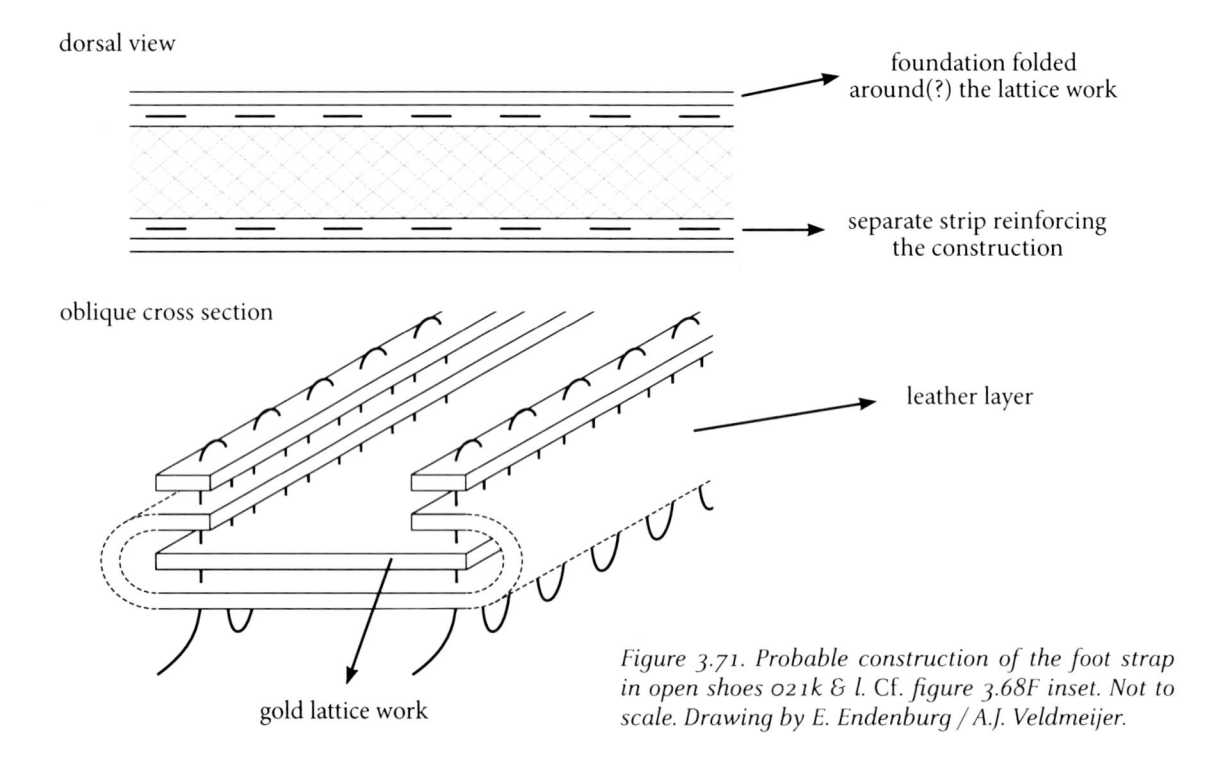

Figure 3.71. Probable construction of the foot strap in open shoes 021k & l. Cf. figure 3.68F inset. Not to scale. Drawing by E. Endenburg / A.J. Veldmeijer.

Figure 3.72. Artist impression of open shoes 270a. The line drawing on the page 133 guides the reader through the text and figures. Drawing by M.H. Kriek.

two while the right one has largely fallen apart. The poor preservation made a detailed study impossible. Unfortunately, Carter did not make notes and consequently some details can no longer be determined.

Sole

The shape of the sole resembles those of the Type C sewn sandals. They consist of an insole and treadsole, both of thin leather. Along the perimeter, in front of the upper, is a leather band with two rows of slits through which narrow gold strips are woven (figure 3.74A). This band is stitched to the sole by means of stitching on the inner side of the innermost golden strip (figure 3.75A). Stitches are also visible on the outside of the outermost golden strip, and so it was not necessary for the leather band to be folded over the edge of the sole. This construction, however, seems to have been used only anterior to the upper: the stitches that fasten the upper probably include the outer edge of the strip. How far it extended is uncertain, but apparently to the beginning of the upper.

Upper

The upper consists of openwork leather, embellished with gold and bead decoration (figures 3.74B-F). It starts at about one quarter of the way from the front relative to the length of the sandal. The beginning of the dorsal edge (*i.e.* the instep) slopes gently but continuously upwards, reaching the highest point at the heel. The upper consists of a closed leather inner layer and an openwork outer layer (figures 3.74B & 3.76). The latter shows two horizontal rows of lotuses, which alternate with lotus buds, separated by a horizontal band between the two rows. Upon this band is attached a separate, slightly narrower strip of leather of a different colour. The gold bosses, neatly positioned between an upper and lower row of lotuses (figure 3.74B), are much like the ones described for other pieces of footwear, and although the fastening could not be observed, it seems only logical that they are also attached in the same way, *i.e.* with split pins. These go through both the inner and outer layers of leather of the horizontal band, but it is uncertain whether it went through the inner layer of the upper or not, although most likely not, as the inner layer would protect the foot from the pins (figure 3.76B). The colour of the leather cannot be determined, but the gold bosses are yellow. Originally the figures were, on their edges, covered with gold foil, as was the central horizontal band, still largely intact in Burton's photograph (figure 1.10). Only small scraps now remain.

Along the top, the upper is decorated with a band of leather containing two horizontal rows of slits through which a narrow gold strip is woven, as was done at the edge of the sole. Note that it contrasts with the other example of this type of decoration: the strips run parallel through the slits rather than alternating. This band is made out of the same sheet of leather; it is not clear if it was folded or not, but possibly it was.

The construction of the sole is more complex (figures 3.74C-E & 3.75B). A gold plate strip is set against the outer side of the upper. The outer surface of the strip is decorated with triangles of leather pointing downwards. Note that lines, impressed in the gold strip, also indicate the triangles. The gold band is fastened to the upper, which was put on the outer side of the gold band but under the triangular decoration. Along the top runs a narrow strip of leather, which contains the running stitches that fasten the different layers, thus obscuring the seam. Likely, the lowest part of the upper is not openwork leather, but closed and consequently it offers a strong attachment. The stitching seems to have been done with leather thong, suggested by remnants.

The ventral surface of the shoe could not be studied as the shoe is stuck to the display panel and so the sole/upper construction is unclear. Certainly there was a strip of leather mounted over the points of the triangular leather decora-

Figure 3.73. Pair of open shoes 270a. Left shoe in dorsal view; right shoe, still in situ *in the box, see figure 1.10 & 2.1). Scale bar is 50 mm. Photography by A.J. Veldmeijer. Courtesy of the Supreme Council of Antiquities / Authorities Egyptian Museum, Cairo.*

tion. It is also evident that the other edge of this leather strip was sandwiched between the two sole layers, and fastened by means of stitches through the leather strips and the holes of the gold strip, likely with a running stitch. The lowest edge of the gold plate strip, even below the row of stitch holes, bends slightly but distinctly inwards. All stitch holes are punched from outside in (figure 3.74C). Note that the triangles at the top edge of the gold strip are irregularly cut (as are all edges of the gold plate strip). The exact function is rather enigmatic, but the suggestion that the protrusions were there to

GUIDE to 021k & l

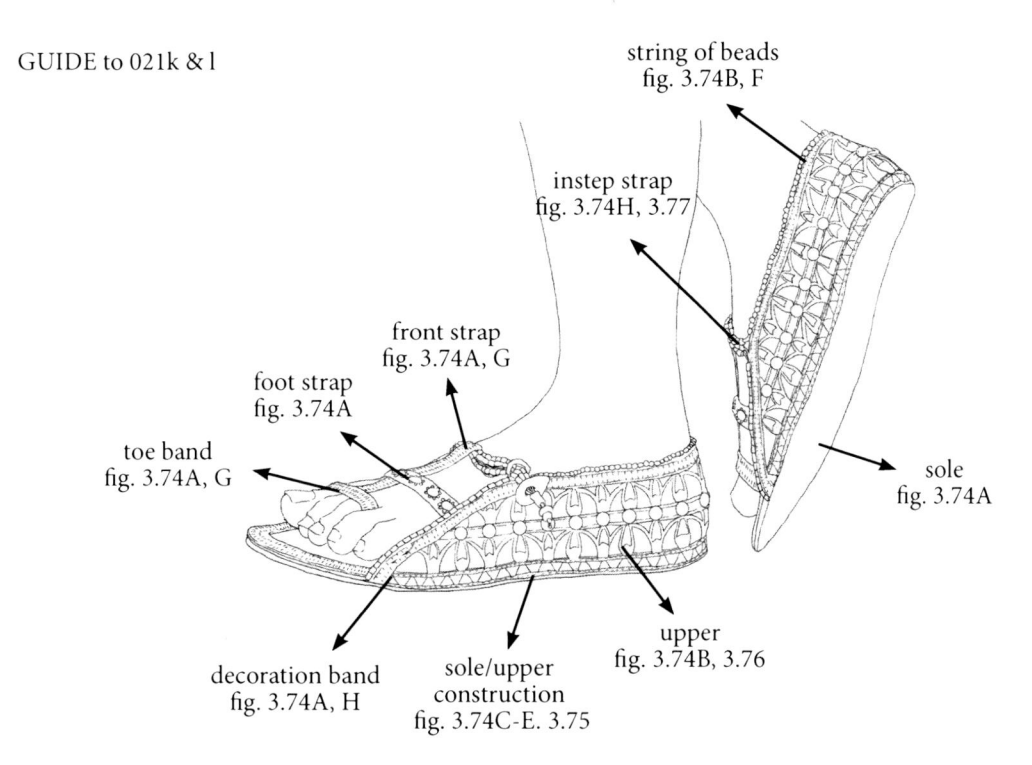

- string of beads fig. 3.74B, F
- instep strap fig. 3.74H, 3.77
- front strap fig. 3.74A, G
- foot strap fig. 3.74A
- toe band fig. 3.74A, G
- sole fig. 3.74A
- decoration band fig. 3.74A, H
- sole/upper construction fig. 3.74C-E, 3.75
- upper fig. 3.74B, 3.76

support the fragile outer layer of the upper, seems plausible. Moreover, the stitch holes in the lower row are sometimes set close to the edge, as they are not punched in a straight line: some of the holes are even punched through the edge, resulting in only half a hole (figure 3.74E). It seems likely that not all stitch holes in the metal strip were used.

Along approximately the back half of the instep, starting at the attachment of the fastening (see below), there is a strand of bright light blue (turquoise), yellow (gold), dark blue (lapis lazuli), gold, red (carnelian), gold beads (figures 3.74B & F). The beads are vaguely disk-shaped, although some are closer to cylinder-shaped. It is interesting to note that not only are the beads strung in the same sequence as the strand of beads in 021k & l, they are actually partially the same in shape and materials. Possibly, the strand of beads in 021f & g was similar as well. A small strip of leather is attached at the instep (how, again, is unclear) and underneath the strand of beads (figure 3.74F). The function is unclear, but it might be there to give support to the string of beads. A narrow leather(?) string protruding from it is looped, on occasion, around the strung thread of the beads. Starting on the other side of the fastening and running to the beginning of the upper are strings (one on each side) of cylindrical beads, all of which seem to be gold (figure 3.74A). Note, however, that alternating (every two or three) gold beads exhibit bright yellow and black colours.[45] They were strung before the attachment to the upper with a separate string looping around the beading thread. The attachment at the beginning of the upper is unclear.

> *Figure 3.74 (next two pages). Details of the left shoe of pair 270a (although the right one is still present, no detail photographs were taken). A) Dorsal view, showing the toe band, first foot strap, front strap and the tube beads lining the front of the upper; B) Upper, showing the openwork outer layer; C-E) The gold plate strip on the lower edge of the upper, showing the triangular impressions, the applied triangular leather decoration and the attachment of the upper (arrows). Note the irregular shape of the strip and the irregular row of stitch holes; F) The heel shows a separate strip of leather, possibly to support the strand of beads; G) The front strap and toe band are one piece (the arrows are explained in the text); H) Top, the fastening in the shoe anno 2008; bottom, a detail from Burton's photograph (figure 1.10). Scale bars are 10 mm. Photography, except H bottom by A.J. Veldmeijer. Courtesy of the Supreme Council of Antiquities / Authorities Egyptian Museum, Cairo. H bottom: Photography by H. Burton. Copyright Griffith Institute, University of Oxford.*

Description

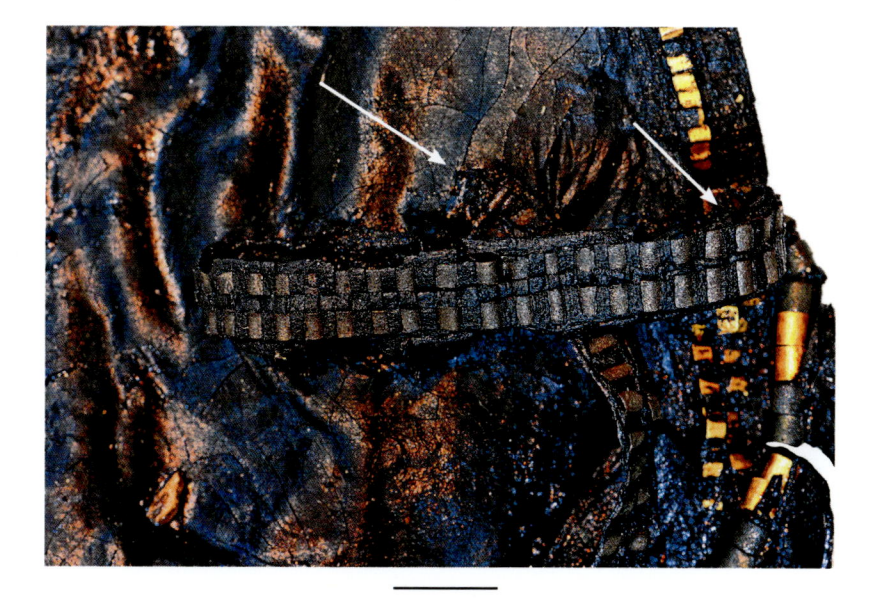

G

H

135

Toe band

A unique type of attachment of the shoe to the foot is the toe band, which is positioned slightly in front of the beginning of the upper, at the medial edge (figures 3.74A & B). The band consists of a single layer of leather with two rows of slits through which thin gold strips are woven parallel to each other instead of alternating, as is usually seen. It forms a loop by both ends of the band being inserted into longitudinal slits in the insole. The slit on the medial side is inserted between the two narrow strips of gold of the decorative leather strip that adorn the sole's perimeter. It must have been fastened (stitched most likely) together with the front strap, but how is not evident. The front strap emerges at about the centre under the toe band, and considering the strange angle, it

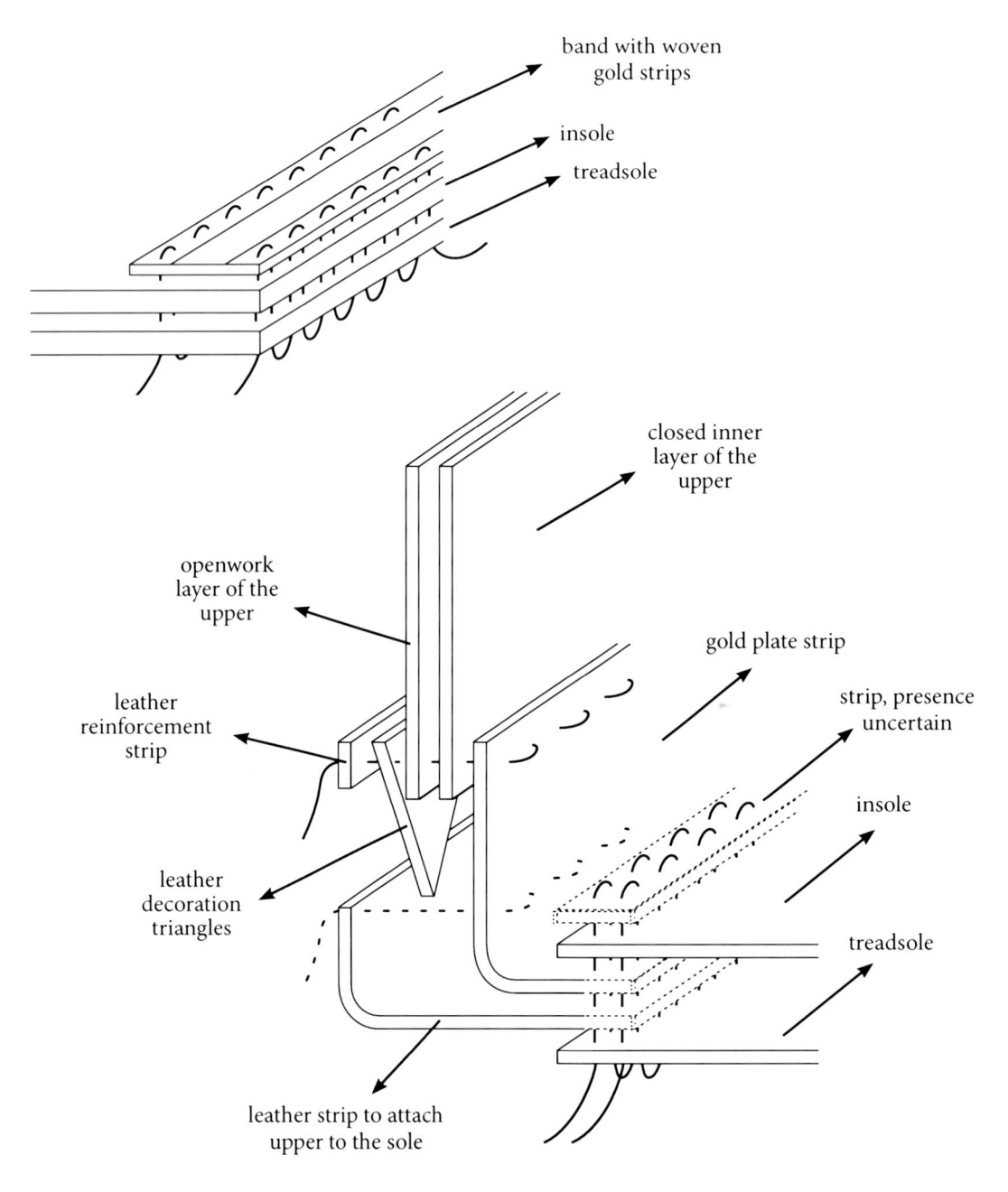

Figure 3.75. The sole/upper construction in open shoes 270a. A) Construction of the sole anterior to the upper; B) Sole/upper construction. The condition of the shoes did not allow confirmation of the continuation of the decorative band seen in A; in Burton's photograph (figure 1.10) it seems, however, that it did not continue. The construction is nevertheless included in dashed line. Extension of the top of the upper is uncertain. Not to scale. Drawing by E. Endenburg / A.J. Veldmeijer.

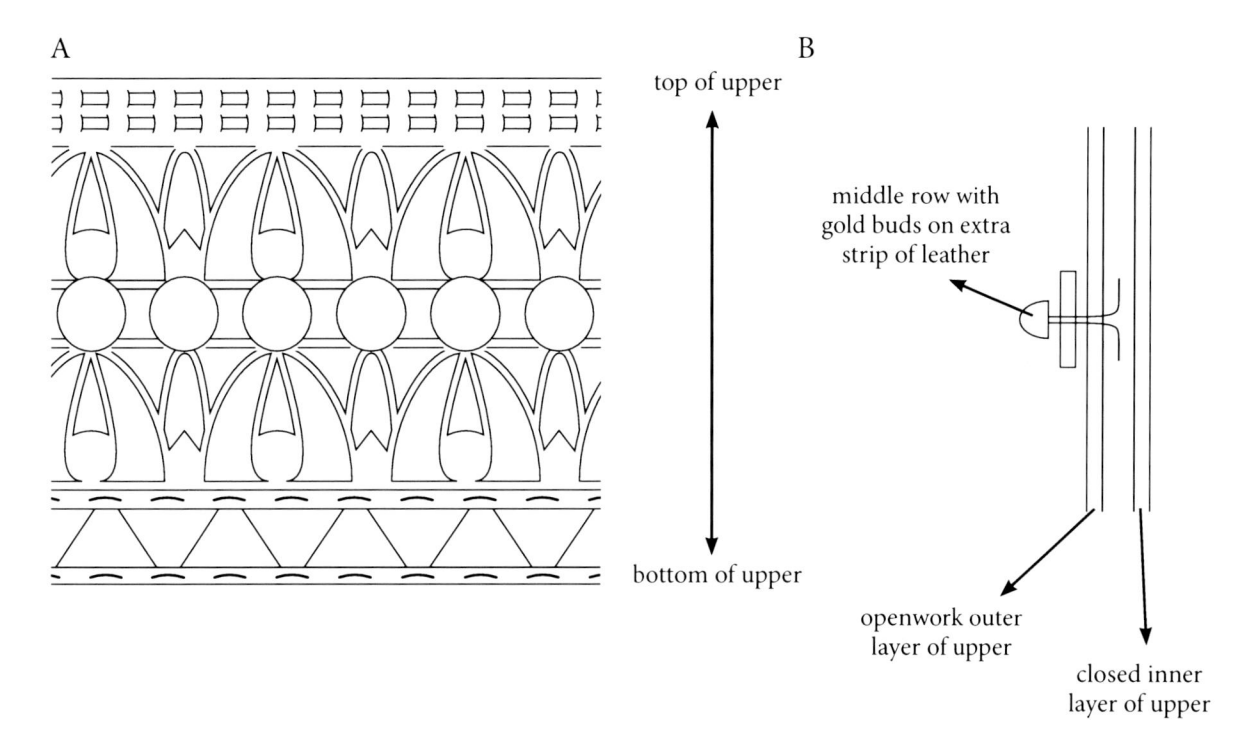

Figure 3.76. The upper in open shoes 270a consists of a closed inner and an openwork outer layer of leather. A) The outer layer of the upper; B) Construction of the two layers of the upper. Not to scale. Drawing by E. Endenburg / A.J. Veldmeijer.

must be the extended part of the lateral end of the toe band. The circle of the toe band is too wide to accommodate the big toe only; likely the second and third toes were also put through it.

Front strap

As indicated, the front strap comes out of the sole at the centre of the toe band (figure 3.74G). The front strap is assumed to be the extended part of the lateral end of the toe band (arrows) because of its similarity to it. It runs under the foot strap and is looped around the fastening. The way the front strap is fastened remains obscure, but the end seems to have been stitched after the small loop around the fastening (figure 3.77).

Foot strap

The foot strap (figures 1.10 & 3.74A) consists of two narrow bands of leather, the top one slightly narrower, thus showing part of the edge of the lower one. Onto it are sewn seven gold bosses, forming the centers of flowers, with painted petals. It is not clear how the foot strap is attached, but most likely it is inserted into the decorative band around the instep.

Instep strap

The fastening (figure 3.74H) is unique but the system, a toggle pulled through an eye,[46] is comparable to the instep strap in 021k & l. Laterally, there are three attachments: the smallest is a strip of leather (1 in figure 3.77), followed by a strand of beads (2). The third element (3) is also a strip of leather, which loops as though to receive the strands of leather and beads with the big toggle-bead at the end. The three are secured by means of a strip of leather at right angles, attached to the edge of the upper (4). A strip of leather, split lengthwise and flanked by three strands of beads, is fastened on the latter side of the upper (5). The loose end has several large beads: a large tube bead, a flat circular bead and a small tube bead at the end. An additional flat,

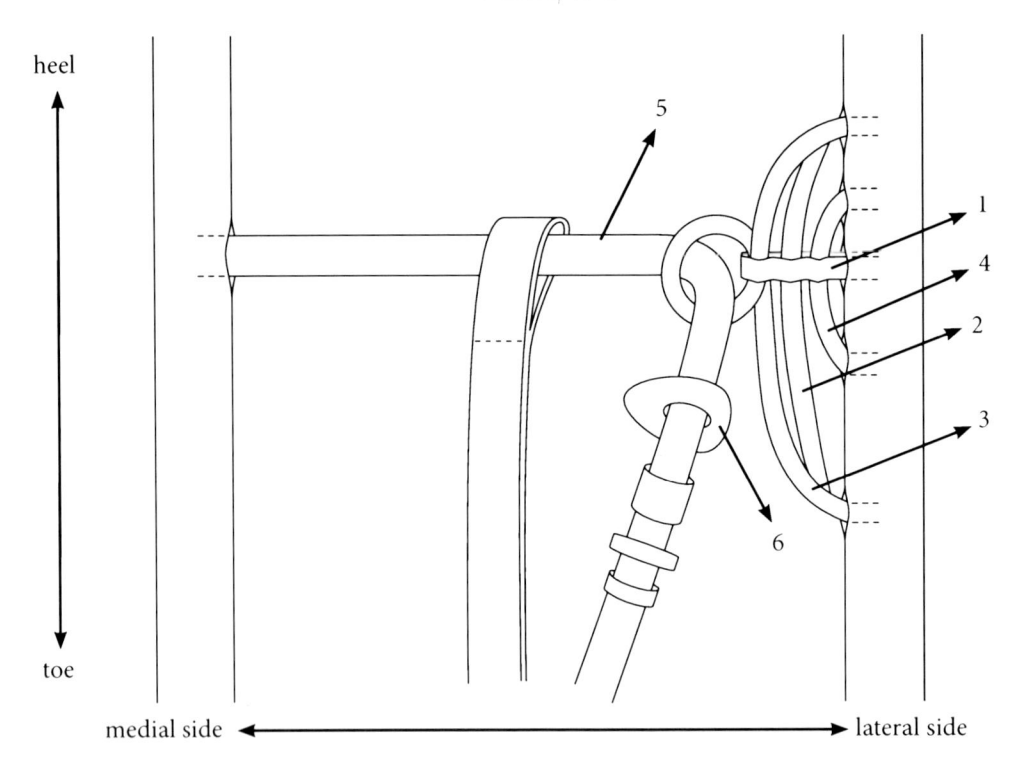

Figure 3.77. The unique fastening in open shoes 270a. The numbers are discussed in the text. Note that 5 actually consists of a leather string with beads, flanked by strings of beads (see figure 3.74H). Not to scale. Drawing by E. Endenburg / A.J. Veldmeijer.

oval bead (6), however, serves as a toggle. To close the shoe, this toggle-bead needed to be inserted through the loop on the lateral side. Additionally in the construction of the left shoe (but not seen in the right one), there is a ring made of unknown material. It is open on one side.

3.4 NOT KEPT OBJECTS

There are several objects, which were in too bad of a condition and were not kept by Carter (table 9). A beadwork sandal, 021j, consisting of "tiny disks of blue, red and yellow faience" (Card No. 021j), lying under leather sandal 021h, had fallen to pieces and "no notes could be obtained either of size or ornamentation" (Card No. 021j). It could very well be that some of the remnants of beadwork, attached to the ventral surfaces of the sandals, are parts of the bead sandals. However, the fragment seen in figure 3.55G is part of another beadwork object, judging by the large circular rosettes, which were not used in the beadwork sandals 087a/147a (*cf.* figure 1.2D).

Carter's entry 085c is a sole of a left sandal, made of leather (Card No. 085c; figure 1.4, table 9). As mentioned, the sandal was in poor condition and not kept,[47] but in Burton's photograph it is clear that the sandal has a rounded, rather small heel and a distinctly constricted waist. Towards the front, the width increases slightly but continuously. At about a quarter of the length, the lateral edge turns sharply inwards, terminating in a rounded toe. The perimeter shows a clear line, which might be a separate leather edge applied onto the sole. Remnants of the pre/back strap might be associated but nothing can be identified with any certainty.

The entry 067b (table 9) might be the right sandal of a pair. Although Carter did not mention it, the fact that there are no additional numbers suggests that the object was not kept and hence not studied first hand by the present author. Carter (Card

No. 067b) mentions "applied decoration in strips of coloured bark" with the main part showing Asiatic and African foes, tied back to back. Both soles are very thin and possibly were part of a multi-layered sole. It is not unlikely that they belong to the same sandal, as they were found close together. In that case, 085c shows the surface, which was attached to the back of 067b. Obviously the decoration would have been on the dorsal surface of the insole.

Sandal 104b, one of a pair (figure 1.7, table 9), was in a very bad condition and hence not kept (Card No. 104b). For a description, see sandal 104a (section 3.2.1.1).

3.5 ADDITIONAL OBSERVATIONS

3.5.1 Size

Tutankhamun's footwear falls in two size categories: those with a length of approximately 220 mm and those with a length of approximately 300 mm. Only the bead sandals are slightly shorter: about 200 mm long. The actual size, however, does not reflect the actual foot size (Van Driel-Murray, 2000: 312). The length of Tutankhamun's right foot is 24.2 cm (Card No. 256ll), which is evidently too large for either the bead sandals or the group of the approximate size of 220 mm. The sandals of the largest group of sewn sandals are roughly 7 cm too long (the big toe only slightly protruding beyond the slit for the front strap), but remember that the toe was usually upturned. A good indication is, of course, the gold sandals on the king's feet, which imitate fibre, sewn sandals (figures 1.8 & 3.60). According to Carter (Card No. 256ll) they measured "29.5; Max. W. 10.3 cents". and fall in the group of the largest size. Moreover, many, if not all three-dimensional representations (see chapter 8) show the sandals oversized, even if not taking the upturned toe into account, which seems therefore a common situation.

The shoes, in contrast, all are about 280-290 mm in length,[48] suggesting a closer fit and therefore supports the assumption made as to the oversized nature of the sandals. The absence of child's footwear is interesting. Several finds, including sewn sandals (figure 3.78),[49] suggest that very small children (some of which could hardly walk) did wear footwear. Assuming Tutankhamun did wear footwear when he was a child, why are they not among the objects in the tomb? Were they not kept for the burial or has it something to do with Amarna where he might have lived as a boy? Or were they worn beyond repair, children being active as they are, and hence not kept? The small sized footwear found in the tomb might fit a boy about 10 years old. Tutankhamun ascended the throne at about that age; possibly the lack of child's sandals has to do with becoming king (more on the possible reasons in chapter 8).

3.5.2 Use and Wear[50]

The interpretation of wear in fibre, sewn sandals is hindered by the fact that not all of them have been photographed by Burton. Some, however, have been photographed and comparison of sandals 094a and 104a clearly shows that much of the damage has occurred after excavation. This observation forces us to be cautious regarding the interpretation of the condition of not-photographed fibre, sewn sandals and hence we cannot know if damage (broken straps for example) is post-depositional or not. Moreover, if the damage occurred before the excavation, we cannot identify the damage as due to use or due to the robber's/priest's activities. This seems especially applicable to the strap complex. In some sandals for example, in which the pre-straps were still in their original place, a third pre-strap was lying on the sole. Note that, even when the sandal is much damaged, the pre-strap is often intact; the attachment of the pre/back straps is always traceable. But if we are certain on the strap complex's history, it is easy to identify

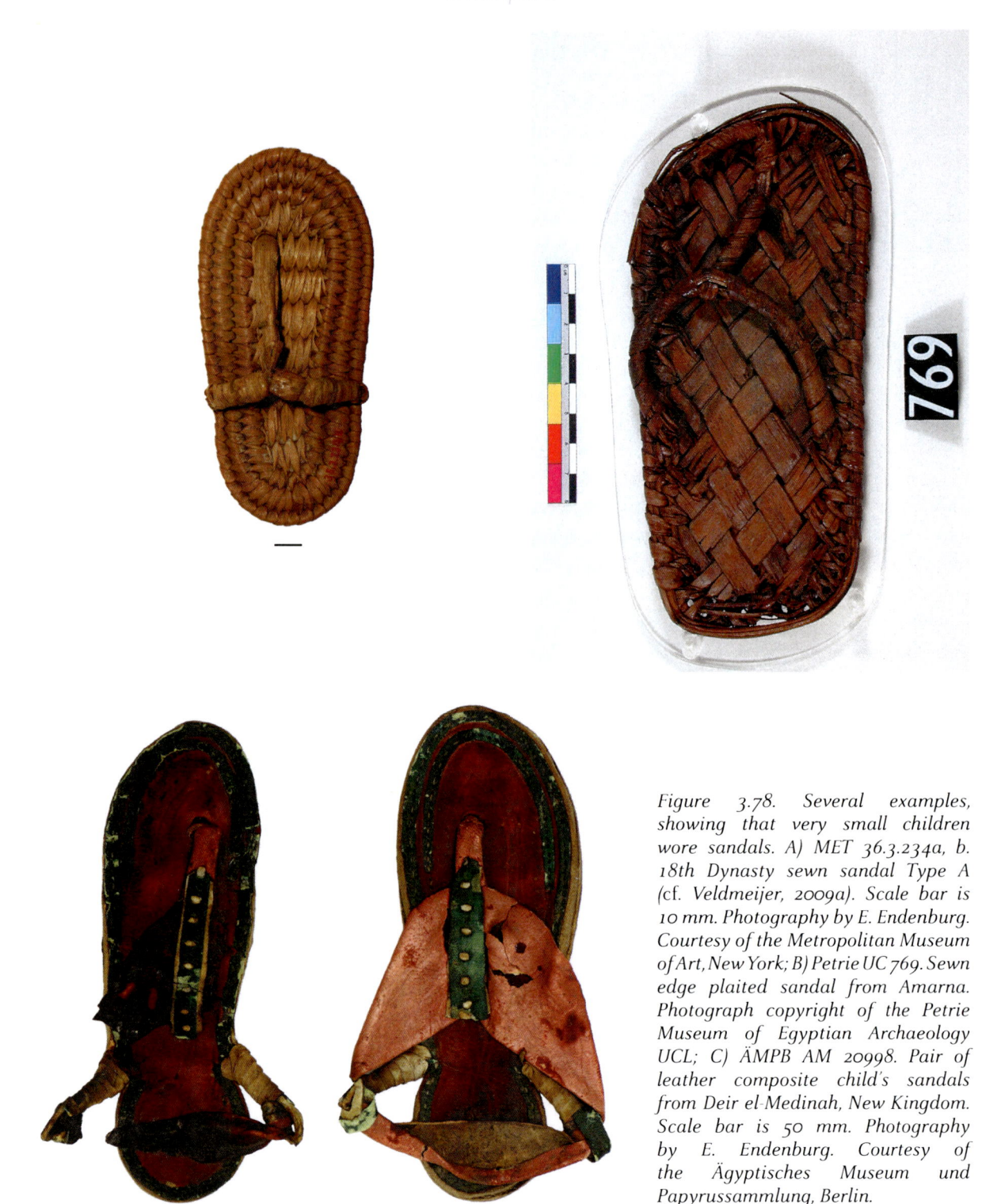

Figure 3.78. Several examples, showing that very small children wore sandals. A) MET 36.3.234a, b. 18th Dynasty sewn sandal Type A (cf. Veldmeijer, 2009a). Scale bar is 10 mm. Photography by E. Endenburg. Courtesy of the Metropolitan Museum of Art, New York; B) Petrie UC 769. Sewn edge plaited sandal from Amarna. Photograph copyright of the Petrie Museum of Egyptian Archaeology UCL; C) ÄMPB AM 20998. Pair of leather composite child's sandals from Deir el-Medinah, New Kingdom. Scale bar is 50 mm. Photography by E. Endenburg. Courtesy of the Ägyptisches Museum und Papyrussammlung, Berlin.

wear: the strap complex of sewn sandals was sometimes repaired when broken. One such an example is the additional papyrus cladding of the front strap in sandal 367b.

Many fibre sandals show damaged sewing strips on the surface of the sole, *i.e.* the parts of the strips that are sandwiched between two rows are still *in situ*. The condition is often limited to several stitches or, in the worst cases, an entire row. It does not occur especially at those parts of the sandal that are in contact with the foot; in contrast, it seems the opposite. Moreover, of a pair, often one of the two shows more severe damage of this type but this might be coincidental. In addition, some sandals of a pair were not together originally. Although it might be that the broken stitch was, for example, a weak spot in the strip of palm leaf, the numbers of this occurrence as well as the fact that it is not common in sewn sandals from other contexts (Veldmeijer, 2009a), seems to exclude the interpretation that it is caused by use. It cannot entirely be ruled out that it is due to storage, but this type of damage can already been seen in the few excavation photographs of fibre, sewn sandals.

There are, however, signs of wear that are undoubtedly due to use. The slight compression of the sewing strips on the ventral surface of 021a is due to the owner's weight and suggests a hard surface to walk on rather than soft surface such as sand. The fibrous condition of the crown sinnet supports such an interpretation. Comparable wear is seen in 4301, but on the dorsal surface, mainly at the heel and ball of the foot. Moreover, these spots show a slight dark patina of the convex surfaces of the sewing strips. This discoloration is even more distinct in other sandals (right one in 4302, 4310). Likely, the discolouration is due to the natural oils that skin produces or oils that were applied to the skin and thus a clear sign the sandal was worn. In 4302 this contradicts with the absence of damaged sewing strips, unless not much rubbing of the foot over the surface occurred. The absence of the patina in the left sandal makes it also questionable whether the sandals were originally a pair.

Another clear indication of wear is the bulging of the dorsal surface of the sole anterior to the crown sinnet that secures the front strap to the sole (JE 62689, JE 62690, 4286, 4287; figure 3.15). This bulging cannot be due to heavy items on top of them during their storage in the tomb, as it requires pressure around the crown sinnet, pushing the sole around the knot forward and downward. Moreover, the straps are intact in some, which makes it unlikely that items were stored on top of them. Therefore, it can only be due to the toes and the weight of the owner. It would be most interesting to see if this feature occurs with walking on all kinds of surfaces and to the same degree or predominantly with one particular type of surface only. One could imagine that it does not occur or far less so when walking in loose sand, as the knot will be pushed in the sand and hence the sole proper finds support on the sand. On harder surfaces, however, this will not happen and the sole will be pushed 'over' the thick knot. Needless to say that it is expected that experiments would shed light on this supposition. The remarkable thing about this feature is that it is lacking in other sandals or is far less noticeable. The crown sinnet, however, is not always as bulky as for example the one in 021a & b (figure 3.9, cf. 4290 in figure 3.8). The absence of this feature in other types of sewn sandals (Veldmeijer, 2009a) can be understood if one realises that the soles in Type A sandals are much thicker and less flexible than those in Type C sewn sandals.

Despite this, however, the degree of wear of the sole is surprisingly little, even when it is clear that they have been worn. The large number of sewn footwear articles seems to indicate that they were regularly replaced.

As explained, the present condition of some of the non-fibre footwear (021f & g, 021h & i, 021k & l, 270a), is such that study of the parts that are most prone to wear proved impossible. Although the open shoes were relatively complete when they were photographed by Burton, they already were (much) damaged. Some of the damage is related to the way the priests dealt with the objects when they cleaned up after the robberies (for example the front strap that has been pushed through the sole in 021f & g), but other damage, such as the incomplete leather upper in 021f & g and 021 k & l does not necessarily have to be due to the priests actions. However, the robbers, throwing the shoes and sandals across the room in search of more precious objects, undoubtedly caused damage too. This might particularly be the case for the tearing of the sole/upper seam as well as the breakage of more fragile parts such as strands of bead and the instep straps in 021k & l. On the other hand, the disconnection of the upper from the sole could also be due to use: there is a good possibility in 021k & l that the stitches that fasten the upper to the sole protruded from the ventral surface of the treadsole and thus extremely prone to wear. However, it is hard to believe that, if the damage is due to wear, the shoes were not repaired. The bad preservation of the leather of 021h & i prohibit firm statements regarding wear but the damaged slits of the edge decoration (through which the narrow strips of gold are pulled) might be wear due to use, as is the bulging of the lowest part of the upper/edge of the sole.

The elaborately decorated dorsal surface of pair 397 - the 'marquetry veneer' sandals - does not show signs of wear. The left sandal shows damage to the medial edge, exposing the wood inner core, but it is hard to believe this is due to use. *If* these sandals were used, it is certain the king would not have walked actively in them, as the fastening of the straps (in holes through the soles[51]) to the sole would not allow this. He might, however, have been carried around.[52] The highly symbolic decoration of the insole makes the pair appropriate to wear when the Pharaoh received foreigners bringing tribute or other foreign visitors. Not all depictions of the king, seated on his throne, however, offer a solution as to the exact type of footwear he wears (see chapter 8). Of course it is possible that, during use, the sandal was bumped into a hard object, which caused the decoration to flake off, but this cannot be proven and might also have happened during the robberies or subsequent clearing by the priests.

3.6 COMPARISON[53]

One pair of sewn sandals from the tomb of Yuya and Tjuiu, described in chapter 6, differs from the rest of the sewn sandals and compares well with Tutankhamun's sewn sandals: MET 10.184 has 63 transverse bundles of an average diameter of 4 mm, which are fastened with very fine sewing. The rest of their sewn sandals, however, differ from the 'classical' Type C, Variant 1 sewn sandal. Within this part of their footwear assemblage, there are again differences to note. In general, the shape is less elongated and the toe is blunter, which results in a more thickset appearance, also when taking the difference in length into account. This thickset appearance is even pronounced by the fact that the transverse bundles are much wider (up to as much as 12.5 mm) and flatter and as a consequence less numerous. Although this is true for all of them, one pair shows an extraordinarily large width (JE 95356 and JE 95318). In this, it compares well with the pair found in Sedment (tomb 136; UC 16555), dated to the reign of Amenhotep III (Petrie & Brunton, 1924: 25; see also Veldmeijer, 2009a). Recent investigation of this pair, which is housed in the Petrie Museum for Egyptian Archaeology UCL, London, shows, interestingly, cores made of a woody material rather than the usual grass and are much flatter (as discussed in section 4.1.1). The material seems to be reed, but detailed analyses are forthcoming (Cartwright *et al*., In preparation). The curvature of the transverse bundles, seen relatively often in Tutankhamun's fibre, sewn sandals is not often observed in the sandals from Yuya and Tjuiu (clear in JE 95348b, 95354a, 95348b, slight in 95353b). The pair of fibre, sewn sandals found in the tomb of Nefertari (Veldmeijer, 2009a) differs from those from Tutankhamun: the pointed toe is more distinct and the waist is less constricted.

What is uncommon with the non-sewn sandals footwear is the fastening/closure methods, which warrant its prominent place in the typology (see chapter 9). The pair of leather sandals 021h & i is unique because of the close imitation of fibre, sewn sandals in combination with the materials used: papyrus and leather (and the added decoration with gold studs): it is the only example of a combination of leather and plant fibre in sandals thus far known. None of the known leather sandals from contemporary Egypt have a comparable, 'sewn sandal strap complex,' the reason for which seems to be related to the importance of sewn sandals. The use of this typical Egyptian type of strap complex (also in pair of shoes 021f & g) is a strong indication that the foot strap, which is combined with it in some shoes, was either borrowed from foreign examples or an invention by the Egyptian themselves and an argument against the import of the shoe from foreign countries. The technology of this pair of sandals is relatively simple and conforms to the technology known (for the sole construction, using decorative, reinforcement strips *cf.* for example ÄM 20998 from Deir el-Medinah in figure 3.78C; Veldmeijer, 2009i). The use of foot straps is common in Mesopotamia, as is seen in the reliefs of Ashurnasirpal II in the British Museum, London or Persepolis (Walser, 1966; see also Kuckertz, 2006: 148-150), although these are of later date.[54] Open shoes with (elaborately) decorated strap complexes, including foot straps, are known from – also much later – Meroitic Nubia. An interesting image is known from Qasr Ibrim (Pyke, in Rose, 2007: 49-50; figure 3.79) showing a foot "with a cross-hatched design and a reclining uraeus on top of the foot". Remarkably, the design looks very similar to the gold-on-leather foot strap in 021k & l (figure 3.71). In contrast to ancient Egypt, where shoes were almost never depicted and the royal family are always shown to be shod with sandals (despite the fact that at least Tutankhamun had shoes), in much later Meroitic Nubia, images of the royal family wearing elaborately decorated open shoes are fairly common (*Ibidem*: 50).

The leather shoes 270a have no equivalent either. Here too, the construction of the sole is of a known type and compares well with the construction in sandals 021h & i. However, the sole/upper construction in which the upper is supported by a decorative gold strip is without parallel even though a comparable construction is seen in the pair of leather shoes BM EA 4408 & 4409. In these, however, a leather strip acts as the connecting element between soles and upper (Veldmeijer, 2009f). Also, the combination of an openwork upper with a closed leather lining is not seen anywhere else, although openwork, decorative leather in footwear is not uncommon (*cf.* Van Driel-Murray, 2000: 315; Veldmeijer, 2009d, for examples of closed shoes with openwork decoration; Veldmeijer, 2009i, for examples of openwork in leather sandals).[55] Another feature without analogy outside the tomb of Tutankhamun is the toe band, which is not known in Egypt and as explained above, might have been taken from foreign examples. This explanation seems more plausi-

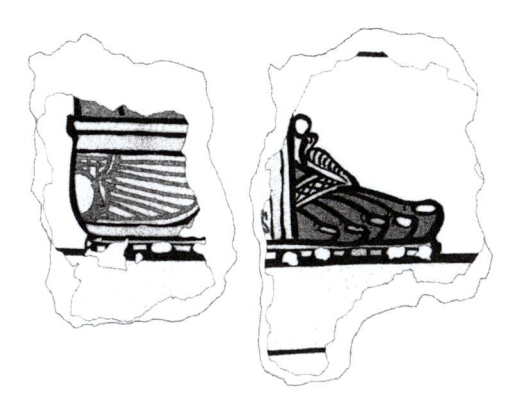

Figure 3.79. Foot of a ruler from Meroitic context (Qasr Ibrim). Note the partial upper (open shoe) with the foot strap. Photography by P.J. Rose. Courtesy of the Egypt Exploration Society. Drawing by G. Pyke.

ble than that the entire shoe was imported: despite the deviant sole/upper construction, the overall technology does not differ from Egyptian footwear/leatherwork technology. Moreover, the openwork decoration shows popular Egyptian motifs. Finally, the daisy-decoration on the foot strap correlates to those on the front strap in 021h & i; the openwork leather of the upper and back strap is also comparable.

There are no close parallels for the shoes 021f & g and 021k & l either. These shoes are not unique because they are shoes: they are unique because of the combination of materials used, the elaborate decoration and, especially in 021k & l, the fastening/closure method. What is true for the foot strap and toe band, is true for the instep strap as well – a feature only seen with the shoes from Tutankhamun. Here too, we can be fairly sure that the shoes are Egyptian products: shoes 021f & g combine sewn sandal features (strap complex) with Egyptian decoration motifs (papyrus, lilies, lotus). The sole construction, combining two sole layers of which the dorsal one is folded around the edge of the lower one, is seen more often in Egyptian footwear (sandals: Veldmeijer, 2009i; open shoes: Veldmeijer, 2009f [see figure 6.20]; closed shoes: Veldmeijer, 2009d [see figure 6.22]). Although the fold at the ventral surface of the sole layer is usually covered by the treadsole or an isolated strip,[56] this is not universal and the construction of Tutankhamun's shoes is therefore not special. Usually, the sole layers are stitched with running stitches, as is likely the case in Tutankhamun's footwear. The attachment of the upper to the soles has most likely also been done with running stitching. In this, it differs from the known examples of curled-toe ankle shoes in which the upper is secured by means of whip stitches (Veldmeijer, 2009d; see figure 6.22). The sole/upper construction in stubbed-toe low ankle shoes (Veldmeijer, In preparation b [see figure 6.24]) differs entirely from those in the curled-toe ankle shoes: the upper is, at the sole, folded outwards and sewn with leather thong running stitches to the sole. In this, it compares more closely to the construction in 021f & g and 021k & l.

Gold tomb sandals are known from the tomb of foreign wives of Tuthmosis III (Winlock, 1948: 45-46, pl. XXVI; Lilyquist *et al.*, 2004: 133-135). These differ from those found on Tutankhamun's feet as the wives' sandals seem to imitate leather sandals (Winlock, 1948: 45; Lilyquist *et al.* 2004: 133; *cf.* Veldmeijer, 2009i) rather than fibre, sewn sandals. It is not clear whether they imitate the sandals common in the wives' homeland, Syria, or sandals worn by the royal family in Tuthmosis' times. If, however, the sandals are a true imitation, than these types of sandals have yet to be found from the archaeological record.

The sandals on the feet of Tjuiu, discussed in chapter 6, were also made of metal and seem to simulate sewn sandals, but if this is combined with leather straps, it differs from other metal tomb sandals. Daressy (1902) mentions the find of small gold fragments on the foot of Maiherpri's mummy, which might be remnants of gold sandals. A pair of gilded copper sandals in the Roemer- und Pelizaeus Museum, Hildesheim (personal observation 2005), possibly from the Old Kingdom (according to the museum's archive from Mastaba G, viii S of Giza's Southern Cemetery), differs in shape: it is roughly rectangular with a T-shaped strap complex, that can be compared with those seen in figure 6.17[57] (except for the attached curled toe part).

CHAPTER 4

THE MATERIALS

With sections by Alan J. Clapham, James A. Harrell, Paul T. Nicholson, Jack M. Ogden & André J. Veldmeijer

4.1 ORGANIC MATERIALS

4.1.1 Fibres

André J. Veldmeijer

Identification of the fibre sandals was not performed by Carter and his team although the cards refer to several vegetable materials, such as rush and papyrus.[1] Modern microscopic identification is hindered by the fact that most of the fibre sandals have been treated (see chapter 2), requiring cleaning of the conservatives before taking samples. This has not been done, but we are fortunate to have comparable sandals in collections elsewhere (Veldmeijer, 2009a), with forthcoming identification using optical and scanning electron microscopy.[2] Moreover, several of the sandals are in excellent condition, allowing for identification by macroscopic investigation, with the aid of a magnifying glass (x 20). Finally, Greiss (1949: 268) published the identification of a sewn sandal, confirming the identification presented here.[3] All of Tutankhamun's sandals are made of transverse bundles of halfa grass (*Desmostachya bipinnata* or *Imperata cylindrica*; figure 4.1A)[4] and the innermost two cores of the edges also seems to have been made predominantly of this material.

Recent research on the sewn sandals in the Petrie Museum of University College, London (UC 16555), suggest that the cores in the bundles are made of a much more woody material, probably a reed (Cartwright *et al.*, In preparation; figure 4.1B; see also sandal JE 95318 from Yuya and Tjuiu in figure 6.5). Halfa grasses are plants

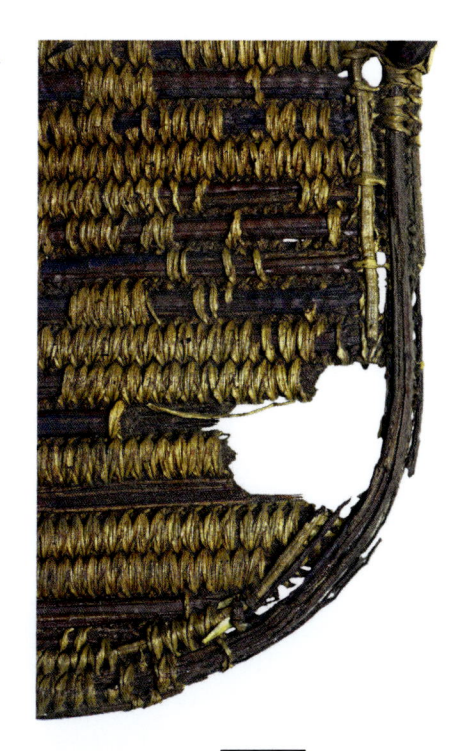

Figure 4.1. Plant fibres used in sewn sandals. A) The cores of the transverse bundles are usually made of halfa grass (104a); B) Examples of reed(?) cores are known from the Yuya and Tjuiu sandals and from an example in the Petrie Museum of Egyptian Archaeology UCL seen here (UC 16555). Scale bars are 10 mm. Photography by A.J. Veldmeijer. Courtesy of the Supreme Council of Antiquities / Authorities Egyptian Museum, Cairo and Petrie Museum of Egyptian Archaeology UCL respectively.

which have been used in Egypt extensively for cordage, basketry and matting from the earliest times onwards (references are abundant, but for a short survey see Greiss, 1949: 252-253) up to the present day (for example Greiss, 1949: 252-253; Wendrich, 1999). However, some specimens show additional fibres, with an appearance which suggests it is the same fibre used for the outermost core, which might be made from the fruit-bearing stalks of the date palm (figure 3.3).[5] The reason for the use of the (split?) stalks as core for the outermost row of the edge, might be because the diameter needed to be very small, rendering the use of a bundle of grass impossible.

The sewing is done with strips of dom palm leaf (*Hyphaene thebaica*; *e.g.* figures 3.3 and 4.1), a plant which is extensively used for basketry, matting and related objects (for example Greiss, 1949: 255-256; Murray, 2000: 620-621; Wendrich, 1999: 274-277). Macroscopic investigations suggest that the innermost core of the front strap (figure 3.7) is made of palm leaf strips (species not identified), with a lengthwise cladding of papyrus (*Cyperus papyrus*). The transverse cladding is done with palm leaf strips, the species of which has not been identified. The back strap (*e.g.* figure 3.5 & 3.34B) and the cladding of the pre- and back strap attachments (figure 3.6) are made of papyrus. The pre-strap itself, however, is made of palm leaf (figure 3.5). Papyrus was much used throughout Egypt's history, but mainly for the production of papyrus sheets that were used for writing (*e.g.* Leach & Tait, 2000: 227-253). As already pointed out by Lucas (1948: 130), papyrus was rarely used for basketry (but did find some use in boxes) and seems to be limited in footwear[6] only to the production of fine, so-called tomb sandals[7] (Petrie, 1889; personal observation 2006) and straps.[8] Another application of papyrus, especially in Pharaonic Egypt, was for the production of cordage, mainly with fairly large diameters (Ryan & Hansen, 1987: 9-13) although this too seems to have been limited: the coils of rope found in Mersa/Wadi Gawasis, for example, which are dated to the Middle Kingdom, are not made of papyrus but of reed (Veldmeijer & Zazzaro, 2008).

Invariably, the first thing to do in manufacturing fibre sandals is the harvesting and preparation of the material (see Wendrich, 1999: 273-282).[9] The halfa grasses did not need much preparation, perhaps comparable to Wendrich's (1999: 283) ethno-archaeological observations that it was dried for three to five days and wetted just before use. It is certain that it was not beaten before use as suggested by Greiss (1949: 252) for the manufacturing of grass cordage,[10] as the fibres are usually still intact and unbroken. Dom palm leaves were dried for a minimum of two weeks, after which the leaves were split (Wendrich, 1999: 275). The culms of papyrus need about ten days to dry and only need soaking in water prior to use (*Ibidem*: 285).

4.1.2 The Presence of Silver Birch (*Betula pendula* Roth)

Alan J. Clapham

According to Carter (Card No. 397) the white material in the marquetry veneer sandals (397) is bark. It has been suggested that this could be the bark of silver birch (*Betula pendula* Roth). The author has only seen photographs of the sandals and his first impression was that birch bark is an unlikely candidate; perhaps some type of animal material is more likely. Closer inspection by Salima Ikram and André J. Veldmeijer enabled them to reject the animal origin hypothesis for the white border; therefore, without the possibility of further analysis, the original identification of silver birch bark must stand for the time being. The sandals seem to have been conserved in the past and this may actually mask any characteristics that indicate birch bark.

Further study of the photographs provided revealed dark lines that appeared across the white border at irregular intervals. If the identification of birch bark is accepted, these dark lines are most likely lenticels which occur in bark, and function like stomata in leaves, permitting the exchange of gases between the atmosphere and the tree trunk.

Silver birch bark has been found covering other artefacts from Tutankhamun's tomb, such as several self bows (McLeod, 1982), composite bows (McLeod, 1970), the bow case (McLeod, 1982), sticks, a fan-handle, goads (Gale *et al.* 2000: 336-337; Hepper 1990: 43) and chariots (A5, see Littauer & Crouwel, 1985).

Silver birch is a tree with a height of up to 30 m. The bark is smooth and silvery-white except towards the base (Walters, 1993: 68). The bark can be removed in large sheets. Its waterproofing and insulating properties are well known and make it a useful material for covering objects (Gale *et al.*, 2000: 336-337; Littauer & Crouwel, 1985: 93). The tree is found mainly on sandy or peaty soils (Walters, 1993: 68) and can be found growing up to 200 m above sea level (Gale *et al.*, 2000: 336-337). It can be found growing all over Europe but is rarely found growing in the south (Walters, 1993: 68). According to Gale *et al.* (2000: 336-337) the furthest south that the tree can be found in any numbers is northern Greece and the Caucasus. The tree is not found in Egypt.

Since the tree is not native to Egypt, the bark must have been imported as a luxury item, possibly coming from northern Greece or traded from further afield. This is supported by the poorly attested use of the birch wood in Egypt (Gale *et al.*, 2000: 337). This, in its turn, might be an indication that the bark was imported rather than a situation where entire logs were imported and then bark removed after arrival in Egypt.

4.1.3 Leather

André J. Veldmeijer

Identification[11] of archaeologically attested leather is a difficult matter and often not possible, even if the leather is in good condition, which, as already mentioned, it was not. Attempts to identify leather from Amarna, which is in a comparable condition to much of the leather from the tomb (Veldmeijer, 2009b; see above) was only partially successful (Trommer, 2005: 141-144). Moreover, the leather continued to deteriorate after excavation, making the identification even more unlikely. Therefore, it was decided not to start the sampling process, although this might be considered in the future if techniques are improved enough to make identification likely. Consequently, we have to rely on the work done in the 1920's by the excavation scientists. Lucas (1927: 176) mentions that "Four specimens of this leather have been kindly examined by Dr. R.H. Pickard, F.R.S., Director of the British Leather Manufacturers' Research Association, and it was found that the specimen from the seat of a stool was unquestionably goat-skin and that of the sandals [shoes 021k & l] was possibly calf-skin." Cow leather is used most often in sandals (Van Driel-Murray, 2000: 302) as many examples from all periods suggest, but other types of leathers have been tentatively identified (Schwarz, 2000: 217). Shoes were, according to Van Driel-Murray (2000: 302), generally made from goatskin, which is confirmed by Veldmeijer (2009d: 14). This, however, is limited to certain types of footwear, as other types have been made of much thicker leather, likely cow as well (Veldmeijer, In preparation b).

Skin processing is rather universal and is relatively well documented for ancient Egypt (Forbes, 1966: 1-21; Schwarz, 2000: 16-64, Van Driel-Murray, 2000: 299-306).[12] Important sources of information are scenes in tombs (one of the most important being the tomb of Rekhmira, see Davies, 1943). In short, the process was as follows. After flaying the skin, the underlying fat was removed, and then the skin was depilated. Curing arrests the degenerative process and was the next step. Curing, and especially oil curing, was the preferred method of skin processing in Pharaonic Egypt; the scholarly view holds that vegetable tanning was introduced by the Greek or Romans (Van Driel-Murray, 2000: 299, 302-306); however, recent research might suggest a slightly more nuanced picture (Friedman, 2007: 60; Veldmeijer, 2007: 24; 2008: 3; Veldmeijer & Laidler, 2008: 1216). Then, the skin was treated to make it supple and was ready for use.[13]

4.2 INORGANIC MATERIALS

4.2.1 Glass and Faience

Paul T. Nicholson

There is no doubt that glass and faience is used in the footwear but the results of the study, based on photographs (021f & g and 021k & l) and viewing the objects through the glass of the display case in combination with photographs (085a/147a and 270a), are, at best, provisional. The study of glass and faience requires an optical microscope, or at least a hand lens, in order to obtain more certainty regarding the identification of the materials. The matter is further complicated because when producing small beads of faience, the silica core of the material is sometimes sufficiently vitrified that the whole item becomes, essentially, a glass, rather than a silica core with glazed (*i.e.* glass) surface. The chemical composition of this 'accidental' glass may be distinct from that of deliberately produced glass, but cannot, of course, be determined without laboratory analyses. Such analyses are essential if the two materials are to be separated conclusively and on unbroken specimens. Finally, as it is, the material belongs to a time when the faience colour palette was expanded as a result of the introduction of glass and the colours of the two materials can overlap considerably.[14] It must be stressed, therefore, that the observations are tentative and that without proper scientific examination, no firm conclusions can be drawn.

At least some of the turquoise-coloured beads in shoes 021f & g seem to be of glass: their thickness varies and there is some pitting to the surfaces of the cylindrical examples which seems to me more characteristic of glass than of faience. The red-brown cylinder section beads share similar pitting as do the purple-blue ones, and these may also be glass, though this attribution is less certain. The dark blue background of the gold floral decorations may be glass but is most likely lapis lazuli. The deep colour and the fragmented nature of the material make it less likely to be faience, which could have been made in large, moulded, pieces. The dark blue of the lotus decoration also seems likely to be lapis lazuli, whilst the other inlays in this are probably semi-precious stones rather than glass or faience (see section 4.2.2).

The white beads in 021k & l may well be glass, and at least one of the red beads seems to have a raised edge as though from piercing with, or trailing around, wire. Some of the turquoise, green and yellow examples might be glass too.

The beadwork in the pair of shoes 270a might, at least in part, be comprised of glass. One of the turquoise blue beads seems to exhibit a slight twist as though it has been wrapped around a wire and includes a small 'tail' of glaze. Such tails are not of themselves unknown in faience since they can be formed where glaze has run, but here the piece looks more likely to be the result of drawing a rod away from the newly formed bead. The thickness of some of the turquoise beads also varies considerably and they look more like glass examples from Amarna than faience ones (see finds catalogue in Nicholson, 2007). The dark blue beads may be of glass coloured with cobalt or of lapis lazuli.

The multi-coloured beadwork in sandal 085a/147a seems most likely to be faience: no clear signs of bubbles in the material have been noted and the size and shape of the beads is consistent with similar small faience beads known from Amarna (see the finds catalogue in Nicholson, 2007; see also section 4.2.2). All of the colours represented are known in faience, and though the same can be said for glass, the red-brown looks more like faience than glass. A possible exception is the white material which in the photographs appears to more glass-like. One example shows bubbles, but it is not clear from the photograph whether these are original or on the surface as a result of some conservation treatment.

4.2.2 Gemstones

James A. Harrell

4.2.2.1 Identification in the Footwear

Three of the four pieces of footwear examined in Cairo's Egyptian Museum (021g & h, 021k & l and 270a) contain gemstone beads or inlays. The fourth, 085a/147a, is made entirely of faience beads (see section 4.2.1). The gemstones are: (1) opaque to slightly translucent, bluish green 'amazonite', a variety of microcline feldspar; (2) translucent, reddish orange to red 'carnelian' (also spelled 'cornelian'), a variety of chalcedonic quartz; (3) opaque, dark blue 'lapis lazuli', which is a rock, rather than a mineral, consisting of blue lazurite with occasional specks of golden pyrite and patches of white calcite; and (4) opaque, bright, light blue 'turquoise'. All these are commonly used gemstones in ancient Egyptian jewellery (Andrews, 1990: 39-52; DePutter & Karlshausen, 1992: 47-48, 130-131, 105-107; Aston et al., 2000: 26-27, 39-40, 45-46, 62-63).

Shoes 021f & g are the only ones with gemstone inlays and these include amazonite, carnelian and lapis lazuli in the central, triangular lotus flower design on the back strap, and lapis lazuli on the sides around the gold daisies (as suggested in section 4.2.1; see also section 4.2.3.5). The blue material on the sides of the two golden duck heads (flanking the aforementioned triangular design) is glass paste imitating lapis lazuli (see also section 4.2.3.5). Beads of the same three gemstones (plus gold) were also used in these shoes as well as for shoes 021k & l and 270a. Shoes 270a additionally has turquoise[15] but no faience beads whereas the pair 021k & l seems to include many glass and/or faience beads, as mentioned previously. The latter shoes may also have rare beads of turquoise but this is uncertain given their small size and similarity in colour to some of the faience beads.

4.2.2.2 Origin

The sources of these gemstones are quite varied. For example, the only known source for lapis lazuli is the ancient mines in the Badakhshan region of northeast Afghanistan (Herrmann, 1968; Von Rosen, 1988: 11-13; Moorey, 1994: 85-92). The turquoise, of course, would have come from the well known mines in the Sinai Peninsula at Serabit el-Khadim and Wadi Maghara (Petrie & Currelly, 1906: 34-193; Barrois, 1932; Chartier-Raymond, 1988; Chartier-Raymond et al., 1994).

The amazonite was probably obtained from the recently discovered 18th Dynasty mine on Gebel Migif in Egypt's Eastern Desert (Harrell & Osman, 2007). This is the only known Dynastic mine for this gemstone but others must exist in the Migif-Hafafit-Nugrus region where numerous small deposits of amazonite have been found.

The source for carnelian, however, is problematic. This is surprising given that carnelian was the most commonly used gemstone throughout the Dynastic period. The only known ancient mine is at Stela Ridge in the Nubian Desert northwest of Abu Simbel, but this dates only to the Middle Kingdom (Murray, 1939: 105; Harrell & Bloxam, 2004; Bloxam, 2006: 289-290). The question then is: where did the carnelian come from both before and after the Middle Kingdom? It is widely rumoured that carnelian pebbles are abundant in the wadis of the Eastern Desert (*e.g.*, Lucas & Harris, 1962: 391) but this is not correct. In fact, no true carnelian of the type used for jewellery has yet been documented from this region. Barring still undiscovered mines in Egypt, the most likely source of carnelian is the gravels on the terraces above the Nile River between the Third and Fourth Cataracts in northern Sudan. Pebbles of carnelian, as well as sard and sardonyx, are relatively common within these deposits (Harrell, In press). It is conceivable that much of the richly-coloured carnelian used during the Dynastic period was artificially produced through a heat treatment process like that employed in the modern production of carnelian beads in Cambay, India (Arkell, 1936; Posselhl, 1981). Yellowish, brownish and pinkish chalcedonic quartz (including sard and pale carnelian) can be given a permanent, deep reddish colour by baking over a fire in a ceramic pot. Heating the stones also has the added benefit of making them easier to work. It is not known if the ancient Egyptians knew of this simple process, but it would be surprising if they did not.

4.2.2.3 Foreign

The Amarna Letters indicate that bejewelled footwear was among the gifts given to Egypt's 18th Dynasty rulers by King Tushratta of the Mitannian Empire (Moran, 1992: 53). The gemstones, at least, do not support such a provenance. There are two reasons for this. First, although amazonite, carnelian, lapis lazuli and turquoise from non-Egyptian sources were used in ancient Mesopotamian jewellery, during the mid-2nd millennium BC, only carnelian was in common usage with the other three gemstones rarely utilized (Moorey, 1994: 75-103). And second, the four gemstones were widely used in Egypt both before and after the 18th Dynasty, and so their appearance in Tutankhamun's shoes would not be unusual if these were made in Egypt.

4.2.2.4 Manufacturing of Gemstone Beads and Inlays

Both gemstone beads and inlays were shaped initially by percussion flaking and then by grinding on a hard stone such as quartzite (Lucas & Harris, 1962: 42-44; Andrews, 1990: 67-81). Polishing may have been done by hand-churning in a mixture of other hard stones and/or quartz sand. For beads, the final step was perforation by drilling and this process is illustrated on the walls of several Theban tombs of the 18th and 19th Dynasties (Andrews, 1990: 74-81; Stocks, 2003: 208-213). An especially informative example comes from the tomb of Sobekhotep and is shown in figure 4.2. Three of the workers are using bow drills to simultaneously perforate three or four beads. The worker at right in the upper register appears to be polishing the beads by hand-churning, and the worker at left in the lower register is stringing the beads for a collar. The bow drills would have been fitted with a bit of either chert (*i.e.* flint) or solid copper or bronze, and used with a quartz sand abrasive that did the actual cutting at the bit (Lucas & Harris, 1962: 42-44; Stocks, 2003: 203-224). The vessels (with spoons) at the feet of four of the workers in the painting undoubtedly hold this abrasive. With a Mohs hardness of 7, quartz is hard enough to cut through carnelian (Mohs = 6.5) or any of the other gemstones used by the Egyptians (for example, amazonite, lapis lazuli and turquoise have, respectively, Mohs hardness values of 6, 5-5.5 and 6). There is thus no need to invoke the much harder corundum (in the form of granular emery) or diamond bits (*e.g.*, Gorelick & Gwinnett, 1983), the use of which are without any archaeological support in ancient Egypt (Lucas & Harris, 1962: 42-43, 69-70). There can be no doubt that the holes through beads were drilled in the manner described as indeed has been demonstrated experimentally (Stocks, 2003: 203-224).

What has not been previously remarked upon by scholars, however, is how the

Figure 4.2. Manufacturing scene for bead jewellery from an 18th Dynasty wall painting in the private Theban tomb of Sobekhotep, 'Mayor of the Southern Lake' (i.e., the Faiyum) during the reign of Tuthmosis IV (BM EA 920). Courtesy of the British Museum, London.

cylindrical beads, which are so common in Tutankhamun's shoes and many other jewelled objects, were made. It seems likely that these beads were drilled out of pieces of raw material using again a bow drill but one fitted with a hollow, tubular bit of copper or bronze. Such bits were certainly employed in ancient Egypt for other types of stone work (Lucas & Harris, 1962: 68-90; Arnold, 1991: 265-266; Stocks, 2003: 103-138). It is possible then that the New Kingdom representations of workers using bow drills to make beads depict both the extraction of cylindrical beads from the raw materials as well as their perforation.

4.2.3 Gold

Jack M. Ogden

4.2.3.1 Introduction

In the context of the spectacular exhibitions and the plethora of ever-better-illustrated books that make the words 'ancient Egypt' and 'Tutankhamun' almost synonymous with 'gold', it is remarkable to find that the development of goldworking technology through almost three millennia of ancient Egyptian Dynastic history has received minimal attention. There are some exceptions, in particular the ground-breaking work of John Heins who provided the technical background to Caroline Ransom Williams'

151

catalogue of the ancient Egyptian jewellery that was in the New York Historical Society, prior to its transfer to the Brooklyn Museum (Williams, 1924). Émile Vernier gave some information about the construction of goldwork in the Cairo Museum (Vernier, 1907-1927) and the late Cyril Aldred also briefly touched on the subject in his 'Jewels of the Pharaohs' (Aldred, 1971). Unfortunately the chemist and conservator at the Cairo Museum, Alfred Lucas, although perhaps having more hands-on experience of Tutankhamun's possessions than anyone else, shows little evidence of an interest in gold manufacturing technology in his published works (Lucas, 1926; 1927), and the notes dealing with ancient Egyptian gold by Harry Garland, a metallurgist and Lawrence of Arabia's explosive expert, were sadly too fragmented to be incorporated in his book on ancient Egyptian metallurgy published by his posthumous editor (Garland & Bannister, 1927).

Recent studies of ancient jewellery technology in general, or focussed on ancient societies other than Egyptian, are more abundant, and have varying degrees of relevance to Egyptian goldwork. The first comprehensive survey of ancient goldworking processes was the present writer's 'Jewellery of the Ancient World' which, incidentally, was prompted by frustration at the lack of ancient jewellery-making information available following a visit to the Tutankhamun exhibition in Paris in 1967 – the first time the boy-kings treasures had been seen outside of Egypt (Ogden, 1982).[16]

What follows are some observations on the goldworking processes as evidenced in Tutankhamun's gold or gold-decorated footwear. These observations are based on photographs: it is greatly to be hoped that a more detailed, hands-on study of at least some of the less fragmentary or fragile gold objects from Tutankhamun's tomb will be possible in the near future. Such a study is very long overdue.

4.2.3.2 Goldwork in Ancient Egypt

The gold incorporated in the sandals has not been analysed, but assuming usual ancient Egyptian practice, most of it was probably employed in its natural as-mined, and thus impure, state – 'native gold' – or alloyed with a little silver or copper or both for practical or aesthetic purposes. Analyses over the last century have shown that most ancient Egyptian goldwork prior to the Late Period is between about 70% and 85% pure, the balance being predominantly silver with a small amount of copper (Ogden, 2000: 162-164). The two components of a little gold button from Egypt, exactly contemporary with Tutankhamun, represented exactly this range – the shank was just over 71% gold, the domed head just over 85% gold (Roberts, 1973a).[17] This is in line with gold as mined. There seems to be a trend, at least by the Late Period, for very thin foils to be of higher purity than the gold used for general goldwork. This makes sense – pure gold is easier to hammer into extremely thin sheets – but whether this was a case of the Egyptians spotting and separating the purer native gold on the basis of its colour or an indication that some form of refining to purify native gold was used remains uncertain.[18]

Mined gold almost invariably contains a proportion of silver, ranging from a fraction of a percent up to 50% or more. When there is more than about 25% silver present, whether naturally or deliberately alloyed with the gold, the alloy has a grey to greenish tinge that increases with silver content until the metal looks like silver. When gold has enough silver present to produce such a recognisable grey to greenish colour it is often termed 'electrum'.

The natural copper content of mined gold seldom ranges much over about 2%. The intentional alloying of copper with the gold was carried out for practical or aesthetic reasons. The predominant practical reason in the earliest times was for casting. Casting of gold was seldom resorted to in antiquity because, generally speaking, gold does not cast well with the processes used in antiquity and casting is almost inevitably wasteful. However, when gold was cast, copper was often added as it greatly improved the ease with which the molten alloy flowed into and filled the mould – thus giving good detail – and it reduced the temperature required for the process. Examples of cast gold-copper alloys from Tutankhamun's time are limited to some of the 'stirrup' signet rings (for example, Ogden, 1982: pl. 2 upper left), but copper-containing gold castings are characteristic of many metallurgically immature cultures, from the Chalcolithic Balkans to Bronze Age Britain to Pre-Colombian South America. Observation by the writer to date suggests that the gold-copper alloy stirrup rings are cast. Those of more usual gold-silver alloys are usually produced from one or more hammered components. Whether the reddish colour of the cast, copper-containing signet rings of the 18th Dynasty was a deliberate aesthetic choice, or the inevitable by-product of using an easy-to-cast copper-containing gold alloy is uncertain, but we do find deliberate use of gold-copper alloys to create colour contrasts as with some of the Mycenaean inlaid dagger blades that are contemporary with the Egyptian New Kingdom (Ogden, 1993).

4.2.3.3 The Gold in the Tomb of Tutankhamun

Throughout the tomb, gold was found of varying colours (Lucas, 1927: 172-274), leading Carter in one instance to believe, initially, that the gold sole of shoes 21f & g was made of "rush (?)".[19] In the 1923 publication, however, he did not mention this and might have identified, when looking at it in more detail, the true nature of the sole. Unfortunately, his preliminary remark on the finds card has found its way into publications (*e.g.* Van Driel-Murray, 2000: 316; Vogelsang-Eastwood, 1994: 140). At present, no footwear is known which consists of a combination of metal and fibre.[20] Lucas (1927: 173) explained the various colours (except for the rose colour) as being "fortuitous, and due to chemical changes that had taken place during the time the objects had been in the tomb." The gold of this sole (note, however, that this colour, albeit to a lesser extent also occurs in shoes 021k & l) is of a dull, brownish hue, and, as described in section 3.2.1 and 3.2.2, does not cover the entire sole. According to Lucas (1927: 173) "The bright yellow gold is evidently fairly pure and doubtless corresponds to the "fine gold" referred to in the ancient records. The dull and tarnished yellow gold contains small proportions of other metals, such as silver and copper, which on the surface have undergone chemical changes and thus caused the tarnishing." (Quotation marks in original). New thoughts on the colour are presented below. Interestingly, sandals from the tomb of Yuya and Tjuiu were made from gold and silver (Lilyquist, 1997: 201; see section 6.2.1).

The red colour of the beads, seen in the shoes 021f & g and 021k & l "proved to be a staining of the gold by organic matter" (Lucas, 1927: 172) in some instances. Since the regular distribution of red gold beads in the outer layer of the uppers of the pairs of shoes, it is unlikely the colour was fortuitous and a result of the tomb's environment, but intentional: the ancient goldsmith deliberately made it in this colour.[21] The red coating of gold in several objects consists of coloured glue, but Carter (1933: 173-174) adds "The amount of material available for examination was too small for the nature of the pigment to be determined, but it is probably of mineral origin."

4.2.3.4 The Gold in the Footwear

The daisies decorating the most elaborate sandals (021f & g) provide examples of the deliberate use of colour-contrasting gold alloys by ancient Egyptian goldsmiths (figure 3.63K). Schorsch (2001: 58) has said that

Figure 4.3. The construction of the daisies in shoes 021f & g. Cf. figure 3.63K. Figure by J.M. Ogden.

"Precious-metal polychromy, as it emerges in Egypt in the Eighteenth Dynasty, is a specific achievement, reflected in the manufacture of royal jewellery of the highest quality". The daisies are constructed as shown in figure 4.3. One of the two petal-shaped gold rosettes on each flower is made from a distinctly different gold alloy, one that presumably contains a significant admixture of silver, copper or both. From the colour and the fact that these components were clearly cut from malleable hammered sheet gold they are probably made from a gold alloy with some 35% or more silver present, but this can only be confirmed by analysis. Their present dull brownish colour is caused by such a silver-rich gold alloy's greater susceptibility to corrosion.[22] Originally these petals would have presented a more silvery or, if copper was the additive, a redder, colour, but not necessarily any less bright or polished than the other gold components.

The same use of colour contrasting gold alloys is seen with two-by-two arrays of cylindrical beads in 270a (figures 3.74A & G). It seems probable that other gold components on this object were also of deliberately varied gold alloys, but this cannot be discerned for certain without close study because of the overlay and discoloration from the degraded organic components and the apparent use of what would seem to be transparent greyish-brown varnishes on other gold components (see below).

The use of gold alloys of contrasting colour on a single object are not unknown in ancient Egypt and became popular in the New Kingdom (see Schorsch, 2001). Perhaps the best known of the many examples from the tomb of Tutankhamun is the electrum moon disk on the so-called rebus pendant (267d [JE 61884]; Carter, 1933: pl. XIX, B top). This forms a strong contrast with the yellow colour of the other gold components. There are other constructional similarities between this rebus pendant and the shoes 021f & g that might point to a common workshop origin (see below).

A more common form of colour contrast in goldwork in New Kingdom Egyptian work is also represented in the pair 021k & l. Here, in the chequerboard pattern of hemispherical and square sheet gold beads, the hemispherical ones have a distinctly reddish colour (figures 3.68C & G). But, as the lesser presence of colour on the more exposed areas shows, this colour is a surface effect. Again, close study and analysis was not possible, but the consistent placing of the redder beads very strongly indicates that the colour variation was deliberate and it seems almost certain that this is an example of the 'rose gold' surface first studied by Lucas (Lucas & Harris, 1962) and, more

154

recently, by Frantz & Schorsch (1990; see also Schorsch, 2001: 67-68). The reader is directed to the latter work, but, in brief, the surface colour is believed to be the result of small iron additions to the gold, which, with subsequent heat treatment, form a bright red oxide layer on the gold surface. This 'rose gold' appears to be an Egyptian phenomenon, limited to royal workshops, and which, to date, we first encountered in the tomb of Queen Tiye and was last seen on a pair of earrings of Rameses XI (Frantz & Schorsch, 1990; Ogden, 2000: 164).

A surface colour difference is also apparent between the gold rosettes on o21f & g and the gold lotus and papyrus motifs amongst which they are dispersed. Possibly the rosettes were deliberately surface coloured, but it should be kept in mind that the lotus and papyrus motifs are of sheet gold with simple pierced attachment holes, while the rosettes have separately made and soldered-on attachment loops (see below). The heat of soldering may well have had some unplanned affect on the surface colour, possibly only manifested after long burial had allowed oxidation, diffusion or both. However, that the deliberate 'rose gold' surface affect could be created on soldered components is shown by the earrings of Rameses XI as well as the beadwork in o21k & l.

The colour differences between the main outer part of the soles of o21f & g and the central shaped sections is noteworthy. The deliberate working of the sheet gold to represent woven rush may well indicate that the greyish brown colour surface to the gold was also deliberately produced to replicate the colour of rushwork. In any case, Lucas' suggestion that the colour was fortuitous and due to chemical action during burial is untenable. The surface appears to have been produced by some sort of applied 'varnish' and, indeed, chemical action in places has removed this leaving the brighter yellow gold revealed. A similar type of 'varnish' might be applied on the soles on o21k & l.

4.2.3.5 The Technology

This brief section is not the place to revisit ancient gold manufacturing technology in detail, but a few observations specific to the gold in the footwear will be made.

Shaped Sheet Gold Components

Designs could be produced on sheet gold in various ways. The simplest was by freehand work using one or more small implements to impress or deform the metal. With thin and relatively high purity sheet gold, these implements could be of such materials as wood or bone. For multiple pieces with the same form, the sheet gold could be shaped by pressing into a shaped depression – a 'die' – or over a raised shaped form – a 'former'. Alternatively, the gold could be placed on a resilient background, such as pitch, wax or lead, and struck with a shaped punch. Subsequent sharpening-up or addition of detail with freehand use of small punches was also common.

All three of the 'mass production' processes were probably in use by the New Kingdom in Egypt, but detailed metal dies, and to a lesser extent formers and punches, had to be made of a tough copper alloy and then required even tougher, sharp metal punches to add detail to them. Thus, sophisticated metal dies were probably an Iron Age phenomenon. Close examination of shaped sheet gold components will sometimes permit the identification of which technique was used to form them. Photographs alone are seldom sufficient to allow such determination and with the present examples, subsequently-added linear detail makes identification of production method impossible without actual examination. However, as a general observation, the quality and care of the work on the embossed sheet gold attachments on the footwear is poorer than that seen in roughly contemporary Mycenaean Greek gold foil attachments and appliqués.

The simple domes on 021h & i were probably made by pressing the sheet gold into a metal, stone, or, perhaps, even wood block with one or more hemispherical depressions – what is termed a 'doming block'. The back edges have a flattened burr, suggesting that they were smoothed by rubbing on a flat abrasive stone. The use of abrasive stone, possibly fine sandstone, as a simple form of file has been noted by the writer on other New Kingdom Egyptian goldwork. The presence of the flattened back implies that these domes were originally intended to decorate footwear (or possibly, originally, some other object) that would be subjected to wear. The narrow gold strips for attachment (see below) were soldered on after the domes had had their backs flattened. The fronts of the domes would then have required cleaning and polishing to remove discolouration caused by the heat of the soldering operation.

The rosettes, primarily the large number of fine examples on 021f & g, had the main dome-like form made with, most likely, a doming block. However, the straight depressions that delineate were added freehand. The papyrus and lotus motifs on 021f & g also seem to have had their basic shape produced with a former or punch of some sort and the detail lines added freehand.

The gold ducks in 021k & l, although solid, were probably not cast but hammered into shape from a cast 'blank' or a cut section of sturdy ingot; the line and dot decoration was certainly added by hand.

Attachment Methods

The embossed components are interesting because of the range of attachment methods used. The simplest attachment methods are the perforations, all rather crudely produced with sharp burred edges and often irregular positioning, as used for lotus and papyrus motifs on 021f & g (figure 4.4) and the dome and square-shaped appliqués on 021k & l.

One of the rows of lotus and papyrus motifs on the left and right shoes of 021f & g were attached by a series of secondary crude piercings (figure 3.63E), reinforcing the view that the craftsman who put together these shoes was using his initiative to best assemble the shoes from the various components placed at his disposal. Perhaps he laid out the gold components on the other parts, flat, prior to assembly, to form a pleasing design or best match a pre-determined one, and then worked out how he might best fasten the components together. The same row of crude perforations is seen on the embossed motifs on 021k & l (see figure 3.68C).

The hemispherical buttons on 021h & i have a split pin attachment – what an engineer would term a 'cotter pin' (figure 4.5). This was a favourite attachment method in antiquity, although these seem to be an early example. A form of cotter pin also provides the attachment for the gold daisy attachments on 021f & g (figure 4.3). The most sophisticated method of attachment is found on the rosettes on 021f & g. These have sheet gold attachment loops soldered in place (figure 4.6). These attachment loops have the added sophistication of doubled-back or rolled edges. This was a common metalworking trick later on, when sturdiness plus a smooth rather than rough edge was required, usually when wear was anticipated, against textile, threads or the skin. The very different approach to attachment found side-by-side on 021f & g – the crudely pierced lotus and papyrus heads, and the well constructed rosettes – might suggest that the rosettes were originally made for another purpose. The same might also be true of the wide strip of gold on 270a that supports the uppers. The holes are punched close to the edge and sometimes even partly through the edge (figure 3.74E), and the protrusions along the upper edge are difficult to explain unless they could be supporting devices for the openwork leather upper.

Figure 4.4. The gold lotus and papyrus beads in 021f & g are crudely perforated. Cf. figure 3.63E. Figure by J.M. Ogden.

Figure 4.5. The split pin attachment ('cotter pin') in the buttons in 021h & i. Cf. figure 3.55F. Figure by J.M. Ogden.

Wire and Components Constructed from Wire

The shoes provide little evidence for ancient Egyptian gold wire-making processes. Wire has been a significant component in goldwork – jewellery in particular – since the early Bronze Age. By the late 18th Dynasty there were several wire manufacturing processes in use. These ranged from simple hammered or cut strips to what is termed strip 'twist wire'. In this technique a narrow cut strip of gold is twisted and then rolled into near-circular cross-section. The wires usually retain observable spiral 'seam lines' (figure 4.7; Ogden, 1991a).

Strip twist wire is first encountered around 2000 BC, for example in some of the goldwork from Troy where it is co-synchronous with the earliest granulation (clearly visible in Antonova *et al.*, 1996: pl. 126, from Troy Treasure F). The present author has recently suggested that the parallel development of these techniques might have related to the availability of hard and tough tin-copper alloy ('bronze') tools at about this time – such implements were necessary for the accurate cutting of thin strips of gold for wire and the small fragments for fusing into individual grains (Ogden, 2008). Perhaps there is also a later correlation between even smaller-scale granulation and filigree and the beginnings

Figure 4.6. The rosettes in o21f & g have soldered attachment loops. Cf. figure 3.63F. Figure by J.M. Ogden.

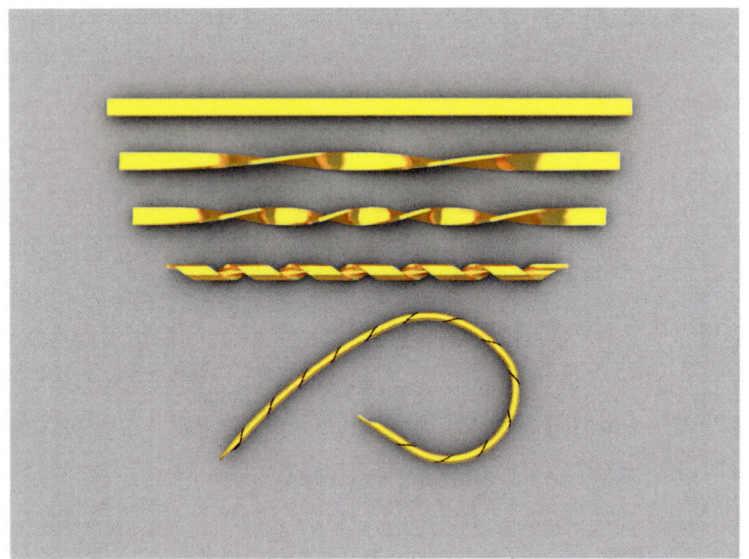

Figure 4.7. Twist wire with observable 'seam lines'. Figure by J.M. Ogden.

of iron technology. Strip twist wire is seen in some Pre-Palatial Minoan jewellery from Crete and had become common throughout the Eastern Mediterranean by the mid 2nd millennium. Unfortunately, the date of the first introduction of this technique into Egypt has not been ascertained, but it was certainly in use by the time of Tutankhamun, as witnessed by its presence on the dagger from Tutankhamun's tomb (clearly visible in Smith, 1983). Whether the presence on the dagger, often assumed to be of 'foreign' manufacture, is significant awaits clarification by further study of other Egyptian goldwork.

Circular section wire on the sandals is limited to the wire used to form the small rings soldered together to create the openwork filigree 'tubes' on o21k & l and o21f & g. In o21k & l these rings were hammered flat after soldering side-by-side but before bending into a tube. Those on o21f & g are flattened to a lesser extent, perhaps only during the bending of the soldered rings into a tube. This flattening has made it impossible to identify the wire-making technique from photographs alone. The 'woven' wire used both flat and also for some of the sections of tubes on o21k & l, used for the attachment panel of the instep strap, was also hammered flat and its mode of manufacture impossible to discern from photographs.

The tubes, originally forming the front strap in o21f & g, warrant some discussion, as does the 'woven band' of the foot strap on 021k & l. The construction of these components is shown in figure 4.8 and 4.9. This almost frivolous use of wire, which stands out from the stricter iconographic nature of most other Egyptian goldwork, does have earlier precedents, such as the Middle Kingdom wire circlet of Senebtisi from Lisht, now in the Metropolitan Museum of Art New York (07.227. 6-7: Muller & Thiem, 1999: 124, pl. 238). However, the closest parallels to the tubes of wire rings in the shoes are the openwork filigree beads

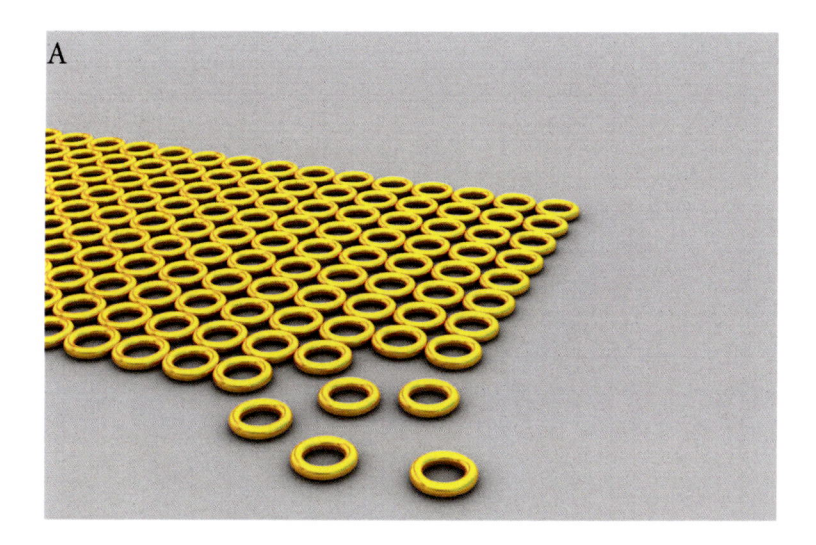

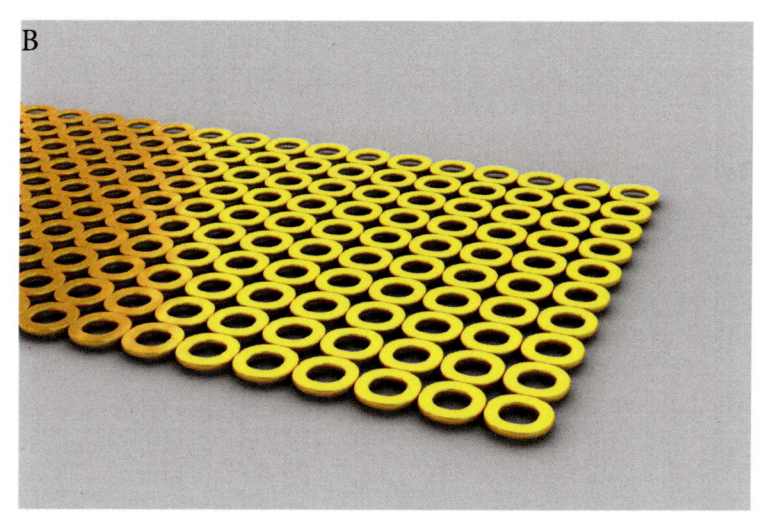

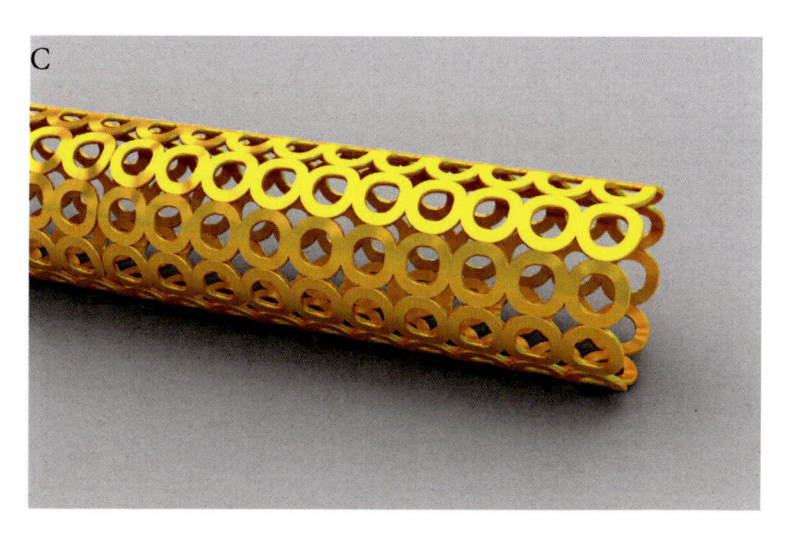

Figure 4.8A-C. The construction of the openwork filigree tubes in 021f & g and 021k & l. Cf. figures 3.63C & 3.68F. Figures by J.M. Ogden.

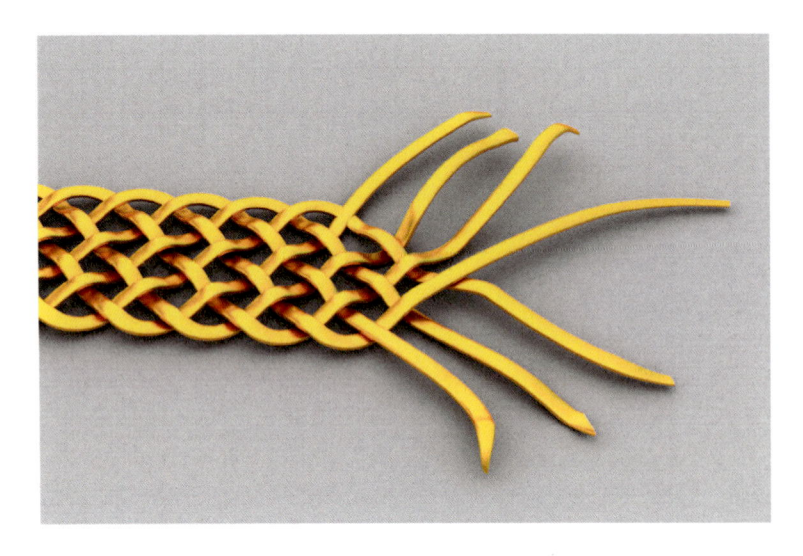

Figure 4.9. The construction of the woven band of the foot strap in 021k & l. Cf. figure 3.68A. Figure by J.M. Ogden.

and seed-pod pendants from the tombs of Seti II and Ta-usret, divided between the Metropolitan Museum of Art and the Cairo Museum (figure 4.10). They are constructed from circular wire rings soldered together.[23] These were recently described as "the earliest example of [openwork] filigree work" from Egypt (Muller & Thiem, 1999: 198),[24] a distinction now better deserved by the sandal components from Tutankhamun's tomb, although earlier examples of openwork filigree include the wire scrolls on some Middle Kingdom uraeus pendants. The woven wire band and its tubular counterparts from 021k & l find their closest match, in appearance although not technique, in the hoops of a pair of earrings now in Berlin (AM 19300; Seipel, 2001: 95, No. 106). These earrings have been variously argued to be of late 18th and 19th Dynasty date. The construction of the tubes that were bent to form the earring hoops is shown in figure 4.11. Incidentally, this construction is remarkably similar to that used on the cage-like gold 'sceptre' from Taranto of early Hellenistic date now on the British Museum (Williams & Ogden, 1994: 204 No. 134).[25] The similarities between the tubular, openwork shoe components and the earring hoops in Berlin might help support an 18th rather than 19th Dynasty date for the earrings, but there are too few surviving 19th Dynasty gold ornaments for comparison to lend much weight to this argument.

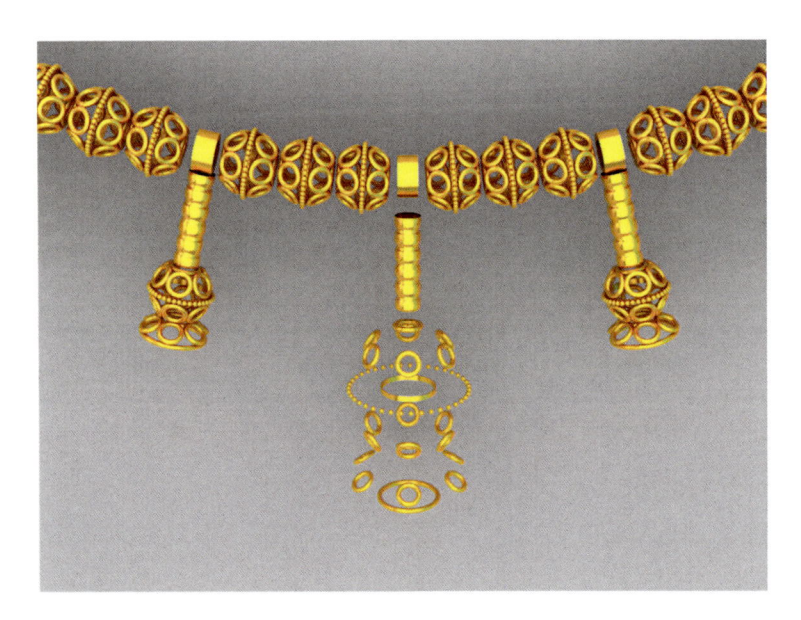

Figure 4.10. The filigree beads and seed-pod pendants from the tomb of Seti II and Ta-usret. Figure by J.M. Ogden.

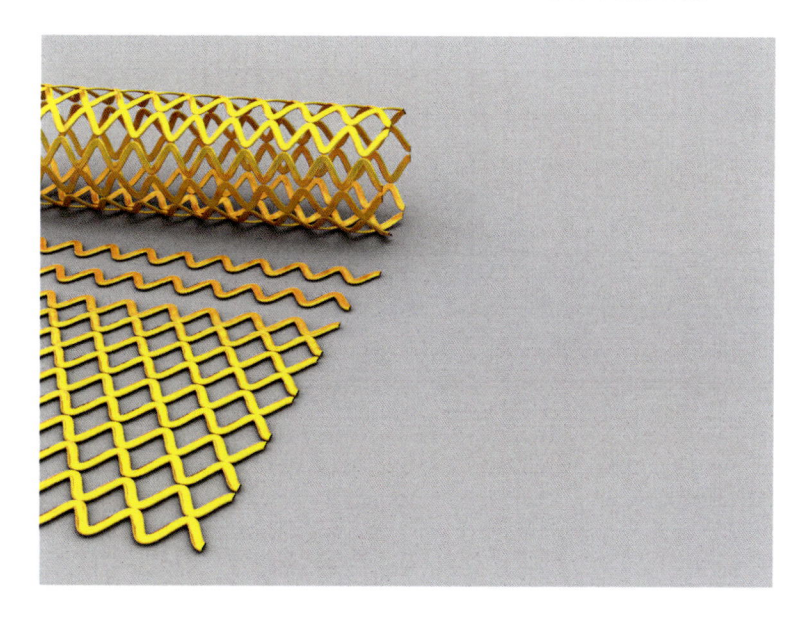

Figure 4.11. Tubes to form earrings in the Berlin Museum (AM 19300). Figure by J.M. Ogden.

Inlaid Components

The inlaid lotus flower ornaments on the shoes 021f & g are perhaps the most quintessentially 'Egyptian' of the shoe components, with their orthodox form and the lapis, carnelian and amazonite inlays used more as blocks of pigments than gems. The construction of these lotus flowers, as shown in figure 4.12, tells us little that we do not already know about mainstream New Kingdom Egyptian technology, but it does suggest that these components may have come from the same workshop as Tutankhamun's famous rebus pendant (267d [JE 61884]) and, perhaps, the scarab pectoral (267n [JE 61890]; Carter, 1933: pl. XIX, B bottom) and triple scarab pectoral (256ooo; Carter, 1927: 124-125, pl. LXXXIVc). These pendants share various features, ranging from their rather free-form openwork design, not constrained by the more usual naos-like frame, to the three-dimensional form of the inlaid lotus flower motifs. We can also note that the sheet gold strips forming the cloisonné walls of the 'petals' were made from a single folded strip, something that facilitated construction and, in particular, helped hold the cloisonné walls vertical during soldering.

The inlaid duck heads on 021f & g also deserve closer study. Their mode of construction is uncertain, but the photographs and comparisons with other ancient goldwork suggest that they were made from

Figure 4.12. The construction of the central piece of the strap complex in 021f & g. Cf. figure 3.63L. Figure by J.M. Ogden.

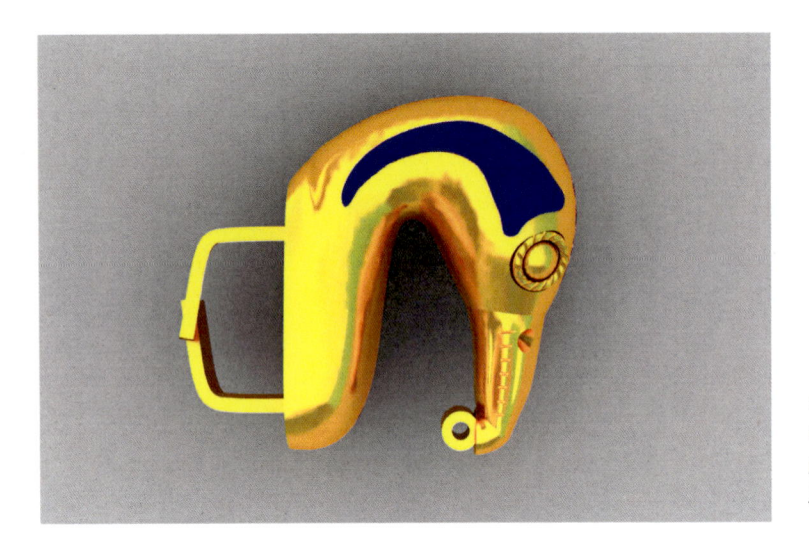

Figure 4.13. The duck heads in 021f & g are attached by means of soldered(?) pegs. Cf. figure 3.63M. Figure by J.M. Ogden.

sheet gold. The pegs that are presumably soldered into the back of the duck heads, as shown in figure 4.13, form the attachment behind the duck head. The shaped recesses of the sides and tops of the heads, contain lapis lazuli or blue glass inlays (see also section 4.2.1 and 4.2.2), but these are far smaller than the recesses and the rest of the spaces are filled with a blue material (figure 3.63M). This material is most likely to be coloured filler, perhaps ground 'Egyptian blue' in a binder. Such fillers are common in Egyptian inlaid goldwork, forming a bedding for the inlaid gem or glass, and filling any gaps between inlay and goldwork relatively unobtrusively. The filler is unlikely to be enamel because the filling material clearly fills right up to and around the inlay, but the heat of enamelling would adversely affect either lapis lazuli or glass. In general, enamelling is not impossible at this period in Egypt, but would be hazardous due to the heat of enamelling being dangerously close to the rather unpredictable melting temperature of ancient Egyptian gold. We can note, however, that close parallels to the duck heads can be seen on the famous bracelets of Rameses II where the very shallow inlay cells bordered by wire, would hardly suit any type of inlay other than an enamel (JE 39873; Ogden, 1990/1991; Ogden, 2000).

Foil Decoration

Gold foil decoration is seen on 397 (figure 3.43) and 1259 (figure 3.58). Thin gold foil was glued onto white birch bark (see section 4.1.2) and then small strips, rectangles and diamond shapes of this were overlaid onto the background. The cuts evident in several places on 397 on the white 'borders' (figure 3.44A & 3.46C) indicate a likely way in which the smaller gold rectangles and diamond-shapes were applied. As shown in figure 4.14, a narrow strip of foil plus backing was laid in place and a chisel-like tool used to both hold it down and cut it. The blade of the chisel also slightly cut the border strips. The pair 397 also shows clear evidence that the gold foil on two sandals was applied by different craftsmen. Compare, for example, the fluidity of line and confidence of the delineation of the African captive on the right sandal and that on the left (see figure 3.44). There are also other differences, including the three 'bindings' on each of the eight bows on the left sandal, and the four on the right. It would be interesting to compare the technique of 397 and 453b with the decorated bow.

The gold strips woven into the leather on 021f & g, 021k & l and 270a are a very distinctive decorative feature (figure 4.15), but without a fuller body of New Kingdom objects, we cannot say it was widespread, or if it points to a single workshop origin.

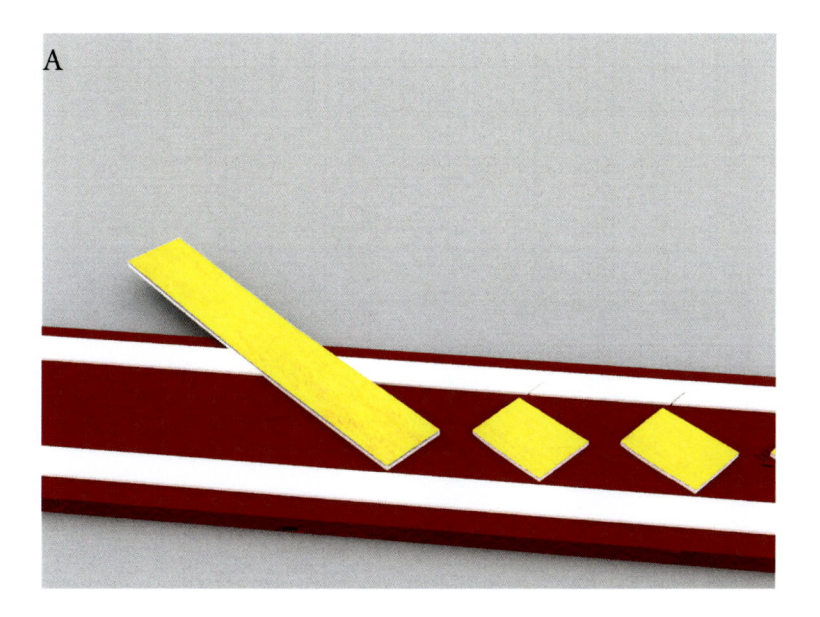

Figure 4.14A-C The application of the gold foil-on-birch-bark-decoration in 397. Cf. figure 3.44 & 3.46. Figure by J.M. Ogden.

163

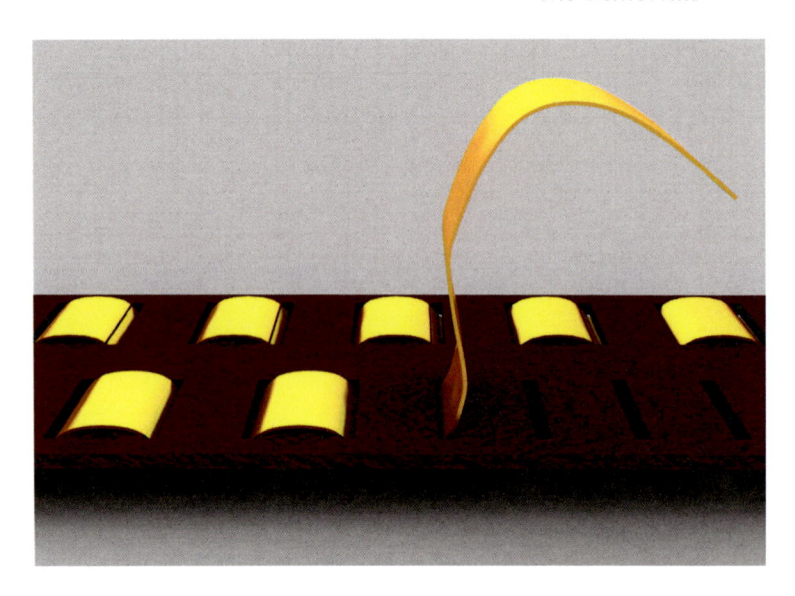

Figure 4.15. Strips of gold, woven through slits in the leather, is a distinctive decorative feature. Cf. figure 3.54A & 3.74A. Figure by J.M. Ogden.

Workshops

Creating three-dimensionally curved and inlaid gold components, as in 021f & g, demanded more from the goldsmith than the more common flat and two-dimensional jewellery forms. Compare the shape and colour schemes of the lotus flowers on the rebus and scarab pendants, as noted as possible comparisons above, with the 021f & g lotus component, and their similar choice of gems – not glass or faience. Also note the similar use of pairs of sheet gold petals overlaying parts of the inlaid design, the cabochon (domed) carnelian inlays in the rebus pendant and the sandal lotus flowers, and the shaped gold overlays on these. Remember, also, that the moon disk in the rebus pendant represents a deliberate use of gold alloys of contrasting colour – like the rosettes in shoes 021f & g. Even without hands-on examination, it is clear that the jewellery in Tutankhamun's burial were produced by different hands. Close study of assembly would undoubtedly provide us with much more information about the variety of jewellery workshops represented in this Pharaoh's objects, and help identify which were older ornaments adapted for him.

Shoes 021f & g and 021k & l have similar, although not identical, soles which might suggest that these at least came from the same craftsman or team of craftsmen. That the pairs do not share similar gold components might indicate that these shoes were not completed at the same time, or were completed by different craftsmen.

The variation in quality of work between different components on the same object raises questions about workshop organisation and the extent to which the footwear incorporate components that were not necessarily originally intended for the same object. Once again, the opportunity for close examination of a wide range of Tutankhamun's goldwork would help provide answers. It is also worth asking whether the level of goldworking skills used on different footwear is commensurate with the working of the leather and other components.

In general, we cannot assume that a goldsmith would have much experience working with organic materials, whereas a leatherworker probably had minimal gold working skills. Both the gold components and the leather and other organic parts demonstrate a high level of skill by the respective craftsmen, but a lack of sophistication is manifested in the way in which some of the gold components are attached to, or incorporated into, the other materials, particularly the crude perforations of some of the embossed sheet-gold components. Perhaps in these rough perforations we see the evidence of the sandal-maker's awl, and thus, as we might expect, a sandal-maker, not a goldsmith, was the assembler.

CHAPTER 5

SOCKS

Gillian Vogelsang-Eastwood

5.1 INTRODUCTION

One of the more unexpected finds from the tomb of Tutankhamun were his socks. Footwear in the form of sandals were expected, but given the range of 'normal' Egyptian clothing from the New Kingdom, somehow socks were an unexpected bonus.

There were several items identified as socks and there were some items that, based on the original excavation notes and photographs, were probably socks. If it is accepted that all of the items in the table below are actually socks, then it would indicate that there were at least four pairs of them in the tomb (figures 5.1-5.4).

The socks come from two find spots, namely the bundle 046, in the Antechamber, and box 089, also in the Antechamber. There is no indication as to whether these items were originally placed together and then were separated following the disturbances and subsequent tidying up by the priests, or not.

5.2 THE CONSTRUCTION OF THE SOCKS

The socks are made of two layers of different qualities of undyed, tabby weave linen. A fine quality linen is on the inside close to the skin, while a second, coarse layer, is on the outside.

Each sock was made out of three elements, namely a sole, a vamp with front ankle/leg section, and an enclosing 'sock' section (figure 5.5). The latter was used to cover the ankle and part of the calf. The various sections were sewn together using a whipped seam with a flax thread.

In addition, there are three pairs of ties made out of very fine linen, which were sewn down on the inside of the sock. These ties were used to fasten the sock in place. At the top of the upper section there is also a loop of cloth through which the highest binding pair of ties passed; this helped to secure the upper ties in place and so keep the sock on the foot. The same construction, namely three pairs of ties and a loop, was also used on the king's 'gauntlets' (089a & b; see below).

Identification	Socks	Condition	Find spot
0460[C]; JE 62676; 1042[E] (figure 5.1)	Yes	Good	Bundle 046, Antechamber
046dd[C]	Yes	Good	Bundle 046, Antechamber
046ee[C]	Probably	Poor	Bundle 046, Antechamber
046hh[C]	Probably	Poor	Bundle 046, Antechamber
046nn[C]; 30 3 + 34 09 [T]; 3267[E]	Probably	Poor	Bundle 046, Antechamber
089a[C]; JE 62670; 1649[E]	Yes	Good	Box 089, Antechamber
089b[C]; 30 3 + 34 16 [T]; 3285[E] (figure 5.4)	Probably	Poor	Box 089, Antechamber

Items identified as socks or socks (?) from the tomb of Tutankhamun. [C] = *Carter's number;* [E] = *Exhibition number;* [T] = *Temporary number.*

Socks

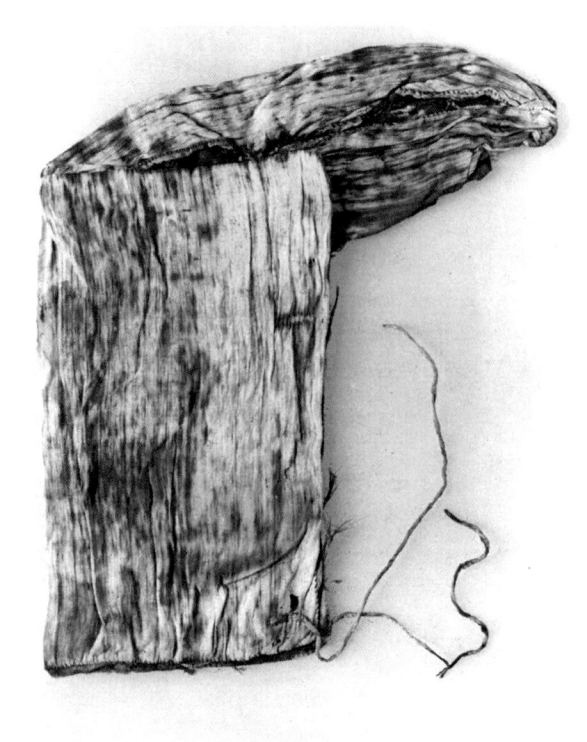

46 O

46 P

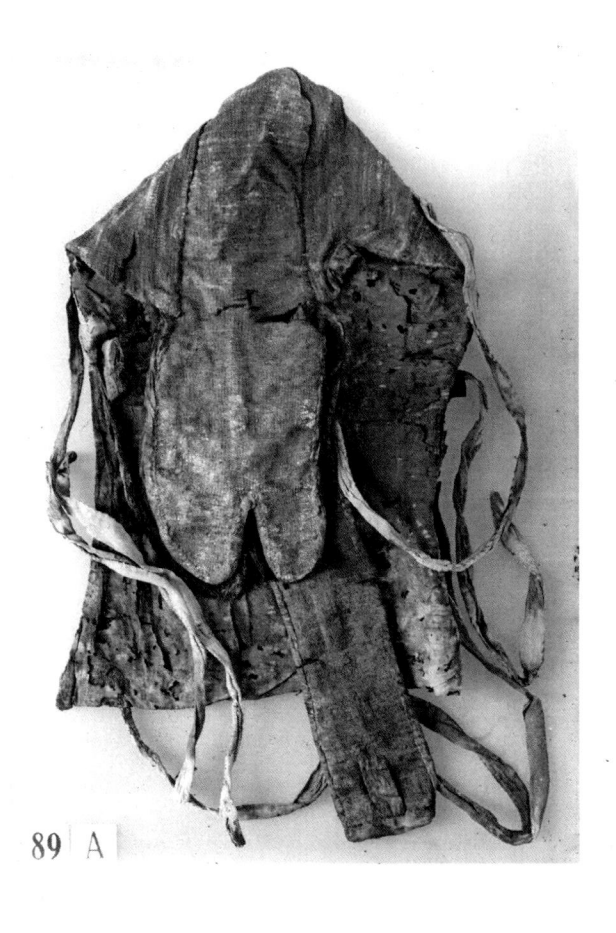

89 A

89 B

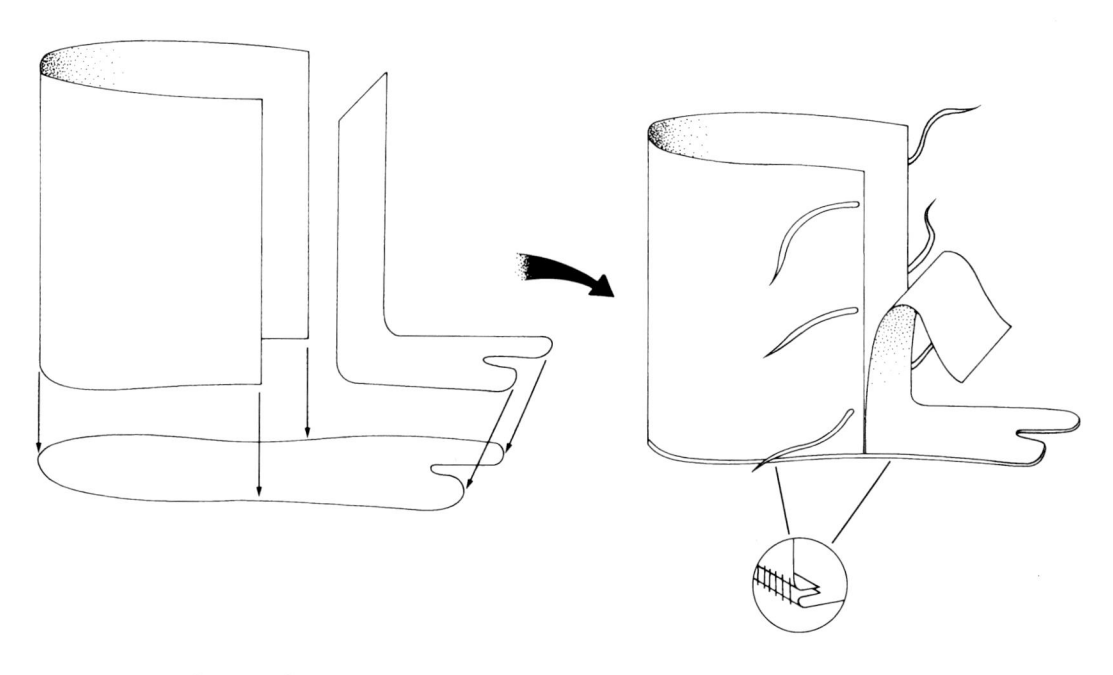

Figure 5.5. Diagram showing the construction of a sock from the tomb of Tutankhamun. Drawing by A.M. Hense.

Both the sole and the vamp have an indentation at the front. This indentation was intentional and designed to accommodate the front strap of a traditional Egyptian sandal, in a very similar manner to traditional Japanese socks.

5.3 SOCKS VERSUS GAUNTLETS

A degree of confusion has arisen about some items as to whether they are socks or gauntlets. This situation seems to have developed because in the original notes written by Carter's team, some pieces were described as gauntlets when they are in fact, socks.

The difference between a gauntlet and a sock lies in how they were made. As noted above, socks were made in three pieces with very different shapes, namely, a sole, a vamp with front section, and the enclosing cloth, all of which were sewn directly together. In contrast, the gloves and gauntlets from the tomb were made in three pieces: an upper and lower glove/gauntlet shape which are identical in shape, and a narrow band of about 1 cm wide that separates the two layers. The upper and lower sections were sewn to the band and not to each other, so creating a 'sandwich' construction. This technical difference helps to make it clear that, for example, 089a (figure 5.3), which is sometimes called a gauntlet, is in fact, a sock, as it has a sole, vamp and enclosing wall that are sewn together. There is no evidence of the narrow band used to make the 'sandwich' construction, which is a characteristic feature of the gloves and gauntlets.

5.4 COMPARATIVE ITEMS

Unfortunately, to date, it would seem that no other ancient Egyptian socks have been recorded or published, nor do there seem to be any depictions of someone either wear-

< *Figure 5.1. Sock 046o (JE 62676; 1042).*
< *Figure 5.2. Sock 046p (JE 62677; 1043).*
< *Figure 5.3. 'Gauntlet' 089a (JE 62670; 1649).*
< *Figure 5.4. 'Gauntlet' 089b (30 3 + 34 16; 3285).*
Photography by H. Burton. Copyright Griffith Institute, University of Oxford.

ing, holding or giving socks.[1] Nevertheless, it would seem likely that the socks, as with the gloves, gauntlets and cloth 'corset', were part of a chariot outfit and that they were used to protect the feet from dust and small stones while hunting or fighting.

It is possible that the origins of Tutankhamun's socks should be sought among the people who regularly gave chariots and related garments, notably tunics, gloves, gauntlets, sandals and shoes, to the Egyptian court (Moran, 1992), namely the Mitanni from what is now northern Syria. The famous 'dalmatica' or more correctly a sleeved tunic of Tutankhamun (367j), for example, has been identified as Mitanni in style, if not origin (Crowfoot & Davies, 1941; Vogelsang-Eastwood, 1999: 80-86).[2]

CHAPTER 6

CONTEMPORARY FOOTWEAR: A SURVEY

6.1 INTRODUCTION

We can rely on the finds from two sites: Amarna, where Tutankhamun must have spent part of his life, and Deir el-Medinah, the village in the cliffs halfway between the Ramesseum and Medinet Habu and inhabited by the workmen who built the royal tombs in the Valley of the Kings during the New Kingdom. Also important is the footwear from Yuya and Tjuiu. As with Tutankhamun's footwear, these were found in their tomb in the Valley of the Kings.

Many isolated finds are housed in collections all over the world, some of which have also been dated. One of the most important of these is the pair of sandals of Nefertari, the principal wife of Ramses II of the 19th Dynasty. The lack of detailed research limits comparison, but fortunately much research is currently in progress. Another problem is the fact that, in general, footwear that is housed in collections suffer from lack of a more precise dating, *i.e.* dating within Dynasties; 'contemporary' should, therefore, be taken as 'New Kingdom' (with a focus on the 18th and 19th Dynasty). Yuya's and Tjuiu's footwear will be described in detail.

6.2 SANDALS

6.2.1 Yuya and Tjuiu

The tomb of Yuya and Tjuiu was found by Theodore Davis in 1905 (Davis *et al.*, 1907; Reeves, 1990b: 148-153; Reeves & Wilkinson, 1996: 174-178) and was largely intact. Davis, however, being more of a treasure hunter than archaeologist decided (Shaw & Nicholson, 1995: 308) "to have the tomb cleared in a matter of days, in the absence of Quibell,[1] [which] meant that virtually no record was made of the positions of the contents, which has greatly diminished the value of the find to archaeology." As we will see, this will become an issue especially for the identification of one pair of so-called sandals. This tomb was entered by robbers, as was the tomb of Tutankhamun, Therefore, it is highly unlikely that the footwear was in their original places when discovered by the archaeologists.

Until the find of Tutankhamun's tomb, the tomb of Yuya and Tjuiu was the most celebrated discovery in Egyptian archaeology. This find is also important for footwear studies in general as well as for Tutankhamun's footwear in particular, as Yuya and Tjuiu had a collection of footwear buried with them, consisting, according to Reeves & Wilkinson (1996: 178), of 24 individual sandals. The list published by Quibell (1908: 58-59) gives 18 as the count, all of which entered the Egyptian Museum, Cairo.[2] This number, however, does not include the pair that is still on Tjuiu's feet (Lilyquist, 1997; personal observation 2009; figure 6.1). Moreover, one additional pair is not listed because this pair went to the Metropolitan Museum of Art, New York.[3] A total of 24 objects have been studied (including the two objects that are not sandals).

Another reason for the importance of their footwear is the fact that Yuya and Tjuiu were the great-grandparents of Tutankhamun (being the parents of Tiye, Amenhotep III's principal wife)[4] and were of non-royal descent.

169

According to Quibell (1908: v): "Two pairs of sandals and the wooden handle of a mirror were on one of the beds: other sandals were on the floor beneath and around them." Another sandal was found in a box in the southeast corner, together with rags, four lids of *ushabti* boxes, one *ushabti* and a clay seal of the box itself (*Ibidem*: vi). We do not know, however, which sandals were on the bed and which one was in the box and whether all of the remaining footwear was lying on the floor.

Surprisingly, the feet of Yuya were bare but possibly not originally. The mummy was thoroughly ransacked by robbers and, if Yuya had a comparable set of sandals to Tjuiu's on her feet (see below), these would have been worthwhile to take. Interestingly, Smith (1908: 70) reports that "The skin is still intact on the greater part of the sole of the foot, but on both feet there is a triangular area devoid of epidermis, the base of which is opposite the second, third and fourth toes" which might well be an indication of the robbers activities. According to him, the mummy of Tjuiu (CG 51190), which he investigated with the assistance of Dr. Derry (*Ibidem*: 72) was far from undisturbed, but the robbers did not get to Tjuiu's feet as "Each sandal has a sole composed of a thin metal (? electrum[5]) plate, which presents three longitudinal grooves alongside each lateral edge, the intervening space being occupied by a series of transverse grooves, so that the whole plate is corrugated. Across the instep there is a band composed of some brittle dark material (? mud), the surface of which is gilded. At its attachment to the metal sole on each side this band is fashioned like a rope, but on the dorsum of the foot it expands on each side into a fusiform plate, the two plates being united by a narrower piece, opposite the cleft between the great and second toes, to which a toe-band was probably attached and passed through the cleft to be attached to the sole in front." Indeed, the old photographs of the mummy do show the sandal clearly on the left foot and although the right foot seems bare in old photographs (Reeves & Wilkinson, 1996: 176, figure at bottom) a sandal is still present nowadays (figure 6.1).

If we compare this description with the golden sandals worn by Tutankhamun (figures 1.8 & 3.60),[6] we cannot but conclude that these are imitations of sewn sandals (*viz.* Type D). The three longitudinal grooves compare with the triple edge in sewn sandals made of fibre and the transverse grooves with the transverse bundles of grass and palm leaf.[7] The 'brittle dark material' could very well be leather, as many examples show that leather can change into this condition,[8] including examples from the tomb of Tutankhamun. Moreover, other examples from Yuya's and Tjuiu's tomb include footwear of gilded leather. If, however, the straps are indeed of leather, combined with a metal sole, it means yet another variant: all known examples of this type of imitation sewn sandals are solely made of metal. The attachment of the straps 'fashioned like a rope' refers to the clad pre-straps. On the dorsal side of the foot, the back strap expands and is held with the narrower loop of the front strap, which, again, fits the early description perfectly. More difficult to explain is the reinforcement of each circumference by silver wire mentioned by Lilyquist (1997: 201), which has not been observed by the present author. This has no parallels in the fibre sandals, unless it is to understand as imitation of the cores of the edge that sandwich the sole. More likely, however, is that these wires are parts of the attachment method of the straps to the sole. The metal soles were, most likely, the insoles, folded over the edge of the, now lost, leather or rawhide treadsole (*cf.* Tutankhamun's 021f & g and 021k & l).

Davis *et al.* (1907: pl. XLIV) shows, far right in the photograph, a pair of leather sandals that has not been studied first hand because the whereabouts is currently unknown. These are not the sandals found on the mummy's feet, but the pair of white leather sandals mentioned by Quibell (1908:

Figure 6.1. The sandals on the feet of Tjuiu. Photography by A.J. Veldmeijer. Courtesy of the Supreme Council of Antiquities / Authorities Egyptian Museum, Cairo.

58): "Edges of soles are turned in below. From one sidestrap to the other a broad strip of leather covering the instep. A stamped ornament on the sole. The pair are still stitched together; both are somewhat eaten by insects."

Smith (1908: 71) reports the length of the feet of Yuya: the maximal length of the right foot is 24.5 cm and the maximal width 8.5 cm. Measurements of Tjuiu's feet are, unfortunately, not given. Given the overall smaller dimensions of Tjuiu, it is possible that the smaller sandals (*i.e.* those with a length of about 24 cm; table 10 & 11) were meant for her and the larger ones (*i.e.* those with a length of about 30 cm; table 10 & 11) for Yuya. But this leaves us with several sandals with a length of around 26 cm, which are impossible to assign to an owner. However, sandals were often oversized if we might deduce this from three-dimensional art (see section 8.2). However if we accept this interpretation, then it turns out that most of the footwear was meant for Tjuiu. Even more so, because all imitation footwear has dimensions comparable to the possible Tjuiu footwear (table 11).

In order to compare Yuya's and Tjuiu's footwear with Tutankhamun's,[9] the former's sandals are described in this chapter. For a general description of the sewn sandals, the reader is referred to the introduction of the description of Tutankhamun's sewn sandals as well as to Veldmeij-er (2009a). In the present work, focus will be on differences. The pristine condition of most of the fibre sandals did not allow for study of the cores of the transverse bundles. In one example, however, much of the sewing strips were damaged, exposing the cores. Without microscopic investigations, it is not possible to identify the fibre, but there can be little doubt that the cores of the sandals with wide transverse bundles, consist of grass. But, in contrast to the cores in Tutankhamun's sandals and, in general, in all sandals with transverse bundles of far smaller diameter, these are not halfa grasses. The fibre is much more woody in nature and does not show the (for halfa grass characteristic) more circular construction, caused by the natural constitution of halfa grasses (*cf.* figure 4.1A & B). Most likely, the cores are made of reeds.[10]

6.2.1.1 Sewn Sandals Type C

MET 10.184

The pair in the Metropolitan Museum of Art, New York (figure 6.2, table 10), which are in pristine condition and completely intact, differs from the rest of the sewn sandals: the sewing is finer and is much more comparable to the sandals from Tutankhamun, including the larger number of transverse bundles. The sole is thinner compared to the other sandals from Yuya and Tjuiu.

JE 91351a & b (CG 51128; SR 128)[11]

Well preserved, intact left and right sandals in beautiful condition (figure 6.3, table 10). The sandals have been registered as a pair, but there are some differences between the two. The toe of the right sandal is distinctly more pronounced whereas the toe in the left sandal is blunter. Moreover, the measurements differ slightly for the sole (except for the average diameter of the transverse bundles), but quite substantially for the strap complex. This is extraordinary, as differences in size within a pair of sandals, even within the less well made Type A, are usually much less (see Veldmeijer, 2009a). The left sole shows a coarsely sewn patch lateral to the front strap (figure 6.3, double arrow), which clearly does not fit with the rest of the sewing, and is interpreted as a repair.

The completeness of the strap complex does not allow exact identification of its construction. Most likely it is constructed in a comparable way to sandals from Tutankhamun, but instead of a transverse cladding of a palm leaf strip, a strip of papyrus

A   B

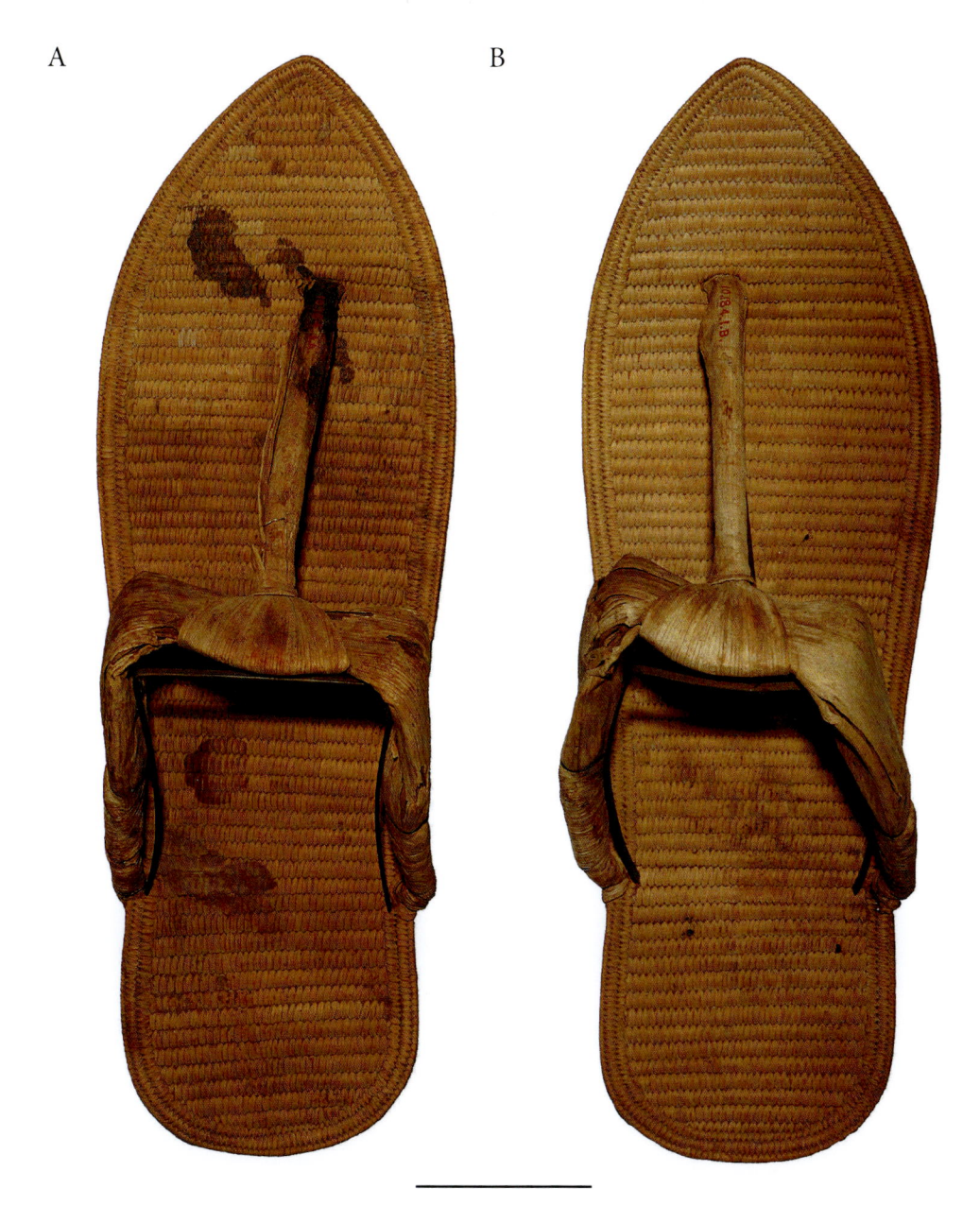

Figure 6.2. Pair of sandals MET 10.184 in dorsal view. These sandals differ from the rest of Yuya's and Tjuiu's fibre sandals even though all are sewn sandals Type C, Variant 1. Scale bar is 50 mm. Photography by E. Endenburg. Courtesy of the Metropolitan Museum of Art, New York.

is used. Note that on the left one, two ends are knotted with a half knot (figure 6.3, arrow); on the right one, the ends are stitched through the front strap. It is tempting to interpret this as another indication that the two sandals were not a pair originally and might even indicate different sandal-makers: is it not unlikely that one sandal-maker uses different ways of finishing one pair of sandals? The other differences might be explained in the same way.

JE 95305 (CG 51127; SR 127)[12]

The pair JE 95305 is, as nearly all footwear from Yuya and Tjuiu and in contrast to most of Tutankhamun's fibre sandals, largely complete and in excellent condition (figure 6.4, table 10). Only slight damage can be detected posterior to the lateral back strap in the left sandal. This allows identification of the core of the outermost row of the edge, which consists of narrow palm leaf strips.

173

A   B

C

Figure 6.3. Pair of sandals JE 91351a & b). A) Dorsal view of the left sandal; B) Dorsal view of the right sandal; C) Right sandal in medial view. The arrow points to the different ways of finishing of the transverse cladding; the double arrow points to the repair of the sewing of the left sole. Scale bar is 50 mm. Photography by A.J. Veldmeijer. Courtesy of the Supreme Council of Antiquities / Authorities Egyptian Museum, Cairo.

A   B

C

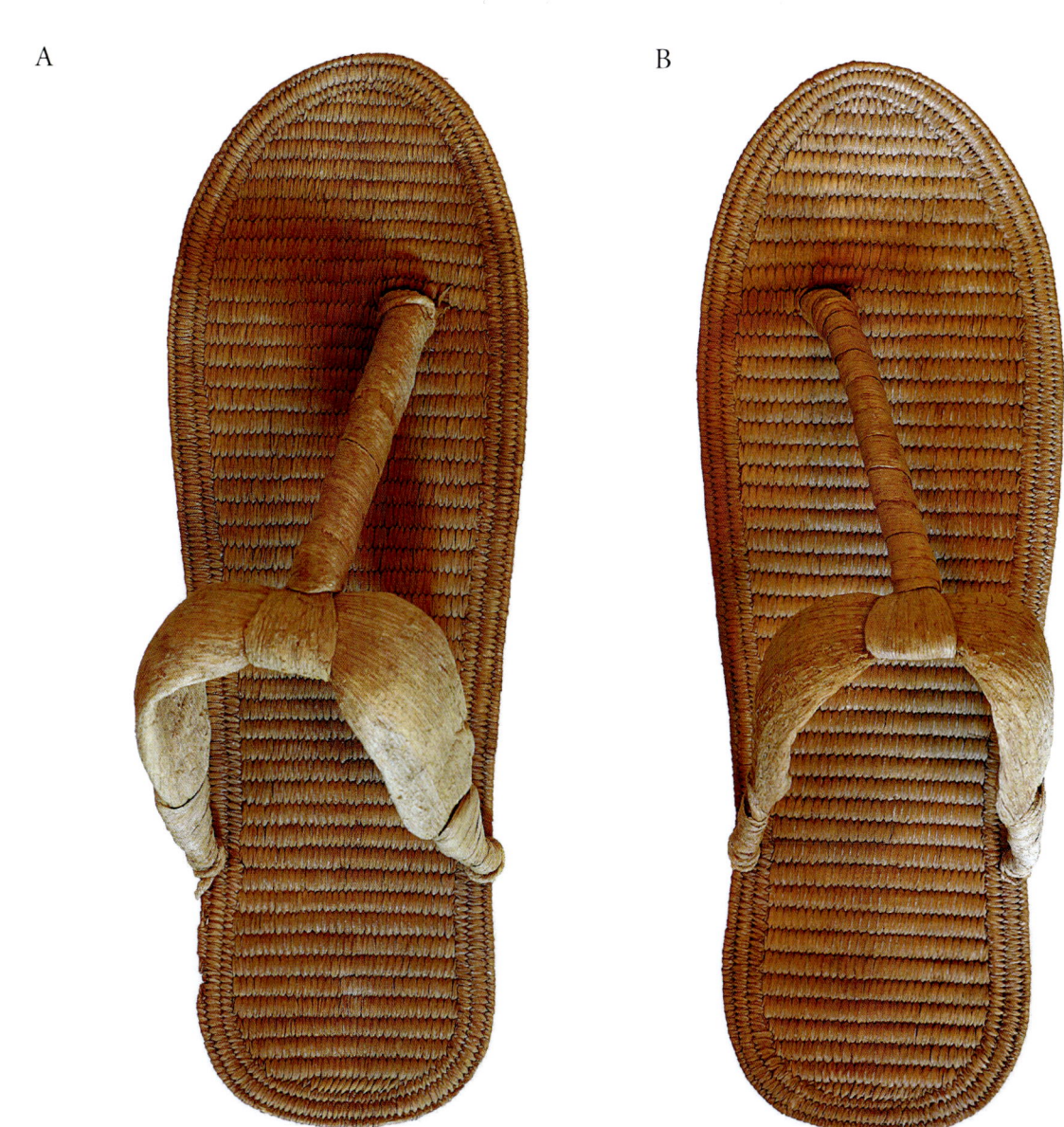

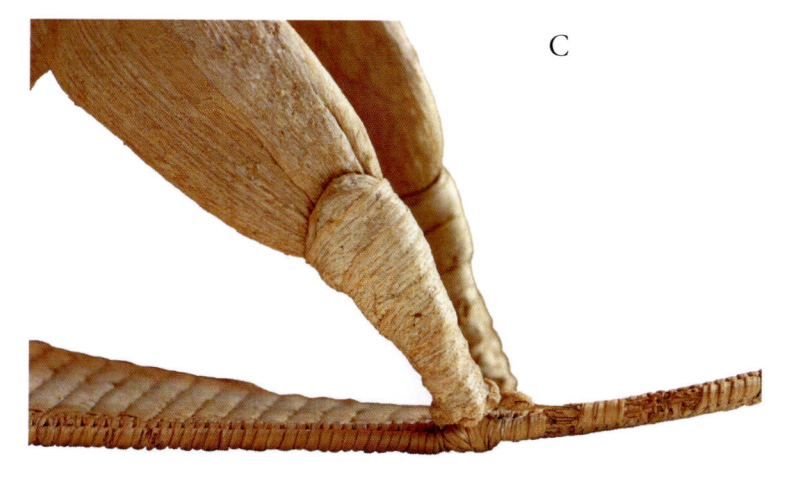

Figure 6.4. Pair of sandals JE 95305a & b. A) Left sandal in dorsal view; B) Right sandal in dorsal view; C) Pre/back strap of the left sandal in lateral view (for scale cf. A & B). Scale bar is 50 mm. Photography by A.J. Veldmeijer. Courtesy of the Supreme Council of Antiquities / Authorities Egyptian Museum, Cairo.

175

Note that the shape of the sole compares well with the left sandal in JE 91351a & b (see above).

The front strap seems of comparable construction; the exact arrangement of the pre/back strap is uncertain. The cladding of this attachment is done, as with all sandals of Yuya and Tjuiu, with papyrus rather than palm leaf but the fastening of the pre-strap to the sole is clearly done with palm leaf, suggesting that it, itself, was made of palm leaf.

JE 95318 (CG 51129; SR 95)

According to Quibell (1908: 59), this entry is a pair but only one sandal in the Egyptian Museum, Cairo with this number is registered. The other sandal is registered as JE 95356 (CG 51129; SR 133 see below). The dorsal surface of this right sandal (figure 6.5, table 10) shows large patches that lack the sewing palm leaf strips, but the transverse cores are complete. The damage to the ventral surface, however, is largely limited to the front part. The triple edge is intact, prohibiting identification of its cores. The attachment of the pre-straps are the only remnants of the strap complex still *in situ*, showing that it is attached to the two outer rows of the edge. The sandal is comparable to, for example, JE 95356 (see below) rather than to the pair in New York (MET 10.184a, described above), including the woody cores of the transverse bundles (reed?, *cf.* petrie UC 16555, see figure 4.1).

JE 95319 (CG 51130; SR 96)

The left sandal shows large holes, predominantly on the medial half (figure 6.6, table 10). It is tempting to conclude that this is due to wear, suggesting the user walked on the inner side of his feet. However, one would

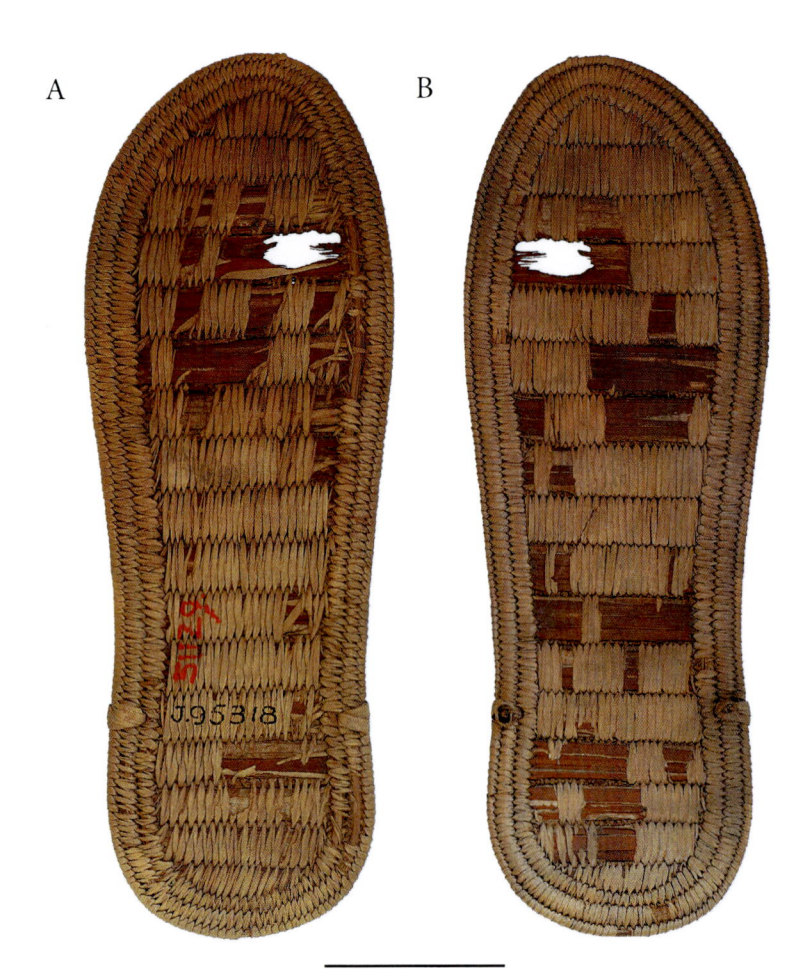

Figure 6.5. The right sandal JE 95318. A) Ventral view; B) Dorsal view. Possibly a pair with JE 95356 (cf. figure 6.10). Scale bar is 50 mm. Photography by A.J. Veldmeijer. Courtesy of the Supreme Council of Antiquities / Authorities Egyptian Museum, Cairo.

A   B

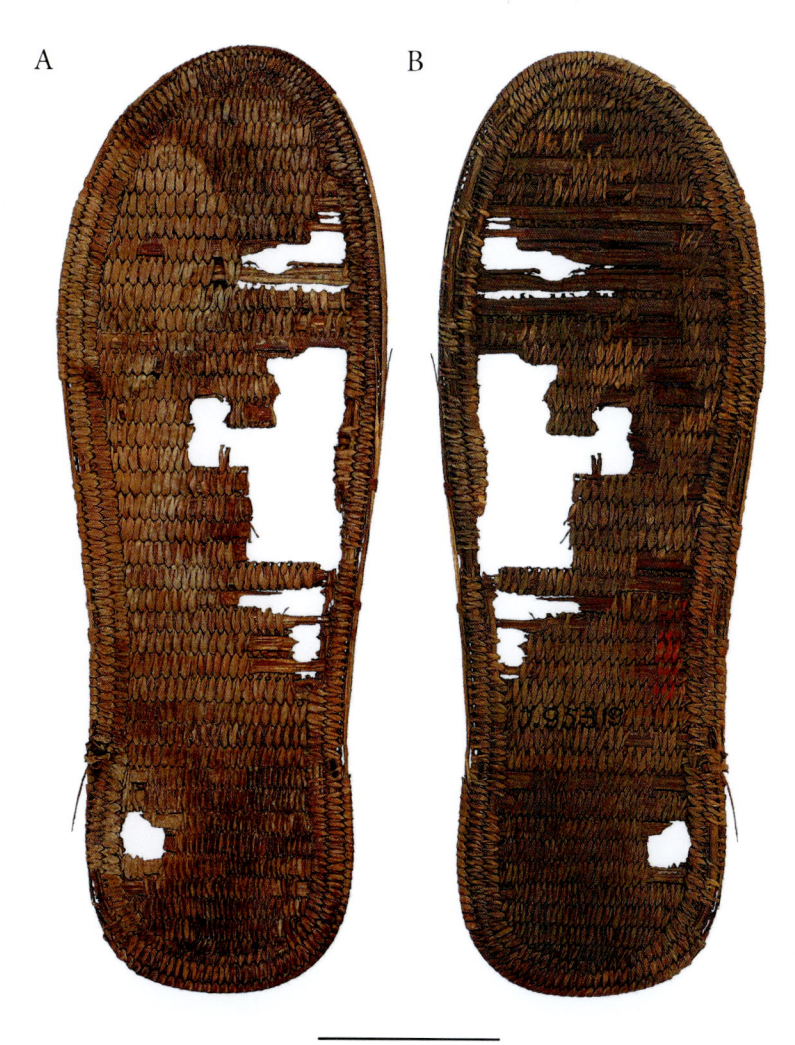

Figure 6.6. The left sandal JE 95319. A) Dorsal view; B) Ventral view. Scale bar is 50 mm. Photography by A.J. Veldmeijer. Courtesy of the Supreme Council of Antiquities / Authorities Egyptian Museum, Cairo.

expect to find more wear of the sewing strips lining the holes, which is not the case for the majority of the hole's edges. The fact that the sandal has been used is, however, apparent from the discoloration of the dorsal surface of mainly the heel part. As explained in section 3.5.2, the damage of the edge, the lack of most of the strap complex (in this case even nothing is left of it, except for the attachment of the lateral pre-strap) and the broken sewing strips should not be too readily taken as obvious example of wear.

JE 95348 (CG 51120; SR 125)

The two sandals, although registered with the same JE-number, are not a pair originally, as both are right sandals (figure 6.7, table 10). Moreover, there are many small differences in overall measurements and the measurements of the strap complex. Most obvious, however, is the big difference in number of transverse bundles as well as their width.

Sandal JE 95348a (figure 6.7A), is in excellent condition and complete. The only damage that could be detected is the posterior edge of the medial half of the back strap, which has split. The sewing is very regular but a small, slight irregularity can be noticed next to the front strap, at the medial half of the sandal. Such an irregularity in the sewing can also be see in the left of JE 91351a & b (figure 6.3), albeit more obvious.

Sandal JE 95348b (figure 6.7B), is complete as well. The colour is slightly darker than JE 95348a. Moreover, the transverse bundles show a distinct curvature mainly in the front and heel part.

A   B

Figure 6.7. Two right sandals, registered as a pair (JE 95348a & b). A) Dorsal view of JE 95348a; B) Dorsal view of JE 95348b. Scale bar is 50 mm. Photography by A.J. Veldmeijer. Courtesy of the Supreme Council of Antiquities / Authorities Egyptian Museum, Cairo.

JE 95353a & b (CG 51125; SR 130)

Pair of sandals in pristine condition (figure 6.8, table 10): they are entirely without damage. Note the slight curvature of the heel's transverse bundles.

JE 95354a & b (CG 51126; SR 131)

Pair of sandals in good condition (figure 6.9, table 10). The left sandal, however, has a spot of red on the front, with a slightly glazy constitution, the origin of which is unknown but it resembles sealing wax. Only a small spot in the middle of the sole (approximately 10 mm long) lacks the palm leaf sewing strip. Note the slight curvature of some of the heel's transverse bundles. The condition of the right sandal is slightly worse, which manifests itself mainly in the strap complex. The transverse cladding of the front strap is loosened and the medial half of the back strap shows two cracks. Moreover, the surface of the entire back strap is slightly worn. In particular, the lateral attachment of the pre- and back strap has become slightly detached.

178

A   B

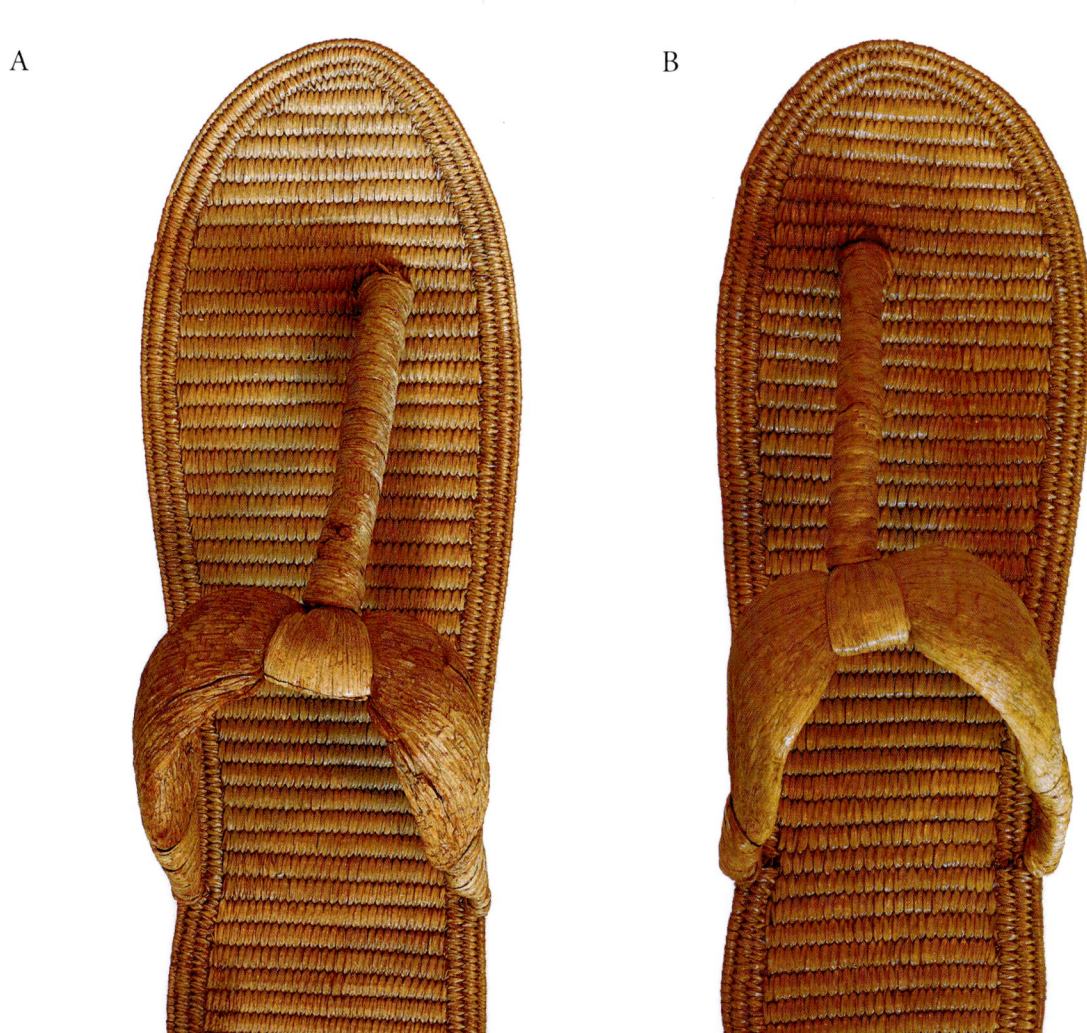

Figure 6.8. Pair of sandals JE 95353a & b. A) Left sandal in dorsal view; B) Right sandal in dorsal view. Scale bar is 50 mm. Photography by A.J. Veldmeijer. Courtesy of the Supreme Council of Antiquities / Authorities Egyptian Museum, Cairo.

JE 95356 (CG 51129; SR 133)

The left sandal of the pair Quibell (1908: 59) refers to: he mentions that most of the grass [sic] is being worn away as well as the loss of the straps in one of them, which fits well with JE 95318 (CG 51129; SR 95, figure 6.5). The sandals are comparable in terms of width and number of the transverse bundles as well as measurements. The width of the bundles suggests that the cores are made of reed(?), as seen in JE 95318 and Petrie UC 16555 (see above).

Left sandal JE 95356 (figure 6.10, table 10) is in pristine condition and no damage has been noted.

JE 95357 (CG 51130?; SR 134)

Isolated, left sandal in pristine condition (figure 6.11, table 10). Note the slight irregularity of the heel's transverse bundles, a feature noted in some of Tutankhamun's sandals too.

179

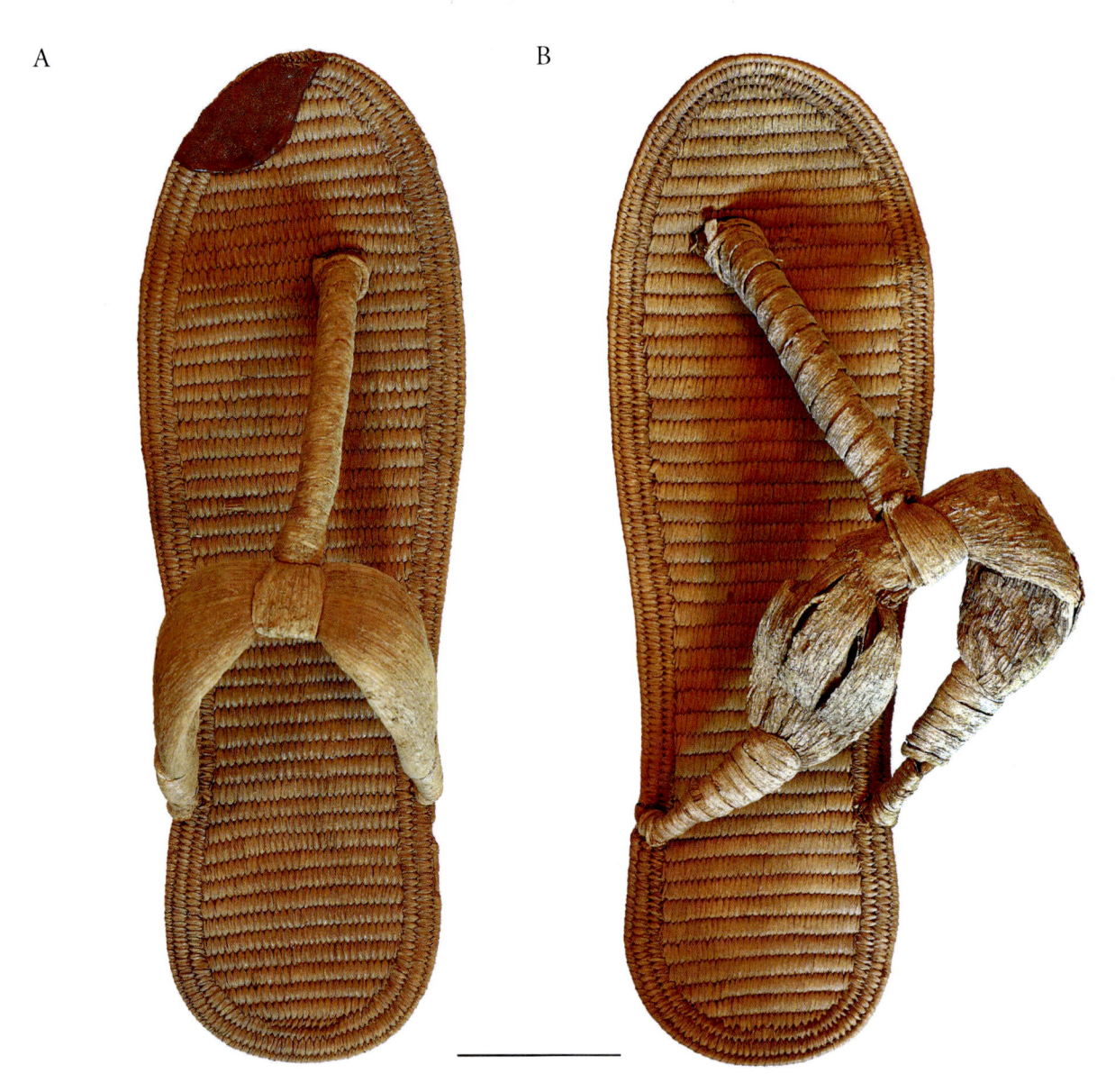

Figure 6.9. Pair of sandals JE 95354a & b. A) Left sandal in dorsal view; B) Right sandal in dorsal view. Scale bar is 50 mm. Photography by A.J. Veldmeijer. Courtesy of the Supreme Council of Antiquities / Authorities Egyptian Museum, Cairo.

6.2.1.2 Sewn Sandals Type D (Imitations)

JE 95349 (CG 51124; SR 126)

An example of Type D (imitations) is the pair JE 95349 (Davis *et al.*, 1907: pl. XLIV; Quibell, 1908: 58-59; figure 6.12, table 11). The shape is much more comparable to Type A sewn sandals, but more elongated. Although the strap complex is detached and incomplete, the sole is without damage, obscuring a view of the cross section. It is likely though, that the sole's construc-

tion is comparable to JE 95355, described below, *i.e.* a layer of rawhide, covered with gesso and gilded. The gold foil, however, covers the ventral surface as well and does not show wrinkles. This contrasts with JE 95355. The transverse-bundle-pattern, so characteristic for fibre, sewn sandals, is stylized in the gesso layer. There are at least 43 transverse bundles in the left one, the exact number of which could not be established because it is obscured by the strap complex, which adheres to the dorsal surface. There are 40 in the right one. The edge consists of

Figure 6.10. Left sandal JE 95356 in dorsal view. Possibly a pair with JE 95318 (cf. figure 6.5). Scale bar is 50 mm. Photography by A.J. Veldmeijer. Courtesy of the Supreme Council of Antiquities / Authorities Egyptian Museum, Cairo.

three rows. The pre-strap as well as the front strap is of the same shape as in JE 95355 and, in contrast to the soles, without details. They are inserted in holes and emerge on the treadsole at the same level as the sole's surface.

JE 95352a & b (CG 51123; SR 129)

Remnants of two objects are referred to by Quibell (1908: 58) as sandals (figure 6.13, table 11). None of the objects are complete, but although one is broken in two, they are of about equal size. The gold foil cover in the broken one ('a') shows large gaps, but this layer is intact in the unbroken object ('b').

Figure 6.11. Left sandal JE 95357 in dorsal view. Scale bar is 50 mm. Photography by A.J. Veldmeijer. Courtesy of the Supreme Council of Antiquities / Authorities Egyptian Museum, Cairo.

Especially well visible on it are hairs, which are undoubtedly remains of the brush that was used to add conservatives to the layer.

It is unlikely that these objects are sandals, as there are no indications of straps. Also, folding a strip of leather over the edge (edge binding) without protecting it with an additional sole against it, is not seen in sandals, although the edge of an entire sole might have been folded over the edge of the underlying sole, thus facing the ground directly (*cf.* Veldmeijer, 2009i). However, this

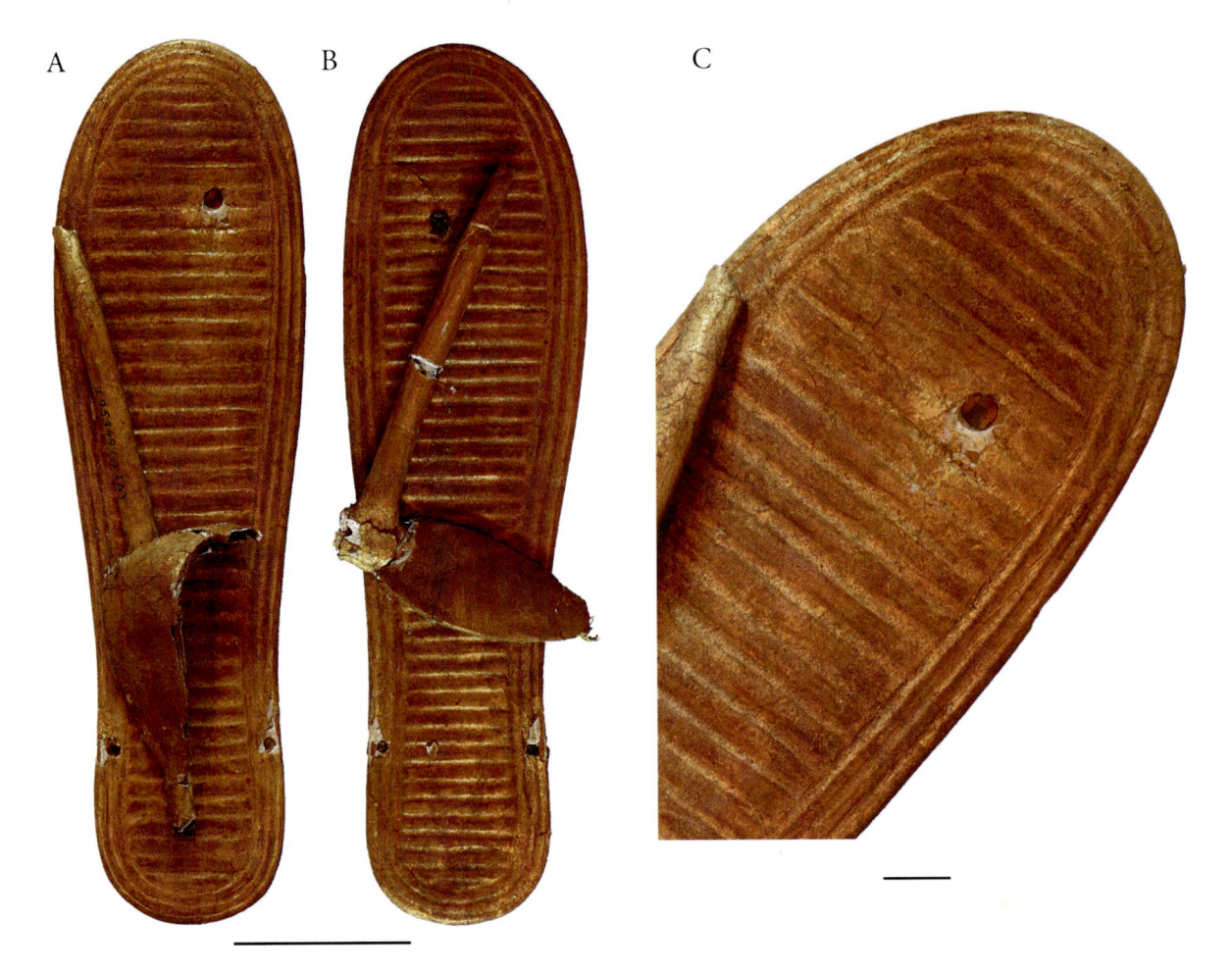

Figure 6.12. Pair of Yuya's and Tjuiu's sewn sandals Type D (imitations) JE 95349. A) Left sandal in dorsal view; B) Right sandal in dorsal view; C) Close up of the front part of the left sandal. Scale bar A & B is 50 mm; scale bar C is 10 mm. Photography by A.J. Veldmeijer. Courtesy of the Supreme Council of Antiquities / Authorities Egyptian Museum, Cairo.

construction does occur in shoes (Veldmeijer, 2009d) and might have been present in some of Tutankhamun shoes (section 3.3). Quibell (1908: 58) mentions several stitches for the attachment of the green strip, but stitches only occur on the short edges and could hardly have functioned as such. It is more likely that these rather coarse stitches were used to attach the object to another surface. The green leather binding might have been glued. Even though the choice of materials and construction is of lesser concern for footwear made specifically for the hereafter, the features seem too 'out of the ordinary' for footwear. A final argument against sandals is the shape, which is elliptical and thus symmetrical longitudinally,[13] which is a shape not seen in Egyptian leather footwear. It does occur, however, in fibre sandals, as the example in the World Museum, Liverpool[14] suggests (Veldmeijer, 2009g). According to the archival records this sandal dates to the New Kingdom. The identification of the objects notwithstanding, description is provided for.

The gold foil, topmost layer is applied directly onto a rawhide layer. The rawhide layer is rather thick and has split in several places, suggesting there were multiple layers, which is not the case. The other surface of this rawhide layer is covered with a thin layer of coarsely woven fabric onto which a relatively thick layer of gesso has been applied. Is not clear whether there is another layer of textile fabric, but there is a small spot of fabric visible that runs under the green leather binding in the broken one.

A B C D

E

F

Figure 6.13. Objects JE 95352. A) Obverse of 'a'; B) Reverse of 'a'; C) Obverse of 'b'; D) Reverse of 'b'; E F) Close up of the obverse of 'b' showing the layers of cloth, gesso and gold foil. Note the absence of stitches to fasten the green leather strip except for the two at one edge. Scale bar A-D is 50 mm; scale bar E & F is 10 mm. Photography by A.J. Veldmeijer. Courtesy of the Supreme Council of Antiquities / Authorities Egyptian Museum, Cairo.

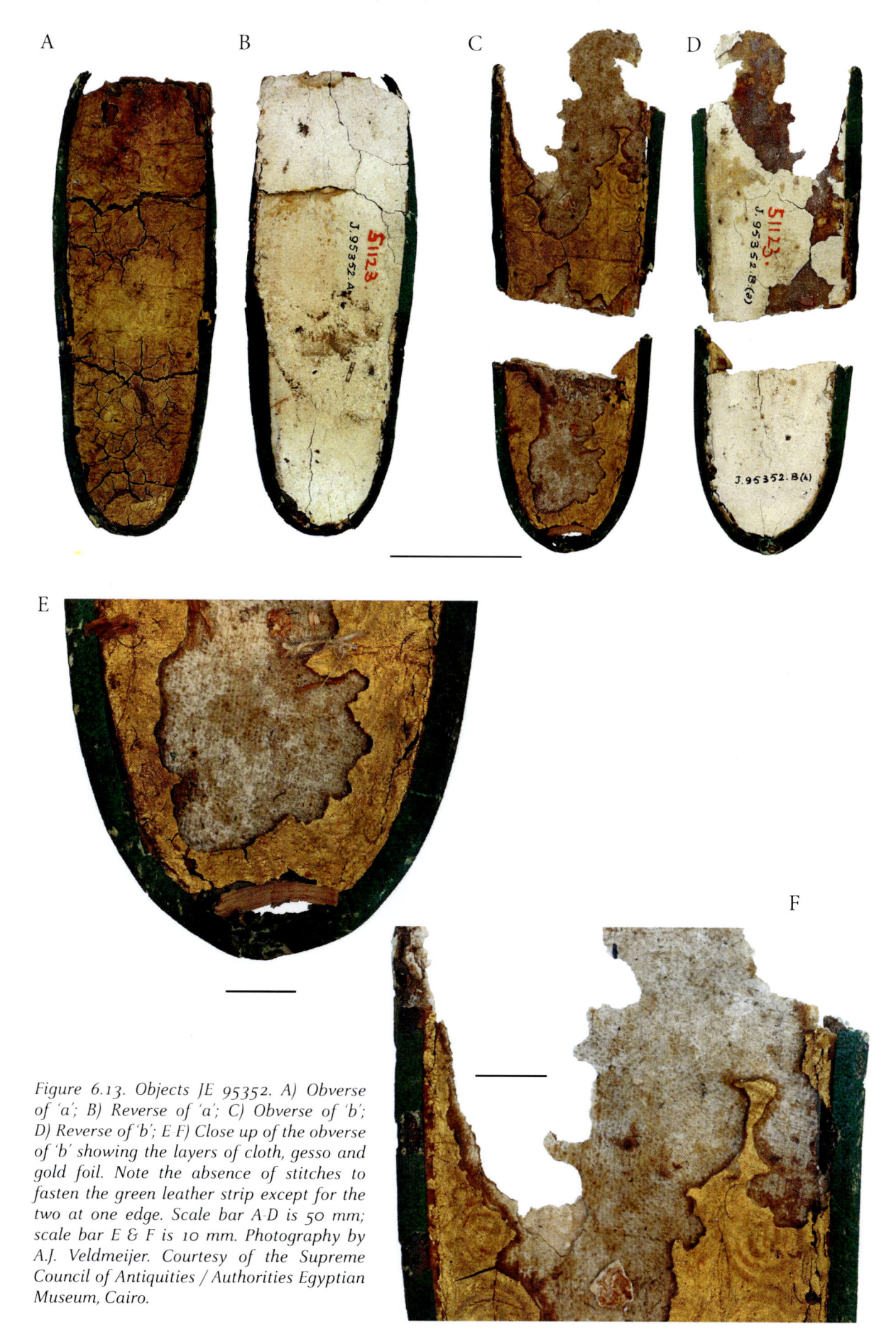

No traces are visible in the more complete specimen. The surface of the gold foil is decorated, according to Quibell (1908: 58) by "a hard pebble or metal point." (figure 6.13F). Since the running spiral design is rather wide, the former seems more plausible than the latter. The design is in itself not extraordinary and is an often-encountered motif in all kinds of decoration, including leatherwork (*e.g.* Veldmeijer, 2009b: ÄM AM 076k, Cat. No. 45).

Smith (1908: 71), in his examinations of the mummies, describes that "Above the uppermost bandage there is a transverse oblong flattened area on the back, between the shoulders. Only small fragments of gold remain on the surface of this." Unfortunately, no measurements are given, but one wonders if this area, not reported for Yuya's mummy, is an area that originally was covered with the objects described here. With the size as reported, it would certainly fit a mummy. The aforementioned stitches, then, served to attach it. Comparable objects are not common but not unheard of either (personal communication Salima Ikram 2008).

JE 95355 (left; CG 51121; SR 132)
& JE 95317 (right; CG 51121; SR 94)

The two sandals (figure 6.14, table 11), presumably forming a pair, show an extreme degree of preservation. The left one is nearly intact with only slight damage on the heel's edge and small areas of the edge of the front half. Small patches of the gold foil of the strap complex are lacking or are loosening. The right sandal, in contrast, has large holes in all sole layers and especially on the front half. The remaining gold foil, again of roughly the front part, has come loose and has crumpled. The straps are entirely missing, but the hole for the front strap as well as the slits for the insertion of the back straps, can still be noted.

The sandals (Davis *et al.*, 1907: pl. XLIV; Quibell, 1908: 58) consists of a sole of rawhide of which the dorsal and ventral surfaces are covered with a thin layer of white gesso, which has turned a greyish hue on the right sandal, and is distinctly thicker on the ventral surface (figures 6.14B & E). The dorsal surface is gilded, the foil of which is folded around the edges but does not cover the ventral surface. Clearly visible are the wrinkles in the foil. In the right sandal, the gesso and gold foil have become largely detached from the rawhide sole layer.

The strap complex probably consists of the same layers (*viz.* rawhide, gesso, gold foil) and in one piece, but this could not be established for certain due to the fact that it is intact and the cross-section could not be examined. The right sandal shows tiny holes in the rawhide sole at the attachment of the 'pre-straps,' but how exactly they were attached is not clear. It is apparent, however, that the gesso layer with gold foil has indents to accommodate the imitation pre-straps.

The shape of the sole falls in Type A of sewn sandals (Veldmeijer, 2009a), although it is more elongated.[15] Further evidence for the imitation of sewn sandals is the fact that the strap complex is the same in shape, including the imitation of the pre-straps.

6.2.2 Nefertari[16]

Ernest Schiaparelli discovered the tomb of Nefertari in 1904, which contained one pair of sewn sandals. The shape of the pair of sandals (figure 6.15, table 12) differs slight-

> *Figure 6.14. Pair of sewn sandals Type D (imitation). A) The left sandal (JE 95355) in dorsal view; B top) Cross section of the sole, showing the gesso upon the rawhide, covered with gold foil; B bottom) The beige/white cross section of the main layer suggests rawhide, rather than leather; C) The right sandal (JE 95317) in dorsal view; D) The right sandal (JE 95317) in ventral view. Note the differences in colour between the two; E) Detail of the anteromedial portion of the right sandal in dorsal view. Scale bar A, C & D is 50 mm; scale bar E is 10 mm. Indication of scale B: the thickness of the sole is 2.7 mm. Photography by A.J. Veldmeijer. Courtesy of the Supreme Council of Antiquities / Authorities Egyptian Museum, Cairo.*

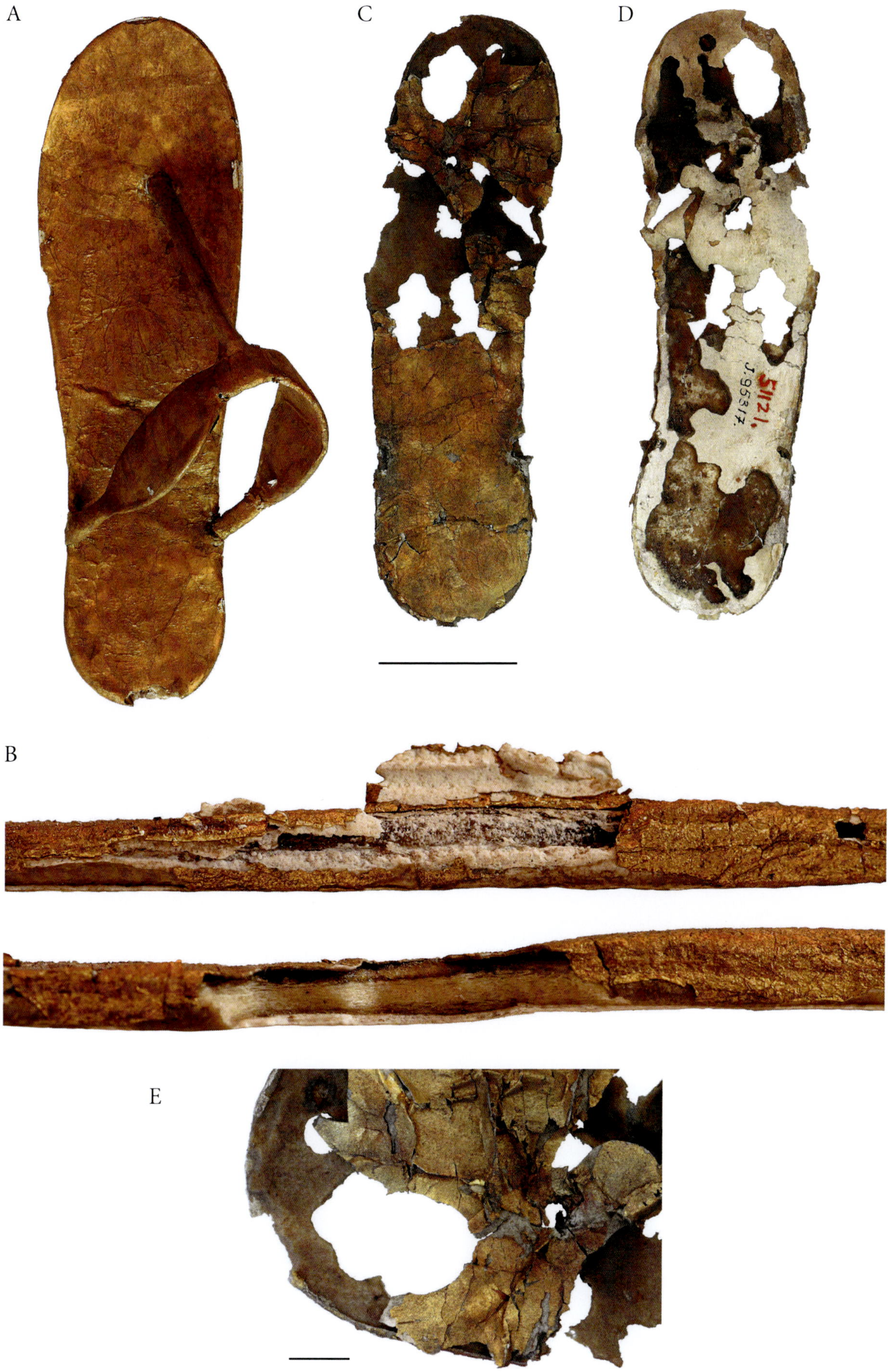
A
C
D
B
E

ly from the most commonly encountered Type C sandals (*i.e.* from Tutankhamun) in that, from the heel towards the front, the width increases slightly but continuously: the waist is not restricted. The toe is slightly elongated. The strap complex, although incomplete, is of comparable layout, but distinctly less bulky and compares well with those seen in sewn sandals Type A. The front strap is referred to as Type 3 (the core is entirely clad by means of winding a strip of papyrus around a core: the cladding is not knotted); the back strap as Type 2 (the back strap is of (almost) equal width; it is pulled through the looped pre-strap outside in, after which the construction is clad). The edge consists of three rows, which are of approximately the same width.

The dorsal surfaces show wear, caused by the movement of the foot. Unfortunately, it was not possible to study the ventral surfaces because they are mounted on a display panel and too fragile to dismount. Consequently, it could not be established whether this ventral surface is worn.

Figure 6.15. Pair of sandals (MEgT S. 5160) from the tomb of Nefertari, found by Ernesto Schiaparelli. A) Left sandal in dorsal view; B) Right sandal in dorsal view. Scale bar is 50 mm. Photography by E. Endenburg. Courtesy of Museo Egizio, Turin.

6.2.3 Amarna

Only several examples of fibre footwear are known from Amarna. The Petrie Museum of Egyptian Archaeology UCL houses a child's sewn-edge plaited sandal (Veldmeijer, Accepted; Freed et al., 1999: 260; figure 3.78B) and the Rosicrucian Egyptian Museum & Planetarium, San Jose, USA, houses a pair of fibre sandals.[17] Wendrich (1989; 1991) does not mention any (remnants of) fibre sandals in her work on Amarna's basketry and cordage, perhaps because of the lack of this type of find. Still we have a relatively large collection of footwear from Amarna, but these are made of leather (Veldmeijer, 2009b[18]). Here, the most common examples are presented in general terms.

The German excavations, lead by Ludwig Borchardt during 1911-1914, recovered quite a substantial amount of leatherwork. Approximately half of the finds, which are currently housed in the Ägyptisches Museum und Papyrussammlung, Berlin, consists of (remnants of) footwear.[19] One type of sandal (figure 6.16A) consists of a one-layer sole, the pre-straps of which are cut from the same sheet of leather (so-called 'eared sandals'). The back (and heel) strap is attached to a slit in the terminal end of the pre-strap. Other types of sandals (figure 6.16B) consist of several sole layers and have a differently shaped pre-strap. Many sandals are cut in a curved shape, which occurs far more often in Amarna than anywhere else.

Two of the most complete examples of leather sandals, besides several less well preserved (parts of) sandals, however, were recovered during the EES expeditions between 1921 and 1936 (Peet & Woolley, 1923: 79, pl. XX, 2, no. 22/119 and 22/120; Veldmeijer, 2009b; cf. Veldmeijer, 2009i). The child's and adult's sandals are comparable in construction and consist of several sole layers, which are stitched together along the perimeter. The child's one has a decorative strip included in the perimeter stitching, which is lacking in the adult's sandal. The strap complexes are also comparable.

6.2.4 Other Sandals

The variation of fibre, sewn sandals have already been mentioned, but the abundance of sandals made in this technique in collections emphasises its importance.[20] But other types of fibre footwear occurred as well, such as sewn-edge plaited sandals (figures 6.17 & 3.78B) known from among others Deir el-Medinah (Gourlay, 1981a: 63-64; 1981b: 56-59, pl. V, D-F, pl. XX, A, C; Veldmeijer, Accepted) and cordage sandals, also from Deir el-Medinah (Gourlay, 1981a: 65-58; 1981b: 41-45; pl. V; cf. Veldmeijer, 2006/2007). Coiled sewn sandals (figure 6.18) are likely to be somewhat older and might be dated to the Middle Kingdom (Veldmeijer, 2009g).

Leather sandals are common in the New Kingdom and range from simple single sole examples (e.g. Van Driel-Murray, 2000: 312-315; Montembault, 2000: 87-91; see also below) to elaborate ones, consisting of several sole layers, padding, decoration and often made in bright colours (figure 6.19; Montembault, 2000: 106; Veldmeijer, 2009i).

6.3 SHOES

The known open shoes are mainly made of fibre (figure 6.20); examples are known from Deir el-Medinah (Gourlay, 1981a: 61-62; 1981b: 55-56; more examples in Veldmeijer, 2009h).[21] Petrie (1890: 28) described several leather variants from 12th Dynasty Kahun,[22] which are similar in layout to the well known fibre ones. An additional pair of leather open shoes, housed in the British Museum, is unprovenanced, but interestingly, these shoes combine the sandal-like straps with laces, usually seen in closed shoes (figure 6.21, see Veldmeijer, 2009f).[23] A comparable shoe, housed in the Egyptian Museum, Cairo, is based on a typical Egyptan eared sandal (Veldmeijer, In press c). The Minoans bringing tribute in the tomb of Rekhmira seem to be wearing open shoes, combined with socks, but the study of these scenes are still in progress.

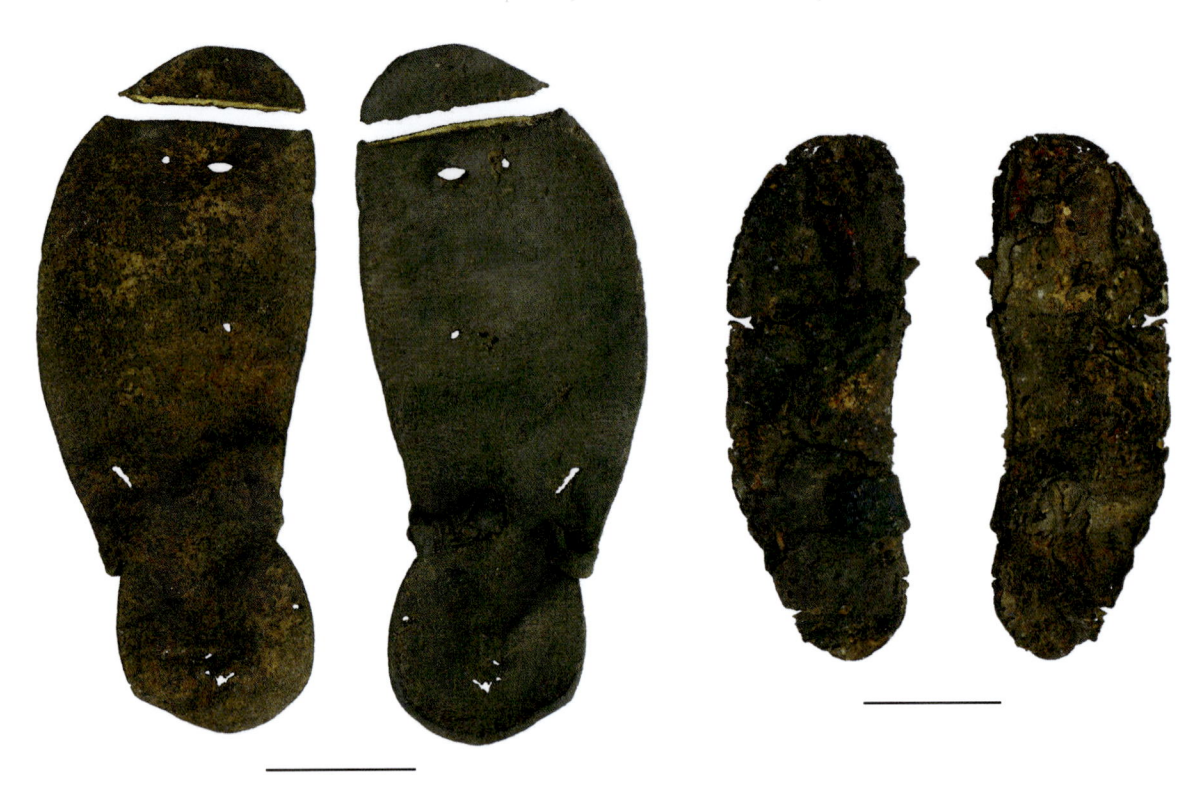

Figure 6.16. Two examples of leather sandals from Amarna. A) ÄMPB AM 046c, an eared-sandal with a single layer sole; B) ÄMPB AM 054a consists of five sole layers. The pre-strap, rectangular in shape, is possibly a separate element. Scale bars are 50 mm. Photography by E. Endenburg. Courtesy of the Ägyptisches Museum und Papyrussammlung, Berlin.

Figure 6.17. Example of sewn-edge plaited sandal (BM EA 4451). Scale bar is 50 mm. Photography by A. 't Hooft. Courtesy of the British Museum London.

The first shoes that entirely cover the foot (closed shoe) appear in the late New Kingdom, possibly introduced by the Hittites (Van Driel-Murray, 2000: 316), but doubt has recently been raised about this, suggesting that closed shoes might have evolved from open shoes and much earlier. Closed shoes were made of leather. Two types of closed leather shoes are relatively abundant in the New Kingdom: the delicate and well made, coloured curled-toe ankle shoes (figure 6.22 & 6.23; Van Driel-Murray, 2000: 313-315; Montembault, 2000: 204-205; Veldmeijer, 2009d), which might be related to chariotry (Veldmeijer, 2009c) and the less delicate but more sturdy stubbed-toe low ankle shoes (figure 6.24; Montembault, 2000: 194; Veldmeijer, In preparation b).

Figure 6.18. Example of a coiled sewn sandal (BM EA 4432). Photography by A. 't Hooft. Courtesy of the British Museum, London.

Figure 6.19. Example of a leather composite sandal (ÄMPB AM 21680). Photography by E. Endenburg. Courtesy of Ägyptisches Museum und Papyrussammlung, Berlin.

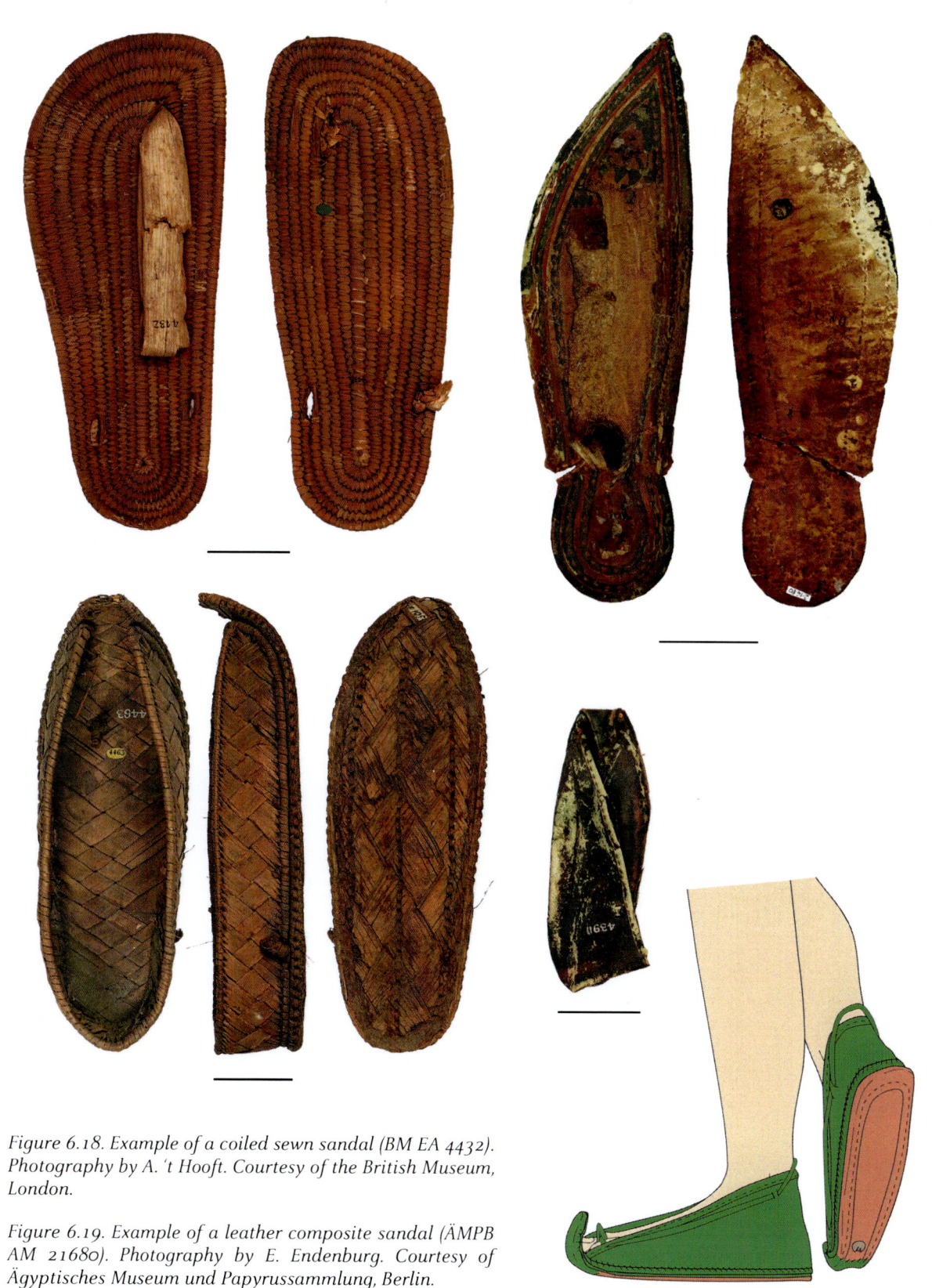

Figure 6.20. Example of a fibre open shoe (BM EA 4463) in dorsal, lateral and ventral views respectively. Photography by A. 't Hooft. Courtesy of the British Museum, London.

Figure 6.21. Artist impression of the leather open shoes, with photograph as inset (BM EA 4391). Drawing (not to scale) by M.H. Kriek. Photography by A. 't Hooft. Courtesy of the British Museum, London.

Scale bars are 50 mm.

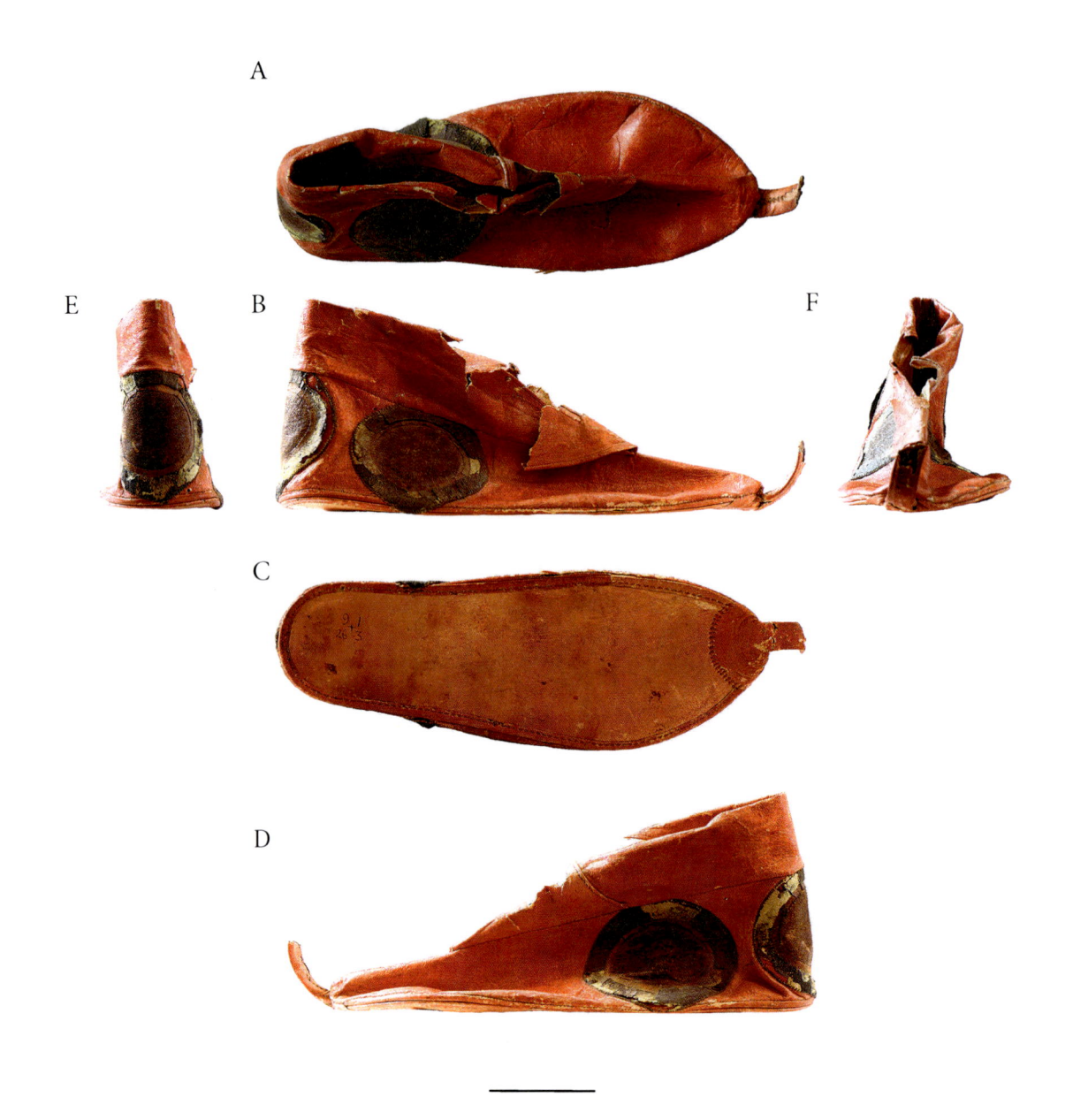

Figure 6.22A-M. Left shoe of the pair EgCa 5174/5 in A) Dorsal; B) Medial; C) Ventral; D) Lateral; E) Posterior and F) Anterior views. > Figure 4G-M) Details of the pair of shoes. G) Anteromedial view of the ventral surface of the treadsole, showing the sole seam and attachment of the cladding of the toe extension; H) Medial view of the front edge of the left shoe; I) Lateral view of the left shoe, showing the seam between ventral and dorsal upper, including the triangular instep flap. Note that the decoration patch is included in the seam as well; J) The top of the dorsal upper is folded, the edge of which is folded too (arrow); K) One end of the lace is simply fastened with an overhand stopper knot; L) The lace runs around the heel through holes in the ventral upper; M) The patches are added after the ventral upper was attached to the sole, evidenced by the fact that the patch runs over the seam (and even under the ventral surface of the treadsole). See Veldmeijer (2009d) for a detailed description. Scale bar A-F is 50 mm; scale bars G-M are 10 mm. Photography by A.J. Veldmeijer. Courtesy of the Supreme Council of Antiquities / Egyptian Museum, Cairo.

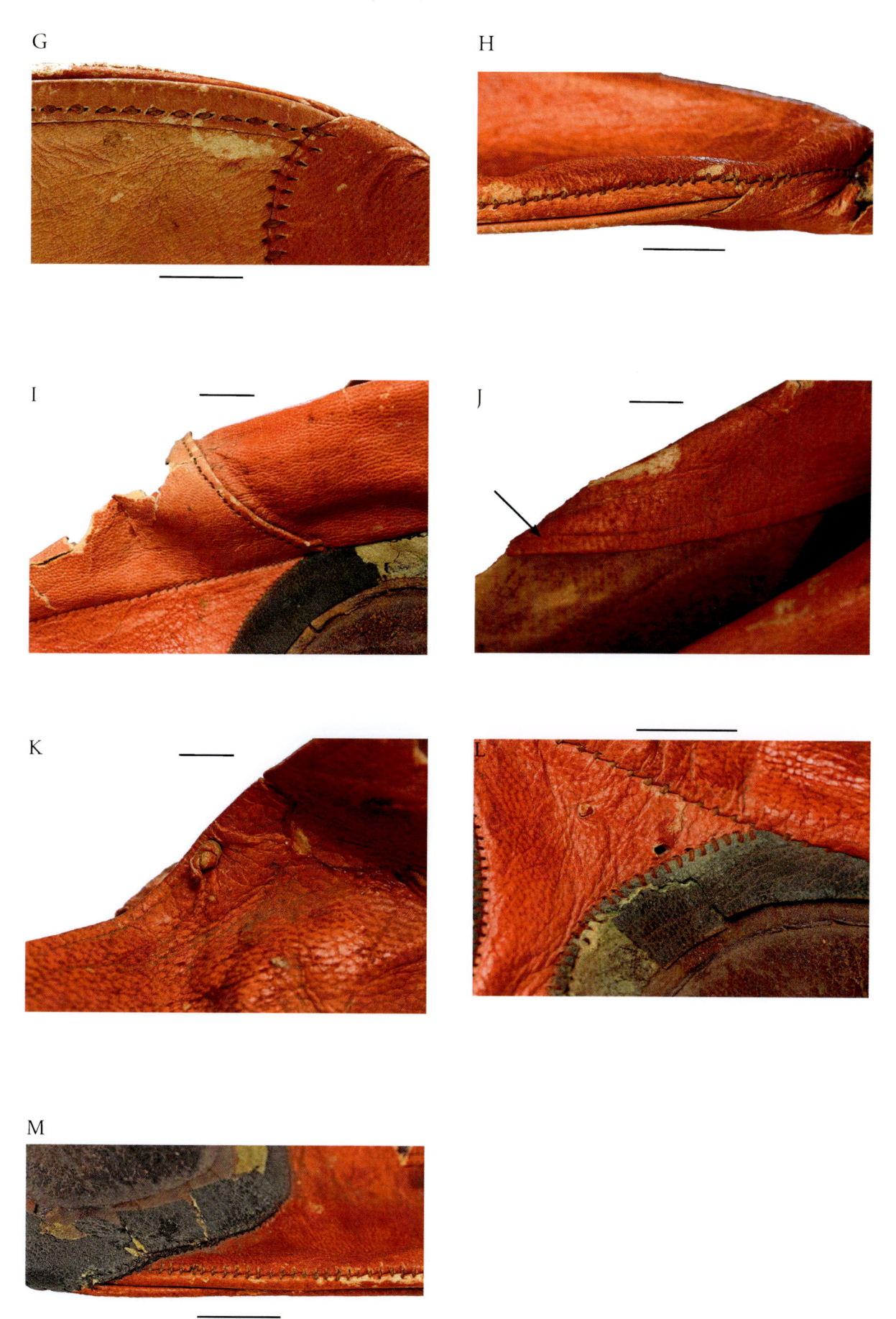

G

H

I

J

K

L

M

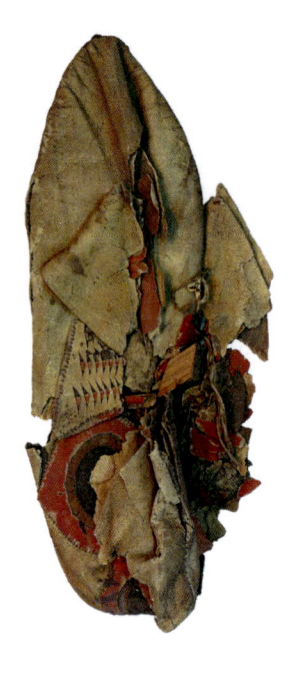

Figure 6.23. Right shoe EgCa JE 30607 in dorsal view. The small piece of wood, possibly put there to give support, could not be removed before consolidation. See Veldmeijer (2009d) for a detailed description. Scale bar is 50 mm. Photography by A.J. Veldmeijer. Courtesy of the Supreme Council of Antiquities / Egyptian Museum, Cairo.

Figure 6.24. Dorsal view of stubbed-toe low ankle shoe (BM EA 4404). Scale bar is 50 mm. Photography by A. 't Hooft. Courtesy of the British Museum, London.

CHAPTER 7

NEW KINGDOM SANDALS: A PHILOLOGICAL PERSPECTIVE

Fredrik Hagen[1]

7.1 INTRODUCTION

Scholars working with textual material from Egypt, be it monumental inscriptions of hieroglyphs or manuscripts in the cursive hieratic script, have lately become more aware of the problems involved in relating language to material culture (Kemp & Vogelsang-Eastwood, 2001: 476; Quirke, 1998: vii–viii). Despite lexicographic projects like the *'Wörterbuch der ägyptischen Sprache'* (Erman & Grapow, 1926-1963), we are frequently on tenuous ground when translating, for example, plant names (Germer, 1998) or different items of clothing (Janssen, 2008). The same is true of footwear, and the first part of this chapter deals with the different types of sandals identifiable in the textual record and their correlation with the archaeological record. The second part deals with the evidence for the manufacture of sandals and their economic role. The abundance of New Kingdom texts mentioning sandals and sandal-makers notwithstanding, the majority of the sources are not particularly informative. They consist of hieratic ostraca, isolated administrative papyri, private and official inscriptions and passages in literary texts, but because of the fragmentary nature of the sources and their uneven survival, it is difficult and perhaps even speculative to synthesise the material into a broad overview. In addition, the nature of the sources frequently imposes restrictions on the kind of information available. For example, most of the hieratic ostraca that mention footwear, over 120 in total, are notes relating to small-scale economic transactions between the Deir el-Medinah villagers, where sandals figure as part of payment along with other objects. In such lists there is little or no information about the appearance of the sandals, their colour or decoration. Because their function is economic, prices are common, and these vary considerably, but without further information about the objects themselves it is impossible to say why some are more expensive than others: it could be due to decoration, size, the quality of the material used, or the quality of the craftsmanship.

7.2 LEXICOGRAPHIC TYPOLOGY AND MATERIAL CULTURE

It has long been recognised that typologies can be helpful in cataloguing and analysing different categories of material objects – in archaeology exemplified by pottery – but such typologies need not correspond to ancient categories and types as conceived of by the Egyptians themselves. In this section, I analyse the vocabulary and semantic categories as presented in the textual sources, and attempt to relate this to the material objects that survive. There is no confusion surrounding the basic word for 'sandal' in New Kingdom, Egypt: this was, 𓏏𓃀𓅱𓋴𓋴 *tiwt* (earlier *ṯbw*). A sub-group was called 𓏏𓃀𓅱𓋴𓋴𓂝𓈖𓅱 , *tiwt ꜥfnw*, meaning literally "enveloping sandals" or "shoes" (Janssen, 1966: 85; 1975: 293), although these are comparatively rare in the textual record.[2] Relating this category to the material culture is not straightforward. There are two categories of shoes known from Pharaonic Egypt: open (figure 6.21 & 6.22) and closed shoes (6.23 & 6.24), but open shoes were the only category of shoes among Tutankhamun's footwear. Open shoes may have been the first to appear, possibly as early as the Middle Kingdom (Petrie, 1890: 28; Veldmeijer, 2009d: 4-6). The closed shoes are shoes in the modern sense, *i.e.* entirely enclosing the foot. It is not clear whether the term "enveloping sandals" referred to such open shoes or to the closed shoes, or both. The former generally retains a similar strap complex to regular sandals (a feature in which some of the open shoes of Tutankhamun differs, see section 3.3), which might indicate that it is this style that is meant – they may still be seen as part of the broader category 'sandals' (*tiwt*).

A second sub-group of sandals are [hieroglyphs], "Nubian sandals" mentioned once in the surviving sources (HO 65.2). If this is a genuine Nubian style of sandal then the rarity is perhaps not surprising; Thebes was some way from Egypt's southern frontier, and sandals may not have been a primary class of object for import.[3] Archaeologically, there is a definite Nubian style of sandals detectable, although there are minor differences between various sites. Perhaps the most prominent Nubian feature is the double front strap, but although these have been identified in the Kerma material (Reisner, 1923: 306-308), they were not found among the finds from Adindan (Williams, 1983: 75).[4] In terms of decoration, the elaborate incised lines such as those seen in the material from Adindan (multiple lines following the perimeter of the front part and, separately, the same decoration following the perimeter of the heel) seems a peculiarly Nubian feature. In contrast, incised decoration in Egyptian leather sandals are limited to one or two lines along the perimeter and/or a decoration in the centre of the dorsal surface which vaguely follows the shape of the sandal (*e.g.* Veldmeijer, 2009i). A C-Group character mentioned by Williams (1983: 73) is the double sole, which is folded at the toe, a type of construction that is not found in New Kingdom Egyptian footwear.

However, two pairs of sandals from an Old Kingdom tomb from Gebelein (14043 and 14044) in the Turin Museum show this construction too (personal communication, Veldmeijer 2008).

An example of another possible category of sandal comes from a fragmentary papyrus letter from Deir el-Medinah (P. DeM 31; figure 7.1):

[To ... of] the necropolis:

When my letter reaches you, you shall arrange for the sandals: [...]

One pair of men's leather shoes (*tiwt ʿfnw ḥꜣwty*), one pair pure-priest's leather sandals (*tiwt n wʿb*), [one pair of] leather sandals [...] and one pair of men's leather shoes (*tiwt ʿfnw ḥꜣwty*). He said: 'I shall bring (them) to him from [...]'. [...] caused to be brought to me a leather sandal sole (*wʿ rd tiwt n dḥri*) [...and they were] sent to him. He did not [give] anything for them, sending [...] shoes (*ʿfnw*). Nothing was given to me for them. Sandals [...], and sent me his leather sandals [...end lost]

(Černý, 1986: pl. 21A+21; *cf.* Wente, 1990: 163-164, no. 262).

What is meant by "pure-priest's sandals" is not clear to me. The determinative used ([hieroglyph]) clearly indicates that they are made of leather, and they may correspond to the white sandals frequently associated with temple service and purity (Schwarz, 1996: 71-76; Goffoet, 1992: 118; *cf.* below).[5] As can be seen in the letter above (P. DeM 31), the sources generally distinguish between "men's sandals" (*tiwt ḥꜣwty / tiwt ṯꜣy*) and "women's sandals" (*tiwt n st / tiwt ḥmt*), which presumably reflects differences in size rather than styles (Janssen, 2008: 101). This conclusion finds support in the archaeological material where no stylistic differences between the two are detectable (on sewn sandals, see Veldmeijer, 2009a: 572; *cf.* Yuya's and Tjuiu's sandals in chapter 6

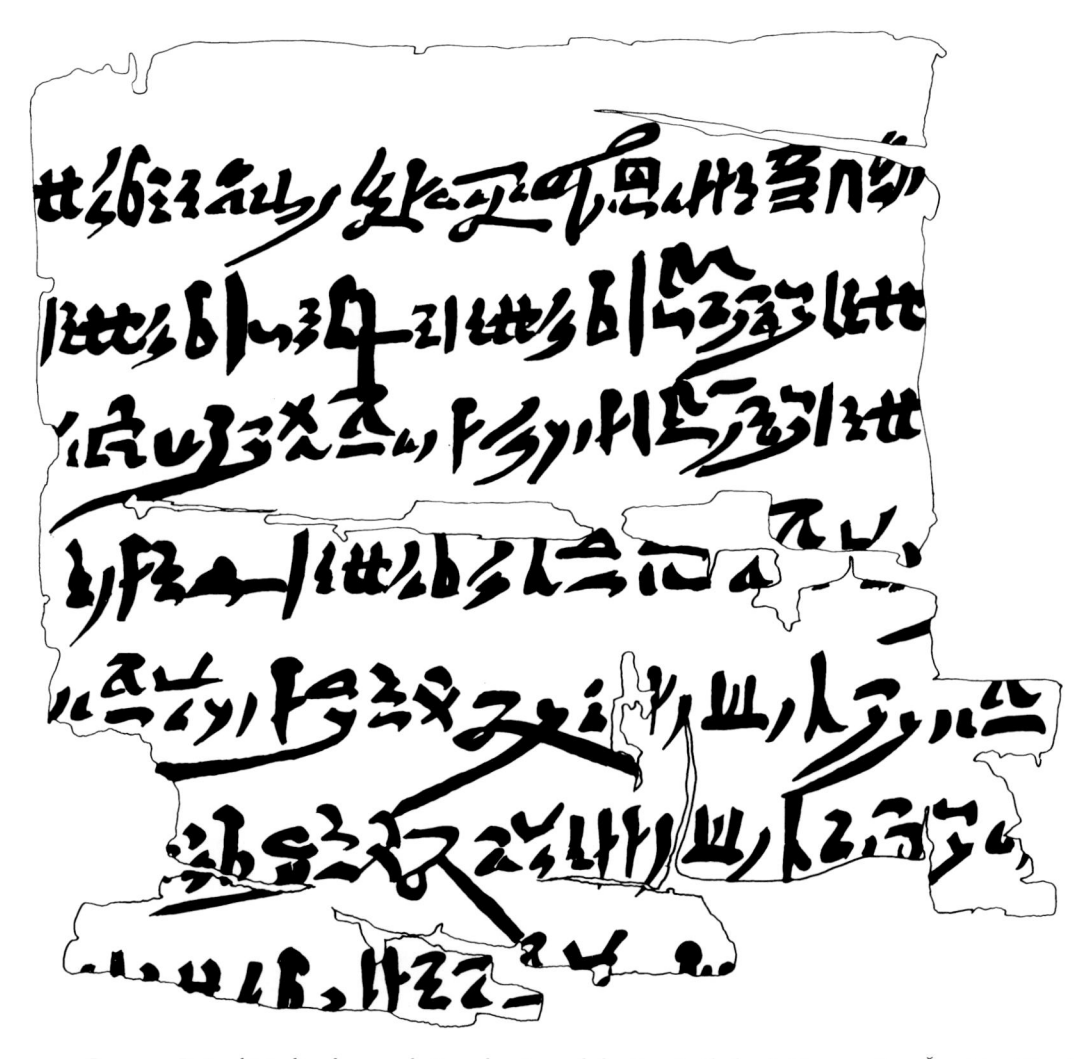

Figure 7.1. Papyrus Deir el-Medinah 31, a letter about sandals. Facsimile by F. Hagen after Černý (1986: pl. 21).

of this volume). If the designations "men's sandals" and "women's sandals" are an indication of size, then that might explain the relative rarity of reference to "large" (ꜥꜣ; O. DeM 240) and "small" (šri; O. DeM 695) sandals. It is occasionally stated that texts mention children's sandals as a separate category (*e.g.* Helck 1961-1969: 941), but this is not the case. The only reference cited in the literature explicitly states that they are ![glyphs], "four pairs of *men's sandals* for the children" (HO 61.3; my emphasis), and so do not constitute a separate category in and of themselves. There may well have been other types of sandals, but these are not mentioned in the surviving texts.[6]

An example that illustrates the difficulties associated with the translation of texts mentioning sandals is the single reference to sandals from the tomb of Tutankhamun. This is a wooden label with two lines of hieratic (figure 7.2), which was originally attached to something, as shown by the round hole at the top of the label, and it carries a short inscription that reads "Papyrus (*dmꜥ*): sandals of his Majesty, life, prosperity and health." Although seemingly trivial, the text raises important questions about the accuracy of our translations when compared to the material finds from the tomb, because no sandals made solely of papyrus were found. The plant fibre sandals in the tomb are, as discussed (chapter 3 and 4), made of bundles of halfa grass and strips

195

Figure 7.2. The only inscription from the tomb related to footwear is a wooden label. A) The wooden label (21nᶜ) with hieratic inscription; B) The text. Photography by H. Burton. Copyright Griffith Institute, University of Oxford. Drawing by F. Hagen after Černý (1965: 15, pl. IX).

of dom palm leaf, with only straps of papyrus, and yet the hieratic label seems to indicate papyrus as the main material. The crux of the matter is our understanding of the Egyptian word *ḏmꜥ*, which is translated "papyrus" in dictionaries of ancient Egyptian (*e.g.* Erman & Grapow, 1926-1963: V, 574.4-9; Hannig, 1995: 1006; 2003: 1503; Lesko, 1982-1990: IV, 159; *cf.* Helck, 1961-1969: 942-943). There is no doubt that in many cases the word does refer to papyrus, particularly where it designates writing material (Erman & Grapow, 1926-1963: V, 574.3-5), but there are many words for papyrus in Egyptian (*e.g.* mḥyt, wꜣḏ, mnḥ, ṯwfi, ḏt), and it is not always clear what the different nuances of meaning might be. This is a perennial problem in translating ancient Egyptian plant names, perhaps in part because we have unrealistic expectations; as Germer (1998: 85) notes, "the ancient Egyptians [...] knew nothing of the classification system of Linné," and our expectations of their vocabulary for plants have to be modified accordingly.

From an archaeological perspective, there are two main categories of material used in sandals during the New Kingdom: leather and plant fibre (but never solely papyrus).[7] The ancient scribe's use of the word *ḏmꜥ* is not a mistake, however, and it appears elsewhere as the most commonly used material in the manufacture of sandals (see below). In fact, there is reason to believe that the Egyptians thought of *ḏmꜥ* as the 'default' material used in sandals. In the Great Harris Papyrus, a document recording temple endowments by Ramesses III, there are two categories of sandals mentioned, *viz.* leather and *ḏmꜥ* (Grandet, 1994: 96), and out of a total of 18830, 80% are said to be of *ḏmꜥ*, and only 20% of leather. This contrasts markedly with the hieratic ostraca, where a survey of the main publications[8] reveals a total of 143 mentions of sandals (or soles of sandals) on 102 individual ostraca. Of the ones where the relevant part of the text is preserved, 76.2% of the entries do not mention the material used,[9] 22.4% specify that they are made of leather,[10] and only in 2.4% of the entries is the material explicitly said to be *ḏmꜥ*.[11] However, the ratio of leather-to-fibre sandals in the Harris Papyrus tallies with the archaeological evidence in the sense that approximately 25% of surviving New Kingdom sandals are made of leather, and 75% of plant fibre (personal communication Veldmeijer 2008).[12] A comparison between these figures and the hieratic ostraca suggests to me that the entries in the latter where the material is not specified (76.2%) in reality correspond to sandals made of plant fibre (the *ḏmꜥ* of P. Harris). The commonly accepted translation of *ḏmꜥ* as "papyrus" thus requires some modification, and a broader definition like 'plant fibre' seems more suitable; this would also account for its application to such a wide range of objects as writing materials (papyrus) and the 15110 (dom palm leaf?) sandals in P. Harris. In view of the 22% of entries in Deir el-Medinah ostraca that specify sandals made of leather, Janssen's (2008: 95) suggestion that leather sandals were worn "mainly or exclusively by priests," and that *ḏmꜥ* sandals were worn by "the lower personnel [in the temples]," seems speculative and does not accord with the archaeological evidence, such as the presence of plant fibre sandals in high-status tombs, or leather sandals for children from Deir el-Medinah (see *e.g.* Veldmeijer, 2009i).[13]

There are some lexicographic problems related to words for constituent parts of sandals, such as 'sole,' 'strap,' and 'cordage.' In many cases, ostraca and papyri mention the ⟨*rd*⟩ of sandals. In cases where the word is spelled out phonetically and/or using an indirect genitive (*e.g.* ⟨*rd n tiwt*⟩) there is no problem identifying *rd* as a separate word,[14] but many references simply add the ⟨⟩ signs after the word for 'sandal' (*e.g.* ⟨⟩). The meaning of this is unclear – it could either be an alternative writing of *rd (n) tiwt* with a direct genitive (*tiwt rd*, "sandal-soles"?), or it could be a scribal convention for the writing of 'sandals' with ⟨⟩ as a second set of determinatives. With Janssen (2008: 100) I consider the former more likely because of numerous examples of the full form (*rd n tiwt*), and because there is a parallel in the way leather sandals are designated: this can either take the full form ⟨*dḥri tiwt*, 'leather-sandals'⟩[15] or the abbreviated ⟨⟩.[16] Janssen (2008: 100) thought *rd* was simply the singular of *tiwt*, "sandal" but this seems unlikely to me in view of O. DeM 554 – also cited by Janssen himself – which specifically mentions "one *rd* of sandals" (*wꜥ n rd n tiwt*).[17] The qualification "one of" would be superfluous if *rd* was inherently singular. A different and more plausible explanation is that *rd* – in the New Kingdom – was simply the word for 'sole,' as both Grandet (*e.g.* 2006: 73-74, 86, 120) and Wente (1990: 163) have suggested. 'Sole' was the original meaning of *ṯbw* in the Old Kingdom (Erman & Grapow 1926-1963: Vol. V, 361.9-362.15), but by the New Kingdom this is the regular word for 'sandal,' which might explain the need for a new word for 'sole.' Its frequent occurrence in economic transactions can be explained by the fact that this is the main component in any sandal.

Another word that seems to refer to part of a sandal is ⟨*sfḫ*⟩, the basic meaning of which in other contexts is "loose" or "unfastened" (Erman & Grapow, 1926-1963: Vol. IV, 116.2-117.5). There are only three references to this part, one of which is certain (O. Gardiner 167; Kitchen, 1975-1989: Vol. VII, 309-310) and two of which are probable (O. Turin 57480, P. Turin 1880; Gardiner, 1948: 48.6), and opinions differ as to what it refers to. Janssen (2008: 103; *cf.* 1975: 298) suggested that it refers to the straps of a sandal, but conceded that in view of the basic meaning of the word in other contexts, this seems uncertain. Other scholars have suggested that it refers to the 'remnants' of sandals, in other words the individual pieces that would be assembled into a complete sandal (Sturtewagen, 1990: 939; Wente, 1967: 53). This seems the most plausible explanation to me. Janssen's objection (2008: 103) to this is the price of one *deben*[18] recorded for a *sfḫ* (O. Turin 57480), which he thinks is rather high for an unfinished object, but this is not necessarily problematic. Prices for sandals commonly range from one to three *deben* per pair (Janssen, 1975: 298), and if the *sfḫ* was of average to good quality, a price of one *deben* (*i.e.* 1/3 of the total price) is not unrealistic. Surviving examples occasionally show great variation in the craftsmanship and complexity of their constituent parts. For example, a sandal from Deir el-Medinah (ÄMPB AM 20998, see figure 3.78C) has very elaborate and decorated straps but basic soles (Veldmeijer, 2009i), and such differences in craftsmanship (and material) would presumably be reflected in the value assigned to these individual parts prior to their assembly.

7.3 SYMBOLISM AND IDEOLOGY

There are few textual sources that deal with the symbolism and ideology of sandals, and scholars are largely dependent on iconographic sources to reconstruct such aspects (see chapter 8). Exceptions include the topos, common in royal inscriptions, of someone being "under the sandals of N." (*ḥr ṯbw N.*), which was a way to express dominance (Lorton, 1974: 129-130) – this also occurs in the Book of the Dead where Isis says to Osiris "I have made you a god; I have placed your enemies under your sandals" (BD 151; Allen, 1974: 148).[19] Sandals formed a barrier to dirt, and elsewhere in the Book of the Dead the deceased proclaims that "I will not step on it (*i.e.* faeces) with my sandals" (BD 51-51; Allen, 1974: 51-52) as way of expressing his purity. The link between white sandals and ritual purity has long been known (*cf.* Schwarz, 1996), exemplified by the advice of Merikare: "A man should do what is good for his soul; performing the monthly purification (*wꜥb.t ꜣbd*), putting on white sandals (*šsp ḥḏ.ti*), joining the temples, keeping the secrets hidden, entering the sanctuary and eating the bread" (Quack, 1992: 38-39, 177). They also occur, with the same connotations of ritual purity, in the funerary literature of the Middle and New Kingdom. Coffin Text Spell 149, for example, should be uttered "by a man shod with white sandals,"[20] and similarly Book of the Dead Spell 125: "Let this spell be recited when he is pure (*wꜥb*) and clean... shod with white sandals and anointed with myrrh" (Allen, 1974: 100). To what extent the "silver sandals" (*ṯbw n ḥḏ*) apparently handed out as a reward to priests (Schwarz, 1996: 77-79), differ from the white sandals referred to above is not clear; both are described by the word *ḥḏ* which can mean both "white" and "silver," and both are associated with "pure-priests" (*wꜥb*). Archaeologically, silver and gold sandals have been found, but only in high status funerary contexts where they can hardly be classified as "gold of praise"-type objects (Schwarz, 1996: 79).

7.4 ECONOMIC ROLE AND MANUFACTURE

There has been some debate about how common sandals would have been amongst the non-elite of New Kingdom Egypt, but the consensus seems to be that they were not unusual (Goffoet, 1992: 120-121; Veldmeijer, 2009a: 561). There is some support for this in texts indicating that sandals were conceptually considered part of the basic outfit of an Egyptian. So for example, in the 'Story of the Two Brothers' when the protagonist goes off in search of his brother, "he took his staff and likewise his sandals, his clothes and his weapons" (P. d'Orbiney 12.10-13; Gardiner, 1932: 22). Similar passages occur in the mortuary literature of both the Middle and the New Kingdom, where the deceased is enjoined to "Take your staff, your kilt and your sandals, and go down to the Tribunal" (Faulkner, 1973-1978: Vol. II, 14-15), or to "Take your staff, your kilt, your sandals and your arrows for the road" (Allen, 1974: 176). Setting off "without sandals" was not advisable ('Letter of Menna'; McDowell, 1999: 144-147, no. 107).

Texts also afford a more detailed view of various economic aspects of footwear. The price of a pair of sandals varied but was generally in the region of one to three *deben* (Janssen, 1975: 298), *i.e.* roughly equivalent to the cost of one sack (circa 78 litres) of grain. This gives some indication of their worth: most were not luxury items, but neither were they insignificant in terms of value. Their moderate value, along with their common occurrence and logistic suitability, explains their frequent use as part-payment in economic transactions recorded on hieratic ostraca. Not all ostraca are records of transactions, and exceptions can be revealing. Many of the sandals that survive in museums and collections today come from funerary contexts, predominantly from tombs, where they appear to have been deposited as part of the mortuary equipment (although not specifically manufactured for that purpose). This is reflected in the textual sources too. O. Vienna 1 contains the records of an official inspection made during the reign of Ramesses III (c. 1185-1153 BC) of a – by then – old and dilapidated tomb, probably of the 18th Dynasty (c. 1550-1300 BC). The text from this ostracon notes, amongst other things, the objects found in the tomb. Along with the coffin of an anonymous Deir el-Medinah resident, the items listed include several pieces of furniture, a scribal palette, bronze objects, jars, a box of papyrus and various other objects of daily life, and two pairs of sandals (McDowell, 1999: 70-71; Zonhoven, 1979).

Sandals formed part of the economy, both at a national level and at the household level. The state provided sandals to workers at Deir el-Medinah, along with their wages and other supplies for the work in the Valley of the Kings. One of the papyri from the village (P. Turin 1898) records deliveries made to the gang of workers of "60 pairs of sandals for the left (side of the gang), and [...] for the right (side)" (Kitchen, 1975-1989: Vol. VI, 687.11). A similar social context is plausible for O. Ashmolean 1945.37 (Černý & Gardiner, 1957: pl. 75), which lists 440 leather sandals, as well as an unpublished ostracon (O. IFAO 827; cited by Janssen, 2008: 95) that mentions 1976 pairs of sandals. In view of the similarly high numbers for other commodities in those texts – the former lists 20,000 $ḥk3t^{21}$ of grain and 424 pieces of various types of clothing, and the latter 23,200 half-litre jars of honey and 2166 sheets of *ifd*-cloth – they are unlikely to relate to private economy. The "sandals of Pharaoh" occasionally mentioned in the ostraca (O. DeM 215, 240, 10073, O. Berlin P 12647) probably belong to the same distributive system as other items of clothing provided by the state to the Deir el-Medinah workmen (Janssen, 2008: 12, 101) and were distinguished from regular sandals in lists of commodities (O. BM EA 65935).

Despite occasional references to sandals being supplied in this manner (and only at Deir el-Medinah), it is difficult to reconstruct the organisation of sandal manufacture by the state. The scale of production must have been considerable, as implied by the numbers of sandals in the texts cited above, as well as the Great Harris Papyrus, where over 18,000 sandals are assigned to temples by Ramesses III (Grandet, 1994: 96). The number is exceptionally high, but not necessarily unrealistic. The priesthood appears to have been a large-scale consumer of sandals (Schwarz, 1996: 71-72), and inscriptions describe them being "shod" (*ṯbw*) by the king (Urk. IV, 1257.6-7; Gardiner, 1952: 19, pl. IX fragment ff). The military would have been another significant consumer of sandals, and several passages from the Late-Egyptian Miscellanies, dealing with the terrible working conditions of the soldier, mention the lack of sandals as a potential problem: "there are no clothes, there are no sandals [...] and during his long marches on the hills he drinks water only every three days, and it is smelly and tastes like salt: his body is broken by dysentery" (P. Lansing 9.10-10.2; Caminos, 1954: 401). The lack of sandals during long marches in inhospitable surroundings could no doubt be a serious issue. Papyrus Chester Beatty V (6.13-7.2) vividly describes the problems facing a soldier without the appropriate footwear when traversing difficult terrain: "[he] is in pain as he [walks] without sandals, hindered(?) by the rushes, while the undergrowth (? *šfnw*) is abundant and thick, and the *wnb*-plants troublesome" (Gardiner, 1935: Vol. I, 48; Vol. II, pl. 25). This is not artistic license: Middle Kingdom expedition inscriptions record sandal-makers as part of the crew, as well as "donkeys laden with sandals" as part of their provisions (Couyat & Montet, 1912: Vol. I, 83 no. 114; 86, no. 127; Vol. II, pl. 31; Goyon, 1957: 81-85, no. 61; Vandersleyen, 1989). New Kingdom pictorial evidence appears to show soldiers having their feet inspected after prolonged marching (McDermott, 2004: 117), although they do not normally wear sandals when shown in battle (Darnell & Manassa, 2007: 82).

The workshops necessary to produce large numbers of sandals would presumably have been associated with major institutions like temples and palaces, but direct evidence is elusive. The numerous tomb-scenes showing work on sandals in small groups is compatible with the existence of institutional workshops (Drenkhahn, 1976: 7; Klebs, 1934: 168–169; *cf.* 1915: 95-96; 1922: 121-122), but it is difficult to extract meaningful information about the organisation of work from such iconographic sources (Eyre, 1987: 192).[22] Nonetheless, the detailed depictions of the workshops of the great temple of Amun at Karnak in the tomb of Rekhmira (Theban Tomb No. 100) show a degree of organisation of craftsmen, including sandal-makers (Davies, 1943: pl. LIII, see figure 8.1).

In the absence of archaeological remains identified as workshops of sandal-makers, we have to rely on categories of evidence that only indirectly shed some light on the organisational models at work. Administrative titles offer one avenue of exploration, but such material has to be evaluated carefully: titles found on monuments are not simplistic reflections of professional organisations and hierarchy (Franke, 1984). The title "overseer of sandal-makers" (*imy-r ṯbw*; Brovarski, 1973: 458; Ward, 1982: no. 417) suggests a degree of formal organisation, perhaps along the lines attested for other types of craftsmen like goldsmiths and carpenters (Eyre, 1987: 192-196). Administrators like the "overseer of sandal-makers of the temple of Amun" (Gardiner, 1910: 99; Porter & Moss, 1994: 139) or "overseer of sandal-makers in the temple" (Jones, 2000: 274-275 no. 988), would presumably have been in charge of the day-to-day management of the workshops. Some of the individuals employed in these can be identified, like Paabunakhte and his colleague Ashaket(?) who are listed as "sandal-makers of the mortuary temple of Ramesses III" in the tomb-robbery papyri (Kitchen, 1975-1989: Vol. VI, 508.9-10, 512.6, *cf.* Vol. VI, 577.7). Evidence from earlier periods suggests that temples of more moderate wealth and status employed the services of sandal-makers who were not part of the temple staff themselves. The administrative archive of the Middle Kingdom mortuary temple of King Senwosret II at Lahun contained records of transactions with sandal-makers:

Copy of a [letter brought] from the pyramid town Hetep-Senwosret which the sandal-maker Werenptah son of Sankhptah brought. Let a cow-skin or, alternatively, a goat-skin (? ꜥwt) be brought. It is to the sandal-maker Werenptah that you should give it, putting it in writing: "A cow-skin has been given to this sandal-maker".

(P. Berlin 10050; Wente, 1990: 73-74)

Regnal year four, fourth month of Shemu, day 17. Let a cow-skin, it being of good quality (*m ḥt nfr*), be brought. Look, it must be suitable for its purpose (*r ḥnt=f*). Now I made the sandal-maker Hetepi come about it, so you will give it to him. [Address:] Scribe of the temple, Horemsaf.

(P. Berlin 10014; Wente, 1990: 74)

Here the sandal-makers are not part of the temple staff, and have to be sent to the temple to collect the raw material for the sandals. The writers are concerned with getting leather "of good quality" suitable for the manufacture of sandals. The two papyri clearly refer to different occasions – the first is a copy of a letter inscribed in the daily journal of the temple dated to regnal year 7, the second is an actual letter of year 4 – but they reveal some of the practical and economic processes underlying the production of sandals. The writer of P. Berlin 10050 clearly prefers cowskin, although goatskin also seems to be acceptable, and the comment about putting the transaction in writing may be an attempt to prevent any economic irregularities arising from the transaction.

Major temples in ancient Egypt had ready access to cowskin in the form of ritual slaughter, and it is therefore not surprising to find them supplying the leather for the sandals. The process of producing leather of a suitable quality was complex and difficult in the Egyptian context, partly because of environmental factors (Van Driel-Murray, 2000: 300). The leather of a sandal-maker was even ascribed medicinal qualities in some cases; it occurs as an ingredient in medical recipes (Wreszinski, 1912: 24 no. 96; 1913: 157 no. 628). A concern for the quality of leather for the production of sandals is also evident in later times. In what appears to be an ironically phrased letter of the late New Kingdom (O. Michaelides 79), a scribe called Hormin writes to a fellow scribe Maanakhtef, wishing that he "attain a long life and a great old age, being a great sandal-maker forever, and possessing good leather and large bright hides (*dḥri nfrt ḥny ꜥꜣ wbḫ*)" (McDowell, 1999: 31; Wente, 1990: 152). If the address naming Maanakhtef as a "scribe" (*sš*) is taken at face value he is unlikely to have been an actual "great sandal-maker," although the title itself appears to be genuine (*cf.* O. Cairo 25519). Nonetheless, the well-wishes by Hormin illustrate the link between good quality leather and sandal manufacture.

There is some doubt surrounding the question of whether sandal-makers worked with both leather and plant fibre, or whether they specialised in one or the other, although the former is perhaps most likely (see also section 4.2.3.5).[23] Certainly texts only mention the title "sandal-maker" without further qualification, regardless of whether the person is producing sandals of plant fibre (O. DeM 240.8-9) or leather (O. IFAO 1395.14-15; unpublished). It has been suggested (*e.g.* Quirke, 2004: 75) that the term 'sandal-maker' might be a term used for leatherworkers in general, and this could well be the case: a passage in P. Anastasi I (26.4) has "craftsmen (*ḥmw*) and sandal-makers (*ṯbw*)" being set to work on a chariot (Fischer-Elfert, 1983: 148; 1986: 227).

The rate of production expected from a sandal-maker – in the context of institutional workshops rather than private production – is revealed in a passage from a mathematical instruction manual known as the Moscow Mathematical Papyrus:

Method of calculating the work-quota (*bꜣkw*) of a sandal-maker:

If one says to you: "The work-quota of a sandal-maker;
If he cuts (*wdꜥ*), it is 10 per day;
If he finishes (*db3*),[24] it is 5 per day.
If he cuts and finishes, how many will it be per day?"
Then you calculate the parts of this 10 together with this 5.
Then the sum results as 3. Then you divide 10 by this.
Then 3 1/3 times is the result.
Look, it is 3 1/3 per day.
What you have found is correct.

(P. Moscow 4676, 42.1-6, no. 23; Imhausen, 2003: 374-377; Struve, 1930: 106-107).

This is one of a rare group of examples called *bꜣkw*-problems which present methods of working out the work-rate of professions such as fowl-catchers (or farmers), carpenters and herdsmen (Imhausen &

Ritter, 2004: 83). It sets out the expected production values of a sandal-maker, depending on whether he is cutting the leather (wdʿ) or putting the different parts together (dbȝ). The latter was obviously a more time-consuming process, because the expected daily quota was five sandals, whereas if he was just cutting, it was 10 sandals per day. The question raised by the problem is how many completed sandals a sandal-maker could be expected to produce per day if he had to do both the cutting and the finishing. The answer is 3 1/3: in other words 10 complete sandals every three days. The calculation does not account for the preparation of leather; this might indicate a certain level of specialisation and division of labour in an institutional context where such work would have been handled by others, but it need not reflect practices outside such institutional workshops (see for example the remark about sandal-makers preparing their leather in the 'Instruction of Khety,' XVIIIa-b, cited below).

The evidence for household economy and the private market in New Kingdom Egypt is sparse (Eyre, 1998; 1999), and the case of sandal-makers is no exception. There are several references to sandal-makers in texts from or relating to the village of Deir el-Medinah (O. Ashm 267; Černý Notebook, 31.61, O. Turin 57382, P. Turin fragment β, lines 2-3; Černý Notebook 152.2, P. Turin 1945 + 2073 + 2076 + 2082 + 2083, section B 5.10; Kitchen 1975-1989: Vol. VI, 577.7), and these indicate a classification of such individuals as specialised craftsmen. In O. DeM 240, two sandal-makers, Mahy and Khau, are said to have produced respectively nine and eight pairs of sandals each (Janssen, 2008: 96-97), perhaps roughly a week's work in light of the Moscow Mathematical Papyrus cited above. In a list of personnel brought to the village in year 2 of Merenptah, alongside draughtsmen, sculptors, carriers and stonemasons are two "craftsmen of sandals" (ḥmwt tiwt), all included under the heading "service personnel (smdt) to the workmen" (O. Cairo 25581). Outside Thebes the documentary record relating to sandal-makers is limited. A Ramesside account papyrus from the palace at Medinet Gurob records the issue of bricks for an unspecified construction project (P. UC 32133G; Gardiner, 1948: 34), and amongst groups of workers like "builders," (ḳd) "copper-smiths" (ḥmt) and "guards of the granary" (sȝw šnwt), "sandal-makers" (ṯbw) are listed. The implication of this is not entirely clear but it would appear that sandal-makers were employed as bricklayers in a building project, possibly fulfilling a work-quota owed to the state. There are parallels for such an arrangement where people with 'professional' titles are used for manual labour: an unpublished papyrus from the same site lists "washermen" (rḫty) as part of a team of cultivators sent out to work in the fields under the authority of a "controller" (rwḏw).[25]

Any attempt at reconstructing the social status and living conditions of sandal-makers finds itself entering the realm of speculation. There are no contemporary accounts by sandal-makers themselves, and the few descriptions that survive are literary in nature, written by the scribal classes, and ideologically charged:

The sandal-maker mixes bḥw; his odour stinks; his hands are red with dye, like one who is smeared with his own blood and looks behind him for the vulture, as a wounded man whose flesh is exposed...

(P. Lansing 4.5-7; Caminos, 1954: 384)

Similarly, the composition known to Egyptologists as the 'Instruction of Khety' or the 'Satire of Trades' – one of the most frequently copied literary texts in New Kingdom Egypt – includes the following passage:

The sandal-maker is worst off by far;
under his jars (of oil) forever,
his health like the health of corpses,
chewing on his skins.

('Instruction of Khety,' XVIIIa-b; Helck, 1970: Vol. II, 104)

Such characterisations are not unproblematic as sources for their living conditions because the descriptions are employed specifically to contrast with the quality of life associated with the scribal profession, and a certain amount of exaggeration is to be expected (Guglielmi, 1994: 45-47, 52-55). They need not be entirely unrealistic, however. The process of preparing skins for use by cleaning and depilating, particularly if the latter was effected by applying urine and ash as has been suggested (Van Driel-Murray, 2000: 302), would explain the reference to the pronounced stink associated with sandal-makers in the texts. The subsequent stage of curing the skins with fat or oil would have involved laborious and messy work, and the chewing of skins (if this method was employed) would have caused long-term damage to teeth and gums. It is likely to have been a hard life from a modern point of view, but it is impossible to compare it meaningfully with other types of craftsmen based on the available evidence; the literary texts quoted above present all non-scribal professions in equally dramatic terms.

CHAPTER 8

FOOTWEAR IN LATE NEW KINGDOM ART

With sections by Aude Gräzer & André J. Veldmeijer

8.1 TWO-DIMENSIONAL ART

8.1.1 Manufacturing Footwear

André J. Veldmeijer

The manufacturing of sandals[1] is often depicted but only the production of leather sandals is represented. Therefore, these images are not really helpful for Tutankhamun's footwear, because these types of sandals have not been encountered in the tomb. The absence of the manufacturing of fibre sandals in two-dimensional art is nevertheless informative despite the fact that, as will be argued below, fibre sandals are sometimes shown above the (leather) sandal-maker. This absence, together with *"Das frei verfügbare Material und die einfache Anfertigungstechnik"* has lead Schwarz (2000:

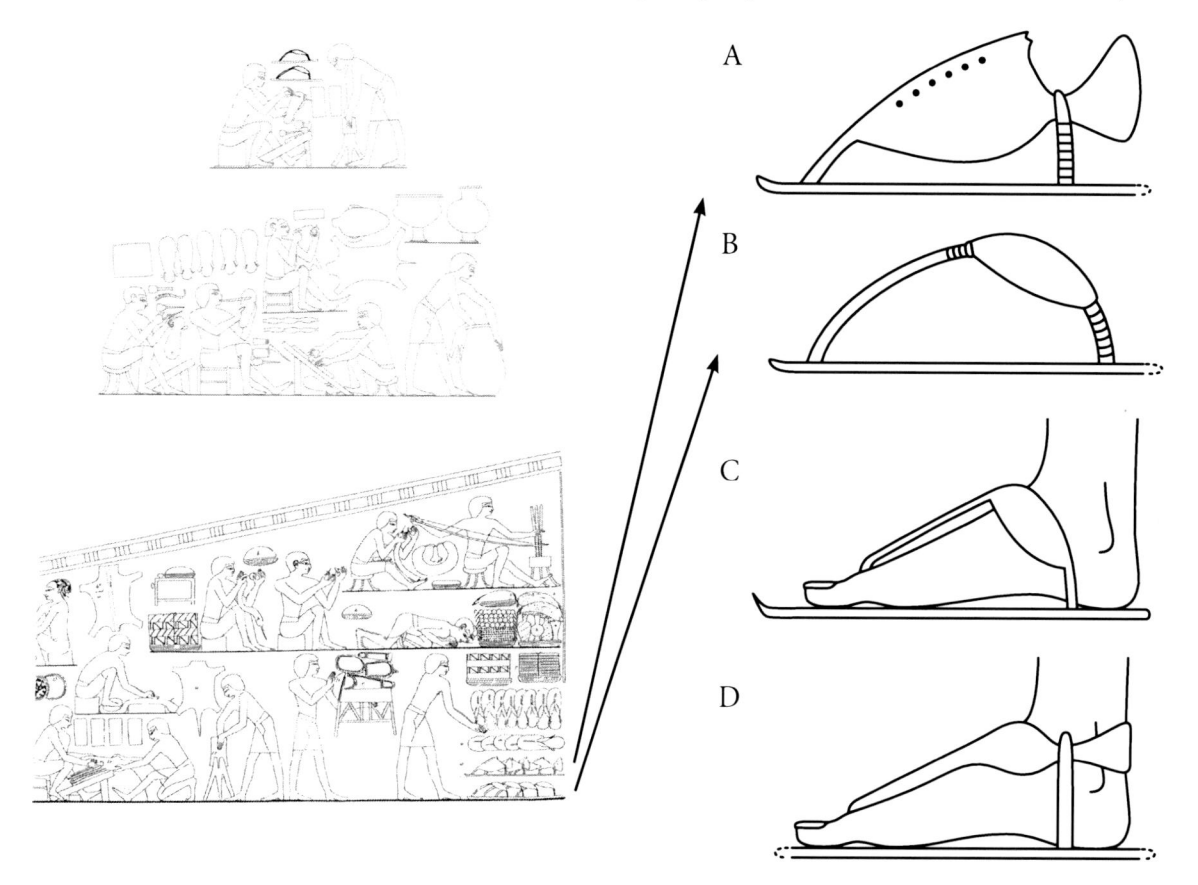

Figure 8.1. Skin processing and the manufacturing of objects from leather. The inset shows the bottom row of sandals. A) Leather composite sandals (cf. figure 3.78C); B) Fibre, sewn sandals (cf. 3.13C); C) Sewn sandal worn by the Pharao in the Amun barque procession in Luxor Temple; D) Leather sandals worn by the priests in the Amun barque procession in Luxor Temple. Figure 8.1, 8.1A & B: Tomb of Rekhmira. Figure 8.1 from Davies (1943: pl. LII, LIII, LIV); 8.1A & B after Davies (1943: pl. LII, LIV); 8.1C & D after Bickel (2004: 51, fig. 11). Figures A-D by E. Endenburg.

215, note 764) to conclude that "*Sandalen aus Papyrus[?] o.ä. jederzeit von dem Tragenden selbst verfertigt wurden und als Produkt einer Werkstatt eher zu vernachlässigen sind.*" But, she remarks (*Ibidem*), "*Trotzdem erscheinen solche sandalen unter den in Magazinen aufbewahrten Gütern*" (figure 8.1, see also section 8.1.3). Veldmeijer (2009a: 572), however, notes that "Statements as these [the simple manufacturing technique], which are not based on detailed study of archaeological material, are premature [...].³ Moreover, the statement that the manufacturing of fibre sandals is simple, which it is in some cases, equally applies to some [types of] leather sandals" although admittedly, the leather was much more difficult to obtain. The high level of craftsmanship of sewn sandals made of fibre, especially of Type C as presented here, together with the regularity of at least part of the footwear corpus from Tutankhamun and Yuya and Tjuiu suggests a (semi-) professional craft.⁴ If the suggestion, on the basis of the storage of fibre sandals in leatherworker's scenes (figure 8.1), that these craftsmen were responsible for the fibre sandals too, there is no question that they were professional.⁵

Despite the fact that manufacturing scenes themselves are of limited use for the topic of the present work, the opportunity is taken to have closer look at these scenes. The scenes, such as those in the tomb of Rekhmira, tend to show only some elements of the whole manufacturing process.⁶ According to Schwarz (2000: 73), only the most important parts of the process are shown. But which part of the sandal is more important: the sole or the straps? Neither can function without the other. It seems more likely that only the most characteristic parts of the process are shown, as Schwarz herself suggests (*Ibidem*): "*Vernachlässigt wird dagegen, was sich nicht so leicht darstellen lässt und was für diesen Bereich wohl als nicht so wichtig erachtet wurde*". In my opinion, "*wichtig*" should be understood as 'not characteristic enough.' The choice of the hides, for example, was important for making good footwear⁷ and yet it is not seen in manufacturing scenes. The manufacturing of another element of sandals – straps – is not shown either, although straps themselves are sometimes depicted. The only handling of straps that is shown is the pulling of the front strap through the sole (figure 8.1; *cf.* Schwarz, 2000: 73). Other examples of missing actions are the stitching of the soles, and application of padding or decoration. This, one can argue, might be because these types of sandals had no decoration, padding or stitched soles and indeed, these sandals are known from the archaeological record (ÄMPB AM 046c is a good example, see Veldmeijer, 2009b). More often,⁸ however, sandals with pre-straps that are cut out of the same sheet(s) of leather as the sole (layers)⁹ consist of multiple stitched sole layers and clad pre-straps.¹⁰ Sandals do sometimes show features of which the manufacturing is not shown. An example is the cladding of pre-straps; the cladding of the pre-strap by the sandal-maker is not depicted, but most sandals in storage in the Rekhmira scene show the cladding (*cf.* figure 8.1A). A reason for this absence is, possibly, that this part of the manufacturing is difficult to show and, indeed, seems to require accompanying texts to explain what is going on. Texts, however, rarely accompany the manufacturing of sandals.

The sandals in the manufacturing scenes are easy recognisable as *sandal*, *i.e.* not a particular *type* of sandal and that seems exactly the reason why the artist has chosen them: he had to convey the message that sandals were made, rather than *which* sandals. Since a larger variety of sandals are shown in representations (figure 8.1A),¹¹ but not their manufacturing, it seems that representations are standardised. This might also explain the lack of the production of the more specialised pieces of footwear (such as shoes), as they are less well known, and less easily recognisable to the public. On the other hand, we might have expected a scene with an accompanying text, saying that the sandal-maker makes sandals for the Pharaoh, but these do not exist either.

8.1.2 The Identification of Depicted Footwear

André J. Veldmeijer

Matching depicted footwear with the archaeological examples seems fairly easy, but there are several problems. In New Kingdom times, only several types of footwear are shown but the archaeological record shows a much larger variety. The depiction of sewn sandals, seen from above (figure 8.2),[12] is easily recognisable due to the transverse bundles that are bordered by the triple edge. Seen from the side, however, it is less easy.

In New Kingdom times people are often depicted wearing sandals with pre- and back straps that look very much like those described for sewn sandals: a clad pre-strap with attached back strap that distinctly widens at the sides of the foot (figures 8.1B & C). There is quite a variety in detail, which is currently being studied,[13] but in many cases, details that are added in paint, suggest the looped construction (*cf.* for example figure 3.5). This is either accompanied with the horizontal lines of the cladding or these latter occur without the looped construction. As suggested elsewhere (Veldmeijer, 2009a: 565), the loop of the pre-strap is important, or, perhaps more likely, characteristic: in archaeological examples they are not visible, being obscured by the cladding.[14]

The straight front strap seen in some of Tutakhamun's sandals (figure 3.14C), in which case the strap lies close to the foot especially at the posterior-most part, can be recognised in the example from the Amun barque procession scene in Luxor Temple (see figure 8.1C). Other examples, such as the ones shown in Rekhmira's scene (figure 8.1B) shows the strong convex curvature, as

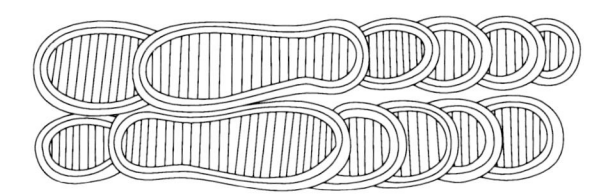

Figure 8.2. Detail from the tribute scene from the tomb of Rekhmira, showing fibre, sewn sandals Type A, seen from above (or below). Note the absence of straps. After Davies (1943: pl. XLIII). Drawing by E. Endenburg.

reported for sandals JE 62689 (figure 3.13C), but lack the upturned toe part. Remarkably enough, the big knot that fasten the front strap is not shown. It could be, however, as is suggested by the bulging of the sole (*cf.* figure 3.15), that the knot is not visible because the sole is pushed around the knot (see section 3.2.1.1).

The representation of the back straps is characteristic enough to identify them. As these shapes of straps do not occur in leather sandals, there can be little doubt. However, some examples of sewn-edge plaited sandals have exactly the same type of straps (ÄMPB AM 1397, MFA 03.1721, NMAL E20/AU9, BM EA 4456, discussed by Veldmeijer, Accepted), although the lack of well preserved examples prohibits the identification of the curvature of the front strap. However, the only well preserved example, seen in figure 8.3, has a straight front strap. As with sewn sandals, the sole slightly turns upwards at the front.[15] In other words, having no additional details of the sole's fabric we cannot be absolutely sure which of the two are meant. But the archaeological record, as well as three-dimensional art (see below), shows that only sewn sandals are associated with people of high social class: no sewn-edge plaited sandals have been recovered from Tutankhamun's or the tomb of Yuya and Tjuiu. Moreover, sewn sandals are much more abundant than the sewn-edge plaited sandals with a comparable strap complex and usually the strap complexes differ. Therefore, I propose to identify the depicted sandals as fibre, sewn sandals Type C.[16]

Figure 8.3. Pair of sewn-edge plaited sandals (MFA 03.1721), with a strap complex that is comparable to the one in fibre, sewn sandals Type C. The side view of this sandal is also the same as in sewn sandals, which hampers identification in two-dimensional art. Scale bar is 50 mm. Photography by E. Endenburg. Courtesy of the Museum of Fine Arts, Boston.

8.1.3 Footwear in Domestic Indoor Spaces: An Incursion into Amarnian Iconography

Aude Gräzer

8.1.3.1 Introduction

During Akhenaten's reign, the artists managed to revitalize Egyptian art. Yet, their innovation did not consist in creating new graphical conventions. It rather rested on the introduction of new iconographical themes pertaining to the ideology initiated by Akhenaten. Hence, when artists during the Amarna period chose to systematically depict the interior structure of buildings, their pictorial production operated according to former pictorial rules but also gave us the possibility to take a new look at temples, magazines, workshops, palaces or houses. Providing us with quite a unique access to the Egyptians' daily life and to their 'indoor' behaviour, this iconographical tendency, which differentiates Amarna art from its predecessors, is interesting in many ways for our investigation into the use of footwear. For instance, it is possible, through Amarnian depictions of the royal palace and private houses, to access the detail of the inside rooms, circulation, furniture, implements, as well as their inhabitants' life and the home staff's activities. The careful scrutiny of these pictures will produce useful information about footwear in domestic areas and might clarify the Egyptians' notion of indoor space. Nevertheless, Amarnian scenes of daily life should not be regarded as simply 'realistic.' Despite their 'picturesque' character, those depictions were not made up of fortuitous elements: they rather consist of a combination of significant elements and express a deliberate idea.[17] Based on this assumption, we can deduce that the decision to depict sandals in a determinate place or portray figures with or without sandals is also meaningful.

8.1.3.2 Footwear in Indoor Spaces

Many domestic indoor scenes occurred among the Amarna tombs reliefs[18] and the scattered decorated blocks and *talatats* found in Karnak,[19] Tell el-Amarna,[20] Medamud[21] and Hermopolis.[22] However, only a part of this material is really useful for the topic of this section since most of the preserved depictions are incomplete: the lower part of the scenes is frequently missing, making it impossible to observe the feet of the figures. Besides this material, a post-Amarnian depiction of private houses found in the Memphite tomb of Horemheb is integrated in the corpus as well. Interestingly, Amarnian iconographical conventions have been conspicuously incorporated in this later document.[23]

A number of questions arise when focusing on the interactions between footwear and domestic space. For instance, was footwear worn inside the house or palace? If so, by whom and where precisely? Did special circumstances lead Egyptians to put on or to take off their sandals? Which types of footwear were used indoors?

In the light of the aforementioned material, a few persons were shod while inside domestic areas. According to the presence or absence of this item, different contexts can be isolated as follows:

a) The king and the queen always wear sandals in the royal palace. They appear shod in many different situations that will be commented on later;

b) The royal princesses are sometimes depicted wearing sandals as well;

c) Likewise, some dignitaries of the royal court occasionally wear sandals inside the palace, even in the presence of the king;

d) In case of private individuals, it is impossible to establish whether they went shod inside their own house or not. Depictions of private houses seldom depict (if ever) their main inhabitant inside: the only picture showing a private master of the house is unfortunately too damaged to be useful here (figure 8.4);[24]

e) All members of the home staff – wherever they were (in the royal palace or in private houses) – are systematically barefoot (see for instance figures 8.4, 8.5, 8.7, 8.9 and 8.11);

f) Sandals also appear arranged with other toilette garments in the elite mansions wardrobe (figures 8.4-8.6) as well as in the royal palace bathroom (figures 8.9-8.11, 8.13).[25]

This first glimpse of footwear in Amarnian depictions raises further questions: first of all, should we infer that only important persons (the master and his family, some of his guests) were allowed to wear sandals inside domestic areas?

Only two types of footwear appear in all the aforementioned cases (a, b, c, f).[26] In the great majority of the depictions, sandals correspond to Type C of the fibre, sewn sandals with large lateral straps and a thin sole ending in a pointed toe (as explained in section 8.1.3). Since Type C is known as the elite's sandal (Veldmeijer, 2009a: 572), its wearing in domestic areas could have been the sign of an elite's prerogative too. In two cases, however, sandals are seemingly depicted as leather sandals, with their straps and sole clearly cut from the same piece of material:

1) In the twin depictions of the royal palace from Ay's tomb (see one of them in figure 8.9, detail),[27] three pairs of leather sandals appear on a stand inside a bathroom. Nonetheless, the location of this room between the royal bedroom and the women's apartments (probably the royal harem) questions their ownership. Should we regard this bathroom and its contents as being assigned to the king himself? This assumption seems inconclusive since no other case of royal leather sandals is known. Should we, rather, link this bathroom

209

master of the house worshipping

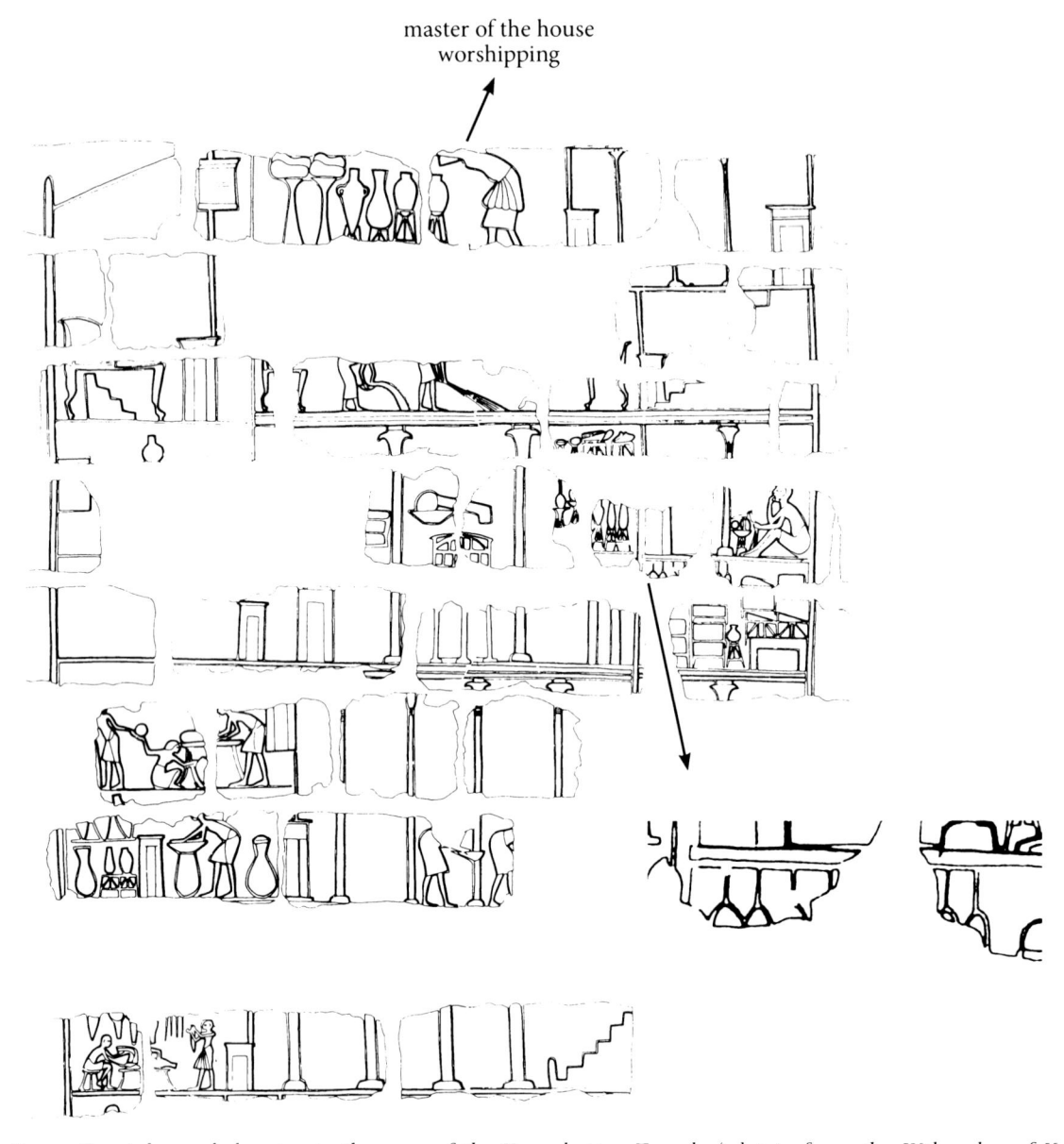

Figure 8.4. A house belonging to the area of the Karnak Aten Temple (talatats from the IXth pylon of Karnak Temple). Detail of the reconstructed wall exhibited in the Luxor Museum. From Lauffray (1980: fig. 1).

with other palace occupiers, for instance, the women from the nearby royal harem? I think this suggestion is more persuasive: the depiction of leather sandals seems to tally with the presence of the harem itself. Moreover, another depiction of the royal palace of Akhenaten, once again with the harem suites, shows similar sanitary spaces (unfortunately too damaged to see their exact content) directly adjoining the women apartments.[28] Finally, as a second group of bathrooms is also recognisable between the two royal dining-rooms (figure 8.9), these could have been the actual royal sanitary spaces;

2) The reconstruction work by Vergnieux with the Karnak *talatats* produced a similar knotty problem – depiction of the royal bathroom containing leather sandals (figure 8.13). First of all, we must emphasize the hypothetical aspect of this kind of reconstruction. Indeed, even if the presence of globular jars and sandals inside the royal bathroom is quite credible,[29] the combination of these different *talatats* remains debatable. In particular, the block showing a row of leather sandals can raise objections. Two preserved columns of text mention the name of queen Nefertiti instead of king

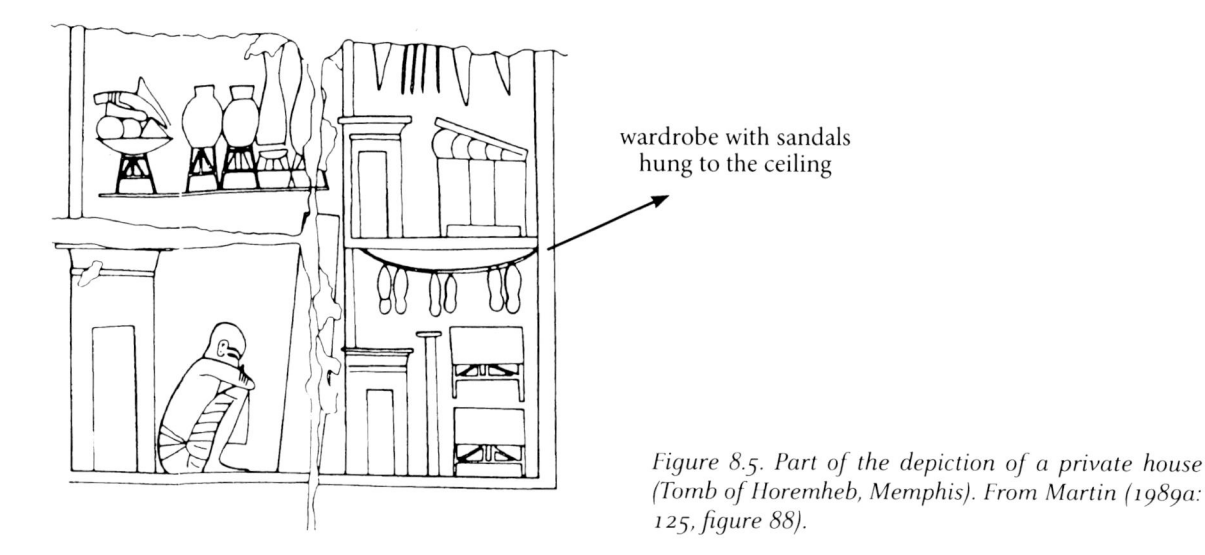

Figure 8.5. Part of the depiction of a private house (Tomb of Horemheb, Memphis). From Martin (1989a: 125, figure 88).

Akhenaten, which suggests two possibilities: a) a second sequence of pictures showing queen Nefertiti's toilette has coexisted with the king's one on the lower register; b) this block mentioning the queen had nothing to do with the depiction of the king's toilette and belonged to a separated sequence, which was completely independent from the king's.

Whatever the solution may be, should we infer that a link existed between leather sandals and women from the king's entourage? Information provided by our material is unfortunately too scarce to allow us to determine what form this link would have taken or what those leather sandals were intended for.

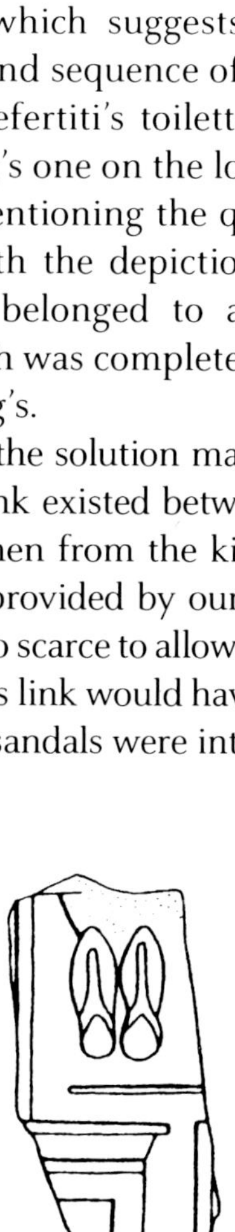

Figure 8.6. Fragment with the depiction of a private wardrobe(?) (Tomb of Horemheb, Memphis). From Martin (1989a: 144, figure 131, m).

If we go back now to the depictions of shod characters inside domestic areas, should we deem that their sandals were used both outside and inside the house or palace, or that specific 'indoor' footwear existed?

A unique scene engraved over an isolated block (figure 8.7) provides some clue to this question. On the right part of the scene, we can recognise a gate leading to a courtyard where a servant is sweeping. A door at the back of this entrance space opens into a now-missing building (but in all likelihood a great mansion[30]). In front of the door remains a quite interesting small construction: a sort of enclosure where five pairs of sandals were left on either side of the entrance, the two upper ones directed towards the house (indoor) while the three lower ones directed away from the house (outdoor).[31] This unprecedented iconographical detail is of particular interest. Even if we cannot be sure whether those sandals were associated to indoor and outdoor use respectively, possibly indicated by their opposite directions (this brings to mind the practice in traditional Japanese houses, figure 8.8), it is clear that they were left at the entrance of the building in an intermediate space separating inside from outside. The presence of such a space in

211

bakeries   private house (see inset)

Outside

Inwards (house)

Courtyard

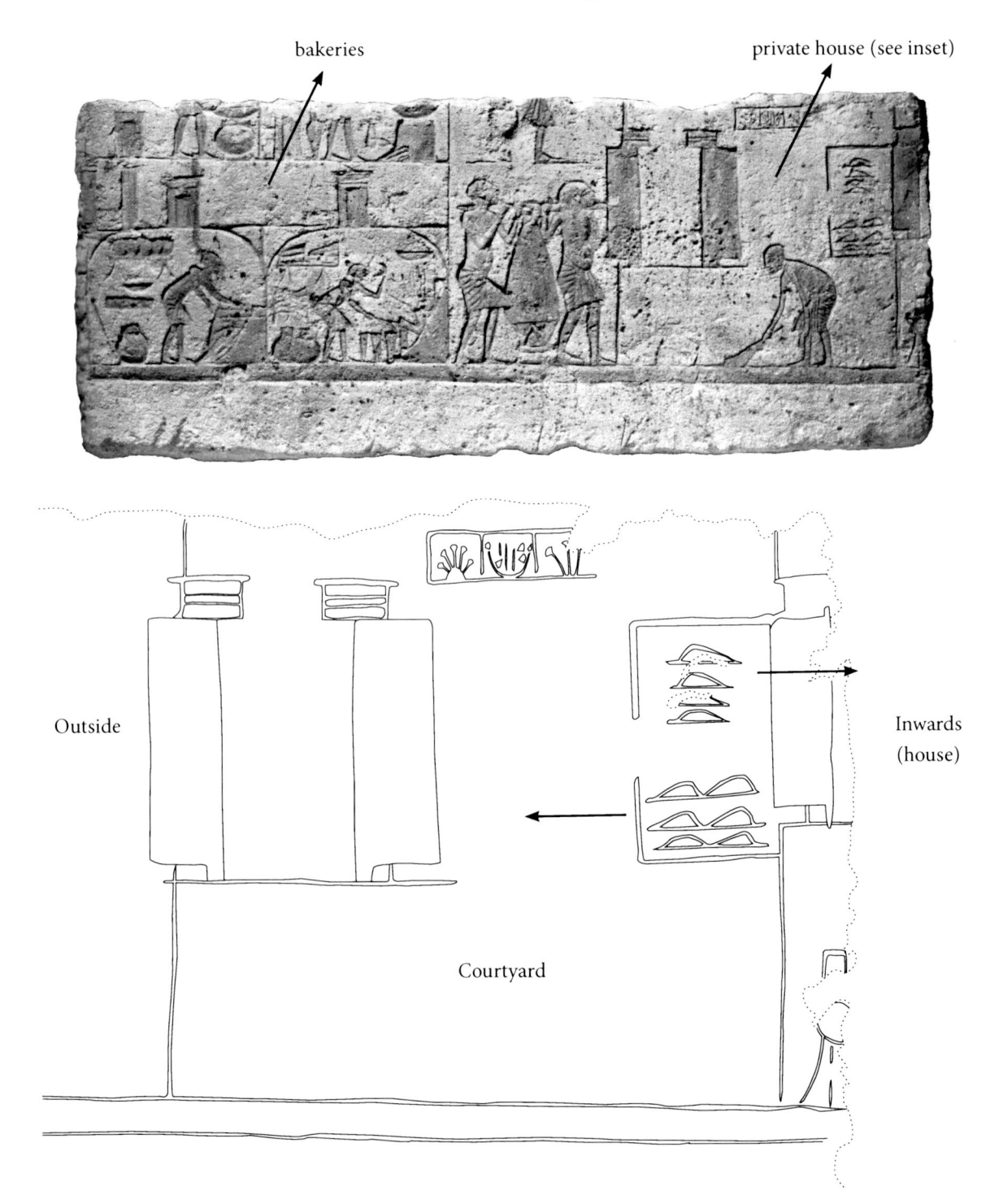

Figure 8.7. Bakeries and the entrance area of a private house(?) (Armanian block from Hermopolis, now kept in the Museum of Fine Arts, Boston, No. 62.149). Photograph from Cooney (1965: 73, figure 46). Drawing by A. Gräzer.

real dwellings is confirmed by coeval archaeological remains.[32] These archaeological remains reveal much about the Egyptians' notion of indoor and outdoor spaces: the discovery of bath slabs found nearby or in the very entrance of New Kingdom royal palaces and private mansions demonstrates that a preliminary purification (for hands, feet or the whole body) ruled the access to indoor space (Gräzer, In press). Presumably, ancient Egyptians conceived each element coming from outside as a vehicle of potential danger to the household. For this reason, dirt must not invade the

212

Figure 8.8. In the genkan, the transition between outside and inside is rendered through a first area at the same level as the outside ground followed by the raised floor of the house. The visitor must, firstly, take off his outside shoes and turn them to face the door, and secondly, put on the indoor slippers which were beforehand arranged by the mistress of the house as to be inward looking. From Fahr-Becker (2005: 25).

dwelling place. Since impure material had to be removed before entering, it is safe to assume that dusty, dirty footwear (*i.e.* used for walking outside the dwelling quarters) were not allowed in ritually pure buildings such as the royal palace or the elite mansions.[33] Conversely, 'clean' footwear (as well as 'clean' feet) might have prevailed inside the domestic space.[34]

Even if functionality of outside footwear (for example the protection of the feet against an uneven or hot sandy surface) can easily be understood, the motive of wearing sandals inside a dwelling area remains less obvious. For instance, why did the royal family and some of its guests wear sandals inside the palace? In order to offer a possible explanation, we have to look at the circumstances in which these figures appear shod and relate them with information provided for by archaeology.

8.1.3.3 The Royal Couple

Thus, in case of the royal couple's depictions, an intriguing observation is that the king and the queen wear sandals in every situation[35]: not only at public appearances (*e.g.* reward ceremonies[36]) but also during private activities, such as meals[37] (figure 8.12), royal toilette (figure 8.13) and bedtime[38] (figure 8.14). Fortunately, Veldmeijer's inquiry devoted to archaeological specimens of royal sandals will help to clue us in regarding this unexpected 'omnipresence.' Indeed, the different types of sandals that Veldmeijer was able to identify – and their intrinsic features – help to enlighten us as to the functions of royal footwear.

Tutankhamun's footwear included numerous Type C sewn sandals of fibre. As explained in the present work (but see also Veldmeijer, 2009a), these differ from other sewn sandals in shape and refinement and were, therefore, probably more expensive. This surely emphasized the social importance of their owner. Consequently, it is clear that wearing Type C sewn sandals, or being followed by a servant carrying them, constituted a way to set oneself apart socially. Likewise, the iconographical choice to depict numerous 'ready-to-use' Type C sewn sandals in the royal bathroom[39] (figure 8.13) might have signalled the high social position of the king compared to his subjects. But despite the relevance of this semiologi-

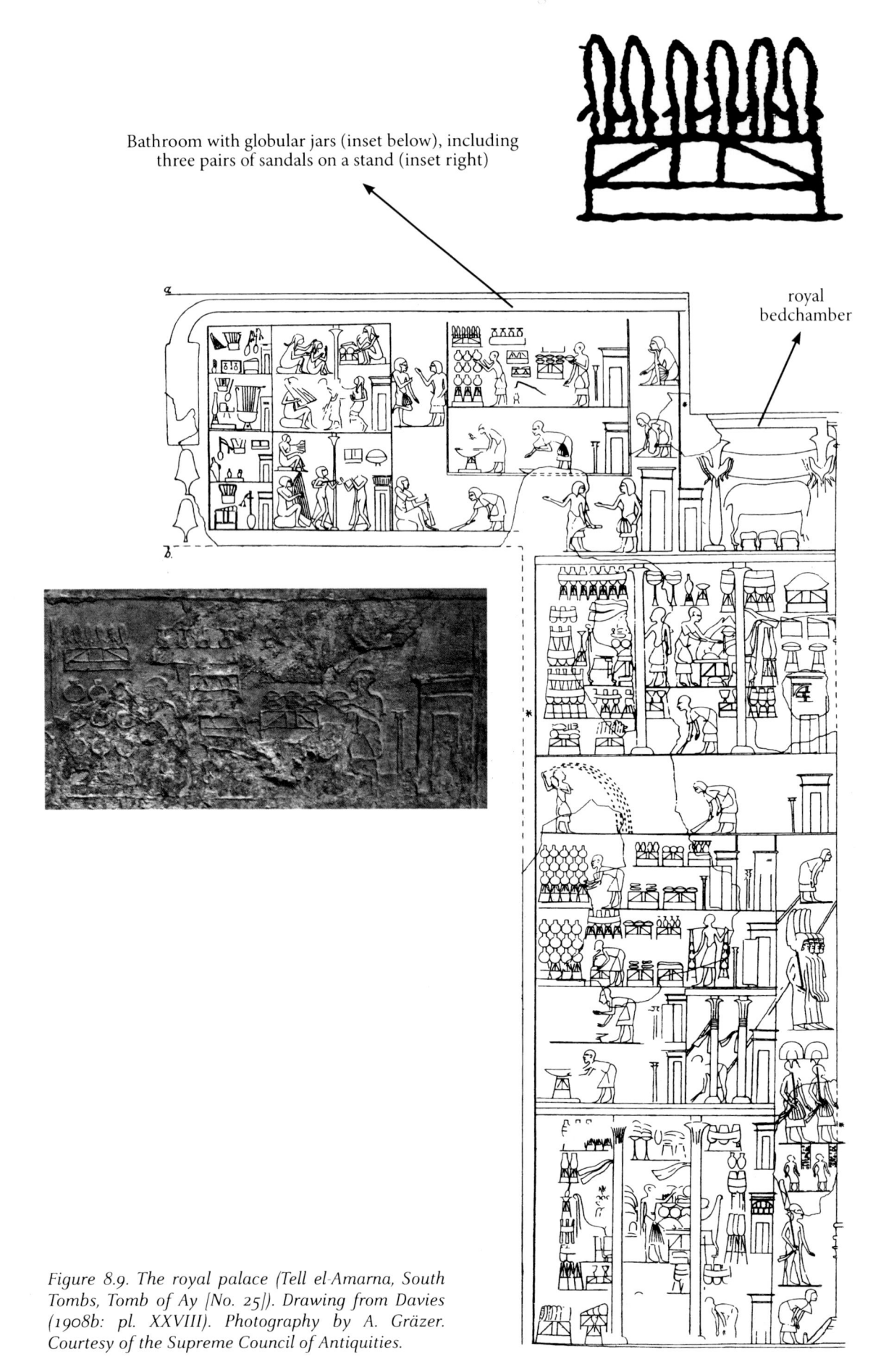

Bathroom with globular jars (inset below), including three pairs of sandals on a stand (inset right)

royal bedchamber

Figure 8.9. The royal palace (Tell el-Amarna, South Tombs, Tomb of Ay [No. 25]). Drawing from Davies (1908b: pl. XXVIII). Photography by A. Gräzer. Courtesy of the Supreme Council of Antiquities.

214

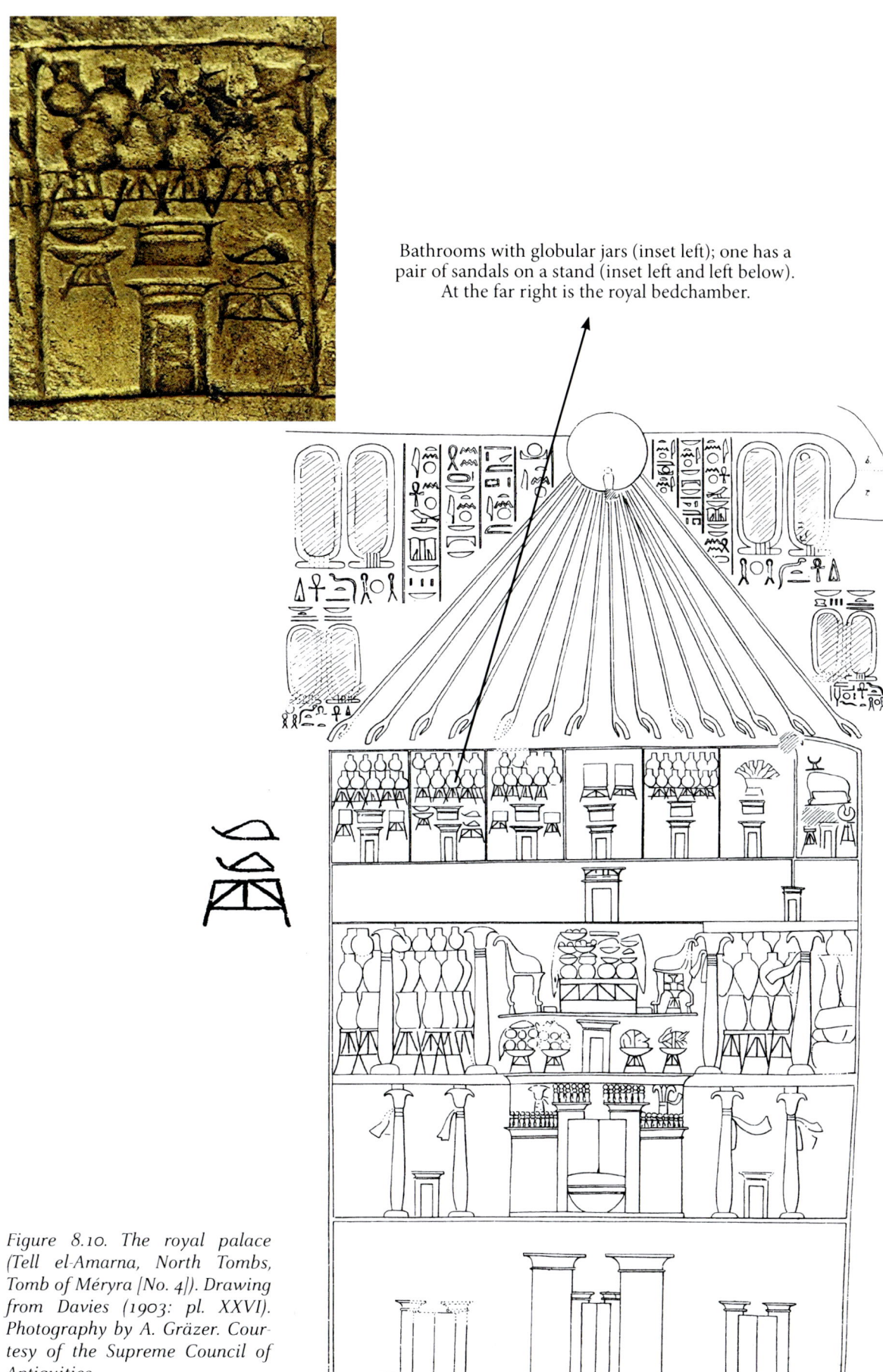

Bathrooms with globular jars (inset left); one has a pair of sandals on a stand (inset left and left below). At the far right is the royal bedchamber.

Figure 8.10. The royal palace (Tell el-Amarna, North Tombs, Tomb of Méryra [No. 4]). Drawing from Davies (1903: pl. XXVI). Photography by A. Gräzer. Courtesy of the Supreme Council of Antiquities.

215

cal approach, it does not cover the intricacy of the king's behaviour towards footwear entirely. For instance, it does not take into account the double nature (human/divine) particular to the Egyptian Pharaoh: on the one hand, as a normal *per se* personage holding a high social status and, on the other hand, as a person in charge of a divine function. Once more, archaeology provides some hints. The marquetry veneer sandals (397, described in section 3.2.2.1) are particularly meaningful. If we consider their general aspects, they do not differ in shape from the fibre ones, making it impossible to distinguish between them in depictions. In the same time, we notice that their material (wood being the main constituent) and construction refutes any use for active walking. They, as well as at least one other pair, bear typical royal symbols such as the bound enemies, emphasising the king's role.[40] Thus, royal footwear could also take on a ritual dimension, whether those sandals were actively (*i.e.* that the owner walked him/herself) worn or not.

The existence of sandals that were symbolic rather than functional seems to suggest that footwear belonged to the royal outfit anyway and might have been a distinctive attribute, in the same way as the regalia. A series of scenes can be interpreted as supporting this hypothesis (figure 8.13): a set of blocks shows the successive stages of the king's toilette that took place inside the *rwd-mnw* bathroom. The king, after having cleansed his body, is gradually putting on elements of the royal outfit. By this concrete means (*i.e.* the wearing of regalia), he is vested with the royal function. If we base our reasoning on Vergnieux's tentative reconstruction (Vergnieux, 1999: pl. XLIa [A0036]: see figure 8.13), it appears that sandals were also put on during this symbolical ceremony.[41] This assertion rests on the following points:

1) In the extreme left of the preserved sequence, the king is depicted barefoot while he appears shod in the next scenes;

2) On the lower register, a large number of sandals were arranged near chests for garments and globular water jars intended for the royal purification.[42]

Ritualised as the royal daily life was, it is hardly surprising that wearing sandals in every context expressed, for the king, much more than a simple social display. A number of questions remain unsolved nevertheless: for instance, were sandals intended for protecting their bearer symbolically from the ground, or conversely for protecting a sacred area from its visitor? A thorough investigation focusing on depictions of Akhenaten inside the temple area would probably help to clarify the exact symbolic and liturgical dimension of royal footwear. This iconographical study remains to be done.[43]

For all that, does it mean that the king and the queen really wore sandals in every daily circumstance? The question is worth being raised since we cannot dismiss the possibility that some restrictive iconographical conventions had interfered with the faithful and accurate reproduction of life. Indeed, the depiction of distinctive attributes (including sandals) might also have worked as visual signs helping to identify the king and his wife in a picture: this could explain why the royal couple always appears fully dressed, even in scenes of purification shower or procreation. Moreover, we must take into account that, in the Egyptian mind, image was always coupled with a virtual dimension. According to the well known Egyptian belief, image was performative: in other words, by means of a picture, it was possible to make something or someone exist forever or make an action fulfilled. To bring such a virtual efficiency, the image had to be detailed and

> *Figure 8.11. The royal palace (Tell el-Amarna, South Tombs, Tomb of Parennefer [No. 7]). Drawing from Davies (1908b: p. IV). Photography by A. Gräzer. Courtesy of the Supreme Council of Antiquities.*

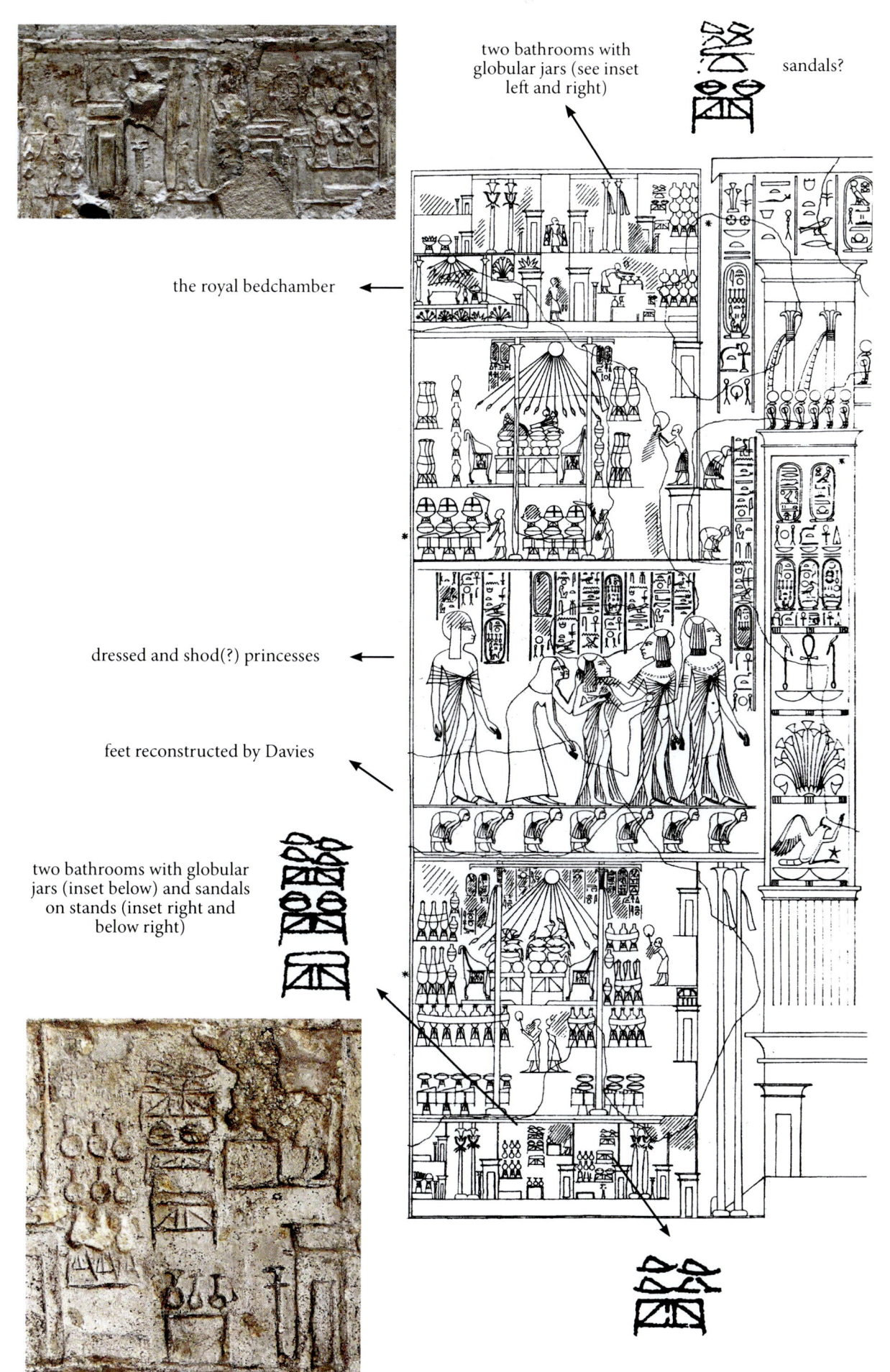

Footwear in Late New Kingdom Art

two bathrooms with globular jars (see inset left and right)

sandals?

the royal bedchamber

dressed and shod(?) princesses

feet reconstructed by Davies

two bathrooms with globular jars (inset below) and sandals on stands (inset right and below right)

217

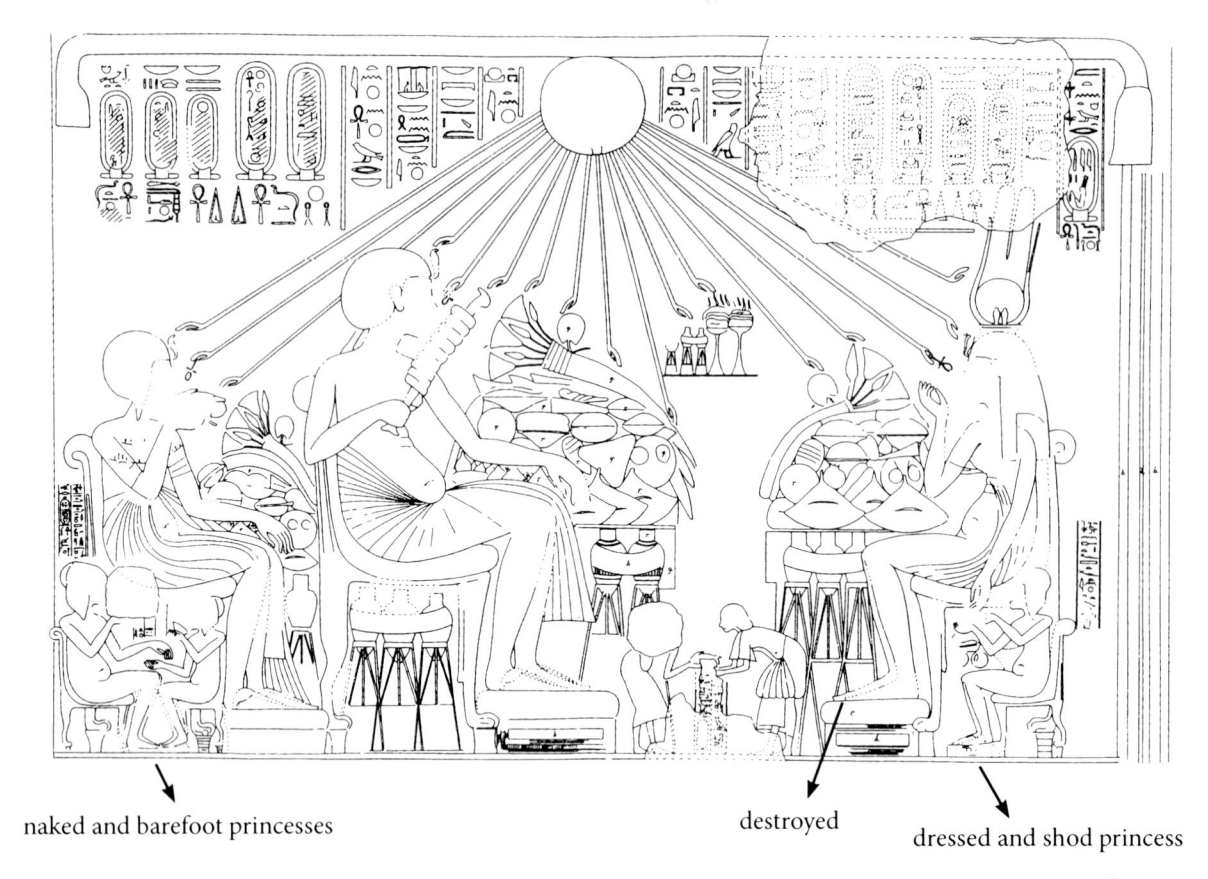

naked and barefoot princesses destroyed dressed and shod princess

Figure 8.12. The royal family having a meal in the palace (Tell el-Amarna, North Tombs, Tomb of Huya [No. 1]). From Davies (1905b: pl. IV).

distinctive. Once more, systematically portraying the king with all his royal attributes, including sandals, did, therefore, make sense. The multifaceted aspect of footwear in Egyptian depictions prompts us, however, to be cautious with a rigid 'realistic' theory. During the deduction process, the commentator must indeed bear in mind the iconographical grammar which sometimes overtakes the principle of mimesis (the mere reproduction of reality). In this way, the Egyptian iconographical study often requires us to put into perspective the plausibility of Pharaonic depictions.[44] To conclude about the nature of royal footwear depicted in Amarnian indoor scenes, it appears that its omnipresence on the king's feet owed to iconographical requisites as much as to social and ritual motives.

8.1.3.4 The Royal Children

If we focus on depictions of the king's daughters, we can observe the same phenomenon as noticed for their parents: the princesses wore Type C sewn sandals and appear shod in both public and private contexts.[45] This parallelism might indicate that Amarnian princesses' footwear conveyed the same triple overtone (social/ritual/iconographical) as royal sandals.

Yet, examining a large corpus of pictures staging the royal princesses inside the palace, we can ascribe a further function to the footwear depiction. Once more, sandals presumably functioned here as an iconographical tool: in a number of cases, the youngest royal daughters appear nude and barefoot (figures 8.12 & 8.15),[46] which suggests that the absence of footwear constituted a visual indicator of child status (like nakedness). Conversely, their presence (combined with other garments) could have characterised nubile princesses (figures 8.11(?) & 8.12 [see Baketaten in the right hand corner of the figure]).[47]

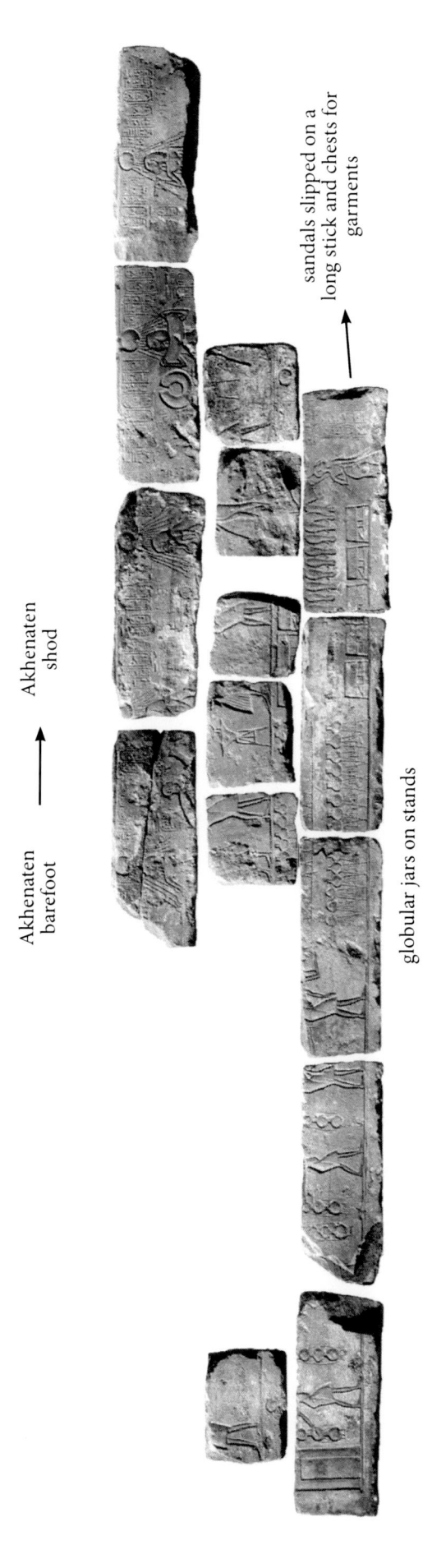

Figure 8.13. The toilette of the king in the royal bathroom (talatats from the IXth pylon of Karnak Amen Temple). From Vergnieux (1999: pl. XLIa [reconstructed A0036]).

Figure 8.14. Akhenaten and Nefertiti standing next to the royal bed (talatats from the IXth pylon of Karnak Amen Temple, Nos. 31/216 and 31/203). Photography by A. Bellod. Courtesy of the Centre Franco Egyptien d'Etude des Temples de Karnak.

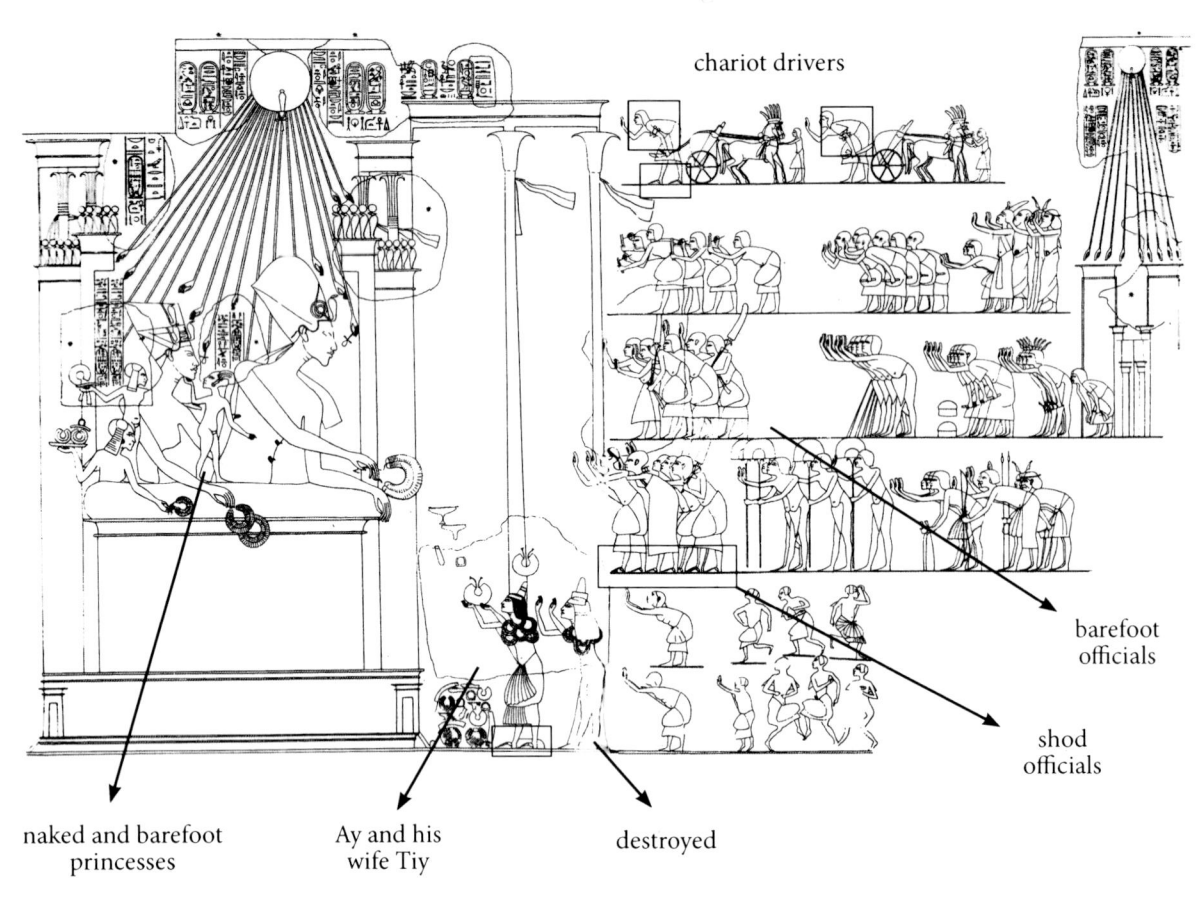

Figure 8.15. Reward ceremony in the royal palace staging Ay and his wife Tiy (Tell el-Amarna, South Tombs, Tomb of Ay [No. 25]). From Davies (1908b: pl. XXIX).

8.1.3.5 Dignitaries

The last category of depictions is that of the Amarnian dignitaries. Surprisingly, however, no intimate scenes were found. The disproportion between the abundance of pictures showing royal intimacy and the lack of scenes staging individuals inside their own houses has to be imputed to the ideology peculiar to Atonism. Indeed, driven by this new religious current, Amarnian artists created unprecedented pictures of the royal family's private life, as so many metaphors of the divine solar mechanism which rules, regulates and regenerates the world every day.[48] Conversely, they restricted individuals' daily life to their active role in running the Egyptian society and in serving the king and his new cult. In all likelihood, non-royal intimacy was of no use for expressing the principles of Atonism. The close connection that links Amarna iconography to Akhenaten's new ideology makes sense when considering our iconographical material. Every character is depicted while accomplishing his assigned task:

1) Domestic staff are running private houses (figures 8.4, 8.5 & 8.7) as well as the king's palace (figures 8.9-8.11 & 8.13);

2) Personages of high social standard are serving the king in his daily life (see Huya in figure 8.12) or participating in royal ceremonies inside the palace court (mainly reward ceremonies; see for instance figure 8.15).

It is in such ceremonial contexts that footwear can be observed on dignitaries' feet. A glance at depictions of reward ceremonies inside the palace (figure 8.15) allows the following observations:

1) In the foreground, the personages rewarded by the king from his 'window of appearance' are wearing Type C sewn sandals together with the famous golden collars[49];

2) In the background of the scene, several unnamed but important figures of the royal court[50] attend the ceremony, some of them appearing shod (Type C sewn sandals) while the others are barefoot;

3) finally, a few servants, such as chariot drivers or bearers,[51] working for the persons mentioned with 1) and 2) also appear shod while waiting for their master. Once more, those figures wear Type C fibre, sewn sandals.

In the absence of distinctive attributes or texts indicating their identity (cases 2 and 3),[52] only the presence of footwear constitutes a means of distinguishing between them. Then, which message are Type C sandals here supposed to convey?

If we base our reasoning upon the coherence of the iconographical construction, sandals introduce a slight social nuance here between characters belonging to a same group. However, could we not go one step further in the grasp of footwear connotation? When comparing the reliefs in Amarna private tombs, we notice that, when the deceased who were honoured by the king chose to be portrayed with their golden collars on either side of their tomb entrance, they also happen to have Type C sewn sandals on their feet.[53] Does this mean that these sandals are a marker displaying royal favour? A further comparison between Panehesy's and Ay's Amarnian tomb reliefs goes in favour of this theory. As already mentioned, Panehesy and Ay were both honoured by the king; they consequently wear sandals in almost every depiction. But, if we consider their wives' feet, we notice that Panehesy's wife is barefoot[54] while Ay's wife, Tiy, appears shod.[55] Yet, we know that Tiy was rewarded together with her husband by king Akhenaten in the palace (figure 8.15). This unusual case tends to prove that a connection existed between wearing these sandals and royal reward.[56]

To conclude, the last part of the survey devoted to footwear inside domestic areas, it seems quite obvious that Type C fibre, sewn sandals constituted a social status marker for individuals, which sometimes helped to emphasize attributes such as the well known golden collars granted to dignitaries who were honoured by the king. I would even dare to suppose that such sandals were only worn during special occasions (for instance, attending official ceremonies inside the palace) and have nothing to do with everyday utilitarian sandals. A possible proof from an archaeological point of view could be the minimal wear on the Type C specimens discovered in tombs (Veldmeijer, 2009a).[57]

8.1.4 Footwear Outside Domestic Areas: Some Remarks

André J. Veldmeijer

The investigation of footwear in two-dimensional art has barely begun, and the present section, therefore, will be limited to some general observations and thus far less elaborate than the previous sections.[58]

The predominance of sewn sandals is also visible but again seen only with high-ranking persons. An example is the Amun procession in the Temple of Luxor. Here, the lower legs of the Pharaoh are just visible, showing he is shod with sewn sandals (figure 8.1C). The priests that carry the barque, however, are shod in leather sandals (figure 8.1D).[59] Scenes, seemingly showing Tutankhamun and his wife in a leisurely activity either shows them unshod, but more often with sewn sandals on their feet.[60] The fact that sewn sandals have a strong connection with official ceremonies, suggests that these scenes might have a similar connotation. In scenes involving gods, royals might go barefoot, but often they are shod. Gods and deities, however, never are. For example in the tomb of Tutankhamun, south wall, west part (the doorway between the Antechamber and the Burial Chamber on the left). Here, Tutankhamun, followed by the god Anubis, receives life from the goddess Hathor, 'Mistress of Heaven, Chieftainess of the West' (text adapted from the website of the Griffith Institute; figure 8.16B). Another example can be seen on the north wall, where Ay, dressed as *sem* priest performs the 'Opening of the Mouth Ceremony'. He is the only one wearing (sewn) sandals (figure 8.16C).

We have already seen that footwear is often mentioned in literature, and Schwarz (2000: 229) lists the professions for which footwear were a commodity, such as travellers and soldiers.[61] Mortals often go unshod but there are, nevertheless, indications (besides those from the archaeological record) that footwear was not as exceptional as sometimes suggested in secondary literature. The depictions suggest that they are predominantly of non-ceremonial nature: for example, people are shown wearing sandals during work. In the tomb of Khaemhat, for example, "a harvesting scene shows men threshing and women with baskets picking up in the field.

Figure 8.16A) East wall (partly above the doorway between the Burial Chamber and the Treasury). 'Friends' and officials of the palace dragging a sledge with the sarcophagus; > B) Tutankhamun, followed by the god Anubis, receives life from the goddess Hathor, 'Mistress of Heaven, Chieftainess of the West.' [The king is shod in sewn sandals; the gods are barefoot]; > C) Tomb of Tutankhamun, North wall. Three scenes, from left; 1) Tutankhamun, followed by his ka, embraced by Osiris; 2) Tutankhamun welcomed by the goddess Nut; 3) King Ay (Tutankhamun's successor) performs the Opening-the-Mouth ceremony on the mummy of Tutankhamun (text from the website of the Griffith Institute; between [ ] inserted by the author). Photography by H. Burton. Copyright Griffith Institute, University of Oxford.

B

C

It contains an odd depiction of a man leaping up to press down the lid on a huge basket of grain." (Pinch-Brock, 2001a: 366). The sandal this man wears shows a pre- and heel strap and most likely are made of leather. Another example is the men catching quail from the tomb of Nebamun (Parkinson, 2008: 118). The men are shod in red sandals that include a pre- and heel strap. The shape as well as colour suggests that they were made of leather.

8.2 THREE-DIMENSIONAL ART

André J. Veldmeijer

The identification of the sandals is unmistakable in all of the three-dimensional art from the tomb in which the Pharaoh is shown shod: sewn sandals. Intriguingly, the degree of detail differs, although the straps are always plain. The guard-statues (022 and 029) have sewn sandals "made in bronze and overlaid with gold" (Card No. 022-4) but without details of the transverse bundles. Other statuettes, which show the king in various manifestations, however, do show details of the sole's fabric, but none of them include details of the sewing. One statuette (275a) is barefoot. Interestingly, the statuettes themselves are made of wood with gesso and gilt, whereas in all statuettes of which Carter mentions the material, the sandals are made of gilded bronze. One wonders if this is to emphasize the importance of sandals or due to a more practical reason. A distinction in detail is also seen in the objects recovered: shoes 021k & l only show the transverse bundles, but shoes 021f & g have added details of the sewing strips. Gods and goddesses are usually depicted without sandals.

CHAPTER 9

DISCUSSION

9.1 TYPOLOGY

The typology in table 9.1 is preliminary and contains only part of the typology thus far developed by the AEFP, but it already demonstrates the enormous variety in footwear. In ancient Egypt, several types of fibre and leather sandals were made, each with their own variants. The fibre sandals from Tutankhamun are all sewn sandals Type C (most are Variant 1, several Variant 2). All other sandals use simulations of the texture of the fibre, sewn sandal (sewn sandals Type D, Imitations).

There are two types of shoes in ancient Egypt (table 9.1), but one should realise that the identification of a piece of footwear as 'shoe' largely depends on definition. The AEFP, as explained in the glossary, regards all footwear with a closed heel as 'shoe'. Two categories can be distinguished: open shoes and closed shoes, with the former being the only category which includes examples made of fibre as well. Since closed shoes are not among the footwear from Tutankhamun, the focus here is on the open shoes. According to Veldmeijer (2009h) within the open shoes, difference can be made between those with a partial upper (which start at about one-quarter of the length from the front of the sole) and those in which the upper runs around the entire perimeter of the sole. These latter, the ones with the full upper, can be divided in two variants: the upright upper (Variant 1) and the flexible upper (Variant 2). Full upper, open shoes were not among Tutankhamun's footwear either. The fibre open shoe, with a full but flexible upper is much younger and appeared as late as the 3rd century AD (Veldmeijer, In press a; see also Veldmeijer & Endenburg, 2008). However, it is possible that these shoes have an earlier (Roman?) precedent, but the research is still in progress and is much hindered by lack of reliable dates.

The origin of closed shoes and its introduction in Egypt is not clear but usually the introduction of the closed shoe is linked with the Hittites in the 18th Dynasty (Van Driel-Murray, 2000: 316). It might, however, be much earlier: it has been suggested (Veldmeijer, 2009c) that certain leather curled-toe ankle shoes (such as seen in figure 6.21) may have been made as part of chariot equipment (including the leather siding of the body itself, quivers and bow cases) and hence introduced together with the chariot.[1] The arrival of the chariot in Egypt is dated to the Second Intermediate Period with the Hyksos. Veldmeijer (2009c: 12) questions if Tutankhamun's open shoes and chariots are related too: "Most of his [Tutankhamun's] chariots are elaborately decorated with inlay work rather than dressed with red-and-green leatherwork. His [Tutankhamun's] footwear is equally elaborately decorated with gold beadwork and, in one case, with inlays of gemstones."

The origin of the open shoe and its first appearance in Egypt is not well understood either. However, Petrie (1890: 28) mentions leather shoes from the 12th Dynasty town of Kahun, which are similar in layout to the well known fibre ones in that "all of them have the leather sandal strap between the toes, and joining to the sides of the heel, to

Kind of footwear	Category	Type	Variant
Fibre Sandal	Sewn	A)	1) Plain
			2) Leather treadsole
		B)	1) Plain
			2) Leather treadsole
		C)	1) Plain
			2) Linen insole
		D) Imitations	1) Wood
			2) Leather / rawhide with covering (incl. beads) (021h & I; 085a/147a; 453b?)
			3) Metal only (256ll)
	Sewn-Edge Plaited	A)	1) - 3)
		B)	1) - 4)
		C)	1) - 2)
		D)	1) - 4)
		E)	
Leather Sandal	Composite	A)	
		B)	1)
			2)
		C)	
Fibre Shoe	Open Shoe	A) Fibre. Partial Upper	1) Sandal-like Strap Complex
		B) Fibre. Full Upper	1) Upright Upper
			2) Flexible Upper
Leather Shoe	Open Shoe	Partial Upper	1) Sandal-like Strap Complex
			2) Combined Lace / Sandal-like Strap Complex
Leather Shoe	Closed Shoe	A) Curled-Toe Ankle	1) i)
			ii)
			2)
			Uncertain
		B) Stubbed-Toe Low Ankle	
Combined materials	Open Shoe	Partial Upper: leather	Front Strap / Toe Band / Foot Straps / Instep Strap (270a)
		Partial Upper: leather & beadwork	Sewn Sandal Strap Complex / Foot strap (021f & g; 453b?)
			Foot Strap / Instep Strap (021k & l)

Table 9.1. Partial, preliminary typology of ancient Egyptian footwear. In bold are those types of which examples are amongst Tutankhamun's footwear. The elaborate combined fastenings in the open shoes play an important role in the typology of the king's footwear.

retain the sole on the foot; the upper leather being stitched on merely as a covering without its being intended to hold the shoe on the foot." The shoes have not been traced yet and hence have not been studied by the author (but see Veldmeijer, 2009f). A possible link between open and closed shoes is suggested by a pair of open shoes in the British Museum, London (*Ibidem*) and a link between leather sandals and open shoes on the basis of a pair of open shoes in the Cairo collection (Veldmeijer, In press c).

The open shoes from Tutankhamun are unique in terms of combination of materials, which warrant a division from the other known open shoes, hence the group 'combined materials' as opposed to 'fibre' and 'leather'. Moreover, the fastening or closure methods differ from anything thus far known from Pharaonic Egypt. Even in the case of the familiar 'sewn sandal strap complex'[2] (021f & g), the combination of used materials is, in itself, extraordinary. The use of this type of strap complex in open shoes is not seen elsewhere: usually the strap complex in open shoes is less elaborate and basically consists of a core, clad with strips of palm leaf and having a circular cross-section throughout. Moreover, the strap complex in Tutankhamun's shoes is combined with other means of fastenings: foot straps. The ancient Egyptians were very reluctant to use anything other than the straps that go between the toes; foot straps are only known from the tomb of Tutankhamun and might very well be borrowed from foreign examples (see below). Differentiation between 021f & g and 021k & l on the one hand, and the 270a on the other is made as the upper of the former pairs are made of an inner layer of leather, which is on the outside, covered with gold beadwork. This differs from the two-layer upper on 270a in the fact that this upper consists of two layers of leather, the outer layer consisting of openwork leather. This is a good example where recognisability is an important characteristic to separate them into two types.

The separation into variants in the type 'partial upper, leather and beadwork' (table 9.1) is made on the basis of the closure method, which are distinctly different (instep strap versus sewn sandal strap complex) and hence warrant the differentiation. The two pairs of shoes in this type share, however, one part of the method, *viz.* the foot strap. Although 270a is separated on the basis of the upper and sole, the closure method is, to a certain extent, comparable with the two variants of the 'partial upper, leather and beadwork' Type: 270a shares with 021k & l the instep strap (although of entirely different layout) and shares a foot strap with 021f & g and 021k & l. Like 021f & g, 270a has a front strap, but again, of an entirely different layout. Unique to 270a is the toe band, a feature not known from Pharaonic Egypt and which strongly suggests foreign influence: in the Near East, open shoes were worn this way.[3]

Often, the shape of soles is used (too) in classifying footwear. For the footwear from Tutankhamun, however, this is less useful: all footwear items have soles that are comparable to the shape of fibre, sewn sandals Type C.

The study of archaeological objects, combined with two-dimensional art, suggests that a typology solely on the basis of representations is of limited use. The archaeological record shows a much larger variety than shown in two-dimensional art, often characterised by small, but significant details. Moreover, many types of footwear have not been depicted at all.[4] Finally, the representations are standardised, focussing on the most characteristic elements and hence miss some parts of the sandals (*e.g.* multiple sole layers). The representations of seemingly the same type of footwear might differ due to other factors: different artists, topic of the scene where the footwear is depicted, relief/painted or both, nature of the surface etc.

9.2 PHILOLOGY

Linking sandals mentioned in texts proved more difficult than one would expect: there are far more types of sandals than words that go with them. The philological sources occasionally differentiate between men's and women's sandals, but the archaeology suggests this difference is only in terms of size. It has been suggested that closed shoes were for women only, but again this is based on their size rather than their context (Van Driel-Murray, 2000: 315). The importance of the identification of the material from which fibre footwear is made is emphasized by the problems of translating Egyptian words for various materials. Identification of parts of sandals in text proved equally problematic. Texts mention sandal-makers but whether they made all footwear is not certain. However, the inclusion of fibre footwear in leatherworking scenes (if they can be regarded as belonging to them) suggests as much. Strangely enough, not much time was spent elaborating on the process of manufacturing fibre footwear in texts (or two-dimensional representations).

It is not clear whether the term 'enveloping sandals' referred to open shoes or to the closed shoes, or both, but one could argue that, taking the usual sandal-like straps of open shoes into account, reference is made to open rather than closed shoes.

9.3 ART

Although linking two-dimensional representations of footwear with archaeological examples often proved difficult if not impossible, one can be fairly certain about the identification of the fibre, sewn sandals, as has been shown in chapter 8. This type of sandal is recognisable beyond doubt in three-dimensional art. The study of footwear in indoor spaces clearly shows the status of this footwear, and a link with other social markers can be detected (see below), which might also explain the fact that they are recognisable in art. The sewing technique to produce sandals is an old tradition (Veldmeijer, 2009a) and no examples are known from outside Egypt. In this respect, it is interesting to see fibre, sewn sandals Type A among the products from the Dakhlah Oasis (rather than from Nubia as suggested by Wendrich, 2000: 266[5]), as depicted in Rekhmira's tomb chapel (Davies, 1943: 46, pl. XLIX; see figure 8.2).[6] The objects were meant as goods assigned to the temple, and included sandals (see chapter 7) along with other goods.

9.4 REVISION OF PREVIOUS WORK

For obvious reasons, there is no need to discuss secondary literature in detail. It is more interesting and productive to look at professional accounts on (Tutankhamun's) footwear.

Van Driel-Murray (2000: 314) notes that the sandals are identical to Old and Middle Kingdom sandals. Indeed, as explained by Veldmeijer (2009a), the *manufacturing technique* of the fibre sandals dates back to at least Middle Kingdom times and possibly earlier but the shape, in combination with the manufacturing technology, does not occur before the New Kingdom. The lack of dated finds seriously hinders the establishment of the rise of the sewn sandal Type C tradition but the peak is seen in the later 18th and early 19th Dynasties.

Although sewn sandals are usually made of cores of halfa grass, sewn with dom palm leaf and straps of papyrus, examples from the tomb of Yuya and Tjuiu, and an isolated find from Sedment currently in the Petrie Museum, London, shows that caution is required when making general statements about the material of a particular type of sandal. The identification of the material in the cores of the edge construction supports this warning: sometimes they seem to have been made of grass, although they are usually made of palm. These elements of the sandals in particular need specialised microscopic analyses.

It is a matter of taste to call a technology 'sophisticated' (Van Driel-Murray, 2000: 314). The close relationship between Tutankhamun's shoes and the curled-toe ankle shoes, mentioned by Van Driel-Murray (*Ibidem*), does not exist, as the two types are clearly different unless both were originally part of the chariot assemblage. The most important difference is the fact that the uppers in the king's shoes only cover the sides and heel of the foot (open shoes) whereas in the ankle shoes, the whole foot is covered (closed shoes).

9.5 NON-FIBRE FOOTWEAR: FOREIGN AND UNIQUE?

It has been suggested that the decorated shoes and sandals might have been foreign. The description of footwear in the Amarna letters (Moran, 1992: 53) could apply to Tutankhamun's footwear. However, the decorated footwear is based on a typically Egyptian footwear category, sewn sandals, and, if decorated, shows Egyptian motifs. However, some motifs did occur in other areas as well. Feldman (2006: 67, 68, 78, 81ff) recognises the voluted palmettes (in the present work referred to as 'lily'), seen in 021f & g, as a hybrid rendering of several plants (*i.e.* the deliberate modification in such a way that it is more generic; still recognisable, but without the details that would link the shape of this motif to a particular region): palm, lily and lotus[7] and are often used in high profile objects that were used as gifts between the so-called 'Great Kings' (international *koiné*). Even though in some cases, hybridization indeed has been convincingly proven by Feldman for high profile objects, the arguments for the lily-motif as a hybrid rendering is less convincing. Moreover, the shoes seem much too Egyptian to be part of an international *koiné*.[8]

The use of gold and some gemstones (such as lapis lazuli and carnelian) surely points to royal items, but it is too early to conclude that these shoes were gifts from abroad. Moreover, according to James Harrell (section 4.2.2) and Jack Ogden (section 4.2.3), there is nothing specifically that suggests foreign craftsmanship and indeed, the quality and techniques of the goldwork fits well with the rest of the goldwork found in the tomb. The same could be said about the construction techniques, which are comparable to other open shoes, except, of course, for the use of different materials. Having said this, the shoes do show remarkably innovative features, expressed mainly in the way they were held to the foot. Some of these, such as the use of straps that run over the foot to either side or the toe strap, through which the toes were inserted, are known from Asia Minor. But whether this has any connection to ones from the tomb is as yet unclear, which is partly due to our lack of knowledge of footwear from these regions. An alternative interpretation to identifying these features as hybrid shoes, is that the Egyptians could have taken elements over to use them in their own types of footwear. As an aside: note the presence of a foot strap in the open shoes in a Meroitic painting from Qasr Ibrim. As explained, in ancient Egypt, closed shoes have not been depicted[9] but they do occur occasionally in Nubian two- and three-dimensional art.

The lack of finds from a comparable context (*i.e.* royal tomb) makes it difficult to know whether the 'non-sewn sandals' were unique for Tutankhamun or not. One can be sure, of course, that such elaborately decorated, expensive footwear are only to be expected in contexts of higher social class, but despite the reference by the excavators to some of the shoes as 'court slippers,' there is no indication at all (be it philological, iconographic or archaeological) as to the more specific (symbolic) use of this footwear (but see above about the possible link with chariots). Thus, one cannot exclude the possibility that this or comparable footwear might also have been worn by other wealthy people and indeed, the footwear found on Tjuiu's feet seems to be such an example. Metal sandals, such as Tutankhamun's golden sandals, might have been much more widespread as is suggested by the finds in several tombs (Lilyquist, 2004: 133).

9.6 STATUS

Tutankhamun, and indeed all royals as far as can be inferred from a survey of 18th and 19th Dynasty two-dimensional art, are only depicted wearing sewn sandals Type C (when shod). Intriguingly, Tutankhamun (or any other king in these times, if one assume that they would have possessed a comparable collection of footwear) has not been depicted wearing the extraordinary footwear.[10] That the sewn sandals have been worn is evident from the wear; wear in the other footwear is difficult to prove due to their inferior preservation, but nevertheless indications of their use has been identified.

Persons of high social class, such as nobles, might have worn sewn sandals too, as is evidenced by the finds from, for example, the tomb of Yuya and Tjuiu. As explained in chapter 7, ordinary footwear was not particularly expensive, but nevertheless valuable enough to repair, as suggested by some of Yuya and Tjuiu's sandals.

As Aude Gräzer concluded "it seems quite obvious that Type C sewn sandals constituted for individuals a social status marker, which sometimes helped to emphasize attributes such as the well known golden collars granted to dignitaries who were honoured by the king. I would even dare to suppose that such sandals were only worn during special occasions (for instance, attending official ceremonies inside the palace) and have nothing to do with everyday utilitarian sandals." If this is true, this might indicate that everyday utilitarian footwear was not buried with the Pharaoh, or that the robbers took these with them.[11] One cannot, however, wholly ignore the possibility that the king used the sewn sandals in a utilitarian way. It is remarkable that seemingly ordinary sandals obtained such a high status: the deliberate working of the sheet gold to represent sewing in 021f & g even seems to replicate the colour of fibre. Exactly why and when these particular sandals made of grass and palm became so important is as yet not understood.

The difference in quality, as suggested by the comparison between the fibre, sewn sandals from Yuya and Tjuiu and Tutankhamun (*i.e.* the coarser ones and more refined ones respectively), cannot be observed in two-dimensional art. However, although the difference in archaeological examples is apparent, it would be convenient to have additional archaeological evidence from persons other than Yuya and Tjuiu, who are not related to the royal family, to be confident about this difference.

Interestingly, Tutankhamun's footwear falls more or less into two size-groups; child-sized footwear (except the pair of beaded leather sandals) is missing. Children's footwear, even for very young children, is not uncommon in Egypt, as is evidenced by finds of sandals in particular, fibre and leather alike. This in itself already suggests that footwear was not just for the 'rich and famous', an observation which is supported by the relatively low price, depictions of 'mortals' wearing sandals when working in the field, and numerous texts mentioning footwear in daily context. The size groups seem to coincide with Tutankhamun's succession to the throne: the group of smallest size footwear might have fit the king when he was about 10, the approximate age when he became king. This suggests that only the footwear he wore as a king was buried with him and not the footwear from before the succession. If this reasoning is correct, it emphasizes the importance of these sandals as social markers. The exception is, however, the pair of leather and bead sandals, for which an explanation is difficult. Could it be that Tutankhamun particularly liked this pair and hence kept them?

9.7 FINALLY

It is a pity that ancient Egyptian footwear has so long been neglected in the field of archaeology of Egypt/Egyptology as well as in more global studies of footwear. Even recently published books that include, for example, Greek footwear (Riello & McNeil, 2006), skip Egyptian footwear or only mention it in passing (Bossan, 2007) or not at all (Roder, 2008[8]). This is strange, as I dare say that the number of finds from Pharaonic Egypt compares to or, perhaps more likely, exceeds the number of finds from most other regions. Note that even footwear from foreign peoples, which have no chance of being preserved in their home country, have been found within the borders of Egypt. Among these are the Persian footwear found at Elephantine, and Nubian footwear.

Footwear is much more than a protective foot covering, and has considerable symbolic content. This is found in all societies, and Egypt was no exception, as the present work clearly shows. Although the systematic study of footwear by the AEFP already provides us with answers to many questions, especially relating to manufacturing technology, it has created many more questions that await answers.

NOTES

INTRODUCTION

1 The story is well known and much has been written about it. Some examples are of course Carter's readable volumes on the find (Carter & Mace, 1923; Carter, 1927; 1933) but more recently Reeves (1990a) and Hoving (1978). James (1992) is a good source of information about Carter himself.

2 The reader might notice that the aims of the Amarna Leatherwork Project (part of the Ancient Egyptian Leatherwork Project) are highly comparable. This is because, as we will see, leatherwork and footwear are intimately linked: leather footwear usually makes up the larger bulk of leather finds from an excavation. On the other hand, it is only a small part of all footwear known from ancient Egypt (see figure 2). The text here is for a large part quoted from Veldmeijer (2009b).

3 The objects in the following collections and from several excavations have been studied first-hand, to show that the conclusions of the AEFP can draw on a large sample. Note that attention is also given to the museological history of the objects (figure 1). Collections: Ägyptisches Museum und Papyrussammlung, Berlin – Ashmolean Museum, Oxford – British Museum, London – Egyptian Museum, Cairo – Kelsey Museum, Michigan (scheduled for 2010) – Luxor Museum, Luxor – The Manchester Museum, University of Manchester (scheduled for 2010) – Metropolitan Museum of Arts, New York – Museo Egizio, Turin – Museum of Fine Arts, Boston – National Museum of Antiquities, Leiden – National Museums of Scotland, Edinburgh – Oriental Institute Museum, Chicago – Petrie Museum of Egyptian Archaeology UCL, London – Roemer- und Pelizaeus-Museum, Hildesheim – Royal Ontario Museum, Toronto – Sammlung des Ägyptologischen Instituts der Universität, Heidelberg – World Museum, Liverpool. Excavations: Amarna Amenhotep II Temple Luxor – Berenike – Deir el-Bachit – Dra Abu el Naga – Elephantine – Hierakonpolis – Mersa/Wadi Gawasis – Qasr Ibrim.

4 The study of the tools, however, is not included here, as it is a project of its own. But see Schwarz (2000: 78-125) for a good overview, even though focussed on the leatherworker (but these might also be the sandal-maker.

5 One of the most important finds if it comes to foreign footwear: in most areas in the Middle East, preservation circumstances are far less favourable for organic materials than in Egypt. The finds from Elephantine have been published; a supplement, discussing lacking details is forthcoming.

6 Alfano (1987) bases a typology on two-dimensional art and distinguish, according to Schwarz (2000: 217-218), four types: "*Typ A und C [...] sind in der Aufmachung sehr ähnlich, indem beide zwei Seitenriemen besitzen, die an einer flachen Sohle ansetzen und sich auf dem Fußrist treffen. Typ A besitzt ein senkrechtes Zwischenstück, das von der Sohle bis an den schräg geführten Ristriemen reicht, während bei Typ C die Riemen direct an der Sohle ansetzen. [...] Typ B wird gekennzeichnet durch eine aufgebogene Spitze [...], während Typ D einen Fersenriemen*

besitzt. Alfano nimmt mit ihrer Einteilung keine Rücksicht auf eine chronologische Abfolge." Cherpion (1999) based a typology of Old Kingdom sandals on representations too. As might be clear from section 8.1.1 and 8.1.2, a typology solely on the basis of iconography suggests a picture which is (largely) unusable in reconstructing the use of footwear in an ancient society. A more detailed discussion is forthcoming.

7   Of seemingly lesser importance for the present work is footwear from Nubia, but since the exact relationship between 'indigenous' and 'foreign' footwear is not well understood (*cf.* the remarks about the 'Nubian' sewn sandals tribute in chapter 9), the work of Williams (1983: 71-75) should be mentioned, who established a typology of sandals from the C-Group.

8   With shoes, this is different, as in appearance comparable shoes can be made in different ways, for example with or without rand (not present in early Egyptian footwear, but see for example the Christian [Veldmeijer & Van Driel-Murray, In preparation] and Ottoman shoes from Qasr Ibrim [Veldmeijer, In preparation a]; see the short overview by Veldmeijer & Endenburg, 2008). This, in its turn, can be originally designed but can also be due to repair, the exact origin of which in many cases cannot be determined anymore. Furthermore, the appearance of a shoe is important, evidenced for example by the fact that inserts are always placed in such a way that they are hard to notice, *i.e.* at the medial side of the shoe (note in this respect the large decorative patches in curled-toe ankle shoes to obscure the back seam [Veldmeijer, 2009d]). In sandals, a good example for the same technology but different shapes are some types of sewn-edge plaited sandals (Veldmeijer, Accepted) and fibre composite sandals.

9   See also Murray & Nuttall (1963).
10 See the annotated glossary (appendix II).
11 The decision to use these terms is to avoid confusion with describing the upper in closed shoes. Although these were not recovered from Tutankhamun's tomb, in order to be consistent throughout the AEFP, the terminology is used here as well. Note, however, that they are not used exclusively (see also the annotated glossary).
12 The reader is referred to Schwarz (2000: 82-83, 101-102) for a more detailed account.

CHAPTER 1: CONTEXT

1   054y=122www=G 54 in Littauer & Crouwel (1985: 44, see pl. XLVII [www]).

2   Card No. 122rrryy. 100d=122rrr=G 49 in Littauer & Crouwel (1985: 44, see pl. XLVII [rrr]).

3   122ttt=122uuu=122vvv=G 51/G 52 & G 53 respectively in Littauer & Crouwel (1985: 44, see pl. XLVII [ttt/uuu/vvv]).

4   This excludes the 10 golden toe stalls.

5   Exhibition Number 1262.

6   As well as the objects that were not footwear, as explained above (054y, 085e and 100d). The number of objects is contra Reeves (1990a: 157), who records 17 pieces.

7   For a description of the box and the views of its contents see Carter & Mace (1923: 110-112; pl. L-LIV); see also Card Nos. 021-1-8 (note the three additional cards by Mrs. de Garis Davies 021-01-03). Beinlich & Saleh (1989: 6-10) and Reeves (1990a: 157) list the contents of the box. The box itself was published by Davies & Gardiner (1962).

8   There is only one. See also card no. 367abc.

CHAPTER 2: PRESERVATION AND CONSERVATION

1   This condition is often referred to as 'melting'.

2   More on the chemical mechanisms of deterioration of leather in Trommer (2005) but see Florian (2006) for an introduction.

3   See also Card No. 85a.

4   It is not entirely sure what Carter means with "tops," but most likely the gold decoration on the openwork back strap.

CHAPTER 3: DESCRIPTION

1 See also section 4.1.1 (and figure 4.1).
2 Most are in excellent condition, prohibiting a view of the cores.
3 There is some variation in the pre/back strap construction in other sewn sandals, see Veldmeijer (2009a).
4 The description of the manufacturing of sewn sandals has been published previously by Veldmeijer (2009a) and is largely quoted here. The text as well as the references are adjusted. Additional remarks can be found with the description of the individual sandals. The manufacturing of the other footwear is inserted in the description.
5 An interesting find from Amarna is a wooden 'shoe-pattern' (Peet & Woolley, 1923: 69, pl. XX, 2), which might have functioned as a template. See Veldmeijer (2009b).
6 Seemingly, the sandals of Yuya and Tjuiu are an exception (table 10) but note the confusion in identifying pairs.
7 This might have been done previously, as suggested by Veldmeijer (2009a: 568) but it would be much easier and more likely that they were applied after the pre-straps were attached to the sole.
8 According to the archive in the Egyptian Museum Cairo, JE 62689 has Museum Number 4293. However, the specimens in the museum are labelled number 4294. To avoid confusion with JE 62690, the JE number is used as identification in the present work, as these are the numbers written on the ventral surface of the sole. Pair; the right sandal is housed in the Luxor Museum (see section 3.2.1.2); the left in the Egyptian Museum Cairo.
9 According to the archive in the Egyptian Museum Cairo, JE 62690 has Museum Number 4294. However, the specimens in the museum are labelled number 4293. To avoid confusion with JE 62689, the JE number is used as identification in the present work, as these are the numbers written on the ventral surface of the sole. The left sandal is in the Luxor Museum; the right in Cairo's Egyptian Museum. It is clear that these 'pairs' are not pairs originally: it seems beyond doubt that the left in 'pair' JE 62689 and the right in 'pair' JE 62690 belong together.
10 Perhaps the oils, either the natural form from that person's foot or perhaps oils applied to the skin as part of a ritual, helped make the palm leaf more supple and less brittle? This interesting suggestion by Joanne Ballard certainly needs further investigation and will be included in the experimental phase.
11 The left one shows evidence of an insole and is discussed in section 3.2.1.2.
12 The right sandal of JE 62690, of which the presence of an insole is uncertain, is discussed in section 3.2.1.1.
13 According to the archive in Cairo's Egyptian Museum, JE 62689 has Museum Number 4293. However, the specimen in the museum has number 4294. To avoid confusion with JE 62690, the JE number is used for identification purposes in the present work, as these are the numbers written on the ventral surface of the sole. The right sandal of the pair is housed in the Luxor Museum; the left in Cairo's Egyptian Museum (described in section 3.2.1.1).
14 The right one is discussed in section 3.2.1.1.
15 The material, however, has not been analysed. Carter refers to the white material as 'stucco' (Card. No. 397) but Lucas (1927: 167, 172) explains that gesso, a white plaster containing glue (but see Aston *et al.*, 2000: 22), was normally used to cover wood before gilding or decoration with other materials (see for example Gale *et al.*, 2000: 367) and, generally, before painting (see also Newman & Halpine, 2001: 23, 25). More generally it was used to adhere thin, decorative surfaces to objects (see for example Ogden, 2000: 160, 164, 166) as well as in the production of *cartonnage* (see for example Leach & Tait, 2000: 243). Since it contains glue, it is more likely to have been used here.

16   However, on the lateral side of the heel of the right sandal, the gesso layer is visible in between the first green strip with diamonds and the second set of white strips, seemingly contradicting the suggestion that the entire dorsal surface is covered with leather. Consequently, it cannot be entirely excluded that this is either damage of the leather layer or something is missing from it.

17   The description is done from outside in.

18   See section 4.2.3.5.

19   Other indications of different craftsmen are explained in section 4.2.3.5.

20   See also section 4.2.3.5.

21   Amazingly, even though Carter's notes are clear about the number of bows, the literature often mentions nine bows (for example Reeves, 1990a: 155; Vogelsang-Eastwood, 1994: 144; Goffoet, 1992: 119; Welsh, 1993: 48).

22   For Tutankhamun's composite bows see McLeod (1970).

23   Bow terminology is after McLeod (1970: 4).

24   See also section 4.2.1.

25   Comparable techniques are used in necklaces (*e.g.* Markowitz & Shear, 2001).

26   More on this in section 4.2.3.5.

27   *Ibidem.*

28   Note that this classification is tentative and based on the close similarity to the strap complex in the so-called marquetry veneer sandals (397). Open shoes 021g & h also have an imitation sewn sandal strap complex. In other words, the strap complex discussed here could originate from a pair of open shoes rather than from sandals.

29   See the remark on 453b in section 3.2.2.2 on the possible identification with this type.

30   As in 021k & l (section 3.3.2) the term 'bead' is used, but they actually are flat cut-out designs of gold, strung by means of holes in their raised edges or applied to the upper by means of soldered loops at their back (see section 4.2.3.5).

31   See section 4.2.3 for a detailed account on the gold beadwork.

32   See section 4.2.2.

33   See section 4.2.3.

34   Discussed in some detail in section 4.2.3.

35   Carter refers to these flower heads as daisies, which is followed here.

36   See also 4.2.3.4.

37   See also 4.2.3.5.

38   Actually, these are squares but strung through holes in the corners so that the beads are orientated with a corner pointing downwards.

39   As in 021f & g (section 3.3.1) the term 'bead' is used, but they actually are flat cut-out designs, with edges bent downward, strung by means of holes in their bent edges.

40   An alternative could be that the thread passed through one layer of the leather inner upper only; the folded-over element with the four rows of slit decoration would run over the stitches and thus protect them from friction with the surface. This construction might have been used in 021f & g as well, although, if the interpretation of an independent decorative band is correct, it would be near-impossible to keep them in place under the treadsole.

41   See section 4.2.3.

42   *Ibidem.*

43   Carter mentions them lying loose in the shoe, but unfortunately not where. They also are not visible in Burton's photographs.

44   The technology of which is discussed in some detail in section 4.2.3.

45   More on this in section 4.2.3.

46   I am indebted to Mikko Kriek for this suggestion.

47   The website of Griffith Institute lists two additional numbers (JE 62686; 747), but these refer to the group 085 (see section 1.1).

48   The measurements are approximate, but the smallest measurements seem more like the original situation, since the soles have partially fallen apart.

49   Another example in Veldmeijer (2008: 5, fig. 7). Note that there is a large number of footwear of small size, especially leath-

er shoes. These, however, are much larger than the child's sandals referred to here and depicted in figure 3.78 and generally are slightly smaller than the smallest sandals of Tutankhamun. For example, the shoe depicted in Veldmeijer (2008: 3, fig. 3) has a length of 160 mm. The small size has led Van Driel-Murray (2000: 315) to suggest that they were women's and/or children's shoes. Although beyond the scope of the present work, the leather sandals in figure 3.78C are of special interest from an iconographic point of view as these might be shown in the Rekhmira relief in figure 8.1A.

50 See also chapter 7 and 8.

51 As in wooden tomb sandals.

52 Not to confuse a wooden sandal with wooden shoes (for example Montembault, 2000: 49) and wooden pattens (for example Veldmeijer, Forthcoming b). Although walking on sandals with a wooden sole is possible and known from several finds in Europe (for example Goubitz, *et al.*, 2001: 263-265, 278), this would be a unique case for ancient Egypt. Moreover, usually wooden-sole-sandals have foot straps rather than a strap complex consisting of a front, back and heel strap.

53 See also chapter 9. For a detailed comparison between sewn sandals Type C and the other types (A and B), see Veldmeijer (2009a).

54 Investigation of foreign footwear is currently being executed by present author.

55 Openwork decoration is also seen in non-footwear leather (see Veldmeijer, 2009b)

56 In sandals 397 (section 3.2.2.1) the layer that is folded around the edge of the sole is secured at the ventral surface of the sole.

57 See Lilyquist *et al.* (2004) for a short overview of metal sandals. Schwarz (1996) has extensively discussed the meaning of silver sandals (see also chapter 7).

CHAPTER 4: MATERIALS

1 For example: 367a: grass/pith/palm-leaf; 373: fruit-bearing stalks of the date-palm/fonds of the date-palm, or possibly the dom-palm/papyrus pith; 104a: reed/papyrus leaf; 21a & b: rush/papyrus.

2 Identification of material in the British Museum, London, The Petrie Museum of Egyptian Archaeology UCL and the Ägyptisches Museum und Papyrussammlung, Berlin together with C.R. Cartwright (Department of Scientific Research, The British Museum) and A.J. Clapham (Worcester Archaeological Services).

3 Vogelsang-Eastwood (1994: 140) also mentions these materials as used for sewn sandals, although she additionally mentions papyrus and palm fibre as core materials. These two, however, have not been identified with the sandals from Tutankhamun (present work) or other sewn sandals (Veldmeijer, 2009a).

4 Based on macroscopic analyses. For basket making these two species of halfa grass are interchangeable (Wendrich, 1999: 147-148). Without microscopic analysis of all sandals, one cannot assume this is true for all footwear, but macroscopic investigation suggests it is true for most of them. Greiss (1949: 268, pl. iii, xiv) identified the material of the sewn sandal from Deir el-Medinah as halfa grass (*Imperata cylindrica*) and dom palm (*Hyphaene thebaica*).

5 These have not been identified microscopically and thus its identification as stalks is uncertain. However, only the first part (*i.e.* the part closest to the tree) could have been used, as the parts carrying the dates are not straight stalks and hence not useable as core. It is certain, however, that it is not halfa grass.

6 See section 7.2 for papyrus funerary sandals. Gourlay (1981b) has identified sandals made of papyrus. However, comparable sandals from several collections have been sampled and although the identification by means of optical and scanning electron mi-

croscopy is in progress, doubts have been raised that the material is papyrus. But one cannot *a priori* assume that all sandals of a certain type are made of the same materials as the one or two which have been identified.

7   Although the identification of the material of these sandals is in progress, it can be safely assumed that these are also not made of papyrus alone.

8   All sewn sandals thus far investigated; other sandals might have papyrus straps as well (Veldmeijer, Accepted; see also section 8.1.2).

9   The harvest of papyrus is shown in reliefs and paintings, but this papyrus is used for the building of the papyrus rafts (for example in the tomb of Anta [Petrie, 1898: pl. IV]) or manufacturing of ropes (for example the tomb of Kaemnofret [Dunham, 1935: fig. 1]).

10   But see Veldmeijer (2009e).

11   Useful are for example Reed (1972) and Haines (2006).

12   See Veldmeijer (2008) and Veldmeijer & Laidler (2008) for overviews and bibliographic notes.

13   More on manufacturing of leather objects in chapter 7 and 8.

14   On adding glass to faience to expand the palette see Kühne (1969).

15   But see section 4.2.1. on the possible glass origin. More on the dark blue beads can be found here as well.

16   Other works in English that deal with relevant aspects of ancient gold technology include Higgins (1980), Hoffmann & Davidson (1965, but must be treated with caution, as many of the objects described were later identified as fake), Ogden (1991a; 1991b; 1992; 1995; 1998), Roberts (1973a), Schorsch (1995), Williams & Ogden (1994).

17   The history of this object, its provenance and evidence for its dating to the time of Tutankhamun were kindly explained to the present author by Philip Roberts (Roberts, 1973b).

18   There appears to have been at least an understanding that gold as mined might be purified by the mid 2nd millennium BC, but little evidence that this was a usual goldsmith's process until a thousands years later (see Ogden, 2000). However, for possible use of refining in early Iron Age Greece, see Verdan (2007).

19   Card No. 021f-19. Probably he thought so due to the fact that, besides the transverse bundles of sewn sandals, the palm leaf sewing strips are also indicated.

20   Except sandals 021h & i which have gold decorative domes and a papyrus strap core.

21   Carter came to a comparable conclusion (Card No. 021-57): "Absolutely impossible that the red discoloration can have been due solely to damp and iron, acting locally, unless quite different alloys were used. ? would different alloys react differently this way."

22   Which confirms Lucas' statement.

23   The central band on these beads and the seed-pods appear from photographs to be granulated and are shown as such here. This, however, requires confirmation.

24   Pendants of exactly this same seed-pod form, but created from circles of yellow glass and described as being of the Amarna Period, have been noted by the present writer in a private collection.

25   There are other net-like gold wire ornaments from the Hellenistic Greek world of apparently similar construction, but the sceptre is the only one that was examined closely by the present author. Any link between a 19th Dynasty Egyptian assembly technique and a Hellenistic Greek one seems highly improbable, but perhaps the potential influence of fortuitously excavated goldwork on later goldsmiths should not be totally disregarded.

CHAPTER 5: SOCKS

1   However, the Minoan people might have worn socks, see section 9.5.
2   This garment is now on display in the Egyptian Museum, Cairo, although the sleeves were cut off at some point and were placed above the garment.

CHAPTER 6: CONTEMPORARY FOOTWEAR: A SURVEY

1   Who discovered the tomb while working for Davis.
2   Assuming that the pair JE 51122 is stored here too: they have not been found (yet) and hence not studied.
3   Strangely enough, although Quibell (1908: 73) mentions the absence of some objects in the Catalogue, no mention is made of this pair of sandals. Are the sandals from this tomb?
4   It is beyond the scope of the present work to discuss the family relations of Tutankhamun. Here, Dodson & Hilton (2004: 144-146, 149-150) is followed, suggesting the king was a son of Akhenaten. Note, however, that "proponents of a long co-regency between Amenhotep III and Amenhotep IV (Akhenaten) continue to suggest that the former might be the prince's [Tutankhamun] father." (*Ibidem*: 150).
5   Lilyquist (1997: 201) refers to the sole as 'silver'.
6   And the general description of sewn sandals (section 3.2) and the accompanying figures.
7   Rather than papyrus sandals with wrapped rush pre-straps as mentioned by Lilyquist (1997: 201).
8   In March 2009 I had the opportunity to examine the sandals, albeit from a distance as the mummy was being conserved (see figure 6.1). Nevertheless, the observations confirm the suggestion that the straps are made of leather and covered with gold foil. A good example of leather that turned black and brittle are the pieces of loincloth(?) from Amarna (ÄM AM 041, Cat. No. 62, see Veldmeijer, 2009b). For gold foil applied directly on leather or rawhide, see the 'gold' sandals from Yuya and Tjuiu (figure 6.14).
9   See Veldmeijer (2009a) for some preliminary remarks.
10 The material is comparable to the core in the pair of sandals in the Petrie Museum of Egyptian Archaeology UCL

(UC 16555). The identification is forthcoming (Cartwright *et al.*).

11   Likely JE 95351. According to Quibell (1908: 59) 51128 is only one sandal. The study in the Egyptian Museum Cairo, however, shows that this number was assigned to a pair of sandals.

12   Likely JE 95359.

13   Although none of them is complete, one is largely preserved, allowing for the reconstruction of the shape.

14   WM 11902.

15   Note the resemblance to Type C sandals.

16   See also Veldmeijer (2009a).

17   It is not clear what kind of fibre sandals; they have not been traced (with thanks to James Allen [IAE] and Joanne Ballard). Attempts to contact the museum have thus far been unsuccessful.

18   Some examples are discussed by Veldmeijer & Endenburg (2007) and Veldmeijer (In press b).

19   Mainly sandals. One entry (ÄM AM 048a) is interpreted as the sole of a shoe. Unfortunately, however, the context is as yet uncertain (for comments on this see Veldmeijer & Endenburg, 2007: 36), but most likely the shoe is of Christian date.

20   Discussed in detail by Veldmeijer (2009a).

21   Possibly, the types with a full, upright upper are a precursor of the shoes with a full, flexible upper (*cf.* figure 9.1) as we know from much later (after the 4th c. AD) Qasr Ibrim (Veldmeijer, In press a).

22   We should bear in mind that Petrie's dating of Kahun is not trustworthy and confirmation by means of provenanced and dated material is badly needed. Tracing the shoes has not been successful yet.

23   It has been suggested that this is an early stage between the open shoes with complete sandal-like straps and the closed shoes with laces only.

CHAPTER 7: NEW KINGDOM SANDALS: A PHILOLOGICAL PERSPECTIVE

1   I am grateful to Jac. J. Janssen who shared his archival material relating to sandals at Deir el-Medinah with me. This formed the basis for his chapter on footwear in a recent book (Janssen, 2008: 95-107) and included much unpublished material from J. Černý's notebooks in the Griffith Institute, Oxford. Janssen's notes provided a convenient starting point, although I draw on a wider range of material and my conclusions occasionally differ from those reached by him; I have noted such cases in the text. Abbreviations are explained in appendix Ia. Text in square brackets [...] are restorations by me. Round brackets (...) are words added by me for clarity in translation but not present in the Egyptian text. <...> designates words inserted by me but missed out by mistake by the ancient scribe.

2   HO 85.1; O. DeM 213; P. Turin 1907/1908 (Janssen, 1966); P. DeM 31 mentions them three times (Černý, 1986).

3   It is interesting to note the fibre, sewn sandals Type A among the products from the Dakhleh Oasis in Rekhmira's tomb chapel (Davies, 1943: 46, pl. XLIX). See also section 8.1.1 and 8.1.2.

4   The double front strap seems much more common and widespread in post-Roman times; almost all sandals from Qasr Ibrim were equipped with them (Veldmeijer, 2006/2007; 2008/2009a, b), but also finds from Kulubnarti exhibit this type of strap complex.

5   In the autobiography of Amenemhat, a high priest of Amun during the 18th Dynasty, the deceased claims to have been a "pure-priest of the sandals of the god" (*wꜥb tiwt nṯr*) early in his career. This is an otherwise unattested title (Gardiner, 1910: 95) that may signify someone responsible for that part of the divine wardrobe, but I would hesitate to associate it with the "pure-priest's sandals" of P. DeM 31.

6   There is a commodity called *tiwt wnš*,

literally "wolf's sandals" which occurs in two Egyptian texts of the New Kingdom, P. Anastasi I, 24.3 (Fischer-Elfert, 1983: 142; 1986: 205) and P. MMA 3569 (Kitchen, 1975-1989: Vol. VII, 271.4). Certainly in the first instance this is a plant, as shown by the context and the determinative ⸗ (Gardiner's sign list M2; "plant"), and despite the determinative ⸗ (Gardiner sign list F27; "leather") in the second instance, this is perhaps most likely also a plant (Hayes, 1959: 369). The latter is in any case measured in *mḫ*, "cubits", whereas sandals are consistently measured in "pairs" (⸗). Fischer-Elfert (1986: 205, with reference to Feinbrun-Dothan, 1977: Vol. I, 156; Vol. II, pl. 258) rejects the original identification of this plant (by Chassinat, 1921: 248) with *Genitana Lutea* L. and proposes *Lycopus europeae* L. instead, a plant that is common in Syria-Palestine. This would agree with the geographical area ascribed to the *tiwt wnš*-plant in P. Anastasi I, and, as Fischer-Elfert points out, the modern Hebrew designation 'wolf's paw' for this plant is suggestive.

7   An exception, although of a much later date (Ptolemaic), is a pair of funerary sandals – presumably never worn – from the Allard Pierson Museum in Amsterdam (APM 1.1988) allegedly made of papyrus (Van Haarlem, 1992). For the 'papyrus' sandals from Deir el-Medinah, see section 4.1.1.

8   For the publications consulted, see the list in the Appendix Ia. I have excluded the unpublished material in Černý's notebooks for the purposes of the following statistics as they cannot easily be checked by colleagues, but this does not distort the overall picture.

9   HO 22.2, 28.4, 32.2 (twice), 36.1 (twice), 45.1, 52.2, 54.2, 56.1, 57.1, 61.3 (four times), 78, 85.1, 87.2 (twice); O. DeM 107, 131, 183, 198, 213, 223, 224, 231, 240 (ten times), 241 (six times), 275, 289, 295 (twice), 321, 371, 423, 424, 428, 446 (twice), 454 (three times), 554, 556, 562, 668, 695, 767 (twice), 772, 787, 929, 1086 (twice), 10044, 10070, 10071 (twice), 10076 (three times), 10077; O. Cairo 25519, 25588, 25585, 25624+25365 (three times), 25677 (twice); O. BM EA 50736 (three times); O. Michaelides 6, 7, 14; O. Ashm 162 (twice), 173; O. Černý 20 (Kitchen, 1975-1989: Vol. VII, 343-344); O. Gardiner AG 104 (Kitchen, 1975-1989: Vol. VII, 323); O. Glasgow D.1925.72 (twice), D.1925.74, D.1925.78, D.1925.81; O. Prague H22 (Kitchen, 1975-1989: Vol. VII, 233-234); O. Strasbourg H133; O. Vienna Aeg. 1 (Zonhoven, 1979), 2 (Kitchen, 1975-1989: Vol. VI, 132-133), O. Berlin P10631, 10665 (twice); O. Qurna 635/3; O. Turin 57349. For publication details *cf.* Appendix Ia.

10 HO 18.5 (probable), 29.3, 56.2 (twice), 57.2, 62.1, 65.2 (five times), 75, 86.2; O. DeM 51, 215, 232, 242, 285, 292, 446, 767, 10073, 10083; O. Cairo 25572, 25583, JdE 72462; O. BM EA 50711, 50736; O. Ashm 194; O. Prague H12 (Kitchen, 1975-1989: Vol. III, 548), O. Qurna 648; O. Turin 57398.

11 O. DeM 115; O. Cairo 25679. The determinative ⸗ (Gardiner's sign list V6), used on O. DeM 10076, normally indicates textiles, but this example is unique to my knowledge and may simply be a scribal mistake.

12 Veldmeijer cautions that this is a rough estimate. The study and publication of several types of sandals is still ongoing, and this hinders more precise evaluations of the statistics relating to the archaeological material. Nonetheless, the overall picture is unlikely to change significantly.

13 Additional support against this theory comes from iconography (see chapter 8).

14 HO 87.2 (*tiwt rd*); O. DeM 51 (*rd n tiwt*), 115 (*rd n tiwt dmꜥ*), 198 (*tiwt rd*), 285 (*tiwt rd*), 295 (*tiwt rd / tiwt st ḥmt rd*), 554 (*rd n tiwt*), 562 (*pꜣ rd ḥr tiwt*), 668 (*rd tiwt*), 762 (*pꜣy=f rd*), 787 (*wꜥt rd n tiwt*), 10070 (*tiwt rd*), 10076 (*tiwt ꜣy rd / [tiwt] st ḥmt rd*), 10083 (*rd n tiwt m dḥri*); O. Cairo 25588 (*pꜣy=f rd tiwt*), 25597 (*pꜣ rd tiwt*), O. Qurna 635/3 (*rd n tiwt*), 648 (*pꜣ rd n tiwt*); P. DeM 31 (*wꜥ rd tiwt n dḥri*).

15 O. Glasgow D.1925.89; HO 75; O. DeM 232, 446; O. Cairo 25572, 25583; O. Ashm 194 (Kitchen 1975-1989: Vol. VII, 311-312).

16 Numerous examples, but see *e.g.* HO 56.2, 65.2, 86.2; O. DeM 215, 242, 285, 292, 10073.

17   Compare O. DeM 787: "one sandal sole" (w῾t rd n tiwt; Grandet, 2006: 120, pl. 321), 668: "one sandal sole" (w῾ rd tiwt), and P. DeM 31: "He sent me one sandal sole of leather" ([iw]=f dit in <n>=i w῾ rd tiwt n dḥri).

18   In the absence of coinage, prices in ancient Egypt were expressed by comparison with a set value of copper. The basic unit for this system was a *deben* of copper, which is approximately 91 grams (Janssen, 1975: 101).

19   *Cf.* the related phrase "to place something under someone's feet" (rdi ḫt ḥr rdwy), which was a judicial term used in the transfer of ownership (Théodoridès, 1972: 188-192).

20   *Cf.* Faulkner (1973: 127), although he misunderstood the context: the phrases are 'stage-instructions' to the performer, as commonly found in Book of the Dead manuscripts.

21   ḥkȝt is an ancient Egyptian measure of 4.54 litres.

22   See also section 8.1.1 and 8.1.2.

23   Note that both fibre and leather sandals are shown in the product area of a leather-working scene in the tomb of Rekhmira (Davies, 1943: pl. LIV), as explained in section 8.1.1 and 8.1.2 (figure 8.1).

24   Peet (1931: 158) was the first to recognise the unusual meaning of ḏbȝ in this context, translating it 'to decorate,' but Imhausen (2003: 376), based on a caption to a tomb scene (Capart, 1907: pl. 33), is no doubt correct in her suggestion that it means 'to finish' (put together the different parts, perhaps also incorporating the decoration of) a sandal.

25   P. BM 10776, verso; the inclusion of these washermen in the total sum of "cultivators" (iḥwty) in column II, line 24 shows that they were not classified as washermen for the purposes of this work, despite being identified by that title in the list itself.

CHAPTER 8: FOOTWEAR IN LATE NEW KINGDOM ART

1   The manufacturing of shoes is not depicted and depictions of shoes themselves are extremely rare, the reason for which is, as yet, unclear. Note, however, that foreigners such as the Minoans (Davies, 1943: pl. XVIII-XX) do wear shoes. Moreover, in much later Meroitic times, depictions of open shoes are much more common (see figure 3.79).

2   Note that papyrus utilitarian sandals, as remarked in chapter 7, have not been identified thus far, despite the fact that this is often stated in secondary and scientific literature (see Cartwright *et al.*, In preparation).

3   Although some types might have been homemade, such as for example certain coiled sandals (*cf.* Veldmeijer, 2006/2007: 73-74).

4   A comparable situation is seen with basketry (Wendrich, 2000: 265-266): the manufacturing of coiled baskets is not depicted. In contrast to the manufacturing of (bed)matting, which is rarely depicted, coiled baskets do not require any special workshop and "since the baskets seem to have been used only inside the houses it seems likely that they were made by women, perhaps mainly for their own use" (*Ibidem*: 265). Vogelsang-Eastwood (1994: 145) suggests that the production of fibre sandals might also have been done by women on a semi-professional basis. But would this apply to the royal sandals as well?

5   See also section 7.4.

6   Showing only some parts of a process is also seen in more general leatherworking-scenes: which leads Van Driel-Murray (2000: 302-303) to suggest that there is a reluctance to show messy things. This might not be true, however: the choice might, as with footwear, be dictated by showing only the most characteristic elements of the process.

7   See also section 7.4.

8   A bias in the archaeological record? If the single-sole sandals were so common as possibly suggested by the manufacturing scenes, and regularly worn, they might not have left any trace, being worn beyond repair, in contrast to the less ordinary types with multiple sole layers and (elaborate) decoration.

9   Often referred to as 'ears.' In the AEFP, however, they are referred to as 'pre-strap' (see Glossary).

10   For example 22/120 (see Veldmeijer, 2009b). In these cases, the pre-straps are usually clad but not always. As said, the process of cladding is not shown in two-dimensional art either. Others with comparable pre-straps have decorated insoles (for example ÄMPB AM 20998 in Veldmeijer, 2009i). Often the terminal end is not pierced, but a slit is cut in them. In some examples, these slits extend all the way to the sole, limited to a small slit by the cladding.

11   No attempts have been made yet to identify the two topmost rows of sandals, which is due to the ongoing nature of the AEFP.

12   Or below, no way to tell when they do not show straps. *Cf.* Davies (1943: pl. XC) where fibre, sewn sandals Type A are depicted with straps.

13   Differences occur in the same period (compare the two examples in figure 8.1A & B with the relief from the tomb of Horemheb in Saqqara [Gnirs, 2004: 37, fig. 16]) but seems to be related to time as well (*cf.* for example the depictions of the footwear of Ramses III and prince Khaemwaset and Amenherkhepshef from the 19th Dynasty (Leblanc, 2001a: 314; 2001b: 316, 317, 319).

14   They might show, when the cladding is done really tight, as bumps. This is, however, not noticeable from a distance.

15   But not in ÄMPB AM 1397.

16   A comparable reasoning as presented for showing only the characteristic parts might apply to the additional insole in fibre, sewn sandals Type C (variant 2): it is not characteristic enough. However, since these are only known from Tutankhamun, this is an exceptional case altogether.

17   Previous studies have already stated that 'picture' was, during the Amarna period, systematically used as a convenient means for conveying sense. See notably the article of Traunecker about the three 'priest' houses depicted on a reconstructed wall in the Luxor Museum (Traunecker, 1988).

18   About indoor scenes in the private tombs of Amarna, see the palace depictions in Davies (1903: pl. XVIII, XXVI; 1905a: pl. XIV, XXXII, XXXIII, XXXIV, XXXV, XLI; 1905b: pl. XIII, XVI, XVII, XVIII, XXXIII, XXXIV; 1906: pl. VIII; 1908b, pl. IV, XVII, XIX, XXVIII, XXIX). Davies' scale drawings of the private Amarnian tomb reliefs require caution: a visit on the spot showed that a new iconographical survey has to be undertaken as well as a discrimination between Davies' copies and his restitutions. I thank the Supreme Council of Antiquities who gave me access to all these tombs (March 2007). Regarding indoor scenes in the royal tombs of Amarna, see Martin (1989b: pl. 58-67).

19   I am grateful to the *Centre Franco-Égyptien d'Étude des Temples de Karnak* which allowed me access to the unpublished database of the *talatats* discovered in the IXth pylon of Karnak Amen Temple (March 2007). A few *talatats* have already been published by Lauffray (1980), Traunecker (1988) and Vergnieux (1999: pl. III [reconstruction A0011], pl. V [A0022, A0024, A0034], pl. XVIIa [A0071], pl. XLIa, c [A0036, A0040], pl. XLIIIb, c [A0041, A0044]). About Amarnian blocks found in Karnak, see Anus (1970: fig. 1 [Block 1], fig. 3 [Block 3], fig. 7 [Block 5] and fig. 9 [Block 7]).

20   See for instance a block depicting part of a private house, currently housed in the Malawi Museum (illustrated in Gräzer, In press [fig. 16]).

21   See Cottevieille-Giraudet (1936: 6, fig. 3 [Block M2410], 21, fig. 30 [M4767], 25, fig. 36 [M5431], 43, fig. 67 [M6044]).

22   In Roeder (1969), see the following blocks which are named according to their discovery numbering: pl. 58 (92-VIII, 494-VII), pl. 59 (27-VIIIA), pl. 60 (436-VIIC,

436-VIIA), pl. 62 (244-VII), pl. 63 (442-VIIA, 261-VIIA, 460-VII), pl. 64 (207-VII, 40-VIIA, 485-VIIIC), pl. 65 (771-VIIID, 290-VIIIB, 673-VIII), pl. 66 (68-VIIIA, 77-VIIIC, 68-VIIIC), pl. 67 (663-VIIIC), pl. 68 (41-VIIIC, 414-VIIC), pl. 70 (242-VII), pl. 71 (282-VIA), pl. 76 (874-VIII, 916-VIII), pl. 78 (126-VIIA), pl. 79 (4-VIII), pl. 80 (1149-VIII), pl. 82 (619-VIIIC, 1115-VIII, 1150-VIII), pl. 83 (64-VIIIA, 64-VIIIC), pl. 84 (852-VIIIC), pl. 85 (137-VI, 173-VI), pl. 86 (729-VIII, 809-VIII), pl. 90 (917-VIII), pl. 98 (907-VIIIC), pl. 100 (426-VIIA, 403-VIIC), pl. 101 (139-VIIIC, 611-VIIC), pl. 102 (437-VIIC, 468-VIIIA), pl. 184 (PC 83, PC 84: this block is currently kept in Boston (see Cooney, 1965: 73-74 [inventory no 62.149], see my figure 8.7), pl. 189 (PC 116, PC 115), pl. 191 (PC 125, PC 127), pl. 192 (PC 138), pl. 207 (PC 264, PC 265), pl. 208 (PC 270, PC 271, PC 269, PC 273) and pl. 209 (PC 283).

23 See Martin (1989a: pl. 125, figure 88) for the whole scene and Martin (*Ibidem*: pl. 144, figure 131, m) for a fragment of a similar depiction).

24 Only the most important house depicted on the reconstructed wall exhibited in Luxor Museum (House III) shows the master of the house (one of the "*directeurs des magasins-ateliers*" of the Aten Temple: see Traunecker, 1988: 88) worshipping the sun on the flat roof. Unfortunately, his feet are missing (figure 8.4).

25 During the Amarna Period, sandals appear hung from the ceiling in private houses (figure 8.4) or arranged on stands in the royal palace (figures 8.9-8.11), pictured from above (allowing to see the sole shape) or from the side (allowing to see the shape of the straps). Hanging things from the ceiling was probably the cheapest way for keeping objects. It is interesting to point out that such a depiction of ready-to-use sandals also appears in post-Amarnian houses (figures 8.5 & 8.6), in a room intended for garments as well.

26 The servant, in the upper dining room of the royal palace (see Ay's tomb, figure 8.9), seems to be wearing sandals of a different type. However, investigation of the relief on site (March 2007) revealed that the 'sandals' are damaged parts of the relief that are wrongly interpreted by Davies.

27 The second depiction is shown in Davies (1908b: pl. XXVIII).

28 See the depiction from Tutu's tomb in Davies (1908b: pl. XIX).

29 Many other similar examples of such a combination are known in the Amarnian tomb iconography as well as through the Amarnian blocks and *talatats*. However, in those cases, the depicted sandals consisted systematically of fibre, sewn sandals.

30 Nothing remains as to the identification of this building. Nevertheless, the presence of food workshops (bakery, brewery) nearby reminds us of the kitchens of a great mansion or of the royal palace area (Cooney, 1965: 73-74).

31 Roman times produced an equivalent depiction (Knötzele, 2008: 61, fig. 6): the excavation of the entrance to a bathhouse (Timgad, Algeria) revealed a unique mosaic showing two pairs of sandals, one pair pointing to the inside and the other to the outside of the bath. However, the iconographical intention could have been slightly different from our Amarnian depiction. The Roman mosaic included two captions (facing each other) by the means of which it "*begrüsste (BENE LAVA – bade gut!) bzw. verabschiedete die Gäste (SALUM LAVISSE – wünsche gut gebadet zu haben)*" (*Ibidem*). The sandals could have been a way to emphasise the text by suggesting the two motions: entering and leaving.

32 See Gräzer (In press) for an annotated list of these archaeological remains.

33 More in Gräzer (In press).

34 We note a quite similar situation inside the temple area where a preliminary purification as well as pure sandals are required before entering (Schwarz, 1996).

35 There are, however, two exceptions: in scenes of *heb-sed* preparation inside the palace the king is depicted barefoot wearing the *heb-sed* coat. He is followed by a

bowed servant carrying the royal sandals slipped on a stick (see unpublished *talatats* from Karnak: *e.g.* blocks No 24/263 and 24/707). The second exception are scenes of mourning inside the palace, in which the king and the queen are lamenting over the lying corpses of a royal family woman who died during childbirth: the royal couple appears barefoot in the bedchamber of queen Kiya(?) (Royal Tomb, Room α, Wall F: see Martin, 1989b: 37-41 and pl. 58, 60, 61) and in the bedchamber of princess Maketaten (Royal Tomb, Room γ, Wall A: see Martin, 1989b: 42-45 and pl. 63, 66). This seems to suggest that some special occasions required being barefoot.

36   See a list of depictions of reward scenes in the palace in note 49.

37   See Davies (1905a: pl. XXXII; 1905b: pl. IV-V, pl. VI-VII and pl. XXXIV; 1908b: pl. VI), Vergnieux (1999: pl. XVIIa [A0071]).

38   Traunecker has already pointed out that such a depiction of the intertwined royal couple standing near the bed probably functioned as a metaphor of the procreative act (Traunecker, 1986: 37-39).

39   Moreover, the choice to depict such sandals hung from the ceiling or arranged on stands is certainly not at random: such precious items were in all likelihood stored not on the ground as to keep them away from vermin; the best way to do this is to hang them from the ceiling.

40   For instance, the theme of the bound enemies which directly refers to the king's ruling role was very popular in the New Kingdom: examples from the tomb of Tutankhamun, besides the two pairs of sandals, are the footstool (Carter, 1933: pl. XXXIII) and examples from outside Tutankhamun's tomb are the royal throne dais found in Merenptah's palace in Memphis (Fischer, 1917: 218, fig. 82; 1921) and a depiction under the window of appearance found in Ramses III's palace in Medinet Habu (Hölscher, 1941: 40, pl. 3).

41   It is clear that the sandals are not imitation sandals such as the marquetry veneer sandals (397): he stands erect, putting on the different elements of his outfit and cleansing parts of his body (hands). He is preparing himself before going to undertake the daily solar service. Imitation sandals would not be very practical and suitable for this.

42   See above on the debatable aspect of this reconstruction, especially the presence of leather sandals in the king's bathroom. However, the coexistence of globular water jars, garment chests and Type C fibre, sewn sandals in the king's bathroom is far from unusual, even in Amarnian *talatats*: see for instance another reconstruction combining these elements in Vergnieux (1999: pl. III [A0011]).

43   Forthcoming by the present author and AJV. Based on textual evidence, Schwarz published an interesting inquiry devoted to footwear in liturgical and funeral contexts (Schwarz, 1996). Gabolde probably took the same sources into account when he wrote (Gabolde, 1988: 69): "*La sandale est d'ailleurs plus qu'un simple élément du vêtement: placée entre le corps et le sol, elle sert de limite entre le pur et l'impur; pharaon place ses ennemis sous ses sandales, mais se déchausse en entrant dans le sanctuaire. Le Livre des Morts, quant à lui, traite de leur usage prophylactique pour repousser les embûches et les abominations semées par des puissances du mal sur la route du défunt.*"

44   See also the comments in the same line related to the identification of the sandals in iconography in section 8.1.2 and 8.1.3.

45   The conclusions only rest upon unequivocal scenes that I was able to check during my stay in Tell el-Amarna.

46   See for instance a naked and barefoot princess attending Ay's reward ceremony from the palace window of appearance (Davies, 1908b: pl. XXIX; see figure 8.15) or another identical one on the queen's lap in Tutu's tomb (Davies, 1908b: pl. XVII). Likewise, two private stelae (Cairo JE 44865 and Berlin 14145) found in Amarnian houses depict royal princesses as young naked children on the royal couple's lap.

47 For more conclusive depictions of dressed and shod princesses see Davies (1905a: pl. X, XXXII and XXXIII).

48 Traunecker (1986: 39-41): "*les nombreuses scènes nous faisant pénétrer dans l'intimité de la famille royale (...) expriment par une série de clichés iconographiques l'harmonie et la fécondité du couple royal en son rôle de Rê et de Hathor et expression terrestre de l'harmonie du monde.*"

49 See the reward ceremonies of Meryra (Davies, 1903: pl. VI, VIII), Huya (Davies, 1905b: pl. XVI, XVII), Parennefer (Davies, 1908b: pl. IV), Tutu (Davies, 1908b: pl. XVII, XIX), Ay (Davies, 1908b: pl. XXIX) and also Ramose in his Theban tomb (Davies, 1941: pl. XXX and XXXIII-XXXVIII). In case of Meryra II (Davies, 1905a: pl. XXXIII, XXXV) should we restore sandals on his feet, given the fact that he appears shod on the next register, when leaving the palace and being cheered by the crowd (Davies, 1905a: pl. XXXVI)? Should we do the same with Panehesy (Davies, 1905a: pl. X; see also Davies' comment on page 12)? As to Mahu, he is depicted barefoot even if he bears the golden collars: should we infer that he took off his sandals in order to pray inside the temple (Davies, 1906: pl. XVIII)? It seems that his chariot driver is waiting for him followed by another man bearing sandals on his arm (Davies, 1906: pl. XIX): are these Mahu's sandals? In figure 8.15, two chariot drivers are waiting (probably for Ay and his wife) with sandals slipped on their left arm. See also post-Amarnian reward scenes, such as Neferhotep's (Davies, 1933: pl. IX-XIII) or Horemheb's (Martin, 1989a: pl. 107, 112, 115).

50 They share the same elaborate outfit, which indicates their high social status.

51 See for instance figure 8.15 but also the reward scene of Ramose (Davies, 1941: pl. XXXV).

52 Except the Vizier who is recognisable with his specific dress: see for instance figure 8.12.

53 See Panehesy (Davies, 1905a: pl. VII, VIII), Meryra II (Davies, 1905a: pl. XXX, XXXI), Huya (Davies, 1905b: pl. II, III and pl. XX [chapel entrance]), Ahmes (Davies, 1905b: pl. XXVII, XXVIII), Sutau (Davies, 1908a: pl. XV), Parennefer (Davies, 1908b: pl. III), Tutu (Davies, 1908b: pl. XVI), Penthu (Davies, 1906: pl. III: the emplacement of the collars is damaged but Penthu is shod), Meryra (Davies, 1903: pl. XLI : ditto, but in the second path (pl. XXXVII), the depiction is complete) and maybe Ay (Davies, 1908b: pl. XXXIX: only the lacing that fasten the collars are preserved). Conversely Mahu (Davies, 1906: pl. XXIX) is not depicted with his golden collars. Is that why he was portrayed barefoot?

54 Panehesy's wife is depicted at her husband's side in a funeral meal scene: her children and she appear barefoot unlike Panehesy (Davies, 1905a: pl. XXIII).

55 Depictions of the couple in their tomb entrance (Davies, 1908b: pl. XXXIX). In the reward scene, unfortunately, Tiy's feet are destroyed (Davies, 1908b: pl. XLIII).

56 This theory requires caution, as a much-damaged post-Amarnian depiction showing the reward of Neferhotep's wife, Merytre, depicts the reward of a barefoot lady under Ay's reign (Davies, 1933: pl. XIV-XV). If our explanation is correct, however, the presence of sandals hung in private wardrobes (such as the third priest house depicted on Luxor Museum reconstructed wall, see figure 8.4) might indicate that the king gratified the master of the house. Based on New Kingdom textual evidence, Schwarz (1996: 79) draws a similar conclusion about silver sandals and rewards for priests: "*Aufgrund des hohen materiellen Wertes dieser Sandalen muss man sie als Gabe in der Art des "Lobgoldes" betrachten. Neben den typischen Gaben für Militärpersonen, wie Prunkwaffen, Land, Fliegen- und Löwenanhänger sowie Schmuck und Ehrengold für Privatpersonen könnte man in den silbernen Sandalen einen beziehungsreichen Gunstbeweis für Priester sehen.*"

57 See section 3.5.2.

58 I, AJV, am indebted to Jac. J. Janssen who shared his archival material relating to

footwear in two- and three-dimensional art. His investigations of the use of footwear in more than 300 tombs(!) forms a strong basis for the study of iconography within the AEFP. Needless to say that the study, interpretation and linkage of these data with the archaeological record will take some time to process. I much benefited from discussions about the preliminary results of Janssen's efforts to gain insight in this topic.

59 Comparable but not exactly identical to the child's sandals in Berlin (ÄMPB AM 20998 in figure 3.78c; see Veldmeijer, 2009i). *Cf.* the Berlin sandals with the sandals depicted in Rekhmira's leatherworking scene (figure 8.1A). Note that in the tomb of Userhat, the owner of the tomb is dressed as a *sem*-priest and makes offerings to Osiris (Pinch-Brock, 2001b: 416-417), wearing sewn sandals. The 'Nine Friends' and two Viziers (and a single figure) that draw the shrine and coffin of Tutankhamun all wear fibre, sewn sandals (figure 8.16A; *cf.* the previous section). More on the identification of other footwear in two- and three-dimensional art in Veldmeijer (Forthcoming a).

60 The so-called 'Golden Throne' depicts the king and his wife. The scene on the inner side of the back seat shows Tutankhamun, sitting on his throne, with Ankhesenamun in front of and bending towards him. A quick glance from a distance at this scene seems to show that Tutankhamun is only wearing a sandal on his left foot; Ankhesenamun only on her right foot. Goffoet (1992: 122) questions whether it could be symbolism, freedom of the artist or damage. Most of the museum guides explain this as symbolism: sharing a pair of sandals, symbolises the marriage and bond between them. It is, however, clear that the Pharaoh does wear a right sandal and Ankhesenamun a left one (Carter mentions on Card No. 091-02 that "The feet have bronze shoes"). Visible under the feet is a small strip, representing the soles. The straps, however, were attached independently and have fallen off the back seat, suggested by the disturbed areas where they once were (Eaton-Krauss, 2008: 39: "[...] the queen's left sandal was missing when Carter removed the throne from the tomb; the strap of the king's right sandal was lost subsequently"). Since Tutankhamun and Ankhesenamun face each other, the other foot of both stick out of the surface and consequently suffered most when leaning with one's back to the back seat. Possibly, this is the reason of the damage (*i.e.* a sign of use): various bits and pieces that had fallen off were restored by the excavators (Card. No. 091-04; see also Eaton-Krauss, 2008: 26). Note that the chair has been repaired in antiquity (Card. No. 091-04: "On the corner of the back r. hand leg are two places where the overlaid gold has been torn off. They are (anciently) marked with black ink and have hieratic notes in red (See note by A.H.G.). Traces of ancient repairs"; see Eaton–Kraus (2008: 37-41) for a detailed discussion on damage, repairs and alteration. It might be that the queen's sandals were damaged during this repair work. Alternately it might be that the parts fell off due to rough handling of the chair by the tomb robbers or the necropolis officials cleaning up the mess. Perhaps more likely, however, is the possibility that they just simply fell off, for example because the way they were fastened to the seat was not sufficient and could not stand much wear (a view shared by Eaton-Krauss, 2008: 40). According to Eaton-Krauss (*Ibidem*: 27) the chair has undergone restoration repeatedly, but none of the work "affected the figures on the backrest."

61 See also chapter 7.

248

CHAPTER 9: DISCUSSION

1   This link is suggested by the leatherworking scenes in two-dimensional art as well as the recent find of near-complete red-and-green leather chariot casing, currently under study by the author, Salima Ikram, Lucy Skinner and Barbara Wills. Moreover, the chariot leather finds from the tomb of Amenhotep III include part of an upper of a shoe (personal observation 2009).

2   Although this strap complex is characteristic for sewn sandals, it is not exclusive for this type of sandal, as it is recognised, albeit rarely, in sewn-edge plaited sandals (explained in section 8.1.2, see also Veldmeijer, Accepted).

3   A detailed analysis is forthcoming, but the Minoans depicted in Rekhmira's tomb may be wearing footwear with this element.

4   The lack of depicted leather curled-toe ankle shoes might be related to the above-suggested link with chariots: if the chariot-owner wears these shoes while standing in the chariot, the feet are not visible.

5   It would have been remarkable: Nubian groups were much more focussed on leather as a material for the production of sandals as many finds suggest (many references of which Reisner, 1923: 306-308 and Williams, 1983: 71-75 are only two); fibre sandals are, to the best of my knowledge, not found during this period but are known from much later periods.

6   See also section 8.1.1 and 8.1.2.

7   The author herself (Feldman, 2006: 84) admits that the lily and the 'hybrid' voluted palmettes are particularly closely connected.

8   One should keep in mind that footwear from abroad is even less well understood than Egyptian footwear. Egypt is fortunate that organic materials have a relatively good chance of surviving; in areas like current Iran and Iraq, organic materials do not survive. Hence, it is unknown whether fibre sandals, for example, such as the 'Egyptian' sewn sandals, did occur or not.

9   Depictions of open shoes (see Alfano, 1987: pl. XIII) are extremely rare. As mentioned in note 3, the analyses of footwear from foreign cultures is in progress, but possibly these do wear closed footwear.

10   But this might be because they were not visible if the shoes were related to chariot as explained above.

11   Note that small remnants suggests the presence of more footwear.

12   But this book is strongly focussed on German footwear history.

BIBLIOGRAPHY

Aldred, C. 1971. Jewels of the Pharaohs. – London, Thames & Hudson.

Allen, T.G. 1974. The Book of the Dead. – Chicago, Oriental Institute (Studies in Ancient Oriental Civilizations 37).

Alfano, C. 1987. I Sandali. Moda e Rituale Nell' Antico Egitto. – Città di Castello, Tibergraph Editrice.

Andrews, C. 1990. Ancient Egyptian Jewelry. – New York, Harry N. Abrams.

Antonova, I., V. Tolstikov & M. Treister. 1996. The Gold of Troy. – London, Thames & Hudson.

Anus, P. 1970. Un domaine thébain d'époque amarnienne. – Le Bulletin de l'Institut Français d'Archéologie Orientale 69: 69-88.

Arnold, D. 1991. Building in Egypt. Pharaonic Stone Masonry. – Oxford, Oxford University Press.

Ashley, C.W. 1993 [1944]. The Ashley Book of Knots. – New York etc., Doubleday.

Arkell, A.J. 1936. Cambay and the Bead Trade. – Antiquity 10: 292–305.

Aston, B.G., J.A. Harrell & I. Shaw. 2000. Stone. In: Nicholson, P.T. & I. Shaw. 2000. Ancient Egyptian Materials and Technology. – Cambridge, Cambridge University Press: 5-77.

Barrois, A. 1932. The Mines of Sinai. – Harvard Theological Review 25: 101-121.

Beinlich, H. & M. Saleh. 1989. Corpus der hieroglyphischen Inschriften aus dem Grab des Tutanchamun. – Oxford, Griffith Institute (Tut'ankhamun's Tomb Series).

Bickel, S. 2004. Theology, Politics and Belief in the 18th Dynasty. In: Wiese, A. & A. Brodbeck. Eds. 2004. Tutankhamun. The Golden Beyond. Tomb Treasures from the Valley of the Kings. – Basel, Antikenmuseum Basel und Sammlung Ludwig: 45-56.

Bloxam, E. 2006. Miners and Mistresses. Middle Kingdom Mining on the Margins. – Journal of Social Anthropology 6, 2: 277-303.

Bossan, M.-J. 2007. The Art of the Shoe. – Rochester, Grange Books.

Brovarski, E.J. 1973. An Unpublished Stele of the First Intermediate Period in the Oriental Institute Museum. – Journal of Near Eastern Studies 32: 453-465.

Caminos, R.A. 1954. Late-Egyptian Miscellanies. – London, Oxford University Press (Brown Egyptological Studies 1).

Capart, J. 1907. Une rue de tombeaux à Saqqarah. – Bruxelles, Vromant.

Carter, H. & A.C. Mace. 1923 [2003]. The Tomb of Tut.ankh.Amen. Search, Discovery and Clearance of the Antechamber. – London, Gerald Duckworth & Co.

Carter, H. 1927 [2001]. The Tomb of Tut.ankh.Amen. The Burial Chamber. – London, Gerald Duckworth & Co.

Carter, H. 1933 [2000]. The Tomb of Tut.ankh.Amen. The Annexe and Treasury. – London, Gerald Duckworth & Co.

Cartwright, C.R., A.J. Clapham & A.J. Veldmeijer. In preparation. Material Identification in Ancient Egyptian Footwear.

Černý, J. 1935a. Catalogue général des antiquités égyptiennes du Musée du Caire: Ostraca hiératiques Nos. 25501-25832. Volume I & II. – Cairo, Institut Français d'Archéologie Orientale.

Černý, J. 1935b. Catalogue des ostraca hiératiques non littéraires de Deir el Médineh, Tome I: Nos. 1-113. – Cairo, Institut Français d'Archéologie Orientale (Documents de fouilles 3).

Černý, J. 1937a. Catalogue des ostraca hiératiques non littéraires de Deir el Médineh, Tome II: Nos. 114-189. – Cairo, Institut Français d'Archéologie Orientale (Documents de fouilles 4).

Černý, J. 1937b. Catalogue des ostraca hiératiques non littéraires de Deir el Médineh, Tome III: Nos. 190-241. – Cairo, Institut Français d'Archéologie Orientale (Documents de fouilles 5).

Černý, J. 1939. Catalogue des ostraca hiératiques non littéraires de Deir el Médineh, Tome IV: Nos. 242-339. – Cairo, Institut Français d'Archéologie Orientale (Documents de fouilles 6).

Černý, J. 1951. Catalogue des ostraca hiératiques non littéraires de Deir el Médineh, Tome V: Nos. 340-456. – Cairo, Institut Français d'Archéologie Orientale (Documents de fouilles 7).

Černý, J. 1965. Hieratic Inscriptions from the Tomb of Tutankhamun. – Oxford, Griffith Institute (Tut'ankhamun's Tomb Series).

Černý, J. 1970. Catalogue des ostraca hiératiques non littéraires de Deir el Médineh, Tome VIII: Nos. 624-705. – Cairo, Institut Français d'Archéologie Orientale (Documents de fouilles 14).

Černý, J. 1986. Papyrus hiératiques de Deir el–Médineh, Tome II: Nos. XVIII-XXXIV. – Cairo, Institut Français d'Archéologie Orientale (Documents de fouilles 22).

Černý, J. & A.H. Gardiner. 1957. Hieratic Ostraca. – Oxford, Oxford University Press.

Chartier-Raymond, M. 1988. Notes sur Maghara (Sinaï). – Cahiers de Recherche de l'Institut de Papyrologie et Egyptologie de Lille 10: 13-22.

Chartier-Raymond, M., M.B. Gratien, C. Traunecker & J.-M. Vincon. 1994. Les sites miniers pharaoniques du Sud–Sinaï: quelques notes et observations de terrain. – Cahiers de Recherche de l'Institut de Papyrologie et Egyptologie de Lille 16: 31-80.

Chassinat, E. 1921. Un papyrus médical copte. – Cairo, Institut Français d'Archéologie Orientale (Mémoires publiés par les membres de l'Institut français d'archéologie orientale du Caire 32).

Cherpion, N. 1999. Sandales et porte-sandales à l'Ancien Empire. In: Ziegler, C. & N. Palayret. Eds. 1999. Lart de l'Ancien Empire égyptien. – Paris, Musée du Louvre: 227–280.

Cooney, J.D. 1965. Amarna Reliefs from Hermopolis in American Collections. – Brooklyn, New York, The Brooklyn Museum.

Cottevieille-Giraudet, R. 1936. Rapport sur les fouilles de Médamoud (1932), Les reliefs d'Aménophis IV Akhenaton. – Cairo, Institut Français d'Archéologie Orientale (Fouilles de l'Institut Français d'Archéologie Orientale 13).

Couyat, J. & P. Montet. 1912. Les inscriptions hiéroglyphiques et hiératiques du Ouâdi Hammâmat. Volume I & II. – Cairo, Institut Français d'Archéologie Orientale (Mémoires publiés par les membres de l'Institut Français d'Archéologie Orientale du Caire 34).

Crowfoot, G.M. & N. de G. Davies. 1941. The Tunic of Tutankhamun. – Journal of Egyptian Archaeology: 113-130.

Daressy, M.G. 1902. Catalogue general des Antiquités Égyptiennes du Musée du Caire. Nos. 24001–24990. Fouilles de la Vallée des Rois. – Cairo, Institut Français d'Archéologie Orientale.

Darnell, J.C. & C. Manassa. 2007. Tutankhamun's Armies. Battle and Conquest during Ancient Egypt's Late Eighteenth Dynasty. – Hoboken, NJ, John Wiley & Sons.

Davis, T.M., H. Carter, G. Maspero & P.E. Newsberry. 1907. Theodore M. Davis' Excavations. The Tomb of Iouiya and Touiyou. – London, Constable.

Davies, N. de G. 1903. The Rock Tombs of El Amarna. Part I. The Tomb of Meryra. – London, Egypt Exploration Society.

Davies, N. de G. 1905a. The Rock Tombs of El Amarna. Part II. The Tombs of Panehesy and Meryra II. – London, Egypt Exploration Society.

Davies, N. de G. 1905b. The Rock Tombs of El Amarna. Part III. The Tombs of Huya and Ahmes. – London, Egypt Exploration Society.

Davies, N. de G. 1906. The Rock Tombs of El Amarna. Part IV. Tombs of Penthu, Mahu, and others. – London, Egypt Exploration Society.

Davies, N. de G. 1908a. The Rock Tombs of El Amarna. Part V. Smaller Tombs and Boundary Stelae. – London, Egypt Exploration Society.

Davies, N. de G. 1908b. The Rock Tombs of El Amarna. Part VI. Tombs of Parennefer, Tutu, and Ay. – London, Egypt Exploration Society.

Davies, N. de G. 1933 [1973]. The Tomb of Nefer–hotep at Thebes. – New York, Metropolitan Museum of Art. Davies, N. de G. 1941. The Tomb of the Vizier Ramose. – London, Egypt Exploration Society.

Davies, N. de G. 1943. The Tomb of Rekhmi-Re at Thebes. Volume I & II. – New York, The Metropolitan Museum of Art (Publications of the Metropolitan Museum of Art, Egyptian Expedition 11).

Davies, N.M. & A.H. Gardiner. 1962. Tutankhamun's Painted Box. – Oxford, Griffith Institute (Tut'ankhamun's Tomb Series).

Demarée, R.J. 2002. Ramesside Ostraca. – London, British Museum Press.

DePutter, T. & C. Karlshausen. 1992. Les pierres utilisées dans la sculpture et l'architecture de l'Égypte pharaonique. Guide pratique illustré. – Bruxelles, Connaissance de l'Égypte Ancienne.

Derry, D.E. 1927 [2001]. Appendix I. Report upon the Examination of Tut.Ankh. Amen's Mummy. In: Carter, H. 1927 [2001]. The Tomb of Tut.ankh.Amen. The Burial Chamber. – London, Gerald Duckworth & Co.: 143-161.

Dodson, A. & D. Hilton. 2004. The Complete Royal Families of Ancient Egypt. – London, Thames & Hudson.

Drenkhahn, R. 1976. Die Handwerker und ihre Tätigkeiten im Alten Ägypten. – Wiesbaden, Otto Harrassowitz (Ägyptologische Abhandlungen 31).

Driel–Murray, van, C. 2000. Leatherwork and Skin Products. In: Nicholson, P.T. & I. Shaw. Eds. 2000. Ancient Egyptian Materials and Technology. – Cambridge, Cambridge University Press: 299-319.

Dunham, D. 1935. A "Palimset" on an Egyptian Mastaba Wall. – American Journal of Archaeology 39: 300-309.

Eaton–Krauss, M. 2008. The Thrones, Chairs, Stools, and Footstools from the Tomb of Tutankhamun. – Oxford, Griffith Institute (Tut'ankhamun's Tomb Series).

Erman, A. & H. Grapow. 1926–1963. Wörterbuch der ägyptischen Sprache. Volume I–V. – Leipzig, J. C. Hinrichs.

Eyre, C.J. 1987. Work and the Organisation of Work in the New Kingdom. In: Powell, M.A. Ed. 1987. Labor in the Ancient Near East. – New Haven, American Oriental Society (American Oriental Series 68): 167-222.

Eyre, C.J. 1998. The Market Women of Pharaonic Egypt. In: Grimal, N. & B. Menu. Eds. 1998. Le commerce en Égypte ancienne. – Cairo, Institut Français d'Archéologie Orientale (Bibliothèque d'Étude 121): 173-191.

Eyre, C.J. 1999. The Village Economy in Pharaonic Egypt. In: Bowman, A. Ed. 1999. Agriculture in Egypt. From Pharaonic to Modern Times. – Oxford, Oxford University Press (Proceedings of the British Academy 96): 33-60.

Fahr-Becker, G. 2005. Ryokan, Séjour dans le Japon traditionnel. Photographies de Narimi Hatano et Klaus Frahm. Traduit de l'allemand par Thomas de Kayser. – Cologne, Könemann.

Faulkner, R.O. 1973-1978. The Ancient Egyptian Coffin Texts. Volumes I-III. – Warminster, Aris & Phillips.

Feinbrun-Dothan, N. 1977. Flora Palaestina III. Volume 1 & 2. – Jerusalem, The Israel Academy of Science and Humanities.

Feldman, M.H. 2006. Diplomacy by Design. Luxury Arts and an "International Style" in the Ancient Near East, 1400-1200 BCE. – Chicago, University of Chicago Press.

Fischer, C.S. 1917. The Eckley B. Coxe Jr. Egyptian Expedition, Memphis. – The Museum Journal, University of Pennsylvania 8, 4: 211-237.

Fischer, C.S. 1921. The Throne Room of Merenptah. – The Museum Journal, University of Pennsylvania 12: 30-34.

Fischer-Elfert, H.-W. 1983. Die satirische Streitschrift des Papyrus Anastasi I: Textzusammenstellung. – Wiesbaden, Otto Harrassowitz.

Fischer-Elfert, H.-W. 1986. Die satirische Streitschrift des Papyrus Anastasi I. Übersetzung und Kommentar. – Wiesbaden, Otto Harrassowitz (Ägyptologische Abhandlungen 44).

Florian, M.-L.E. 2006. The Mechanisms of Deterioration in Leather. In: Kite, M. & R. Thomson. Eds. 2006. Conservation of Leather and Related Materials. – Amsterdam etc., Butterworth-Heinemann (Elsevier): 36-57.

Forbes, R. 1966. Studies in Ancient Technology. Volume V. – Leiden, Brill.

Franke, D. 1984. Probleme der Arbeit mit altägyptischen Titeln des Mittleren Reiches. – Göttinger Miszellen 83: 103-124.

Frantz, J.H. & D. Schorsch. 1990. Egyptian Red Gold. – Archaeomaterials 4: 133-152.

Freed, R.E., Y.J. Markowitz & S.H. D'Auria. 1999. Pharaohs of the Sun. Akhenaten, Nefertiti, Tutankhamen. – Boston, Museum of Fine Arts.

Friedman, R. 2007. The Nubian Cemetery at Hierakonpolis, Egypt. Results of the 2007 Season. The C-Group Cemetery at Locality HK27C. – Sudan & Nubia 11: 57-71.

Gabolde, M. 1988. Le monde des vivants. In: [no editor specified]. Les réserves de Pharaon, L'Égypte dans les collections du Musée des Beaux-arts de Lyon (Exposition, Musée des Beaux-Arts, Lyon, à partir du 15 décembre 1988). – Lyon, Musée des Beaux-Arts: 55-75.

Gale, R., P. Gasson, N. Hepper & G. Killen. 2000. Wood. In: Nicholson, P.T. & I. Shaw. Eds. 2000. Ancient Egyptian Materials and Technology. – Cambridge, Cambridge University Press: 334-371.

Gardiner, A.H. 1910. The Tomb of Amenemhat, High-Priest of Amon. – Zeitschrift für Ägyptische Sprache und Altertumskunde 47: 87-99.

Gardiner, A.H. 1932. Late-Egyptian Stories. – Bruxelles, Fondation Égyptologique Reine Élisabeth (Bibliotheca Aegyptiaca 1).

Gardiner, A.H. 1935. Hieratic Papyri from the British Museum, Third Series. The Chester Beatty Gift. Volume I & II. – London, British Museum Press.

Gardiner, A.H. 1948. Ramesside Administrative Documents. – Oxford, Griffith Institute.

Gardiner, A.H. 1952. Tuthmosis III Returns Thanks to Amun. – Journal of Egyptian Archaeology 38: 6-23.

Gardiner, A.H. & G. Möller. 1911. Hieratische Papyrus aus den Königlichen Museen zu Berlin, Band III, Schriftstücke der VI. Dynastie aus Elephantine, Zaubersprüche für Mutter und Kind, Ostraka. – Leipzig, J.C. Hinrich.

Garland, H. & C.O. Bannister. 1927. Ancient Egyptian Metallurgy. – London, Griffin.

Gasse, A. 1990. Catalogue des ostraca littéraires de Deir-el-Médina, Tome IV, fasc. 1: Nos. 1676-1774. – Cairo, Institut Français d'Archéologie Orientale (Documents de fouilles 25).

Gasse, A. 2005. Catalogue des ostraca littéraires de Deir al–Médina, Tome V: Nos. 1775–1873 et 1156. – Cairo, Institut Français d'Archéologie Orientale (Documents de fouilles 43).

Germer, R. 1998. The Plant Remains Found by Petrie at Lahun and Some Remarks on the Problems of Identifying Egyptian

Plant Names. In: Quirke, S. Ed. 1998. Lahun Studies. – New Malden, Sia Publishing: 84-91.
Goedicke, H. & E.F. Wente. 1962. Ostraka Michaelides. – Wiesbaden, Otto Harrassowitz.
Gnirs, A.M. 2004. The 18th Dynasty. Light and Shadow of an International Era. In: Wiese, A. & A. Brodbeck. Eds. 2004. Tutankhamun. The Golden Beyond. Tomb Treasures from the Valley of the Kings. – Basel, Antikenmuseum Basel und Sammlung Ludwig: 27-44.
Goffoet, J. 1992. Notes sur les sandales et leur usage dans l'Égypte Pharaonique. In: Obsomer, C. & A.-L. Oosthoek. 1992. Amosiadès. Mélanges offerts au Professeur Claude Vandersleyen par ses anciens étudiants. – Louvain, Catholic University: 111-123.
Gorelick, L. & A.J. Gwinnett. 1983. Ancient Egyptian Stone–Drilling. An Experimental Perspective on a Scholarly Disagreement. – Expedition 25: 40-47.
Goubitz, O., C. van Driel–Murray & W. Groenman–van Waateringe. 2001. Stepping through Time. Archaeological Footwear from Prehistoric Times until 1800. – Zwolle, Stichting Promotie Archeologie.
Gourlay, Y.J.-L. 1981a. Les sparteries de Deir el–Médineh. XVIIIe-XXe dynasties. I. Catalogue des techniques de sparterie. – Cairo, L'Institut Français d'Archéologie Orientale.
Gourlay, Y.J.-L. 1981b. Les sparteries de Deir el–Médineh. XVIIIe-XXe dynasties. II. Catalogue des objets de sparterie. – Cairo, L'Institut Français d'Archéologie Orientale.
Goyon, G. 1957. Nouvelles inscriptions rupestres du Wadi Hammamat. – Paris, Imprimerie nationale.
Grandet, P. 1994. Le Papyrus Harris I: BM 9999. Volume 1 & 2. – Cairo, Institut Français d'Archéologie Orientale (Bibliothèque d'Étude 109).

Grandet, P. 2000. Catalogue des ostraca hiératiques non littéraires de Deîr el-Médineh, Tome VIII: Nos. 706-830. – Cairo, Institut Français d'Archéologie Orientale (Documents de Fouilles 39).
Grandet, P. 2003. Catalogue des ostraca hiératiques non littéraires de Deîr el-Médineh, Tome IX: Nos. 831-1000. – Cairo, Institut Français d'Archéologie Orientale (Documents de Fouilles 41).
Grandet, P. 2006. Catalogue des ostraca hiératiques non littéraires de Deîr el-Médineh, Tome X: Nos. 10001-10123. – Cairo, Institut Français d'Archéologie Orientale (Documents de Fouilles 46).
Gräzer, A. In press. Hygiène et sécurité dans l'habitat égyptien d'époque pharaonique. In: Boussac, M.F., T. Fournet & B. Redon. Eds. In press. Actes du colloque Balnéorient "Le bain collectif en Égypte, origine évolution et actualité des pratiques", Alexandrie, 1-4 déc. 2006, Études Urbaines. – Cairo, Institut Français d'Archéologie Orientale/Institut Français du Proche-Orient.
Greiss, E.A.M. 1949. Anatomical Identification of Plant Material from Ancient Egypt. – Bulletin de l'Institut d'Égypte: 249-277.
Guglielmi, W. 1994. Berufssatiren in der Tradition des Cheti. In: Bietak, M., J. Holaubek, H. Mukarovsky & H. Satzinger. Eds. 1994. Zwischen den beiden Ewigkeiten: Festschrift Gertrude Thausing. – Vienna, Institut für Ägyptologie der Universität Wien: 44-72.
Haarlem, van, W.M. 1992. A Pair of Papyrus Sandals. – Journal of Egyptian Archaeology 78: 294-295.
Haines, B.M. 2006. The Fibre Structure of Leather. In: Kite, M. & R. Thomson. Eds. 2006. Conservation of Leather and Related Materials. – Amsterdam etc., Butterworth-Heinemann (Elsevier): 11-21.
Hannig, R. 1995. Grosses Handwörterbuch Ägyptisch-Deutsch (2800-950 v. Chr.). Die Sprache der Pharaonen. – Mainz, Phillip von Zabern (Kulturgeschichte der antiken Welt 64).

Hannig, R. 2003. Ägyptisches Wörterbuch 1, Altes Reich und Erste Zwischenzeit. – Mainz, Phillip von Zabern (Kulturgeschichte der antiken Welt 98).

Harrell, J.A. In press. Archeaological Geology of Hosh el-Guruf, Fourth Nile Cataract, Sudan. – Gdansk Archaeological Museum African Reports.

Harrell, J.A. & E.G. Bloxam. 2004. Stela Ridge Carnelian Mine, Nubian Desert. – Annual Meeting of the American Research Center in Egypt, Tucson, AZ. Program and Abstracts: 52.

Harrell, J.A. & A.F. Osman. 2007. Ancient Amazonite Quarries in the Eastern Desert. – Egyptian Archaeology 30: 26-28.

Hayes, W.C. 1959. The Sceptre of Egypt. Volume 1 & 2. – New York, Metropolitan Museum of Art.

Helck, W. 1955-1958. Urkunden der 18. Dynastie. – Berlin, Akademie Verlag.

Helck, W. 1961-1969. Materialien zur Wirtschaftsgeschichte des Neuen Reiches. Volume 1-5. – Wiesbaden, Akademie der Wissenschaften und der Literatur in Mainz.

Helck, W. 1970. Die Lehre des Dua-khety. Volume I & II. – Wiesbaden, Otto Harrassowitz.

Hepper, F.N. 1990. The Pharoah's Flowers. Botanical Treasures from Tutankhamun's Tomb. – London, HMSO.

Herrmann, G. 1968. Lapis lazuli. The Early Phases of its Trade. – Iraq 30: 21-57.

Higgins, R. 1961 [1980]. Greek and Roman Jewellery. – London, Methuen.

Hoffmann, H. & P. Davidson. 1965. Greek Gold. Jewelry from the Age of Alexander. – Boston, Museum of Fine Arts.

Hölscher, U. 1941. The Excavation of Medinet Habu III. The Mortuary Temple of Ramses III. – Chicago, Oriental Institute (Oriental Institute Press 54).

Hoving, T. 1978. Tutankhamun. The Untold Story. – New York, Simon & Schuster.

Imhausen, A. 2003. Egyptian Mathematical Texts and Their Contexts. – Science in Context 16: 367-389.

Imhausen, A. & J. Ritter. 2004. Mathematical Fragments: UC 32114B, UC 21118B, UC 32134A+B, UC 32159-UC 32162. In: Collier, M. & S. Quirke. Eds. 2004. The UCL Lahun Papyri. Religious, Literary, Legal, Mathematical and Medical. – Oxford, Archaeopress (British Archaeological Reports International Series 1209): 71-98.

James, T.G.H. 1992 [2001]. Howard Carter. The Path to Tutankhamun. – Cairo, American University in Cairo Press.

Janssen, J.J. 1966. A Twentieth-Dynasty Account Papyrus (Pap. Turin no. Cat. 1907/8). – Journal of Egyptian Archaeology 52: 81-94.

Janssen, J.J. 1975. Commodity Prices from the Ramesside Period. – Leiden, Brill.

Janssen, J.J. 2008. Daily Dress at Deir el-Medîna. Words for Clothing. – London, Golden House Publishing (Egyptology 8).

Jones, D. 2000. An Index of Ancient Egyptian Titles, Epithets and Phrases of the Old Kingdom. Volume I & II. – Oxford, Archaeopress (British Archaeological Reports International Series 866).

Kemp, B.J. & G. Vogelsang-Eastwood. 2001. The Ancient Textile Industry at Amarna. – London, Egypt Exploration Society (Excavation Memoirs 68).

Kitchen, K.A. 1975-1989. Ramesside Inscriptions. Volume 1-7. – Oxford, Blackwell.

Klebs, L. 1915. Die Reliefs des alten Reiches. – Heidelberg, Carl Winters Universitätsbuchhandlung.

Klebs, L. 1922. Die Reliefs und Malereien des mittleren Reiches. – Heidelberg, Carl Winters Universitätsbuchhandlung.

Klebs, L. 1934. Die Reliefs und Malereien des neuen Reiches. – Heidelberg, Carl Winters Universitätsbuchhandlung.

Knötzele, P. 2008. Römische Schuhe. In: Roder, H. Ed. 2008. Schuhtick. Von kalten Füßen und heißen Sohlen. – Mainz, Philipp von Zabern: 57-64.

Koenig, Y. 1997. Les ostraca hiératiques inédits de la Bibliothèque Nationale et Universitaire de Strasbourg. – Cairo, Institut Français d'Archéologie Orientale (Documents de Fouilles 33).

Kuckert, J. 2006. Schuhe aus der persischen Militärkolonie von Elephantine, Oberägypten, 6.-5. Jhdt. V. Chr. – Mitteilungen der Deutschen Orient-Gesellschaft zu Berlin 138: 109-156.

Kühne, J. 1969. Zur Kenntnis silikatischer Werkstoffe und der Technologie ihrer Herstellung im 2. Jahrtausend vor unserer Zeitrechnung. – Berlin, Abhandlung der Deutschen Akademie der Wissenschaften zu Berlin.

Lauffray, J. 1980. Les talatates du IXe pylône de Karnak et le 'tenymenou'. – Cahiers de Karnak VI: 67-89.

Leach, B. & J. Tait. 2000. Papyrus. In: Nicholson, P.T. & I. Shaw. Eds. 2000. Ancient Egyptian Materials and Technology. – Cambridge, Cambridge University Press: 227-253.

Leblanc, C. 2001a. The Tombs of the Sons of Rameses III. In: Weeks, K.R. Ed. 2001. The Treasures of the Valley of the Kings. – Cairo, The American University in Cairo Press: 312-315.

Leblanc, C. 2001b. The Tomb of Amenherkhepshef. In: Weeks, K.R. Ed. 2001. The Treasures of the Valley of the Kings. – Cairo, The American University in Cairo Press: 316-319.

Lesko, L. 1982–1990. A Dictionary of Late Egyptian. – Berkeley, BC Scribe.

Leguilloux, M. 2006. Les objects en cuir de Didymoi. *Praesidium* de la route caravanière Coptos-Bérénice. – Cairo, Institut Français d'Archéologie Orientale (Fouilles de l'Institut Français d'Archéologie Orientale 53).

Lilyquist, C. 1997. Descriptive Notes from the Valley. In: Goring, E., N. Reeves & J. Ruffle. 1997. Chief of Seers. Egyptian Studies in Memory of Cyril Aldred. – London, Kegan Paul International.

Lilyquist, C. 2004. With contributions by: J.E. Hoch & A.J. Peden. The Tomb of Three Foreign Wives of Tuthmosis III. – New York, Metropolitan Museum of Art.

Littauer, M.A. & J.H. Crouwel. 1985. Chariots and Related Equipment from the Tomb of Tut'ankhamun. – Oxford, Griffith Institute (Tut'ankhamun's Tomb Series).

Lorton, D. 1974. The Juridical Terminology of International Relations in Egyptian Texts Through Dyn. XVIII. – Baltimore, Johns Hopkins University Press.

López, J. 1978. Ostraca ieratici. N. 57001-57092. – Milan, La Goliardica (Catalogo del Museo Egizio di Torino. Serie seconda–collezioni. Volume 3. Fascicolo 1).

López, J. 1980. Ostraca ieratici. N. 57093-57319. – Milan, La Goliardica (Catalogo del Museo Egizio di Torino. Serie seconda-collezioni. Volume 3. Fascicolo 2).

López, J. 1982. Ostraca ieratici. N. 57320-57449. – Milan, La Goliardica (Catalogo del Museo Egizio di Torino. Serie seconda-collezioni. Volume 3. Fascicolo 3).

López, J. 1984. Ostraca ieratici. N. 58001-58007. – Milan, La Goliardica (Catalogo del Museo Egizio di Torino. Serie seconda-collezioni. Volume 3. Fascicolo 4).

Lucas, A.E. 1926. Ancient Egyptian Materials. – London, Longmans, Green and Co.

Lucas, A.E. 1927. [2001] Appendix II. The Chemistry of the Tomb. In: Carter, H. 1927 [2001]. The Tomb of Tut.ankh.Amen. The Burial Chamber. – London, Gerald Duckworth & Co.: 162-188.

Lucas, A.E. 1948. Ancient Egyptian Materials and Industries. Third Revised Edition. – London, Edward Arnold.

Lucas, A.E. & J.R. Harris. 1962. Ancient Egyptian Materials and Industries. Fourth Edition. – London, Edward Arnold.

Markowitz, Y.J. & S.B. Shear. 2001. New Thoughts on an Old Egyptian Necklace. – Adornment 3, 2: 1-2, 19-21.

Martin, G.T. 1989a. The Memphite Tomb of Horemheb, Commander-in-Chief of Tut'ankhamûn I. The Reliefs, Inscriptions and Commentary. – London, Egypt Exploration Society.

Martin, G.T. 1989b. The Royal Tomb at El-'Amarna II. The Reliefs, Inscriptions, and Architecture. – London, Egypt Exploration Society.

McDermott, B. 2004. Warfare in Ancient Egypt. – Stroud, Sutton Publishing.

McDowell, A.G. 1991. Hieratic Ostraca in the Hunterian Museum Glasgow (The Colin Campbell Ostraca). – Oxford, Griffith Institute.

McDowell, A.G. 1999. Village Life in Ancient Egypt. Laundry Lists and Love Songs. – Oxford, Oxford University Press.

McLeod, W. 1970. Composite Bows from the Tomb of Tut'ankhamun. – Oxford, Griffith Institute (Tut'ankhamun's Tomb Series).

McLeaod, W. 1982. Self Bows and Other Archery Tackle from the Tomb of Tut'ankhamun. – Oxford, Griffith Institute (Tut'ankhamun's Tomb Series).

Montembault, V. 2000. Catalogue des chaussures de l'Antiquité Égyptienne. – Paris, Réunion des Musées Nationaux.

Moorey, P.R.S. 1994. Ancient Mesopotamian Materials and Industries. – Oxford, Clarendon Press.

Moran, W.L. 1992. The Amarna Letters. – Baltimore/London, Johns Hopkins University Press.

Muller, H.W. & E. Thiem. 1999. The Royal Gold of Acient Egypt. – London, Tauris.

Murray, G.W. 1939. The Road to Chephren's Quarries. – The Geographical Journal 94, 2: 97-114.

Murray, M.A. 2000. Fruits, Vegetables, Pulses and Condiments. In: Nicholson, P.T. & I. Shaw. Eds. 2000. Ancient Egyptian Materials and Technology. – Cambridge, Cambridge University Press: 609-655.

Murray, H. & M. Nuttall. 1963. A Handlist to Howard Carter's Catalogue of Objects in Tut'ankhamun's Tomb. – Oxford, Griffith Institute (Tut'ankhamun's Tomb Series).

Newman, R. & S.M. Halpine. 2001. The Binding Media of Ancient Egyptian Painting. In: Davis, W.V. Ed. 2001. Colour and Painting in Ancient Egypt. – London, The British Museum Press: 22-32.

Nicholson, P.T. 2007. Brilliant Things for Akhenaten. The Production of Glass Vitreous Materials and Pottery at Amarna Site O45.1. – London, Egypt Exploration Society.

Ogden, J.M. 1982. Jewellery of the Ancient World. – London, Trefoil books.

Ogden, J.M. 1990/1991. Gold in a Time of Bronze and Iron. – The Journal of the Ancient Chronology Forum 4: 6-14.

Ogden, J.M. 1991a. Classical Gold wire. Some Aspects of its Manufacture and Use. – Jewellery Studies 5: 95-105

Ogden, J.M. 1991b. Casting Doubt. Economic and Technological Considerations regarding Metal Casting in the Ancient World. In: Vandiver, P.B., J. Druzik & G.S. Wheeler. Eds. 1991. Material Issues in Art and Archaeology. Materials Research Society. – Pittsburgh, Geology and Planetary Science University of Pittsburgh: 713-717.

Ogden, J.M. 1992. Interpreting the Past. Ancient Jewellery. – London, British Museum Press.

Ogden, J.M. 1993. Aesthetic and Technical Considerations Regarding the Colour and Texture of Ancient Goldwork. In: La Niece, S. & P.T. Craddock. Eds. 1993. Metal Plating and Patination. Cultural, Technical and Historical Developments. – London, Butterworth-Heinemann: 39-49.

Ogden, J.M. 1995. The Gold Jewellery. In: Bennett, C.-M. & P. Bienkowski. Eds. 1995. Excavations at Tawilan in Southern Jordan. – Oxford Oxford University Press: 69-78.

Ogden, J.M. 1998. The Jewellery of Dark Age Greece. Construction and Cultural Connections. In: Williams, D. Ed. 1998. The Art of the Greek Goldsmith. – London, British Museum Press.

Ogden, J.M. 2000. Metals. In: Nicholson, P.T. & I. Shaw. Eds. 2000. Ancient Egyptian Materials and Technology. – Cambridge, Cambridge University Press: 148-176.

Ogden, J.M. 2008. Granulation. Gold, Bronze and Iron. – Gems and Jewellery 17, 3: 13.

Parkinson, R. 2008. The Painted Tomb Chapel of Nebamun. Masterpieces of Ancient Egyptian Art in the British Museum. – London, The British Museum Press.

Peet, T.E. 1931. Notices of Recent Publications. Mathematischer Papyrus des Staatlichen Museums der Schönen Künste in Moskau. Von W.W. Struve. Berlin, 1930 (Quellen und Studien zur Geschichte der Mathematik. Abteilung A. Quellen, Band 1). – Journal of Egyptian Archaeology 17: 154-160.

Peet, T.E. & C.L. Woolley. 1923. The City of Akhenaten. Part I. Excavations of 1921 and 1922 at El-'Amarneh. – London, Egypt Exploration Society (Thirty-eighth Memoir).

Petrie, W.M.F. 1890. Kahun, Gurob and Hawara. – London, Kegan Paul, Trench, Trübner, and Co.

Petrie, W.M.F. 1889. Hawara, Biahmu, and Arsinoe. – London, Trübner.

Petrie, W.M.F. 1898. Deshasheh. – London, Egypt Exploration Society.

Petrie, W.M.F. & C.T. Currelly. 1906. Researches in Sinai. – London, John Murray.

Petrie, W.M.F & G. Brunton. 1924. Sedment II. – London, British School of Archaeology in Egypt.

Pinch–Brock, L. 2001a. The Tomb of Khaemhat. In: Weeks, K.R. Ed. 2001. The Treasures of the Valley of the Kings. – Cairo, The American University in Cairo Press: 365-375.

Pinch–Brock, L. 2001b. The Tomb of Userhat. In: Weeks, K.R. Ed. 2001. The Treasures of the Valley of the Kings. – Cairo, The American University in Cairo Press: 414-417.

Porter, B. & R.L.B. Moss. 1994. Topographical Bibliography of Ancient Egyptian Hieroglyphic Texts, Reliefs and Paintings. I. The Theban Necropolis, Part One. Private Tombs. – Oxford, Griffith Institute (Second Edition, revised and augmented).

Possehl, G.L. 1981. Cambray Bead Making. An Ancient Craft in Modern India. – Expedition 23: 39-47.

Posener, G. 1934. Catalogue des ostraca hiératiques littéraires de Deir el Médineh, Tome I: Nos. 1001-1108. – Cairo, Institut Français d'Archéologie Orientale (Documents de Fouilles 1).

Posener, G. 1951-1952-1972. Catalogue des ostraca hiératiques littéraires de Deir el Médineh, Tome II: Nos. 1109-1266. – Cairo, Institut Français d'Archéologie Orientale (Documents de Fouilles 18).

Posener, G. 1977-1978-1980. Catalogue des ostraca hiératiques littéraires de Deir el Médineh, Tome III: Nos. 1267-1675. – Cairo, Institut Français d'Archéologie Orientale (Documents de Fouilles 20).

Quack, J.F. 1992. Studien zur Lehre für Merikare. – Wiesbaden, Otto Harrassowitz (Göttinger Orientforschungen, Reihe IV. Ägypten, Band 23).

Quibell, J.E. 1908. Catalogue Général Égyptiennes du Musée du Caire. Nos 51001-51191. Tomb of Yuiaa and Thuiu. – Cairo, Institut Français d'Archéologie Orientale.

Quirke, S. 1998. Word and Object. Problems of Translation. In: Quirke, S. Ed. 1998. Lahun Studies. – New Malden, Sia Publishing: vii-viii.

Quirke, S. 2004. Titles and Bureaux of Egypt 1850-1700 BC. – London, Golden House Publications (Egyptology 1).

Reed, R. 1972. Ancient Skins, Parchments and Leathers. – London, Seminar Press Ltd.

Reeves, N. 1990a. The Complete Tutankhamun. The King. The Tomb. The Royal Treasure. – London, Thames & Hudson.

Reeves, N. 1990b. Valley of the Kings. The Decline of a Royal Necropolis. – London/New York, Kegan Paul International.

Reeves, N. & R.H. Wilkinson. 1996 [2005]. The Complete Valley of the Kings. Tombs and Treasures of Egypt's Greatest Pharaohs. – London, Thames & Hudson.

Reisner, G.A. 1923. Excavations at Kerma, IV-V. – Cambridge, MA, Peabody Museum of Harvard University.

Riello, G. & P. McNeil. 2006. Shoes. A History from Sandals to Sneakers. – Oxford/New York, Berg.

Roberts, P.M. 1973a. Gold Brazing in Antiquity. – Gold Bulletin 6, 4: 112-119.

Roberts, P.M. 1973b. Private Communication 1973 Including a Copy of 'Ancient Egyptian Gold Button', Probe Report 1973 by J.M. Notton, Johnson, Matthey & Co. Ltd. London 1973, Unpublished.

Roder, H. Ed. 2008. Schuhtick. Von kalten Füßen und heißen Sohlen. – Mainz, Philipp von Zabern.

Roeder, G. 1969. Amarna-Reliefs aus Hermopolis II. Ausgraben der Deutschen Hermopolis-Expedition in Hermopolis 1929-1939. – Hildesheim, Gerstenberg (Wissenschaftliche Veröffentlichung 6; herausgegeben von Rainer Hanke).

Rose, P.J. With contributions by D.N. Edwards, G. Pyke, P. Wilson, J. Hallof and S.-A. Ashton. 2007. The Meroitic Temple Complex at Qasr Ibrim. – Egypt Exploration Society (Excavation Memoir 84).

Rosen, von, L. 1988. Lapis Lazuli in Geological Contexts and in Ancient Written Sources. – Kungälv, Goterna Press (Studies in Mediterranean Archaeology and Literature 65).

Ryan, D.P. & D.H. Hansen. 1987. A Study of Ancient Egyptian Cordage in the British Museum. –London, British Museum (Occasional Paper no. 62).

Sauneron, S. 1959. Catalogue des ostraca hiératiques non littéraires de Deir el-Médineh, Tome VII: Nos. 550-623. – Cairo, Institut Français d'Archéologie Orientale (Documents de fouilles 13).

Schorsch, D. 1995. The Gold and Silver Necklaces of Wah. A Technical Study of an Unusual Metallurgical Joining Method. In: Brown, C.E., F. Macalister & M. Wright. Eds. 1995. Conservation in Ancient Egyptian Collections. – London, Archetype Publications Ltd: 127–135.

Schorsch, D. 2001. Precious-Metal Polychromy in Egypt in the Time of Tutankhamun. – Journal of Egyptian Archaeology 87: 55-71.

Schwarz, S. 1996. Zur Symbolik weißer und silberner Sandalen. – Zeitschrift für Ägyptische Sprache und Altertumskunde 123: 69-84.

Schwarz, S. 2000. Altägyptisches Lederhandwerk. – Frankfurt am Main, Peter Lange.

Seibels, R. 1996. The Wearing of Sandals in Old Kingdom Tomb Decorations. – Bulletin of the Australian Centre for Egyptology 7: 75-88.

Seipel, W. 2001. Gold der Pharaonen. – Vienna, Kunsthistorischen Museums.

Sethe, K. 1905-1906. Urkunden der 18. Dynastie. – Leipzig, J.C. Hinrichs.

Shaw, I. & P. Nicholson. 1995. The British Museum Dictionary of Ancient Egypt. – London, The British Museum Press.

Smith, C.S. 1983. A Search for Structure. Selected Essays on Science, Art, and History. – Cambridge, MA, MIT Press.

Smith, G.E. 1908. Mummy of Yuaa. In: Quibell, J.E. 1908. Catalogue Général Égyptiennes du Musée du Caire. Nos 51001-51191. Tomb of Yuaa and Thuiu. – Cairo, Institut Français d'Archéologie Orientale: 68-71.

Stocks, D.A. 2003. Experiments in Egyptian Archaeology. – London, Routledge, Taylor & Francis Group.

Strecker, C. & P. Heinrich. 2007. Eine Innovative Restaurierung - eine Neuartige Präsentation. In: [no editor specified]. Ägyptische Mumien. Unsterblichkeit im Land der Pharaonen. – Stuttgart, Landesmuseum Württemberg/Mainz am Rhein, Philipp von Zabern.

Struve, V.V. 1930. Mathematischer Papyrus des Staatlichen Museums der Schönen Künste in Moskau. – Berlin, J. Springer (Quellen und Studien zur Geschichte der Mathematik, Abteilung A. Quellen 1).

Sturtewagen, C. 1990. Studies in Ramesside Administrative Documents. In: Israelit-

Groll, S. Ed. 1990. Studies in Egyptology Presented to Miriam Lichtheim. – Jerusalem, Magnes Press. Volume 2: 933-942.

Théodoridès, A. 1972. Mettre des biens sous les pieds de quelqu'un. – Revue d'Egyptologie 24: 188-192.

Thomas, E. 1966. The Royal Necropoleis of Thebes. – Princeton, Princeton University.

Traunecker, C. 1986. Amenophis IV et Néfertiti, le couple royal d'après les talatates du IXe pylône de Karnak. – Bulletin de la Sociéte Française d'Égyptology 107: 17-44.

Traunecker, C. 1988. Les maisons du domaine d'Aton à Karnak. – Cahiers de Recherches de l'Institut de Papyrologie et Égyptologie de Lille 10: 73-93.

Trommer, B. 2005. Die Kollagenmatrix archäologischer Funde im Vergleich zu künstlich gealterten Ledermustern historischer Gerbverfahren (Dissertation.) – Freiberg, Technischen Universität Bergakademie (online at https://fridolin.tu-freiberg.de/).

Vandersleyen, C. 1989. Les inscriptions 114 et 1 du Ouadi Hammamât (11e dynastie). – Chronique d'Égypte 64: 148-158.

Veldmeijer, A.J. 2005. Archaeologically Attested Cordage. Terminology on the Basis of the Material from Ptolemaic and Roman Berenike (Egyptian Red Sea coast). – Eras 7 (online at: www.arts.monash.edu.au/eras/edition_7; visited 16 June 2009).

Veldmeijer, A.J. 2005/2006. With contributions by A.J. Clapham and C.R. Cartwright. Studies of Ancient Egyptian Footwear. Technological Aspects. Part II. Wooden Pattens from Ottoman Qasr Ibrim. – Journal of the American Research Centre in Egypt 42: 147-152.

Veldmeijer, A.J. 2006. Knots, Archaeologically Encountered. A Case Study of the Material from the Ptolemaic and Roman Harbour at Berenike (Egyptian Red Sea Coast). – Studien zur Altägyptischen Kultur 35: 337-366.

Veldmeijer, A.J. 2006/2007. Studies of Ancient Egyptian Footwear. Technological Aspects. Part I. Cordage Sandals from Qasr Ibrim. – Jaarberichten Ex Oriental Lux 40: 61-75.

Veldmeijer, A.J. 2007. The World of Leather. – Nekhen News Fall: 24.

Veldmeijer, A.J. 2008. Leatherwork. – UCLA Encyclopedia of Egyptology: 1-10 (online at: http://repositories.cdlib.org/nelc/uee/1045; visited 16 June 2009).

Veldmeijer, A.J. 2008/2009a. Studies of Ancient Egyptian Footwear. Technological Aspects. Part III. Leather or String-Reinforced Plaited Sandals from Qasr Ibrim. – Jaarberichten Ex Oriental Lux 41: 105-125.

Veldmeijer, A.J. 2008/2009b. Studies of Ancient Egyptian Footwear. Technological Aspects. Part IV. Plain Plaited Sandals from Qasr Ibrim. – Jaarberichten Ex Oriental Lux 41: 127-150.

Veldmeijer, A.J. 2009a [in press 2010]. Studies of Ancient Egyptian Footwear. Technological Aspects. Part VI. Sewn Sandals. In: Ikram, S. & A. Dodson. Eds. 2009. Beyond the Horizon: Studies in Egyptian Art, Archaeology and History in Honour of Barry J. Kamp. – Cairo, Supreme Council of Antiquities: 554-580.

Veldmeijer, A.J. 2009b [in press 2010]. Amarna's Leatherwork. Part I. Preliminary Analysis and Catalogue. – Norg, DrukWare.

Veldmeijer, A.J. 2009c. Note on the Possible Relation between Shoes and Chariots. – Archaeological Leather Group Newsletter 29: 11-12.

Veldmeijer, A.J. 2009d. Studies of Ancient Egyptian Footwear. Technological Aspects. Part XV. Leather Curled-Toe Ankle Shoes. – PalArch's Journal of Archaeology of Egypt/Egyptology 6, 4: 1-21 (online at: http://www.palarch.nl/category/egypt/; visited 16 June 2009).

Veldmeijer, A.J. 2009e. Cordage and Netting Production. – UCLA Encyclopedia of Egyptology: 1-9 (online at: http://repositories.cdlib.org/nelc/uee/1059; visited 16 June 2009).

Veldmeijer, A.J. 2009f. Studies of Ancient Egyptian Footwear. Technological Aspects. Part XVI. Leather Open Shoes. – British Museum Studies in Ancient Egypt and Sudan 11: 1-10 (online at: http://www.britishmuseum.org/research/online_journals/bmsaes.aspx; visited 16 June 2009).

Veldmeijer, A.J. 2009g. Studies of Ancient Egyptian Footwear. Technological Aspects. Part VII. Coiled Sewn Sandals. – British Museum Studies in Ancient Egypt and Sudan 14:85-96.

Veldmeijer, A.J. 20009h. Studies of Ancient Egyptian Footwear. Technological Aspects. Part XII. Fibre Shoes. – British Museum Studies in Ancient Egypt and Sudan 14:97-129.

Veldmeijer, A.J. 2009i. Studies of Ancient Egyptian Footwear. Technological Aspects. Part X. Leather Composite Sandals. – PalArch's Journal of Archaeology of Egypt/Egyptology 6, 9:1-27.

Veldmeijer, A.J. In press. a Studies of Ancient Egyptian Footwear. Technological Aspects. Part V. Fibre Open Shoes from Qasr Ibrim. In: Godlewski, W. & A. Lajtar. Eds. In press. Acts of the 11th Conference of Nubian Studies, Warsaw, 27 August-2 September 2006, Vol. II. Session Papers. – Warsaw, Warsaw University Publishers (Polish Centre of Mediterranean Archaeology of Warsaw University, Supplement Volume 4/5).

Veldmeijer, A.J. In press b. Leatherwork. In: Kemp, B.J. & A.K. Stevens. Busy Lives at Amarna. Excavations in a Housing Neighbourhood (Grid 12) in the Main City. – London, Egypt Exploration Society.

Veldmeijer, A.J. In press c. Studies of Ancient Egyptian Footwear. Technological Aspects. Part XVI: Additional Pair of Leather Open Shoes. – Journal of the American Research Center in Egypt.

Veldmeijer, A.J. Accepted. Studies of Ancient Egyptian Footwear. Technological Aspects. Part XI. Sewn-Edge Plaited Sandals. – Jaarberichten Ex Oriental Lux.

Veldmeijer, A.J. In preparation a. Leatherwork from Qasr Ibrim. Volume I. Ottoman. – Norg, DrukWare.

Veldmeijer, A.J. In preparation b. Studies of Ancient Egyptian Footwear. Technological Aspects. Part XVII. Leather Stubbed-Toe Low Ankle Shoes.

Veldmeijer, A.J. Forthcoming a. [Footwear in Ancient Egypt. A History.] – Norg, DrukWare.

Veldmeijer, A.J. Forthcoming b. Studies of Ancient Egyptian Footwear. Technological Aspects. Supplement: A Pair of Wooden Pattens.

Veldmeijer, A.J. & C. van Driel-Murray. In preparation. Leatherwork from Qasr Ibrim. Volume II. The Pharaonic Period to the Age of Christianity. – Norg, DrukWare.

Veldmeijer, A.J. & E. Endenburg. 2007. Amarna Leatherwork in Berlin. – Egyptian Archaeology 31: 36-37.

Veldmeijer, A.J. & E. Endenburg. 2008. Footwear from Qasr Ibrim. – Egyptian Archaeology 33: 18-20.

Veldmeijer, A.J. & J. Laidler. 2008. Leatherwork in Ancient Egypt. In: Selin, H. Ed. 2008. Encyclopedia of the History of Science, Technology, and Medicine in Non-Western Cultures. – Heidelberg, Springer Verlag: 1215-1220.

Veldmeijer, A.J. & C. Zazzaro. With contributions by A.J. Clapham, C.R. Cartwright & F. Hagen. 2008. The 'Rope Cave' at Mersa/Wadi Gawasis. – Journal of the American Research Center in Egypt 44: 9-39.

Verdan, S. 2007. Eretria. Metalworking in the Sanctuary of Apollo Daphnephoros during the Geometric Period. In: Mazarakis Ainian, A. Ed. 2007. Oropos and Euboea in the Early Iron Age. Acts of an International Round Table, University of Thessaly (June 18-20, 2004). – Volos, University of Thessaly: 345-361.

Vergnieux, R. 1999. Recherches sur les monuments thébains d'Amenhotep IV à l'aide d'outils informatiques, Méthodes et résultats. Volume I & II. – Geneva, Société d'Égyptologie (Cahiers de la Société d'Egyptologie, Vol. 4).

Vernier, É. 1907-1927. Catalogue Général des Antiquités égyptiennes du Musée du Caire. Bijoux et orfèvreries. – Cairo, Institut Français d'Archéologie Orientale.

Vernier, É. 1907. La bijouterie et la joaillerie égyptiennes. – Cairo, Institut Français d'Archéologie Orientale.

Vogelsang-Eastwood, G.M. 1999. Tutankhamun's Wardrobe. Garments from the Tomb of Tutankhamun. – Rotterdam, Barjesteh and Meeuwes.

Vogelsang-Eastwood, G.M. 1994. De Kleren van de Farao. – Amsterdam, De Bataafsche Leeuw.

Walser, G. 1966. Die Völkerschaften auf den Reliefs von Persepolis. – Berlin, Mann (Teheraner Forschungen II).

Walters, S.M. 1993. Fagales: 34. Betulaceae. In: Tutin, T.G., N.A. Burges, A.O. Chater, J.R. Edmondson, J.R. Heywood, D.M. Moore, D.H. Valentine, S.M. Walters & D.A. Webb. Eds. 1993. Flora Europaea. Volume 1. Psilotaceae to Plantanaceae (2nd Edition). – Cambridge, Cambridge University Press: 68.

Ward, W.A. 1982. Index of Egyptian Administrative and Religious titles of the Middle Kingdom. – Beirut, American University of Beirut.

Welsh, F. 1993. Tutankhamun's Egypt. – Buckinghamshire, Shire Publications Ltd.

Wendrich, W.Z. 1989. Preliminary Report on the Amarna Basketry and Cordage. In: Kemp, B.J. Ed. 1989. Amarna Reports V. – London, Egypt Exploration Society (Occasional Publications 6): 169-201.

Wendrich, W.Z. 1991. Who's Afraid of Basketry. A Guide to Recording Basketry and Cordage for Archaeologists. – Leiden, Centre of Non-Western Studies.

Wendrich, W.Z. 1999. The Word According to Basketry. An Ethno-Archaeological Interpretation of Basketry Production in Egypt. – Leiden, Centre of Non-Western Studies.

Wendrich, W.Z. 2000. Basketry. In: Nicholson, P.T. & I. Shaw. Eds. 2000. Ancient Egyptian Materials and Technology. – Cambridge, Cambridge University Press: 254-267.

Wente, E.F. 1967. Late Ramesside Letters. – Chicago, Oriental Institute (Studies in Ancient Oriental Civilizations 33).

Wente, E.F. 1990. Letters from Ancient Egypt. – Atlanta, Scholars Press.

Williams, B. 1983. C-Group, Pan Grave, and Kerma Remains at Adindan Cemeteries T, K, U, and J. – Chicago, The Oriental Institute of the University of Chicago (The University of Chicago Oriental Institute Nubian Expedition Volume V. Excavations between Abu Simbel and the Sudan Frontier).

Williams, C.R. 1924. Catalogue of Egyptian Antiquities. Numbers 1-60. Gold and Silver Jewelry and Related Objects. – New York, New York Historical Society.

Williams, D. & J.M. Ogden. 1994. Greek Gold. Jewellery of the Classical World. – London, British Museum Press.

Winlock, H.E. 1948. The Treasure of Three Egyptian Princesses. – New York, The Metropolitan Museum of Art

Wreszinski, W. 1912. Der Londoner medizinische Papyrus (Brit. Museum Nr. 10059) und der Papyrus Hearst in Transkription, Übersetzung und Kommentar. – Leipzig, J.C. Hinrichs.

Wreszinski, W. 1913. Der Papyrus Ebers. Umschrift, Übersetzung und Kommentar. – Leipzig, J.C. Hinrichs.

Zonhoven, L.M.J. 1979. The Inspection of a tomb at Deir el-Medina (O. Wien Aeg. 1). – Journal of Egyptian Archaeology 65: 89–98.

APPENDICES

I ABBREVIATIONS

I.A Abbreviations Used in Chapter 7

HO
Ostraca published by Černý & Gardiner (1957); numbers refer to plates.

O.
Ostracon

O. Ashm
Ostraca in the Ashmolean Museum, Oxford (previously O. Gardiner), published by Kitchen (1975-1989).

O. Berlin
Ostraca in the Egyptian Museum, Berlin, published by Gardiner & Möller (1911).

O. BM
Ostraca in the British Museum, London, published by Demarée (2002).

O. Cairo
Ostraca in the Egyptian Museum, Cairo, published by Černý (1935a).

O. DeM
Ostraca from Deir el-Medinah at the Institut Français d'Archéologie Orientale, Cairo; nos. 1-456 published by Černý (1935b; 1937a, b; 1939; 1951); nos. 550-623 by Sauneron (1959); nos. 624-705 by Černý (1970); nos. 1001-1675 by Posener (1934; 1951-1952-1972; 1977-1978-1980); nos. 1676-1873 by Gasse (1990; 2005); nos. 10001-10123 by Grandet (2000; 2003; 2006).

O. Glasgow
Ostraca in the Hunterian Museum, Glasgow, published by McDowell (1991).

O. Michaelides
Ostraca from the Michaelides collection, originally in Cairo, published by Goedicke & Wente (1962).

O. Qurna
Ostraca from Qurna (Thebes), published with transliteration, translation and photographs as part of Universität München's Deir el-Medine Online project at http://obelix.arf.fak12.uni-muenchen.de/cgi-bin/mmcgi2mmhob/mho-1/hobmain/.

O. Strasbourg
Ostraca in the Bibliothéque Nationale and Universitaire de Strasbourg, published by Koenig (1997).

O. Turin
Ostraca in the Museo Egizio, Turin, published by López (1978; 1980; 1982; 1984).

P.
Papyrus

P. DeM
Papyri from Deir el-Medina, published by Černý (1986).

***Urk*. IV**
Urkunden der 18. Dynastie, 1-1226 published by Sethe (1905-1906), 1227-2179 by Helck (1955-1958).

I.B Other Abbreviations

ÄMPB
Ägyptisches Museum und Papyrussammlung, Berlin.

ASH
Ashmolean Museum, Oxford

BM
British Museum, London

EgCa
Egyptian Museum, Cairo

MEgT
Museo Egizio, Turin

MET
Metropolitan Museum of Arts, New York

MFA
Museum of Fine Arts, Boston

NMAL
National Museum of Antiquities, Leiden

Petrie
Petrie Museum of Egyptian Archaeology University College, London

II GLOSSARY

The glossary is taken from Goubitz *et al.* (2001) with, between square brackets, additions made by the present author. The difference between sewing and stitching used by Goubitz *et al.* is not followed here: 'sewing' is used in vegetable sandals and 'stitching' in leather footwear because the partially passing of the leather's thickness ('sewing' according to Goubitz *et al.*) does not occur in Tutankhamun's footwear.

Ankle shoe
[Type of closed] "Shoe with uppers that reach just to or over the ankle" (Goubitz *et al.*, 2001: 317). Note that open shoes, such as described in the present work, are excluded.

Anterior
Front or toe part of a foot or piece of footwear (figure 3 of the introduction).

Back strap
"The strap which holds the rear part of the sandal to the foot" (Goubitz *et al.*, 2001: 318).

Closed shoe
Shoe with an upper that entirely encloses the foot. In ancient Egypt, this type of shoe was only made in leather.

Combined fastening
"A shoe fastening consisting of more than one method, *e.g.* a combination of lace and buckle or toggle and lace" (Goubitz *et al.*, 2001: 318). In open shoes, this could mean for example the combination of a traditional strap complex, combined with a instep strap.

Curing (leather)
Method of arresting the degenerative process of skin. This is a reversible condition, in contrast to vegetable tanning. Curing can be done with oil, fat or minerals.

Cutting pattern
"Al the main components of the upper or entire shoe laid out flat so that the overall design can be seen; the pieces in their original position as cut out by the shoe maker" (Goubitz et al., 2001: 318).

Decoration
"Designs, cuts, or added materials that are meant to beautify the shoe" (Goubitz et al., 2001: 318).

Dorsal
The dorsal surface of a foot or a piece of footwear is the surface that faces upwards (figure 3 of the introduction).

Edge
Imprecisely defined outer rim of a sandal or shoe's sole. In fibre, sewn sandals: the bundles at right angle to the fabric that is made of transverse bundles.

Ear
Type of pre-strap. Some types of leather sandals (so-called 'eared sandals') have a pre-strap that is cut out from the same sheet of leather as the sole itself. They protrude at the start of the heel. Two-dimensional art showing the production of sandals show sandal types with these 'ear' pre-strap (*cf.* figure 8.1).

Fastening
System to keep a shoe attached to the foot.

Fibre
Strictly speaking, the basic structural unit of which plants are made. However, the term is used in literature and daily language in broader sense to indicate plant material, such as the leaf. In order to avoid confusion, the term is used in the present work as such. When the structural unit is meant, this is explicitly stated. See also 'Palm leaf fibre.'

Foot strap
"The strap on the forepart of a patten [a wooden sandal with stilts, see for examples from Egypt Veldmeijer, 2005/2006] or sandal" (Goubitz et al., 2001: 319). But the open shoes from Tutankhamun have a comparable strap, emphasising the close relation between open shoes and sandals.

Front strap
The strap that holds the front part of the sandal to the foot by running between two toes (or, in the case of a double front strap, the straps that run between the first/second and third/fourth toe) towards the back straps.

Heel
"The backmost part of the foot [...], also the component under the heel seat of a shoe" (Goubitz et al., 2001: 319). Here, this term is used in its general meaning, as explained below with 'heel seat.' True heels did not occur in ancient Egypt until after the Pharaonic era.

Heel seat
"The area in the shoe or on the insole on which the heel of the foot rests" (Goubitz et al., 2001: 319). Since this term, in daily language, is never used, I choose to use 'heel' for this area in footwear (thus not only for shoes but also for sandals, pattens etc.)

Heel strap
Here: the strap that runs from the pre-strap behind the heel of the foot.

Insole
"Sole upon which the foot rests, found in the interior of the shoe" (Goubitz et al., 2001: 320). Note that the term 'insole' is also used in sandals.

Instep
"A rather imprecisely defined area on top of the foot between the rear of the toes and the ankle joint" (Goubitz et al., 2001: 320).

Instep strap
Strap in open shoes that lies over the instep and fasten the two sides of the upper. It is attached at one side and closes, in Tutankhamun's open shoes, by means of a toggle at the other side.

Lateral
The side of a foot or a piece of footwear that faces outwards (figure 3 in the introduction).

Medial
The side of a foot or a piece of footwear that faces inwards (figure 3 in the introduction).

Midsole
"The sole layer or any of the sole layers found between the insole and treadsole" (Goubitz *et al.*, 2001: 320).

Model
"The total shape, cut, and style of a [piece of footwear]" (Goubitz *et al.*, 2001: 320). The original definition referred to shoes only, but the term is applicable to other footwear, such as sandals, too.

Open shoe
Shoe with an upper that covers the sides of the foot only. The dorsal surface of the foot is not covered. Open shoes occur in fibre as well as leather and can be differentiated in those with a partial and full upper (see figure 9.1).

Openwork decoration
"Designs made by cutting or punching shapes and figures out of the leather" (Goubitz *et al.*, 2001: 321).

Painted decoration
"Decoration made by using pigment to ornament the leather surface" (Goubitz *et al.*, 2001: 321).

Palm leaf fibre
The leaf sheat at the base of the leaf midribs in date palms, which turns into a fibrous material after decaying, usually referred to as 'palm fibre'.

Posterior
Back or heel part of a foot or piece of footwear (figure 3 in the introduction).

Pre-strap
The connecting element of the back and / or heel strap to the sole.

Rand
"Strip of leather included in the sole seam of turnshoes, placed between the sole and upper (Goubitz *et al.*, 2001: 321).

Rawhide
Hide which has not been treated to increase its durability.

Reconstruction
"Object that is made in new leather or other materials, to show how its original would have appeared when new and complete. Reconstruction can also apply to a drawing of how the object must have looked when in use" (Goubitz *et al.*, 2001: 322).

Running stitch
"Single thread that follows a serpentine course in and out [the material]" (Goubitz *et al.*, 2001: 322). Originally, only reference to leather was made but it equally applies to other materias (for example plant fibre)

Sandal
"A sole only, which is made of one material or a combination of different materials (among which are leather, vegetable fibre or wood) with a back strap, and / or heel strap and / or front strap. The sole can consist of various layers. This means that footwear with a closed heel are excluded (shoe); the same counts for footwear with a closed front part (slippers)." (Veldmeijer, 2006/2007: 62).

Sewing or stitch hole
"Round or oval holes left in the leather [or other material] after the sewing or stitch thread has disintegrated" (Goubitz et al., 2001: 322-323).

Shoe
Sole with an upper that encloses the heel only (open shoe) or the entire foot (closed shoe).

Skin processing
The action of obtaining skin, cleaning it and increasing its durability. This can be curing, resulting in pseudo-tannages, or vegetable tanning, resulting in true leather.

Sole
"All-inclusive term for the parts of the shoe under the foot" (Goubitz et al., 2001: 322). A sole might consist of several sole layers: insole, treadsole and midsole(s).

Sole/upper construction
"The way in which the sole layers are built up; and the method used to attach the sole to the uppers [or, in sandals, to attach the strap complex to the soles]" (Goubitz et al., 2001: 322).

Sole layer
See 'sole'.

Stitching
"When the awl, and subsequently the thread, pass straight through the thickness of the leather; the leathers can be overlapping or facing each other" (Goubitz et al., 2001: 323).

Straight sole
"Sole with a [longitudinally] symmetrical shape, i.e. neither left- or right-foot oriented" (Goubitz et al., 2001: 323).

Strap complex
The entire system of straps in sandals: usually, front strap, back strap, pre-strap, heel strap. These four not necessarily occur together in one sandal: this differs per type, as do their shape and construction. Less common are toe band and foot strap.

Swayed [...] sole
"Sole matching the right or left curving of the foot". [These soles are asymmetrical longitudinally] (Goubitz et al., 2001: 323).

Toe band
Part of the strap complex. A looped construction through which the big toe (and, possibly, additional toes) was put to keep the piece of footwear attached to the foot.

Transverse bundle
In sewn sandals the parallel grass cores, which are wrapped and sewn to each other with narrow palm leaf strips.

Treadsole
"The undermost sole of footwear, facing the ground" (Goubitz et al., 2001: 324).

Upper
"All the leather [or vegetable fibre] above the sole and covering parts or the [sic] all of the foot and leg" (Goubitz et al., 2001: 324).

Vegetable tanning
Process of arresting the degenerative process of skin in such a way that chemically stable and water resistant leather is created. This process is not reversible, in contrast to curing.

Ventral
The ventral surface in a foot or a piece of footwear is the surface that faces downwards (figure 3 in the introduction).

Waist
"The narrow middle part of the [...] shoe or the sole, corresponding with the instep and the arch of the foot" (Goubitz et al., 2001: 324).

III CONCORDANCES

III.A FOOTWEAR TUTANKHAMUN

III.A.1 Carter's Number

Carter's Number	Exhibition Number	Special Registry Number	Temporary Number	JE Number	Table	Figures
397	565	2822	-	62692	3	3.43-3.46
021a & b	910	2823	-	62688	1	1.2A, B; 2.2; 3.9
021f & g	341	2818	-	62680	6	1.2D; 2.3; 3.61-3.65
021h & i	-	4276	-	62684	5	1.2C; 2.5; 3.52-3.57
021j	-	-	-	-	9	
021k & l	912/913	2820	-	62681	7	1.2D; 2.4; 3.66-3.71
0367b	1261	2821	-	62692	2	1.11; 3.6; 3.41
067b	-	-	-	-	9	1.3; 1.4
085a	747	2825	-	62686	4	1.5; 3.47A, B-3.51
085c	-	-	-	-	9	1.4
094a	3395	4284	30 3 + 34 27	-	1	1.6; 2.6; 3.10
104a	3413	4293bis	30 3 + 34 45	-	1	1.7; 2.7; 3.11; 4.1A
104b	-	-	-	-	9	1.7
147a	747	2825	-	62686	4	1.5; 3.47C-3.51
256ll	327	3503/3504	-	60678 / 60679	5	1.8; 3.60
270a	904	2819	-	62682	8	1.10; 2.1; 3.72-3.77
453b	1259	2816	-	62683	5	1.13; 3.58; 3.59
587c(?)	1263	2824	-	62687	1	1.14; 3.5; 3.12
620 (119)	1262	2816	-	62691	2	3.42
620 (119)	3387	4285	30 3 + 34 19A, B	-	1	3.16
620 (119)	3388	4291	30 3 + 34 20A, B	-	1	3.22
620 (119)	3389	4289	30 3 + 34 21A, B	-	1	3.20
620 (119)	3390	4288	30 3 + 34 22A, B	-	1	3.19
620 (119)	-	4294? See text	-	62690	2	3.14; 3.7A
620 (119)	3391	4290	30 3 + 34 23A, B	-	1	3.21
620 (119)	3392	4287	30 3 + 34 24B	-	1	3.18
620 (119)	3393	4292	30 3 + 34 25A, B	-	1	3.23
620 (119)	3394	4286	30 3 + 34 26A	-	1	3.17
620 (119)	3396	4304	30 3 + 34 28A, B	-	1	3.34
620 (119)	3397	4298	30 3 + 34 29A, B	-	1	3.28
620 (119)	3398	4308	30 3 + 34 30A, B	-	1	3.38
620 (119)	3399	4307	30 3 + 34 31A, B	-	1	3.37
620 (119)	3400	4310	30 3 + 34 32A, B	-	1	3.40
620 (119)	3401	4301	30 3 + 34 33A, B	-	1	3.31

Carter's Number	Exhibition Number	Special Registry Number	Temporary Number	JE Number	Table	Figures
620 (119)	3402	4303	30 3 + 34 34B	-	1	3.33
620 (119)	3402	4303	30 3 + 34 34A	-	2	3.33
620 (119)	3403	4300	30 3 + 34 35A, B	-	1	3.30
620 (119)	3404	4295	30 3 + 34 36A, B	-	1	3.25
620 (119)	3405	4297	30 3 + 34 37A, B	-	1	3.27
620 (119)	3406	4299	30 3 + 34 38A, B	-	1	3.29
620 (119)	3407	4306	30 3 + 34 39A, B	-	1	3.36
620 (119)	3408	4296	30 3 + 34 40A, B	-	1	3.26
620 (119)	3409	4294bis	30 3 + 34 41A, B	-	1	3.24
620 (119)	3410	4309	30 3 + 34 42A, B	-	1	3.39
620 (119)	3411	4305	30 3 + 34 43A, B	-	1	3.35
620 (119)	3412	4302	30 3 + 34 44A, B	-	1	3.32
620 (119)	-	4294	-	62690	1	3.14; 3.7A
620 (119)	-	4293? See text	-	62689	1/2	3.13

III.A.2 Exhibition Number

Exhibition Number	Carter's Number	Special Registry Number	Temporary Number	JE Number	Table	Figures
327	256ll	3503/3504		60678 / 60679	5	1.8; 3.60
341	021f & g	2818	-	62680	6	1.2D; 2.3; 3.61-3.65
565	397	2822	-	62692	3	3.43-3.46
747	085a	2825	-	62686	4	1.5; 3.47A, B-3.51
747	147a	2825	-	62686	4	1.5; 3.47C-3.51
904	270a	2819	-	62682	8	1.10; 2.1; 3.72-3.77
910	021a & b	2823	-	62688	1	1.2A, B; 2.2; 3.9
1259	453b	2816	-	62683	5	1.13; 3.58; 3.59
1261	0367b	2821	-	62692	2	1.11; 3.6; 3.41
1262	620 (119)	2816	-	62691	2	3.42
1263	587c(?)	2824	-	62687	1	1.14; 3.5; 3.12
3387	620 (119)	4285	30 3 + 34 19A, B	-	1	3.16
3388	620 (119)	4291	30 3 + 34 20A, B	-	1	3.22
3389	620 (119)	4289	30 3 + 34 21A, B	-	1	3.20
3390	620 (119)	4288	30 3 + 34 22A, B	-	1	3.19
3391	620 (119)	4290	30 3 + 34 23A, B	-	1	3.21
3392	620 (119)	4287	30 3 + 34 24B	-	1	3.18
3393	620 (119)	4292	30 3 + 34 25A, B	-	1	3.23
3394	620 (119)	4286	30 3 +34 26A	-	1	3.17
3395	094a	4284	30 3 + 34 27	-	1	1.6; 2.6; 3.10
3396	620 (119)	4304	30 3 + 34 28A, B	-	1	3.34
3397	620 (119)	4298	30 3 + 34 29A, B	-	1	3.28
3398	620 (119)	4308	30 3 + 34 30A, B	-	1	3.38

Exhibition Number	Carter's Number	Special Registry Number	Temporary Number	JE Number	Table	Figures
3399	620 (119)	4307	30 3 + 34 31A, B	-	1	3.37
3400	620 (119)	4310	30 3 + 34 32A, B	-	1	3.40
3401	620 (119)	4301	30 3 + 34 33A, B	-	1	3.31
3402	620 (119)	4303	30 3 + 34 34B	-	1	3.33
3402	620 (119)	4303	30 3 + 34 34A	-	2	3.33
3403	620 (119)	4300	30 3 + 34 35A, B	-	1	3.30
3404	620 (119)	4295	30 3 + 34 36A, B	-	1	3.25
3405	620 (119)	4297	30 3 + 34 37A, B	-	1	3.27
3406	620 (119)	4299	30 3 + 34 38A, B	-	1	3.29
3407	620 (119)	4306	30 3 + 34 39A, B	-	1	3.36
3408	620 (119)	4296	30 3 + 34 40A, B	-	1	3.26
3409	620 (119)	4294bis	30 3 + 34 41A, B	-	1	3.24
3410	620 (119)	4309	30 3 + 34 42A, B	-	1	3.39
3411	620 (119)	4305	30 3 + 34 43A, B	-	1	3.35
3412	620 (119)	4302	30 3 + 34 44A, B	-	1	3.32
3413	104a	4293bis	30 3 + 34 45	-	1	1.7; 2.7; 3.11; 4.1A
-	021h & i	4276	-	62684	5	1.2C; 2.5; 3.52-3.57
-	021j	-	-	-	9	
-	067b	-	-	-	9	1.3; 1.4
-	085c	-	-	-	9	1.4
-	104b	-	-	-	9	1.7
-	620 (119)	4294	-	62690	1	3.14; 3.7A
-	620 (119)	4293? See text	-	62689	1/2	3.13
-	620 (119)	4294? See text	-	62690	2	3.14; 3.7A
912/913	021k & l	2820	-	62681	7	1.2D; 2.4; 3.66-3.71

III.A.3 Special Registry Number

Special Registry Number	Carter's Number	Exhibition Number	Temporary Number	JE Number	Table	Figures
2816	453b	1259	-	62683	5	1.13; 3.58; 3.59
2816	620 (119)	1262	-	62691	2	3.42
2818	021f & g	341	-	62680	6	1.2D; 2.3; 3.61-3.65
2819	270a	904	-	62682	8	1.10; 2.1; 3.72-3.77
2820	021k & l	912/913	-	62681	7	1.2D; 2.4; 3.66-3.71
2821	0367b	1261	-	62692	2	1.11; 3.6; 3.41
2822	397	565	-	62692	3	3.43-3.46
2823	021a & b	910	-	62688	1	1.2A, B; 2.2; 3.9
2824	587c(?)	1263	-	62687	1	1.14; 3.5; 3.12
2825	085a	747	-	62686	4	1.5; 3.47A, B-3.51
2825	147a	747	-	62686	4	1.5; 3.47C-3.51
4276	021h & i	-	-	62684	5	1.2C; 2.5; 3.52-3.57

Special Registry Number	Carter's Number	Exhibition Number	Temporary Number	JE Number	Table	Figures
4284	094a	3395	30 3 + 34 27	-	1	1.6; 2.6; 3.10
4285	620 (119)	3387	30 3 + 34 19A, B	-	1	3.16
4286	620 (119)	3394	30 3 +34 26A	-	1	3.17
4287	620 (119)	3392	30 3 + 34 24B	-	1	3.18
4288	620 (119)	3390	30 3 + 34 22A, B	-	1	3.19
4289	620 (119)	3389	30 3 + 34 21A, B	-	1	3.20
4290	620 (119)	3391	30 3 + 34 23A, B	-	1	3.21
4291	620 (119)	3388	30 3 + 34 20A, B	-	1	3.22
4292	620 (119)	3393	30 3 + 34 25A, B	-	1	3.23
4294	620 (119)	-	-	62690	1	3.14; 3.7A
4295	620 (119)	3404	30 3 + 34 36A, B	-	1	3.25
4296	620 (119)	3408	30 3 + 34 40A, B	-	1	3.26
4297	620 (119)	3405	30 3 + 34 37A, B	-	1	3.27
4298	620 (119)	3397	30 3 + 34 29A, B	-	1	3.28
4299	620 (119)	3406	30 3 + 34 38A, B	-	1	3.29
4300	620 (119)	3403	30 3 + 34 35A, B	-	1	3.30
4301	620 (119)	3401	30 3 + 34 33A, B	-	1	3.31
4302	620 (119)	3412	30 3 + 34 44A, B	-	1	3.32
4303	620 (119)	3402	30 3 + 34 34B	-	1	3.33
4303	620 (119)	3402	30 3 + 34 34A	-	2	3.33
4304	620 (119)	3396	30 3 + 34 28A, B	-	1	3.34
4305	620 (119)	3411	30 3 + 34 43A, B	-	1	3.35
4306	620 (119)	3407	30 3 + 34 39A, B	-	1	3.36
4307	620 (119)	3399	30 3 + 34 31A, B	-	1	3.37
4308	620 (119)	3398	30 3 + 34 30A, B	-	1	3.38
4309	620 (119)	3410	30 3 + 34 42A, B	-	1	3.39
4310	620 (119)	3400	30 3 + 34 32A, B	-	1	3.40
-	021j	-	-	-	9	-
-	067b	-	-	-	9	1.3; 1.4
-	085c	-	-	-	9	1.4
-	104b	-	-	-	9	1.7
3503/3504	256ll	327		60678 / 60679	5	1.8; 3.60
4293? See text	620 (119)	-	-	62689	1/2	3.13
4293bis	104a	3413	30 3 + 34 45	-	1	1.7; 2.7; 3.11; 4.1A
4294? See text	620 (119)	-	-	62690	2	3.14; 3.7A
4294bis	620 (119)	3409	30 3 + 34 41A, B	-	1	3.24

III.A.4 Temporary Number

Temporary Number	Carter's Number	Exhibition Number	Special Registry Number	JE Number	Table	Figures
-	397	565	2822	62692	3	3.43-3.46
-	021a & b	910	2823	62688	1	1.2A, B; 2.2; 3.9
-	021f & g	341	2818	62680	6	1.2D; 2.3; 3.61-3.65
-	021h & i	-	4276	62684	5	1.2C; 2.5; 3.52-3.57
-	021j	-	-	-	9	
-	021k & l	912/913	2820	62681	7	1.2D; 2.4; 3.66-3.71
-	0367b	1261	2821	62692	2	1.11; 3.6; 3.41
-	067b	-	-	-	9	1.3; 1.4
-	085a	747	2825	62686	4	1.5; 3.47A, B-3.51
-	085c	-	-	-	9	1.4
-	104b	-	-	-	9	1.7
-	147a	747	2825	62686	4	1.5; 3.47C-3.51
-	270a	904	2819	62682	8	1.10; 2.1; 3.72-3.77
-	453b	1259	2816	62683	5	1.13; 3.58; 3.59
-	587c(?)	1263	2824	62687	1	1.14; 3.5; 3.12
-	620 (119)	1262	2816	62691	2	3.42
-	620 (119)	-	4294	62690	1	3.14; 3.7A
-	620 (119)	-	4293? See text	62689	1/2	3.13
-	620 (119)	-	4294? See text	62690	2	3.14; 3.7A
30 3 + 34 19A, B	620 (119)	3387	4285	-	1	3.16
30 3 + 34 20A, B	620 (119)	3388	4291	-	1	3.22
30 3 + 34 21A, B	620 (119)	3389	4289	-	1	3.20
30 3 + 34 22A, B	620 (119)	3390	4288	-	1	3.19
30 3 + 34 23A, B	620 (119)	3391	4290	-	1	3.21
30 3 + 34 24B	620 (119)	3392	4287	-	1	3.18
30 3 + 34 25A, B	620 (119)	3393	4292	-	1	3.23
30 3 + 34 27	094a	3395	4284	-	1	1.6; 2.6; 3.10
30 3 + 34 28A, B	620 (119)	3396	4304	-	1	3.34
30 3 + 34 29A, B	620 (119)	3397	4298	-	1	3.28
30 3 + 34 30A, B	620 (119)	3398	4308	-	1	3.38
30 3 + 34 31A, B	620 (119)	3399	4307	-	1	3.37
30 3 + 34 32A, B	620 (119)	3400	4310	-	1	3.40
30 3 + 34 33A, B	620 (119)	3401	4301	-	1	3.31
30 3 + 34 34A	620 (119)	3402	4303	-	2	3.33
30 3 + 34 34B	620 (119)	3402	4303	-	1	3.33
30 3 + 34 35A, B	620 (119)	3403	4300	-	1	3.30
30 3 + 34 36A, B	620 (119)	3404	4295	-	1	3.25
30 3 + 34 37A, B	620 (119)	3405	4297	-	1	3.27
30 3 + 34 38A, B	620 (119)	3406	4299	-	1	3.29
30 3 + 34 39A, B	620 (119)	3407	4306	-	1	3.36

Temporary Number	Carter's Number	Exhibition Number	Special Registry Number	JE Number	Table	Figures
30 3 + 34 40A, B	620 (119)	3408	4296	-	1	3.26
30 3 + 34 41A, B	620 (119)	3409	4294bis	-	1	3.24
30 3 + 34 42A, B	620 (119)	3410	4309	-	1	3.39
30 3 + 34 43A, B	620 (119)	3411	4305	-	1	3.35
30 3 + 34 44A, B	620 (119)	3412	4302	-	1	3.32
30 3 + 34 45	104a	3413	4293bis	-	1	1.7; 2.7; 3.11; 4.1A
30 3 +34 26A	620 (119)	3394	4286	-	1	3.17
	256ll	327	3503/3504	60678 / 60679	5	1.8; 3.60

III.A.5 JE Number

JE Number	Carter's Number	Exhibition Number	Special Registry Number	Temporary Number	Table	Figures
62680	021f & g	341	2818	-	6	1.2D; 2.3; 3.61-3.65
62681	021k & l	912/913	2820	-	7	1.2D; 2.4; 3.66-3.71
62682	270a	904	2819	-	8	1.10; 2.1; 3.72-3.77
62683	453b	1259	2816	-	5	1.13; 3.58; 3.59
62684	021h & i	-	4276	-	5	1.2C; 2.5; 3.52-3.57
62686	085a	747	2825	-	4	1.5; 3.47A, B-3.51
62686	147a	747	2825	-	4	1.5; 3.47C-3.51
62687	587c(?)	1263	2824	-	1	1.14; 3.5; 3.12
62688	021a & b	910	2823	-	1	1.2A, B; 2.2; 3.9
62689	620 (119)	-	4293? See text	-	1/2	3.13
62690	620 (119)	-	4294	-	1	3.14; 3.7A
62690	620 (119)	-	4294? See text	-	2	3.14; 3.7A
62691	620 (119)	1262	2816	-	2	3.42
62692	397	565	2822	-	3	3.43-3.46
62692	0367b	1261	2821	-	2	1.11; 3.6; 3.41
-	021j	-	-	-	9	-
-	067b	-	-	-	9	1.3; 1.4
-	085c	-	-	-	9	1.4
-	094a	3395	4284	30 3 + 34 27	1	1.6; 2.6; 3.10
-	104a	3413	4293bis	30 3 + 34 45	1	1.7; 2.7; 3.11; 4.1A
-	104b	-	-	-	9	1.7
-	620 (119)	3387	4285	30 3 + 34 19A, B	1	3.16
-	620 (119)	3388	4291	30 3 + 34 20A, B	1	3.22
-	620 (119)	3389	4289	30 3 + 34 21A, B	1	3.20
-	620 (119)	3390	4288	30 3 + 34 22A, B	1	3.19
-	620 (119)	3391	4290	30 3 + 34 23A, B	1	3.21
-	620 (119)	3392	4287	30 3 + 34 24B	1	3.18
-	620 (119)	3393	4292	30 3 + 34 25A, B	1	3.23
-	620 (119)	3394	4286	30 3 +34 26A	1	3.17
-	620 (119)	3396	4304	30 3 + 34 28A, B	1	3.34

JE Number	Carter's Number	Exhibition Number	Special Registry Number	Temporary Number	Table	Figures
-	620 (119)	3397	4298	30 3 + 34 29A, B	1	3.28
-	620 (119)	3398	4308	30 3 + 34 30A, B	1	3.38
-	620 (119)	3399	4307	30 3 + 34 31A, B	1	3.37
-	620 (119)	3400	4310	30 3 + 34 32A, B	1	3.40
-	620 (119)	3401	4301	30 3 + 34 33A, B	1	3.31
-	620 (119)	3402	4303	30 3 + 34 34B	1	3.33
-	620 (119)	3402	4303	30 3 + 34 34A	2	3.33
-	620 (119)	3403	4300	30 3 + 34 35A, B	1	3.30
-	620 (119)	3404	4295	30 3 + 34 36A, B	1	3.25
-	620 (119)	3405	4297	30 3 + 34 37A, B	1	3.27
-	620 (119)	3406	4299	30 3 + 34 38A, B	1	3.29
-	620 (119)	3407	4306	30 3 + 34 39A, B	1	3.36
-	620 (119)	3408	4296	30 3 + 34 40A, B	1	3.26
-	620 (119)	3409	4294bis	30 3 + 34 41A, B	1	3.24
-	620 (119)	3410	4309	30 3 + 34 42A, B	1	3.39
-	620 (119)	3411	4305	30 3 + 34 43A, B	1	3.35
-	620 (119)	3412	4302	30 3 + 34 44A, B	1	3.32
60678/60679	256ll	327	3503/3504		5	1.8; 3.60

III.B FOOTWEAR YUYA AND TJUIU

III.B.1 JE Number

JE Number	Identification	CG Number	Special Registry Number	Table	Figures
95317	-	51121	94	11	6.14
95318	-	51129	95	10	6.5
95319	-	51130	96	10	6.6
95355	-	51121	132	11	6.14
95356	-	51129	133	10	6.10
95357	-	51130(?)	134	10	6.11
-	10,184a, b	-	-	10	6.2
91351a (= 95351?)	-	51128	128	10	6.3
91351b (= 95351?)	-	51128	128	10	6.3
95305a (= 95350?)	-	51127	127	10	6.4
95305b (= 95350?)	-	51127	127	10	6.4
95348a	-	51120	125	10	6.7
95348b	-	51120	125	10	6.7
95349(c)a	-	51124	126	11	6.12
95349(c)b	-	51124	126	11	6.12
95351 (= 91351a?)	-	51128	128	10	6.3

JE Number	Identification	CG Number	Special Registry Number	Table	Figures
95351 (= 91351b?)	-	51128	128	10	6.3
95352a	-	51123	129	11	6.13
95352b(a)	-	51123	129	11	6.13
95353a	-	51125	130	10	6.8
95353b	-	51125	130	10	6.8
95354a	-	51126	131	10	6.9
95354b	-	51126	131	10	6.9

III.B.2 CG Number

CG Number	JE Number	Identification	Special Registry Number	Table	Figures
51120	95348a	-	125	10	6.7
51120	95348b	-	125	10	6.7
51121	95317	-	94	11	6.14
51121	95355	-	132	11	6.14
51123	95352a	-	129	11	6.13
51123	95352b(a)	-	129	11	6.13
51124	95349(c)a	-	126	11	6.12
51124	95349(c)b	-	126	11	6.12
51125	95353a	-	130	10	6.8
51125	95353b	-	130	10	6.8
51126	95354a	-	131	10	6.9
51126	95354b	-	131	10	6.9
51127	95305a (= 95350?)	-	127	10	6.4
51127	95305b (= 95350?)	-	127	10	6.4
51128	91351a (= 95351?)	-	128	10	6.3
51128	91351b (= 95351?)	-	128	10	6.3
51128	95351 (= 91351a?)	-	128	10	6.3
51128	95351 (= 91351b?)	-	128	10	6.3
51129	95318	-	95	10	6.5
51129	95356	-	133	10	6.10
51130	95319	-	96	10	6.6
-	-	10,184a, b	-	10	6.2
51130(?)	95357	-	134	10	6.11

III.B.3 Special Registry Number

Special Registry Number	JE Number	Identification	CG Number	Table	Figures
94	95317	-	51121	11	6.14
95	95318	-	51129	10	6.5
96	95319	-	51130	10	6.6

Special Registry Number	JE Number	Identification	CG Number	Table	Figures
125	95348a	-	51120	10	6.7
125	95348b	-	51120	10	6.7
126	95349(c)a	-	51124	11	6.12
126	95349(c)b	-	51124	11	6.12
127	95305a (= 95350?)	-	51127	10	6.4
127	95305b (= 95350?)	-	51127	10	6.4
128	91351a (= 95351?)	-	51128	10	6.3
128	91351b (= 95351?)	-	51128	10	6.3
128	95351 (= 91351a?)	-	51128	10	6.3
128	95351 (= 91351b?)	-	51128	10	6.3
129	95352a	-	51123	11	6.13
129	95352b(a)	-	51123	11	6.13
130	95353a	-	51125	10	6.8
130	95353b	-	51125	10	6.8
131	95354a	-	51126	10	6.9
131	95354b	-	51126	10	6.9
132	95355	-	51121	11	6.14
133	95356	-	51129	10	6.10
134	95357		51130(?)	10	6.11
-	-	10,184a, b	-	10	6.2

IV TABLES

Table 1. The technological details of Tutankhamun's sewn sandals Type C, Variant 1. Measurements (in mm) are as the object is preserved (see text); those which could not be taken, have not been mentioned. The measurements of the '32 pairs of sandals' are not inserted. According to Carter (Card No. 620 (119) the 21 pairs of large basketwork sandals have maximal length of 31 cm and a maximal width of 11.5 cm. The 11 pairs of small basketwork sandals a maximal length of 21.5 cm and a maximal width of 8.0 cm. The diameters of the rows of the sole relative to each other are in the sequence innermost/middle (if present)/outermost. Abbreviations to identify the numbers: ^{C} = Carter's number; ^{E} = Exhibition number; ^{S} = Special register number; ^{T} = Temporary number. Other abbreviations: app. = approximate; D = diameter; e = equal (edge); l = large (edge) L= length; max = maximal; s = small (edge); T = thickness; W = width.

Collection	Position tomb / identification	Sole					Strap complex			Remarks
		Measurements	No. of rows	W row	Quality	Edge (Ø)	Front strap / fastening	Back strap	Measurements	
Egyptian Museum, Cairo	Antechamber / 021a^C (2823^S; JE 62688; 910^E; left)	W heel: 92; W waist: 87.4; W front: 112.1. L: 325. T: 4.5.	66	4.0	fine	triple l/l/s	type 5? / crown sinnet	common type	L front strap: 105; D front strap: 12.5. W pre strap: 12.5-20.5. W back strap (max): 40.	Pair with 911. Measurements Carter (Card No. 021ab): L circa 30 cm. W circa 10 cm. The first and last transverse rows are narrower.
Egyptian Museum, Cairo	Antechamber / 021b^C (2823^S; JE 62688; 911^E; right)	W heel: 90.3; W waist: 87.4; W front: 112.2. L: 325. T: 4.	66	4.0	fine	triple l/l/s	type 5 / crown sinnet	common type	L front strap: 105; D front strap: 10.5. W pre strap: 11-16. W back strap (max): 42.5.	Pair with 910. Measurements Carter (Card No. 021ab): L circa 30 cm. W circa 10 cm. Back strap glued to sandal, obscuring part of fabric. The number of rows by measuring the sandal's width and divide it by the average width of the horizontal rows.

Collection	Position tomb / identification	Sole Measurements	No. of rows	W row	Qua-lity	Edge (Ø)	Front strap / fastening	Back strap	Measurements	Remarks
Egyptian Museum, Cairo	Antechamber / 104a[C] (4293bis[S]; 30 3 + 34 45[T]; 3413[L], left)	W heel: 91.8; W waist: 90.2; W front: 106.8. L: 320. T: 4.9.	69	4.2	fine	triple l/l/s	?	common type (based on remaining pre strap)	?	For 104b, see table 6. Measurements Carter (Card No. 104ab): L (max): 31 cm. W (max): 11 cm; W instep: 8.7 cm; W heel 9 cm. Edge: some spots are s/l/s. Width front: slightly damaged.
Egyptian Museum, Cairo	Annexe / 094a[C] (4284[S]; 30 3 + 34 27[T]; 3395[L], right)	W heel: 68.5; W waist: 66.5; W front: 82.4. L: 225. T: 4.2.	45	4.0	fine	triple l/l/s	?	common type	W pre-strap: 5.8.	Measurements Carter (Card No. 094a): L (max): 22 cm. W widest point: 8 cm; W instep: 6.5 cm; W heel: 7 cm. W pre-strap: At attachment with the sole; rest is too damaged for representative measurement.
Egyptian Museum, Cairo	Annexe / 587c[C](?) (2824[S]; JE 62687; 1263[L], left)	W heel: 66.0; W waist: 62.0; W front: 79.1. L: 220. T: 4.0.	49	3.0	fine	triple l/l/s	type 5 / crown sinnet	common type	L front strap: 93.0; D front strap: 8.7.	L front strap: repaired.
Egyptian Museum, Cairo	Annexe / 587c[C](?) (2824[S]; JE 62687; 1263[L]; right)	W heel: 63.6; W waist: 62.6; W front: 77.8. L: 210. T: 4.0.	46	3.0	fine	triple l/l/s	type 5 / crown sinnet	common type	L front strap: 84.0; D front strap: 10.4. W pre-strap: 6.7-12.6.	The sandal is distorted, due to which the measurements are less reliable. L front strap: including the loop to the back strap. W pre-strap: broken.
Egyptian Museum, Cairo	Annexe / 4285[S] (620 (119)[C]; 30 3 + 34 19A[T]; 3387[L], right)	W heel: 67.8; W waist: 65.6; W front: 81.3. L: 215. T: 4.1.	47	3.8	fine	triple l/l/s	?	?	?	Differences in diameter transverse bundles and rows of the edge.
Egyptian Museum, Cairo	Annexe / 4285[S] (620 (119)[C]; 30 3 + 34 19B[T]; 3387[L], left)	W heel: 64.3; W waist: 62.7; W front: 78.5. L: 215. T: 3.8.	44	3.8	fine	triple l/l/s	?	?	?	

Collection	Position tomb / identification	Sole Measurements	No. of rows	W row	Quality	Edge (Ø)	Front strap / fastening	Back strap	Measurements	Remarks
Luxor Museum, Luxor	Annexe/ 4286^S (620 (119)^C; 30 3 + 34 26A^T; 3394^L, right)	W heel: 68.1; W waist: 64.7; W front: 77.5 . L: 220. T: 4.8.	48	4.0	fine	triple l/l/s	type 5 / crown sinnet	-	L front strap: app. 75; D front strap: 6.5-8.2.	W front: slightly damaged.
Luxor Museum, Luxor	Annexe / 4287^S (620 (119)^C; 30 3 + 34 24B^T; 3392^L, right)	W heel: 68.2; W waist: 65.8; W front: 78.1. L: 218. T: 4.2.	46	3.5	fine	triple l/l/s	type 5 / crown sinnet	-	D front strap: 10.0.	-
Egyptian Museum, Cairo	Annexe / 4288S (620 (119)^C; 30 3 + 34 22A^T; 3390^L, left)	W heel: 69.3; W waist: 62.8; W front: 80.0. L: 225. T: 3.9.	49	4.0	fine	triple l/l/s	?	?	?	
Egyptian Museum, Cairo	Annexe / 4288^S (620 (119)^C; 30 3 + 34 22B^T; 3390^L, right)	W heel: 67.7; W waist: 64.0; W front: 78.0. L: 220. T: 3.8.	53	4.0	fine	triple l/l/s	?	common type (based on remaining pre-strap)	?	The outer row is slightly narrower than the middle core, but still wider than the outer row.
Egyptian Museum, Cairo	Annexe / 4289^S (620 (119)^C; 30 3 + 34 21A^T; 3389^L, right)	W heel: 64.0; W waist: 62.0; W front: 75.1. L: 220. T: 3.8.	45	4.0	fine	triple l/l/s	?	?	?	Registered as a pair but both are right sandals.
Egyptian Museum, Cairo	Annexe / 4289^S (620 (119)^C; 30 3 + 34 21B^T; 3389^L, right)	W heel: 69.5; W waist: 66.0; W front: 75.5. L: 220. T: 3.5.	44	4.0	fine	triple l/l/s	?	?	?	Broken in two. Registered as a pair but both are right sandals.
Egyptian Museum, Cairo	Annexe / 4290^S (620 (119)^C; 30 3 + 34 23A^T; 3391^L, left)	W heel: 68.7; W waist: 66.1; W front: 80.1. L: 225. T: 3.3.	52	4.0	fine	triple l/l/s	type 5 / crown sinnet	common type	L front strap: app. 80; D front strap: 9.1.	D front strap: repaired; due to incompleteness, no measurements of the back and pre-strap.
Egyptian Museum, Cairo	Annexe / 4290^S (620 (119)^C; 30 3 + 34 23B^T; 3391^L, right)	W heel: 68.2; W waist: 66.3; L: 225. T: 3.8.	51	4.0	fine	triple l/l/s	type 5 / crown sinnet	common type	L front strap: app. 80; D front strap: approximately 7.	-

Collection	Position tomb / identification	Sole					Strap complex			Remarks
		Measurements	No. of rows	W row	Quality	Edge (Ø)	Front strap / fastening	Back strap	Measurements	
Egyptian Museum, Cairo	Annexe / 4291^S (620 (119)^C; 30 3 + 34 20A^T; 3388^L, right)	W heel: 67.9; W waist: 63.2; W front: 78.6. L: 215. T: 3.4.	45	4.0	fine	triple l/l/s	?	?	?	-
Egyptian Museum, Cairo	Annexe / 4291^S (620 (119)^C; 30 3 + 34 20B^T; 3388^L, left)	W heel: 69.2; W waist: 67.1; W front: 81.3. L: 220. T: 4.5.	46	3.5	fine	triple l/l/s	?	common type (based on remaining pre-strap)	?	Differences in width transverse rows.
Egyptian Museum, Cairo	Annexe / 4292^S (620 (119)^C; 30 3 + 34 25A^T; 3393E; left)	W heel: 64.0; W waist: 62.3; W front: 76.2. L: 215. T: 4.1.	47	3.5	fine	triple l/l/s	type 5 / crown sinnet	common type (based on remaining pre-strap)	?	-
Egyptian Museum, Cairo	Annexe / 4292^S (620 (119)^C; 30 3 + 34 25B^T; 3393^L; right)	W heel: 70.5; W waist: 64.8; W front: 79.3. L: 225. T: 4.3.	48	3.5	fine	triple l/l/s	type 5 / ?	common type (based on remaining pre-strap)	?	-
Luxor Museum, Luxor	Annexe / 4294^S (620 (119)^C; 30 3 + JE 6269O; left)	W heel: 93.4; W waist: 91.0; W front: 112.4. L: 320. T: 4.2.	66	4.2	fine	triple l/l/s	type 5 / crown sinnet	common type (strap pulled through pre-strap?)	L front strap: app. 110; D front strap: 10.7. W pre-strap: 8.5-18.7. T pre-strap: 10.2. W back strap (max): 42.4.	-
Egyptian Museum, Cairo	Annexe / 4294bis^S (620 (119)^C; 30 3 + 34 41A^T; 3409^L, right)	W heel: 95.8; W waist: 91.4; W front: 113.2. L: 320. T: 4.0.	64	3.6-4.8	fine	triple l/l/s	?	?	?	-

Appendices

Collection	Position tomb / identification	Sole Measurements	No. of rows	W row	Quality	Edge (Ø)	Front strap / fastening	Back strap	Measurements	Remarks
Egyptian Museum, Cairo	Annexe/ 4294bis[S] (620 (119)[C]; 30 3 + 34 41B[T]; 3409[E], left)	W heel: 92.6; W waist: 87.7; W front: 113.1. L: 325. T: 4.7.	66	4.0-4.8	fine	triple l/l/s	?	common type (based on remaining pre-strap)	?	The inner row of the edge is slightly narrower than the middle, but still wider than the outer row. W waist and heel: approximate, because of the malformation of the sandal.
Egyptian Museum, Cairo	Annexe / 4295[S] (620 (119)[C]; 30 3 + 34 36A[T]; 3404[E], left)	W heel: 95.8; W waist: 91.8; W front: 113.1. L: 5.6.	65	4.0	fine	triple l/l/s	type 5 / crown sinnet	common type	L front strap: appr. 130; D front strap: 12.7.	L front strap: Including the loop for attachment to the back strap.
Egyptian Museum, Cairo	Annexe / 4295[S] (620 (119)[C]; 30 3 + 34 36B[T]; 3404[E], right)	W heel: 94.4; W waist: 88.5; W front: 112.5. L: 4.7.	63	3.8-4.7	fine	triple l/l/s	?	common type (based on remaining pre-strap)	?	
Egyptian Museum, Cairo	Annexe / 4296[S] (620 (119)[C]; 30 3 + 34 40A[T]; 3408[E], left)	W heel: 86.8; W waist: 81.4; W front: 101.5. L: 3.9.	63	4.0	fine	triple l/l/s	?	common type (based on remaining pre-strap)	?	Last transverse row is narrow.
Egyptian Museum, Cairo	Annexe / 4296[S] (620 (119)[C]; 30 3 + 34 40B[T]; 3408[E], right)	W heel: 86.7; W waist: 80.4; W front: 103.0. L: 4.3.	62	4.2	fine	triple l/l/s	?	common type (based on remaining pre-strap)	?	Last transverse row is narrow.
Egyptian Museum, Cairo	Annexe / 4297[S] (620 (119)[C]; 30 3 + 34 37A[T]; 3405[E], left)	W heel: 94.4; W waist: 88.2; W front: 111.7. L: 4.7.	64	4.0	fine	triple l/l/s	type 5 / crown sinnet	?	?	First and last transverse rows are narrow.
Egyptian Museum, Cairo	Annexe / 4297[S] (620 (119)[C]; 30 3 + 34 37B[T]; 3405[E], right)	W heel: 92.1; W waist: 89.7; W front: 111.7. L: 5.1.	69	4.0	fine	triple l/l/s	type 5? / ?	?	?	Last transverse row is narrow.

283

Collection	Position tomb / identification	Sole Measurements	No. of rows	W row	Quality	Edge (Ø)	Front strap / fastening	Back strap	Strap complex Measurements	Remarks
Egyptian Museum, Cairo	Annexe / 4298^S (620 (119)^C; 30 3 + 34 29A^T; 3397^L; right)	W heel: 93.9; W waist: 91.3; W front: 114.5. L: 325. T: 4.0.	70	3.6-4.6	fine	triple l/l/s	type 5 / ?	common type	D front strap: 8.7. W pre-strap: 9.8. T pre-strap: 8.0.	Number of bundles: uncertain, because the strap complex obscures part of the dorsal surface. This is also the reason this surface could not be thoroughly studied. Stitching quality: from front to heel increasing in width.
Egyptian Museum, Cairo	Annexe / 4298^S (620 (119)^C; 30 3 + 34 29B^T; 3397^L; left)	W heel: 93.8; W waist: 88.7; W front: 112.2. L: 325. T: 4.6.	69	4.0	fine	triple l/l/s	type 5 / ?	common type	L front strap: app. 135; D front strap: 7.2.	Number of bundels: uncertain, because the strap complex obscures part of the dorsal surface. This is also the reason this surface could not be thoroughly studied.
Egyptian Museum, Cairo	Annexe / 4299^S (620 (119)^C; 30 3 + 34 38A^T; 3406^L; left)	W heel: 93.5; W waist: 85.0; W front: 111.3. L: 315. T: 4.5.	65	4.5	fine	triple l/l/s	?/?	?	?	W waist: uncertain because broken.
Egyptian Museum, Cairo	Annexe / 4299^S (620 (119)^C; 30 3 + 34 38B^T; 3406^L; right)	W heel: 93.9; W waist: 88.5; W front: 112.2. L: 325. T: 4.7.	63	4.5	fine	triple l/l/s	?/?	?	?	
Egyptian Museum, Cairo	Annexe / 4300^S (620 (119)^C; 30 3 + 34 35A^T; 3404^L; right)	W heel: 88.7; W waist: 87.3; W front: 109.4. L: 310. T: 3.8.	67	4.0	fine	triple l/l/s	?	common type	?	Last transverse row is narrow.
Egyptian Museum, Cairo	Annexe / 4300^S (620 (119)^C; 30 3 + 34 35B^T; 3403^L; left)	W heel: 91.1; W waist: 90.0; W front: 111.1. L: 320. T: 4.4.	68	3.5-4.0	fine	triple l/l/s	type 5 / ?	common type	L front strap: app. 130; D front strap: 9.5. W pre-strap: 9.4. T pre-strap: 8.6.	First and last transverse rows are narrower.

Collection	Position tomb / identification	Sole					Strap complex			Remarks
		Measurements	No. of rows	W row	Qua-lity	Edge (Ø)	Front strap / fastening	Back strap	Measurements	
Egyptian Museum, Cairo	Annexe / 4301^S (620 (119)^C; 30 3 + 34 33A^T; 3401^E; right)	W heel: 97.2; W waist: 91.9; W front: 116.5. L: 325. T: 4.3.	65	4.5	fine	triple l/l/s	type 5 / crown sinnet	common type (based on remaining pre-strap)	D front strap: 12.2.	The first and last transverse rows are narrow.
Egyptian Museum, Cairo	Annexe / 4301^S (620 (119)^C; 30 3 + 34 33B^T; 3401^E; left)	W heel: 93.8; W waist: 88.2; W front: 111.4. L: 330. T: 5.2.	66	4.3	fine	triple l/l/s	?	common type	?	The first and last ones are narrow.
Egyptian Museum, Cairo	Annexe / 4302S (620 (119)^C; 30 3 + 34 44A^T; 3412^E; right)	W heel: 85.5; W waist: 78.7; W front: 101,0. L: 305. T: 4.0.	59	app. 4.5	fine	triple l/l/s	?	?	?	The first and last transverse rows are narrow.
Egyptian Museum, Cairo	Annexe / 4302^S (620 (119)^C; 30 3 + 34 44B^T; 3412^E; left)	W heel: 84.0; W waist: 78.6; W front: 99.3. L: 300. T: 4.7.	60	3.8	fine	triple l/l/s	? / crown sinnet	?	?	The last transverse row is rather narrow.
Egyptian Museum, Cairo	Annexe / 4303^S (620 (119)^C; 30 3 + 34 34B^T; 3402^E; right)	W heel: 94.0; W waist: 90.2; W front: 112.5. L: 325. T: 4.4.	60	4.6	fine	triple l/l/s	? / crown sinnet	common type (based on remaining pre-strap)	?	-
Egyptian Museum, Cairo	Annexe / 4304^S (620 (119)^C; 30 3 + 34 28A^T; 3396^E; right)	W heel: 92.1; W waist: 88.5; W front: 112.2. L: 320.	68	4.1	fine	triple l/l/s	type 5 / ?	common type	D front strap: 10.6. W pre strap: 7.5-10.8; T pre strap: 11.8. W back strap (max): ?	First and last transverse rows are narrower. The inner row of the edge is slightly narrower than the middle core, but still wider than the outer row. The condition did not allow measuring the width of the back strap.

Collection	Position tomb / identification	Sole Measurements	No. of rows	W row	Quality	Edge (Ø)	Front strap / fastening	Back strap	Strap complex Measurements	Remarks
Egyptian Museum, Cairo	Annexe / 4304[S] (620 (119)[C]; 30 3 + 34 28B[T]; 3396[L], left)	W heel: 91.8; W waist: 86.5; W front: 110.9. L: 318. T: 3.8.	67	4.0	fine	triple l/l/s	type 5 / ?	common type	D front strap: 10.4. W pre strap: 8.0-14.0; T pre-strap: 15.5. W back strap (max): 36.2.	The first transverse row is narrower.
Egyptian Museum, Cairo	Annexe / 4305[S] (620 (119)[C]; 30 3 + 34 43A[T]; 3411[L], left)	W heel: 93.5; W waist: 91.9; W front: 111.3. L: 320. T: 4.4.	67	3.6	fine	triple l/l/s	?	common type	-	First and last transverse rows are narrower.
Egyptian Museum, Cairo	Annexe / 4305[S] (620 (119)[C]; 30 3 + 34 43B[T]; 3411[L], right)	W heel: 92.2; W waist: 88.1; W front: 112.0. L: 320. T: 4.5.	68	3.5-4.6	fine	triple l/l/s	?	?	-	Last transverse row is narrower.
Egyptian Museum, Cairo	Annexe / 4306[S] (620 (119)[C]; 30 3 + 34 39A[T]; 3407[L], left)	W heel: 95.0; W waist: 90.1; W front: 114.2. L: 320. T: 4.5.	66	3.8	fine	triple l/l/s	type 5 / ?	common type (based on remaining pre-strap)	D front strap: 12.2.	Last transverse row is narrower.
Egyptian Museum, Cairo	Annexe / 4306[S] (620 (119)[C]; 30 3 + 34 39B[T]; 3407[L], right)	W heel: 95.8; W waist: 91.4; W front: 113.6. L: 320. T: 4.0.	65	3.5-4.0	fine	triple l/l/s	?	common type (based on remaining pre-strap)	?	First and last transverse rows are narrower.
Egyptian Museum, Cairo	Annexe / 4307[S] (620 (119)[C]; 30 3 + 34 31A[T]; 3399[L], left)	W heel: 90.7; W waist: 85.2; W front: 112.2. L: 320. T: 4.2.	64	4.0-4.5	fine	triple l/l/s	?	common type	?	Registered as a pair but both are right sandals. Last transverse row is narrower.
Egyptian Museum, Cairo	Annexe / 4307[S] (620 (119)[C]; 30 3 + 34 31B[T]; 3399[L], left)	W heel: 94.3; W waist: 90.0; W front: 112.7. L: 320. T: 4.2.	63	4.0	fine	triple l/l/s	?	?	?	Registered as a pair but both are left sandals. First and last transverse rows are narrower.

Collection	Position tomb / identification	Sole Measurements	No. of rows	W row	Quality	Edge (Ø)	Front strap / fastening	Back strap	Measurements	Remarks
Egyptian Museum, Cairo	Annexe / 4308^S (620 (119)^C; 30 3 + 34 30A^T; 3398^E; right)	W heel: 96.6; W waist: 91.8; W front: 115.1. L: 315. T: 4.5.	68	3.3-4.0	fine	triple l/l/s	?	?	?	
Egyptian Museum, Cairo	Annexe / 4308^S (620 (119)^C; 30 3 + 34 30B^T; 3398^E; left)	W heel: 96.2; W waist: 92.0; W front: 115.1. L: 320. T: 4.2.	66	3.4-4.0	fine	triple l/l/s	type 5 / ?	common type	D front strap: 9.7. W pre-strap: 8.6. T pre-strap: 7.2. W back strap (max): 40.1.	
Egyptian Museum, Cairo	Annexe / 4309^S (620 (119)^C; 30 3 + 34 42A^T; 3410^E; right)	W heel: 96.5; W waist: 91.3; W front: 114.0. L: 320. T: 4.2.	66	4.0	fine	triple l/l/s	?	?	?	
Egyptian Museum, Cairo	Annexe / 4309^S (620 (119)^C; 30 3 + 34 42B^T; 3410^E; left)	W heel: 93.8; W waist: 93.3; W front: 116.2. L: 315. T: 3.7.	63	4.7	fine	triple l/l/s	?	common type (based on remaining pre-strap)	?	The inner row of the edge is slightly narrower than the middle one, but still wider than the outer row. Width waist is approximate as the edge here is damaged. The length is approximate too because of distortion.
Egyptian Museum, Cairo	Annexe / 4310^S (620 (119)^C; 30 3 + 34 32A^T; 3400^E; right)	W heel: 95.4; W waist: 91.8; W front: 112.5. L: 315. T: 5.3.	69	4.0	fine	triple l/l/s	?	common type (based on remaining pre-strap)	?	First and last transverse rows are narrower.
Egyptian Museum, Cairo	Annexe / 4310^S (620 (119)^C; 30 3 + 34 32B^T; 3400^E; left)	W heel: 97.3; W waist: 89.1; W front: 113.4. L: 320. T: 4.5.	63	3.6-4.0	fine	triple l/l/s	type 5 / crown sinnet	common type	?	First and last transverse rows are narrower.

Table 2. The technological details of Tutankhamun's sewn sandals Type C, Variant 2. Measurements (in mm) are as the object is preserved (see text); those which could not be taken, have not been mentioned. The measurements of the '32 pairs of sandals' are not inserted. According to Carter (Card No. 620 (119) the 21 pairs of large basketwork sandals have maximal length of 31 cm and a maximal width of 11.5 cm. The 11 pairs of small basketwork sandals a maximal length of 21.5 cm and a maximal width of 8.0 cm. The diameters of the rows of the edge of the sole relative to each other are in the sequence innermost/middle (if present)/outermost. Abbreviations to identify the numbers: [C] = Carter's number; [E] = Exhibition number; [S] = Special register number; [T] = Temporary number. Other abbreviations: app. = approximate; D = diameter; e = equal (edge); l = large (edge); L = length; max = maximal; s = small (edge); T = thickness; W = width.

Collection	Position tomb / identification	Sole Measurements	No. of rows	W row	Quality	Edge (ø)	Front strap / fastening	Back strap	Strap complex Measurements	Remarks
Egyptian Museum, Cairo	Annexe / 367b[C] (2821[S]; JE 62692; 1261[E], right)	W heel: 95.2; W waist: 91.1; W front: 112. L: 325. T: 7.5.	64	?	fine	triple l/l/s	type 5 / crown sinnet	common type (pre-strap outside back strap?)	L front strap: 110.0; D front strap: 9.6-11.3. W pre-strap: 9.2-20.6. T pre-strap: 8.6. W back strap (max): 42.8.	Measurements Carter (Card No. 367abc): L (max): 30.0 cm. Thickness sole includes the stiff linen insole. Width of row not possible due to insole. Length front strap excluding loop to back strap. Differences diameter front strap due to repair.
Egyptian Museum, Cairo	Annexe / 2816[S] (620 (119)[C]; JE 62691; 1262[E])	W heel: 93; W waist: 88.7; W front: 112.3. L: 320. T: 5.3.	68	4.0	fine	triple l/l/s	type 5(?) / crown sinnet	common type though covered with linen	L front strap: 105; D front strap: 9.8. W pre-strap: 11.5-16. T pre-strap: 11.5. W back strap (max): 35.	Linen insole with decoration. Thickness of sole includes the insole.
Egyptian Museum, Cairo	Annexe / JE 62690 (620 (119)[C], right)	W heel: 94.5; W waist: 92.3; W front: 111.5. L: 315. T: 4.5.	64	4.0-4.5	fine	triple l/l/s	type 5 / ?	common type	L front strap: app. 12.5; D front strap: 11.1. W pre-strap: 11.8-18.9. T pre-strap: 8.7. W back strap (max): 35.9.	See text on [S]-number. First transverse row is narrow. Length front strap includes loop to the back strap

Collection	Position tomb / identification	Sole					Strap complex			Remarks
		Measurements	No. of rows	W row	Qua-lity	Edge (ø)	Front strap / fastening	Back strap	Measurements	
Egyptian Museum, Cairo	Annexe / JE 62689 (620 (119)^C; left)	W heel: 94.7; W waist: 92.7; W front: 112.6. L: 320. T: 4.1.	67	3.5	fine	triple l/l/s	type 5 / crown sinnet	common type	L front strap: app. 100; D front strap: 11.8. W pre-strap: 10.7. T pre-strap: 6.3. W back strap (max): 28.6.	See text on ^{s}-number. One of pair? See text. Length front strap is incomplete. The outer row of the edge is slightly narrower than the middle, but still wider than the outer row.
Luxor Museum, Luxor	Annexe / JE 62689 (620 (119)^C; right)	W heel: 95.5; W waist: 92.5; W front: 115.0. L: 315. T: 4.2.	64	4.2	fine	triple l/l/s	type 5 / crown sinnet	common type: (pre-strap outside back strap)	L front strap: app. 145; D front strap: 8.6. W pre-strap: 8.3-17.3. T pre-strap: 8.8. W back strap (max): 37.2.	See text on ^{s}-number. One of pair? See text.
Egyptian Museum, Cairo	Annexe / 4303^S (620 (119)^C; 30 3 + 34 34A^T; 3402^L; left)	W heel: 95.0; W waist: 93.2; W front: 113.2. L: 325. T: 4.7.	66?	3.2-4.0	fine	triple l/l/s	type 5? / crown sinnet	common type	L front strap: app. 75; D front strap: 4.4. W pre-strap: 8.5-16.8; T pre-strap: 8.7. W back strap (max): 31.5.	First and last transverse rows are narrower. Number of rows is uncertain because the dorsal surface is partially obscured by the back strap.

Table 3. The technological details of Tutankhamun's marquetry veneer sandals, 397^C (2822^S; JE 62692; 565^E), Egyptian Museum, Cairo. Measurements (in mm) are as the object is preserved (see text); those which could not be taken, have not been mentioned. Abbreviations to identify the numbers: C = Carter's number; E = Exhibition number; S = Special register number. Other abbreviations: D = diameter; L = length; max = maximum; T = thickness; W = width.

Element	Construction	Shape	Measurements (left/right resp.)	Measurements Carter (Card No. 397)
sole	wood, bark, leather, gold foil		L: 290.0/290.0 W front: 93.9/93.0 W waist: 62.7/74.6 W heel: 75.3/79.0 T: 7.1/6.4	L max: 28.4 cm. W max: 9.2 cm.
strap complex	wood, bark, leather, gold foil	cf. sewn sandals Type C	L front strap: 7.8/7.5 D front strap: 7.8/7.5 L x W loop front strap: 28.5x17.6/23.9x16.8 W maximal back strap: 29.9/31.5 D 'pre strap': 6.3-9.8x1.6/7.3-9.7x11.0	

290

Table 4. The technological details of sandals 085a^C [left]/147a^C [right] (2825^S; JE 62686; 747^E), Egyptian Museum, Cairo. Measurements (in mm) are as the object is preserved (see text); those which could not be taken, have not been mentioned. Abbreviations to identify the numbers: ^{C} = Carter's number; ^{E} = Exhibition number; ^{S} = Special register number; ^{T} = Temporary number. Other abbreviations: D = diameter; L = length; T = thickness; W = width.

Element	Construction	Shape	Measurements (left/right resp.)	Measurements Carter (all of left one; Card No. 085a)
sole	leather treadsole and beadwork insole		L: 203/195 W front: 78.4/80.0 W waist: 54.9/56.8 W heel: 55.2/? T: 2.3/4.5 (the leather is bulging; the original thickness will have been between the measurement of the left and right.) D beads: approximately 1.0x2.0	L maximal: 20.5 cm W maximal: 8 cm W instep: 5.5 cm W heel: 5.5 cm
strap complex	beadwork on leather	cf. sewn sandals Type C	D front strap: 6.9/approximately 7 W back strap maximal: 28.0/approximately 30 D 'pre strap': 7.7/approximately 7	D front strap: 0.7 cm W centre piece back strap: 2.7 cm W back strap maximal: 2.5 cm D 'pre strap': 0.7 cm L 'pre strap': 4 cm

Table 5. The technological details of strap complex 453b[E], leather sandals 256ll[C], Egyptian Museum, Cairo. Measurements (in mm) are as the object is preserved (see text); those which could not be taken, have not been mentioned. Abbreviations to identify the numbers: [C] = Carter's number; [E] = Exhibition number; [S] = Special register number; [T] = Temporary number. Other abbreviations: D = diameter; H = height; L = length; T = thickness; W = width.

Identification	Construction	Shape	Measurements	Carter's Measurements
021h & i[C] (4276[S]; JE 62684)	leather soles palm leaf and papyrus front strap, lengthwise covered with leather papyrus and leather back/pre-strap, all decorated with gold	sewn sandals Type D, Variant 2 *cf.* fibre, sewn sandals Type C	Too fragile to measure. Fragmented.	*Card No. 021gh* L: 30.5 cm. W heel: 8 cm. W instep: 7.5 cm. W maximal: 9.5 cm. W gold wire: 2 mm. D gold bosses: 3 & 7 mm. *Card No. 021i* L front strap: 6 cm. D front strap: 8 mm. W back strap: 8.2 cm. H back strap: 2.5-3.5. L pre strap: 4.0 cm.
453b[C] (2816[S]; JE 62683; 1259[E])	rawhide, bark, leather, gold foil	sewn sandals Type D, Variant 2 *cf.* fibre, sewn sandals Type C	W total: 114.4 L front strap: 111.0 D front: 8.2-12.8 W maximal back strap: 31.2 T back strap: 6.0	—
256ll[C] (3503/3504[S]; JE 60678/60679; 327[E])	gold	sewn sandals Type D, Variant 3 *cf.* fibre, sewn sandals Type C	Not studied first hand	*Card No. 256ll* L: 29.5 cm. W maximal: 10.3 cm. (note L. of right foot of mummy from extreme back of heel to tip of great toe 24.2 cm).

Table 6. The technological details of shoes 021[C] [left]/021g[C] [right] (2818[S]; JE 6268o; 341[E]), Egyptian Museum, Cairo, including measurements. Measurements (in mm) are as the object is preserved (see text); those which could not be taken, have not been mentioned. Measurements with * are approximate. Abbreviations to identify the numbers: [C] = Carter's number; [E] = Exhibition number; [S] = Special register number; [T] = Temporary number. Other abbreviations: D = diameter; e = equal (edge); l = large (edge); L = length; s = small (edge); T = thickness; W = width.

Element	Construction	Shape	No. Bundles / Edge	Measurements (left / right resp.)	Carter's Measurements
sole	leather treadsole; gold insole, leather cover of centre		about 67/ triple	L: 295*/285* W front: 104.7*/108.0* W waist: 89.8*/84.2* W heel: 88.5/87.8 L centre: ?/240.0 W centre: -/16.2 (heel); 10.7 (waist); 27.0 (front) W bundles: 4.3/4.5 W edge: 12.7/12.8	Card Nos. 21/19-21, 21-57 L: 29 cm. W widest part: 10 cm. W heel: 8 cm.
upper	leather inner layer with beadwork outer layer; string of beads along the instep	shape see figure 3.61		W leather decoration strip top: 7.8 (from here on, measurements of one of the pair) W leather decoration strip bottom: 9.8 W gold strips: 1.1 Size metal beads outer upper: 5.2 (rosettes); 5.0x7.5 (lotuses)	
pre-strap	gold tapering tubes	cf. sewn sandals: appearing towards sole		L: 65.5 D at attachment: 6.7x7.8/5.3x8.2 W: 8.5-18.2 T: 6.2	L: 6 cm W at attachment: 0.7 cm W (max): 1.5 cm
back strap	wood, textile, leather, metal and various decoration	cf. sewn sandals		W (max=height): 38.5/39.2*	W (max=height): 3.8 cm
foot strap	six rows of beads on leather	rectangular		W total: 12.2 L (reconstructed): 105.0 D beads: 1.5	

Table 7. *The technological details of shoes 021k^C [right]/021l^C [left];(2820^S; JE 62681; 912/913^t), Egyptian Museum, Cairo. Measurements (in mm) are as the object is preserved (see text); those which could not be taken, have not been mentioned. Abbreviations to identify the numbers: ^C = Carter's number; ^t = Exhibition number; ^s = Special register number; ^T = Temporary number. Other abbreviations: D = diameter; L = length; T = thickness; W = width.*

Element		Construction	Shape	No. Bundels / Edge	Measurements (912 / 913 resp.)	Carter's Measurements Card Nos. 021k-25 & 26	Remarks
sole		leather treadsole; gold insole, leather cover of centre		?/triple	L: 280*/295* W front: 114.0/103.0 W waist: 83.6/85.0* W heel: 89.2/89.9 L centre: 220*/220* W centre: 30.5 (front)/31.0 Folds at ventral surface sole: ?/? W bundles: 3.5/? W edge: 10.7/?	L: 30.5 cm W (max): 10.5 cm	W centre is approximately, because good measuring is prohibited due to the fact that the upper of the shoe rests on the sole. For the same reason no measurements of the heel and waist of the centre part. Regarding folds at ventral surface of the sole: the shoes are too fragile to study and measure the ventral surface.
upper		leather inner layer with beadwork outer layer; string of beads along the instep	*shape* see figure 3.66		L one side: ?/? H at heel: 54.0/? H halfway: 41.5/? H front: 28.0/? W folded top inner: 10.0/10.8 W strip bottom: 10.7 *(from here on, measurements are limited to one of the pair)* W gold strips: 1.3 Size metal beads outer upper: 5.0x5.0		Regarding H halfway: preserved, but reliable measurement impossible. Regarding H front: about 10 mm before the front attachment to the sole.
instep strap		one, consistent of three gold / leather and two cylinders leather	semi-circular		D metal cylinders: 4.0 D leather cylinders: 4.0	W total: 5 cm H: 2.5 cm	
		one gold / leather cylinder of semi-circular closing panel	cylinder		D: 5.4 L (reconstructed): 95*		Regarding D: this is the golden tube that is part of the closing panel.
foot strap		gold lattice work on leather	rectangular		W total: 12.5 L (reconstructed): approximately 100	W lattice work: 1.2 cm	
other	bird				L: 21.0 W: 12.8	1.9 cm long by 1.2 cm wide	

Table 8. The technological details of shoes 270a[C] (2819[S]; JE 62682; 904[E]), Egyptian Museum, Cairo. Measurements (in mm) are as the object is preserved (see text) and are only taken of the left shoe as the right one is too badly preserved; those which could not be taken, have not been mentioned. Measurements with * are approximate. Abbreviations to identify the numbers: [C] = Carter's number; [E] = Exhibition number; [S] = Special register number. Other abbreviations: D = diameter; L = length; W = width.

Identification	Construction	Shape	Measurements (left)	Carter's Measurements Card No. 270a	Remarks
sole	leather insole and treadsole		L: 280 W front: 100.0 W waist: ? W heel: 84.1 W (total): ? W decoration strip edge: 8.7 W gold strip pulled through edge: 2.1	L: 28 cm W sole: approximately 95 cm	Regarding W waist: not measurable due to overlapping upper. W (total): not measurable due to the fact that the sandal is concreted to the bord on which it is exposed.
upper	openwork leather outer with gold and beadwork on closed leather inner layer; string of beads along the instep	see figure 3.72	L one side: 210.0 H at heel: 53.0 H halfway: 44.5* H front: 22.3 W decoration strip top: 9.8 W decoration strip bottom: 13.0 W gold strips: 2.2		L one side: at lateral side, approximately. Regarding H at heel: taken slightly before the heel proper.
foot strap	two strips of leather, decorated with daisies	narrow strip	W: 13.6 D gold bosses: 7.2		
instep strap	strings of beads and leather	transverse strings	W: 11.0* D beads: 2.5x3.2		
toe band	leather band with gold strip	narrow transverse band	W: 9.0		
front strap	leather band with gold strip	narrow band running from front to second transverse front attachment	W: 9.2		

Table 9. The technological details of not kept objects (021f[c] is not included, see text). Abbreviations to identify the numbers: [c] = Carter's number. Other abbreviations: D = diameter; e = equal (edge); l = large (edge); L = length; s = small (edge); T = thickness; W = width.

Identification	Construction	Shape	Measurements	Carter's Measurements
085[c]	leather	Rounded heel, constricted waist. Towards the front, the width increases, terminating in a rounded toe.	?	Card No. 085c L maximal: 21 cm. W maximal: 6.5 cm. W instep 5 cm. W heel: 5.4 cm.
067b[c]	leather, bark	Rounded heel, constricted waist. Towards the front, the width increases, terminating in a rounded toe.	?	Card No 067b L: ?. W: about 6 cm.
104b[c]	see table 1, 104a	see table 1, 104a	?	Card No. 104b L: about 21 cm. W maximal: about 7 cm.

296

Table 10. The technological details of the sewn sandals from Yuya and Tjuiu. Measurements (in mm) are as the object is preserved (see text); those which could not be taken, have not been mentioned. Measurements with * are approximate. The diameters of the rows of the edge of the sole relative to each other are in the sequence innermost/middle (if present)/outermost. Abbreviations: D = diameter; e = equal (edge); l = large (edge); L = length; max = maximal; s = small (edge); T = thickness; W = width.

Collection	Identification/ orientation	Sole					Strap complex (Back strap is common type)		Remarks
		Measurements	No. of rows	W row	Quality	Edge (∅)	Front strap / fastening	Measurements	
Egyptian Museum, Cairo	JE 91351a (= 95351?) CG 51128, SR 128 left, pair with JE 91351b	W heel: 73.1; W waist: 70.8; W front: 89.5. L: 260.0. T: 5.0.	39	5.7	fine	triple s/l/s	type 3; crown sinnet	D front: 10.3. W back (maximal): 39.8.	According to Quibell (1908: 59), 51128 is only one sandal. The study in the Egyptian Museum Cairo however, shows this number assigned to a pair of sandals.
Egyptian Museum, Cairo	JE 91351b (= 95351?) CG 51128, SR 128 right, pair with JE 91351a	W heel: 75.4; W waist: 72.4; W front: 92.8. L: 260.0. T: 4.9.	39	5.0	fine	triple s/l/s	type 3; crown sinnet	D front: 8.5. W back (maximal): 29.1.	-
Egyptian Museum, Cairo	JE 95305a (= 95350?) CG 51127, SR 127 right, pair with JE 95305b	W heel: 81.7; W waist: 79.7; W front: 99.4. L: 285.0. T: 5.3.	46	4.7	fine	triple l/l/s	type 3; crown sinnet	D front: 10.5. W back (maximal): 34.9.	Edge: the difference between the two inner and the outer bundles is small and is slightly more distinct in EgCa J 95305b.
Egyptian Museum, Cairo	JE 95305b (= 95350?) CG 51127, SR 127 left pair with JE 95305a	W heel: 87.9; W waist: 84.6; W front: 103.8. L: 295.0. T: 5.6.	48	4.7	fine	triple l/l/s	type 3; crown sinnet	D front: 13.5. W back (maximal): 38.5.	-

Collection	Identification/ orientation	Sole					Strap complex (Back strap is common type)		Remarks
		Measurements	No. of rows	W row	Quality	Edge (Ø)	Front strap / fastening	Measurements	
Egyptian Museum, Cairo	JE 95318 CG 51129, SR 95 right, pair with JE 95356	W heel: 73.1; W waist: 69.5; W front: 84.8. L: 235.0. T: 6.4.	17	12.1	fine	triple l/l/s	-		
Egyptian Museum, Cairo	JE 95319 CG 51130, SR 96 left	W heel: 74.1; W waist: 70.9; W front: 90.0. L: 255.0. T: 5.1.	39	4.8	fine	triple l/l/s	-		
Egyptian Museum, Cairo	JE 95348a CG 51120, SR 125 right	W heel: 74.5; W waist: 73.8; W front: 92.5. L: 263.0. T: 5.8.	36	5.8	fine	triple l/l/s	type 3; crown sinnet	D front: 10.7. W back (maximal): 36.4.	The entry number suggests EgCa J 95348a and EgCa J 95348b are a pair but in fact they are both a right sandal.
Egyptian Museum, Cairo	JE 95348b CG 51120, SR 125 right	W heel: 77.1; W waist: 74.4; W front: 93.8. L: 275.0. T: 6.0.	48	4.8	fine	triple l/l/s	type 3; crown sinnet	D front: 12.5*. W back (maximal): 36.0.	The entry number suggests EgCa J 95348a and EgCa J 95348b are a pair but in fact they are both a right sandal. Regarding the edge: the layout is not consistent throughout and parts are s/l/s.
Egyptian Museum, Cairo	JE 95353a CG 51125, SR 130 left, pair with JE 95353b	W heel: 86.8; W waist: 83.8; W front: 104.4. L: 300.0. T: 6.3.	48	5.3	fine	triple l/l/s	type 3; crown sinnet	D front: 12.8. W back (maximal): 41.4.	W row: average composed by relatively large low and high value.
Egyptian Museum, Cairo	JE 95353b CG 51125, SR 130 right, pair with JE 95353a	W heel: 89.2; W waist: 84.7; W front: 103.0. L: 300.0. T: 6.3.	46	5.4	fine	triple l/l/s	type 3; crown sinnet	D front: 12.6. W back (maximal): 44.3.	-

Collection	Identification/ orientation	Sole					Strap complex (Back strap is common type)		Remarks
		Measurements	No. of rows	W row	Quality	Edge (Ø)	Front strap / fastening	Measurements	
Egyptian Museum, Cairo	JE 95354a CG 51126, SR 131 left, pair with JE 95354b	W heel: 85.6; W waist: 81.1; W front: 100.6. L: 300.0. T: 5.6.	50	4.5	fine	triple l/l/s	type 3; crown sinnet	D front: 12.4. W back (maximal): 40.2.	–
Egyptian Museum, Cairo	JE 95354b CG 51126, SR 131 right, pair with JE 95354a	W heel: 81,8; W waist: 77.8; W front: 96.8. L: 300.0. T: 5.4.	47	4.5	fine	triple l/l/s	type 3; crown sinnet	D front: 13.5. W back (maximal): app. 42.0.	Edge: The difference between the two inner and the outer bundles is small and is slightly more distinct in EgCa J 95354a.
Egyptian Museum, Cairo	JE 95356 CG 51129, SR 133 left, pair with JE 95318	W heel: 77.5; W waist: 73.4; W front: 86.4. L: 240.0. T: 6.8.	16	12.5	fine	triple s/l/s	type 3; crown sinnet	D front: 9.6. W back (maximal): 31.5.	Edge: not consistent throughout; parts are l/l/s.
Egyptian Museum, Cairo	JE 95357 CG 51130(?), SR 134 left	W heel: 83,5; W waist: 84.5; W front: 100.8. L: 295.0. T: 5.4.	47	4.8	fine	triple l/l/s	type 3; crown sinnet	D front: 11.8. W back (maximal): 41.3.	Regarding W row: note the relatively big difference between the width of the bundles of the heel part and front part.
Metropolitan Museum of Arts New York	10.184a, b, pair	W heel: 84.5; W waist: 82.5; W front: 113.0. L: 300.0. T: -.	63	4	fine	triple l/l/s	type 5; crown sinnet	D front: 9.0. W back (maximal): 39.0.	Measurements of left sandal (10.184a). Regarding T: not measured: the sandals are mounted and it was decided not to free them.

Table 11. The technological details of the sewn sandals Type D (imitations) from Yuya and Tjuiu. Measurements (in mm) are as the object is preserved (see text); those which could not be taken, have not been mentioned. Measurements with * are approximate. Abbreviations: D = diameter; L = length; T = thickness; W = width.

Collection	Identification / Orientation	Sole Measurements	No. of rows	W row	Edge	Strap complex	Remarks
Egyptian Museum, Cairo	JE 95349(c)a CG 51124, SR 126 left, pair with JE 95349(c)b	W heel: 53.5; W waist: 50.8; W front: 70.5. L: 240.0.	40	34*	triple	As in JE 95355	The numbers at the sole are sometimes very badly visible, due to which Veldmeijer (2009a) erroneously listed this sandal as 95347.
Egyptian Museum, Cairo	JE 95349(c)b CG 51124, SR 126 left, pair with JE 95349(c)a	W heel: 51.7; W waist: 48.6; W front: 68.5. L: 240.0.	43+	35*	triple	As in JE 95355	The fragile condition did not allow the removal of the strap complex, which rests on the dorsal surface of the sole obscuring probably two or three transverse bundles.
Egyptian Museum, Cairo	JE 95352a CG 51123, SR 129 left(?), see text	W heel: 44.1; W front: 63.1. L: 180. T: app. 2.7.	Most likely not sandals (see text)				
Egyptian Museum, Cairo	JE 95352b(a) CG 51123, SR 129 right(?), see text	W heel: 51.8; W front: 66.5. L: app 175. T: app. 2.6	Most likely not sandals (see text)				
Egyptian Museum, Cairo	JE 95355 CG 51121, SR 132 left	W heel: 57.9; W waist: 56.0; W front: 73.7. L: 240.0. T: 2.7.					The sole consists of a layer of white leather, covered with plaster and, at the dorsal surface and edge, covered with gold foil. No indication of transverse bundles, but the shape and especially the layout of the strap complex strongly suggests an imitation of sewn sandals. Strap are inserted in holes and not secured at the ventral surface (which is not covered with gold foil). Note the longitudinally curvature in medial direction of the right sandal.
Egyptian Museum, Cairo	JE 95317 CG 51121, SR 94 right	W heel: 56.5; W waist: 53.8; W front: 64.0. L: app. 220. T: app. 3					

Table 12. The technological details of Nefertari's sewn sandals Type C. Measurements (in mm) are as the object is preserved (see text); those which could not be taken, have not been mentioned. The diameters of the rows of the edge of the sole relative to each other are in the sequence innermost/middle (if present)/outermost. Abbreviations: D = diameter; e = equal (edge); L = length; T = thickness; W = width.

Collection/ Identification	Provenance / Date	Sole					Strap complex		
		Measurements (right sandal)	No. of rows	W row	Quality	Edge (ø)	Front strap / Fastening	Back strap	Measurements
Museo Egizio, Turin, 5160 (pair)	Valley of the Queens, Tomb of Nefertari 19th Dynasty, Ramesses II	W heel: 82.2. W front: 97.7. L: 293.0.	66	3.5	fine	triple e	type 3 / ?	common type	D. front: 10.8. W back (maximal): 20.0.

INDEX

(Entries in bold are explained in Glossary)

A

Adindan 194, 263
AEFP 5, 11, 12, 13, 15, 225, 231, 233, 234, 244, 248
AELP 12, 13
African prisoner/foe 89, 92, 93, 139
Akhenaten 208, 210, 211, 216, 219, 220, 221, 240, 252, 254, 258, 259
alloy 152, 153, 154, 155, 157, 164, 239
Amarna 6, 14, 17, 139, 140, 147, 148, 149, 150, 169, 187, 188, 208, 209, 214, 215, 218, 220, 221, 229, 233, 236, 240, 244, 245, 246, 252, 253, 256, 258, 260, 261, 262, 263
amazonite 118, 119, 128, 149, 150, 161, 256
Amenhotep III 142, 169, 240, 249
Amun 200, 205, 207, 221, 241, 254
amyl acetate 35, 40
Ancient Egyptian Footwear Project (AEFP) see AEFP
Ancient Egyptian Leatherwork Project (AELP) see AELP
Ankhesenamun 248
anklet 26
Annexe 15, 19, 26, 29, 31, 251
Antechamber 15, 19, 21, 25, 29, 41, 165, 222, 251
antiquity 34, 152, 153, 156, 248, 260
appliqué 12, 155, 156
archaeological record 12, 13, 14, 144, 193, 206, 207, 222, 227, 244, 248
Ashurnasirpal 143
Asiatic prisoner/foe 84, 89, 92, 93, 139
atonism 220
Ay 214, 220, 221, 222, 247, 253

B

back strap 16, 35, 45, 46, 47, 49, 50, 51, 53, 55, 56, 57, 58, 60, 63, 66, 67, 68, 70, 71, 73, 76, 78, 80, 83, 84, 85, 86, 93, 94, 97, 98, 100, 102, 104, 105, 106, 107, 108, 111, 117, 118, 120, 121, 138, 144, 146, 149, 170, 173, 175, 176, 177, 178, 186, 207, 235, 236, 266, 268, 269, 279, 280, 282, 283, 285, 286, 287, 288, 289, 290
bag 23, 99
band 95, 98, 111, 117, 118, 119, 123, 124, 128, 129, 131, 132, 133, 136, 137, 158, 160, 167, 170, 237, 239
barefoot 12, 209, 216, 218, 219, 220, 221, 222, 224, 245, 246, 247
bark 17, 25, 87, 89, 91, 92, 94, 95, 105, 107, 139, 146, 147, 162, 163
basketry 13, 146, 187, 243, 263
basketry maker 13
bathroom 209, 210, 213, 214, 215, 216, 217, 219, 246
bead 6, 21, 23, 25, 26, 35, 40, 95, 96, 97, 98, 99, 102, 109, 111, 117, 118, 119, 120, 121, 122, 123, 124, 127, 128, 129, 131, 133, 137, 138, 139, 148, 149, 150, 151, 153, 154, 157, 159, 160, 226, 230, 237, 239, 251, 259
beadwork 5, 23, 96, 99, 102, 109, 111, 117, 118, 119, 121, 123, 124, 128, 129, 130, 138, 148, 149, 155, 225, 226, 227, 237
bed 25, 170, 219, 243, 246
Berenike 15, 233, 261
binding 14, 124, 162, 165, 181, 182, 258
birch 6, 91, 92, 94, 95, 105, 146, 147, 162, 163
bit 150, 151
boss 99, 102, 104, 120, 121, 131, 132, 137
bow 89, 92, 94, 147, 162, 225, 237, 258
bow drill 150, 151
box 21, 23, 25, 26, 29, 30, 31, 35, 36, 37, 39, 99, 102, 120, 132, 146, 165, 170, 199, 235, 253
Bronze Age 153, 157
burial 17, 139, 155, 164
Burial Chamber 15, 19, 222, 251, 253, 257
Burton, Harry 9, 11, 15, 21, 23, 25, 26, 27, 29, 30, 31, 36, 37, 39, 40, 41, 49, 108, 110, 117, 118, 120, 122, 124, 130, 132, 133, 136, 138, 139, 141, 167, 196, 222, 237
button 152, 156, 157, 260

C

Canada balsam 37
carnelian 118, 119, 128, 133, 149, 150, 161, 164, 229, 256
Carter, Howard 5, 7, 11, 15, 16, 17, 19, 21, 25, 26, 27, 29, 31, 34, 35, 36, 37, 39, 40, 47, 49, 50, 51, 84, 91, 98, 99, 102, 105, 107, 108, 110, 117, 118, 119, 120, 122, 124, 128, 129, 130, 131, 138, 139, 145, 146, 153, 154, 161, 165, 167, 224, 233, 235, 236, 237, 239, 246, 248, 251, 252, 253, 256, 257, 258
cast 152, 153, 156

category 15, 43, 193, 194, 195, 220, 225, 226, 229
Caucasus 147
celluloid 35, 40
C-Group 194, 234, 254, 263
chariot 19, 25, 26, 147, 168, 188, 201, 220, 221, 225, 229, 247, 249, 257, 261
chemical analyses 12, 35
chemical composition 148
child 7, 14, 139, 140, 187, 195, 197, 218, 230, 238, 246, 247, 248
cladding 45, 46, 49, 50, 51, 53, 55, 57, 58, 60, 63, 68, 71, 76, 78, 80, 83, 84, 86, 104, 121, 140, 146, 172, 174, 176, 178, 186, 190, 206, 207, 244
cloisonné 161
closed shoe (see also curled-toe ankle shoe and stubbed-toe low ankle shoe) 13, 143, 144, 187, 188, 193, 194, 225, 226, 227, 228, 229, 234, 241, 266, 269
cloth 21, 23, 25, 55, 120, 165, 167, 168, 183, 199
clothing 19, 165, 193, 199, 256
coiled sewn sandal 187, 189, 262
colour 16, 23, 25, 35, 49, 51, 53, 63, 69, 71, 84, 87, 94, 95, 98, 105, 110, 111, 117, 119, 120, 121, 124, 129, 130, 131, 132, 133, 139, 148, 149, 150, 152, 153, 154, 155, 156, 162, 164, 177, 184, 187, 188, 193, 224, 230, 258
combined fastening 226, 266
commodity 222, 241, 256
community 13, 14
conservation 5, 35, 37, 39, 40, 149, 235, 254, 255, 260
consolidation 99, 109, 121, 192
construction 6, 16, 44, 45, 46, 47, 49, 55, 71, 72, 77, 84, 92, 95, 97, 98, 104, 105, 107, 111, 119, 120, 121, 124, 127, 129, 130, 131, 132, 133, 136, 137, 138, 143, 144, 152, 154, 159, 160, 161, 165, 167, 172, 176, 180, 182, 186, 187, 194, 202, 207, 211, 216, 221, 228, 229, 236, 237, 239, 258, 269
context 5, 12, 14, 16, 17, 26, 143, 151, 199, 201, 202, 216, 228, 229, 230, 241, 242, 243
copper 144, 150, 151, 152, 153, 154, 155, 157, 243
Coptos 15, 257
cordage 13, 14, 16, 146, 187, 197, 260, 261, 263
core 45, 46, 47, 50, 51, 55, 56, 57, 58, 60, 61, 63, 67, 68, 71, 77, 80, 84, 86, 91, 94, 97, 98, 102, 104, 120, 121, 124, 129, 130, 142, 146, 148, 173, 186, 227, 238, 239, 240
cowskin 200, 201
craftsmen 14, 92, 156, 162, 164, 193, 198, 200, 201, 202, 203, 206, 237
culm 146
curing 35, 95, 130, 132, 148, 203, 266, 269
curled-toe ankle shoe 144, 188, 226, 229, 234, 249, 261
cylinder 98, 120, 129, 130, 133, 148

D

dagger 153, 158
daily life 13, 199, 208, 216, 220
daisy 111, 120, 121, 144, 149, 153, 154, 156, 237
dalmatica 168
decay 23, 29, 35, 268
decoration 12, 25, 35, 82, 84, 85, 89, 91, 92, 94, 99, 102, 104, 105, 107, 111, 119, 120, 124, 128, 131, 132, 133, 136, 139, 142, 143, 144, 148, 156, 162, 163, 184, 187, 190, 194, 235, 236, 237, 238, 243, 244, 260, 267, 268
Deir el-Bachit 14
Deir el-Medinah 14, 17, 140, 143, 169, 187, 193, 194, 195, 197, 198, 199, 202, 238, 241, 242, 252, 254, 255, 263, 265
Desmostachya bipinnata 45, 145
Didymoi 15, 257
document 17, 196, 209, 252, 254, 255, 257, 259, 260
domestic indoor space 7, 17, 208
doorway 15, 29, 222
dress 89, 94, 217, 218, 222, 225, 247, 248, 256
duckhead 111, 118, 120, 121, 124, 129, 149, 156, 161, 162
Dynasty 140, 149, 150, 151, 153, 157, 160, 169, 187, 199, 225, 230, 239, 241, 244, 251, 252, 255, 256

E

eared sandal 187, 188, 267
earring 155, 160, 161
edge binding (see binding)
Egyptian blue 162
electrum 152, 154, 170
Elephantine 14, 231, 233, 254, 257
enamel 162
Europe 15, 147, 238

F

faience 6, 17, 23, 25, 29, 31, 95, 99, 121, 138, 148, 149, 164, 239
fashion 14
fastening 15, 47, 55, 60, 71, 95, 118, 120, 124, 129, 131, 133, 137, 138, 142, 144, 176, 226, 227, 266, 267
fat 35, 71, 148, 203, 266
fibre, sewn sandal 5, 6, 15, 16, 17, 29, 31, 35, 43, 44, 45, 46, 47, 49, 70, 80, 82, 86, 94, 95, 96, 98, 99, 102, 104, 105, 107, 108, 109, 111, 120, 121, 131, 139, 140, 141, 142, 143, 144, 145, 170, 172, 173, 180, 182, 184, 186, 187, 189, 194, 205, 206, 207, 208, 209, 213, 218, 221, 222, 224, 225, 226, 227, 228,

229, 230, 234, 236, 237, 238, 293, 240, 241, 244, 245, 246, 248, 249, 261, 267, 269
filigree 124, 129, 157, 158, 159, 160
filler 162
flax 53, 82, 84, 95, 117, 118, 120, 165
floor 19, 25, 26, 29, 31, 34, 35, 170, 213
flower 95, 102, 104, 118, 137, 149, 154, 161, 164, 237, 256
foil 44, 49, 91, 92, 94, 95, 105, 107, 132, 152, 155, 162, 163, 180, 181, 182, 183, 184
foot strap 5, 37, 39, 109, 111, 119, 121, 124, 130, 133, 137, 143, 144, 158, 160, 226, 227, 229, 238, 267, 269
foreign 6, 7, 11, 12, 13, 14, 142, 143, 144, 150, 158, 227, 229, 231, 233, 234, 238, 243, 249, 257
former 155, 156
front strap 5, 37, 40, 45, 46, 47, 49, 50, 51, 53, 55, 57, 58, 60, 63, 66, 67, 71, 72, 73, 76, 78, 80, 83, 84, 86, 93, 94, 97, 98, 102, 104, 105, 106, 107, 108, 111, 119, 120, 121, 129, 130, 133, 136, 137, 139, 140, 141, 144, 146, 158, 167, 170, 172, 173, 176, 177, 178, 181, 184, 186, 194, 206, 207, 226, 227, 241, 267, 268, 269
funerary 198, 199, 238, 242
furniture 19, 199, 208

G

garment 23, 25, 85, 168, 209, 216, 218, 219, 240, 245, 246, 263
gauntlet 6, 23, 165, 167, 168
Gebelein 194
gemstone 6, 17, 119, 149, 150, 225, 229
gesso 87, 91, 94, 95, 180, 182, 183, 184, 224, 236, 237
Giza 144
glass 6, 16, 17, 29, 121, 148, 149, 162, 164, 239, 258
glove 23, 29, 167, 168
glue 35, 91, 102, 153, 162, 182, 236
goatskin 147, 201
gold 6, 16, 17, 19, 21, 26, 29, 35, 44, 49, 86, 91, 92, 94, 95, 99, 102, 104, 105, 107, 108, 109, 110, 111, 117, 118, 119, 120, 121, 123, 124, 127, 128, 129, 130, 131, 132, 133, 136, 137, 139, 142, 143, 144, 148, 149, 151, 152, 153, 154, 155, 156, 157, 158, 159, 160, 161, 162, 163, 164, 170, 180, 181, 182, 183, 184, 198, 224, 225, 227, 229, 230, 235, 237, 239, 240, 247, 248, 251, 254, 255, 256, 258, 260, 263
gold foil (see 'foil')
goldsmith 153, 164, 200, 239, 258
goldwork 6, 17, 151, 152, 154, 156, 157, 158, 159, 161, 162, 164, 229, 239, 258
granulation 157, 259
grass 45, 46, 47, 50, 51, 53, 55, 57, 60, 63, 66, 71, 72, 77, 84, 142, 145, 146, 170, 172, 179, 195, 228, 230, 238, 269

Greece 147, 239, 258
Griffith Institute 9, 15, 16, 21, 23, 25, 26, 27, 29, 30, 31, 36, 37, 39, 40, 41, 108, 124, 133, 167, 196, 222, 237, 241
guest 209, 213

H

harem 209, 210
head-rest 21, 23
heel 16, 31, 37, 40, 43, 44, 50, 53, 56, 57, 58, 60, 63, 65, 66, 70, 71, 73, 76, 77, 79, 80, 82, 84, 85, 89, 93, 94, 95, 96, 99, 100, 107, 111, 124, 127, 131, 133, 138, 141, 177, 179, 184, 186, 187, 190, 194, 225, 229, 237, 267, 268, 269
heel seat 267
heel strap 189, 224, 238, 267, 268, 269
hole 47, 49, 60, 63, 65, 71, 76, 108, 120, 121, 123, 127, 128, 129, 132, 133, 142, 150, 155, 156, 176, 177, 181, 184, 190, 195, 237, 269
hook 104, 111, 120, 121
household 199, 202, 212
Hyphaene thebaica 45, 146, 238

I

iconography 7, 11, 12, 208, 220, 234, 242, 245, 246, 248
imitation 5, 6, 25, 45, 86, 142, 144, 170, 172, 180, 182, 184, 225, 237, 246
Imperata cylindrica 45, 145, 238
import 143, 194
inlay 120, 121, 162, 225
insole 21, 31, 44, 53, 55, 75, 80, 82, 83, 84, 85, 86, 94, 95, 97, 98, 99, 108, 109, 111, 117, 118, 119, 120, 121, 122, 128, 131, 136, 139, 142, 170, 226, 236, 244, 267, 268, 269
instep 117, 118, 123, 128, 129, 131, 133, 137, 170, 172, 267, 268, 269
instep strap 5, 37, 42, 121, 124, 129, 130, 133, 137, 144, 158, 226, 227, 266, 268
instruction of Khety 202, 256

J

jewellery 149, 150, 151, 152, 154, 157, 158, 164, 256, 258, 259, 263

K

Kahun 187, 225, 241, 259
Karnak 200, 209, 210, 219, 244, 246, 257, 261
Kerma 194, 260, 263
Khaemhat 222, 259
knot 16, 57, 84, 120, 129, 141, 251, 173, 190, 207, 261

L

language 193, 267
lapis lazuli 118, 119, 120, 121, 128, 133, 148, 149, 150, 162, 229, 256, 260, 261
lattice 130
lead 155, 187, 205, 209
leather composite sandal 15, 123, 189, 205, 262
leatherwork 11, 12, 13, 144, 164, 184, 187, 201, 225, 228, 237, 243, 248, 249, 253, 261
letter 150, 194, 195, 198, 200, 201, 229, 258, 263
lily 118, 144, 229, 249
linen 21, 23, 25, 26, 44, 47, 80, 82, 83, 84, 85, 111, 165, 226
linguistic 17
Lisht 159
literary text 193, 202, 203
loop 45, 51, 53, 57, 58, 60, 63, 67, 71, 80, 84, 94, 104, 105, 107, 111, 118, 120, 121, 136, 137, 138, 165, 170, 207
lotus 84, 94, 95, 104, 120, 131, 144, 148, 149, 155, 156, 157, 161, 164, 229
Lucas, Alfred 11, 35, 146, 147, 150, 151, 152, 153, 154, 155, 236, 239, 257
Luxor Museum 9, 53, 54, 55, 57, 58, 210, 233, 236, 244, 245, 247

M

mansion 209, 211, 212, 213, 245
manufacturing technique (see also 'technology') 12, 14, 15, 206, 228
marquetry veneer 16, 29, 31, 40, 87, 89, 91, 105, 107, 142, 146, 216, 237, 246
mass production 155
material culture 6, 12, 17, 193
Medinet Habu 169, 246, 256
Mediterranean 11, 13, 14, 158, 260, 262
melt 37, 50, 73, 95, 130, 162, 235
Meroitic 143, 229, 243, 260
Mersa/Wadi Gawasis 146, 233, 262
Mesopotamia 143, 150, 258
metal 13, 35, 44, 133, 144, 152, 153, 154, 155, 156, 170, 184, 226, 230, 238, 258, 260

Methodology 5, 16
Middle Kingdom 146, 149, 159, 160, 187, 194, 200, 228, 251, 263
midsole 268, 269
mimesis 218
mine 149, 150, 251, 256
mineral 149, 153, 266
Minoan 158, 187, 240, 243, 249
model 26, 200, 268
Mohs 150
motif 144, 155, 156, 161, 184, 229
mummy 15, 19, 26, 29, 96, 107, 108, 144, 170, 184, 222, 240, 253, 260
mummy sandals 16

N

necropolis 17, 34, 194, 248, 259
needlework 84
nefer 105, 106, 107
Nefertari 6, 142, 169, 184, 186, 301
Nefertiti 210, 211, 219, 254, 261
New Kingdom 6, 7, 13, 17, 140, 151, 153, 154, 155, 156, 161, 162, 165, 169, 182, 187, 188, 193, 194, 196, 197, 198, 200, 201, 202, 205, 207, 212, 228, 241, 242, 243, 246, 247, 253
Nubia 11, 13, 14, 143, 149, 194, 228, 229, 231, 234, 249, 254, 256, 262, 263

O

Old Kingdom 144, 194, 197, 234, 256, 260
open shoe 5, 13, 14, 37, 39, 109, 110, 111, 119, 122, 123, 124, 129, 130, 131, 132, 136, 137, 138, 141, 143, 144, 187, 188, 189, 193, 194, 225, 226, 227, 228, 229, 237, 241, 243, 262, 266, 267, 268, 269
openwork (see also 'decoration') 130, 131, 132, 133, 136, 137, 143, 156, 159, 160, 161, 227, 235
ostraca 193, 196, 197, 199, 251, 252, 253, 254, 255, 257, 258, 259, 260, 265
overseer 200

P

padding 187, 206
paint 12, 207
palace 21, 26, 137, 200, 202, 208, 209, 210, 211, 212, 213, 214, 215, 216, 218, 220, 221, 222, 227, 230, 244, 245, 246, 247, 253, 258, 268
palm fibre 238, 268
palm leaf 45, 46, 50, 51, 55, 63, 67, 71, 80, 82, 83, 84, 86, 102, 104, 110, 141, 146, 170, 172, 173, 176, 178, 195, 197, 227, 228, 236, 239, 267, 269

panel 122, 124, 128, 129, 130, 132, 158, 186
papyrus 14, 21, 23, 26, 45, 46, 49, 51, 53, 55, 60, 63, 83, 84, 86, 95, 102, 104, 105, 118, 140, 142, 144, 145, 146, 155, 156, 157, 172, 176, 186, 194, 195, 196, 197, 199, 201, 202, 206, 228, 238, 239, 240, 242, 243, 252, 254, 255, 256, 257, 259, 260, 263, 265, 292
paraffin wax 35
patina 71, 141, 258
patten 238, 261, 262, 267
pectoral 161
pendant 23, 154, 160, 161, 164, 239
perimeter 44, 45, 56, 82, 84, 91, 92, 94, 99, 120, 131, 136, 138, 187, 194, 225
Persepolis 143, 263
Persian 14, 231
Pharaoh 15, 18, 142, 146, 148, 152, 164, 193, 199, 205, 207, 216, 218, 221, 224, 227, 230, 231, 248, 251, 252, 253, 254, 255, 259, 262, 267
philology 6, 7, 11, 12, 17, 193, 228, 229, 241
pigment 12, 153, 261, 268
plaster 44, 91, 236
post-Amarna 13
post-excavation 17, 29
preservation 5, 14, 35, 118, 130, 142, 184, 230, 233, 235
pre-strap 18, 40, 47, 45, 49, 51, 50, 55, 56, 57, 58, 60, 63, 65, 66, 67, 68, 71, 73, 76, 78, 79, 80, 84, 86, 89, 92, 94, 98, 100, 105, 107, 121, 139, 146, 172, 176, 177, 181, 186, 187, 188, 206, 207, 244, 267, 268, 269
priest 14, 120, 139, 141, 142, 165, 194, 197, 198, 205, 221, 222, 241, 244, 247, 248, 254
princess 209, 217, 218, 220, 246, 247, 263
profession 11, 13, 18, 200, 202, 203, 206, 228, 243
provenance 15, 150, 239, 241
punch 110, 117, 118, 212, 122, 132, 133, 155, 156, 268

Q

Qasr Ibrim 14, 143, 229, 233, 234, 241, 260, 261, 262
quartz 149, 150

R

Rameses 155, 162, 196, 199, 200, 202, 253, 254, 256, 257, 260, 263
Ramesseum 169
rand 234, 268
rawhide 35, 94, 105, 109, 120, 121, 170, 180, 182, 184, 226, 240, 268
reconstruction 99, 109, 210, 216, 241, 244, 246, 268

reed 25, 142, 145, 146, 172, 176, 179, 238
Rekhmira 148, 187, 200, 205, 206, 207, 228, 238, 241, 243, 248, 249
relief 84, 143, 209, 221, 227, 238, 239, 244, 245, 252, 256, 259, 260, 263
repair 14, 51, 55, 60, 63, 68, 83, 139, 142, 172, 174, 230, 234, 244, 248, 288
reward 198, 213, 220, 221, 246, 247
ring 138
ritual 198, 201, 216, 218, 236
robber 34, 139, 141, 142, 169, 170, 200, 230, 248
robe 21, 23, 25, 26, 29, 85
rope 94, 146, 170, 239, 262
rosette 99, 118, 138, 154, 155, 156, 158, 164
running stitch 82, 117, 118, 119, 123, 130, 132, 144, 268
rush 21, 29, 145, 153, 155, 199, 238, 240

S

sandal-maker 12, 13, 14, 164, 173, 193, 200, 201, 202, 203, 205, 206, 207, 228, 233
sard 150
sardonyx 150
Satire of Trades 202
seam 85, 95, 132, 142, 157, 158, 165, 190, 234, 268
Sedment 142, 228, 259
Senebtisi 159
servant 211, 213, 221, 245, 246
Seti II 160
sewing 40, 44, 46, 47, 49, 50, 51, 53, 56, 57, 58, 60, 61, 63, 65, 66, 67, 70, 71, 72, 73, 76, 77, 79, 80, 84, 86, 108, 109, 122, 127, 129, 140, 141, 142, 146, 172, 174, 176, 177, 178, 224, 228, 230, 239, 245, 266, 269
sewn-edge plaited sandal 140, 187, 188, 207, 208, 226, 234, 249, 262
semi-circular side panel (see 'panel')
shoe (see 'open shoe' and 'closed shoe')
showcase 16, 39
silver 152, 153, 154, 170, 198, 238, 240, 247, 260, 263
size 5, 12, 14, 17, 23, 26, 50, 70, 94, 123, 138, 139, 149, 172, 181, 184, 193, 194, 228, 230, 238
skin 25, 71, 141, 148, 156, 165, 170, 200, 236, 253, 266, 269
skin processing 12, 147, 148, 205, 269
slipper 16, 21, 213, 229, 268
slit 45, 47, 53, 58, 60, 63, 66, 67, 71, 72, 73, 76, 80, 86, 99, 104, 117, 118, 124, 127, 128, 129, 130, 131, 132, 136, 139, 142, 164, 184, 187, 237, 244
socio-cultural aspects 12, 13
sock 6, 17, 165, 167, 168, 187, 240
soldier 199, 200, 222
sole layer 99, 117, 121, 132, 144, 184, 187, 188, 206, 268, 269

sole/upper construction 111, 119, 124, 127, 129, 132, 133, 136, 142, 143, 144, 269
spacer bead 111, 120
split pin 131, 156, 157
statue 224
status 7, 13, 14, 18, 197, 198, 200, 202, 216, 218, 221, 228, 230, 247
stitch (see also 'running stich' and 'whip stich') 12, 46, 47, 50, 53, 60, 61, 85, 95, 99, 102, 119, 121, 117, 118, 128, 131, 132, 141, 145, 182, 201, 221, 268, 269
stitch hole 31, 53, 55, 75, 84, 86, 109, 110, 111, 117, 118, 119, 122, 124, 128, 132, 133, 269
straight sole 43, 269
strap complex 5, 29, 31, 40, 45, 50, 51, 53, 56, 58, 60, 63, 65, 67, 71, 72, 73, 75, 76, 78, 79, 80, 83, 84, 86, 94, 95, 105, 106, 108, 109, 226, 139, 143, 144, 161, 172, 176, 177, 180, 184, 185, 187, 194, 207, 208, 227, 237, 241, 249
string 92, 118, 119, 133, 138, 261, 293, 294, 295
stubbed-toe low ankle shoe 144, 188, 192, 262
stucco 236
swayed sole 44, 47, 107, 269
symbolism 6, 14, 18, 198, 248, 269
Syria 144, 168, 242

T

talatat 209, 210, 219, 244, 245, 246, 257, 261
tanning 35, 148, 266, 269
Taranto 160
Ta-usret 160
technology 6, 15, 44, 143, 144, 151, 152, 155, 158, 161, 228, 229, 231, 234, 237, 239, 251, 253, 254, 257, 258, 262, 263
Tell el-Amarna (see 'Amarna')
temple 194, 196, 197, 198, 199, 200, 201, 205, 207, 208, 210, 216, 219, 221, 228, 233, 244, 245, 247, 256, 260
terminology 16, 234, 237, 257, 261
textile 35, 53, 55, 156, 182, 242, 256, 293
Thebes 150, 151, 194, 200, 202, 247, 251, 253, 259, 261, 262, 265
thread 23, 35, 95, 96, 118, 119, 122, 124, 127, 128, 133, 156, 165, 237, 268, 269
three-dimensional art 7, 17, 172, 161, 164, 207, 224, 228, 229, 248
throne 25, 26, 29, 139, 142, 230, 246, 248, 253, 254
tin 157
Tiye 155, 169
Tjuiu 6, 7, 17, 142, 144, 145, 153, 169, 170, 171, 172, 173, 176, 206, 207, 228, 230, 236, 240
toe band 5, 130, 133, 136, 137, 143, 144, 170, 226, 227, 269
toggle 137, 138, 266, 268

toilette 209, 211, 213, 216, 219
tomb 5, 6, 9, 11, 13, 15, 17, 19, 21, 34, 35, 44, 47, 57, 84, 130, 139, 141, 142, 143, 144, 146, 147, 150, 151, 152, 153, 154, 155, 158, 160, 165, 167, 169, 170, 184, 186, 187, 194, 195, 196, 197, 199, 200, 205, 206, 207, 209, 211, 214, 215, 216, 218, 220, 221, 222, 224, 227, 228, 229, 230, 234, 238, 239, 240, 241, 243, 244, 245, 246, 247, 248, 249, 251, 252, 253, 254, 255, 256, 257, 258, 259, 260, 263
tool 12, 13, 16, 26, 157, 162, 218, 233
transverse bundle 40, 44, 45, 46, 50, 60, 71, 72, 73, 79, 80, 84, 108, 109, 110, 121, 142, 145, 170, 172, 176, 177, 178, 179, 180, 207, 224, 239, 267, 269
treadsole 43, 44, 82, 83, 84, 85, 91, 94, 95, 97, 98, 99, 109, 117, 118, 119, 120, 121, 122, 124, 128, 131, 136, 142, 144, 170, 181, 190, 226, 237, 268, 269
treasure 152, 157, 169, 251, 255, 256, 257, 259, 263
Treasury 15, 19, 26, 30, 222, 251
Troy 157, 251
tube 98, 105, 120, 124, 129, 133, 137, 158, 159, 160, 161
turquoise 29, 133, 148, 149, 150
two-dimensional art 7, 17, 127, 164, 205, 208, 221, 227, 228, 230, 233, 244, 249, 267
typology 6, 7, 12, 14, 15, 18, 142, 193, 225, 226, 227, 233, 234

U

upper 5, 14, 35, 37, 109, 111, 117, 118, 119, 120, 121, 122, 123, 124, 127, 128, 129, 130, 131, 132, 133, 136, 137, 141, 142, 143, 144, 150, 153, 156, 165, 167, 190, 225, 226, 227, 229, 234, 237, 241, 245, 249, 266, 267, 268, 269

W

waist 43, 44, 63, 99, 107, 138, 142, 186, 269
wardrobe 209, 211, 241, 247, 263
wear 5, 12, 14, 16, 17, 31, 49, 60, 63, 65, 71, 76, 78, 79, 80, 128, 139, 141, 142, 156, 176, 177, 186, 221, 230, 243, 248
Wedjet-eye 105, 106
wire 102, 108, 124, 130, 148, 157, 158, 159, 160, 162, 170, 239, 258
wood 13, 44, 86, 87, 91, 94, 120, 142, 147, 155, 156, 192, 216, 224, 226, 236, 254, 268
workshop 12, 13, 154, 155, 161, 162, 164, 200, 201, 202, 208, 243, 245

X

xylene 37

Y

Yuya 6, 7, 17, 44, 142, 145, 153, 169, 170, 172, 173, 176, 182, 184, 194, 206, 207, 228, 230, 236, 240

AUTHORS

André J. Veldmeijer studied archaeology at Leiden University, The Netherlands, and received his Ph.D from Utrecht University, The Netherlands. He has worked in Egypt since 1995 as a leather, footwear and cordage specialist on various expeditions. He has also worked in many collections all over the world, studying ancient Egyptian leatherwork and footwear, and is the director of two ongoing research projects: the Ancient Egyptian Leatherwork Project (including the Egyptian Museum Chariot Project) and the Ancient Egyptian Footwear Project. He has published extensively on these three topics in scientific as well as popular journals, among which is the monograph *Amarna's Leatherwork* (2010). Veldmeijer is one of the founders and current chairman of the PalArch Foundation (www.palarch.nl).

Alan J. Clapham holds a Ph.D from Liverpool John Moores University on the palaeoecology of submerged forests and has been studying archaeobotany for over 25 years. He has studied plant remains from the British Isles, Spain, Jordan, Madagascar, Sudan and Egypt, where he mainly works on material from Amarna, Qasr Ibrim and the Kharga Oasis. He is currently employed as a Senior Environmental Archaeologist at Worcestershire Historic Environment and Archaeology Service.

Ing. Erno Endenburg has worked in Egypt on many excavations, including Amarna, Qasr Ibrim and Deir el-Bachit, and in collections all over the world as a photographer and illustrator of leatherwork and footwear. His work is published in numerous scientific and popular publications.

Aude Gräzer is about to finish her Ph.D in Egyptology under the supervision of Pr. emeritus Claude Traunecker (University of Strasbourg and UMR 7044 Laboratory, CNRS, France). Her work focuses on Egyptians concept of domestic comfort in all its facets (criteria, concrete implementation and socio-ideological implications) by studying archaeological remains of Pharaonic houses and palaces as well as iconographic and textual evidence.

Fredrik Hagen received his Ph.D from the University of Cambridge, where he was subsequently designated the Lady Wallis Budge Junior Research Fellow at Christ's College. He is currently Associate Professor of Egyptology at the University of Copenhagen, where his research focuses on papyri and ostraca of the New Kingdom.

James A. Harrell is Professor Emeritus of Geology at the University of Toledo in Toledo, Ohio, USA. For the past 20 years he has been conducting geo-archaeological research on the varieties, sources and uses of rocks and minerals employed by ancient Middle Eastern civilizations, including the Egyptian in Egypt, the Napatan and Meroitic in Sudan, and the South Arabian in Yemen and Saudi Arabia.

Mikko H. Kriek works as illustrator and graphic designer at VU University, Amsterdam, The Netherlands. Besides contributing work to a wide variety of projects in Dutch archaeology, he also works as an illustrator for several international projects in Syria and Egypt. As freelancer he is the principal illustrator for the Ancient Egyptian Leatherwork and Footwear Projects. Mikko is a full member of the board of the Association of Archaeological Illustrators and Surveyors.

Paul T. Nicholson is a reader in Archaeology, School of History and Archaeology, Cardiff University, Wales, U.K. He specialises in early technology, especially vitreous materials and has worked widely on projects in Egypt.

Jack M. Ogden, currently CEO of the Gemmological Association of Great Britain, is a specialist in the history of jewellery materials and technology. His 1982 'Jewellery of the Ancient World' is still the standard work on ancient jewellery technology. His Doctoral Thesis (Durham University) dealt with the jewellery industry in Hellenistic and Roman Egypt. He has written and lectured widely on early jewellery including teaching courses at The J. Paul Getty Museum, Smithsonian Institution, Institute of Fine Arts (NY) and Institute of Archaeology (London). He is an elected Fellow of the Society of Antiquaries of London.

Dr. Gillian Vogelsang-Eastwood, director of the Textile Research Centre (TRC, www.texdress.nl), Leiden, The Netherlands, is a textile and dress historian specializing in Middle Eastern dress. The TRC specializes in dress and identity: what people wear in order to say who they are. She has published various books and articles on the subject of clothing in ancient Egypt, as well as more specific works on the clothing found in the tomb of Tutankhamun.